Group Cognition

Acting with Technology
Bonnie Nardi, Victor Kaptelinin, and Kirsten Foot, editors

Group Cognition

Computer Support for Building Collaborative Knowledge

Gerry Stahl

The MIT Press
Cambridge, Massachusetts
London, England

MIT Press books may be purchased at special quantity discounts for business or sales promotional use. For information, please e-mail <special_sales@mitpress.mit.edu> or write to Special Sales Department, The MIT Press, 55 Hayward Street, Cambridge, MA 02142.

This book was set in Sabon by SNP Best-set Typesetter Ltd., Hong Kong.
Printed and bound in the United States of America.

Library of Congress Cataloging-in-Publication Data

Stahl, Gerry.
Group cognition : computer support for collaborative knowledge building / Gerry Stahl.
  p. cm.—(Acting with technology)
Includes bibliographical references and index.
ISBN 0-262-19539-9 (hc : alk. paper)
1. Computer-assisted instruction. 2. Computer networks. I. Title. II. Series.

LB1028.5.S696 2006
371.33′4—dc22

2005052047

10 9 8 7 6 5 4 3 2 1

Contents

Series Foreword

The MIT Press Acting with Technology series is concerned with the study of meaningful human activity as it is mediated by tools and technologies. The goal of the series is to publish the best new books—both research monographs and textbooks—that contribute to an understanding of technology as a crucial facet of human activity enacted in rich social and physical contexts.

The focus of the series is on tool-mediated processes of working, playing, and learning in and across a wide variety of social settings. The series explores developments in postcognitivist theory and practice from the fields of sociology, communication, education, organizational studies, science and technology studies, human-computer interaction studies, and computer-supported collaborative work. It aims to encompass theoretical frameworks developed through cultural-historical activity theory, actor-network theory, distributed cognition, ethnomethodology, and grounded theory.

In *Group Cognition: Computer Support for Building Collaborative Knowledge*, Gerry Stahl challenges us with the provocative notion that "small groups are the engines of knowledge building." He notes that research on learning has focused on either individual cognition or the larger community. Based on his extensive experience in teaching and system building, Stahl points to the "decisive role of small groups" in learning. Stahl's contribution is to alert us to the need for a theoretical representation of small groups and their pivotal role in group cognition. He explores this theme in varied ways—empirical, theoretical, philosophical—each persuasive and thoughtful in its own way.

Stahl pushes hard on the notion of group cognition, proposing that we view discourse as a "substrate for group cognition." *Discourse* is defined broadly to include spoken words, inscriptions, and body language. Using these notions, Stahl hopes to position cognition in that zone of small groups where he feels it belongs, moving it away from individual "brains" but not too far into less precise entities such as community. Stahl notes that adopting such a notion would change education profoundly in terms of classroom practice, testing, assessment, and teacher training.

Group Cognition is a welcome addition to the Acting with Technology series. It is highly recommended for readers interested in education, human-computer inter-action, and computer-supported collaborative work.

Group Cognition

Introduction: Essays on Technology, Interaction, and Cognition

The promise of globally networked computers to usher in a new age of universal learning and sharing of human knowledge remains a distant dream; the software and social practices needed have yet to be conceived, designed, and adopted. To support online collaboration, our technology and culture have to be reconfigured to meet a bewildering set of constraints. Above all, this requires understanding how digital technology can mediate human collaboration. The essays gathered in this volume document one path of exploration of these challenges. They include efforts to design software prototypes featuring specific collaboration-support functionality, to analyze empirical instances of collaboration, and to theorize about the issues, phenomena, and concepts involved today in supporting collaborative knowledge building.

The studies in this book grapple with the problem of how to increase opportunities for effective collaborative working, learning, and acting through innovative uses of computer technology. From a technological perspective, the possibilities seem endless and effortless. The ubiquitous linking of computers in local and global networks makes possible the sharing of thoughts by people who are separated spatially or temporally. Brainstorming and critiquing of ideas can be conducted in many-to-many interactions, without being confined by a sequential order imposed by the inherent limitations of face-to-face meetings and classrooms. Negotiation of consensual decisions and group knowledge can be conducted in new ways.

Collaboration of the future will be more complex than just chatting—verbally or electronically—with a friend. The computational power of personal computers can lend a hand here; software can support the collaboration process and help to manage its complexity. It can organize the sharing of communication, maintaining both sociability and privacy. It can personalize information access to different user perspectives and can order knowledge proposals for group negotiation.

Computer support can help us transcend the limits of individual cognition. It can facilitate the formation of small groups engaged in deep knowledge building. It can empower such groups to construct forms of group cognition that exceed what the group members could achieve as individuals. Software functionality can present, coordinate, and preserve group discourse that contributes to, constitutes, and represents shared understandings, new meanings, and collaborative learning that is not attributable to any one person but that is achieved in group interaction.

Initial attempts to engage in the realities of computer-supported knowledge building have, however, encountered considerable technical and social barriers. The transition to this new mode of interaction is in some ways analogous to the passage from oral to literate culture, requiring difficult changes and innovations on multiple levels and over long stretches of time. But such barriers signal opportunities. By engaging in experimental attempts at computer-supported, small-group collaboration and carefully observing where activity breaks down, researchers can identify requirements for new software.

The design studies presented in this book explore innovative functionality for collaboration software. They concentrate especially on mechanisms to support *group formation, multiple interpretive perspectives,* and the *negotiation of group knowledge.* The various applications and research prototypes reported in the first part of this book span the divide between cooperative work and collaborative learning, helping us to recognize that contemporary knowledge workers must be lifelong learners and also that collaborative learning requires flexible divisions of labor.

The attempt to design and adopt collaboration software led to a realization that we need to understand much more clearly the social and cognitive processes involved. In fact, we need a multifaceted theory for computer-supported collaboration, incorporating empirically based analyses and concepts from many disciplines. This book, in its central part, pivots around the example of an empirical micro-analysis of small-group collaboration. In particular, it looks at *how the group constructs intersubjective knowledge that appears in the group discourse itself,* rather than theorizing about what takes place in the minds of the individual participants.

The notion that it is important to take the group, rather than the individual, as the unit of analysis ultimately requires developing, from the ground up, a new *theory of collaboration* in the book's final part. This theory departs from prevalent cognitive science, grounded as it is on mental representations of individuals. Such a theory builds on related efforts in social-cultural theory, situated cognition, and ethnomethodology, as well as their post-Kantian philosophical roots.

Collaboration as Group Cognition

This book does not aspire to the impossible task of describing all the ways that technology does or could affect working and learning. I work and I learn in innumerable ways and modes—and everyone else works and learns in additional ways, many different from mine. Working and learning with other people mixes these ways into yet more complex varieties. Technology multiplies the possibilities even more. So this book chooses to focus on a particular form of working and learning—one that seems especially attractive to many people and may be particularly responsive to technological support but one that is also rather hard to point out and observe in the current world. It is the holy grail of cooperative knowledge work and collaborative learning—*the emergence of shared group cognition* through effective collaborative knowledge building.

The goal of collaborative knowledge building is much more specific than that of e-learning or distance education generally, where computer networks are used to communicate and distribute information from one teacher to several students who are geographically dispersed. Collaborative knowledge building stresses supporting interactions among the students themselves, with a teacher playing more of a facilitating than instructing role. Moreover, knowledge building involves the construction or further development of some kind of knowledge artifact. That is, the students are not simply socializing and exchanging their personal reactions or opinions about the subject matter but might be developing a theory, model, diagnosis, conceptual map, mathematical proof, or presentation. These activities require the exercise of high-level cognitive activities. In effective collaborative knowledge building, the group must engage in thinking together about a problem or task and produce a knowledge artifact such as a verbal problem clarification, a textual solution proposal, or a more developed theoretical inscription that integrates their different perspectives on the topic and represents a shared group result that they have negotiated.

We all know from personal experience—or think we know based on our tacit acceptance of prevalent folk theories—that individual people can think and learn on their own. It is harder to understand how a small group of people collaborating online can think and learn as a group and not just as the sum of the people in the group thinking and learning individually.

Ironically, the counterintuitive notion of group cognition turns out to be easier to study than individual learning. Whereas individual cognition is hidden in private mental processes, group cognition is necessarily publicly visible. This is because any ideas involved in a group interaction must be displayed for the members of the group to participate in the collaborative process. In this book, I try to take advantage of such displays to investigate group cognition without reducing it to an epiphenomenon of individual cognition. This does not mean that I deny that individuals have private thoughts: I simply do not rely on our commonsense intuitions and introspections about such thoughts. In the end, consideration focused on the group unit may have implications for understanding individual cognition as a socially grounded and mediated product of group cognition.

How does a group build its collective knowing? A noncognitivist approach avoids speculating on psychological processes hidden in the heads of individuals and instead looks to empirically observable group processes of interaction and discourse. The roles of individuals in the group are not ignored but are viewed as multiple interpretive perspectives that can conflict, stimulate, intertwine, and be negotiated. The spatiotemporal world in which collaborative interactions are situated is not assumed to be composed of merely physical as opposed to mental ideas but is seen as a universe filled with meaningful texts and other kinds of artifacts—human-made objects that embody shared meanings in physical, symbolic, digital, linguistic, and cultural forms.

The concern with the processes and possibilities of building group knowing has implications for the choice of themes investigated in this book. The software prototypes reported on in part I, for instance, were attempts to support the formation of teams that had the right mix for building knowledge as a group, to represent the multiple perspectives involved in developing group ideas, and to facilitate the negotiation of group knowledge that arose. Certainly, there are other important processes in online collaboration, but these are of particular concern for small-group knowledge building. Similarly, the empirical analysis in part II zooms in on the way in which the participants in an observed group of students constructed knowledge in their discourse that could not be attributed to any simple conjunction of their individual contributions. Finally, the theoretical reflections of part III try to suggest a conceptual framework that incorporates these notions of "interpretive perspectives" or "knowledge negotiation" within a coherent view of how group cognition takes place in a world of discourse, artifacts, and computer media.

Rather than centering on practical design goals for *computer-supported cooperative work* (CSCW) industrial settings or *computer-supported collaborative learning* (CSCL) classrooms, the following chapters explore foundational issues of how small groups can construct meaning at the group level. The ability of people to engage in effective group cognition in the past has been severely constrained by physical limits of the human body and brain. We can really relate to only a small number of individual people at a time or follow only one primary train of thought at a time, and most business meetings or classroom activities are structured, moderated, and delimited accordingly. Moreover, we quickly forget many of the details of what was said at such meetings. Collaboration technology has enormous potential to establish many-to-many interactions, to help us manage them, and to maintain logs of what transpired. Figuring out how to design and deploy collaboration technologies and social practices to achieve this still-distant potential is the driving force that is struggling to speak through these essays.

The structure of the book follows the broad strokes of my historical path of inquiry into computer-supported group cognition. Part I reports on several attempts to design online technologies to support the collaborative building of knowing—that is, computer-mediated group sense making—in which I was involved. Part II shows how I responded to the need I subsequently felt to better understand phenomena of collaboration—such as group formation, perspective sharing, and knowledge negotiation through microanalysis of group interaction—in order to guide such software design. In turn, part III indicates how this led me to formulate a conceptual framework and a research methodology: a theory of collaboration, grounded in empirical practice and exploration. Although theory is typically presented as a solid foundational starting point for practice, this obfuscates its genesis as a conceptual reflection in *response* to problems of practice and their circumstances. I have tried to avoid such reification by presenting theory at the end of the book because it emerged as a result of design efforts and empirical inquiry.

The Problematic of CSCL and the Approach of This Book

This book documents my engagement with the issues of CSCL as a research field. Although I believe that much of the group-cognition approach presented is also applicable to CSCW, my own research during the decade represented here was more explicitly oriented to the issues that dominated CSCL at the time. In particular, CSCL is differentiated from related domains in the following ways:

• *Group*   The focus is not on individual learning but on learning in and by small groups of students.

• *Cognition*   The group activity is not one of working but of constructing new understanding and meaning within contexts of instruction and learning.

• *Computer support*   The learning does not take place in isolation but with support by computer-based tools, functionality, microworlds, media, and networks.

• *Building*   The concern is not with the transmission of known facts but with the construction of personally meaningful knowledge.

• *Collaborative*   The interaction of participants is not competitive or accidental but involves systematic efforts to work and learn together.

• *Knowledge*   The orientation is not to drill and practice of specific elementary facts or procedural skills but to discussion, debate, argumentation, and deep understanding.

The fact that these points spell out the title of this book is an indication that the book consists of an extended reflection on the defining problems of CSCL.

The history of CSCL research and theory can be schematically viewed as a gradual progression of ever-increasing critical distance from its starting point, consisting of conceptualizations of learning inherited from dominant traditions in the fields of education and psychology. Much of the early work in CSCL started from this individualistic notion of learning and cognition. For instance, the influence of artificial intelligence (AI) on CSCL—which can be seen particularly clearly in my first three studies—often relied on computational cognitive models of individual learners. For me, at least, dramatic shifts away from this tradition came from the following sources:

• *Mediated cognition*   Vygotsky's work from the 1920s and 1930s only became available in English 50 years later, when it proposed a radically different view of cognition and learning as socially and collaboratively mediated.

• *Distributed cognition*   This alternative, developed by a number of writers (including Suchman, Winograd, Pea, and Hutchins), also stressed the importance of not viewing the mind as isolated from artifacts and other people.

• *Situated learning*   Lave's work applied the situated perspective to learning, showing how learning can be viewed as a community process.

• *Knowledge building*   Scardamalia and Bereiter developed the notion of community learning with a model of collaborative knowledge building in computer-supported classrooms.

• *Meaning making*   Koschmann argued for reconceptualizing knowledge building as meaning making, drawing on theories of conversation analysis and ethnomethodology.

• *Group cognition*   This book arrives at a theory of group cognition by pushing this progression a bit further with the help of a series of software-implementation studies, empirical analyses of interaction, and theoretical reflections on knowledge building.

The notion of group cognition emerged out of the trajectory of the research that is documented in this volume. The software studies in the early chapters attempted to provide support for collaborative knowledge building. They assumed that collaborative knowledge building consisted primarily of forming a group, facilitating interaction among the multiple personal perspectives brought together, and then encouraging the negotiation of shared knowledge. When the classroom use of my software resulted in disappointing levels of knowledge building, I tried to investigate in more detail how knowledge building occurs in actual instances of collaborative learning.

The explorative essays in the middle of the book prepare the way for that analysis and then carry out a microanalysis of one case. The fundamental discovery made in that analysis was that, in small-group collaboration, *meaning is created across the utterances of different people.* That is, the meaning that is created is not a cognitive property of individual minds but a characteristic of the group dialogue. This is a striking result of looking closely at small-group discussions; it is not so visible in monologues (although retrospectively these can be seen as internalized discourses of multiple voices), in dialogues (where the utterances each appear to reflect the ideas of one or the other member of the dyad), or in large communities (where the joint meaning becomes fully anonymous). I call this result of collaborative knowledge building *group cognition.*

For me, this discovery—already implied in certain social science methodologies like conversation analysis—led to a conception of group cognition as central to understanding collaboration and consequently required a rethinking of the entire theoretical framework of CSCL: collaboration, knowledge, meaning, theory building, research methodology, design of support. The paradigm shift from individual cognition to group cognition is challenging—even for people who think they already accept the paradigms of mediated, distributed, and situated cognition. For this reason, the essays in the last part of the book not only outline what I feel is necessary for an appropriate theory but also provide a number of reflections on the perspective of group cognition itself. While the concept of group cognition that I develop is closely related to findings from situated cognition, dialogic theory, symbolic interactionism, ethnomethodology, and social psychology, I think that my focus on small-group collaboration casts it in a distinctive light particularly relevant to CSCL. Most important, I try to explore the core phenomenon in more detail than other writers, who tend to leave some of the most intriguing aspects as mysteries.

Accomplishing this exposition on group cognition requires spelling out a number of interrelated points, each complex in itself. A single conference or journal paper can enunciate only one major point. This book is my attempt to bring the whole argument together. I have organized the steps in this argument into three major book parts:

Part I, Design of Computer Support for Collaboration, presents eight studies of technology design. The first three apply various AI approaches (abbreviated as DODE, LSA, CBR) to typical CSCL or CSCW applications, attempting to harness the power of advanced software techniques to support knowledge building. The next two shift the notion of computer support from AI to providing collaboration media. The final three try to combine these notions of computer support by creating computational support for core collaboration functions in the computational medium. The chapters discuss how to

1. Support teacher collaboration for constructivist curriculum development (written in 1995),

2. Support student learning of text production in summarization (1999),

3. Support the formation of groups of people who can work effectively together (1996),

4. Define the notion of personal interpretive perspectives of group members (1993),

5. Define the role of computational media for collaborative interactions (2000),

6. Support group and personal perspectives (2001),

7. Support group work in collaborative classrooms (2002), and

8. Support the negotiation of shared knowledge by small groups (2002).

Part II, Analysis of Collaborative Knowledge Building, consists of five essays related to research methodology for studying small-group interaction. First, a process model of knowledge building shows how utterances from multiple perspectives may be negotiated to produce shared knowledge. Second, methodological considerations argue that the most important aspects of collaboration are systematically obscured by the approach taken by many leading CSCL studies. A solution is then proposed that integrates knowledge building and merged perspectives with artifacts from distributed cognition theory and the close interpretation of utterances from conversation analysis. This solution is applied to an empirical case of collaboration. This case reveals how group cognition creates shared meaning through the thick interdependencies of everyone's utterances. It also shows how the group builds knowledge about meaning in the world. In particular, these chapters provide

9. A process model of collaborative knowledge building, incorporating perspectives and negotiation (2000),

10. A critique of CSCL research methodologies that obscure the collaborative phenomena (2001),

11. A theoretical framework for empirical analysis of collaboration (2001),

12. Analysis of five students who are building knowledge about a computer simulation (2001), and

13. Analysis of the shared meaning that they built and its relation to the design of the software artifact (2004).

Part III, Theory of Group Cognition, includes eight chapters that reflect on the discovery of group meaning in chapter 12 and its further analysis in chapter 13. As preliminary context, previous theories of communication are reviewed to see how they can be useful, particularly in contexts of computer support. Then a broad-reaching attempt is made to sketch an outline of a social theory of collaborative knowledge building based on the discovery of group cognition. A number of specific issues are taken up from this, including the distinction between meaning making at the group level versus interpretation at the individual level and a critique of the popular notion of common ground. Chapter 18 develops the alternative research methodology hinted at in chapter 10. Chapters 19 and 20 address philosophical possibilities for group cognition, and the final chapter complements chapter 12 with an initial analysis of computer-mediated group cognition, as an indication of the kind of further empirical work needed. The individual chapters of this final part offer

14. A review of traditional theories of communication (2003),

15. A sketch of a theory of building collaborative knowing (2003),

16. An analysis of the relationship of group meaning and individual interpretation (2003),

17. An investigation of group meaning as common ground versus as group cognition (2004),

18. A methodology for making group cognition visible to researchers (2004),

19. Consideration of the question, "Can groups think?" in parallel to the AI question, "Can computers think?" (2004),

20. Exploration of philosophical directions for group-cognition theory (2004), and

21. A wrap-up of the book and an indication of future work (2004).

The discussions in this book are preliminary studies of a science of computer-supported collaboration that is methodologically centered on the group as the primary unit of analysis. From different angles, the individual chapters explore how meanings are constituted, shared, negotiated, preserved, learned, and interpreted socially by small groups within communities. The ideas these essays present themselves emerged out of specific group collaborations.

Situated Concepts

The studies of this book are revised forms of individual papers that were undertaken during the decade between my dissertation at the University of Colorado and my research at Drexel University and were published on various specific occasions. In bringing them together, I have tried to retain the different voices and perspectives that they expressed in their original situations. They look at issues of online collaboration from different vantage points, and I wanted to retain this diversity as a sort of collaboration of me with myself—a collection of selves that I had internalized under the influences of many people, projects, texts, and circumstances. The format of the book thereby reflects the theory it espouses: that knowledge emerges from situated activities involving concrete social interactions and settings and that such knowledge can be encapsulated in vocabularies and texts that are colored by the circumstances of their origins.

Thus, the main chapters of this book are self-contained studies. They are reproduced here as historical artifacts. The surrounding apparatus—this overview, the part introductions, the chapter lead-ins, and the final chapters—has been added to make explicit the gradual emergence of the theme of group cognition. When I started to assemble the original essays, it soon became apparent that the whole collection could be significantly more than the sum of its parts, and I wanted to bring out this interplay of notions and the implications of the overall configuration. The meaning of central concepts, like *group cognition*, are not simply defined; they evolve from chapter to chapter in the hope that they will continue to grow productively in the future.

Concepts can no longer be treated as fixed, self-contained, eternal, universal, and rational, for they reflect a radically historical world. The modern age of the last several centuries may have questioned the existence of God more than the medieval age, but it still maintained an unquestioned faith in a god's-eye view of reality. For Descartes and his successors, an objective physical world was knowable in terms of a series of facts that were expressible in clear and distinct propositions using terms defined by necessary and sufficient conditions. While individuals often seemed to act in eccentric ways, one could still hope to understand human behavior in general in rational terms.

The twentieth century changed all that. Space and time could henceforth be measured only relative to a particular observer; position and velocity of a particle were in principle indeterminate; observation affected what was observed; relatively simple mathematical systems were logically incompletable; people turned out to be poor judges of their subconscious motivations and unable to articulate their largely tacit knowledge; rationality frequently verged on rationalization; revolutions in scientific paradigms transformed what it meant in the affected science for something to be a fact, a concept, or evidence; theories were no longer seen as absolute foundations but as conceptual frameworks that evolved with the inquiry; and knowledge (at least in most of the interesting cases) ended up being an open-ended social process of interpretation.

Certainly, there are still empirical facts and correct answers to many classes of questions. As long as one is working within the standard system of arithmetic, computations have objective answers—by definition of the operations. Some propositions in natural language are also true, like "This sentence is declarative." But others are controversial, such as "Knowledge is socially mediated," and some are even paradoxical: "This sentence is false."

Sciences provide principles and methodologies for judging the validity of propositions within their domain. Statements of personal opinion or individual observation must proceed through processes of peer review, critique, evaluation, argumentation, negotiation, refutation, and so on to be accepted within a scientific community; that is, to evolve into knowledge. These required processes may involve empirical testing, substantiation, or evidence as defined in accord with standards of the field and its community. Of course, the standards themselves may be subject to interpretation, negotiation, or periodic modification.

Permeating this book is the understanding of knowledge, truth, and reality as products of social labor and human interpretation rather than as simply given independently of any history or context. *Interpretation* is central. The foundational essay of part I (chapter 4) discusses how it is possible to design software for groups (groupware) to support the situated interpretation that is integral to working and learning. Interpretation plays the key analytic role in the book, with the analysis of collaboration that forms the heart of part II (chapter 12) presenting an interpretation of a moment of interaction. And in part III (particularly chapter 16), the concepts of interpretation and meaning are seen as intertwined at the phenomenological core of an analysis of group cognition. Throughout the book, the recurrent themes of multiple interpretive perspectives and of the negotiation of shared meanings reveal the centrality of the interpretive approach.

There is a philosophy of interpretation, known since Aristotle as *hermeneutics*. Hans-Geory Gadamer (1988) formulated a contemporary version of philosophical hermeneutics, based largely on ideas proposed by his teacher, Martin Heidegger (1996). A key principle of this hermeneutics is that the meaning of a term should be interpreted based on the history of its effects in the world. Religious, political, and philosophical concepts, for instance, have gradually evolved their meanings as they have interacted with world history and been translated from culture to culture. Words like *being, truth, knowledge, learning,* and *thought* have intricate histories that are encapsulated in their meaning but that are hard to articulate. Rigorous interpretation of textual sources can begin to uncover the layers of meaning that have crystallized and become sedimented in these largely taken-for-granted words.

If we now view meaning making and the production of knowledge as processes of interpretive social construction within communities, then the question arises of whether such fundamental processes can be facilitated by communication and computational technologies. Can technology help groups to build knowledge? Can computer networks bring people together in global knowledge-building communities and support the interaction of their ideas in ways that help to transform the opinions of individuals into the knowledge of groups?

As an inquiry into such themes, this book eschews an artificially systematic logic of presentation and, rather, gathers together textual artifacts that view concrete investigations from a variety of perspectives and situations. My efforts to build software systems were not applications of theory in either the sense of foundational principles or predictive laws. Rather, the experience gained in the practical efforts of part I motivated more fundamental empirical research on computer-mediated collaboration in part II, which in turn led to the theoretical reflections of part III that attempt to develop ways of interpreting, conceptualizing, and discussing the experience. The theory part of this book was written to develop themes that emerged from the juxtaposition of the earlier, empirically grounded studies.

The original versions of the chapters were socially and historically situated. Concepts they developed while expressing their thoughts were, in turn, situated in the contexts of those publications. In being collected into the present book, these papers have been only lightly edited to reduce redundancies and to identify cross-references. Consistency of terminology across chapters has not been enforced as much as it might be to allow configurations of alternative terminologies to bring rich complexes of connotations to bear on the phenomena investigated.

These studies strive to be *essays* in the postmodern sense described by Theodor Adorno (1984, p. 160):

In the essay, concepts do not build a continuum of operations, thought does not advance in a single direction, rather the aspects of the argument interweave as in a carpet. The fruitfulness of the thoughts depends on the density of this texture. Actually, the thinker does not think, but rather transforms himself into an arena of intellectual experience, without simplifying it. . . . All of its concepts are presentable in such a way that they support one another, that each one articulates itself according to the configuration that it forms with the others.

In Adorno's book *Prisms* (1967), essays on specific authors and composers provide separate glimpses of art and artists, but there is no development of a general aesthetic theory that illuminates them all. Adorno's influential approach to cultural criticism emerged from the book as a whole, implicit in the configuration of concrete studies but nowhere in the book articulated in propositions or principles. His analytic paradigm—which rejected the fashionable focus on biographical details of individual geniuses or eccentric artists in favor of reflection on social mediations made visible in the artworks or artifacts themselves—was too incommensurable with prevailing habits of thought to persuade an audience without providing a series of experiences that might gradually shift the reader's perspective. The metaphor of prisms—that white light is an emergent property of the intertwining of its constituent wavelengths—is one of bringing a view into the light by splitting the illumination itself into a spectrum of distinct rays.

The view of collaboration that is expressed in this book itself emerged gradually, in a manner similar to the way that *Prisms* divulged its theories, as I intuitively pursued an inquiry into groupware design, communication analysis, and social philosophy. While I have made some connections explicit, I also hope that the central meanings will emerge for each reader through his or her own interpretive interests.

In keeping with hermeneutic principles, I do not believe that my understanding of the connotations and interconnections of this text is an ultimate one; certainly, it is not a complete one, the only valid one, or the one most relevant to a particular reader. To publish is to contribute to a larger discourse, to expose one's words to unanticipated viewpoints. Words are always open to different interpretations.

The chronology of the studies has generally been roughly maintained within each of the book's parts, for they document a path of discovery, with earlier essays anticipating what was later elaborated. The goal in assembling this collection has been to provide readers with an intellectual experience open-ended enough that they can collaborate in making sense of the enterprise as a whole—to open up "an arena of intellectual experience" without distorting or excessively delimiting it so that it can be shared and interpreted from diverse perspectives.

The essays were written from my own particular and evolving perspective. They are linguistic artifacts that were central to the intellectual development of that perspective and should be read as situated within that gradually developing interpretation. It may help the reader to understand this book if some of the small groups that incubated its ideas are named.

Collaborating with Groups

Although most of the original papers were published under my name, they are without exception collaborative products, artifacts of academic group cognition. Acknowledgments in the notes section at the end of the book indicate the most immediate intellectual debts. Due to collaboration technologies like the Web and e-mail, our ideas are ineluctably the result of global knowledge building. Considered individually, there is little in the way of software features, research methodology, or theoretical concept that is completely original here. Rather, available ideas have been assembled as tools or intellectual resources for making sense of collaboration as a process of constituting group knowing. If anything is original, it is the mix and the twist of perspectives. Rather than wanting to claim that any particular insight or concept in this book is absolutely new, I would like to think that I have pushed rather hard on some of the ideas that are important to CSCL and brought unique considerations to bear. In knowledge building, the configuration of existing ideas and the intermingling of a spectrum of perspectives on those ideas count.

In particular, the ideas presented here have been developed through the work of certain knowledge-building groups or communities:

• The very notion of knowledge-building communities was proposed by Scardamalia and Bereiter and the Computer-Supported International Learning

Environment (CSILE) research group in Toronto. They pioneered CSCL, working on pedagogical theory, system design, and evaluation of computer-supported classroom practices.

• They cited the work of Lave and Wenger on situated learning, a distillation of ideas brewing in an active intellectual community in the San Francisco Bay area that had a formative impact on CSCW in the 1970s.

• The sociocultural theory elaborated there, in turn, had its roots in Vygotsky and his circle, which rose out of the Russian revolution. The activity theory that grew out of that group's thinking still exerts important influences in the CSCW and CSCL communities.

The personal experience behind this book is perhaps most strongly associated with:

• McCall, Fischer, and the Center for LifeLong Learning and Design in Colorado, where I studied, collaborated, and worked on Hermes and CIE in the early 1990s (see chapters 4 and 5);

• The Computers and Society research group led by Herrmann at the University of Dortmund (now at Bochum), which collaborated on WebGuide and negotiation support (chapters 6 and 9);

• Owen Research, Inc., where TCA and the Crew software for NASA were developed (chapters 1 and 3);

• The Institute for Cognitive Science at Boulder, where State the Essence was created (chapter 2);

• The Innovative Technology for Collaborative Learning and Knowledge Building (ITCOLE) project in the European Union (2001–2002), in which I designed BSCL and participated as a visiting scientist in the CSCW group at Fraunhofer-FIT (chapters 7 and 8);

• The research community surrounding the conferences on computer support for collaborative learning, where I was program chair in 2002 (chapter 11); and

• The Virtual Math Teams (VMT) project that colleagues and I launched at Drexel University in 2003 (chapter 21).

But today knowledge building is a global enterprise, and most of the foundational concepts—like knowledge, learning, and meaning—have been forged in the millennia-long discourse of Western philosophy, whose history is reviewed periodically in the following chapters.

Technology as Mediation

When I launched into software development with a fresh degree in artificial intelligence, I worked eagerly at building cognitive aids—if not directly machine cognition—into my systems, developing rather complicated algorithms using search procedures, semantic representations, case-based reasoning, fuzzy logic, and an involved system of hypermedia perspectives. These mechanisms were generally intended to enhance the cognitive abilities of individual system users. When I struggled to get my students to use some of these systems for their work in class, I became increasingly aware of the many barriers to the adoption of such software. In reflecting on this, I began to conceptualize my systems as artifacts that mediated the work of users. It became clear that the hard part of software design was dealing with its social aspects. I switched my emphasis to creating software that would promote group interaction by providing a useful medium for interaction. This led me to study collaboration itself and to view knowledge building as a group effort.

As I became more interested in software as mediator, I organized a seminar with colleagues and graduate students from different fields on computer mediation of collaborative learning. I used the software discussed in chapter 6 and began the analysis of the moment of collaboration that over the years evolved into chapter 12. We tried to deconstruct the term *mediation,* as used in CSCL, by uncovering the history of the term's effects that are sedimented in the word's usage today. We started with its contemporary use in Jean Lave and Etienne Wenger's *Situated Learning* (1991, p. 50): "Briefly, a theory of social practice emphasizes the relational interdependency of agent and world, activity, meaning, cognition, learning and knowing. . . . Knowledge of the socially constituted world is socially mediated and open ended."

This theory of social practice can be traced back to Lev Vygotsky. Vygotsky described what is distinctive to human cognition, psychological processes that are not simply biological abilities, as *mediated cognition.* He analyzed how both signs (words, gestures) and tools (instruments) act as artifacts that mediate human thought and behavior—and he left the way open for other forms of mediation: "A host of other mediated activities might be named; cognitive activity is not limited to the use of tools or signs" (Vygotsky, 1978, p. 55).

Vygotsky attributes the concept of indirect or mediated activity to Hegel and Marx. Where Hegel loved to analyze how two phenomena constitute each other dialectically—such as the master and slave, each of whose identity arises through their relationship to each other—Marx always showed how the relationships arose in concrete socioeconomic history, such as the rise of conflict between the capitalist class and the working class with the establishment of commodity exchange and wage labor. The minds, identities, and social relations of individuals are mediated and formed by the primary factors of the contexts in which they are situated.

In this book, mediation plays a central role in group cognition, taken as an emergent phenomenon of small-group collaboration. The computer support of collaboration is analyzed as a mediating technology whose design and use forms and transforms the nature of the interactions and their products.

Mediation is a complex and unfamiliar term. In popular and legal usage, it might refer to the intervention of a third party to resolve a dispute between two people. In philosophy, it is related to *media*, *middle*, and *intermediate*. So in CSCL or CSCW, we can say that a software environment provides a *medium* for collaboration or that it plays an *intermediate* role in the *midst* of the collaborators. The contact between the collaborators is not direct or *im-mediate* but is *mediated* by the software. Recognizing that when human interaction takes place through a technological medium the technical characteristics influence—or *mediate*—the nature of the interaction, we can inquire into the effects of various media on collaboration. For a given task, for instance, should people use a text-based, asynchronous medium? How does this choice both facilitate and constrain their interaction? If the software intervenes between collaborating people, how should it represent them to each other to promote social bonding and understanding of each other's work?

The classic analyses of mediation will reappear in the theoretical part of the book. The term *mediation*—perhaps even more than other key terms in this book—takes on a variety of interrelated meanings and roles. These emerge gradually as the book unfolds; they are both refined and enriched—mediated—by relations with other technical terms. The point for now is to start to think of group-collaboration software as artifacts that mediate the cognition of their individual users and support the group cognition of their user community.

Mediation by Small Groups

Small groups are the engines of knowledge building. The knowing that groups build up in manifold forms is what becomes internalized by their members as individual learning and externalized in their communities as certifiable knowledge. At least, that is a central premise of this book.

The last several chapters of this book take various approaches to exploring the concept of group cognition because this concept involves such a difficult, counterintuitive way of thinking for many people. This is because cognition is often assumed to be associated with psychological processes contained in individual minds.

The usual story, at least in Western culture of the past three hundred years, goes something like this: an individual experiences reality through his senses (the para-

Figure 1
Auguste Rodin, The Thinker, 1881, bronze, Rodin Museum, Philadelphia, PA. Photo: G. Stahl, 2004.

digmatic rational thinker in this tradition is often assumed to be male). He thinks about his experience in his mind; *cognition*, stemming from the Latin *cogito* for "I think," refers to mental activities that take place in the individual thinker's head (see figure 1). He may articulate a mental thought by putting it into language, stating it as a linguistic proposition whose truth value is a function of the proposition's correspondence with a state of affairs in the world. Language, in this view, is a medium for transferring meanings from one mind to another by representing reality. The recipient of a stated proposition understands its meaning based on his own sense experience as well as his rather unproblematic understanding of the meanings of language.

The story based on the mediation of group cognition is rather different: here, language is an infinitely generative system of symbolic artifacts that encapsulate and embody the cultural experiences of a community. Language is a social product of the interaction of groups—not primarily of individuals—acting in the world in culturally mediated ways. Individuals who are socialized into the community learn to speak and understand language as part of their learning to participate in that community. In the process, they internalize the use of language as silent self-talk, internal dialogue, rehearsed talk, narratives of rational accountability, senses of morality, conflicted dream lives, habits, personal identities, and their tacit background knowledge largely preserved in language understanding. In this story, cognition initially takes place primarily in group processes of interpersonal interaction, which include parent and child, friend and friend, husband and wife, teacher and student, boss and employee, extended family, social network, gang, tribe, neighborhood, community of practice, and so on. The products of cognition exist in discourse, symbolic representations, meaningful gestures, patterns of behavior; they persist in texts and other inscriptions, in physical artifacts, in cultural standards, and in the memories of individual minds. Individual cognition emerges as a secondary effect, although it later seems to acquire a dominant role in our introspective narratives.

Most people have trouble accepting the group-based story at first and viewing collaborative phenomena in these terms. Therefore, the group emphasis emerges gradually in this book rather than being assumed from the start. Indeed, that is what happened during my decade-long inquiry that is documented in these studies.

Although one can see many examples of the decisive role of small groups in the CSCW and CSCL literature, their pivotal function is rarely explicitly acknowledged and reflected on. For instance, the two prevailing paradigms of learning in CSCL—which are referred to in chapter 17 as the acquisition metaphor and the participation metaphor—focus on the individual and the community, respectively, not on the intermediate small group. In the former paradigm, learning consists in the acquisition of knowledge by an individual; for instance, a student acquires facts from a teacher's lesson. In the later, learning consists in knowledgeable participation in a community of practice; for instance, an apprentice becomes a more skilled practitioner of a trade. But if one looks closely at the examples typically given to illustrate each paradigm, one sees that there is usually a small group at work in the specific learning situation. In a healthy classroom there are likely to be cliques of students learning together in subtle ways, even if the lesson is not organized as collaborative learning with formal group work. Their group practices may or may not be structured in ways that support individual participants to learn as the group builds knowledge. In apprenticeship training, a master is likely to work with a few apprentices, and they work together in various ways as a small group; it is not as though all the apprentice tailors or carpenters or architects in a city are being trained together. The community of practice functions through an effective division into small working groups.

Some theories, like activity theory, insist on viewing learning at both the individual and the community levels. Although their examples again typically feature small groups, the general theory highlights the individual and the large community but has no theoretical representation of the critical small groups in which the individuals carry on their concrete interactions and into which the community is hierarchically structured (see chapter 21).

My own experiences during the studies reported here and in my apprenticeships in philosophy and computer science that preceded them impressed on me the importance of working groups, reading circles, and informal professional discussion occasions for the genesis of new ideas and insights. The same can be seen on a world-historical scale. Quantum jumps in human knowledge building emerge from centers of group interaction: the Bauhaus designers at Weimar, the postimpressionist artists in Paris salons, the Vienna Circle, the Frankfurt School—in the past, these communities were necessarily geographic locations where people could come together in small groups at the same time and place.

The obvious question once we recognize the catalytic role of small groups in knowledge building is whether we can design computer-supported environments to create effective groups across time and space. Based on my experiences, documented in part I, I came to the conclusion that to achieve this goal we need a degree of understanding of small-group cognition that does not currently exist. To design effective media, we need to develop a theory of mediated collaboration through a design-based research agenda of analysis of small-group cognition. Most theories of knowledge building in working and learning have focused primarily on the two extreme scales: the individual unit of analysis as the acquirer of knowledge and the community unit of analysis as the context within which participation takes place. We now need to focus on the intermediate scale: the small-group unit of analysis as the discourse in which knowledge actually emerges.

The size of groups can vary enormously. This book tends to focus on small groups of a few people (say, three to five) meeting for short periods. Given the seeming importance of this scale, it is surprising how little research on computer-supported collaboration has focused *methodologically* on units of this size. Traditional approaches to learning—even to collaborative learning in small groups—measure effects on individuals. More recent writings talk about whole communities of practice. Most of the relatively few studies of collaboration that do talk of groups look at dyads, where interactions are easier to describe but qualitatively different from those in somewhat larger groups. Even in triads, interactions are more complex, and it is less tempting to attribute emergent ideas to individual members than in dyads.

The emphasis on the group as unit of analysis is definitive of this book. It is not just a matter of claiming that it is time to focus software development on groupware. It is also a methodological rejection of individualism as a focus of empirical analysis and cognitive theory. The book argues that software should support cooperative work and collaborative learning, should be assessed at the group level, and should be designed to foster group cognition.

This book provides different perspectives on the concept of group cognition, but the concept of group cognition *as discourse* is not fully or systematically worked out in detail. Neither are the complex layers of mediation presented, by which interactions at the small-group unit of analysis mediate between individuals and social structures. This is because it is premature to attempt this; much empirical analysis is needed first. The conclusions of this book simply try to prepare the way for future studies of group cognition.

The Promise of Collaborating with Technology

Online workgroups are becoming increasingly popular, freeing learners and workers from the traditional constraints of time and place for schooling and employment. Commercial software offers basic mechanisms and media to support collaboration. However, we are still far from understanding how to work with technology to support collaboration in practice. Having borrowed technologies, research methodologies, and theories from allied fields, it may now be time for the sciences of collaboration to forge their own tools and approaches, honed to the specifics of the field.

This book tries to explore how to create a science of collaboration support grounded in a fine-grained understanding of how people act, work, learn, and think together. It approaches this by focusing the discussion of software design, interaction analysis, and conceptual frameworks on central, paradigmatic phenomena of small-group collaboration, such as multiple interpretive perspectives, intersubjective meaning making, and knowledge building at the group unit of analysis.

The view of group cognition that emerges from the following essays is one worth working hard to support with technology. Group cognition is presented in stronger terms than previous descriptions of distributed cognition. Here it is argued that high-level thinking and other cognitive activities take place in group discourse and that these are most appropriately analyzed at the small-group unit of analysis. The focus on mediation of group cognition is presented more explicitly than elsewhere, suggesting implications for theory, methodology, design, and future research generally.

Technology in social contexts can take many paths of development in the near future. Globally networked computers provide a promise of a future of worldwide collaboration founded on small-group interactions. Reaching such a future will require overcoming the ideologies of individualism in system design, empirical methodology, and collaboration theory, as well as in everyday practice.

This is a tall order. Today, many people react against the ideals of collaboration and the concept of group cognition based on unfortunate personal experiences, the inadequacies of current technologies, and deeply ingrained senses of competition. Although so much working, learning, and knowledge building takes place through teamwork these days, goals, conceptualizations, and reward structures are still oriented toward individual achievement. Collaboration is often feared as something that might detract from individual accomplishments, rather than valued as something that could facilitate a variety of positive outcomes for everyone. The specter of group-think—where crowd mentality overwhelms individual rationality—is used as an argument against collaboration rather than as a motivation for understanding better how to support healthy collaboration.

We need to continue designing software functionality and associated social practices; continue analyzing the social and cognitive processes that take place during successful collaboration; and continue theorizing about the nature of collaborative learning, working, and acting with technology. The studies in this book are attempts to do just that. They are not intended to provide final answers or to define recipes for designing software or conducting research. They do not claim to confirm the hypotheses, propose the theories, or formulate the methodologies they call for. Rather, they aim to open up a suggestive view of these bewildering realms of inquiry. I hope that by stimulating group efforts to investigate proposed approaches to design, analysis, and theory, they can contribute in some modest measure to our future success in understanding, supporting, and engaging in effective group cognition.

I

Design of Computer Support for Collaboration

Studies of Technology Design

The chapters of this book were written over a number of years while I was finding my way toward a conception of group cognition that could be useful for computer-supported collaborative learning and cooperative work (CSCL and CSCW). Only near the end of that period, in editing the essays into a unified book, did the coherence of the undertaking become clear to me. In presenting these writings together, I think it is important to provide some guidance to the readers. Therefore, I provide brief introductions to the three parts and the 21 chapters to resituate the essays in the book's mission.

Theoretical Background to Part I

The theory presented in this book comes at the end, emanating out of the design studies and the empirical analysis of collaboration. This does not mean that the work described in the design studies of the first section had no theoretical framing. On the contrary, in the early 1990s when I turned my full-time attention to issues of CSCL, my academic training in computer science, artificial intelligence (AI), and cognitive science, which immediately preceded these studies, was particularly influenced by two theoretical orientations: situated cognition and domain-oriented design environments.

Situated Cognition   As a graduate student, I met with a small reading group of fellow students for several years, discussing the then recent works of situated cognition (Brown & Duguid, 1991; Donald, 1991; Dreyfus, 1991; Ehn, 1988; Lave & Wenger, 1991; Schön, 1983; Suchman, 1987; Winograd & Flores, 1986), which challenged the assumptions of traditional AI. These writings proposed the centrality of tacit knowledge, implicitly arguing that AI's reliance on capturing explicit knowledge was inadequate for modeling or replacing human understanding. They showed that people act based on their being situated in specific settings with particular activities, artifacts, histories, and colleagues. Shared knowledge is not a stockpile of fixed facts that can be represented in a database and queried on all occasions but an ongoing accomplishment of concrete groups of people engaged in continuing communication and negotiation. Furthermore, knowing is fundamentally perspectival and interpretive.

Domain-Oriented Design Environments   I was at that time associated with the research lab of the Center for Lifelong Learning and Design (L3D) directed by Gerhard Fischer, which developed the domain-oriented design environment (DODE) approach to software systems for designers (Fischer et al., 1993; Fischer, 1994; Fischer et al., 1998). The idea was that one could build a software system to support designers in a given domain—say, kitchen design—by integrating such components as a drawing sketchpad, a palette of icons representing items from the domain (stovetops, tables, walls), a set of critiquing rules (sink under a window, dishwasher to the right), a hypertext of design rationale, a catalog of previous designs or templates, a searching mechanism, and a facility for adding new palette items, among others. My dissertation system, Hermes, was a system that allowed one to put together a DODE for a given domain and to structure different professional perspectives on the knowledge in the system. I adapted Hermes to create a DODE for lunar-habitat designers. Software designs contained in the studies of part I more or less start from this approach: TCA was a DODE for teachers designing curriculum and CIE was a DODE for computer-network designers.

This theoretical background is presented primarily in chapter 4. Before presenting that, however, I wanted to give a feel for the problematic nature of CSCL and CSCW by providing examples of designing software to support constructivist education (chapter 1), computational support for learning (chapter 2), or algorithms for selecting group members (chapter 3).

The Studies in Part I

The eight case studies included in part I provide little windows on illustrative experiences of designing software for collaborative knowledge building. They are not controlled experiments with rigorous conclusions. These studies hang together rather like the years of a modern-day life, darting off in unexpected directions but without ever losing the connectedness of one's identity—one's evolving yet enduring personal perspective on the world.

Each study contains a parable: a brief, idiosyncratic, and inscrutable tale whose moral is open to—indeed begs for—interpretation and debate. The parables describe fragmentary experiments that pose questions and that, in their specificity and materiality, allow the feedback of reality to be experienced and pondered.

Some of the studies include technical details that may not be interesting or particularly meaningful to all readers. Indeed, it is hard to imagine many readers whose backgrounds would allow them to follow in detail all the chapters of this book. This is an unavoidable problem for interdisciplinary topics. The original papers for part I were written for specialists in computer science, and their details remain integral to the argumentation of the specific study but not necessarily essential to the larger implications of the book.

The book is structured so that readers can feel free to skip around. There is an intended flow to the argument of the book—summarized in these introductions to the three parts—but the chapters are each self-contained essays that can largely stand on their own or be visited in accordance with each reader's particular needs.

Part I explores, in particular ways, some of the major forms of computer support that seem desirable for collaborative knowledge building, shared meaning making, and group cognition. The first three chapters address the needs of individual teachers, students, and group members, respectively, as they interact with shared resources and activities. The individual perspective is then systematically matched with group perspectives in the next three chapters. The final chapters of part I develop a mechanism for moving knowledge among perspectives. Along the way, issues of individual, small-group, and community levels are increasingly distinguished and supported. Support for group formation, perspectives, and negotiation is prototyped and tested.

Study 1, Teachers Curriculum Assistant (TCA)   The book starts with a gentle introduction to a typical application of designing computer support for collaboration. The application is the Teachers Curriculum Assistant (TCA), a system for helping teachers to share curriculum that responds to educational research's recommendation of constructivist learning. It is a CSCW system in that it supports communities of professional teachers as they cooperate in their work. At the same time, it is a CSCL system that can help to generate, refine, and propagate curriculum for collaborative learning by students, either online or otherwise. The study is an attempt to design an integrated knowledge-based system that supports five key functions associated with the development of innovative curriculum by communities of teachers. Interfaces for the five functions are illustrated.

Study 2, State the Essence   The next study turns to computer support for students, either in groups or singly. The application, State the Essence, is a program that gives students feedback on summaries they compose from brief essays. Significantly increasing students' or groups' time on task and encouraging them to create multiple drafts of their essays before submitting them to a teacher, the software uses a statistical analysis of natural-language semantics to evaluate and compare texts.

Rather than focusing on student outcomes, the study describes some of the complexities of adapting an algorithmic technique to a classroom educational tool.

Study 3, CREW   The question in this study is how software can predict the behavior of a group of people working together under special conditions. Developed for the American space agency to help the agency select groups of astronauts for the international space station, the Crew software modeled a set of psychological factors for subjects participating in a prolonged space mission. Crew was designed to take advantage of psychological data being collected on outer-space, under-sea, and Antarctic winter-over missions confining small groups of people in restricted spaces for prolonged periods. The software combined a number of statistical and AI techniques.

Study 4, Hermes   This study was actually written earlier than the preceding ones, but it is probably best read following them. It describes at an abstract level the theoretical framework behind the design of the systems discussed in the other studies. It is perhaps also critical of some assumptions underlying their mechanisms. It develops a concept of situated interpretation that arises from design theories and writings on situated cognition. These sources raised fundamental questions about traditional AI, based as it was on assumptions of explicit, objective, universal, and rational knowledge. Hermes tried to capture and represent tacit, interpretive, situated knowledge. It was a hypermedia framework for creating domain-oriented design environments. It provided design and software elements for interpretive perspectives, end-user programming languages, and adaptive displays, all built on a shared knowledge base.

Study 5, CIE   A critical transition occurs in this study—away from software that is designed to amplify human intelligence with AI techniques and instead toward the goal of software designed to support group interaction by providing structured media of communication, sharing, and collaboration. While TCA attempted to use an early version of the Internet to allow communities to share educational artifacts, CIE aimed to turn the Web into a shared workspace for a community of practice. The specific community supported by the CIE prototype was the group of people who design and maintain local area computer networks (LANs)—for instance, at university departments.

Study 6, WebGuide   WebGuide was a several-year effort to design support for interpretive perspectives focusing on the key idea proposed by Hermes (computational perspectives) and trying to adapt the perspectivity concept to asynchronous threaded discussions. The design study was situated within the task of providing a shared guide to the Web for small workgroups and whole classrooms of students, including the classroom where Essence was developed. Insights gained from adoption hurdles with this system motivated a push to better understand collaboration and computer-mediated communication, resulting in a WebGuide-supported seminar on mediation, which is discussed in this study. This seminar began the theoretical reflections that percolate throughout part II and then dominate in part III. The WebGuide system was a good example of trying to harness computational power to support the dynamic selection and presentation of information in accordance with different user perspectives.

Study 7, Synergeia   Several limitations of WebGuide led to the Synergeia design undertaking. The WebGuide perspectives mechanism was too complicated for users, and additional collaboration supports were needed, particularly support for group negotiation. An established CSCW system was redesigned for classroom usage, including a simplified system of class, group, and individual perspectives and a mechanism for groups to negotiate agreement on shared knowledge-building artifacts. The text of this study began as a design scenario that guided development of Synergeia and then morphed into its training manual for teachers.

Study 8, BSCL   This study takes a closer look at the design rationale for the negotiation mechanism of the previous study. The BSCL system illustrates designs for several important functions of collaborative learning: formation of groups (by the teacher); perspectives for the class, small workgroups, and individuals; and negotiation of shared knowledge artifacts. These functions are integrated into the mature BSCW software system, with support for synchronous chat and shared whiteboard, asynchronous threaded discussion with note types, social-awareness features, and shared workspaces (folder hierarchies for documents). The central point of this study is that negotiation is not just a matter of individuals voting based on their preconceived ideas; it is a group process of constructing knowledge artifacts and then establishing a consensus that the group has reached a shared understanding of this knowledge and that it is ready to display it for others.

The chapters of part I demonstrate a progression that was not uncommon in CSCL and CSCW around the turn of the century. A twentieth-century fascination with technological solutions reached its denouement in AI systems that required more effort than expected and provided less help than promised. In the twenty-first century, researchers acknowledged that systems needed to be user-centric and should concentrate on taking the best advantage of human and group intelligence. In this new context, the important thing for groupware was to optimize the formation of effective groups, help them to articulate and synthesize different knowledge-building perspectives, and support the negotiation of shared group knowledge. This shift should become apparent in the progression of software studies in part I.

1

Share Globally, Adapt Locally

For this project,[1] I worked with several colleagues in Boulder, Colorado, to apply what we understood about educational theory and about approaches to computer support of collaboration to the plight of classroom teachers. Constructivist approaches to learning were well established as being favored by most educational researchers. The problem was disseminating this to teachers in the actual classrooms. Even when teachers were trained in the theory, they had no practical instructional materials to help them implement the new approach on a daily basis. Few textbooks or other resources were available, and teachers had to spend vast amounts of time they did not have to integrate those few materials into classroom practices and institutional requirements.

The Internet was just starting to reach public schools, so we tried to devise computer-based supports for disseminating constructivist resources and for helping teachers to adapt and apply them. We prototyped a high-functionality design environment for communities of teachers to construct innovative lesson plans together, using a growing database of appropriately structured and annotated resources. This was an experiment in designing a software system for teachers to engage in collaborative knowledge building.

This study provides an example of a real-world problem confronting teachers. It tries to apply the power of artificial intelligence and domain-oriented design environment technologies to support collaboration at a distance. The failure of the project to move beyond the design phase suggests that the institutional context of schooling and the intricacies of potential interaction among classroom teachers need further examination.

Many teachers yearn to break through the confines of traditional textbook-centered teaching and present activities that encourage students to explore and construct their own knowledge. But this requires developing innovative materials and curriculum tailored to local students. Teachers have neither the time nor the information to do much of this from scratch.

The Internet provides a medium for globally sharing innovative educational resources. School districts and teacher organizations have already begun to post curriculum ideas on Internet servers. However, just storing unrelated educational materials on the Internet does not by itself solve the problem. It is too hard to find the resources to meet specific needs. Teachers need software for locating material-rich sites across the network, searching the individual curriculum sources, adapting retrieved materials to their classrooms, organizing these resources in coherent lesson plans, and sharing their experiences across the Internet.

In response to these needs, I designed and prototyped a Teacher's Curriculum Assistant (TCA) that provides software support for teachers to make effective use of educational resources posted to the Internet. TCA maintains information for finding educational resources distributed on the Internet. It provides query and browsing mechanisms for exploring what is available. Tools are included for tailoring retrieved resources, creating supplementary materials, and designing innovative curricula. TCA encourages teachers to annotate and upload successfully used curricula to Internet servers and thereby share their ideas with other educators. In this chapter, I describe the need for such computer support and discuss what I have learned from designing TCA.

The Internet's Potential for Collaboration Support

The Internet has the potential to transform educational curriculum development beyond the horizons of our foresight. In 1994, the process was just beginning as educators across the country started to post their favorite curriculum ideas for others to share. This first tentative step revealed the difficulties inherent in using such potentially enormous, loosely structured sources of information. As the Internet becomes a more popular medium for sharing curricula, teachers, wandering around the Internet looking for ideas to use in their classrooms, confront a set of problems that will not go away on its own. On the contrary,

1. Teachers have to *locate* sites of curriculum ideas scattered across the network; there is currently no system for announcing the locations of these sites.

2. They have to *search* through the offerings at each site for useful items. While some sites provide search mechanisms for their databases, each has different interfaces, tools, and indexing schemes that must be learned before the curricula can be accessed.

3. They have to *adapt* items they find to the needs of their particular classroom: to local standards, the current curriculum, their own teaching preferences, and the needs or learning styles of their various students.

4. They have to *organize* the new ideas within coherent curricula that build toward long-term pedagogical goals.

5. They have to *share* their experiences using the curriculum or their own new ideas with others who use the resources.

In many fields, professionals have turned to productivity software—like spreadsheets for accountants—to help them manage tasks involving complex sources of information. I believe that teachers should be given similar computer-based tools to meet the problems listed above. If this software is designed to empower teachers—perhaps in conjunction with their students—in open-ended ways, opportunities will materialize that we cannot now imagine.

In this chapter, I consider how the sharing of curriculum ideas over the Internet can be made more effective in transforming education. I advance the understanding of specific issues in the creation of software designed to help classroom teachers develop curricula and increase productivity and introduce the Teacher's Curriculum Assistant (TCA) that I built for this purpose. First, I discuss the nature of constructivist curriculum, contrasting it with traditional approaches based on behaviorist theory. Then I present an example of a problem-solving environment for high school mathematics students. The example illustrates why teachers need help to construct this kind of student-centered curriculum. I provide a scenario of a teacher developing a curriculum using productivity software like TCA and conclude by discussing some issues I feel will be important in *maximizing the effectiveness of the Internet* as a medium for the dissemination of innovative curricula for educational reform.

The Problem of Curriculum in Educational Reform

The distribution of curriculum over the Internet and the use of productivity software for searching and adapting posted ideas could benefit any pedagogical approach. However, it is particularly crucial for advancing *reform* in education.

The barriers to educational reform are legion, as many people since John Dewey have found. Teachers, administrators, parents, and students must all be convinced that traditional schooling is not the most effective way to provide an adequate foundation for life in the future. They must be trained in the new sensitivities required. Once everyone agrees and is ready to implement the new approach, there is still a problem: what activities and materials should be presented on a day-to-day basis? This concrete question is the one that Internet sharing can best address. I generalize the term *curriculum* to cover this question.

Consider curricula for mathematics. Here, the reform approach is to emphasize the qualitative understanding of mathematical ways of thinking rather than to stress rote memorization of quantitative facts or "number skills." *Behaviorist* learning theory supported the view that one method of training could work for all students; reformers face a much more complex challenge. There is a growing consensus among educational theorists that different students in different situations construct their understandings in different ways (Greeno, 1993). This approach is often called *constructivism* or *constructionism* (Papert, 1993). It implies that teachers must creatively structure the learning environments of their students to provide opportunities for discovery and must guide individual learners to reach insights in their own ways.

Behaviorism and constructivism differ primarily in their views of how students build their knowledge. Traditional, rationalist education assumed that there was a logical sequence of facts and standard skills that had to be learned successively. The problem was simply to transfer bits of information to students in a logical order, with little concern for how students acquire knowledge. Early attempts at designing educational software took this approach to its extreme, breaking down curricula into isolated atomic propositions and feeding these predigested facts to the students. This approach to education was suited to the industrial age, in which workers on assembly lines performed well-defined, sequential tasks.

According to constructivism, learners *interpret* problems in their environments using *conceptual frameworks* that they developed in the past (Roschelle, 1996). In challenging cases, problems can require changes in the frameworks. Such conceptual change is the essence of learning: people's understanding evolves so that they can comprehend their environment. To teach a student a mathematical method or a scientific theory is not to place a set of propositional facts into her mind but to give her a new tool that she can make her own and use in her own ways in comprehending her world.

Constructivism does not entail the rejection of a curriculum. Rather, it requires a more complex and flexible curriculum. Traditionally, a curriculum consisted of a textual theoretical lesson, a set of drills for students to practice, and a test to evaluate if the students could perform the desired behaviors. In contrast, a *constructivist curriculum* might target certain cognitive skills, provide a setting of resources and activities to serve as a catalyst for the development of these skills, and then offer opportunities for students to articulate their evolving understandings (NCTM, 1989). The cognitive skills in math, for example, might include qualitative reasoning about graphs, number lines, algorithms, or proofs.

My colleagues on the project and I believe that the movement from viewing a curriculum as fact-centered to viewing it as cognitive-tool-centered is appropriate for the postmodern (postindustrial, postrationalist, postbehaviorist) period. Cognitive tools include *alternative knowledge representations* (Norman, 1993). As researchers in artificial intelligence, we know that knowledge representations are key to characterizing or modeling cognition. We have also found that professionals working in typical contemporary occupations focus much of their effort on developing and using alternative knowledge representations that are adapted to their tasks (Sumner, 1995). Curricula to prepare people for the next generation of jobs would do well to familiarize students with the creation and use of alternative conceptual representations.

A Diverse Learning Ecology

Teachers need help to create learning environments that stimulate the construction and evolution of understanding through student exploration using multiple conceptual representations. *A stimulating learning environment is one with a rich ecology in which many elements interact in subtle ways.* In this section, I present an illustration of a rich ecology for learning mathematical thinking that includes inductive reasoning, recursive computation, spreadsheet representation, graphing, simultaneous equations, and programming languages.

A typical curriculum suggestion that might be posted on an educational resources listing on the Internet is the *problem of regions of a circle*: Given n points on the circumference of a circle, what is the maximum number of regions one can divide the circle into by drawing straight lines connecting the points? (See figure 1.1.) For instance, connecting two points divides the circle into two regions; connecting three points with three lines creates four regions. This is a potentially fascinating problem because its subtleties can be explored at length using just algebra and several varieties of clear thinking.

The problem with this curriculum offering as an Internet posting is that it has not been placed in a rich setting. To be useful, a fuller curriculum providing a set of conceptual tools is needed. For instance, a discussion of inductive reasoning brings out some of the character of this particular problem. If one counts the number of regions, $R(n)$, for $n = 1$ to 6, one obtains the doubling series 1, 2, 4, 8, 16, 31. Almost! One expects the last of these numbers to be 32, but that last region is nowhere to be found. For larger n, the series diverges completely from the powers of 2. Why? Here, *inductive reasoning* can come to the rescue of the hasty inductive assumption—if, that is, the problem is accompanied by a discussion of inductive reasoning.

Consider the general case of n points. Assume that the answer is known for $n - 1$ points, and think about how many new regions are created by adding the

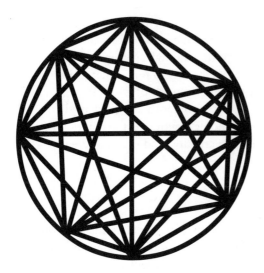

Figure 1.1
Regions of a circle; $n = 8$.

nth point and connecting it to each of the $n - 1$ old points. There is a definite pattern at work here. It may take a couple days of careful thought to work it out. It would also help if the *sigma notation* for sums of indexed terms is explained as a representational tool for working on the problem. Perhaps a collaborative group effort will be needed to check each step and avoid mistakes.

At this point, a teacher might introduce the notion of *recursion* and relate it to induction. If the students can program in Logo or Pascal (programming languages that can represent recursive processes), they could put the general formula into a simple but powerful program that could generate results for hundreds of values of n very quickly without the tedious and error-prone process of counting regions in drawings. It would be nice to formalize the derivation of this result with a *deductive proof*, if the method of formulating proofs has been explained.

Now that students are confident that they have the correct values for many n, they can enter these values in a *spreadsheet* to explore them. The first representation they might want to see is a *graph* of $R(n)$ and n. On the spreadsheet, they could make a column that displays the difference between each $R(n)$ and its corresponding $R(n - 1)$. Copying this column several times, they would find that the fourth column of differences is constant. This result means that $R(n)$ follows a fourth-order equation, which can be found by solving *simultaneous equations*.

The point of this example is that sharing the isolated statement of the problem is not enough. The rich learning experience involves being introduced to alternative representations of the problem: induction, recursion, spreadsheet differences, graphs, computer languages, simultaneous equations, and so on. There is not one correct method for tackling a problem like this; a mathematically literate person needs to be able to view the problem's many facets through several conceptual frameworks.

A curriculum in the new paradigm typically consists of stimulating problems immersed in environments with richly interacting ecologies, including cognitive skills, knowledge representations, computational tools, related problems, and reference materials. Perhaps a creative teacher with unlimited preparation time could put these materials together. However, the reality is that teachers deserve all the support they can get if they are to prepare and present the complex learning ecologies that constructivist reforms call for. Computer support for curriculum development should make the kinds of resources shown in figure 1.2 readily available.

From Database to Design Environment

Curriculum planning for learning ecologies is not a simple matter of picking consecutive pages out of a standard textbook or of working out a sequential presentation of material that builds up to fixed learning achievements. Rather, it is a matter of *design*. To support teachers in developing curriculum that achieves this, we must go beyond databases of isolated resources to provide *design environments for curriculum development*.

It may seem to be an overwhelming task to design an effective learning environment for promoting the development of basic cognitive skills. However, dozens of reform curricula have already been created. *The problem now is to disseminate these in ways that allow teachers to adapt them* to their local needs and to reuse them as templates for additional new curricula. It is instructive to look at a recent attempt to make this type of curriculum available. The CD-ROM *MathFinder Sourcebook: A Collection of Resources for Mathematics Reform* excerpts materials from 30 new math curricula (Kreindler & Zahm, 1992). Like the posting of curriculum ideas at several Internet sites, this is an important early step at electronic dissemination.

Unfortunately, MathFinder has a number of serious limitations due to its CD-ROM (read-only) format. It relies on a fixed database of resources that allows resources to be *located* but not expanded or revised. Its indexing is relatively simple—primarily oriented toward illustrating a particular set of math standards—yet its *search mechanism is cumbersome* for many teachers. Because its resources are stored in bitmap images, they *cannot be adapted* in any way by teachers or students. Moreover, MathFinder provides *no facility for organizing resources into curricula*—despite the fact that most of the resources it includes are excerpted from

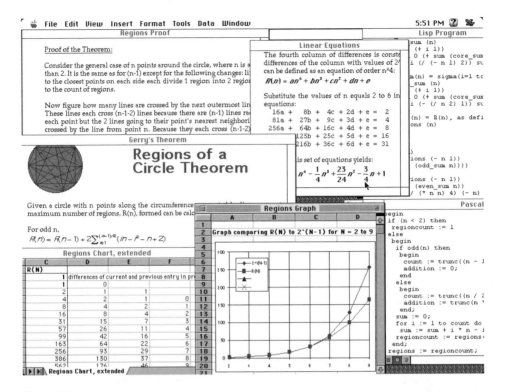

Figure 1.2
A number of multimedia resources related to the "regions of a circle" problem. These include textual documents, drawings, equations, spreadsheets, graphs, and computer-program source code.

carefully constructed curricula. Because it is sold as a read-only commodity, Math-Finder *does not allow teachers to share* their experiences with annotations or to add their own curricular ideas. Thus, of the five issues listed in the introduction to this chapter—locating, searching, adapting, organizing, and sharing—MathFinder provides only a partial solution to the issues of location and search.

An alternative approach is suggested by our work on *domain-oriented design environments* (Fischer et al., 1993; Fischer et al., 1998; Repenning & Sumner, 1995; Stahl, McCall, & Peper, 1992; Stahl, 1993a). A software design environment provides a flexible workspace for the construction of artifacts and places useful design tools and materials close at hand. A design environment for curriculum development goes substantially beyond a database of individual resources. Based on this approach, we built a prototype version of a Teacher's Curriculum Assistant (TCA).

TCA includes a *catalog* of previously designed curricula that can be reused and modified. It has a *gallery* of educational resources that can be inserted into partial curriculum designs. There is a *workspace*, into which curricula from the catalog can be loaded and resources from the gallery inserted. It is also possible for a teacher to specify criteria for the desired curriculum. *Specifications* are used for searching the case base of curricula, adapting the resources, and *critiquing* new designs.

TCA allows teachers to download curricular resources from the Internet and to create coherent classroom activities tailored to local circumstances. In particular, TCA addresses the set of five issues identified in the introduction:

1. TCA is built on a database of information about educational resources posted to the Internet, so it provides a mechanism for teachers to *locate* sources of curriculum ideas at scattered Internet sites.

2. The TCA database indexes each resource in a uniform way, allowing teachers to *search* for all items meeting desired conditions.

3. TCA includes tools to help teachers *adapt* items they find to the needs of their classroom.

4. TCA provides a design workspace for *organizing* retrieved ideas into lesson plans that build toward long-term goals.

5. TCA lets teachers conveniently *share* their experiences through the Internet.

The TCA Prototype

Based on preliminary study of these issues, a TCA prototype has been developed. Six interface screens have been designed for teacher support: Profiler, Explorer, Versions, Editor, Planner, and Networker.

The Profiler, Explorer, and Versions interfaces work together for information retrieval (figure 1.3). The Profiler helps teachers define classroom profiles and locates curricula and resources that match the profile. The Explorer displays these items and allows the teacher to search through them to find related items. Versions then helps the teacher select from alternative versions that have been adapted by other teachers. Through these interfaces, teachers can locate the available materials that most closely match their personal needs; this makes it easier to tailor the materials to individual requirements.

The Planner, Editor, and Networker help the teacher to prepare resources and curricula and to share the results of classroom use (figure 1.4). The Planner is a design environment for reusing and reorganizing lesson plans. The Editor allows the teacher to modify and adapt resources. This is a primary means of personaliz-

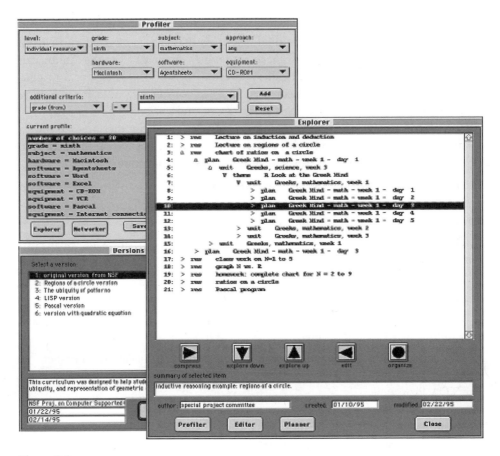

Figure 1.3
The TCA software interface for locating, searching, and selecting resources and curricula: Profiler, Explorer, and Versions.

ing a curriculum to individual classroom circumstances. Finally, the Networker supports interactions with the Internet, providing a two-way medium of communication with a global community of teachers. Using the Networker, a teacher can share personalized versions of standard curricula with other teachers who might have similar needs.

To illustrate how TCA works, each of the five issues is discussed in the following sections. These sections present a scenario of a teacher using TCA to locate resources, search through them, adapt selected resources, organize them into a curriculum, and share the results with other teachers.

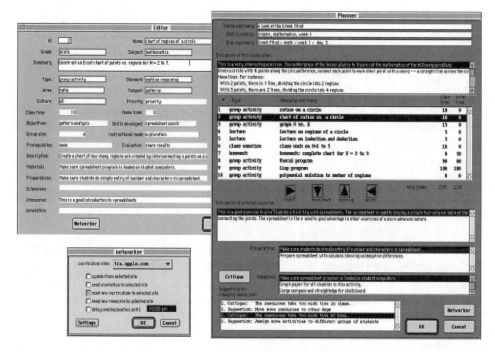

Figure 1.4
The TCA interface for adapting, organizing, and sharing resources and curricula: Planner,
Editor, and Networker.

Scenario Step 1: Locating Curriculum

Imagine a high school mathematics teacher using TCA. In the coming year, she has
to introduce some geometric concepts like Pythagoras's theorem and deductive
proofs. More generally, she might want to discuss the ubiquity of patterns and ways
to represent them mathematically. TCA lets her browse for semester themes and
their constituent weekly units and lesson plans related to these topics.

TCA distinguishes four levels of curricula available on the Internet:

• A *theme* is a major curriculum, possibly covering a semester or a year of school and
optionally integrating several subjects. A theme consists of multiple teaching units.

• A weekly *unit* is part of a theme, typically one week of lessons for a single subject.
A unit is described by its constituent daily lesson plans.

• A *plan* is one day's lesson for a class. A lesson plan might include a number of
resources, such as a lecture, a reading, an exercise, or a project, and perhaps a quiz
and a homework assignment.

▪ A *resource* is an element of a lesson plan. It might be a text, available as a word processing document. It could also be a video clip, a spreadsheet worksheet, a graphic design, or a software simulation. Resources are the smallest units of curricula indexed by TCA.

TCA lets the teacher locate relevant curricula by analyzing information stored on her computer about items available on the Internet. Along with the TCA software on her computer, there is a case base of summaries (indexes) of curricula and resources that can be downloaded. These summary records reference curricula and resources that have been posted to Internet nodes around the world. In addition to containing the Internet address information needed for downloading an item, a record contains a description of the item so that the teacher can decide whether it is of interest.

After a set of interesting items has been selected based on the information in the case base, TCA downloads the items to the teacher's computer. This happens without her having to know where they were located or how to download them. The items are then available for modification, printing, or distribution to her students. If Internet traffic is slow, she may opt to download batches of curriculum and resources overnight and then work with them the next day.

Scenario Step 2: Searching for Resources

TCA provides a combination of query and browsing mechanisms to help a teacher select curricula of interest and to find resources that go with it. She can start in the Profiler (figure 1.3) by specifying that she wants a curriculum for ninth-grade mathematics. Then she can browse through a list of themes in the Explorer that meet the specification. If the list is too long, she can narrow down her search criteria.

The *theme* named "A Look at the Greek Mind" is summarized as "This is an integrated curriculum that explores myth, patterns, and abstract reasoning." It emphasizes patterns and is likely to include Pythagoras's theorem. The teacher can click on this theme in the list. Her computer now displays summaries of the *units* that make up the curriculum for that theme. This list shows three weekly units. Select week 1, described as "Abstract thinking: number theory and deductive reasoning."

She now sees summaries of that week's five daily *lesson plans*. She looks at the geometry example for day 3: "Inductive reasoning example: regions of a circle." She selects that one, and the screen changes to show the lesson plan in the Planner (figure 1.4). It lists all the *resources* suggested for that period: two lecture topics, a class exercise, several alternative activities for small groups, and a homework assignment.

The screenshot of Explorer illustrates how a teacher can browse from a given resource, like "chart of regions on a circle," up to all the lesson plans, units, and themes that include that resource and then back down to all the associated units, plans, and resources. This is one way to locate related resources within curricular contexts. The teacher can also turn to the Versions component to find variations on a particular resource and comments about the resource and its different versions by teachers who have used it.

Notice the second resource in the Planner, where students create a spreadsheet chart: "Group activity: Chart of ratios on a circle." When the teacher selects it with the mouse, the Editor shows the detail for that resource, including its index values.

The description contained in the case base for each posted resource is organized as a set of 24 indexes and annotations, such as recommended grade level, content area, pedagogical goal, instructional mode, prerequisites, materials used, required time, and the like. Note that total class time and homework time are computed and teacher preparations for the resources are listed below the workspace.

The TCA Profiler allows a teacher to specify her curricular needs using combinations of these indexes. Resources are also cross-referenced so that she can retrieve many different resources that are related to a given one. Thus, once she has found the "problem of regions of a circle," she can easily locate discussions of inductive reasoning, formal proofs, recursion, simultaneous equations, sample programs in Logo or Pascal, spreadsheet templates for analyzing successive differences, and graphing tools. She can also find week-long units that build on geometric problems like this one, with variations for students with different backgrounds, learning styles, or interests. TCA allows her to search both top down from themes to resources and bottom up from resources to curricula.

Scenario Step 3: Adapting to Local Needs

Adaptation tools are available in TCA for resources that have been downloaded from the Internet. The Planner component provides a design workspace for assembling a custom lesson plan, and the Editor helps a teacher to adapt individual resources to her local needs. The TCA system can often *make automated suggestions* for adapting a resource to the specification given in the search process. For instance, if she retrieves a resource that was targeted for eleventh grade when she is looking for tenth-grade material, then TCA might suggest allowing her students more time to do the tasks or might provide more supporting and explanatory materials for them. In general, she will need to make the adaptations; even where the software comes up with suggestions, she must use her judgment to make the final decision.

While TCA can automate some adaptation, most tailoring of curricula requires hands-on control by an experienced teacher. Sometimes TCA can support her efforts by *displaying useful information.* For instance, if she is adapting resources organized by national standards to local standards, she might like her computer to display both sets of standards and to associate each local standard with corresponding national standards. In other situations, perhaps involving students whose first language is not English, TCA might link a resource requiring a high level of language understanding to a supplementary visual presentation.

The adaptation process relies on alternative *versions* of individual resources being posted. The TCA Versions component helps a teacher adjust to different student groups, teaching methods, and time constraints by retrieving alternative versions of resources that provide different motivations, use different formats, or go into more depth. She can substitute these alternative resources into lesson-plans; they can then be modified with multimedia editing software from within TCA.

Included in the Editor is a reduced image of the spreadsheet. If a teacher clicks on this image, TCA brings up the commercial software application in which the document was produced. So she can now *edit and modify* the copy of this document that appears on her screen. She need not leave TCA to do this. Then she can print out her revised version for her students or distribute it directly to their computers. In this way, she can use her own ideas or those of her students to modify and enhance curricular units found on the Internet.

Just as it is important for teachers to adapt curricula to their needs, it is desirable to have resources that students can tailor. Current software technology makes this possible, as illustrated by a number of simulations in the Agentsheets Exploratorium (Ambach, Perrone, & Reppening, 1995; Stahl, Sumner, & Repenning, 1995).

Scenario Step 4: Organizing Resources into Lesson Plans

The lesson-plan is a popular representation for a curriculum. It provides teachers a system for organizing classroom activities. TCA uses the *lesson-plan metaphor* as the basis for its design workspace. A teacher can start her planning by looking at downloaded lesson plans and then modifying them to meet her local needs.

The TCA Planner workspace for designing lesson plans was shown in figure 1.4. In addition to summaries of each resource, the workspace lists the time required by each resource, both in class and at home. These times are totaled at the bottom of the list of resources in the Planner. This provides an indication of whether there is too much or too little instructional material to fill the period. The teacher can then decide to add or eliminate resources or adjust their time allowances. The total homework time can be compared to local requirements concerning homework amounts.

TCA incorporates computational *critics* (Fischer et al., 1993; Fischer et al., 1998). Critics are software rules that monitor the curriculum being constructed and verify that specified conditions are maintained. For instance, critics might automatically alert the teacher if the time required for a one-day curriculum exceeds or falls short of the time available.

Scenario Step 5: Sharing New Experiences

Once a teacher has developed curricula and used them successfully in the classroom, she may want to share her creations with other teachers. This way, *the pool of ideas on the Internet will grow and mature*. TCA has facilities for her to annotate individual resources and curricular units at all levels with descriptions of how they worked in her classroom. This is part of the indexing of the resource or unit.

Assume that a teacher downloaded and used the "regions of a circle" resource and modified it based on her classroom experiences. Now she wants to upload her version back to the Internet. The TCA Networker component automates that process, posting the new resource to an available server and adding the indexes for it to the server used for distributing new indexes. Because the indexing of her revision would be similar to that of the original version of the resource, other teachers looking at the "regions of a circle" resource would also find her version with her comments. In this way, the Internet pool of resources serves as a medium of communication among teachers about the specific resources. It is in such ways that I hope the use of the Internet for curriculum development will go far beyond today's first steps.

What I Have Learned

I conceptualize the understanding I have reached through my work on TCA in five principles:

1. Most resources should be *located* at distributed sites across the Internet, but carefully structured summaries (indexes) of them should be maintained on teachers' local computers or in centralized catalogs.

2. The *search* process should be supported through a combination of query and browsing tools that help teachers explore what is available.

3. *Adaptation* of tools and resources to teachers and students is critical for developing and benefiting from constructivist curriculum.

4. Resources must be *organized* into carefully designed curriculum units to provide effective learning environments.

5. The Internet should become a medium for *sharing* curriculum ideas, not just accessing them.

A system to assist teachers in developing curricula for educational reform has been designed and prototyped. All aspects of the system must now be refined through further work with classroom teachers and curriculum developers. While the approach of TCA appeals to teachers who have participated in its design, its implementation must still be tuned to the realities of the classroom.

The distribution of resources and indexes prototyped in TCA has attractive advantages. Because the actual multimedia resources (text, pictures, video clips, spreadsheet templates, HyperCard stacks, software applications) are distributed across the Internet, there is no limit to the quantity or size of these resources and no need for teachers to have large computers. Resources can be posted on network servers maintained by school districts, regional educational organizations, textbook manufacturers, and other agencies. Then the originating agency can maintain and revise the resources as necessary.

However, the approach advocated here faces a major institutional challenge: the standardization of resource indexing. The difficulty with this approach is the need to index every resource and to distribute these indexes to every computer that runs TCA. This involves implementing a distribution and updating system for the case-base index records and then establishing the TCA indexing scheme as a standard.

The distribution and updating of indexes can be handled by tools within TCA and support software for major curriculum contributors. However, the standard-ization requires coordination among interested parties. Before any teachers can use TCA, there must be useful indexed resources available on the network with com-prehensive suggested lesson plans. It is necessary to establish cooperation among federally funded curriculum development efforts, textbook publishers, software publishers, and school districts. If successful, this will establish a critical mass of curriculum on the Internet accessible by TCA. Then the Internet can begin to be an effective medium for the global sharing of locally adaptable curriculum.

2

Evolving a Learning Environment

Chapter 2 offers another fairly typical attempt to use the power of computer technology to support learning.[1] Students need iterative practice with timely expert feedback for developing many skills, but computer-based practice is not easy to implement in ways that are fun and educationally effective when the task involves interpreting semantics of free text. The State the Essence software used latent semantic analysis to solve this problem. It shows how a computer can provide a partial mentoring function, relieving teachers of some of the tedium while increasing personalized feedback to students.

The software evolved through a complex interplay with its user community during classroom testing to provide effective automated feedback to students learning to summarize short texts. It demonstrates the collaboration among researchers, teachers, and students in developing educational innovations. It also suggests collaborative group use of such software.

This case study is interesting not only for describing software design, implementation, and adoption within a social context involving researchers, teachers, and students but also for its assessment of latent semantic analysis, which is often proposed as a panacea for automated natural language understanding in CSCW and CSCL systems. It is an idea that at first appears simple and powerful but turns out to require significant fine-tuning and a very restricted application. Success also depends on integration into a larger activity context in which the educational issues have been carefully taken into account. In this case, well-defined summarization skills of individual students are fairly well understood, making success possible.

Interactive learning environments promise to enrich the experience of students in classrooms by allowing them to explore information under their own intrinsic motivation and to use what they discover to construct knowledge in their own words. To date, a major limitation of educational technology in pursuing this vision has been the inability of computer software to interpret unconstrained free text by students so that the computer can interact with the students without having the students' behavior and expression limited.

In a project at the University of Colorado's Institute of Cognitive Science, a research group I worked with developed a system named State the Essence that provides feedback to students on summaries that they compose in their own words from their understanding of assigned instructional texts. This feedback encourages the students to revise their summaries through many drafts, to reflect on the summarization process, to think more carefully about the subject matter, and to improve their summaries prior to handing them in to the teacher. Our software uses a technology called latent semantic analysis (LSA) to compare the student summary to the original text without having to solve the more general problem of computer interpretation of free text.

LSA has frequently been described from a mathematical perspective, and the results of empirical studies of its validity are widely available in the psychological literature.[2] This report on our experience with State the Essence is not meant to duplicate those other sources but to convey a fairly detailed sense of what is involved in adapting LSA for use in interactive learning environments. To do this, I describe how our software evolved through a two-year development and testing period.

In this chapter, I explain how our LSA-based environment works. There is no magic here. LSA is a statistical method that has been developed by tuning a numeric representation of word meanings to human judgments. Similarly, State the Essence is the result of adapting computational and interface techniques to the performance of students in the classroom. Accordingly, this chapter presents an evolutionary view of the machinery we use to encourage students to evolve their own articulations of the material they are reading.

The chapter begins by discussing the goals and background of our work and then takes a look at our interactive learning environment from the student perspective—the evolving student-computer interface. The multiple ways in which LSA is used to assess a student summary and formulate feedback raise questions about how LSA's semantic representation contained in our software evolved to the point where it can support decisions comparable to human judgments. These questions are addressed in the conclusion, which also summarizes our process of software design in use as a coevolution and suggests directions for continuing development.

Evolution of Student Articulations

Educational theory emphasizes the importance of having students construct their own understanding in their own terms. Yet most schooling software that provides automatic feedback to students requires them to memorize and repeat exact wordings. Although the new educational standards call for helping students to develop high-level critical-thinking skills, such as interpretation and argumentation, current tutoring and testing software tools still look for correct answers to be given by particular keywords. In the attempt to assess learning more extensively without further overburdening the teachers, schools increasingly rely on computer scoring, typically involving multiple-choice or single-word answers. This may be appropriate under certain conditions, but it fails to assess more open-ended communication and reflection skills—and may deliver the wrong implicit message about what kind of learning is important. Encouraging learners to be articulate requires overcoming this limitation of computer support.

The underlying technical issue involves the inability of computer software to understand normal human language. Programs can decide if a multiple-choice or single-word selection matches an option or keyword stored in the program, but software generally cannot decide if a paragraph of English is articulating a particular idea. This is known as the problem of *natural-language understanding* in the field of artificial intelligence (AI). Some researchers have been predicting since the advent of computers that the solution to this problem is just around the corner (Turing, 1950), while others have argued that the problem is in principle unsolvable (Dreyfus, 1972; Searle, 1980).

The software technique called latent semantic analysis promises a way to finesse the problem of natural-language understanding in many situations. LSA has proven to be almost as good as human graders in judging the similarity of meaning of two school-related texts in English in a number of restricted contexts. Thus, LSA can be used to compare a student text to a standard text for semantic similarity without having to interpret the meaning of either text explicitly.

The technique underlying LSA was originally developed in response to the "vocabulary problem" in information retrieval (Furnas et al., 1987). The retrieval problem arises whenever information may be indexed using different terms that mean roughly the same thing. A search using one term should retrieve the information indexed by that term's synonyms as well. LSA maintains a representation of words that are similar in meaning so that it can retrieve information about a given topic regardless of which related index terms are used. The representation of which words are similar in meaning may be extended to determine which texts (sentences, paragraphs, essays) are similar in topic. The way that LSA does all this should become gradually clearer as this chapter unfolds.

Because LSA has often proven to be effective in judging similarities in meaning between texts, it should be able to be used for judging student summaries. The idea seems startlingly simple: submit two texts to LSA—an original essay and a student attempt to summarize that essay—and the LSA software returns a number whose magnitude represents how close the two texts are semantically (how much they express what humans would judge as similar meanings). All that would be needed would be to incorporate this technique in a motivational format where the number is displayed as a score. Students would see the score and try to revise their summaries to increase their scores.

In 1996, we (see note 1) were a group of cognitive scientists who had been funded to develop educational applications of LSA to support articulate learners. We were working with a team of two teachers at a local middle school. We recognized that summarization skills were an important aspect of learning how to be articulate and discovered that the teachers were already teaching these skills as a formal part of their curriculum. We spent the next two years trying to implement and assess this simple-sounding idea. We initially called our application State the Essence to indicate the central goal of summarization.

A companion paper (Kintsch et al., 2000) reports on the learning outcomes of middle-school students using our software during two years of experimentation. This approach also has potential in a different context—collaborative learning at the college level. I conducted an informal experiment in an undergraduate computer science course on AI. The instructor wanted to give the students a hands-on feel for LSA, so we held a class in a computer lab with access to State the Essence. Prior to class, the students were given a lengthy scholarly paper about LSA (Landauer, Foltz, & Laham, 1998) and were asked to submit summaries of two major sections of the paper as homework assignments. Once in the lab, students worked both individually and in small teams. First, they submitted their homework summary to State the Essence, and then they revised it for about half an hour. The students who worked on the first section individually worked on the second section in groups for the second half hour, and vice versa.

I cannot compare the number of drafts done online with the original homework summaries because the latter were done without feedback and presumably without successive drafts. Nor have I assessed summary quality or student time on task. However, informal observation during the experiment suggests that engagement with the software maintained student focus on revising the summaries, particularly in the collaborative condition. In writing summaries of the first section, collaborative groups submitted 71 percent more drafts than individual students—an average of 12 compared to 7. For the second section (which was more difficult and was done when the students had more experience with the system), collaborative groups submitted 38 percent more drafts—an average of 22 drafts as opposed to 16 by individuals. Interaction with the software in the collaborative groups prompted stimulating discussions about the summarization process and ways of improving the final draft—as well as an impressive number of revisions. Computer support of collaboration opens up a new dimension for the evolution of student articulations beyond what we have focused on in our research to date. Developing interface features, feedback mechanisms, and communication supports for collaboration would help to exploit the potential of collaborative learning.

Evolution of the Student-Computer Interface

What did students view on the computer screen that motivated them to keep revising their summaries? The companion paper discusses in detail our shifting rationale for the design of the State the Essence interface. However, it may be useful to show here what the screen looked like after a summary draft was submitted. In the first year of our testing, we built a fairly elaborate display of feedback. Figure 2.1 shows a sample of the basic feedback.

Note that the main feedback concerns topic coverage. The original text was divided into five sections with headings. The feedback indicates which sections the students' summaries cover adequately or inadequately. A link points to the text section that needs the most work. Other indications show which sentences are considered irrelevant (off topic for all sections) and which are redundant (repeating content covered in other sentences of the student summary). In addition, spelling problems are noted. Finally, warnings are given if the summary is too long or too short. The focus of the feedback is an overall score, with a goal of getting 10 points.

The evolution of the interface was driven primarily by the interplay of two factors: our ideas for providing helpful feedback (see next section) and students' cognitive ability to take advantage of various forms of feedback (see the companion paper).

We found that some feedback provides too little help and excessive feedback is overwhelming, depending on student maturity, level of writing skills, class preparations for summarization tasks, classroom supports, and software presentation styles.

For our second year, we simplified the feedback, making it more graphical and less detailed. Following a student suggestion, we renamed the system Summary Street. Figure 2.2 is a sample of feedback provided for a student summary: here the dominant feature is a series of bars, whose length indicates how well the summary covers each of the original text's sections. The solid vertical line indicates the goal to be achieved for coverage of each section. Dashed lines indicate the results of the previous trial and show progress. Spelling errors are highlighted within the summary text for convenient correction. The detailed information about irrelevant and redundant sentences has been eliminated, and the length considerations are not presented until a student has achieved the coverage goals for every section (these different forms of feedback are described in the next section).

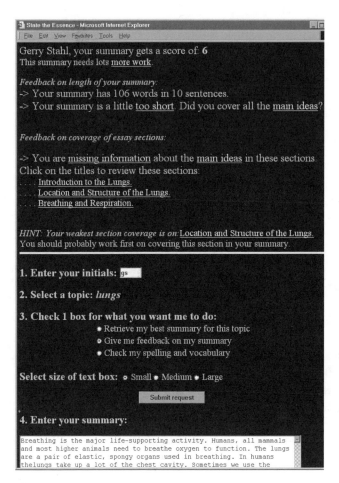

Figure 2.1
View of the early interface showing feedback for a draft summary at the bottom of the screen.

Naturally, the AI college students in our recent experiment were curious about how the system computed its feedback. They experimented with tricks to tease out the algorithms and to try to foil LSA. Surprisingly, many of the sixth graders did the same thing. In general, learning to use the system involves coming to an understanding of what is behind the feedback. Interacting across an interface means attributing some notion of agency to a communication partner. Even sixth graders know that there is no little person crouching in their computer and that computers can only manipulate strings of characters.

The blue dashed lines show how much information your **previous** summary contained, so you can see if y
are improving or not.

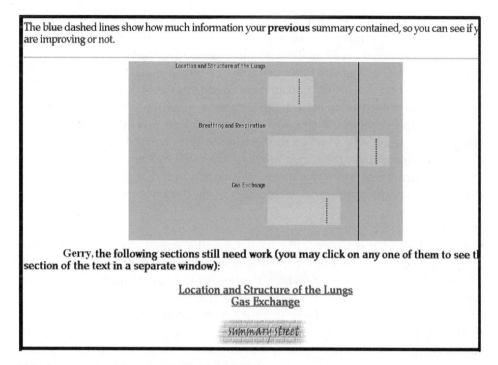

Gerry, the following sections still need work (you may click on any one of them to see t
section of the text in a separate window):

Location and Structure of the Lungs
Gas Exchange

summary street

Figure 2.2
View of the later interface showing feedback for a draft summary.

Evolution of Feedback Techniques

So how does State the Essence figure out such matters as topic coverage? In designing the software, we assumed that we had at our disposal a technology—the LSA
function—that could judge the similarity in meaning between any two texts about
as well as humans can agree in making such judgments. When given any two texts
of English words, the function returns a number between −1.0 and 1.0 such that
the more similar the meaning of the two texts, the higher the result returned. For
instance, if two identical copies of the same essay are submitted, the function will
return 1.0. If an essay and a summary of that essay are submitted, the function will
return a number whose value is closer to 1.0 as the summary better expresses the
same composite meaning as the essay itself. This section reports on how our use of
the LSA function in State the Essence evolved during our research. This provides a
detailed example of how the LSA technology can be adapted to an educational
application.

In the course of our research, we had to make a number of key strategic design decisions and revise them periodically. One was how to structure the software's feedback to provide effective guidance to the students. The feedback had to be useful to students in helping them to think critically about their summaries, recognize possible weaknesses, and discover potential improvements to try. Another decision was how to measure the overlap in meaning between a summary and the original essay. For this we had to somehow represent the essence of the essay that we wanted the summaries to approach. This led to the issue of determining thresholds, or standards of cut-off values for saying when a summary had enough overlap to be accepted. Then we had to define a feedback system to indicate clearly for the students how good their summaries were and how much they were improving.

Providing Guidance

Given the LSA function, we could have developed a simple form on the Web that accepts the text of a student's summary, retrieves the text of the original essay, submits the two texts to the function, multiplies the result of the function by 10, and returns that as the student's score. Unfortunately, such a system would not be of much help to a student who is supposed to be learning how to compose summaries. True, it would give the student an objective measure of how well the summary expressed the same thing as the essay, but it would not provide any guidance on how to improve the summary. Providing guidance—scaffolding the novice student's attempt to craft a summary—is the whole challenge to the educational software designer.

To design our software, we had to clearly define our pedagogical focus. We operationalized the goal of summary writing to be "coverage." That is, a good summary is one that faithfully captures the several major points of an essay. A summary also should cover these points "concisely"—in perhaps a quarter the number of words of the original.

We considered and tried other factors in various versions of the software. For instance, students should progress beyond the common "copy and delete" strategy where they excerpt parts of the original verbatim and then erase words to be more concise; learning to be articulate means saying things in your own words. However, even learning to manipulate someone else's words can be valuable. We generally felt that the most important thing was for students to be able to identify the main points in an essay. It is also necessary that students learn to use the words that they come across in an essay. For instance, a technical article on the heart and lungs has many medical terms that must be learned and that should probably be used in writing a summary. So avoiding plagiarism and reducing redundancy were less primary goals in a system for sixth graders than focusing on coverage.

Spelling is always a concern, although we would not want a focus on spelling to inhibit articulation and creativity. In a software feedback system, correct spelling is necessarily required, if only because misspelled words will not be recognized by the software. Other issues of composition had to be ignored in our software design. We made no attempt to provide feedback on logic or coherence of argument, literary or rhetorical style, and other aspects of expository writing. These were left for the teacher. Our system focused on helping students to "state the essence" of a given text by optimizing their coverage of the main points prior to submitting their compositions to a teacher for more refined and personal feedback. The power of LSA is limited, and the limitations must be taken into account when designing its use context by balancing automated and human feedback appropriately.

Representing the Essence

The first question in defining our system algorithm was how to represent the main points of an essay so that we would have a basis for comparison with student summaries. Most educational essays are already fairly well structured: pages are divided into paragraphs, each of which expresses its own thought; an essay that is a couple pages long is generally divided into sections that discuss distinct aspects of the topic. For our classroom interventions, we worked closely with the teachers to select or prepare essays that were divided into four or five sections, clearly demarcated with headings. We avoided introduction or conclusion sections and assumed that each section expressed one or more of the major points of the essay as a whole. This allowed us to have the software guide the students by telling them which sections were well covered by their summaries and which were not. That is the central heuristic of our design.

So the idea is to compare a student summary with the main points of each section of the original text and then provide feedback based on this. The question is how to formulate the main points of a section for LSA comparison. There are several possible approaches:

- Use previously graded student summaries of text sections and determine how close a new summary is to any of the high-ranked old summaries. This method works only when a text has been previously summarized by comparable students and has been carefully graded. This was not possible for most of our experiments.

- Have adults (researchers or teachers) craft a "golden" summary of each section. This was our original approach. Typically, we had two summaries by the teachers and a couple by researchers; we then created one golden summary for each section that synthesized all of the ideas contained in the adult summaries. We would then use this summary as a section target. In addition, each adult's complete set of section summaries was conglomerated for use as a target for the summary as a whole. The software compared the entire student summary to the target summary for each section and selected the highest LSA score to determine how well the student covered that section's points. It also compared the entire student summary to each of the expert whole summaries to compute the student's score. That gave students a number of alternative adult summaries to target. This approach worked well. However, it required too much preparatory work. Each time we wanted to use a new essay in a classroom, we had to prepare between a dozen and two dozen section summaries. This used too much teacher and researcher time and clearly would not scale up.

• Use the original text for comparison. This did not allow for feedback on coverage of each section.

• Use each section of the original text for a series of comparisons. The problem with this approach was setting thresholds. It is much easier to write a summary that gets a high LSA rating for some texts than it is for others. How do we know what score to consider good enough to praise or bad enough to criticize? Where adults crafted expert target summaries we understood roughly what a 0.75 versus a 0.30 LSA score meant, but this was not the case for an arbitrary page of text. This led to our other major challenge—how to set standards of achievement in cases where we did not have a large base of experience.

Setting Standards

Setting thresholds is always an issue. The easier the method of defining comparison texts, the harder it is to set effective thresholds for them.

One idea we considered was to use past student summaries as a statistical basis for scoring new attempts. But that worked only for essays that had been used in past trials, and most of our experiments introduced new texts. So as an alternative to past summaries, we tried comparing hundreds of randomly selected short texts to the essay section to gain a measure of how hard the essay is to summarize (the random texts were selected from the corpus used for the LSA scaling space; see next section). We found that if a student summary does, say, four or five standard deviations better than a random text, it is probably fairly good. This approach was easy to automate, and we adopted it. However, significant discrepancies sometimes arose between reaching these thresholds for one essay section compared to reaching them for another. We could adopt the attitude that life is just that way and that students need to learn that some things are harder to say than others. But we have some ideas on how to address this issue and revisit the issue in the conclusion to this chapter.

Computing the Basic Feedback

Whatever approach we use to represent the sections and the whole text for LSA comparisons and whatever method we use to set the thresholds for what is considered an adequate or an inadequate comparison, we always compare a given student draft to each section and to the whole text in order to derive a score.

In our early version of State the Essence, we took the best LSA result from comparing the student summary to each expert whole summary. We multiplied this by 10 to give a score from 0 to 10. In addition to calculating this score, we computed feedback on coverage of individual sections. For each essay section, we took the best LSA result from comparing the student summary to each expert section summary. We compared this to thresholds to decide whether to praise, accept, or require more work on the section. Praised sections increased the student's score; criticized sections decreased it. We made additional adjustments for problems with summary length, redundancy, irrelevance, and plagiarism.

In the later version of the system, SummaryStreet, we compared the student summary draft with each section of the original text, as well as with the whole essay. The results of the LSA evaluations of the sections are compared to the automatically generated thresholds for the sections, and the results are displayed graphically.

Refining the Summary

For a human, constructing a summary is a complex design problem with manifold constraints and subgoals. Sixth graders vary enormously in their ability to do this and to respond to standardized guidance feedback. Telling a student that a particular section has not been covered adequately provides some guidance but does not specify clearly what has to be done. How does the student identify the main points of the section that are not yet covered in the summary? Primarily, the feedback points the student back to a confined part of the text for further study. The system also provides a hypertext link to that section so the student can reread it on their computer screen. The student can then try adding new sentences to the summary and resubmitting to see what happens. By comparing the results of subsequent trials, the student can learn what seems to work and what does not. The principle here is that instant and repeated feedback opportunities allow for learning through student-directed trial, with no embarrassing negative social consequences to the student for experimenting.

Repeated additions of material by a student, driven by the coverage requirement, inevitably lead to increasing length, soon exceeding the boundaries of a concise summary. In our early system, we continuously gave length feedback—a word count and a warning if the maximum length was being approached or exceeded. The composite score was also affected by excessive length, so it fluctuated in complex ways as more material was added. Dealing with the tradeoff that was implicitly required between coverage and conciseness seemed to be more than most sixth graders could handle—although it might be appropriate for older students. So in our later system, SummaryStreet, we withheld the length feedback until the coverage thresholds were all met, letting students pursue one goal at a time.

To help with the conciseness goal, we gave additional, optional feedback on relevance and repetition at the sentence level. This provided hints for the students about individual sentences in their summaries. They could view a list of sentences—or see them highlighted in their summary—that were considered irrelevant to the original essay or were considered redundant with other sentences in the summary. These lists were computed with many more LSA comparisons.

For the relevance check, each sentence in the student draft summary was compared (using LSA) with each section of the essay. A sentence whose comparison was well above the threshold for a section was praised as contributing significantly to the summary of that section. A sentence whose comparison was below the thresholds for all the sections was tagged as irrelevant.

To check for overlapping, redundant content, each sentence in the student draft summary was compared with each other sentence of the summary. Where two sentences were highly correlated, they were declared redundant. Similarly, summary sentences could be compared with each sentence in the original to check for plagiarism, where the correlation approached 1.0. Again, this detailed level of feedback is difficult for most sixth graders to use effectively.

A final form of feedback concerns spelling. This does not make use of the LSA function but merely checks each word to see if it is in the lexicon that LSA uses. Because the LSA vocabulary combines a general K through 12 textual corpus with documents related to the essay being summarized, most correctly spelled words used in student summaries are included in it.

As the preceding review indicates, the techniques for computing feedback in State the Essence evolved considerably over a two-year period. Perhaps most interesting is the variety of LSA computations that can be integrated into the feedback. From the original idea of doing a single LSA comparison of student summary to original essay, the system evolved to incorporate hundreds or even thousands of LSA computations. These comparisons are now used to automatically set a variety of system thresholds and to evaluate summaries at the sentence, section, and holistic levels.

At least at the current state of the technology, testing and fine tuning of many factors are always necessary. The final product is an opaque system that returns reasonable feedback in about a second and seems simple. But to get to that point, each component of the system had to be carefully crafted by the researchers, reviewed by the teachers, and tested with students. This includes the style of the text, its division into sections, the representation of the essence of each section, the values of multiple thresholds, the presentation of the feedback, and various factors discussed in the next section, including the composition of the scaling space and the choice of its dimensionality.

Another conclusion to be drawn from the history of the evolution of our techniques is the importance of tuning system feedback to the needs and abilities of the audience rather than trying to exploit the full power that is computationally possible. I reflect on this process in the next section and take a closer look at how the LSA function can do what it does in the computations just described.

Coevolution of the Software in Use

This chapter adopts an evolutionary view of software development. The experience of our project with State the Essence can be summed up by saying that a *coevolution* has taken place among the various participants. Research goals, software features, teacher pedagogy, student attitudes, and classroom activities changed remarkably over two years. They each changed in response to the other factors to adapt to each other effectively. Such an effective *structural coupling* (Maturana & Varela, 1987) between the development of the software and the changing behavior of the user community may constitute a significant indicator for a successful research effort.

Some of these changes and interactions among the researchers, teachers, and students have been documented elsewhere (Kintsch et al., 2000). This chapter focuses more on the software-development process in relation to student cognition. The educational point of the project is to promote evolution at the level of the individual student's ability to articulate his or her understanding of instructional texts. Preliminary impressions suggest that collaborative uses of the software may be even more powerful than individual uses. On a larger scale, significant changes in the classroom as a community were informally observed in the interactions during single classroom interventions as well as during the school year, even when the software was nominally being used by students on an individual basis. Students tended to interact with friends around use of the software as they helped each other and shared experiences or insights. The software interface evolved as it adjusted to student difficulties, and this can be traced back to shifts in approaches at the level of the underlying algorithms. One can go a step deeper and see the use of the basic LSA technology in our software as a product of a similar evolutionary adaptation.

Evolution of the Semantic Representation

At one level, the semantic representation at the heart of LSA is the result of a learning process that is equivalent to the connections in AI neural networks that learn to adjust their values based on experiences with training data. An LSA analysis of a corpus of text has arguably learned from that corpus much of what a child learns from the corpus of text that the child is exposed to (Landauer & Dumais, 1997). One difference is that LSA typically analyzes the corpus all at once rather than sequentially, but that does not make an essential difference. In certain applications, it might be important for LSA to continually revise its values—to continue learning. For instance, in State the Essence, it might be helpful to add new student summaries to the corpus of analyzed text as the system is used to take into account the language of the user community as it becomes available.

The mathematical details of LSA have been described elsewhere, as have the rigorous evaluations of its effectiveness. To understand the workings of State the Essence in a bit more depth and to appreciate both the issues that we addressed as well as those issues that remain open, it is necessary to review some of the central concepts of LSA at a descriptive level. These concepts include scaling space, co-occurrence, dimensionality reduction, cosine measure, and document representation.

Scaling Space   The representation of meaning in LSA consists of a large matrix or high-dimensionality mathematical space. Each word in the vocabulary is defined as a point in this space—typically specified by a vector of about 300 coordinates. The space is a *semantic space* in the sense that words that people would judge to have similar meanings are located proportionately near to each other in the space. This space is what is generated by LSA's statistical analysis of a corpus of text. For State the Essence, we use a large corpus of texts similar to what K through 12 students encounter in school. We supplement this with texts from the domain of the essays being summarized, such as encyclopedia articles on the heart or on Aztec culture. The semantic space is computed in advance and then used as a *scaling space* for determining the mathematical representations of the words, sentences, and texts of the student summaries. It may seem counterintuitive that a mathematical analysis of statistical relations among words in written texts could capture what people understand as the meaning of those words. It seems somewhat akin to learning language from circular dictionary definitions alone. Yet experiments have shown that across a certain range of applications, LSA-based software produces results that are comparable to those of foreign students, native speakers, or even expert graders.

Cooccurrence   The computation of semantic similarity or nearness (in the space) of two words is based on an analysis of the cooccurrence of the two words in the same documents. The corpus of texts is defined as a large number of documents, usually the paragraphs in the corpus. Words that cooccur with each other in a large number of these documents are considered semantically related or similar. The mathematical analysis does not simply count explicit cooccurrences, but takes full account of latent semantic relationships—such as two words that may never cooccur themselves but that both cooccur with the same third word or set of words. Thus, synonyms, for instance, rarely occur together but tend to occur in the same kinds of textual contexts. The LSA analysis takes full advantage of latent relationships hidden in the corpus as a whole and scales similarities based on relative word frequencies. The success of LSA has shown that cooccurrence can provide an effective measure of semantic similarity for many test situations when the cooccurrence relationships are manipulated in sophisticated ways.

Dimensionality Reduction The raw matrix of cooccurrences has a column for every document and a row for every unique word in the analyzed corpus. For a small corpus, this might be 20,000 word rows × 2,000 document columns. An important step in the LSA analysis is dimensionality reduction. The representation of the words is transformed into a matrix of, say 20,000 words × 300 dimensions. This compression is analogous to the use of hidden units in AI neural networks. That is, it eliminates a lot of the statistical noise from the particular corpus selection and represents each word in terms of 300 abstract summary dimensions. The particular number 300 is somewhat arbitrary and is selected by comparing LSA results to human judgments. Investigations show that about 300 dimensions usually generate significantly better comparisons than either higher or lower numbers of dimensions. This seems to be enough compression to eliminate noise without losing important distinctions.

Cosine Measure If the LSA representation of words are visualized as a high-dimensionality mathematical space with 300 coordinate axes, then the vector representing each word can be visualized as a line from the origin to a particular point in the space. The semantic similarity of any two words can be measured as the angle between their vectors. In LSA applications like State the Essence, this angle is measured by its cosine. For two points close to each other with a very small angle between their vectors, this cosine is about 1.0. The larger the angle between the two words, the lower the cosine. While it might seem that nearness in a multidimensional space should be measured by Euclidean distance between the points, experience with LSA has shown that the cosine measure is generally the most effective. In some cases, vector length is also used (the combination of cosine and vector length is equivalent to Euclidean distance). We are considering adopting vector-length measures in

State the Essence, as well, to avoid problems we have encountered (discussed in the next section).

Document Representation   In our software, LSA is used not to compare the meanings of individual words but to assess content overlap between two documents (sentences, summaries, essay sections, and whole essays). It is standard practice in LSA applications to represent the semantics of a document with the vector average of the representations of the words in the document, massaged by some factors that have proven effective empirically. Thus the two documents we are comparing are taken to be at the centroid (vector average) of their constituent words within the same scaling space as their individual words. We then use the cosine between these two centroid points as the measure of their semantic content similarity. On language theoretic grounds, this may be a questionable way to compute sentence semantics. It could be argued, for instance, that "there is no way of passing from the word as a lexical sign to the sentence by mere extension of the same methodology to a more complex entity" (Ricoeur, 1976, p. 7) because words may have senses defined by other words, but sentences refer to the world outside text and express social acts. In response to such an argument, the confines of our experiment might be presumed to protect us from theoretical complexities. State the Essence is looking only for overlapping topic coverage between two documents. Because of this operational focus, the simple similar inclusion of topical words (or their synonyms) might be said to produce the desired experimental effect. However, we have done some informal investigations that indicate that topical words alone are not what influence LSA's judgments; the inclusion of the proper mix of "syntactic glue" words is important as well. Nevertheless, it may be that the LSA-computed centroid of a well-formed sentence performs on average adequately for practical purposes in the tasks we design for them because these tasks need not take into account external reference (situated deixis) or interactional social functions. For instance, we do not expect LSA to assess the rhetorical aspects of a summary.

This overview of the key concepts of the LSA technology suggests that LSA has evolved through iterative refinement under the constant criterion of successful adaptation to comparison with human judgment. The force driving the evolution of the LSA technology as well as that of our application has always been the statistical comparison with human judgments at a performance level comparable to interhuman reliability. In its application to summarization feedback, our use of LSA has evolved significantly to a complex use of many LSA-based measures that have been blended into an interaction style carefully tuned to the intended audience through repeated user trials.

Evolution into the Future

The use of LSA in State the Essence is not fixed as a result of our past work. A number of technical issues must be further explored, and practical improvements are needed, if this software is to be deployed for classroom use beyond the research context.

At least four technical issues that have already been mentioned in passing need further attention: space composition, threshold automation, vector-length measurement, and plagiarism flagging.

Space Composition   As noted, our scaling spaces for middle-school students were based on a corpus of documents that included both generic K through 12 texts and domain-specific texts related to the essay being summarized. It is still not clear what the optimal mix of such texts is and the best way of combining them. Clearly, some domain-specific material needs to be included so that the space includes meaningful representations of technical terms in the essay. It is also important to have the general vocabulary of the students well represented to give valid feedback when they express things in their own words. The problem is that two distinct corpora of text are likely to emphasize different senses of particular words, given the considerable polysemy of English words. Mathematical techniques have been proposed for combining two LSA spaces without disrupting the latent relationships determined for each space, and we must explore these techniques under experimental conditions. The creation and testing of an LSA scaling space is the most computationally intensive and labor-intensive part of preparing an intervention with State the Essence. If this learning environment is to be made available for a wide range of essays in classrooms, we must find a way of preparing effective scaling spaces more automatically.

Threshold Automation   The other technical aspect that needs to be further automated is the setting of reasonable thresholds for a diversity of texts and for different age levels of students. We have already experimented with some approaches to this as described above. Yet we still find unacceptable divergences in how easy it is for students to exceed the automatically generated thresholds of different texts. We have noticed that some texts lend themselves to high LSA cosines when compared to a very small set of words—sometimes even a summary a couple of words long. These are texts whose centroid representation is very close to the representation of certain key words from the text. For instance, a discussion of Aztecs or solar energy might include primarily terms and sentences that cluster around the term "Aztec" or "solar energy." According to LSA measurements, these texts are well summarized by an obvious word or two.

Vector-Length Measurement   We suspect that the use of vector lengths and cosines to measure overlapping topic coverage between two texts will address the threshold problem just discussed—at least partially. But we need to experiment with this. The rationale for this approach is that vector length corresponds to how much a text has to say on a given topic, whereas cosine corresponds to what the topic is. Thus, a document consisting of the single word "Aztec" might be close to the topic of an essay on the Aztecs and therefore have a high cosine, but it would not be saying much about the topic and thus would have a small vector length. The inclusion of vector lengths within LSA-based judgments would allow State the Essence to differentiate between a quick answer and a more thoughtful or complete summary. Here, again, the software must evolve in response to tricks that students might use to achieve high scores without formulating quality summaries.

Plagiarism Flagging   The simplest way to get a good LSA score is to copy the whole essay. This is a winning strategy for topic coverage. If the length is too long, then the unnecessary details must be cut. Here, the sixth grader faces a task that requires distinguishing essential points from inessential details—a task that many sixth graders are still learning. A related alternative approach is to copy topic sentences from each section or paragraph of the original and use them for a summary. Again, this requires an important skill that State the Essence is intended to help teach—identifying topic ideas. So it is probably a decision best left to the teacher to decide how much copying of vocabulary, phrases, and even whole sentences is acceptable in a given exercise. Perhaps for older students, such as college undergraduates, the system should object to any significant level of plagiarism. It is still necessary to define the boundaries of what is considered to be plagiarism, such as reusing or reordering sentence clauses. In the end, such matters may have to be automatically flagged for subsequent teacher review and judgment.

There is still much else to do before State the Essence is ready for widespread deployment. In addition to wrapping up these open research issues and continuing to refine the system's functionality and interface, there is the whole matter of packaging the software for easy use by teachers and of integration with curriculum. Another possibility is to include State the Essence as a tool within larger interactive learning environments like CSILE (van Aalst et al., 1999) or WebGuide (see chapter 6). Perhaps all that can be said now is that we have taken State the Essence far enough to suggest its potential educational utility and to demonstrate how LSA technology can be integrated into an interactive, constructivist, student-centered approach to facilitating student articulation.

3

Armchair Missions to Mars

The matching of people to form groups that will work together closely over periods of time is a subtle task. The Crew software described in this study aimed to advise planners at the National Aeronautics and Space Administration on the selection of teams of astronauts for long missions.[1] The problem of group formation is important for computer support of collaboration in small groups but has not been extensively investigated. This study explores the application of case-based reasoning to this task. This software adapted a variety of AI techniques in response to a complex problem entailing high levels of uncertainty. Like the previous chapter's task of analyzing student writing and the following chapter's task of managing intertwined hypertext perspectives, this involved tens of thousands of calculations—illustrating how computers can provide computational support that would not otherwise be conceivable.

Modeling a Team of Astronauts

The prospect of a manned mission to Mars has been debated for 25 years—since the first manned landing on the moon (American Astronomical Society, 1966). It is routinely argued that this step in human exploration is too costly and risky to undertake, particularly given our lack of experience with lengthy missions in space (McKay, 1985).

During the period of space exploration around 1993, planners at the National Aeronautics and Space Administration (NASA) (the U.S. space agency) were concerned about interpersonal issues in astronaut crew composition. The nature of astronaut crews was beginning to undergo significant changes. In the past, astronauts had been primarily young American males with rigorous military training. Missions were short, and crews were small. Prior to a mission, a crew trained together for about a year, so that any interpersonal conflicts could be worked out in advance. The future, however, promised crews that would be far less homogeneous and regimented. International crews would speak different languages, mix genders and generations, be larger, and go on longer missions. This was the start of Soviet-American cooperation and planning for an international space station. While there was talk of a manned expedition to Mars, the more likely scenario was the creation of an international space station with six-month crew rotations.

NASA did not have much experience with the psychology of crews confined in isolated and extreme conditions for months at a time. Social scientists had explored the effects of *analog* missions under extreme conditions of isolation and confinement, such as Antarctic winter-overs, submarine missions, orbital space missions, and deep-sea experiments (Harrison, Clearwater, & McKay, 1991). This research had produced few generalized guidelines for planning a mission to Mars or an extended stay aboard a space station (Collins, 1985).

The data from submarines and Antarctic winter-overs were limited, inappropriately documented, and inconsistent. NASA was beginning to conduct some experiments to collect the necessary kinds of data, but it required a way to analyze such data, generalize it, and apply it to projected scenarios.

Computer simulations of long missions in space can provide experience and predictions without the expense and risk of actual flights. Simulations are most helpful if they can model the psychological behavior of the crew over time rather than simply predict overall mission success. Because of the lack of experience with interplanetary trips and the problems of generalizing and adapting data from analog missions, it was not possible to create formal rules that were adequate for building an expert system to model extended missions such as this one.

NASA wanted a way to predict how a given crew—with a certain mix of astronauts—might respond to mission stress under different scenarios. This would require a complex model with many parameters. There would never be enough relevant data to derive the parameter values statistically. Given the modest set of available past cases, the method of case-based reasoning suggested itself (Owen, Holland, & Wood, 1993). A case-based system requires (1) a mechanism for retrieving past cases similar to a proposed new case and (2) a mechanism for adapting the data of a retrieved case to the new case based on the differences between the two (Riesbeck & Schank, 1989).

For the retrieval mechanism, my colleagues at Owen Research and I defined a number of characteristics of astronauts and missions. The nature of our data and these characteristics raised several issues for retrieval, and we had to develop innovative modifications of the standard case-based reasoning algorithms, as described in detail below.

For the adaptation mechanism, I developed a model of the mission based on a statistical approach known as *interrupted time-series analysis* (McDowall et al.,

1980). Because there was too little empirical data to differentiate among all possible options, the statistical model had to be supplemented with various adaptation rules. These rules of thumb were gleaned from the social science literature on small-group interactions under extreme conditions of isolation and confinement. The non-quantitative nature of these rules lends itself to formulation and computation using a mathematical representation known as *fuzzy logic* (Cox, 1994).

The application domain presented several technical issues for traditional case-based reasoning: there is no natural hierarchy of parameters to use in optimizing installation and retrieval of cases, and there are large variations in behavior among similar missions. These problems were addressed by custom algorithms to keep the computations tractable and plausible. Thus, the harnessing of case-based reasoning for this practical application required the crafting of a custom, hybrid system.

We developed a case-based reasoning software system named Crew. Most of the software code consisted of the algorithms described in this chapter. Because Crew was intended to be a proof-of-concept system, its data-entry routines and user interface were minimal. The user interface consisted of a set of pull-down menus for selecting a variety of testing options and a display of the results in a graph format (figure 3.1). Major steps in the reasoning were printed out so that the automated reasoning process could be studied.

We were working with staff at the psychology labs of NASA's astronaut support division, so we focused on psychological factors of the crew members, such as stress, morale, and teamwork. NASA had begun to collect time-series psychological data on these factors by having crew members in space and analog missions fill out surveys on an almost daily basis. By the conclusion of our project (June 1995), NASA had analyzed data from an underwater mission designed to test a data-collection instrument, the Individualized Field Recording System (IFRS) survey, and was collecting data from several Antarctic traverses. The IFRS survey was scheduled to be employed on a joint Soviet-American shuttle mission. Its most likely initial use would be as a tool for helping to select crews for the international space station.

Our task was to design a system for incorporating eventual IFRS survey results in a model of participant behavior on long-term missions. Our goal was to implement a proof-of-concept software system to demonstrate algorithms for combining AI techniques like case-based reasoning and fuzzy logic with a statistical model of IFRS survey results and a rule base derived from the existing literature on extreme missions.

By the end of the project, we successfully demonstrated that the time-series model, the case-based reasoning, and the fuzzy logic could all work together to perform as designed. The system could be set up for specific crews and projected missions, and it would produce sensible predictions quickly. The next step was to enter real data

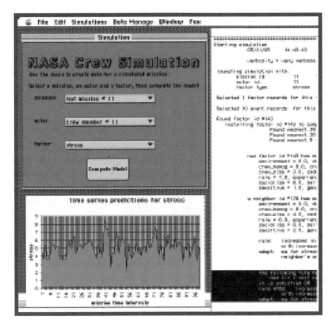

Figure 3.1
A view of the Crew interface. Upper left allows selection of mission characteristics. Menu allows input of data. Lower left shows magnitude of a psychological factor during 100 points in the simulated mission. To the right is a listing of some of the rules taken into account.

that NASA was just beginning to collect. Because of confidentiality concerns, this had to be done within NASA, and we turned over the software to NASA for further use and development.

This chapter reports on our system design and its rationale—the time-series model, the case-based reasoning system, the case-retrieval mechanism, the adaptation algorithm, the fuzzy-logic rules, and our conclusions. The Crew system predicts how crew members in a simulated mission would fill out their IFRS survey forms on each day of the mission; that is, how they would self-report indicators such as stress and motivation. As NASA collects and analyzes survey data, the Crew program can serve as a vehicle for assembling and building on the data—entering empirical cases and tuning the rule base. Clearly, the predictive power of Crew will depend on the eventual quantity and quality of the survey data.

Modeling the Mission Process

NASA is interested in how psychological factors such as those tracked in the IFRS surveys evolve over time during a projected mission's duration. For instance, it is not enough to know what the average stress level will be of crew members at the end of a nine-month mission. We need to know if any crew member is likely to be particularly stressed at a critical point in the middle of the mission when certain actions must be taken. To obtain this level of prediction detail, I created a *time-series* model of the mission.

The model is based on standard statistical time-series analysis. McDowall et al. (1980) argue for a stochastic autoregressive integrated moving-average (ARIMA) model of interrupted time series for a broad range of phenomena in the social sciences. The most general model takes into account three types of considerations: trends, seasonality effects, and interventions. An observed time series is treated as a realization of a stochastic process. The ideal model of such a process is statistically adequate (its residuals are white noise) and parsimonious (it has the fewest parameters and the greatest number of degrees of freedom among all statistically equivalent models).

• *Trends* The basic model takes into account a stochastic component and three structural components. The stochastic component conveniently summarizes the multitude of factors that produce the variation observed in a series, which cannot be accounted for by the model. At each time t, there is a stochastic component α_t which cannot be accounted for any more specifically. McDowall, et al. (1980) claim that most social science phenomena are properly modeled by first-order ARIMA models. That is, the value Y_t of the time series at time t may be dependent on the value of the time series or of its stochastic component at time $t - 1$ but not (directly) on the values at any earlier times. The first-order expressions for the three structural components are as follows:

Autoregressive $\quad Y_t = \alpha_t + \phi Y_{t-1}$
Differenced $\qquad\quad Y_t = \alpha_t + Y_{t-1}$
Moving average $\quad\; Y_t = \alpha_t + \theta\, a_{t-1}$.

I have combined these formulas to produce a general expression for all first-order ARIMA models:

$$Y_t = \alpha_t + \phi Y_{t-1} + \theta a_{t-1}.$$

This general expression makes clear that the model can take into account trends and random walks caused by the inertia (or momentum) of the previous moment's stochastic component or by the inertia of the previous moment's actual value.

• *Seasonality* Many phenomena in economics and nature have a cyclical character, often based on the 12-month year. It seems unlikely that such seasonality effects would be significant for NASA missions; the relevant cycles (daily and annual) would be too small or too large to be measured by IFRS time-series data.

• *Interventions* External events are likely to affect modeled time series. Their duration can be modeled as exponential decay, where the nth time period after an event at time e will have a continuing impact of $Y_{e+n} = \delta^n\omega$, where $0 <= \delta <= 1$. Note that if $\delta = 0$, then there is no impact, and if $\delta = 1$, then there is a permanent impact. Thus, δ is a measure of the rate of decay, and ω is a measure of the intensity of the impact.

I have made some refinements to the standard time-series equations to tune them to our domain and to make them more general. First, the stochastic component $\alpha_i(t)$ consists of a mean value $\mu_i(t)$ and a normal distribution component governed by a standard deviation $\sigma_i(t)$. Second, mission events often have significant effects of anticipation. In general, an event j of intensity ω_{ij} at time t_j will have a gradual onset at a rate ε_{ij} during times $t < t_j$ as well as a gradual decay at a rate δ_{ij} during times $t > t_j$. The following equation incorporates these considerations:

$$Y_{i(t)} = \alpha_{i(t)} + \phi_i Y_{i(t-1)} + \theta_i \alpha_{i(t-1)} + \sum\nolimits_{j=1}^{n} \underbrace{\left[\varepsilon_{ij}^{\ (t_j-t)}\omega_{ij}\right]}_{(for\ t < t_j)} + \sum\nolimits_{j=1}^{n} \underbrace{\left[\delta_{ij}^{\ (t-t_j)}\omega_{ij}\right]}_{(for\ t \geq t_j)}$$

where

$Y_i(t)$ = value of factor i for a given actor in a given mission at mission time t,

t_j = time of occurrence of the jth of n intervening events in the mission,

α = noise, a value is generated randomly with mean μ and standard deviation σ,

μ = mean of noise value, $0 <= \mu <= 10$,

σ = standard deviation of noise, $0 <= \sigma <= 10$,

ϕ = momentum of value, $-1 <= \phi <= 1$,

θ = momentum of noise, $-1 <= \theta <= 1$,

ε = rise rate of interruption, $0 <= \varepsilon <= 1$,

δ = decay rate of interruption, $0 <= \delta <= 1$, and

ω = intensity of interruption, $-10 <= \omega <= 10$.

The model works as follows. Using IFRS survey data for a given question answered by a given crew member throughout a given mission and knowing when significant events occurred, one can use standard statistical procedures to derive the parameters of the preceding equation: μ, σ, ϕ, and θ as well as ε, δ, and ω for each event in the mission. Conversely, these parameters can be used to predict the results of a new proposed mission. Once the parameters have been obtained for a particular psychological factor, a crew member, and each event, one can predict the values that the crew member would enter for that survey question i at each time period t of the mission by calculating the equation with those parameter values.

This model allows us to enter empirical cases into a case base by storing the parameters for each *factor* (a psychological factor for a given crew member during a given mission) or *event* (an intervention event in the given factor time series) with a description of that factor or event. To make a time-series prediction of a proposed factor with its events, I retrieve a similar case, adapt it for differences from the proposed case, and compute its time-series values from the model equation.

Using Case-Based Reasoning

The time-series model is complex in terms of the number of variables and factors. It must produce different results for each time period, each kind of mission, each crew member personality, each question on the IFRS survey, and each type of intervention event. To build a rule-based expert system, we would need to acquire thousands of formal rules capable of computing predictive results for all these combinations. But there are no experts on interplanetary missions who could provide such a set of rules. Nor are there data that could be analyzed to produce these rules. So we took a case-based reasoning approach by taking actual missions— including analog missions—and computing the parameters for their time series.

Each survey variable requires its own model (values for parameters μ, σ, ϕ, and θ), as does each kind of event (values for parameters ε, δ, and ω). Presumably, the 107 IFRS survey questions can be grouped into several *factors*, although this itself is an empirical question. We chose six psychological factors that we thought underlay the IFRS questionnaire: crew teamwork, physical health, mental alertness, psychological stress, psychological morale, and mission effectiveness. In addition, we selected a particular question from the survey that represented each of these factors. The Crew system currently models these 12 factors: six composites and six specific IFRS questions.

There is no natural taxonomy of *events*. Our approach assumes that some categories of events can be modeled consistently as interventions with exponential onsets and decays at certain impact levels and decay rates. Based on the available data, we decided to model eight event types: start of mission, end of mission, emergency, conflict, contact, illness, discovery, and failure.

The case base consists of instances of the 12 factors and the eight event types. Each instance is characterized by its associated mission and crew member and is annotated with its parameter values. Missions are described by 10 *characteristics* (variables), each rated from 0 to 10. The mission characteristics are harshness of environment, duration of mission, risk level, complexity of activities, homogeneity of crew, time of crew together, volume of habitat, crew size, commander leadership, and commander competence. The 12 crew-member *characteristics* are role in crew, experience, professional status, commitment, social skills, self-reliance, intensity, organization, sensitivity, gender, culture, and voluntary status. In addition, events have three characteristics: event type, intensity, and point in mission.

Because there are only a small handful of cases of actual IFRS data available at present, additional cases are needed to test and to demonstrate the system. Approximate models of time series and interventions can be estimated based on space and analog missions reported in the literature, even if raw time-series data are not available to derive the model statistically. Using these, we generated and installed supplemental demo cases by perturbating the variables in these cases and adjusting the model parameters in accordance with rules of thumb gleaned from the literature on analog missions. This database is not rigorously empirical but should produce plausible results during testing and demos. The database can be recreated at a later time when sufficient real data are available. At that point, NASA might change which factor and event types to track in the database or the set of variables to describe them. Then the actual case data would be analyzed using interrupted time-series analysis to derive empirical values for μ, σ, ϕ, and θ for the factors.

Users of Crew enter a *scenario* of a proposed mission, including crew composition and mission characteristics. They also enter a series of n anticipated events at specific points in the mission period. From the scenario, the system computes values for μ, σ, ϕ, and θ for each behavioral factor. For events $j = 1$ through n, it computes values for δ_j, ε_j, and ω_j. The computation of parameters is accomplished with case-based reasoning rather than statistically. The missions or events in the case base that most closely match the hypothesized scenario are retrieved. The parameters associated with the retrieved cases are then adjusted for differences between the proposed and retrieved cases, using rules of thumb formulated in a rule base for this purpose. Then, using the model equation, Crew computes values of Y_t for each behavioral factor at each time slice t in the mission. These values can be graphed to present a visual image of the model's expectations for the proposed mission. Users can then modify their descriptions of the crew, the mission scenario, or the sequence of events and rerun the analysis to test alternative mission scenarios.

Crew is basically a database system, with a system of relational files storing variable values and parameter values for historical cases and rules for case adaptation. For this reason, it was developed in the FoxPro database-management system, rather than in Lisp, as originally planned. FoxPro is extremely efficient at retrieving items from indexed database files, so that Crew can be scaled up to arbitrarily large case bases with virtually no degradation in processing speed. Crew runs on Macintosh and Windows computers.

The Case-Retrieval Mechanism

A key aspect of case-based reasoning (CBR) is its case-retrieval mechanism. The first step in computing predictions for a proposed new case is to retrieve one or more similar cases from the case base. According to Roger Schank (1982), CBR adopts the dynamic-memory approach of human recall.

As demonstrated in exemplary CBR systems (Riesbeck & Schank, 1989), this involves a hierarchical storage and retrieval arrangement. Thus, to retrieve the case most similar to a new case, one might, for instance, follow a tree of links that begins with the mission characteristic "harshness of environment." Once the link corresponding to the new case's environment is chosen, the link for the next mission characteristic is chosen, and so on until one arrives at a particular case. The problem with this method is that not all domains can be meaningfully organized in such a hierarchy. Janet Kolodner (1993) notes that some CBR systems need to define nonhierarchical retrieval systems. In the domain of space missions, there is no clear priority of characteristics for establishing similarity of cases.

A standard nonhierarchical measure of similarity is the n-dimensional Euclidean distance, which compares two cases by adding the squares of the differences between each of the n corresponding variable values. The problem with this method is that it is intractable for large case bases because a new case must be compared with every case in the database.

Crew adopts an approach that avoids the need to define a strict hierarchy of variables as well as the ultimately intractable inefficiency of comparing a new case to each historic case. It prioritizes which variables to compare initially to narrow down to the most likely neighbors using highly efficient indices on the database files. But it avoids strict requirements even at this stage.

The retrieval algorithm also responds to another problem of the space-mission domain that is discussed in the section on adaptation below—the fact that large random variations exist among similar cases. This problem suggests finding several similar cases instead of just one to adapt to a new case. The case-retrieval algorithm in Crew returns n nearest neighbors, where n is a small number specified by the user. Thus, parameters for new cases can be computed using adjusted values from several near neighbors rather than just from the one nearest neighbor as is traditional in CBR. This introduces a statistical flavor to the computation to soften the variability likely to be present in the empirical case data.

The case-retrieval mechanism consists of a procedure for finding the n most similar factors and a procedure for finding the n most similar events, given a proposed factor or event, a number n, and the case-base file. These procedures, in turn, call various subprocedures. Each of the procedures is of computational order n, where n is the number of neighbors sought, so it will scale up with no problem for case bases of arbitrary size. Here are outlines of typical procedures:

nearest_factor (new_factor, **n,** *file)*

1. Find all factor records with the same factor type, using a database index.

2. Of these, find the $4n$ with the **nearest_mission.**

3. Of these, find the n with the **nearest_actor.**

nearest_mission (new_mission, **n,** *file)*

1. Find all mission records with environment = new mission's environment $\pm$ 1 using an index.

2. If less than $20n$ results, then find all mission records with environment = new mission's environment $\pm$ 2 using an index.

3. If less than $20n$ results, then find all mission records with environment = new mission's environment $\pm$ 3 using an index.

4. Of these, find the $3n$ records with minimal |mission's duration − new mission's duration| using an index.

5. Of these, find the n records with minimal $\Sigma\ dif_i^2$.

nearest_actor (new_actor, **n,** *file)*

1. Find up to n actor records with minimal $\Sigma\ dif_i^2$.

Note that in these procedures there is a weak sense of hierarchical ordering. It includes only a couple of levels and usually allows values that are not exactly identical, depending on how many cases exist with identical matches. Note, too, that the n-dimensional distance approach is used (indicated by "minimal $\Sigma\ dif_i^2$"), but only with $3*n$ cases, where n is the number of similar cases sought. The only operations that perform searches on significant portions of the database are those that can be accomplished using file indexes. These operations are followed by procedures that progressively narrow down the number of cases, thereby maintaining a balance that avoids both rigid prioritizing and intractable computations.

Case-based reasoning often imposes a hierarchical priority to processing that is hidden behind the scenes. It makes case retrieval efficient without exposing the priorities to scrutiny. The preceding algorithms employ a minimum of prioritizing. In each instance, priorities are selected that make sense in the domain of extreme missions based on our understanding of the relevant literature and discussions with domain experts at NASA. As understanding of the domain evolves with increased data and experience, these priorities will have to be reviewed and adjusted.

The Adaptation Algorithm

Space and analog missions exhibit large variations in survey results due to the complexity and subjectivity of the crew members' perceptions as recorded in survey forms. Even among surveys by different crew members on relatively simple missions with highly homogeneous crews, the recorded survey ratings varied remarkably. To average out these effects, Crew retrieves n nearest neighbors for any new case rather than the unique nearest one as is traditional in CBR. The value of n is set by the user.

The parameters that model the new case are computed by taking a weighted average of the parameters of the n retrieved neighbors. The weight used in this computation is based on a similarity distance of each neighbor from the new case. The similarity distance is the sum of the squares of the differences between the new and the old values of each variable. So if the new case and a neighbor differed only in that the new case had a mission complexity rating of 3 while the retrieved neighbor had a mission complexity rating of 6, then the neighbor's distance would be $(6 - 3)^2 = 9$.

The weighting actually uses a term called *importance* that is defined as (sum − distance)/(sum * ($n − 1$)), where *distance* is the distance of the current neighbor as just defined, and *sum* is the sum of the distances of the n neighbors. This weighting gives a strong preference to neighbors that are very near to the new case, while allowing all n neighbors to contribute to the adaptation process.

Rules and Fuzzy Logic

Once n similar cases have been found, they must be adapted to the new case. That is, we know the time-series parameters for the similar old cases, and we now need to adjust them to define parameters for the new case, taking into account the differences between the old and the new cases. Because the database is relatively sparse, it is unlikely that we will retrieve cases that closely match a proposed new case. Adaptation rules play a critical role in spanning the gap between the new and the retrieved cases.

The rules have been generated by our social science team, which has reviewed much of the literature on analog missions and small-group interactions under extreme conditions of isolation and confinement, e.g. (Radloff & Helmreich, 1968). They have determined what variables have positive, negligible or negative correlations with which factors. They have rated these correlations as either *strong* or *weak*. The Crew system translates the ratings into percentage correlation values. For instance, the rule "Teamwork is strongly negatively correlated with commander competence" would be encoded as a −80 percent correlation between the variable *commander competence* and the factor *teamwork*.

What follow are examples of the general way that the rules function in Crew. One rule, for instance, is used to adjust predicted *stress* for a hypothetical mission of length *new-duration* from the stress measured in a similar mission of length *old-duration*. Suppose that the rule states that the correlation of psychological *stress* to mission *duration* is +55 percent. All mission factors, such as stress, are coded on a scale of 0 to 10. Suppose that the historic mission had its duration variable coded as 5 and a stress factor rating of 6 and that the hypothetical mission has a duration rating of 8. We use the rule to adapt the historic mission's stress rating to the hypothetical mission given the difference in mission durations (assuming all other mission characteristics to be identical). Now, the maximum that stress could be increased and still be on the scale is 4 (from 6 to 10), the *new-duration* is greater than the old by 60 percent (8 − 5 = 3 of a possible 10 − 5 = 5), and the rule states that the correlation is 55 percent. So the predicted stress for the new case is greater than the stress for the old case by $4 \times 60\% \times 55\% = 1.32$, for a predicted stress of $6 + 1.32 = 7.32$. Using this method of adapting outcome values, the values are proportional to the correlation value, to the difference between the new and old variable values and to the old outcome value, without ever exceeding the 0 to 10 range.

Many rules are needed for the system. Rules for adapting the four parameters (μ, σ, ϕ, and θ) of the 12 factors are needed for each of the 22 variables of the mission and actor descriptions, requiring 1,056 rules. Rules for adapting the three parameters (ε, δ, and ω) of the eight event types for each of the 12 factors are needed for each of the 24 variables of the mission, actor, and intervention descriptions, requiring 6,912 rules. Many of these 7,968 required rules have correlations of 0, indicating that a difference in the given variable has no effect on the particular parameter.

The rules gleaned from the literature are rough descriptions of relationships rather than precise functions. Because so many rules are applied in a typical simulation, it was essential to streamline the computations. We therefore made the simplifying assumption that all correlations were linear from zero difference between the old and new variable values to a difference of the full 10 range, with only the strength of the correlation varying from rule to rule.

However, it is sometimes the case that such rules apply more or less, depending on values of other variables. For instance, the rule "Teamwork is strongly negatively correlated with commander competence" might be valid only if "Commander leadership is very low, and the crew member's self-reliance is low." This might capture the circumstance where a commander is weak at leading others to work on something, the crew is reliant on him, and the commander can do everything himself. It might generally be good for a commander to be competent but problematic under the special condition that he is a poor leader and that the crew lacks self-reliance.

Note that the original rule has to do with the difference of a given variable (*commander competence*) in the old and the new cases, while the condition on the rule has to do with the absolute value of variables (*commander leadership, crew member's self-reliance*) in the new case. Crew uses fuzzy logic (Cox, 1994) to encode the conditions. This allows the conditions to be stated in English language terms, using values like *low*, *medium*, or *high*; modifiers like *very* or *not*; and the connectives *and* or *or*. The values like *low* are defined by fuzzy set-membership functions, so that if the variable is 0, it is considered completely *low*, but if it is 2, it is only partially *low*. Arbitrarily complex conditions can be defined. They compute to a numeric value between 0 and 1. This value of the condition is then multiplied by the value of the rule so that the rule is applied only to the extent that the condition exists.

The combination of many simple linear rules and occasional arbitrarily complex conditions on the rules provides a flexible yet computationally efficient system for implementing the rules found in the social science literature. The English language statements by the researchers are translated reasonably into numeric computations by streamlined versions of the fuzzy-logic formalism, preserving sufficient precision considering the small effect that any given rule or condition has on the overall simulation.

Conclusions and Future Work

The domain of space missions poses a number of difficulties for the creation of an expert system:

- Too little is known to generalize formal rules for a rule-based system.
- A model of the temporal mission process is more needed than just a prediction of final outcomes.
- The descriptive variables cannot be put into a rigid hierarchy to facilitate case-based retrieval.
- The case base is too sparse and too variable for reliable adaptation from one nearest-neighbor case.

- The rules that can be gleaned from available data or relevant literature are imprecise.

Therefore, we have constructed a hybrid system that departs in several ways from traditional rule-based as well as classic case-based systems. Crew creates a time-series model of a mission, retrieving and adapting the parameters of the model from a case base. The retrieval uses a multistage algorithm to maintain both flexibility and computational tractability. An extensive set of adaptation rules overcomes the sparseness of the case base, with the results of several nearest neighbors averaged together to avoid the unreliability of individual cases.

Our proof-of-concept system demonstrates the tractability of our approach. For testing purposes, Crew was loaded with descriptions of 50 hypothetical missions involving 62 actors. This involved 198 intervention parameters, 425 factor parameters and 4,047 event parameters. Based on our reading of the relevant literature, 7,968 case-adaptation rule-correlation figures were entered. A number of fuzzy-logic conditions were also included for the test cases. Given a description of a crew member and a mission, the Crew system predicts a series of 100 values of a selected psychological factor in a minute or two on a standard desktop computer.

Future work includes expanding the fuzzy-logic language syntax to handle more subtle rules. Our impression from conflicting conclusions within the literature is that it is unlikely that many correlation rules hold uniformly across entire ranges of their factors.

We would also like to enhance the explanatory narrative provided by Crew to increase its value as a research assistant. We envision our system serving as a tool to help domain experts select astronaut crews rather than as an automated decision maker. People will want to be able to see and evaluate the program's rationale for its predictions. This would minimally involve displaying the original sources of cases and rules used by the algorithms. The most important factors should be highlighted. In situations strongly influenced by case-adaptation rules or fuzzy-logic conditions derived from the literature, it would be helpful to display references to the sources of the rules if not the relevant excerpted text itself.

Currently, each crew member is modeled independently; it is undoubtedly important to take into account interactions among them as well. While crew interactions indirectly affect survey results of individual members (especially to questions like "How well do you think the crew is working together today?"), additional data would be needed to model interactions directly. Two possible approaches suggest themselves—treating crew interaction as a special category of event and subjecting data from crew members on a mission together to statistical analyses to see how their moods and other factors affect one another. Taking interactions into account would significantly complicate the system and would require data that are not currently systematically collected.

Use of the system by NASA personnel will suggest changes in the variables tracked and their relative priority in the processing algorithms; this will make end-user modifiability facilities desirable. To quickly develop a proof-of-concept system, we hard-coded many of the algorithms described in this chapter. However, some of these algorithms make assumptions about, for instance, what are the most important factors to sort on first. As the eventual system users gain deeper understanding of mission dynamics, they will want to be able to modify these algorithms. Future system development should make that process easier and less fragile.

Data about individual astronauts, about group interactions, and about mission progress at a detailed level is not public information. For a number of personal and institutional reasons, such information is closely guarded. Because NASA was just starting to collect the kind of time-series data that Crew is based on, we were not able to use empirical data in our case base. Instead, we incorporated the format of the IFRS surveys and generated plausible data based on the statistical results of completed IFRS surveys and the public literature on space and analog missions. When NASA has collected enough empirical cases to substitute for our test data, it will have to enter the new parameters, review the rule base, and reconsider some of the priorities embedded in our algorithms based on a new understanding of mission dynamics. However, NASA should be able to do this within the computational framework we have developed and remain confident that such a system is feasible. As NASA collects more time-series data, the Crew database will grow and become increasingly plausible as a predictive tool that can assist in the planning of expensive and risky interplanetary missions.

4

Supporting Situated Interpretation

This chapter opens up themes of computer support for collaboration, design theory, and situated cognition.[1] It also introduces the importance of interpretive perspectives as stressed in the hermeneutic tradition. Anticipating the book's recurrent discussion of perspectives, it argues that collaboration software should support multiple interpretive design perspectives, represent the context of work, and provide shared language elements. The Hermes software that illustrates these principles was part of my dissertation research on computer-supported cooperative work support for NASA lunar-habitat designers.

The chapter discusses the role of interpretation in innovative design and proposes an approach to providing computer support for interpretation in design. According to situated-cognition theory, most of a designer's knowledge is normally tacit. Situated interpretation is the process of explicating something that is tacitly understood, within its larger context. The centrality of interpretation to nonroutine design is demonstrated by a review of the design methodology of Alexander, Rittel, and Schön; a protocol analysis of a lunar-habitat design session; and a summary of Heidegger's philosophy of interpretation. These show that the designer's articulation of tacit knowledge takes place on the basis of an understanding of the design situation, a focus from a particular perspective, and a shared language. As knowledge is made explicit through the interpretive processes of design, it can be captured for use in computer-based design-support systems. A prototype software system is described for representing design situations, interpretive perspectives, and domain terminology to support interpretation by designers. This chapter introduces the concept of interpretation, which plays a central role in each part of this book: software support for interpretive perspectives, interpretation as a rigorous methodology for computer-supported collaborative learning, and interpretation as integral to collaborative meaning making and knowledge building. The hermeneutic philosophy of interpretation introduced here reappears in the later, more theoretical essays.

The Need for Computer Support

The volume of information available to people is increasing rapidly. For many professionals, this means that the execution of their jobs requires taking into account far more information than they can possibly keep in mind. Consider lunar-habitat designers, who serve as a key example in this chapter. In working on their high-tech design tasks, they must take into account architectural knowledge, ergonomics, space science, NASA regulations, and lessons learned in past missions. Computers seem necessary to store these large amounts of data. However, the problem is how to capture and encode information relevant to novel future tasks and how to present it to designers in formats that support their mode of work.

A framework for clarifying the respective roles for computers and people in tasks like lunar-habitat design is suggested by the theory of *situated cognition*. Several influential books (Dreyfus, 1991; Ehn, 1988; Schön, 1983; Suchman, 1987; Winograd & Flores, 1986) have argued that human cognition is fundamentally different from computer manipulations of formal symbol systems. These differences imply that people need to retain control of the processes of nonroutine design, although computers can provide valuable computational, visualization and external memory aids for the designers, and support interpretation by them.

From the viewpoint of situated cognition, the greatest impediment to computer support of innovative design is that designers make extensive use of *tacit* knowledge while computers can use only *explicit* representations of information. This chapter discusses the role of tacit understanding in design to motivate an approach to computer support of design tasks. It focuses on three themes: the need to represent novel design situations, the importance of viewing designs from multiple perspectives, and the utility of formulating tacit knowledge in explicit language.

The following sections discuss how these three themes figure prominently in analyses of interpretation in design methodology and in a study of interpretation in lunar-habitat design. Following a discussion of the tacit basis of understanding, the philosophy of interpretation defines interpretation as the articulation of tacit understanding. Then consequences for computer support for interpretation are drawn, and they are illustrated by the Hermes system, a prototype for supporting interpretation in the illustrative task of lunar-habitat design.

Interpretation in Design Methodology

The centrality of interpretation to design can be seen in seminal writings of design methodologists. The following summaries highlight the roles of appropriate representations of the design situation, alternative perspectives, and linguistic explications of tacit understanding within the processes of interpretation in design.

Christopher Alexander (1964) pioneered the use of computers for designing. He used them to compute diagrams or patterns that decomposed the structural dependencies of a given problem into relatively independent substructures. In this way, he developed explicit interpretations for understanding a task based on an analysis of the unique design *situation*.

For Horst Rittel (Rittel and Webber, 1973), the heart of design is the deliberation of issues from multiple *perspectives*. Interpretation in design is "an argumentative process in the course of which an image of the problem and of the solution emerges gradually among the participants, as a product of incessant judgment, subjected to critical argument" (p. 162). Rittel's idea of using computers to keep track of the various issues at stake and alternative positions on those issues led to the creation of issue-based information systems.

Donald Schön (1983) argues that designers constantly shift perspectives on a problem by bringing various professionally trained tacit skills to bear, such as visual perception, graphical sketching, and vicarious simulation. By experimenting with tentative design moves within the tacitly understood situation, the designer discovers consequences and makes aspects of the structure of the problem explicit. Certain features of the situation come into focus and can be named or characterized in *language*. As focus subsequently shifts, what has been interpreted may slip back into an understanding that is once more tacit but is now more developed.

Interpretation in Lunar-Habitat Design

As part of an effort at developing computer support for lunar-habitat designers working for the National Aeronautics and Space Administration (NASA, the U.S. space agency), I videotaped 30 hours of design sessions (Stahl, 1993a). The specified task was to accommodate four astronauts for 45 days on the moon in a cylindrical module 23 feet long and 14 feet wide.

Analysis of the designers' activities shows that much of the design time consisted of processes of *interpretation*—that is, the explication of previously tacit understanding. As part of this interpretation, representations were developed for describing pivotal features of the design situation that had not been included in the original specification; perspectives were evolved for looking at the task; and terminology was defined for explicitly naming, describing, and communicating shared understandings.

The designers felt that a careful balance of public and private space would be essential given the crew's long-term isolation in the habitat. An early design sketch proposed private crew areas consisting of a bunk above a workspace for each astronaut. Space constraints argued against this. The traditional conception of private space as a place for one person to get away was made explicit and criticized as taking up too much room. As part of the interpretive designing process, this concept was revised into a reinterpretation of privacy as a gradient along the habitat from quiet sleep quarters to a public activity area. This notion of degrees of privacy permitted greater flexibility in designing.

In another interchange related to privacy, the conventional American idea of a bathroom was subjected to critical deliberation when it was realized that the placement of the toilet and that of the shower were subject to different sets of constraints based on life in the habitat. The tacit acceptance of the location of the toilet and shower together was made explicit by comparing it to alternative European perspectives. The revised conception, permitting a separation of the toilet from the shower, facilitated a major design reorganization.

In these and other examples, the designers needed to revise their representations for understanding the design *situation*. They went from looking at privacy as a matter of individual space to reinterpreting the whole interior space as a continuum of private to public areas.

The conventional American notion of a bathroom was compared with other cultural models and broken down into separable functions that could relate differently to habitat usage patterns. Various *perspectives* were applied to the problem, suggesting new possibilities and considerations. Through discussion, the individual perspectives merged and novel solutions emerged.

In this interpretive process, previously tacit features of the design became explicit by being named and described in the *language* that developed. For instance, the fact that quiet activities were being grouped toward one end of the habitat design and interactive ones at the other became a topic of conversation at one point and the term *privacy gradient* was proposed to clarify this emergent pattern.

The Tacit Basis of Understanding

Situated cognition theory disputes the prevalent view that all human cognition is based on explicit mental representations such as goals and plans. Terry Winograd and Fernando Flores (1986) hold that "experts do not need to have formalized representations in order to act" (p. 99). Although manipulation of such representations is often useful, there is a background of preunderstanding that cannot be fully formalized as explicit symbolic representations subject to rule-governed manipulation. This tacit preunderstanding underlies people's ability to understand representations when they do make use of them. Lucy Suchman (1987) concurs that goals and plans are secondary phenomena in human behavior, usually arising only after action has been initiated: "when situated action becomes in some way problematic, rules and procedures are explicated for purposes of deliberation and the action, which is otherwise neither rule-based nor procedural, is then made accountable to them" (p. 54).

Philosophers like Michael Polanyi (1962), John Searle (1980), and Hubert Dreyfus (1991) suggest a variety of reasons why tacit preunderstanding cannot be fully formalized as data for computation. First, it is too vast: background knowledge includes bodily skills and social practices that result from immense histories of life experience and that are generally transparent to us. Second, it must be tacit to function: we cannot formulate, understand, or use explicit knowledge except on the basis of necessarily tacit preunderstandings.

This is not to denigrate conceptual reasoning and rational planning. Rather, it is to point out that the manipulation of formal representations alone cannot provide a complete model of human understanding. Rational thought is an advanced form of cognition that distinguishes humans from other organisms. Accordingly, an evolutionary theorist of consciousness such as Merlin Donald (1991) traces the development of symbolic thought from earlier developmental stages of tacit knowing, showing how these earlier levels persist in rational human thought as the necessary foundation for advanced developments, including language, writing, and computer usage.

The most thorough formulation of a philosophical foundation for situated cognition theory is given by Martin Heidegger (1996), the first to point out the role of tacit preunderstanding and to elaborate its implications. For Heidegger, we are always knowledgeably embedded in our world; things of concern in our situations are already meaningful in general before we engage in cognitive activity. We know how to behave without having to think about it. For instance, without having to actively think about it, an architect designing a lunar habitat knows how to lift a pencil and sketch a line or how to look at a drawing and see the rough relationships of various spaces pictured there. The architect understands what it is to be a designer, to critique a drawing, to imagine being a person walking through the spaces of a floor plan.

Heidegger defines the *situation* as the architect's context—the physical surroundings, the available tools, the circumstances surrounding the task at hand, the architect's own personal or professional aims, and so on. The situation constitutes a network of significance in terms of which each part of the situation is already meaningful (Stahl, 1975b). That is, the architect has tacit knowledge of the situation as a whole; if something becomes a focus for the architect, it is perceived as already understood, and its meaning is defined by its relation to the rest of the situation.

To the architect, a rectangular arrangement of lines on a piece of paper is not perceived as meaningless lines, but given the design situation, it is already understood as a bunk for astronauts. The bunk is implicitly defined as such by the design task, the shared intentions of the design team, the other elements of the design, the sense of space conveyed by the design, and so on indefinitely. This network of significance is background knowledge that allows the architect to think about features of the design, to make plans for changes, and to discover problems or opportunities in the evolving design. At any given moment, the background is already tacitly understood and does not need to be an object of rational thought manipulating symbolic representations.

At some point, the architect might realize that the bunk is too close to a source of potential noise, like the flushing of the toilet. The explicit concern about this physical adjacency arises and becomes something important against the background of relationships of the preunderstood situation. Whereas a commonsensical view might claim that the bunk and toilet were already present and therefore their adjacency was always there by logical implication, Heidegger proposes a more complex reality in which things are ordinarily hidden from explicit concern. In various ways, they can become uncovered and discovered, only to resubmerge soon into the background as our focus moves on.

In this way, our knowledge of the world does not consist primarily in mental models that represent an objective reality. Rather, our understanding of things presupposes a tacit preunderstanding of our situation. Only as situated in our already interpreted world can we discover things and construct meaningful representations of them. Situated cognition is not a simplistic theory that claims our knowledge lies in our physical environment like words on a sign post: it is a sophisticated philosophy of interpretation.

The Philosophy of Interpretation

Human understanding develops through interpretive explication. According to Heidegger, interpretation provides the path from tacit, uncritical preunderstandings to reflection, refinement, and creativity. The structure of this process of interpretation reflects the inextricable coupling of the interpreter with the situation—that is, of people with their worlds. Our situation is not reducible to our preunderstanding of it; it offers untold surprises, which may call for reflection but which can be discovered and comprehended only thanks to our preunderstanding. Often, these surprise occasions signal *breakdowns* in our skillful, transparent behavior, although we can also make unexpected discoveries in the situation through conversation, exploration, natural events, and other occurrences.

A discovery breaks out of the preunderstood situation because it violates or goes beyond the network of tacit meanings that make up the preunderstanding of the situation. To understand what we have discovered, we must explicitly *interpret* it *as* something, as having a certain significance, as somehow fitting into the already understood background. Then it can merge into our comprehension of the meaningful situation and become part of the new background. Interpretation of something *as* something is always a reinterpretation of the situated context.

For instance, the lunar-habitat designers discovered problems in their early sketches that they interpreted as issues of privacy. Although they had created the sketches themselves, they were completely surprised to discover certain conflicts among the interactions of adjacent components, like the bunks and the toilet. The discoveries could only occur because of their understanding of the *situation*, represented in their drawings. The designers paused in their sketching to discuss the new issues. First they debated the matter from various *perspectives*—experiences of previous space missions, cultural variations in bathroom designs, technical acoustical considerations. Then they considered alternative conceptions of privacy, gradually developing a shared *vocabulary* that guided their revisions and became part of their interpretation of their task. They reinterpreted their understanding of privacy and represented their new view as a "privacy gradient."

These themes of representing the situation, changing perspectives, and using explicit language correspond to the threefold structure of interpretation in Heidegger's philosophy. He articulates the preconditions of interpretation as *prepossession* of the situation as a network of preunderstood significance, *preview* or expectations of things in the world as being structured in certain ways, and *preconception*, a language for expressing and communicating.

In other words, interpretation never starts from scratch or from an arbitrary assignment of representations but is an evolution of tentative preunderstandings and anticipations. Sets of prejudices have been handed down historically, and the interpretive process allows one to reflect on these preunderstandings methodically and to refine new meanings, perspectives, and terminologies for understanding things more appropriately.

Computer Support for Interpretation

The theory of situated cognition and the philosophy of interpretation stress how different human understanding is from computer manipulations of arbitrary symbols. These theories suggest the approach of *augmenting* (rather than automating) human intelligence. According to this approach, software can at best provide computer representations for people to interpret based on their tacit understanding of what is represented.

Representations used in computer programs must be carefully structured by human programmers who thoroughly understand the task being handled because the computer itself simply follows the rules it has been given for manipulating symbols, with no notion of what these symbols represent. People who understand the domain must sufficiently codify their background knowledge into software rules to make the computer algorithms generate results that will be judged correct when interpreted by people. Only if a domain can be strictly delimited and its associated knowledge exhaustively reduced to rules can it be completely automated.

Many tasks, like lunar-habitat design, that call for computer support do not have such strictly delimited domains with fully catalogued and formalized knowledge bases. These domains may require exploration of problems never before considered, assumption of creative viewpoints, or formulation of innovative concepts. Software to support designers in such tasks should provide facilities for the creation of new representations and flexible modification of old ones. As the discussion of Alexander emphasized, the ability to develop appropriate representations dynamically is critical. Because they capture understandings of the *situation* that evolve through processes of interpretation, representations need to be modifiable during the design process itself and cannot adequately be anticipated in advance or provided once and for all.

The concept of an objective, coherent body of domain knowledge is misleading. As Rittel said, nonroutine design is an argumentative process involving the interplay of unlimited perspectives, reflecting differing and potentially conflicting technical concerns, personal idiosyncrasies, and political interests. Software to support design should capture these alternative deliberations on important issues, as well as document specific solutions. Furthermore, because all design knowledge may be relative to perspectives, the computer should be used to define a network of overlapping *perspectives* by which to organize issues, rationale, sketches, component parts, and terminology.

As Schön emphasizes, interpretive design relies on moving from tacit skills to explicit conceptualizations. Additionally, design work is inherently communicative and increasingly collaborative, with high-tech designs requiring successive teams of designers, implementers, and maintainers. Software to support collaborative design should provide a *language* facility for designers to develop a formal vocabulary for expressing their ideas, for communicating them to future collaborators, and for formally representing them within computer-executable software. An end-user language is needed that provides an extensible domain vocabulary, is usable by nonprogrammers, and encourages reuse and modification of expressions.

Heidegger's analysis of interpretation suggests that most of the information that would be useful to designers may be made explicit at some moment of interpretation during designing. One strategy for accumulating a useful knowledge base is to have the software capture knowledge that becomes explicit while the software is being used. As successive designs are developed on a system, issues and alternative deliberations can accumulate in its issue base; new perspectives can be defined containing their own modifications of terminology and critic rules; the language can be expanded to include more domain vocabulary, conditional expressions, and query formulations. In this way, potentially relevant information is captured in formats useful for designers because it is a product of human interpretation.

This is an evolutionary, bootstrap approach, where the software supports individual design projects but also simultaneously facilitates the accumulation of expertise and viewpoints in open-ended, exploratory domains. This means that the software should make it easy for designers to formalize their knowledge as it becomes explicit, without requiring excessive additional effort. The software should reward its users for increasing the computer knowledge base by performing useful tasks with the new information, like providing documentation, communicating rationale, and facilitating reuse or modification of relevant knowledge.

The Hermes System

In Greek mythology, Hermes supported human interpretation by providing the gift of spoken and written language and by delivering the messages of the gods. A prototype software system named Hermes has been designed to support the preconditions of interpretation by representing the design construction situation for *prepossession*, by providing alternative perspectives for *preview*, and by including an end-user language for *preconception*.

It supports tacit knowing by encapsulating mechanisms for analyzing design situations using interpretive critics (Fischer et al., 1993), alternative sets of information organized in named perspectives (Stahl, 1993a), and hypermedia computations expressed in language terms (Stahl et al., 1992). In each of these cases, the hidden complexities can be made explicit on demand, so the designer can reflect on the information and modify (reinterpret) it.

Hermes is a knowledge-representation substrate for building computer-based design assistants (like that in figure 4.1). It provides various media for designers to build formal representations of design knowledge. The hypermedia network of knowledge corresponds to the design *situation*. Nodes of the knowledge representation can be textual statements for the issue base, CAD graphics for sketches, or language expressions for critics and queries.

Hermes supports the collaborative nature of design by multiple teams through its *perspectives* mechanism. This allows users to organize knowledge in the system into overlapping collections. Drawings, definitions of domain terms in the language, computations for critic rules, and annotations in the issue base can all be grouped

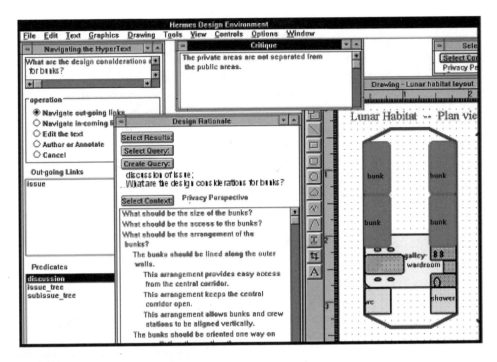

Figure 4.1
A view of the Hermes design environment, showing (left to right) a dialogue for browsing, a view of the issue base, a critic message, a construction area, and a button for changing interpretive perspectives.

together for a project, a technical specialty, an individual, a team, or an historical version. Every action in Hermes takes place within some defined perspective, which determines what versions of information are currently accessible.

The Hermes *language* pervades the system, defining mechanisms for browsing, displaying, and critiquing all information. This means that designers can refine the representations, views, and expressions of all forms of domain knowledge in the system. Vocabulary in the language is modifiable and every expression can be encapsulated by a name. The syntax is English-like, in an effort to make statements in the language easily interpretable. The language is declarative, so users need not be bothered with explicit sequential programming concerns. Combined with the perspectives mechanism, the language permits designers to define and refine their own interpretations. This allows the Hermes substrate to support multiple situated interpretations.

Conclusion

The theory of situated cognition argues that only people's tacit preunderstanding can make data meaningful in context. Neither people nor computers alone can take advantage of huge stores of data; such information is valueless unless designers use it in their interpretations of design situations. The data-handling capabilities of computers should be used to support the uniquely human ability to understand. The philosophy of interpretation suggests that several aspects of human understanding and collaboration can be supported with mechanisms like those in Hermes, such as refining representations of the design situation, creating alternative perspectives on the task, and sharing linguistic expressions. Together, situated cognition theory and Heidegger's philosophy of interpretation provide a theoretical framework for a principled approach to computer support for designers' situated interpretation in the information age.

5

Collaboration Technology for Communities

In the age of information overload, lifelong learning and collaboration are essential aspects of most innovative work.[1] Fortunately, the computer technology that drives the information explosion also has the potential to help individuals and groups learn, on demand, much of what they need to know. In particular, applications on the Internet can be designed to capture knowledge as it is generated within a community of practice and to deliver relevant knowledge when it is useful.

Computer-based design environments for skilled domain workers have recently graduated from research prototypes to commercial products, supporting the learning of individual designers. Such systems do not, however, adequately support the collaborative nature of work or the evolution of knowledge within communities of practice. If innovation is to be supported within collaborative efforts, these domain-oriented design environments must be extended to become collaborative information environments, capable of providing effective community memories for managing information and learning within constantly evolving collaborative contexts. In particular, collaborative information environments must provide functionality that facilitates the construction of new knowledge and the shared understanding necessary to use this knowledge effectively within communities of practice.

This chapter reviews three stages of work on artificial (computer-based and Web-based) systems that augment the intelligence of people and organizations. NetSuite illustrates the domain-oriented design environment approach to supporting the work of individual designers with learning on demand. WebNet extends this model to collaborative information environments that support collaborative learning by groups of designers, and WebGuide shows how a computational perspectives mechanism for these environments can support the construction of knowledge and of shared understanding within groups. According to recent theories of cognition, human intelligence is the product of tool use and of social mediations as well as of biological development. Collaborative information environments are designed to enhance this intelligence by providing computationally powerful tools that are supportive of social relations.

This chapter carries out a transition from systems that use artificial intelligence techniques and computational power to computer-based media that support communication and collaboration. In part, this is a difference of emphasis, as the media may still incorporate significant computation. However, it is also a shift in the locus of intelligence from clever software to human group cognition.

Introduction: The Need for Computer Support of Lifelong Collaborative Learning

The creation of innovative artifacts and helpful knowledge in our complex world—with its refined division of labor and its flood of information—requires continual learning and collaboration. Learning can no longer be conceived of as an activity confined to the classroom and to an individual's early years. Learning must continue while we are engaged with other people as workers, citizens, and adult learners for many reasons:

- Innovative tasks are ill-defined; their solution involves continual learning and the creative construction of knowledge whose need could not have been foreseen (Rittel & Webber, 1984).

- There is too much knowledge, even within specific subject areas, for anyone to master it alone or all in advance (Zuboff, 1988).

- The knowledge in many domains evolves rapidly and often depends on the context of the task situation, including the support community (Senge, 1990).

- Frequently, the most important information has to do with a work group's own structure and history, its standard practices and roles, and the details and design rationale of its local accomplishments (Orr, 1990).

- People's careers and self-directed interests require various new forms of learning at different stages as their roles in communities change (Argyris & Schön, 1978).

- Learning—especially collaborative learning—has become a new form of labor, an integral component of work and organizations (Lave & Wenger, 1991).

- Individual memory, attention, and understanding are too limited for today's complex tasks; divisions of labor are constantly shifting, and learning is required to coordinate and respond to the changing demands on community members (Brown & Duguid, 1991).

- Learning necessarily includes organizational learning: social processes that involve shared understandings across groups. These fragile understandings are both reliant on and in tension with individual learning, although they can also function as the cultural origin of individual comprehension (Vygotsky, 1978).

The pressure on individuals and groups to continually construct new knowledge out of massive sources of information strains the abilities of unaided human cognition. Carefully designed computer software promises to enhance the ability of communities to construct, organize, and share knowledge by supporting these processes. However, the design of such software remains an open research area.

The contemporary need to extend the learning process from schooling into organizational and community realms is known as *lifelong learning*. Our past research at the University of Colorado's Center for LifeLong Learning and Design explored the computer support of lifelong learning with what we call *domain-oriented design environments* (DODEs). This chapter argues for extending that approach to support work within communities of practice with what it will term *collaborative information environments* (CIEs) applied both to design tasks and to the construction of shared knowledge. This chapter illustrates three stages that our efforts with illustrative software systems have evolved through during the 1990s.

The second section of this chapter highlights how computer support for lifelong learning has already been developed for individuals such as designers. It argues, however, that DODEs—such as the commercial product NetSuite—that deliver domain knowledge to individuals when it is relevant to their task are not sufficient for supporting innovative work within collaborative communities. The next section sketches a theory of how software productivity environments for design work by individuals can be extended to support organizational learning in collaborative work structures known as communities of practice; a scenario of a prototype system called WebNet illustrates this. Finally, the chapter discusses the need for mechanisms within CIEs to help community members construct knowledge in their own personal perspectives while also negotiating shared understanding about evolving community knowledge; this is illustrated by the perspectives mechanism in WebGuide, discussed in terms of three learning applications. A concluding section locates this discussion within the context of broader trends in computer science.

Augmenting the Work of Individual Designers

In this section, I discuss how our DODE approach, which has now emerged in commercial products, provides support for individual designers. However, because design (such as the layout, configuration, and maintenance of computer networks) now typically takes place within communities of practice, it is desirable to provide computer support at the level of these communities as well as at the individual designer's level and to include local community knowledge as well as domain knowledge. Note that much of what is described in this section about our DODE systems applies to a broad family of design critiquing systems developed by others for domains such as medicine (Miller, 1986), civil engineering (Fu, Hayes, & East, 1997), and software development (Robbins & Redmiles, 1998).

Domain-Oriented Design Environments

Many innovative work tasks can be conceived of as *design* processes: elaborating a new idea, planning a presentation, balancing conflicting proposals, or writing a visionary report, for example. While designing can proceed on an intuitive level based on tacit expertise, it periodically encounters breakdowns in understanding where explicit reflection on new knowledge may be needed (Schön, 1983). Thereby, designing entails learning.

For the past decade, we have explored the creation of DODEs to support workers as designers. These systems are *domain-oriented*: they incorporate knowledge specific to the work domain. They are able to recognize when certain breakdowns in understanding have occurred and can respond to them with appropriate information (Fischer et al., 1993). They support learning on demand.

To go beyond the power of pencil-and-paper representations, software systems for lifelong learning must "understand" something of the tasks they are supporting. This is accomplished by building knowledge of the domain into the system, including capturing design objects and design rationale. A DODE typically provides a computational workspace within which a designer can construct an artifact and represent components of the artifact being constructed. Unlike a CAD system, in which the software only stores positions of lines, a DODE maintains a *representation* of objects that are meaningful in the domain. For instance, an environment for local-area network (LAN) design (a primary example in this chapter) allows a designer to construct a network's design by selecting items from a palette representing workstations, servers, routers, cables, and other devices from the LAN domain and configuring these items into a system design. Information about each device is represented in the system.

A DODE can contain domain knowledge about constraints, rules of thumb, and design rationale. It uses this information to respond to a current design state with active advice. Our systems use a mechanism we call *critiquing* (Fischer et al., 1998). The system maintains a representation of the semantics of the design situation, which is usually the two-dimensional location of palette items representing design components. Critic rules are applied to the design representation. When a rule "fires," it posts a message alerting the designer that a problem might exist. The message includes links to information such as design rationale associated with the critic rule.

For instance, a LAN DODE might notice that the length of a cable in a design exceeds the specifications for that type of cable, that a router is needed to connect two subnets, or that two connected devices are incompatible. At this point, the system could signal a possible design breakdown and provide domain knowledge relevant to the cited problem. The evaluation of the situation and the choice of action is up to the human designer, but now the designer has been given access to information relevant to making a decision (Fischer, Lemke, McCall, & Morch, 1996).

NetSuite: A Commercial Product
Many of the ideas in our DODEs are now appearing in commercial products, independently of our efforts. In particular, there are several environments for designing LANs. As an example, consider NetSuite, a highly rated system that illustrates current best practices in LAN design support. This is a high-functionality system for skilled domain professionals who are willing to make the effort required to learn to use its rich set of capabilities (figure 5.1). NetSuite contains a wealth of domain knowledge. Its palette of devices, which can be placed in the construction area, numbers over 5,000, with more available for download from the vendor every month. Each device has associated parameters defining its characteristics, limitations, and compatibilities—domain knowledge used by the critics that validate designs.

In NetSuite, one designs a LAN from scratch, placing devices and cables from the palette. As the design progresses, the system validates it, critiquing it according to rules and parameters stored in its domain knowledge. The designer is informed about relevant issues in a number of ways: lists of devices to substitute into a design are restricted by the system to compatible choices, limited design rationale is displayed with the option of linking to further details, and technical terms are defined with hypertext links. In addition to the construction area, there are LAN tools, such as an automated internet protocol (IP) address generator and utilities for reporting on physically existing LAN configurations. When a design is completed, a bill of materials can be printed out, and a Web page of it can be produced for display on the Internet. NetSuite is a knowledgeable, well-constructed system to support an individual LAN designer.

The Need to Go Further
Based on our understanding of organizational learning and our investigation of LAN design communities, we believe that in a domain like LAN management no closed system will suffice. The domain knowledge required to go beyond the

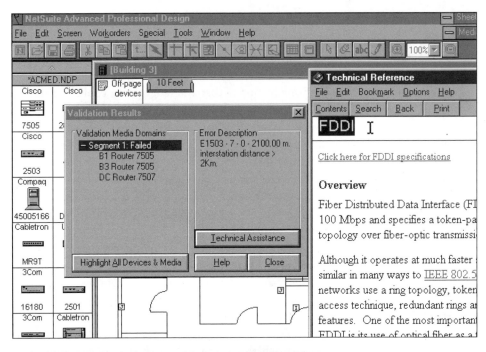

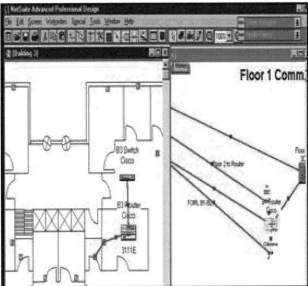

Figure 5.1

Two views of NetSuite. *Top:* The system has noted that a cable-length specification for a fiber distributed data interface (FDDI) network has been exceeded in the design, and the system has delivered information about the specification and affected devices. *Bottom:* Parts of the network viewed in physical and logical representations are connected.

functionality of NetSuite is too open-ended, too constantly changing, and too dependent on local circumstances. The next generation of commercial DODEs will have to support extensibility by end-users and collaboration within communities of practice. While a system like NetSuite has its place in helping to design complex networks from scratch, most work of LAN managers involves extending existing networks, debugging breakdowns in service, and planning for future technologies.

Many LAN management organizations rely on home-grown information systems because they believe that critical parts of their local information are unique. Each community of practice has its own ways of doing things. Generally, these local practices are understood tacitly and are propagated through apprenticeship (Lave & Wenger, 1991). This causes problems when the old-timer who set things up is gone and when a newcomer does not know who to ask or even what to ask. A community memory is needed that captures local knowledge when it is generated (such as when a device is configured) and delivers knowledge when it is needed (when there is a problem with that device) without being explicitly queried.

The burden of entering all this information in the system must be distributed among the people doing the work and must be supported computationally to minimize the effort required:

• The DODE knowledge base should be integrated with work practices in ways that capture knowledge as it is created.

• The benefits of maintaining the knowledge base have to be clearly experienced by participants.

• There may need to be an accepted distribution of roles related to the functioning of the organizational memory.

• The software environment must be thoroughly interactive so that users can easily enter data and comments.

• The information base should be seeded with basic domain knowledge so that users do not have to enter everything and so that the system is useful from the start.

• As the information space grows, there should be ways for people to restructure it so that its organization and functionality keep pace with its evolving contents and uses (Fischer et al., 1999).

DODEs must be extended in these ways to support communities of practice and not just isolated designers. This reflects a shift of emphasis from technical domain knowledge to local, social-based community knowledge.

Supporting Communities of Practice

In this section, I briefly define *community of practice*—a level of analysis increasingly important within discussions of computer-supported cooperative work (CSCW)—and suggest that these communities need group memories to carry on their work. The notion of DODEs must be extended to support the collaborative learning that needs to take place within these communities. A scenario demonstrates how a CIE prototype named WebNet can do this.

Community Memories
Communities of Practice   All work within a division of labor is social (Marx, 1976). The job that one person performs is also performed similarly by others and relies on vast social networks. That is, work is defined by social practices that are propagated through socialization, apprenticeship, training, schooling, and culture (Bourdieu, 1995; Giddens, 1984a; Lave & Wenger, 1991), as well as by explicit standards. Often, work is performed by collaborating teams that form communities of practice within or across organizations (Brown & Duguid, 1991). These communities evolve their own styles of communication and expression, or genres (Bakhtin, 1986b; Yates & Orlikowski, 1992).

For instance, interviews we conducted showed that computer network managers in different departments at our university work in concert. They need to share information about what they have done and how it is done with other team members and with other LAN managers elsewhere. For such a community, information about their own situation and local terminology may be even more important than generic domain knowledge (Orr, 1990). Support for LAN managers must provide memory about how individual local devices have been configured, as well as offer domain knowledge about standards, protocols, compatibilities, and naming conventions.

Communities of practice can be colocated within an organization (such as at our university) or across a discipline (such as all managers of university networks). Before the World Wide Web existed, most computer support for communities of practice targeted individuals with desktop applications. The knowledge in the systems was mostly static domain knowledge. With intranets and dynamic Web sites, it is now possible to support distributed communities and also to maintain interactive and evolving information about local circumstances and group history. Communities of practice need to be able to maintain their own memories. The problem of adoption of organizational memory technologies by specific communities involves complex social issues beyond the scope of this chapter. For a review of common adoption issues and positive and negative examples of responses, see

Grudin (1990), Orlikowski (1992), and Orlikowski, Yates, Okamura, & Fujimoto (1995).

Digital Memories for Communities of Practice Human and social evolution can be viewed as the successive development of increasingly effective forms of memory for learning, storing, and sharing knowledge. Biological evolution gave us episodic, mimetic, and mythical memory; then cultural evolution provided oral and written (external and shared) memory; and finally modern technological evolution generates digital (computer-based) and global (Internet-based) memories (Donald, 1991; Norman, 1993).

At each stage, the development of hardware capabilities must be followed by the definition and adoption of appropriate skills and practices before the potential of the new information technology can begin to be realized. External memories, incorporating symbolic representations, facilitated the growth of complex societies and sophisticated scientific understandings. Their effectiveness relied on the spread of literacy and industrialization. Similarly, while the proliferation of networked computers ushers in the possibility of capturing new knowledge as it is produced within work groups and delivering relevant information on demand, the achievement of this potential requires the careful design of information systems, software interfaces, and work practices. New computer-based organizational memories must be matched with new social structures that produce and reproduce patterns of organizational learning (Giddens, 1984a; Lave & Wenger, 1991).

Community memories are to communities of practice what human memories are to individuals. They embody organizational memory in external repositories that are accessible to community members. They make use of explicit, external, symbolic representations that allow for shared understanding within a community. They make organizational learning possible within the group (Ackerman & McDonald, 1996; Argyris & Schön, 1978; Borghoff & Parechi, 1998; Buckingham Shum & Hammond, 1994; Senge, 1990).

Integrative Systems for Community Memory Effective community memory relies on integration. Tools for representing design artifacts and other work tasks must be related to rich repositories of information that can be brought to bear when needed. Communication about artifacts under development should be tied to that artifact so they retain their context of significance and their association with each other. Also, members of the community of practice must be integrated with each other in ways that allow something one member learned in the past to be delivered to other members when they need it in the future. One model for such integration—on an individual level—is the human brain, which stores a wealth of memories over a lifetime of experience, thought, and learning in a highly interrelated associative network that permits effective recall based on subjective relevance. This—and not the traditional model of computer memory as an array of independent bits of objective information—is the model that must be extended to community memories.

Of course, we want to implement community memories using computer memory. Perhaps the most important goal is integration to allow the definition of associations and other interrelationships. For instance, in a system using perspectives (like those to be discussed in the section below on Perspectives on Shared, Evolving Knowledge Construction), it is necessary for all information to be uniformly structured with indications of perspective and linking relationships. A traditional way to integrate information in a computer system is with a relational database. This allows associations to be established among arbitrary data. It also provides mechanisms like structured query language (SQL) queries to retrieve information based on specifications in a rather comprehensive language. Integrating all the information of a design environment in a unified database makes it possible to build bridges from the current task representation to any other information. Certainly, object-oriented or hybrid databases and distributed systems that integrate data on multiple computers can provide the same advantages. Nor does an underlying query language like SQL have to be exposed to users; front-end interfaces can be much more graphical and domain-oriented (Buckingham Shum, 1998).

Communities themselves must also be integrated. The Web provides a convenient technology for integrating the members of a community of practice, even if they are physically dispersed or do not share a homogeneous computer platform. In particular, intranets are Web networks designed for communication within a specific community rather than worldwide. WebNet, for instance, is intranet-based software that we prototyped for LAN management communities. It includes a variety of communication media as well as community memory repositories and collaborative productivity tools. It is discussed later in this section.

Dynamic Web pages can be interactive in the sense that they accept user inputs through selection buttons and text entry forms. Unlike most forms on the Web that only provide information (like product orders, customer preferences, or user demographics) to the Web master, intranet feedback may be made immediately available to the user community that generated it. For instance, the WebNet scenario below includes an interactive glossary. When someone modifies a glossary definition, the new definition is displayed to anyone looking at the glossary. Community members can readily comment on the definitions or change them. The history of the changes and comments made by the community is shared by the group. In this way, intranet technology can be used to build systems that are CIEs in which community members deposit knowledge as they acquire it so that other members can learn when they need or want to and can communicate with others about their learning. This model illustrates computer support for collaborative learning with digital memories belonging to communities of practice.

Extending the DODE Approach to CIEs for Design

To provide computer support for collaborative learning with CIEs, we first have to understand the process of collaborative learning. Based on this analysis, we can see how to extend the basic characteristics of a DODE to create a CIE.

The Process of Collaborative Learning   The ability of designers to proceed based on their existing tacit expertise (Polanyi, 1962) periodically breaks down, and they have to rebuild their understanding of the situation through explicit reflection (Schön, 1983). This reflective stage can be helped if they have good community support and effective computer support to bring relevant new information to bear on their problem. When they have comprehended the problem and incorporated the new understanding in their personal memories, we say they have learned. The process of *design* typically follows this cycle of breakdown and reinterpretation in learning (figure 5.2, cycle on left).

When design tasks take place in a collaborative context, the reflection results in articulation of solutions in language or in other symbolic representations. The articulated new knowledge can be shared within the community of practice. Such knowledge, created by the community, can be used in future situations to help a member overcome a breakdown in understanding. This cycle of collaboration is called *organizational learning* (see figure 5.2, upper cycle). The personal reflection and the collaborative articulation of shared perspectives interacting together make innovation possible (Boland & Tenkasi, 1995; Tomasello, Kruger, & Ratner, 1993).

Organizational learning can be supported by computer-based systems of organizational memory if the articulated knowledge is captured in a digital symbolic representation. The information must be stored and organized in a format that facilitates its subsequent identification and retrieval. To provide *computer support*, the software must be able to recognize breakdown situations when particular items of stored information might be useful to human reflection (see figure 5.2, lower cycle). DODEs provide computer support for design by individuals. They need to be extended to collaborative information environments to support organizational learning in communities of practice.

Extending the DODE Approach to CIEs for Design   The key to active computer support that goes significantly beyond printed external memories is to have the system deliver the right information at the right time in the right way (Fischer

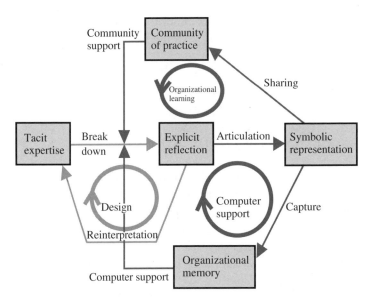

Figure 5.2
Cycles of design, computer support, and organizational learning. Adapted from Stahl (1993).

et al., 1998). To do this, the software must be able to analyze the state of the work being undertaken, identify likely breakdowns, locate relevant information, and deliver that information in a timely manner.

Systems like NetSuite and our older prototypes used critics based on domain knowledge to deliver information relevant to the current state of a design artifact being constructed in the design environment work space (see figure 5.3, left).

One can generalize from the critiquing approach of these DODEs to arrive at an overall architecture for organizational memories. The core difference between a DODE and a CIE is that a DODE focuses on delivering domain knowledge, conceived of as relatively static and universal, while a CIE is built around forms of community memory, treated as constantly evolving and largely specific to a particular community of practice. Where DODEs relied heavily on a set of critic rules predefined as part of the domain knowledge, CIEs generalize the function of the critiquing mechanisms.

In a CIE, it is still necessary to maintain some representation of the task as a basis for the software to take action. This task representation plays the role of the design artifact in a DODE, triggering critics and generally defining the work context to decide what is relevant. This is most naturally accomplished if work is done within

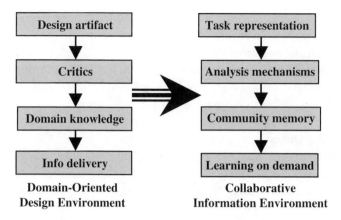

Figure 5.3
Generalization of the domain-oriented design environment (DODE) architecture (left) to a collaborative information environment (CIE) (right).

the software environment. For instance, if communication about designs takes place within the system where the design is constructed, then annotations and e-mail messages can be linked directly to the design elements they discuss. This reduces problems of deixis (comments referring to "that" object "over there"). It also allows related items to be linked together automatically. In an information-rich space, there may be many relationships of interest between new work artifacts and items in the organizational memory. For instance, when a LAN manager debugs a network, links between network diagrams, topology designs, LAN diary entries, device tables, and an interactive glossary of local terminology can be browsed to discover relevant information.

The general problem for a CIE is to define analysis mechanisms that can bridge the gap from task representation to relevant community memory information items to support learning on demand (see figure 5.3, right).

To take a very different example, suppose a student is writing a paper within a software environment that includes a digital library of papers written by her and her colleagues. An analysis mechanism to support her learning might compare sentences or paragraphs in her draft (which functions as a task representation) to text from other papers and from e-mail discussions (the community memory) to find excerpts of potential interest to her. We use latent semantic analysis (Landauer & Dumais, 1997) to mine our e-mail repository (Lindstaedt & Schneider, 1997) and are exploring similar uses of this mechanism to link task representations to textual information to support organizational learning. Other retrieval mechanisms might be appropriate for mining catalogs of software agents or components, design elements, and other sorts of organizational memories.

Using our example of LAN design, I next show how a CIE might function in this domain. I present a scenario of use of WebNet, a prototype I developed to extend our DODE concept to explicitly support communities of LAN designers.

WebNet: Scenario of a CIE for Design

Critiquing and Information Delivery   Kay is a graduate student who works part-time to maintain her department's LAN. The department has a budget to extend its network and has asked Kay to come up with a design. Kay brings up WebNet in her Web browser. She opens up the design of her department's current LAN in the LAN Design Environment, an Agentsheets (Repenning, 1994) simulation applet. Kay starts to add a new subnet. Noticing that there is no icon for an Iris graphics workstation in her palette, Kay selects the WebNet menu item for the Simulations Repository Web page (figure 5.4, left frame). This opens a Web site that contains simulation agents that other Agentsheets users have programmed. WebNet opens the repository to display agents that are appropriate for WebNet simulations. Kay locates a simulation agent that someone else has created with the behavior of an Iris workstation. She adds this to her palette and to her design.

When Kay runs the LAN simulation, WebNet proactively inserts a router (see figure 5.4, upper right) and informs Kay that a router is needed at the intersection of the two subnets. WebNet displays some basic information about routers and suggests several Web sites with details about different routers from commercial vendors (see figure 5.4, lower right). Here, WebNet has signaled a breakdown in Kay's designing and provided easy access to sources of information for her to learn what she needs to know on demand. This information includes generic domain knowledge like definitions of technical terms, current equipment details like costs, and community memory from related historical e-mails.

WebNet points to several e-mail messages from Kay's colleagues that discuss router issues and how they have been handled locally. The Email Archive includes all e-mails sent to Kay's LAN management workgroup in the past. Relevant e-mails are retrieved and ordered by the Email Archive software (Lindstaedt, 1996) based on their semantic relatedness to a query. In Kay's situation, WebNet automatically generates a query describing the simulation context, particularly the need for a router. The repository can also be browsed, using a hierarchy of categories developed by the user community.

Kay reviews the e-mail to find out which routers are preferred by her colleagues. Then she looks up the latest specs, options, and costs on the Web pages of router

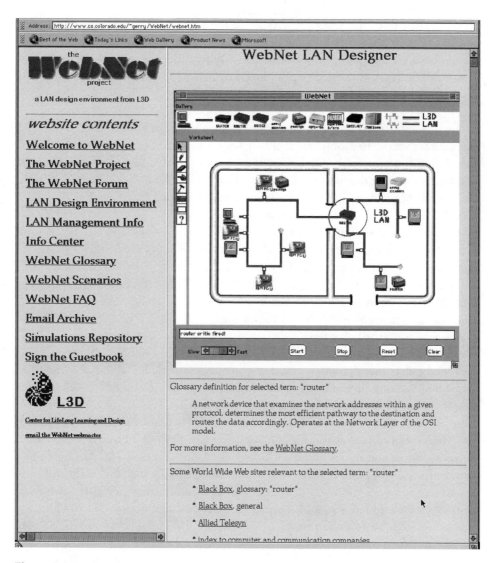

Figure 5.4
The WebNet local area network (LAN) design and simulation workspace (upper-right frame) and information delivered by a critic (lower-right frame). Note table of contents to the Web site (left frame).

suppliers. Kay adds the router she wants to the simulation and reruns the simulation to check it. She saves her new design in a catalog of local LAN layouts. Then she sends an e-mail message to her coworkers telling them to take a look at the new design in WebNet's catalog. She also asks Jay, her mentor at Network Services, to check her work.

Interactive and Evolving Knowledge   Jay studies Kay's design in his Web browser. He realizes that the Iris computer that Kay has added is powerful enough to perform the routing function itself. He knows that this knowledge has to be added to the simulation to make this option obvious to novices like Kay when they work in the simulation. Agentsheets includes an end-user programming language that allows Jay to reprogram the Iris workstation agent (Repenning, 1994). To see how other people have programmed similar functionality, Jay finds a server agent in the Simulations Repository and looks at its program. He adapts it to modify the behavior of the Iris agent and stores this agent back in the repository. Then he redefines the router critic rule in the simulation. He also sends Kay an e-mail describing the advantages of doing the routing in software on the Iris; WebNet may make this e-mail available to people in situations like Kay's in the future.

When he is finished, Jay tests his changes by going through the process that Kay followed. This time, the definition of router supplied by WebNet catches his eye. He realizes that this definition could also include knowledge about the option of performing routing in workstation software. The definitions that WebNet provides are stored in an interactive glossary. Jay goes to the WebNet glossary entry for "Router" and clicks on the Edit Definition button. He adds a sentence to the existing definition, noting that routing can sometimes be performed by server software. He saves this definition and then clicks on Make Annotations. This lets him add a comment suggesting that readers look at the simulation he has just modified for an example of software routing. Other community members may add their own comments, expressing their views of the pros and cons of this approach. Any glossary user can quickly review the history of definitions and comments—as well as contribute their own thoughts.

Community Memory   It is now two years later. Kay has graduated and been replaced by Bea. The subnet that Kay had added crashed last night due to print queue problems. Bea uses the LAN Management Information component of WebNet to trace back through a series of e-mail trouble reports and entries in LAN diaries. The LAN Management Information component of WebNet consists of four integrated information sources: a Trouble Queue of reported problems, a Host Table listing device configurations, a LAN Diary detailing chronological modifications to the LAN, and a Technical Glossary defining local hardware names and aliases. These four sources are accessed through a common interface that provides for interactivity and linking of related items.

The particular problem that Bea is working on was submitted to her through the Trouble Queue. Bea starts her investigation with the Host Table, reviewing how the printer, routers, and servers have been configured. This information includes links to LAN Diary entries dating back to Kay's work and providing the rationale for how decisions were made by the various people who managed the LAN. Bea also searches the Trouble Queue for incidents involving the print queue and related device configurations. Many of the relevant entries in the four sources are linked together, providing paths to guide Bea on an insightful path through the community history. After successfully debugging the problem using the community memory stored in WebNet, Bea documents the solution by making entries and new cross links in the LAN Management Information sources: the Trouble Queue, Host Table, LAN Diary, and Glossary.

In this scenario, Kay, Jay, and Bea have used WebNet as a design, communication, and memory system to support both their immediate tasks and the future work of their community. Knowledge has been constructed by people working on their own but within a community context. Their knowledge has been integrated within a multicomponent community memory that provides support for further knowledge building. This scenario—in which simulations, various repositories, electronic diaries, communication media, and other utilities are integrated with work processes—suggests how complexly integrated CIEs can support communities of practice.

Perspectives on Shared, Evolving Knowledge Construction

In this section, I propose a mechanism designed to make a CIE, like WebNet, more effective in supporting the interactions between individuals and groups in communities of practice. I call this mechanism *perspectives*. The perspectives mechanism permits a shared repository of knowledge to be structured in ways that allow for both individual work and the negotiation of shared results. To illustrate this approach to collaboration, I describe a CIE called WebGuide, which is an example of computer-supported collaborative learning (CSCL) (Crook, 1994; Koschmann, 1996a; O'Malley, 1995). The approach of interpretive, computational perspectives was proposed in chapter 4; the description of WebGuide continues in chapter 6.

Perspectives: A Collaboration Support Mechanism

The concept of perspectives comes from the hermeneutic philosophy of interpretation of Heidegger (1996) and Gadamer (1988). According to this philosophy, all understanding is situated within interpretive perspectives: knowledge is fundamentally perspectival. This is in accord with recent work in cognitive science that argues for theories of socially situated activity (Lave & Wenger, 1991; Winograd & Flores, 1986). These theories extend the hermeneutic approach to take into account the role of social structures in contributing to molding the construction of knowledge (Vygotsky, 1978). Communities of practice play an important role in the social construction of knowledge (Brown & Duguid, 1991).

Knowledge here is the interpretation of information as meaningful within the context of personal or group perspectives. Such interpretation by individuals is typically an automatic and tacit process of which people are not aware (see chapter 4). It is generally supported by cultural habits (Bourdieu, 1995) and partakes of processes of social structuration (Giddens, 1984b). This tacit and subjective personal opinion evolves into shared knowledge primarily through communication and argumentation within groups (Habermas, 1984).

Collaborative work typically involves both individual and group activities. Individuals engage in personal *perspective making* and also collaborate in *perspective taking* (Boland & Tenkasi, 1995). That is, individuals construct elements of domain knowledge and also their own "take" on the domain, a way of understanding the network of knowledge that makes up the domain. An essential aspect of creating a perspective on a domain of knowledge is to take on the perspectives of other people in the community. Learning to interpret the world through someone else's eyes and then adopting this view as part of one's own intellectual repertoire is a fundamental mechanism of learning. Collaborative learning can be viewed as a dialectic between these two processes of perspective making and perspective taking. This interaction takes place at both the individual and group units of analysis—and it is a primary mode of interchange between the two levels.

While the Web provides an obvious medium for collaborative work, it provides no support for the interplay of individual and group understanding that drives collaboration. First, we need ways to find and work with information that matches our personal needs, interests, and capabilities. Then we need means for bringing our individual knowledge together to build shared understanding and collaborative products. Enhancing the Web with perspectives may be an effective way to accomplish this.

As a mechanism for computer-based information systems, the term *perspective* means that a particular, restricted segment of an information repository is being considered, stored, categorized, and annotated. This segment consists of the information that is relevant to a particular person or group, possibly personalized in its display or organization to the needs and interests of that individual or team. Computer support for perspectives allows people in a group to interact with a shared community memory; everyone views and maintains his or her own perspective on the information without interfering with content displayed in the perspectives of other group members.

One problem that typically arises is that isolated perspectives of group members tend to diverge instead of converge as work proceeds. Structuring perspectives to encourage perspective taking, sharing, and negotiation offers a solution to this by allowing members of a group to communicate about what information to include as mutually acceptable. The problem with negotiation is generally that it delays work on information while potentially lengthy negotiations are underway. Here, a careful structuring of perspectives provides a solution, allowing work to continue within personal perspectives while the contents of shared perspectives are being negotiated. I believe that a perspectives approach structured for negotiation can provide powerful support for collaborative use of large information spaces on the Web.

The idea of computer-based perspectives traces its lineage to hypertext ideas like "trail blazing" (Bush, 1945), "transclusion" (Nelson, 1981), and "virtual copies" (Mittal, Bobrow, & Kahn, 1986)—techniques for defining and sharing alternative views on large hypermedia spaces. At the University of Colorado, we have been building desktop applications with perspectives for the past decade (see McCall et al., 1990, and chapters 1 and 4) and are now starting to use perspectives on the Web.

Earlier versions of the perspectives mechanism defined different contexts associated with items of information. For instance, in an architectural DODE, information about electrical systems could be grouped in an "electrical context" or "electrician's perspective." In a CIE, this mechanism is used to support collaboration by defining personal and group perspectives in which collaborating individuals can develop their own ideas and negotiate shared positions. These informational contexts can come to represent perspectives on knowledge. While some collaboration support systems provide personal and group workspaces (Scardamalia & Bereiter, 1996), the perspectives implementation described below is innovative in supporting hierarchies or graphs of perspective inheritance.

This new model of perspectives has the important advantage of letting team members inherit the content of their team's perspective and other information sources without having to generate it from scratch. They can then experiment with this content on their own without worrying about affecting what others see. This is advantageous as long as the goal is simply to use someone else's information for developing one's own perspective. It has frequently been noted in computer science literature (Boland & Tenkasi, 1995; Floyd, 1992) that different stakeholders engaged in the development and use of a system (e.g., designers, testers, marketing, management, end-users) always think about and judge issues from different perspectives and that these differences must be taken into account.

However, if the goal is influencing the content of team members' perspectives, then this approach is limited because someone else's content cannot be changed directly. To support collaborative work, the perspectives need to maintain at least a partial overlap of their contents to reach successful mutual understanding and coordination. The underlying subjective opinions must be intertwined to establish intersubjective understanding (Habermas, 1984; Tomasello et al., 1993). In the late 1990s, our research explored how to support the intertwining of perspectives using the perspectives mechanism for CIEs.

Designing a System for Collaborative Knowledge Construction

We designed a system of computational support for interpretive perspectives in which the content of one perspective can be automatically inherited into perspectives connected in a perspective hierarchy or graph. This subsection recounts the motivation and history of the design of our integration of the perspectives mechanism into a CIE named WebGuide. It discusses a context in which student researchers in middle school learn how to engage in collaborative work and how to use computer technologies to support their work.

In summer 1997, we decided to apply our vision of intertwining personal and group perspectives to a situation in middle-school classrooms. The immediate presenting problem was that students (12-year-old sixth graders) could not keep track of Web site addresses they found during their Web research. The larger issue was how to support team projects. We focused on a project-based curriculum (Blumenfeld et al., 1991) on ancient civilizations of Latin America (Aztec, Inca, Maya) used at the school.

In compiling a list of requirements for WebGuide, we focused on how computer support can help structure the merging of individual ideas into group results. Such support should begin early and continue throughout the student research process. It should scaffold and facilitate the group decision-making process so that students can learn how to build consensus. WebGuide combines displays of individual work with the emerging group view. Note that the topic on Aztec religion in figure 5.5 was added to the team perspective by another student (Bea). Also note that Kay has made a copy of a topic from Que's perspective so she can keep track of his work related to her topic. The third topic is an idea that Kay is preparing to work on

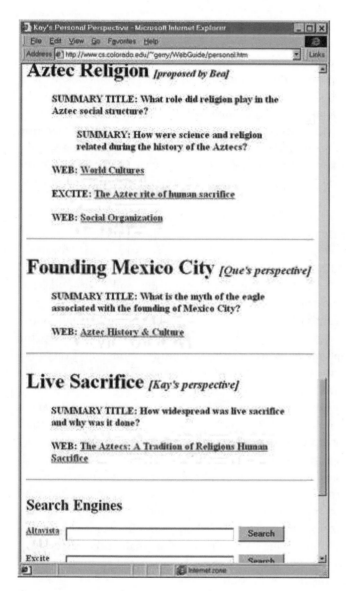

Figure 5.5
Part of Kay's personal perspective. Three topics are visible in this view. Within each topic are short subheadings or comments, as well as Web bookmarks and search queries. At the bottom is access to search engines.

herself. Within her personal electronic workspace, Kay inherits information from other perspectives (such as her team perspective) along with her own work.

It soon became clear to us that each student should be able to view the notes of other team members as they work on common topics and should not have to wait until after certain notes are accepted by the whole team and copied to the team perspective. Students should be able to adopt individual items from the work of other students into their own perspective to start the collaboration and integration process. From early on, they should be able to make proposals for moving specific items from their personal perspective (or from the perspective of another) into the team perspective, which will eventually represent their team product, the integration of all their work.

The requirement that items of information can be copied, modified, and rearranged presupposes that information can be collected and presented in small pieces—at the granularity of a paragraph or an idea. This is also necessary for negotiating which pieces should be accepted, modified, or deleted. We want the CIE to provide extensive support for collecting, revising, organizing, and relating ideas as part of the collaborative construction of knowledge.

The Web pages of a student's personal perspective should contain live link bookmarks, search queries, categories, comments, and summaries authored by the student. Comments can optionally be attached to any information item. Every item is tagged with the name of the person who created or last modified it. Items are also labeled with perspective information and time stamps.

Students each enter notes in their personal perspectives using information available to them: the Web, books, encyclopedias, CD-ROMs, discussions, or other sources. Students can review the notes in the class perspective, their team perspective, and the personal perspectives of their teammates. All of these contents are collected in comparison perspectives, where they are labeled by their perspective of origin. Students extract from the group research the items that are of interest to them and, within their personal perspectives, organize and develop the data they have collected by categorizing, summarizing, labeling, and annotating. The stages of investigating, collecting, and editing can be repeated as many times as desired. Team members then negotiate which notes should be promoted to the team perspective to represent their collaborative product.

The class project ends with each team producing an organized team perspective on one of the civilizations. These perspectives can be viewed by members of the other teams to learn about the civilizations that they did not personally research. The team perspectives can also provide a basis for additional class projects, like narrative reports and physical displays. Finally, this year's research products can be used to create next year's class perspective starting point, so new researchers can pick up where the previous generation left off—within a Web information space that will have evolved substantially in the meantime.

Supporting Perspective Making

The application of a CIE to the problem of supporting middle-school students conducting Web research on the Aztec, Maya, and Inca civilizations drove the original concept of WebGuide. Since then, the basic functionality of the CIE has been implemented as a Java applet and applied in two other applications: *Gamble Gulch*, a set of middle-school teams constructing conflicting perspectives on a local environmental problem, and *Readings '99*, a university research group exploring cognitive science theories that have motivated the WebGuide approach. These two applications further illustrate how perspective making and perspective taking can be supported within a CIE. They are discussed briefly here and in more detail in chapter 6.

We first used an early implementation of WebGuide in a classroom at the Logan School for Creative Learning in Denver (figure 5.6). For the previous five years, this class of middle-school students had researched the environmental damage done to mountain streams by acid mine drainage from deserted gold mines in the Rocky Mountains above Denver. They actually solved the problem at the source of a stream coming into Boulder from the Gamble Gulch mine site by building a wetlands area to filter out heavy metals. Now they were investigating the broader ramifications of their past successes; they were looking at the issue of acid mine drainage from various alternative—and presumably conflicting—perspectives. The students interviewed adult mentors to get opinions from specific perspectives: environmental, governmental, mine owner, and local landowners.

As an initial field test of the WebGuide system, this trial resulted in valuable experience in the practicalities of deploying such a sophisticated program to young students over the Web. The students were enthusiastic users of the system and offered (through WebGuide) many ideas for improvements to the interface and the functionality. Consequently, WebGuide benefited from rapid cycles of participatory design. The differing viewpoints, expectations, and realities of the software developers, teachers, and students provided a dynamic field of constraints and tensions within which the software, its goals, and the understanding of the different participants coevolved within a complex structural coupling.

The Readings '99 application of WebGuide the following year stressed the use of perspectives for structuring collaborative efforts to build shared knowledge. The goal of the graduate seminar was to evolve sophisticated theoretical views on computer mediation within a medium that supports the sharing of tentative positions and documents the development of ideas and collaboration over time. A major

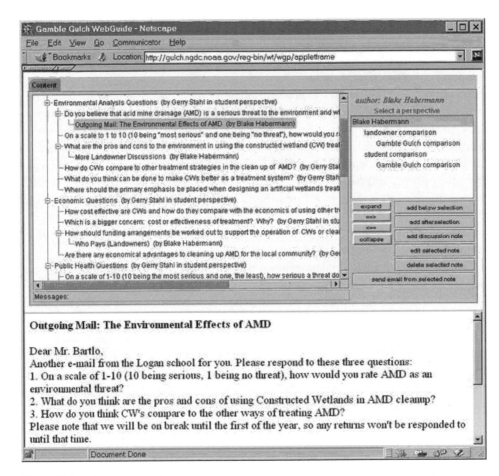

Figure 5.6
WebGuide for negotiating environmental perspectives.

hypothesis to be explored by the course was that software environments with perspectives—like WebGuide—can provide powerful tools for coordinated intellectual work and collaborative learning. For instance, it explored how the use of a shared persistent knowledge-construction space can support more complex discussions than ephemeral face-to-face conversations.

This is not the place to evaluate the effectiveness of the WebGuide perspective mechanism. The story of its development is continued in chapter 6. Here I simply suggest the possibility of computational support for collaboration that goes beyond what is now commercially available. The perspectives mechanism allows people to work collaboratively by intertwining their personal and group perspectives on shared ideas.

Extending Human Cognition

Our early work on domain-oriented design environments was an effort to augment human intelligence within the context of professional design activities. At a practical level, our focus on building systems for experts (rather than expert systems) contrasted with much research at the time, which emphasized either artificial intelligence heuristics intended to automate design tasks or user-friendly, idiot-proof, walk-up-and-use systems that were oriented toward novices. In theoretical terms, we acted on the view that human intelligence is not some biologically fixed system that can be modeled by and possibly even replaced by computationally analogous software systems. Rather, human intelligence is an open-ended involvement in the world that is fundamentally shaped by the use of tools (Donald, 1991; Heidegger, 1996; Vygotsky, 1978). In this view, computer-based systems can extend the power of human cognition. Like any effective tools, software systems like DODEs mediate the cognitive tasks, transforming both the task and the cognitive process (Norman, 1993; Winograd & Flores, 1986). In addition, computer-based systems enhance the capabilities of their users by encapsulating the derived human intentionality of their developers (Stahl, 1993a). In this light, we saw the emergence of the Web as offering an enabling technology for allowing communities of DODE users to embed their own collective experience in the critics and design rationale components of DODE knowledge bases.

The movement in our work from DODEs to collaborative information environments was driven by the potential of Web technology and the increasing awareness of the socially situated character of contemporary work, including the important role of communities of practice (Brown & Duguid, 1991; Lave & Wenger, 1991; Orr, 1990). The fact that much work and learning is overtly collaborative these days is not accidental (Marx, 1976). Just as the cognitive processes that are engaged in work and learning are fundamentally mediated by the tools that we use to acquire, store, and communicate knowledge, they are equally mediated by social phenomena (Giddens, 1984a; Habermas, 1984). In fact, tools, too, have a social origin, so that the mediation of human cognition results from complex interactions between the artifactual and the social (Orlikowski et al., 1995; Vygotsky, 1978). CIEs are designed to serve as social-imbued, computationally powerful tools. They make the social character of knowledge explicit and support collaborative knowledge building.

The notion of a perspectives mechanism such as the one prototyped in WebGuide is to provide tool affordances that support the social nature of mediated cognition.

Collaborative work and learning involve activities at two units of analysis: the individual and the group (Boland & Tenkasi, 1995; Orlikowski, 1992). Personal perspectives and team perspectives provide a structure for distinguishing these levels and create workspaces in which the different activities can take place. The crux of the problem is to facilitate interaction between these levels: the perspectives mechanism lets individuals and teams copy notes from one space to another, reorganize the ideas, and modify the content. Communities of practice are not simple, fixed structures, and so the graph of perspective inheritance must be capable of being interactively extended to include new alliances and additional levels of intermediate subteams.

The perspectives mechanism (more fully discussed in chapter 6) has not been proposed as a complete solution; it is meant to be merely suggestive of computationally intensive facilities to aid collaboration. Systematic support for negotiating consensus building and for the promotion of agreed on ideas up the hierarchy of subteams is an obvious next step (see chapters 7 and 8). Collaborative intelligence places a heavy cognitive load on participants; any help from the computer in tracking ideas and their status would free human minds for the tasks that require interpretation of meaning (see chapter 16).

The concept of intelligence underlying the work discussed in this chapter views human cognition, software processing, and social contexts as complexly and inseparably intertwined. In today's workplaces and learning milieus, neither human nor machine intelligence exists independently of the other. Social concerns about AI artifacts are not secondary worries that arise after the fact but symptoms of the fundamentally social character of all artifacts and of all processes of material production and knowledge creation (Marx, 1976; Vygotsky, 1978). I am trying to explore the positive implications of this view by designing collaborative information environments to support knowledge construction by small groups within communities.

6
Perspectives on Collaborative Learning

After the exploration of computer support for personal and small-group perspectives described in chapters 4 and 5, I pushed as hard as I could a model of threaded discussion with perspectives.[1] I developed a Web-based tool called WebGuide, designed to mediate and structure collaborative learning. This software defined a flexible system of perspectives on a shared knowledge-construction space. WebGuide provides an electronic and persistent workspace for individuals and teams to develop and share distinctive points of view on a topic. The software and associated usage practices were designed by trials in a middle-school classroom and in an advanced graduate seminar. Experience in these use situations raised a range of questions concerning theoretical and practical issues, which drove further research.

This chapter is a reflection on what was collaboratively learned about how software artifacts can mediate learning and shared cognition. Its multifaceted discussion of the design of the WebGuide collaboration system reflects the intricate relationship between theory, design, and usage evaluation. It demonstrates the interplay of considerations required in designing support for the intertwining of personal and group perspectives, arguably that aspect of collaboration most in need of computational support. This design study reflects on the emergence of abstract theory from practical implementation issues.

WebGuide was probably my most intensive software development effort. I tried to create a system that would support group cognition in the sense of collaborative knowledge building. Threaded discussion seemed to be an appropriate medium, but its use always tended to be limited to the exchange of personal opinions, at best. I developed a computational system to support the sharing of interpretive perspectives, but it turned out to be too complicated to use fluidly, despite repeated attempts to make its interface more intuitive. Theoretical reflections related to WebGuide led me to bring in communication specialists and to undertake the analyses of part II of this book and the reflections of part III.

Introductory Narrative

For some years now, I have been interested in how to personalize the delivery of information from knowledge repositories to people based on their preferred *perspectives* on the information (Stahl, 1995, 1996b). For instance, designers often critique an evolving design artifact from alternative technical points of view; different designers have different personal concerns and styles, requiring considerations based on access to different rules of thumb, rationales, constraints, standards, and other forms of domain knowledge. Computer design environments should support these important interpretive perspectives. I am now primarily interested in applying similar mechanisms of perspectival computer support within contexts of collaborative learning.

In 1997, Ted Habermann—an information architect at the National Oceanic and Atmospheric Administration (NOAA) who makes geophysical data available to schoolchildren over the Web—suggested to me that we try to develop some computer support for a project at his son's middle school. Dan Kowal, the environmental sciences teacher at the Logan School for Creative Learning in Denver, was planning a year-long investigation of alternative perspectives on the issue of acid mine drainage (AMD)—the pollution of drinking-water supplies by heavy metals washed out of old gold mines. The fact that Dan and I were interested in perspectives seemed to provide a basis for fruitful collaboration. Ted obtained National Science Foundation (NSF) funding for the project, and we all spent the summer of 1998 planning the course and its perspectives-based software. Each of us brought in colleagues and worked to create a Java application (WebGuide), assemble a set of auxiliary Web pages, and put together a group of adult mentors representing different perspectives on AMD and a course curriculum.

The class started in September, and the software was deployed in October. The students in Dan's class were aware of the experimental nature of the software they were using and were encouraged to critique it and enter their ideas into WebGuide. Feedback from these 12-year-old students provided initial experience with the usability of WebGuide and resulted in a reimplementation of the interface and optimization of the algorithms over the school's winter vacation.

In January 1999, I organized an interdisciplinary seminar of doctoral students from cognitive, educational, and computational sciences to study theoretical texts that might provide insight into how to support collaborative learning with perspectives-based software. The seminar used WebGuide as a major medium for communication and reflection, including reflection on our use of the software. This provided a second source of experience and raised a number of issues that needed to be addressed in software redesign.

In this chapter, I begin a reflection on the issues that have arisen through our WebGuide experiences because I think they are critical to the ability to support collaborative learning with computer-based environments. The potential for computer mediation of collaboration seems extraordinary, but experience warns us that the practical barriers are also enormous. Certainly, our experiences are not unique, and similar projects at the universities of Toronto, Michigan, Berkeley, Northwestern, Vanderbilt, and Georgia Tech have run into significant obstacles for years. Indeed, we observed many of these issues in a seminar in the year prior to the implementation of WebGuide (dePaula, 1998; Koschmann & Stahl, 1998). However, I believe that perspectives-based software addresses or transforms some of the issues and raises some of its own.

Let me describe how computer support for perspectives has evolved in WebGuide. I first discuss the preliminary implementation as used in Dan's middle-school environmental course and explain how perspectives are supported in that version. A number of design issues led to an extended attempt to bring theory to the aid of reflection on practice. This included the graduate seminar that used a revised version of WebGuide. Finally, following the original part of this chapter is a condensed version of the dialogue that took place between the *Journal of Interactive Media in Education* (*JIME*) reviewers and me, where responses from winter 2000 and spring 2001 bring in reflections from subsequent design iterations.

Practice I: Environmental Perspectives

An early implementation of WebGuide was in use in Dan's classroom at the Logan School. For the previous five years, his class had researched the environmental damage done to mountain streams by the Gamble Gulch mine site. Then they investigated the social issue of acid mine drainage from various perspectives: environmental, governmental, mine owner, and local landowner. Working in teams corresponding to each of these perspectives, they articulated the position of their perspective on a set of shared questions.

The Gamble Gulch application of WebGuide served as the medium through which the students collaboratively researched these issues with their mentors and with teammates. Each student and mentor had a personal display perspective, and each display perspective inherited from one of the content-based team perspectives (for example, environmental protection or governmental regulation), depending on which intellectual perspective they were working on constructing.

Figure 6.1 shows one student's (Blake) personal perspective on the class discourse. The tree of discussion threads was "seeded" with question categories, such as "Environmental Analysis Questions." Within these categories, the teacher and I posted

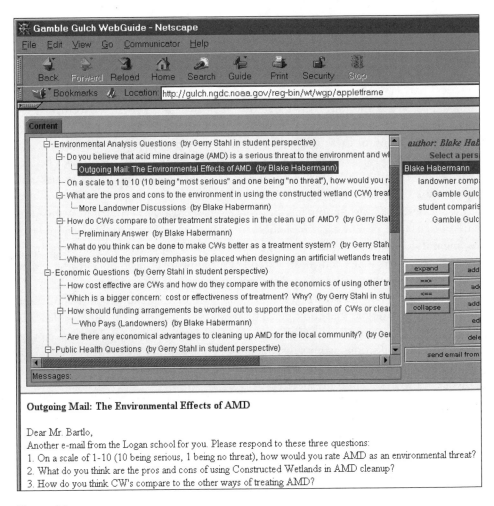

Figure 6.1
The Gamble Gulch version of WebGuide viewed in a Web browser. The top part is a Java applet displaying an outline view of note titles. The content of the selected note is displayed in an HTML frame below. To the right are buttons for navigating the outline and changing the content in the shared knowledge space. The view shown is from the personal perspective of one student.

specific questions for the students to explore, such as "Do you believe that AMD is a serious threat to the environment?" Here, Blake has sent an e-mail to a mentor asking for information related to this question. E-mail interactions happen through WebGuide and are retained as notes in its display perspectives. When replies are sent back, they are automatically posted to the discussion outline under the original e-mail. When someone clicks on a title, the contents of that note are displayed in a hypertext markup language (HTML) frame below the applet (as is the body of the student's e-mail in figure 6.1).

Blake is working in his personal perspective, which inherits from the Class, Student team, and Landowner team perspectives (see the dashed arrows in figure 6.2). Note that the display of his personal perspective (in figure 6.1) includes notes that Dan and I entered in the Student perspective to structure the work of all the students. Blake can add, edit, and delete ideas in his perspective, as well as send e-mail in it. Because he is a member of the Landowner team, the Student team, and the Class team, he can browse ideas in the Student comparison, the Landowner comparison, and the Gamble Gulch Class comparison perspectives (see list of perspectives accessible to him on the right of figure 6.1).

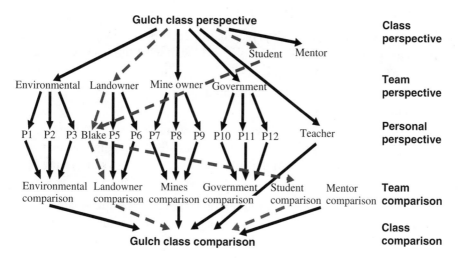

Figure 6.2
The web of perspectives in Gamble Gulch. Information is automatically inherited downward in the diagram. Blake's perspective includes all the notes entered in the Gulch Class, Landowner, and Student perspectives. His notes also show up in the Landowner, Student, and Gulch class comparison perspectives.

For this application, the teacher has decided that perspective comparing and negotiation will take place in live classroom discussions rather than in WebGuide. After a team or the whole class reaches a consensus, the teacher will enter the statements that students have agreed on into the team or class perspective.

The goals of the year-long course are to negotiate within teams to construct the various positions and among the positions to reach consensus or to clarify differences. Dan designed this class—with its use of WebGuide—to teach students that knowledge is perspectival, that different people construct different views, and that compilations of facts and arguments differ depending on the social situation from which they arise. He hopes that his students will learn to evaluate statements as deriving from different perspectives and to negotiate the intertwining of perspectives to the extent that this is possible.

Computer Support of Perspectives

The term *perspectives* is overloaded with meanings. It frequently produces confusion even when it is intended to tacitly exploit in one domain aspects of the perspectives metaphor from a different domain. It may be helpful at this point to distinguish three types of perspectives:

- *Literal perspectives* are optical or perceptual orientations: we see objects from the specific angle or vantage point of the physical location of our eyes.

- *Figurative perspectives* take metaphorical license and refer to, for instance, different ways of conceptualizing a theme, as in adopting a skeptical view of a conversational claim.

- *Computational perspectives* are the result of software mechanisms that classify elements in a database for selective display. In WebGuide, for example, if I enter a note in my personal perspective, then that note will be displayed whenever my perspective is displayed but not when someone else's personal perspective is displayed.

WebGuide implements a system of computational (that is, computer-supported, automated) perspectives designed to utilize the perspective metaphor to support characteristics of collaboration and collaborative learning. It is unique in a number of ways that distinguish it from other software systems that may use the term *perspectives*:

- Other systems refer to different *representations* of information as perspectives. They might have a graphical view and a textual view of the *same* data. In WebGuide, different data is literally displayed in different perspectives while using the same representation—hierarchically structured titles of textual notes.

• In WebGuide, the perspectives mechanism is neither a simple tagging of data nor a database view but is a dynamic computation that takes into account a *web of inheritance* among perspectives. Thus, Blake's perspective includes information that he entered in his perspective and also information inherited from the Class, Student, and Landowner perspectives.

• The web of perspectives can be extended by users *interactively*, and the inheritance of information is always computed on the fly, based on the current configuration of this web.

• The information in a perspective has a user-maintained structure in which each note has one or more "parent" notes and may have "child" notes, creating a *web of notes* within each perspective. The order of child notes displayed under a parent note is user defined and maintained so that WebGuide can be used to *organize ideas* within outline structures.

The computational perspectives mechanism we have been exploring incorporates the following features:

• Individual community members have access to their own information source. This is called their *personal perspective*. It consists of notes from a shared central information repository that are tagged for display within that particular perspective (or in any perspective inherited from that perspective).

• Notes can be created, edited, rearranged, linked together, or deleted by users within their own personal perspective without affecting the work of others.

• Another student, Annie, can integrate a note from Blake's perspective into her own personal perspective by creating a *link* or *virtual copy* of the note. If Blake modifies the original note, then it changes in Annie's perspective as well. However, if Annie modifies the note, a new note is actually created for her, so that Blake's perspective is not changed. This arrangement generally makes sense because Annie wants to view (or inherit) Blake's note, even if it evolves. However, Blake should not be affected by the actions of someone who copied one of his notes.

• Alternatively, Annie can *physically copy* the contents of a note from Blake's perspective. In this case, the copies are not linked to each other in any way. Since Annie and Blake are viewing physically distinct notes now, either can make changes without affecting the other's perspective.

• There is an inheritance web of perspectives; descendent perspectives inherit the contents of their ancestor perspectives. Changes (additions, edits, deletions) in the ancestor are seen in descendent perspectives, but not vice versa. New perspectives can be created by users. Perspectives can inherit from existing perspectives. Thus, a team comparison perspective can be created that inherits and displays the contents of the perspectives of the team members. A hierarchy of team, subteam, personal, and comparison perspectives can be built to match the needs of a particular community (see figure 6.2).

This model of computational perspectives has the important advantage of letting team members inherit the content of their team's perspective and other information sources without having to generate it from scratch. They can then experiment with this content on their own without worrying about affecting what others see.

Types of Perspectives

WebGuide provides several levels of perspectives (see figure 6.2) within a web of perspective inheritance to help students compile their individual and joint research:

- The *class perspective* is created by the teacher to start each team off with an initial structure and some suggested topics. It typically establishes a framework for classroom activities and defines a space used to instantiate the goal of collecting the products of collaborative intellectual work.

- The *team perspective* contains notes that have been accepted by a team. This perspective can be pivotal; it gradually collects the products of the team effort.

- The student's *personal perspective* is an individual's workspace. It inherits a view of everything in the student's team's perspective. Thus, it displays the owner's own work within the context of notes proposed or negotiated by the team and class— as modified by the student. Students can each modify (add, edit, delete, rearrange, link) their virtual copies of team notes in their personal perspectives. They can also create completely new material there. This computational perspective provides a personal workspace in which a student can construct his or her own figurative perspective on shared knowledge. Other people can view the student's personal perspective, but they cannot modify it.

- The *comparison perspective* combines all the personal perspectives of team members and the team perspective, so that anyone can compare all the work that is going on in the team. It inherits from personal perspectives and, indirectly, from the team and class perspectives. Students can go here to get ideas and copy notes into their own personal perspective or propose items for the team perspective.

There is not really a duplication of information in the community memory. The perspectives mechanism merely displays the information differently in the different perspectival views, in accordance with the relations of inheritance.

Issues for Perspectives

The first issues to hit home when we deployed WebGuide were the problems of response time and screen real estate. The student computers were slower, had smaller monitors, had poorer Internet connections, and were further from the server than the computers of the developers. We were already familiar with these issues from other Web applications, but classroom conditions are the final determinant of how things will work out and how they will be accepted.

A prerelease prototype of WebGuide used dynamic HTML pages. This meant that each time a student expanded a different part of the outline of titles, it was necessary to wait for a new page to be sent across the Internet. The dynamic HTML pages also greatly constrained the interface functionality. However, when we moved to a Java applet, we had to wait several minutes to download the applet code to each student computer. Furthermore, it entailed running all the perspectives computations on the slow student computers. To reduce the download time significantly, we first rewrote the interface using standard Java Swing classes that can be stored on the student machines. Then we split the applet into a client (the interface) and a server (the perspectives computations and database access). By downloading only the client part to the classroom, we not only reduced the download time further but also ran the time-consuming computations on our faster server computers.

Such technical problems can be solved relatively easily by optimizing algorithms or by adjusting tradeoffs based on local conditions. Issues of social practice are much more intransigent. There seem to be two major problems for software for threaded discussions and collaborative knowledge construction like WebGuide:

1. Lack of convergence was apparent among the ideas developed in the supported discussions.

2. System use was avoided in favor of e-mail, face-to-face conversation, or inaction.

WebGuide introduces its computational perspectives mechanism as a structural feature to facilitate the articulation of convergent ideas, and it even incorporates e-mail. In attempting to address the problems posed above, it raises a new set of issues:

3. Is the perspectives metaphor a natural one (or can it be made natural) so that people will use computational perspectives to construct their figurative perspectives?

4. Can the web of perspectives be represented in a convenient and understandable format?

In our trials of WebGuide, we have tried to create learning situations that would encourage the use of the software, yet we have observed low levels of usage and underutilization of the system's full functionality. This raises the following additional issues:

5. How can learning situations be structured to take better advantage of the presumed advantages of the software?

6. How can the system's various capabilities—such as its support for threaded discussions and for perspective making—be distinguished?

To answer questions of this magnitude, it was necessary to gather more experience, to be more closely involved in the daily usage of the system, and to develop a deeper theoretical understanding of collaborative learning and of computer mediation. Having defined these goals, I announced a seminar on the topic of computer mediation of collaborative learning, open to interested researchers from a number of disciplines—primarily education, cognitive psychology, and computer science. The goal of the seminar was stated to be an experiment in the use of WebGuide to construct knowledge collaboratively, based on careful reading of selected texts. The texts traced the notion of *computer mediation* (Boland & Tenkasi, 1995; Caron, 1998; Hewitt, Scardamalia, & Webb, 1998; Scardamalia & Bereiter, 1996) back to *situated learning theory* (Bruner, 1990; Cole, 1996; Lave, 1991; Lave & Wenger, 1991; Lave, 1996)—and from there back to the notion of *mediated consciousness* in Vygotsky (1978) and its roots in Hegel (Habermas, 1971; Hegel, 1967; Koyeve, 1969) and Marx (1967a, 1967b, 1976).

Later in this chapter I comment on our current understanding of the six issues listed above. But first it is necessary to describe the ways in which the seminar attempted to make use of WebGuide and the conceptualization of the theory of computer mediation that arose in the seminar.

Practice II: Theoretical Perspectives

The seminar on computer mediation of collaborative learning was designed to use WebGuide in several ways:

• *As the primary communication medium for internal collaboration*   The seminar took place largely online. Limited class time was used for people to get to know each other, to motivate the readings, to introduce themes that would be followed up online, and to discuss how to use WebGuide within the seminar.

• *As an example collaboration support system to analyze*   Highly theoretical readings on mediation and collaboration are made more concrete by discussing them in terms of what they mean in a system like WebGuide. The advantage of using a locally developed prototype like WebGuide as our example was that we knew how it worked in detail and could modify its functionality or appearance to try out suggestions that arose in the seminar.

• *As an electronic workspace for members to construct their individual and shared ideas*   Ideas entered into WebGuide persist there, where they can be revisited and annotated at any time. Ideas that arose early in the seminar would be available in full detail later so that they could be related to new readings and insights. The record of discussions over a semester or a year would document how perspectives developed and interacted.

• *As a glossary and reference library*   This application of WebGuide was seeded with a list of terms that were likely to prove important to the seminar and with the titles of seminar readings. Seminar members could develop their own definitions of these terms, modifying them based on successive readings in which the terms recur in different contexts and based on definitions offered by other members. Similarly, the different readings were discussed extensively within WebGuide. This included people giving their summaries of important points and asking for help interpreting obscure passages. People could comment on each other's entries and also revise their own. New terms and references could easily be added by anyone.

• *As a brainstorming arena for papers*   The application was seeded with themes that might make interesting research papers drawing on seminar readings and goals. WebGuide allows people to link notes to these themes from anywhere in the information environment and to organize notes under the themes. Thus, both individuals and groups can use this to compile, structure, and refine ideas that may grow into publishable papers. Collaborative writing is a notoriously difficult process that generally ends up being dominated by one participant's perspective or being divided up into loosely connected sections, each representing somewhat different perspectives. WebGuide may facilitate a more truly collaborative approach to organizing ideas on a coherent theme.

• *As a bug report mechanism or feature request facility*   Seminar participants could communicate problems they found in the software as well as propose ideas they had for new features. By having these reports and proposals shared within the WebGuide medium, they can be communicated to other seminar participants, who can then be aware of the bugs (and their fixes) and can join the discussion of suggestions.

The seminar version of WebGuide incorporates a built-in permissions system that structures the social practices surrounding the use of the system. Each seminar participant can have a personal perspective in which he or she can manipulate notes without affecting the views in other perspectives. They can add quick discussion notes or other kinds of statements. They can edit or delete anything within their personal perspective. They can also make multiple copies or links (virtual copies) from notes in a personal perspective to other notes there. Anyone is free to browse in any perspective. However, if browsers are not in their own perspective, then they cannot add, edit, or delete notes there (as in figure 6.3). To manipulate notes freely, one must first copy or link the note into one's own personal perspective. The copy or link can optionally include copying (or virtual copying) all the notes below the selected note in the tree as well. These rules are enforced by the user interface, which checks whether someone is in their personal perspective and allows only the legal actions.

Students in the class can form subgroups either within or across their different disciplines. They develop ideas in their personal perspectives. They debate the ideas

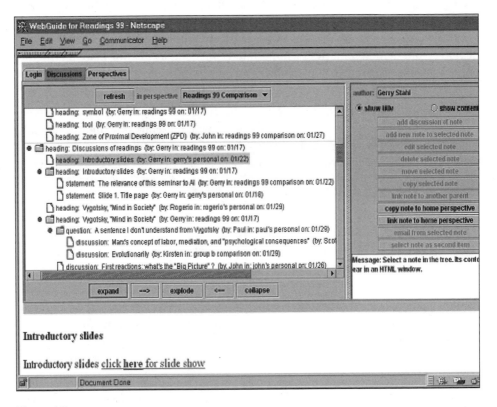

Figure 6.3
The version of WebGuide used in the seminar. Note that some of the control buttons on the right are not functional when the logged-in author is not working in his own personal perspective. This enforces certain social practices. Also note that many headings have been inserted to structure the discussion space.

of other people by finding notes of interest in the class comparison perspective (or in a subgroup comparison perspective) and copying these notes into their own personal perspective, where they can comment on them. The clash of perspectives is visible in the comparison perspectives, while the personal perspectives allow for complete expression and organization of a single perspective. This supports the "taking" of other people's perspectives and the use of shared ideas in the "making" of one's own perspectives (Boland & Tenkasi, 1995).

The seminar application of WebGuide stresses the use of perspectives for structuring collaborative efforts to build shared knowledge. The goal of the seminar is to evolve theoretical views on computer mediation—and to do so within a medium that supports the sharing of tentative positions and documents the development of ideas and collaboration over time. A major hypothesis investigated by the seminar is that software environments with perspectives—like WebGuide—can provide powerful tools for coordinated intellectual work and collaborative learning. It explores how the use of a shared persistent knowledge-construction space can support more complex discussions than ephemeral face-to-face conversation. Many of the desires and concerns in this chapter originated as seminar notes in WebGuide. In particular, the seminar's focus on theory has actually problematized our understanding of the role of theory.

Theory in Practice

Our initial application of WebGuide in the middle-school environmental course raised a number of issues that led us to seek theoretical understanding through a seminar, which served as a second application of WebGuide. We began to see our research differently as a result of the theories we incorporated into our discussions within the seminar. One thing that changed was the relation we see of this theory to our research practice.

My paper proposal to the American Educational Research Association (AERA) (the first draft of this chapter) was written prior to our seminar explorations. I described our approach by following the narrative order implied by conventional wisdom about the relation of theory to practice. After stating the goal or purpose of the work, I provided a theoretical framework, followed by sections on techniques, evidence, conclusions, and educational and scientific import. The assumption here was that theory suggests a solution, and then theory is "applied" to some situation—either the problem situation or an experimental test context. After designing the solution based on the preexisting theory and applying it to the test situation, the researcher gathers evaluative data and analyzes them to measure success. The evaluation then implies whether the solution has a general import.

But such an approach is not in keeping with our current experience or with our emerging theory. We started with an opportunity to explore some vague notions we had about something we called "perspectives." We experimented with ever-evolving techniques through a complex collaborative process involving many people, each with their own concerns, understandings, and insights. As part of this process, some of us turned to theory—but the selection of theoretical texts and our interpretations of them were determined by the processes and issues we observed in our practical strivings.

In this draft of the chapter (still not considered a static final document but a recapitulation from one particular moment in an ongoing process), I am trying to narrate a story about how theory and practice have been comingled in our research. We began with an idea for a concrete classroom curriculum and worked on designing tools and structures to support the practical needs of that curriculum. Once we had a working software prototype that could be used over the Web, we deployed it in the middle-school classroom. We immediately confronted the problems of response speed and monitor-screen real estate that we had been worried about from the start. Students started asking for new functionality, and it became clear that they were not using the implemented functions the way they were designed to be used. A dance commenced between the technicians, the educators, the students, the curriculum, and the software; as we circled each other, we all changed and became more compatible.

There was no point in trying to evaluate the success of our experiment by gathering data under controlled conditions. We needed to figure out how to make things work better, not to measure precisely how well they were (or were not) already working. Beyond the relatively clear technical usability issues, there were deeper questions of how software can mediate interpersonal and cognitive relations within collaboration (Hewitt et al., 1998). This led us to look for a theory of computer mediation—and for that matter, a theory of collaborative learning—in the graduate seminar. It turned out that there are no adequate theories on these topics sitting on the bookshelf. Rather, we had to undertake the construction of such theory, building on hints strewn about in texts from many disciplines and guided by the problematic, in which we are involved firsthand.

Trusting in our intuition that software like WebGuide could facilitate group theory building, we set out to use WebGuide in our theoretical investigations and thereby further drive the development of the software through additional practical experience even as we were developing theoretical justifications for our design. In reflecting on our experience, I have tried to organize this draft of the chapter in accordance with a nontraditional theory about the relation of theory and practice—an understanding of this relationship more in keeping not only with our practice but with our hermeneutic, dialectical, socially situated activity theory.

Thus, we started out from our vague, only partially articulated background understanding of perspectives as an interesting and promising concept for learning and for computer support (see chapter 4). We set up a real-world situation in which we could explore what happens when this idea is implemented. In this situation, we nurtured a process of "structural coupling" (Maturana & Varela, 1987) in which the different actors evolve toward a workable synthesis or homeostasis. Rapid prototyping cycles and participatory design sessions helped facilitate this process. As breakdowns in the intention of our design were recognized, we engaged in reflection in action (Schön, 1983) to make our tacit preunderstanding explicit, to understand what has happened, and to project corrective actions. This process of explication raises broad issues and calls for theory. But despite the generality of the issues, the theory is understood not in a completely abstract way but in terms of its relevance to our situation and to the specific barriers we have uncovered in that concrete situation.

Theory—like everyday thought—often arises after the fact (or well into the complex process of practical investigations) to justify situations that would otherwise be too messy to comprehend and remember. Then, at the first chance it gets, theory reverses the order of things and presents itself as a guiding *a priori* principle. As Hegel (1967) said, "The owl of Minerva flies only at night": the wisdom of theory arrives on the scene only after the practical events of the day (which theory retroactively captures in concepts) have been put to bed. *Theory* is a cherished way to capture an understanding of what has been learned, even if it distorts the picture by claiming that the practice out of which theory arose was a simple application of the theory's preexisting abstract principles.

But as is pointed out by the analyses of mediated cognition that our seminar studied, there are other *artifacts* in which experience can be captured, preserved, and transmitted (Cole, 1996). *Narrative* is one (Bruner, 1990). In this chapter, I have tried to project a voice that does not redefine the temporality of the experience I am reporting.

Sculpture is another way in which people impose meaningful form on nature and, as Hegel would say, externalize their consciousness through the mediation of wood, clay, plaster, or stone, sharing it with others and preserving it as part of their culture's spirit. Sculptures like that in figure 6.4 are such artifacts. They create spaces that project their own perspectives while at the same time being perceived from observational vantage points. Moore's sculptures are not the result of some primordial experience of self-consciousness interacting with unmediated nature. They are late twentieth-century explorations of form and material. Here, organic three-dimensional forms are showcased to contrast with socially prevalent two-dimensional representations and with the geometric shapes produced

Figure 6.4
Henry Moore, *Three Piece Sculpture: Vertebrae*, 1968–69, bronze, Hirschhorn Sculpture Garden, Washington, DC. Photo: G. Stahl, 2004.

by machinery. The characteristics of the materials of nature are brought forth, in contrast to the plastic substances that retreat from our consciousness as commodities. Also, the pragmatic representational function of symbolic objects is sublimated in the study of their abstracted physical forms and materiality. In negating the commonplace characteristics of signs—which point away from themselves—the nonrepresentational sculptures obtrusively confront their creator and viewers with the nature of the artifact as intentionally formed material object.

Polished *software* is a very different way of objectifying experience. Buried in the source code and affordances of a software artifact are countless lessons and insights—those of the particular software developer and those of the traditions (congealed labor) of our technological world on which that developer built (Marx, 1976). This is as true of the current version of WebGuide as it is of any software application. So the software application is such an artifact; one that mediates classroom collaboration. But WebGuide strives to preserve insights explicitly as well, within the notes displayed in its perspectives and within their organization, including their organization into personal and group perspectives. The discussions that evolve within this medium are also artifacts, captured and organized by the perspectives.

Perhaps when we understand better how to use WebGuide in collaborative learning contexts it will maintain the knowledge that people construct through it in a way that preserves (in the sense of Hegel's synthesis or *aufheben*) the construction *process* as well as the resultant theory. Then we may have a type of artifact or a medium *that does not reify and alienate the process by which it developed*—that permits one to reconstruct the origin of collaborative insights without laboriously deconstructing artifacts that are harder than stone. Eventually, collaborative practice and software design may coevolve to the point where they can integrate the insights of multiple perspectives into group views that do not obliterate the insights of conflicting perspectives into the multifaceted nature of truth.

Issues for Mediation

We conclude this chapter with an attempt to sort out what we are collaboratively learning through our use of WebGuide. The six issues for perspectives-based software like WebGuide that arose during the middle-school application appeared in the graduate seminar's usage of the software as well—and were articulated by seminar participants in their notes in WebGuide. These are important and complex issues that other researchers have raised as well. They are not problems that we have solved but rather foci for future work. They define central goals for our redesign of WebGuide and goals for structuring the mediation of collaborative practices.

Here is a summary of our current understanding of these issues, based on our two practical experiences and our reflections on the theory of computer mediation of collaborative learning.

Divergence among Ideas

In his review of computer-mediated collaborative learning, Rogério dePaula (1998) identified divergence of ideas to be a common problem. He argued that the tree structure imposed by standard threaded discussion support was inappropriate for collaboration. The idea of a threaded discussion is that one contribution or note leads to another, so that each new idea is connected to its "parent" to preserve this connection. The problem is that there is often no effective way to bring several ideas together in a summary or synthesis because that would require a particular note to be tied to several parent notes—something that is typically not supported by discussion software. The result is that discussions proceed along ever diverging lines as they branch out and there is no systematic way to promote convergence (Hewitt, 1997). It seems clear, however, that collaboration requires both divergence (for example, during brainstorming) and convergence (for example, during negotiation and consensus).

WebGuide tries to avoid this common structural problem of threaded discussion media at three levels:

• The note-linking mechanism in WebGuide allows notes to be *linked* to multiple parents so that they can act to bring together and summarize otherwise divergent ideas. As in threaded discussions, every note is situated in the workspace by being identified and displayed as the child of some other note. However, WebGuide allows multiple parents so that the web of notes is not restricted to a tree.

• Similarly, the graph of perspectives allows for *multiple inheritance*, so that "comparison" perspectives can be defined that aggregate or converge the contents of multiple perspectives. The Logan School application was seeded with comparison perspectives corresponding to the class and subgroup perspectives. Its overall perspectives graph has a structure in which the inheritance of notes first diverges from the class to the subgroup and then the personal perspectives and then converges through the subgroup comparison perspectives to the class comparison perspective (as shown in figure 6.2). The web of perspectives forms a directed acyclical graph rather than a strict hierarchy.

• Another effective way to encourage a well-structured discussion is to seed the workspace with a set of headings to scaffold the discourse. By introducing carefully conceived *headings* high in the perspective inheritance network, a facilitator (such as a teacher) can define an arrangement of topics that will be shared by the participants and will encourage them to arrange related ideas close to each other.

Although WebGuide provided these three convergence mechanisms in both of our usage situations, most participants were not adept at using any of them. This is probably related to the other issues below and is something that needs to be explored further in the future.

Avoidance of System Use

Media competition poses a barrier to acceptance of new communication software. People are naturally hesitant to adopt yet another communication technology. In a world inundated with pagers, cell phones, voicemail, e-mail, and faxes, people are forced to limit their media or be overwhelmed. They must calculate how much of a burden the new medium will impose in terms of learning how to use it, acquiring the equipment, checking regularly for incoming messages, and letting people know that they are communicating through it. A *critical mass* of adoption by one's communication partners is necessary as well.

In a classroom context, some of these problems are minimized: all one's partners are required to use WebGuide, and the hardware is made available. Yet the Logan School students have to communicate with mentors who may not have Internet access or the proper hardware. Communication with classmates is much easier face to face than typing everything (knowing it has to be done carefully for grading). In the graduate seminar, most participants did not have convenient access to the necessary equipment and had to go out of their way to a special lab. This means that they communicated through WebGuide once a week (at most) and therefore could not enter into lively ongoing interchanges.

We will have to make WebGuide more accessible by increasing the number of platforms or browsers that it can run on and making it work over slow home modems. Further, we need to improve its look and feel to increase people's comfort level in wanting to use it: speed up response time, allow drag-and-drop rearrangement of notes, permit resizing of the applet and fonts for different monitors and different eyes, support searching and selective printouts, and provide graphical maps of the webs of perspectives and nodes.

Naturalness of the Perspectives Metaphor

Despite the fact that WebGuide has been designed to make the perspectives metaphor seem natural and simple to navigate, people express confusion about how to use the perspectives. What perspective should I be working in, browsing for other people's ideas, or entering for discussions? The metaphor of perspectives as a set of alternative (yet linked and overlapping) textual workspaces is a new notion when made operational, as in WebGuide.

The fact that an individual note may have different edited versions and different linking structures in different perspectives, that notes may have multiple parents within the discussion threads, and that new perspectives can be added dynamically and may inherit from multiple other perspectives sets WebGuide apart from simple threaded discussion media. It also makes the computations for displaying notes extremely complex. This is a task that definitely requires computers. By relieving people of the equivalent of these display computations, computer support may allow people to collaborate more fluidly. This is the goal of WebGuide. Although the software now hides much of the complexity, it is not yet at the point where people can operate smoothly without thinking explicitly about the perspectives.

Representation of the Web of Perspectives

One problem that aggravates acceptance of the perspectives metaphor is that the web of inheritance of content from perspective to perspective is hard to represent visually within WebGuide. The WebGuide interface relies on an *outline* display, with hiding or expansion of subnotes. This has many advantages, allowing users to navigate to and view notes of interest in an intuitive way that is already familiar. However, an outline display assumes a strictly hierarchical tree of information. Because the web of perspectives has multiple inheritance, its structure is not visible in an outline, which always shows a perspective under just one of its parents at a time. Thus, for instance, there is no visual representation of how a comparison perspective inherits from several personal perspectives.

The same is true at the level of notes. A note that has been linked to several other notes that it may summarize is always displayed as the child of just one of those notes at a time.

Two solutions suggest themselves for future exploration. One is to provide an alternative representation such as a *graphical map* in place of the outline view. As appealing as this idea sounds, it may be technically difficult to do on the fly. A bigger problem is that graphical maps are notoriously poor at scaling up. Already in our two trial situations—in which there are on the order of twice as many perspectives as participants—it would be hard to clearly label a graphical node for every perspective within the applet's confined display area. The second alternative is to indicate additional links with some kind of *icon* within the outline view. This would require more understanding on the part of the users in interpreting and making use of this additional symbolic information.

Structuring of Learning Situations

We have argued based on previous experience that the crucial aspect of supporting collaborative learning has to do with structuring social practices (Koschmann, Ostwald, & Stahl, 1998). *Practice,* in the sense of Bourdieu's concept of *habitus* (Bourdieu, 1995), is the set of generally tacit procedures that are culturally adopted by a community. In introducing WebGuide into its two user communities, we have tried to establish certain usage practices, both by instruction and by enforcement in the software. Looking back at figure 6.1, one can see that Logan students are allowed to navigate only to certain perspectives—namely, their personal perspective and those group perspectives that inherit from that perspective. Seminar participants were originally given *permission* to navigate throughout the system and to make changes anywhere. That was subsequently modified (as shown in figure 6.3) to restrict their abilities when not in their personal perspective. The governing principle was that all participants should be able to do anything they want within their personal perspective but no one should be able to affect the display of information in someone else's personal perspective.

When the ability to enter notes everywhere was restricted, facilities for copying and linking notes from other computational perspectives into one's own computational perspective were introduced. This was intended to encourage people to integrate the ideas from other figurative perspectives into their own figurative perspective by making a conscious decision about where the new note should go in their existing web of notes. However, this added a step to the process of communication. One could no longer simply select a note that one wanted to comment on and press the "Add discussion" button.

To facilitate discussion of notes that were not necessarily going to be integrated into one's own perspective, the Add Discussion (annotation) button was then made active in all comparison perspectives. This led to minor problems, in that one could then not edit discussion notes that one had contributed in these perspectives. This could be fixed at the cost of additional complexity in the rules by allowing the author of a note to edit it in comparison perspectives.

More significantly, our experiments with changing permission rules pointed out that people were using WebGuide primarily as a threaded discussion medium for superficial opinions and socializing—and rarely as a *knowledge*-construction space. Furthermore, their ability to construct shared group perspectives on discussion topics was severely hampered by the lack of support for *negotiation* in the system.

Distinguishing the System's Capabilities
In iterating the design of WebGuide it became increasingly clear that what the system "wanted to be" (the design vision) was a *medium for construction of knowledge*. Yet users were more familiar with discussion forums and tended to ignore the perspectives apparatus in favor of engaging in threaded discussion. These are very different kinds of tasks. Collaborative knowledge construction generally requires a prolonged process of brainstorming alternative ideas, working out the implications of different options, and negotiating conclusions; discussion can be much more spontaneous.

This suggests that more clarity is needed on the question: what is the *task*? If people are going to use WebGuide for collaborative knowledge construction, then they need to have a clear sense of pursuing a shared knowledge-construction task. The Logan students had such a task in articulating positions on acid mine drainage. However, much of their knowledge construction took place in classroom discussion. They used WebGuide largely as a repository for their ideas. The seminar was concerned with understanding a series of readings, so its participants were more interested in exchanging isolated questions or reactions than in formulating larger integrative positions.

Our experience to date already suggests the complexity of trying to support collaborative learning. We should probably distinguish the software interface functions that support discussion from those that support knowledge construction. But this should be done in a way that allows spontaneously discussed ideas to be readily integrated into longer-term knowledge construction processes. Similarly, additional functionality—most notably, support for group negotiation—must be added, differentiated, and integrated. New capabilities and uses of WebGuide can increase its value, as long as confusions and conflicts are not introduced. For instance, providing facilities for people to maintain lists of annotated Web bookmarks, things to do, favorite references, and upcoming deadlines within their personal perspectives might not only give them familiarity with using the system but would also build toward that critical mass of usage necessary for meaningful adoption.

Computer mediation does have the potential to revolutionize communication, just as the printing press did long ago, but widespread literacy required gradual changes in skills and practices so that people could take full advantage of the technological affordances of the printing press. In fact, the transition from oral tradition to literacy involved a radical change in how people think and work (Ong, 1998). Although social as well as technical changes can be propagated much faster now, suitable mixes of practices and systems still must evolve to support the move from predominantly individual construction of knowledge to a new level of *collaborative cognition*.

Our investigation of the above six issues will guide the next stage of our ongoing exploration of the potentials and barriers of perspectives-based computer mediated collaborative learning on the Web.

Dialogue with *JIME* Reviewers

In fall 2000, the preceding part of this chapter was reviewed through the *Journal of Interactive Media In Education* (*JIME*) online review process. The reviews brought out what the paper was trying to do and added, in a generally supportive way, confirmation of one person's experiences from much broader backgrounds. The reflections on key issues significantly enriched the discussion.

The reviewers' comments and inquiries and my responses are presented below. This serves as another layer of reflection from a somewhat later vantage point.

Question: A slight doubt, which I think it would be hard to understand without using the system for a while, would be if it could feel or be restrictive. When computer-mediated collaboration is well used, users systematically attend to convergence (using the divergent discussion as a resource) by writing summaries and essays based on the shared material. Would WebGuide confine learner freedom to synthesize or converge because of the complexity of its linking systems? Just a doubt.

While WebGuide's interface has improved considerably since its first usage, problems remain of trying to think about ideas on a computer monitor—still a less convivial environment than paper for playing with complexly interrelated ideas. There is also the difficult tradeoff between the interface's simplicity and clarity and the users' need for complicated functionality. The mechanisms to support convergence are only partly automatic, transparent, and natural. And yet if we want to think and write collaboratively, then paper will not suffice.

Question: Does this WebGuide software provide a straightforward discussion area to be used beside the work on perspectives? Somewhere here there seems to be confusion between a virtual collaborative discussion space and a tool to aid collaborative work. Another point that confused me was the idea of the software as artifact in the same way as a piece of sculpture or a narrative, even if, as the author points out, software "represents a very different way of objectifying experience." Can various perspectives be represented with a single graphical image? Perhaps cubist painting rather than sculpture makes a better analogy?

As detailed below, I have subsequently added a discussion perspective that provides a space for threaded discussion. Previously, threaded discussion took place directly in the comparison perspectives—leading people to ignore their personal perspectives and aggravating the conflict between discussion and construction. One of the hardest things I have had to figure out as a designer is how to integrate this into the perspectives framework so that ideas entered one place would be available for the rest of the knowledge-building process. I have just now implemented this and have not yet released it to my users. I have still not implemented the sorely needed negotiation procedures. Discussions with Thomas Herrmann and his colleagues in Germany have helped me to understand the issues related to these new perspectives and the reasons that the system should include explicit discussion and negotiation perspectives.

An artifact is never a simple object. A sculpture, for instance, opens up a rich world: it structures physical space, offers a sensuous surface, and evokes other objects, meanings, and works. Software is yet harder to characterize: what is its form and substance, and where are its resistances and affordances? A communication and collaboration artifact like WebGuide makes possible new forms of interaction and knowledge building—but how do people learn how to take advantage of this without being overloaded? The artifact here is not so much the buttons and windows of the user interface as the discussion content that gets built up through the interface. These issues have led me to another iteration of theory with a seminar in fall 2000 on how artifacts embody meaning and subsequent analysis of empirical data on how people learn to understand and use meaningful artifacts (see chapter 12 as well).

I like the cubist image. But sculptures also encourage and facilitate viewing from different visual perspectives. I have thought of replacing the monoperspectival pictures in the chapter with video clips that could be run in the *JIME* publication. Perhaps I could just use animated graphic interchange format (gif) files of each sculpture that cycle through several views—creating an effect that cubism anticipated before perspectival technology was available.

Question: This article gives us a lot of good, clear, qualitative description of the two situations in which this software is being looked at. At some point, though, there seems to be a need for firmer ground and a few numbers.

The middle-school classroom had 12 students. During the several months of sporadic usage, 835 notes were entered (including revisions of old notes). This count includes guiding questions and organizing headings that the teacher and I entered.

The graduate seminar had eight active students. During the semester, 473 notes were entered.

This semester (which is half over as I draft this response), there are 11 active participants. We have entered 497 notes already, but many of these are headings, modifications, or entry of data to be shared. This probably represents an average of two entries per week per student. While I work on some technical problems that have arisen, I am not encouraging heavy use of WebGuide. Most entries are comments and questions on the class readings, with some follow-up discussion. If I defined some collaborative tasks, we might get much higher usage.

I try to hold class in a computer lab at the beginning of the semester so that we can learn the systems together and students can help each other. Most students can now access WebGuide from home, although this remains problematic. When we all use WebGuide at the same time in the lab, the worst technical problems come up (multiuser issues that are hard to test without class usage). Also, problems arise of how the entries are organized (how to find what a neighbor just said she put in) and how discussion relates to a personal perspective. The main beneficiary of class usage of WebGuide is still the designer, who sees what problems need to be solved and what new functionality is desirable. For the students, this is a glimpse into the future but not yet a powerful cognitive and collaborative tool. In each class that uses WebGuide, the students participate in reflecting on the process of designing the software artifact—and this is integral to the course curriculum as an experiment in collaborative learning.

Question: I see an advantage of being able to see the work of other roles in progress. Figure 6.2 shows that joining of perspectives takes place (too) late—

namely, in Gulch class comparison. It means that students are not having enough time to prepare counterarguments and that they miss out on constructing their perspectives along the same lines as that of other groups. In addition, I doubt whether it is desirable to have students think only about their own role or perspective since this is rather unrealistic. I may have this wrong, I am not sure how the system actually was used in practice.

I fear there is still some confusion on how perspectives work. The inheritance diagrammed in figure 6.2 takes place continually as notes are added, not just when perspectives are somehow complete. Every user of WebGuide can visit every perspective and read what is there at any time. The restriction is that you can modify (edit, delete, rearrange) only the notes in your own perspective. Recently, I have added private notes that users can add in any perspective but are viewable only by the user. This way, you can annotate any notes in the system privately.

I have also added discussion notes that can be added in any perspective. Rather than staying in that perspective (and thereby modifying someone else's perspective), the discussion note and the note it is discussing are copied to a new discussion perspective. The new discussion (and a new negotiation) perspective provides a space for interpersonal discussions to take place. Your contributions in the discussion perspective are also copied into your personal perspective so that you have a complete record of all the ideas you have entered into WebGuide and so that you can integrate these ideas with others in your working perspective.

These changes are part of a rather radical redesign—or at least extension—of the WebGuide perspectives system that has not yet been tried out by users. However, it is worth presenting here in some detail because it shows my response to the worrisome issues that have come up about conflicts between discussion and knowledge building. It brings the presentation up to date as of spring 2001.

Figure 6.5 shows the new interface of WebGuide. It now consists of two separate windows, a Java applet interface, and an HTML window. Previous interfaces included an HTML frame within a fixed-size main interface window. The user can now resize and overlap the two windows to optimize and personalize use of screen real estate. The main interface consists of (1) an expandable hierarchy of notes (either their titles or the first line of their content is displayed in the hierarchy: the full content of the currently selected note is displayed in the HTML window), (2) a bar of buttons for selecting a perspective across the top, and (3) a control panel of function buttons on the right side.

Figure 6.6 shows a closeup of the perspectives buttons, which provide direct access to the most common perspectives and a pull-down list of all defined perspectives in the current database. Note that in addition to the *group* (or class) perspective, the current user's *personal* perspective, and the (group or class) *comparison*

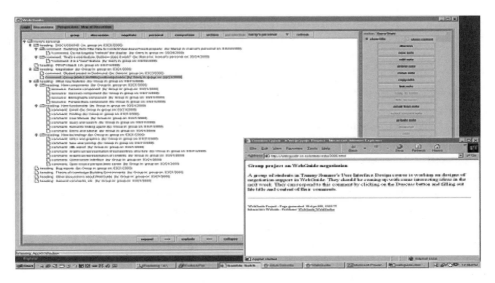

Figure 6.5
The new interface to WebGuide 2000.

Figure 6.6
The new bar of perspectives buttons in WebGuide 2000.

perspective, there are now perspectives for *discussion*, *negotiation*, and *archive*. We show how these are interrelated in figure 6.8 below.

Figure 6.7 shows a closeup of the function controls, with restricted options gray. The Comment button allows a user to enter a quick comment below the selected note. The New Note button is similar to the Comment but allows the user to choose a label for the kind of note and to position the new note after (that is, at the same level of hierarchy) the selected note rather than indented below it (that is, as a child of it). Subsequent buttons let the user Edit, Delete, Move, and Copy or Link a selected note. Copy to Home or Link to Home is used when a user has selected a note that is not in his or her personal perspective and wants to create a physical or virtual copy of it there. Email lets a user send an e-mail and have the content of the e-mail and its responses inserted below the selected note. Search conducts a simple string text search across all notes (their author, title, and content) in the database

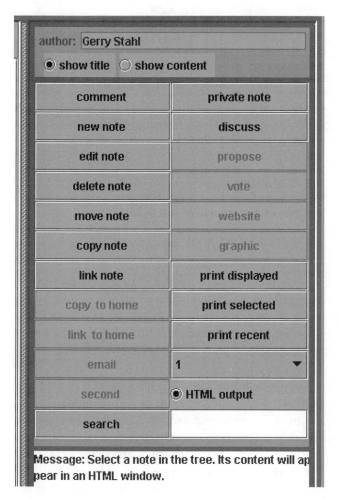

Figure 6.7
The new knowledge management control panel in WebGuide 2000.

and displays the resulting notes in the HTML window (where they can be easily printed out). Private Note is similar to Comment, except that it can be inserted in any perspective and that it will be displayed only when the author is logged in as the current user. Discuss and Promote create notes in the discussion and negotiation perspectives; they are described in the next paragraph. The Vote, Website, and Graphic buttons are for adding votes on negotiation issues, live links to URLs and graphic (multimedia) URLs to be displayed in the HTML window; these functions are not yet implemented. The Print Displayed button causes all notes whose titles are currently displayed in the hierarchy display to have their content shown in the HTML window for printing. The Print Selected button lets a user select multiple notes that are not sequential and have their content displayed in the HTML window. Finally, the Print Recent button displays in the HTML window the content of all notes that were created in the past *n* days, where a value for *n* is selected below this button. These search and print buttons are important steps toward providing tools for more effective knowledge management—offering convenient access to selected notes.

How should the Discuss and Propose buttons work? A user should be able to start a discussion based on any other user's note found in the system. The resulting discussion should be available to everyone in the group. The two perspectives available to everyone are the group and the comparison perspectives. The comparison perspective quickly becomes overcrowded and confusing, so I decided to create a new discussion perspective derived from the group perspective. Similarly, proposals for negotiations should be able to build on anyone's notes and should be generally available, so I also created a negotiation perspective linked to the group perspective. Recall that the group (or class) perspective contains notes agreed to by the group at large (or seeded by the teacher to provide a shared starting point). The group perspective therefore provides an overall context for collaborative discussion and negotiation, as well as for individual efforts at knowledge building. So while we do not want discussion and negotiation notes that have not yet been adopted by the whole group to show up directly in the group perspective (and therefore to be inherited into all other perspectives), we do want to have the discussion and negotiation perspectives inherit from the group perspective to provide some context and structure. Moreover, we want the negotiation to inherit from the discussion so that a note in a discussion thread can be proposed for negotiation and so that discussion threads can be viewed in relation to negotiation proposals. As shown in figure 6.8, individual personal perspectives should inherit from the group but not from the discussion or negotiation perspectives.

The trick with putting notes in the discussion and negotiation perspectives is to situate them meaningfully in the hierarchy with at least some context. Suppose you have entered a note that I want to comment on and to present for group discussion. Your note is in your personal perspective, and I may have found it in the comparison perspective. So I either select your note in the comparison perspective or go to your personal perspective and select it there. I click on the Discuss button. The system then wants to start a thread in the discussion perspective starting with your note, which would then be followed by my note. To do this, the system finds your note's (the one that I want to comment on) parent note (the note that your note is threaded from in the hierarchy of your personal perspective) and designates that

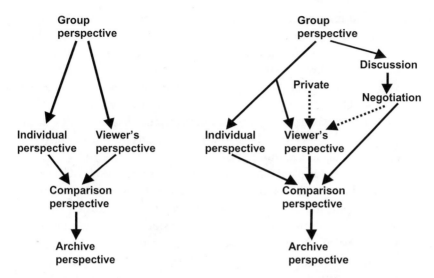

Figure 6.8
The old inheritance structures for perspectives in WebGuide (left) and new structures (right).

note the anchor note. If the anchor note happens to already appear in the discussion perspective (which inherits the whole group perspective), then everything is simple, and the system simply makes a copy of your note below the anchor in the discussion perspective and attaches my note below that. Alternatively, if an ancestor of your note appears within the discussion perspective in the notes hierarchy, then that closest ancestor is used as the anchor. Otherwise, the system attaches a copy of your note to a special Discussions heading note in the discussions perspective and then attaches my note below that. Then we have a discussion thread that anyone can add to in the discussions perspective.

In addition to setting up the new thread in the discussions perspective, the system makes a copy of your note with mine attached to it and places them below the anchor note (which I inherit from the group) in my own personal perspective. This is so that my personal perspective contains all of my contributions to discussions and negotiations. That way, I see all of my ideas, and I can conveniently manipulate them in my own workspace. The dotted line in figure 6.8 from negotiation to viewer's perspective indicates that these entries will appear in my perspective when I am viewing it.

Similarly, figure 6.8 indicates that private notes that I created with the private note button will appear in whatever perspective I created them in when—and only when—I am viewing them. Finally, the archive perspective is simply the group comparison perspective, including notes that have been deleted. This is primarily for the convenience of researchers who want to view old versions of work. Figure 6.8 shows how the inheritance structure has changed with the recent addition of the discussion, negotiation, private, and archive perspectives. The possibility of extending the perspectives metaphor and the underlying computational mechanism to include new perspectives like these confirms the power and generality of the approach.

Table 6.1 summarizes the relationships of the buttons and display modes to the different perspectives. The top of the chart (buttons) indicates the perspectives in which each of the buttons is active (not gray).

The bottom of the chart (displays) indicates which notes are displayed in each type of perspective (and in some cases to whom it is displayed). Statements are notes created with the Comment or New Note button; Discussions are created with the Discuss button; Proposals with the Propose button; Decisions with the Vote button; and Privates with the Private Note button. The viewer is the currently logged-in user; the owner is the person to whom the personal perspective belongs.

This is the designer's story. I think it is premature to give a user's story. For a number of reasons that are my fault (technical problems and poor definition of tasks), WebGuide has been at best used as a threaded discussion forum. I hope that the new structures of Negotiation, Discussion, and Private perspectives will help users to engage in personal and group knowledge building. Perhaps then we will see some insightful user scenarios.

Question: Which ideas led to WebGuide? The author did not start to work on WebGuide with zero theory, but unfortunately, the author did not make his starting notions (theory) very clear in the design narrative. I think this is an omission that should be corrected. If I presume correctly, the author has detected some real-life problem for which there was no adequate solution. This triggered WebGuide development.

As for forerunner systems, I make no claims that WebGuide is superior to other research prototypes or even commercial systems for supporting collaborative learning. It is consciously based on Scardamalia and Bereiter's extensive theoretical, technical, and pedagogical work on knowledge-building communities and their CSILE (now Knowledge Forum) system that is used in schools around the world. WebGuide's only attempted innovation is perspectives. The idea of perspectives grows out of my dissertation work with Ray McCall and is based on ideas cited in this chapter and chapter 4.

Where did the original impetus for WebGuide itself come from? This is another story, told briefly in chapter 5. While introducing the software from chapter 2 in another local middle school, I observed problems of students collecting and

Table 6.1
Table of permissions for WebGuide 2000 buttons and displays.

	Group Perspective	Discussion (Group)	Negotiation (Group)	Personal Perspective	Other's Perspective	Comparison Perspective	Archive (Deleted)
Buttons							
Discuss		X	X	X	X	X	X
Propose			X				
Vote			X	X			
Private note	X	X	X	X	X	X	X
New note				X			
Edit				X			
Delete				X			
Move				X			
Copy				X			
Link				X			
Copy home		X	X		X	X	X
Link home		X	X		X	X	X
E-mail				X			
Search	X	X	X	X	X	X	X
Print	X	X	X	X	X	X	X
Displays							
Statement	X	X	X	X	X	X	W. deleted
Discussion		X	X	Viewer's	Owner's	X	W. deleted
Proposal			X	Viewer's	Owner's	X	W. deleted
Decision			X	Viewer's	Owner's	X	W. deleted
Private	Viewer's	Viewer's	Viewer's	Viewer's	Viewer's	Viewer's	Viewer's

retaining Web site addresses as part of their Web research projects. I thought it would be nice to let them save these addresses on the Web rather than on disks or floppies that never seemed to be available when they needed them. So WebGuide was originally conceived of as their personal guide to the Web, with their collected Web site links. Then I wanted them to be able to share their links and negotiate class-adopted lists of links. Then I added the idea of annotating and eventually discussing the links and finally categorizing and reorganizing them. Soon, the superstructure took over, and I have still not made it easy to store links in WebGuide. The WebGuide interface has always included an HTML window as well as the Java applet display. The content of notes is displayed in the HTML window—specifically so that Web site links can be live and one can click on them and go to the site. This also means that graphics and other media can be stored in WebGuide and viewed and that HTML markup can be used in the content. As for the philosophy behind WebGuide, the notion of perspectives goes back to a former life when I studied Heidegger and hermeneutics (Stahl, 1975b), as well as to my more recent computer science dissertation (Stahl, 1993a) that argued for this kind of software perspectives mechanism—warranted by reference to ideas of design theorists Rittel, Alexander, and Schön (see chapter 4). So persistent questioning pushes the horizon of context further and further back through forgotten cycles of practice and theory, complexly evolving trajectories of inquiry that had no clean starting point *ex nihilo*.

Question: The problem of system underutilization is worldwide and well known. Which functionalities that you consider to be key functions did users underutilize?

I do not care if students do not use all the features of WebGuide, and I do not provide a lot of formatting. But I would like to see them get beyond mere threaded discussion—the superficial exchange of off-the-cuff opinions—to deeper collaborative knowledge building. Seriously taking up each other's ideas and formulations, worrying about terminological disagreements, negotiating innovative insights that merge multiple perspectives: these would be exciting to see emerge from the more sophisticated use of WebGuide's functionality, which allows notes to be modified, copied, and rearranged across perspectives.

Question: I wondered whether the author has worked in a situation in which there were not enough computers for all students forcing the formation of groups.

Periodically, students have teamed up on computers. This is nice for collaboratively learning how to use the system. It is also useful if I want to videotape the usage and analyze the discourse within the little group for a fine-grained view of what is going on from the user perspective. The problem with doing this with WebGuide is that it is text-based and only one person can type text into the shared computer at a time.

Question: Perspectives? How should I fit in the notion of role (such as that of landowner) within the typology of literal, figurative, and computational? And what should I think about different points of view within roles? Are these perspectives too (as seen from the designer's point of view)? And what about class perspective and team perspective?

The perspectives mechanism of automatic inheritance of content down the hierarchy is very general. In some cases, I have used it to define a hierarchy of domain knowledge (my dissertation), of roles (the middle-school Gulch project), of academic disciplines (the interdisciplinary seminar), or just of different people (Fall 2000). The group or class perspective is supposed to display the state of knowledge that has been mutually agreed on and thus requires the still-missing negotiation support. So now it contains mostly what the teacher has defined by fiat as the shared knowledge structure to get the process going in an organized way. This is all hard to explain or comprehend, especially when readers have not actually used the system.

Conclusion

I found the *JIME* reviews very heartening. The reviewers clearly understood and appreciated what I was trying to do with my narrative approach to reporting on recent research. Furthermore, they added important critical perspectives. My concluding response to the reviews consists of a brief overview of the adventure of composing this chapter.

The chapter grew out of a submission to AERA '99 (the annual conference of the American Educational Research Association). To have a paper accepted for this conference, one simply submits an abstract. When my abstract was accepted, I felt free to write in whatever vein I chose. The freedom from having to write to traditional reviewers with narrow paradigms of scholarly publication allowed me to experiment stylistically as well as to think about what format would be most appropriate to the level of experience with WebGuide that I wanted to report.

The paper session at AERA was coordinated by Ricki Goldman-Segall, who served as the discussant as well. She shares my enthusiasm for "perspectivity software." I had just read her book (Goldman-Segall, 1998), which has a "thick description" style of interwoven themes and which begins each chapter with one of her photographs. This gave me the impetus to tell my story by talking about diverse themes that were important to me. I also decided to introduce a decorative element to the page and to tie my ideas about sculpture loosely to my content. (In the book version, I have removed pictures of my own sculpture and added figure 6.4.)

It was clear to me that providing a traditional analysis of the software usage would have been wildly premature. The use of WebGuide by one teacher and his dozen students over several months made a number of technical and social issues painfully clear to me, and the experiment had been an experience for the students, but there was nothing entered into the database to illustrate the ultimate vision I had for the software approach. Similarly, in my graduate seminar with about eight students for a semester, WebGuide served more as an example of what we were thinking about than as a tool that let us think about it more deeply. What was interesting was not the empirical data about the software usage but the process ("dance," "structural coupling") by which our understanding of what was needed developed in the classroom settings where a crude version of WebGuide was used.

The work on WebGuide continues to be the focus of my activities in Colorado. Many of the weaknesses pointed out in the reviews are being gradually addressed in new software functions, theoretical papers, and funding proposals. This evolving article remains my fullest discussion of perspectives and their inheritance, a topic that is devilishly hard to explain clearly. WebGuide 2000 is now being used in my seminar on CSCL. Every month I produce a new version with additional improvements. However, while some students are starting to use it regularly to formulate and discuss ideas, its use still falls far short of the goal.

It has become clearer to me that WebGuide needs to be a *collaborative knowledge-management environment*. It needs to better support the browsing, modifying, and reorganizing of interrelated ideas. Knowledge building has become a more central concept for me, and I am trying to understand how it proceeds or could proceed: what activities are involved and what tools could support these interpersonal activities. Talking about knowledge building (a concept I attribute to Scardamalia and Bereiter) seems to be a productive way to think about learning in a social and collaborative framework. The subtle intertwining of group and personal perspectives is a central structure of collaborative knowledge building.

The notion of artifacts has become ever more central to my theoretical interests. My seminar this semester is on the question of how artifacts—particularly computer-based artifacts like WebGuide—affect our cognitive abilities. How do artifacts embody meaning, how do people design that meaning into them, and how do others learn what that meaning is? What are the implications for designing new media to support thinking and collaborating? Heidegger discusses how works of art like sculpture make explicitly visible their forms, meanings, and material but also open up whole new worlds in which human activities can take place. What kind of world do we want to create for future WebGuide users? What kinds of intellectual worlds do we want students to construct collaboratively for themselves?

The problems of getting communities of students to adopt Web media like WebGuide are daunting. Look at our use of the *JIME* technology in reviewing the journal version of this essay. The idea that the online *JIME* discussion medium might support a back-and-forth knowledge-building discussion among the reviewers and with the author—grounded in the artifact of the submitted article, section by section—was not realized. None of the reviewers knew how to use it effectively. They probably first typed up typical reviews in their word processors and then pasted them into the top of the discussion hierarchy. Then they broke them up and stuck some pieces under different headings but never in the places that were linked to article sections. Months later, the author had to respond in a similar way. The editor of the reviews did not even post his thoughtful contributions to the online *JIME* site at first, but e-mailed them to me separately. Unfortunately, this is typical not only of *JIME* and WebGuide but of groupware in general (Lenell & Stahl, 2001). These are the pressing issues—more pressing than details of technology and statistical assessment methodology—that need to be discussed at this stage.

7

Groupware Goes to School

In this chapter, the idea of computational perspectives from chapter 6 is implemented in a simpler way and supplemented with the negotiation support that was missing there.[1] WebGuide was always designed to include negotiation support, but I never had a chance to implement it until I went to work on the Synergeia software in Europe. The theory of online knowledge negotiation is further elaborated in chapter 8. This completes the exploration of support for three central aspects of group cognition: group formation (chapter 3), interpretive perspectives (chapters 4, 5, and 6), and knowledge negotiation (chapters 7 and 8).

Groupware for computer-supported cooperative work and for computer-supported collaborative learning has many important commonalities as well as different requirements. By transforming a generic collaboration platform into an environment to support a particular vision of education as collaborative knowledge building, I experienced how functionality had to be adopted, transformed, and refined to meet the specific educational social setting. By "taking groupware to school," I discovered the need to extend the original system into an application that could facilitate collaborative learning, knowledge building, perspective intertwining, knowledge negotiation, portfolio sharing, and knowledge artifacts in active, structured, virtual learning places. In this chapter, I describe the resulting system and reflect on issues of design and implementation that differentiate our collaborative-learning (BSCL or Synergeia groupware) approach from its closely related cooperative-work basis (BSCW groupware).

From CSCW to CSCL

With widespread use of the Internet, collaboration software promises to provide the kind of support to networked groups that individual productivity software like word processors and spreadsheets grant individuals. The potential of computer support for groups is perhaps even higher than that for individuals because communication within groups has until now suffered from severe constraints that may be eased by computer support. The question must still be addressed as to what software for groups should aim at, beyond the reproduction of precomputer forms of group interaction.

We need a vision of how networked computers can facilitate the discussion of *all with all* that does not require the coordination of a manager or teacher and can support the collaborative building of knowledge that is not restricted to the skills, memories, and efforts of individuals. Perhaps when we take groupware into the schools in a principled and explorative way, we may see how computer support can be designed to transform teacher-centric learning into collaborative learning and transcend knowledge management with knowledge building. In this way, what we learn about computer-supported collaborative learning (CSCL) could provide an informative model for the design of computer-supported cooperative work (CSCW).

Academically, the exploration of groupware has historically been split into two separate domains of collaboration: CSCW and CSCL, which address issues of work and learning, respectively. Each domain has its own conferences, journals, and adherents. The Cyted-Ritos International Workshop on Groupware (CRIWG) (where an earlier version of this chapter was presented in September 2002) is one of the few places that these two fields come together. This distinction has not been based on a conceptual analysis that might motivate and justify such a division. Certainly, the two domains have at least sufficient commonalities that they can borrow extensively from one another.

Why should CSCW and CSCL be distinguished? There is at least a superficial rationale for this. CSCW is concerned with the world of work, where people must accomplish commercially productive tasks, while CSCL is concerned with the world of schooling, where students must learn basic skills that will in the end allow them to function effectively in the world of work and in adult society generally. These are very different social contexts. Perhaps the clearest lesson of CSCW research to date has been the importance of taking into account the social context—the motivations, prevailing practices, political constraints—in which software is to be used (Greenbaum & Kyng, 1991; Grudin, 1990; Kling, 1999; Orlikowski et al., 1995). By this criterion, the two domains are indeed distinct and should be treated so.

However, it is also true that in today's knowledge society work is often knowledge work that requires constant learning (Brown & Duguid, 1991; Zuboff, 1988). In the interesting cases, work—whether individual or cooperative—is not the repetitive carrying out of well-known tasks that were learned once and for all in school but itself centrally involves various learning tasks. Work may require just-in-time learning, where existing information must be found to solve a current problem. Or it may involve inquiry learning, where solving a wicked (Rittel & Webber, 1984), ill-structured (Simon, 1981), or nonroutine problem requires the building of new knowledge. Similarly, the learning that is needed to prepare students for an effective role in tomorrow's knowledge society cannot consist merely in the transfer of existing knowledge into passively receptive minds but must guide students to develop personal and social skills that will allow them to find information relevant to unanticipated problems and to engage in inquiry processes. In this sense, the application domains of CSCW and CSCL are closely related; it is not just a matter of both having to support the activities of groups.

This chapter reports on the results of trying to extend a basic CSCW system for a typical CSCL application. We started with BSCW (Basic Support for Cooperative Work), a well-known and widely used groupware system (Appelt, 1999; Appelt & Klöckner, 1999; Klöckner, 2001). Used by over 200,000 people since 1995 when it was developed at the Institute for Applied Information Technology (FIT, previously a GMD Institute, now a Fraunhofer Institute near Bonn, Germany), BSCW provides a system of autonomously managed Web-based workspaces that can be used by members of a workgroup to organize and coordinate their work. These workspaces are central access points for shared documents, including folders for organizing them and a wealth of functionality for knowledge management.

Although BSCW has been used in many classrooms, especially at universities in Europe, it is clearly a CSCW application: it provides generic support for work groups to share documents in an organized and accessible way. The BSCW development team wanted to adapt it specifically for the social setting of schools; to see what it would mean to transform it into a CSCL application. I joined them for a year to undertake this within a European Union project named Innovative Technology for Collaborative Learning and Knowledge Building (ITCOLE) (Leinonen et al., 2001). With its emphasis on collaborative knowledge building, this project aims primarily at supporting group discourse. It differs from many other online educational approaches that strive to convey information in the form of curriculum content or videotaped lectures, which can perhaps be done with a CSCW system. In ITCOLE, we assume that students can find information on the Internet or in documents uploaded into the system and that the following kinds of activities need CSCL support:

- The collaborative reflection on this information (sharing and annotating),

- The building of group knowledge (discussion from perspectives), and

- The determination of what is to count as produced knowledge artifacts (knowledge negotiation).

The aim of the ITCOLE project differs from that of BSCW, which focuses on the archiving and sharing of existing knowledge artifacts. While we wanted to take advantage of important forms of CSCW support, like knowledge sharing and social awareness, we also wanted to go beyond the management of established knowledge to the creation of innovative knowledge within a learning community that develops, defines, sanctions, and shares its knowledge.

This chapter reports on how we designed a CSCL system by transforming a CSCW system. It begins with a scenario illustrating the vision of how our new system, called *Synergeia*, might be used to facilitate collaborative knowledge building in a typical collaborative classroom. The system is named Synergeia in recognition that the whole can be much more than the sum of its parts. Thus, *the system strives to support the synergistic construction of knowledge at the group level that is quite distinct from what any of the students could produce individually.* The scenario anticipates the pedagogical concepts that are then presented in the next section. For instance, the "folders" of BSCW are referred to as "virtual learning places" in Synergeia because the metaphor is one not of passive storage containers but of locations where active knowledge building takes place. The functionality associated with the pedagogical concepts is described with the respective concepts. Other Synergeia functions for students, teachers, administrators, and researchers are then summarized, and following a brief discussion of the system infrastructure, reflections on the attempt to adapt CSCW to CSCL are presented.

The Synergeia groupware is already going to school. Teachers and students in Italy, Greece, the Netherlands, and Finland began in early 2002 to use an initial version within the ITCOLE project. Additional classrooms in these countries were scheduled to use the revised version described in this chapter starting in fall 2002. The revisions are based on early feedback from pedagogic researchers, teachers, and students to the initial version, which was itself based on extensive experience with related systems in both CSCW and CSCL contexts.

Synergeia is designed to support collaborative knowledge building. However, it must also be flexible enough that teachers in various countries can use it for a broad spectrum of educational approaches. The following scenario illustrates what might be called the "default usage" of Synergeia. This means that Synergeia was designed to make it especially easy for teachers to set Synergeia up for structuring knowledge building this way, although other ways of using it are also supported.

Scenario of CSCL Support

Meet Carla, a student in the course "The Human Brain." Her teacher has enrolled her in the course and assigned her to a workgroup on the role of vision. When Carla first logs in, she can see a folder called "The Human Brain" for her course. In addition, there is a "personal knowledge-building perspective" for her to jot down her own ideas (figure 7.1).

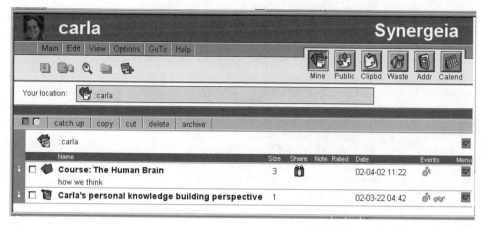

Figure 7.1
Carla's computer screen after she logs in. Her personal learning place includes access to the learning places associated with her courses and to her private knowledge-building area.

Carla clicks on her course to view its contents. She sees a folder called "The Vision Team" for her project group within the overall course. She notices in the size column that there are already some items in the group learning place, so she clicks on Group: The Vision Team and goes there (figure 7.2). Carla works with the other students in her project team to collect Web sites and other documents about how vision works as part of the human brain.

As they collect new information, the team members discuss what they have found and begin to build theories about vision in the group knowledge-building perspective (figure 7.3). This discussion motivates them to do more Web searches and to try to answer questions that they pose to each other. Gradually, they converge on an understanding of their topic and put together a portfolio of what they have learned to share with the other members of the course.

As they begin to explore the physiology of vision, different students find different explanations. Some find discussions of vision in terms of light dynamics, lenses, and the stimulation of the retinal sensors, others read about chemical reactions in the sensors and nerve connections, while others discover presentations involving electrical charges in neurons. As these different findings come together in the group knowledge-building perspective, the concepts and claims in the notes interact. Efforts to question one another and to synthesize multiple notes raise new questions, hypotheses, and insights.

Carla is a shy girl who does not normally participate much in face-to-face class discussions. She is afraid that her ideas are not good, and she hesitates to share them

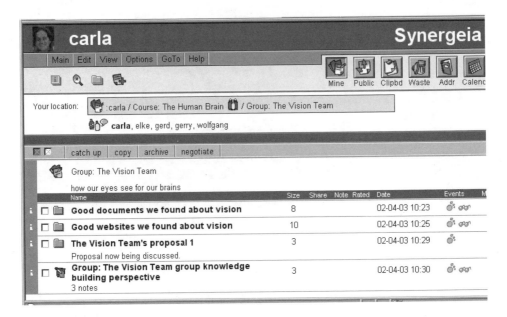

Figure 7.2
The group learning place. Here is where collaboration takes place. Documents, Web sites, and other forms of information are collected, shared, organized, analyzed, and critiqued.

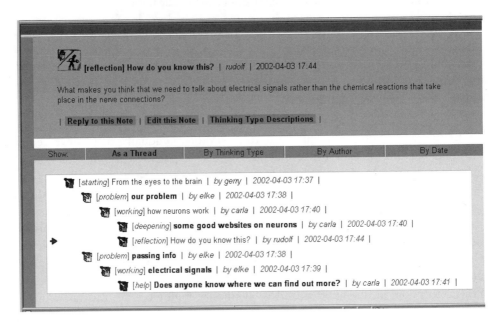

Figure 7.3
The group knowledge-building area. This area provides an overview of the discussion within a group and offers an interface for engaging in the knowledge-building process.

until she has had time to think about them and to compare them with other ideas or to check them out by collecting more information. So when she sees an interesting idea in the group learning place, she often copies it into her personal perspective and works on it there, where no one else will see it right away. During the week, her personal area fills with the results of new Web searches, documents she has collected or edited, notes that she has copied from the group area, and ideas she has jotted down in her own knowledge-building area. When she is happy with some of her ideas, she copies her notes and related documents into the group area to see what her teammates will say. Now she has some confidence that her ideas are thought through and can stand up to inspection by others. Even if her suggestions are not adopted unchanged in the end, they will be taken into the group discourse as serious contributions.

At some point in the collaborative knowledge-building process, Carla thinks that the group members have something almost ready to present to the course as a *knowledge artifact* or part of their team's *knowledge portfolio*. So she puts this information together in folders named "Good documents/Web sites we found about vision" and makes a proposal to share this with the course as the group's portfolio (figure 7.4). Now the group area contains a proposal folder named "Vision Team portfolio of documents and websites."

In addition to the folders with proposed content, the proposal folder contains a voting interface and a knowledge-building area for discussing what changes are needed before the group members are ready to agree to send this folder to the course learning place as their "knowledge portfolio."

Once the team has decided to send its portfolio to the course learning area, it can be discussed by everyone in the course and evaluated by the teacher as a product of the group's knowledge-building effort. This might be the end of a curriculum unit, or it might lead to further inquiry and knowledge building. The same groups might continue to work together, or the teacher and students might create new groups in new learning places. Our scenario ends here, but the learning continues.

Pedagogical Requirements for Synergeia

The adaptation of BSCW for school classrooms involves responding to a particular pedagogical vision and providing support for the particulars of that vision. To understand the difference that the CSCL setting makes to system design, one must understand the pedagogical concepts that drive the adaptation. The central concepts of collaborative knowledge building are presented in the current section, along with a description of the support implemented for them in Synergeia.

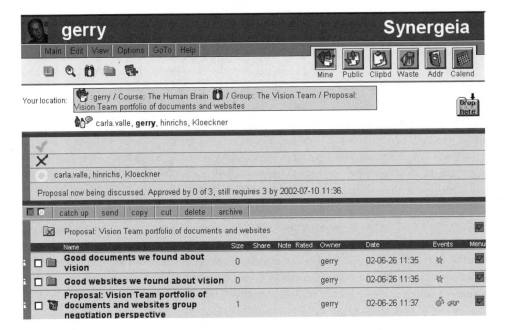

Figure 7.4
The proposal folder. This collects a number of documents or subfolders that are the content of the proposal, as well as a group negotiation perspective for discussing the proposal and debating possible changes to it. It also includes a voting interface displaying the present status of the proposal—who has voted for it, voted against it, or not yet voted.

Note that although Synergeia is most useful and powerful if used to support what is here called "collaborative knowledge building," the system has been designed to be flexible so that teachers with different curricular goals and pedagogical approaches can adjust it to their needs. The design process tried to incorporate the following influences:

• Adoption of pedagogical principles of collaborative knowledge building and progressive inquiry;

• Incorporation of effective functionality from related CSCL and CSCW systems, both commercial and research;

• Adaptation to the social settings of constructivist European classrooms;

• Support for social practices involved in collaborative learning, such as that described in the preceding scenario; and

• Flexibility for teachers in different countries and pedagogical cultures to adapt the system to their varying approaches.

Collaborative Knowledge Building

The design of Synergeia is guided by an educational approach that stresses the construction of knowledge within a learning community, typically including students and more experienced teachers. The idea is that new knowledge will be created through the investigations and discourse of the group. While there are important roles for individual student thinking as well as for teacher guidance, there is also emphasis on sharing, critiquing, and building on others' ideas to arrive at a deeper knowledge of a topic within the community (Bereiter, 2002; Scardamalia & Bereiter, 1996). *Group learning* is to be understood here in an emphatic sense: it is the group that learns; knowledge is constructed by the group itself. Whereas CSCW supports the sharing and archiving of knowledge that is contributed by cooperating individuals, CSCL supports the functioning of a collaborative group to build knowledge that is the shared creation and property of the group. Primarily, group knowledge arises in discourse and is preserved in linguistic artifacts, whose meaning is interpreted within group processes (see chapters 12 and 13 for an analyzed example of this).

Because knowledge building proceeds largely through discussion, each personal, group, and course perspective automatically contains its own knowledge-building area in Synergeia. These knowledge-building areas have extended the basic threaded discussion facility of BSCW. While threaded discussion support is derived from CSCW, it requires more nuanced and specialized support in CSCL. Notes from one perspective can now be copied to other virtual learning places in other perspectives, and notes from elsewhere can be pasted here. Notes in these areas are now included in system searches because they form an important part of the knowledge in the system.

The user interface of the threaded discussion areas in Synergeia has been carefully designed to encourage thoughtful, focused, deep knowledge building. Below the current note is a display of all other notes entered in the same knowledge-building area. The notes can be displayed as indented threads, indicating which notes reply to which other notes. Alternatively, the notes can be sorted by author, date, or thinking type. Sorting by author shows quickly who is contributing the most, by date shows the order in which ideas were written, and by thinking type indicates which parts of the knowledge-building process have or have not been emphasized so far. In each of the sorted displays, the display of the content of the notes can be toggled on and off so that one can see either just the list of the notes or the full content of the whole discussion. This is useful so that one can quickly get an overview of the structure of complex discussions or see (or print) the full content of brief discussions.

As shown in figure 7.3, the note that is currently being read is at the top of the screen. With it are a number of buttons for building further knowledge, such as

Reply to This Note. The background color of this part of the display corresponds to the note's thinking type. The different thinking types are described on a help page reached with the Thinking Type Descriptions button; the corresponding background colors can be seen there.

Thinking Types

Thinking types take on a much more important role in Synergeia than in BSCW, where they were limited and rarely used. Students need to reflect on the role that a note they are entering will play in the knowledge-building process. Both note titles and categories should be chosen carefully (Gerosa, Fuks, & de Lucena, 2001).

Discussion within the knowledge-building areas is scaffolded with a set of thinking-type categories for the notes. Before someone can enter a note, they have to decide what category of note they want to add to the existing discussion. For instance, do they want to state the problem that is to be pursued, propose a working theory, deepen the knowledge that is already there, or make a metacomment about the knowledge-building process that is taking place? It is possible to have different sets of thinking types for different approaches to knowledge building. For instance, the preceding examples illustrate categories of "inquiry" learning notes. Other categories are appropriate for brainstorming, debate, design rationale, and so on.

A teacher or other user may select a thinking-type set for a given knowledge-building area when that area is defined or when the first note is written in that area. The following six sets of thinking types (table 7.1) were defined for version 2 of Synergeia: knowledge building, debate, discussion, brainstorming, negotiation, and scientific theory.

Virtual Learning Places

The most basic function that Synergeia offers is a set of workspaces on the Internet where people can share ideas, documents, Web links, and other objects. Whether people using Synergeia are in the same room during the same class period or are in different countries working at different times, they can share their work and collaborate within these virtual learning places. Teachers and students can create new places whenever they want for any special needs they have. Places can be created to store new collections of documents. Synergeia offers several special kinds of learning places—such as Courses, Groups, Proposals, and Knowledge-building areas—that have special features. Although these virtual learning places are based on BSCW folders for storing documents where they can be accessed by other group members, these places are structured to support specific collaborative knowledge-building activities like negotiation of group knowledge. The CSCW workspaces are appropriated and specialized to support a variety of specific CSCL activities.

Table 7.1
Sets of thinking types.

Knowledge Building	Debate	Discussion
Starting note	Starting note	Starting note
Problem statement	Position	Greeting
Working theory	Argument	Comment
Deepening knowledge	Pro	Opinion
General comment	Con	Like
Reflection on process	Evidence	Dislike
Summary statement	Question	Story
Help request	Clarify	Question
Brainstorming	Negotiation	Scientific Theory
Starting theme	Topic	Phenomenon
Suggestion	Proposal	Hypothesis
Clarification	Counter	Experiment
Process guidance	Agree	Proposal
Distinction	Disagree	Analysis
Generalization	Ask	Argument
Example	Question	Evidence
Summary	Summary	Theory

A major advantage of Synergeia over threaded discussion systems used by commercial groupware systems is that the discussions in Synergeia are separated into personal, group, and course perspectives in different virtual learning places. This means that different topics are not mixed together, and it is easier to keep up with relevant discussions without being overwhelmed by contributions of many other people who are investigating other issues. The same is true of the documents and Web links, for example, that are collected in the various learning places.

The network of learning places needs to be structured in a way that seems natural to the students using those places. The basic structure of learning places follows the normal structure of schools, with students in projects within courses. It should be easy to see what is available and relevant and to navigate to it easily. Therefore, when a student logs in, that student's personal learning place is displayed; the personal place includes a list of the student's courses and the course learning place includes the student's groups. It should also be easy to copy documents and ideas from one place to another. At the same time, because these places are generally shared, it is also important to protect the contents so that one person cannot change or delete someone else's work arbitrarily—as can occur in BSCW.

By default, Synergeia defines appropriate connections between places and reasonable access rights to them when people are registered for courses and groups. Each user, group, and course automatically has its own knowledge-building area—additional areas can be added or the automatic ones can be deleted. Also, plain places that do not have the special characteristics of groups and courses can easily be added. Thus, the structures, navigation paths, access rights, and facilities within Synergeia are designed for usage within the social practices prevailing in school settings, with adequate flexibility to allow for broad variations within these settings.

Perspectives

The approach to building knowledge in Synergeia is based on the idea of intertwining personal and group perspectives (Stahl & Herrmann, 1999). All knowledge involves interpretation from specific perspectives (Nygaard & Sørgaard, 1987) (see chapter 4). In collaboration, personal interpretations of what is said in group discourse interact to form shared understandings (see chapter 12).

The default structure of Synergeia provides a network of virtual learning places that are set up for personal, group, and course uses. These perspectives support a range of pedagogical models that are favored in the research groups participating in the ITCOLE project from different countries:

- *Community of learners (Italy)*   The areas in which work, communication, and learning take place are structured to reflect the structure of the community, with its subgroups and members.

- *Progressive inquiry (Finland)*   The inquiry process progresses through collaborative discourse within groups as well as through reflection by individuals.

- *Conceptual change (Greece)*   Learning is treated as a social process in which the understanding of individuals is affected by and grounded in the discourse of the community.

- *Shared and individual regulation process (Netherlands)*   The intertwining of shared group and individual ideas leads to new understandings at all levels.

Thus, there are private *personal learning places* where only one person can add notes, documents, or subfolders; review and modify them; or copy them to a group place. These are places to develop your personal perspective on a topic without worrying what other people will think about what you are doing. Because your personal ideas and documents are in Synergeia, they can be easily related to ideas in other learning places. Allowing a system for group work to also be used for personal reflection has two major advantages. First, it encourages system use and familiarity. A major problem with groupware systems can be that they require users to log in every day to see what is new; if people do not use the system for their normal activities, then they tend not to log in frequently. Also, if people have to use too many different systems for their work, then it is difficult to become proficient in all of them. Second, by conducting both personal and group work in the same system, people can easily move ideas and documents back and forth between the two. In particular, Synergeia is designed to allow quick cutting and pasting of items and sets of items from any visible learning place to any other.

Then there are the *group learning places* where most of the collaboration and knowledge building gets done. Here everything is shared with the other members of the team or workgroup. Students who are not in the group cannot modify or comment on work in the group until the group decides to share something with the whole course. Knowledge usually emerges from a group perspective (see chapter 11).

And there are also *course learning places*, where all the smaller workgroups or project teams within the course contribute the knowledge they have built up. For instance, a teacher who has a course with 30 students might divide them into six or seven teams. Perhaps each team would develop a portfolio to present its ideas to the course. Each team might have the same task, or team members might divide up different aspects of the larger course topic. After they develop their group portfolios, individual members can share and debate within the whole course perspective. While CSCW systems provide support within a generic group, a CSCL system should support various levels from individual to large group, with fluid navigation and transfer of contents among the levels.

Negotiating Knowledge Artifact Portfolios

Sometimes it is pedagogically important for groups to negotiate the promotion of knowledge from one perspective to another, such as making products of a group available to the larger course. A teacher can set up course learning places so that the only way that new documents, concept maps, and folders can be added is by a group developing a knowledge portfolio or knowledge artifact in a group learning place and then deciding to move this into the course place. Making this kind of group decision is called *knowledge negotiation* in Synergeia. There is a negotiation mechanism to help a group reach this decision and move the knowledge they have created into the course learning place, where it can be shared and discussed by all members of the course. By specifying the negotiation option for a course, the teacher in effect declares that the only knowledge allowed in this learning place is knowledge created by groups.

In CSCW negotiation, such as in Herrmann's or Wulf's model (Herrmann, Wulf, & Hartmann, 1996; Stahl & Herrmann, 1999; Wulf, Pipek, & Pfeifer, 2001), commenting on one's voting serves the purpose of expressing one's supposedly pre-existing opinion. By contrast, within Synergeia, engaging in negotiation of knowledge building is participating in a group reflection on shared knowledge. This can be seen in the thinking types of the notes contributed. In CSCW the note format stresses who the author is and may characterize the notes as a pro or con opinion (for example, in BSCW). In Synergeia, the note must first of all be determined to be a particular aspect of the knowledge-building process, such as a problem statement, a working theory, or a summary statement. Knowledge negotiation is thereby explicitly structured as a collaborative group effort, where notes written by individuals must fit into the group process and are categorized by their function in the group thinking, not in individual opinions.

Negotiation in a knowledge-building context is essentially different from that in a knowledge-management or group-decision situation (see chapter 8). In other groupware settings, negotiation is conceived of as a straw vote to determine how people's preexisting opinions are distributed on alternative options that have been proposed (Herrmann et al., 1996; Kraemer & Pinsonneault, 1990; Wulf et al., 2001). In a collaborative knowledge-building setting, however, it is a matter of further refining the proposed knowledge artifact. Voting serves just to signify that the participants are generally satisfied that the artifact represents their group knowledge, and it can be shared at the course level as a knowledge portfolio contributed by their group. The important part of the negotiation process is the evolution of the knowledge itself in parallel with the group discourse about it.

When members of a group learning place have built a knowledge artifact—such as a collection of Web sites, a PowerPoint slide presentation, a concept map, or a portfolio of texts and pictures—they can decide to copy it to their course learning place to share with members of other groups in their course. This result of their collaborative work as a group may be a final product that the teacher will evaluate, or it may be an intermediate product that they want to share and get feedback on from other people.

If a course has been defined to require negotiation, then students in that course must go through the formal negotiation procedure to copy a proposed knowledge artifact portfolio to the course learning place. The purpose of this is to ensure that all or most people in the group agree to have the proposed portfolio represent the knowledge that the group has built together (if negotiation is not required in the course, anyone can simply copy an item from the group place into the course learning place). To use the negotiation procedure, a student must select items for his or her portfolio and execute the "Negotiate" command. This will create a portfolio proposal in the group place.

The portfolio proposal interface includes a voting area that allows group members to vote on submitting the portfolio when they are happy with it. Within the portfolio are the selected portfolio knowledge artifacts and a negotiation knowledge-building area for discussing changes that should be made to the proposed portfolio.

Students use the negotiation knowledge-building area to negotiate changes that they think should be made within the portfolio. They make changes in the portfolio that they think will make it acceptable to all or most people in their group. When they like the way the portfolio looks, they vote to approve it. Each person who submits an approval or disapproval vote must enter a statement justifying their vote. This statement is automatically incorporated into the negotiation knowledge-building area where it is included in the negotiation discourse and can be discussed. When all or most of the people in the group have voted positively for the portfolio, it is automatically copied to the course learning place. The negotiation knowledge-building area is copied with the portfolio folder so that members of the whole course can see what the group said about the portfolio. Group members may want to make summary comments in this area to say what they think is important in the portfolio. If they still have criticisms of the portfolio or if they would like course members to discuss certain ideas about it, they can put them in this area as well.

Concept Maps, Multimodality, and Social Awareness

In building knowledge, it is often useful for a group to discuss how the concepts they are using are related to each other. One method for doing that is for the group to construct a concept map that diagrams these relationships. Synergeia provides a whiteboard called MapTool for people to work together simultaneously to sketch a concept map. The whiteboard is accompanied by a chat window to support coordination of this task and interpretation of the symbols in the map.

Students and teachers can open the MapTool in course and group learning places and in proposal portfolios. To work with other members of a proposed portfolio, workgroup, or course, they go to the learning place for that portfolio, group, or course. At the top of the screen is a list of all members of that particular place. Those who are currently logged in to Synergeia have their names shown in bold; if they are active in MapTool, their name is shown in red. This form of social awareness has been added to BSCW to let people know who is involved in MapTool in this learning place.

Each proposed portfolio, group, and course learning place has its own version of MapTool. When a MapTool session is first started, the last map for that place is automatically opened so that work on it can be continued if desired. One can also reset the MapTool to start with a blank whiteboard. When other members join an active MapTool session, they see the current state of the whiteboard and the chat window, so they can catch up on what has already been done in there.

At any time, the current state of the work in MapTool can be saved. Then a student can go into the learning place and make a copy of this map. The saved map can be opened as a jpeg (Joint Photographic Experts Group) graphics file. The student can save this file in a Word document, a PowerPoint slide show, a larger graphic file, or simply a jpeg-Compressed Images file in a subfolder. This way, collaborative work in MapTool can be documented as part of a report or knowledge portfolio.

The MapTool module was included in Synergeia as an experiment in combining synchronous communication (the whiteboard and the chat) with asynchronous (the knowledge-building threaded discussion). BSCW did not include any synchronous communication, and many learning support systems like CSILE are also exclusively asynchronous. While asynchronous is considered a more thoughtful, reflective mode for knowledge building, synchronous communication can be much more time-efficient for intense interaction, such as brainstorming or working out details of a drawing—assuming that the participants can get together online at the same time. Threaded discussion has its problems (Hewitt, 1997), and sometimes chat can overcome them. Working out the interplay between MapTool and the BSCW database was complicated (sending information between the modules and storing MapTool sessions in the database and in the asynchronous interface). However, it provides a good demonstration of how this can be done successfully.

The social awareness implemented with MapTool is just a first step toward what is possible. The need to meet synchronously in MapTool made it important to know who else was currently online in a group. A further function requested by early users but not yet implemented is the ability to invite specific people to participate in a current or future MapTool session—for example, through an announcement highlighted in the Synergeia interface or with e-mail.

In general, as the CSCL medium becomes richer, it becomes more important to provide awareness about who is doing what, what has been done in the system, and how to find existing information. As users become more sophisticated, they can use different modes of interaction that are appropriate and that are tuned to different undertakings. Synergeia takes just a first exploratory step in this direction.

Roles and Personalization

Synergeia defines roles for students, teachers, guests, and mentors. This gives people in these roles the power to execute certain menu functions, such as to read, edit, or delete objects in a learning place. When someone is invited into or registered for a particular learning place (such as a course or group), they are invited or registered as a member with a specific role (such as student). It is possible to change a user's role, to define new roles, and to add new subfolders where the user has a different role. Whereas roles in BSCW were generic and rarely used, in Synergeia they capture important distinctions between people based on power and knowledge in school settings. These roles must be adapted to different kinds of learning places.

For youthful users, software needs to be fun to use. Personalization and customization facilities allow users to adapt the system to their own preferences and to feel that the system is "theirs." Synergeia users can personalize the user interface by including a picture of themselves in the upper left-hand corner of the screen next to their username. This picture will represent them at other places in the Synergeia interface as well, such as when knowledge-building notes are sorted by author.

There are many functions for customizing the Synergeia interface. A student can do the following:

· Specify which columns to display for details related to subfolders and documents,
· Change the size of the displayed text,
· Sort the listed subfolders and documents in different orders,
· Toggle on and off the display of menu shortcut icons below the main menu,
· Toggle the descriptions below the names of subfolders and documents, and
· Toggle the contents below the titles of knowledge-building notes.

Students can set a variety of details about how the Synergeia system will work for them, including the following:

· Change their password,
· Set the location for their picture,
· Enter their e-mail address or home page, and
· Set their system preferences.

Students are automatically considered beginner Synergeia users when they start using the system. This means that the menus they see are not full of options that are intended for more experienced users. They can change to advanced or expert status when they feel ready to access more menu items. For younger students in primary school, a new primary profile has been defined; it makes the interface simpler by removing many menu items and shortcuts to make student usage simpler.

Additional Functionality in Synergeia

The previous section describes the pedagogical requirements for Synergeia that distinguish it from related work. Synergeia is focused on the needs of small collaborative groups of students who are guided by teachers who structure and facilitate their interactions. By contrast, most commercial educational software systems are oriented to administrative concerns such as delivering predefined content, tracking attendance and test results, handling homework assignments, and conducting student evaluations. At best, systems like LearningSpace and WebCT provide basic CSCW functionality for sharing documents and communicating. Because systems like Lotus Notes cater to corporate and professional training applications, they provide generic discussion forums, without specialized thinking types or workgroup perspectives structured in response to classroom cultures. Alternative approaches like "Swiki" (Guzdial & Turns, 2000) systems also lack the tailoring to classroom needs due to the generality of their functionality. At the other extreme are CSCL systems that are more specialized for particular pedagogies, like the STEP system to support problem-based learning (Steinkuehler et al., 2002). CSILE/Knowledge-Forum (Scardamalia & Bereiter, 1996) is very similar to Synergeia because its developers began the tradition in which the ITCOLE project is firmly planted. Synergeia also incorporated features from FLE (Muukkonen, Hakkarainen, & Leinonen, 2000) and WebGuide (see chapter 6), research prototypes that led to its conception and prototyped much of the functionality incorporated in it. Synergeia is unique in combining the features of perspectives, multiple thinking-type sets and negotiation with threaded discussion to support collaborative knowledge building. It also features a rare integration of synchronous and asynchronous support.

In addition to the pedagogically motivated features, Synergeia provides a wealth of functions from BSCW. Some of these have been modified or extended to allow students, teachers, administrators, and researchers to take advantage of the core Synergeia functionality.

Student actions have been modified to simplify the uploading of the user's picture; uploading, archiving, and versioning of documents, images, and Web sites is already well supported by the inherited BSCW commands. Likewise, the ability to search the Web, review hits, rate URLs, and store shared bookmarks was already available. Students can set up new virtual learning places and invite friends to join them, as well as start new knowledge-building areas and initiate MapTool sessions. Social awareness is well supported with BSCW's info, events, and history systems. In addition, Synergeia added displays of the names of course and group members, with indications of who is currently active in Synergeia or MapTool.

Considerable support for teachers has been added. Teachers can register lists of students in the system and assign them to courses and workgroups easily. Students no longer have to have their own e-mail addresses to be registered. Teachers can define course and group learning places, with a number of options for negotiation and access; this gives teachers considerable control in structuring the use of

Synergeia. They can, of course, seed a learning place with documents and a knowledge-building area with starting questions for discussion. When a new knowledge-building area is created, the teacher can select which set of thinking type categories will be used: "knowledge building," "scientific theory," "negotiation," "debate," "discussion," or "brainstorming." Teachers can revise the parameters for negotiation, such as the percentage needed for a majority vote. They can also override the voting process to move proposals from group to course places or vice versa.

Although Synergeia is currently run on a central server in Germany, it can be downloaded to local sites to overcome Internet delays in schools with slow connections. The system administrator registers an initial set of teachers and researchers to use Synergeia. The administrator can also translate all terminology in the interface, including the sets of thinking type categories, as well as redefine the actions associated with various user roles. The entire Synergeia interface has been translated into Italian, Greek, Dutch, and Finnish from the English original. Administrators can modify the translation files. Users select the language they want: by default it corresponds to their browser language setting.

In addition, functionality has been added to assist researchers who want to analyze the usage of Synergeia. There are now log files that track all actions in BSCL, the contents of all knowledge-building areas, and all actions in MapTool. The log files can be analyzed with special tools or copied into a spreadsheet. Knowledge-building areas can be printed out in various formats.

The Synergeia Architecture

The present section briefly indicates how the technological infrastructure of BSCW was extended in response to the needs of the classroom setting. Technically, Synergeia consists of the following three components: BSCW, BSCL, and MapTool.

BSCW

This is the Basic Support for Cooperative Work system. It is a Web-based system designed to support teams of adult professionals working together and sharing documents. It provides mechanisms for uploading, downloading, versioning, and archiving many kinds of documents. It also supports Web searches, annotations, and ranking. BSCW is written in Python as an object-oriented set of CGI scripts. It includes a persistent store for objects. The server runs in Windows or Unix, and the client can be displayed in any Web browser. The BSCW technology is literally a technology of extensibility; the CGI scripts extend the functionality of a core Web server like Apache or IIS by means of standard HTTP calls. This makes BSCW an attractive basis for further, open-ended extensions.

BSCL

This is the set of functions and interfaces that adapts the BSCW software to collaborative knowledge building in K through 12 classrooms. It includes the functions to create personal, group, and course learning places and to register users in these with specific roles. It also includes the knowledge-building interface, sets of thinking types, and support for negotiation. BSCL is implemented as a Python package that extends BSCW and that interfaces with MapTool. Packages are a flexible technology for modular extensibility in object-oriented languages like Python. BSCL is one of several packages that extend BSCW, and it is possible to create new packages that extend BSCL itself.

MapTool

This is a collaborative whiteboard that students in a group or course can work on simultaneously (synchronously) to construct concept maps and other simple diagrams. It includes a chat window for coordinating and discussing the drawing. The maps are stored in BSCL learning places. Synchronous support for the MapTool Java applet client is provided by the Ants system, using the Elvin server. The inclusion of MapTool in the Synergeia system involved extending BSCW with synchronous components, where user information, drawings, and chat data must be stored in and retrieved from BSCL's database by MapTool.

What Groupware Can Learn by Going to School

Much has already been learned about the differences and similarities of CSCW and CSCL groupware support through the process of designing and implementing Synergeia. The school setting has special characteristics that make certain functionality particularly important and that require specific transformations of other functions. Many such adaptations and extensions have been illustrated in the preceding sections of this chapter.

One unanticipated technical finding was the importance of mechanisms for setting specific *access rights* for various kinds of folders. A new version of BSCW (4.0) that was released during the beginning of the ITCOLE project included mechanisms for defining *roles*. These mechanisms—which to date have been explored only in the development of Synergeia—proved particularly helpful. From an implementation standpoint, many extensions to BSCW for Synergeia were largely accomplished through the definition of special domain-specific roles, with particular access rights within various kinds of learning places.

A straightforward application of the role mechanism was to define roles for teachers, mentors, students, administrators, and guests. New users are registered in Synergeia with one of these roles. The role determines what actions the user can undertake within his or her personal learning place. For instance, a user who is registered as a teacher may create courses and groups or redefine negotiation parameters, a student user may upload documents, and a guest may view contents only in Synergeia. A teacher has special powers to delete offensive materials and so on. A mentor also has many of these powers that students do not have but does not have the ability to create courses and groups. Users have more control over objects that they created than they do over objects that others created, such as the ability to edit or delete them. A user can invite other users to folders, can reset or modify roles, but can never assign abilities that exceed that user's own existing abilities.

In addition to the standard roles, special roles were defined for "course mates" and "restricted students." These are used for special circumstances. For instance, course mates can view, from their course learning places, groups to which they do not belong. Depending on the option set by the teacher when the group was defined, users who had student roles are reassigned "course mate" roles that allow them to see the name of the group listed, or else they are reassigned the "restricted student" role, which allows them to enter the group learning place and view or copy—but not add to or modify—the content there.

Similarly, in a course where the negotiation option was selected, all student users are reassigned the role of restricted student. This means that they can see and copy all content but cannot add or modify anything (except indirectly through the group negotiation procedure) within that course perspective. This reassigned role is inherited down into all subfolders, subsubfolders, and so on contained in the group perspective (as is usual for roles). This automatically prevents students in a course from changing the contents of a group's negotiated portfolio, although they can view the contents and copy them elsewhere to continue working on them. In a course knowledge-building area, the restricted student roles are changed back to normal student roles, so that students can participate in knowledge-building discussions within the course perspective.

The school setting requires much more complex control over access rights than is instituted in the normal BSCW system. The role mechanism provides a convenient, flexible, and elegant means for defining and instituting the needed sets of access controls.

This chapter reflects the design of version 2 of Synergeia, which was scheduled to be released to European elementary and secondary schools within the ITCOLE project in fall 2002. It has already benefited substantially from informal feedback from the review of version 1 by pedagogic partners in the project and from the use of version 1 by teachers and students in winter and spring 2002. The use of version 1 is currently being subjected to extensive evaluation in each of the participating countries. It is expected that this will reveal additional groupware requirements of the school setting.

Version 2 of Synergeia was scheduled to "go to school" in courses in Italy, Greece, the Netherlands, and Finland during fall 2002. This was to be subjected to formal evaluation using a variety of survey instruments. Data from the log files and classroom observations were to be analyzed with a mix of quantitative and qualitative methods. Results of these evaluations should provide important insight into the effectiveness of the Synergeia adaptations and extensions to groupware mechanisms presented in this chapter.

There are many fundamental commonalities between CSCW and CSCL groupware requirements, and the two can build on each other's accomplishments. However, the school setting, seen from a specific pedagogical perspective, brings with it considerations that call for particular treatments. In the case of the development of Synergeia within the ITCOLE project, we have seen that it was necessary to develop a suite of functionality that adapted generic CSCW forms of support to help define a unique educational environment. As the CSCL extensions mature through testing and usage, they are likely to feed back into suggestions for CSCW itself.

8

Knowledge Negotiation Online

Negotiation processes are important to group knowledge building but are rarely supported in online systems. The negotiation of what is to count as mutually acceptable collaborative knowledge is difficult to conduct when participants cannot interact face to face. In this chapter, I go into more detail about negotiation support in BSCL.[1] I review related work on negotiation support, primarily by my German colleagues, and develop a concept of "knowledge negotiation" that is appropriate for collaborative learning in school courses. This concept is situated within the framework of collaborative knowledge building viewed at the small-group unit of analysis; it contrasts with negotiation as the reconciliation of multiple personal opinions through voting. I then describe the implementation of support for knowledge negotiation in BSCL. After this essay was published, I tried using the BSCL negotiation system in my own classes back in the United States. The failure to have this negotiation support used as intended convinced me of the need for detailed empirical study of how negotiation is actually conducted in online collaborative knowledge building as a central phase of group cognition.

Negotiation—specifically, the negotiation of what is to count as new shared knowledge—is a central phenomenon in cooperative work and collaborative learning. Although there has been considerable research conducted on computer-supported collaborative learning (CSCL), this has not been accompanied by discussion of computer software mechanisms to support negotiation within learning contexts.

CSCL systems are designed to support the building of shared knowledge but rarely provide adequate support for establishing and identifying agreement on achieved knowledge artifacts. Such negotiation is conceptually different from the forms of negotiation supported in computer-supported cooperative work (CSCW), group decision-support systems (GDSS), and other business-oriented systems because in classroom collaborative learning it is a matter of groups constructing new knowledge interactively rather than making decisions based on predefined options and existing opinions of individuals.

Consideration of computer support for negotiation has arisen in the past primarily in relation to group decision-support systems for use in industry (Connolly, 1997; Kraemer & Pinsonneault, 1990; Vogel, Nunamaker, Applegate, & Konsynski, 1987). GDSS is a subarea of computer-supported cooperative work. Although CSCW is a sister field to CSCL, its decision support, knowledge management, and social awareness mechanisms have not yet been adapted for CSCL applications. This chapter continues the preceding discussion in chapter 7 of how a CSCW approach can be adapted to a CSCL context by a rethinking of the nature of the interactions within these differing contexts. It focuses on adapting the role of negotiation and arguing for a concept of "knowledge negotiation."

The approach to knowledge negotiation support in the revised version of BSCL (or Synergeia) is integrated within a set of software components designed for collaborative learning, including virtual learning spaces, perspectives, community roles, knowledge building, thinking types, and concept maps. Knowledge negotiation is implemented to control the publication and transfer of ideas, documents, drawings, and other artifacts or sets of items from a small-project group perspective into the perspective of a larger community of learners in a course.

Knowledge negotiation involves evolving a group knowledge artifact to a mutually acceptable status for publication, rather than reaching consensus on a pre-existing choice of personal opinions. Asynchronous support for such negotiation must allow for the following:

- Proposal of a set of items for consideration as a shared knowledge artifact,

- Discussion of desired modifications to this artifact,

- Carrying out of the actual changes to the items,

- Discussion of remaining misgivings, and

- Signaling of a readiness to accept and publish the artifact for access by a larger community.

The question I faced as designer of BSCL (the asynchronous component of Synergeia) was how to support negotiation among students. Collaborative learning in classrooms has different requirements for sharing knowledge than what is supported by BSCW for professional teams. For instance, BSCW is used primarily for knowledge management (the sharing and manipulation of knowledge that already exists somewhere within the workgroup), while BSCL is intended to support knowledge building (the collaborative construction of knowledge that is new within the community).

This chapter follows the historical sequence of my approach. I began by considering relevant explorations of *negotiation in CSCW*, particularly those of Thomas

Herrmann and Volker Wulf that had been used in systems related to BSCW. Then I reflected on *the role of negotiation in collaborative learning,* based on the major theoretical frameworks for CSCL. From this, I identified various *concepts of negotiation* associated with alternative possible support mechanisms. I developed a concept of knowledge negotiation that seemed most suited for BSCL *as an adaptation of* BSCW to learning scenarios. This notion may be relevant for many CSCW contexts as well. I implemented *support for knowledge negotiation* among students in small workgroups and then *studied negotiation in classrooms* using BSCL.

Negotiation in CSCW

Negotiation is a process by which a group of people who are working together arrive at a group decision. The usual approach to conceptualizing and supporting this process within CSCW was not quite what I wanted for my concept of collaborative knowledge building. I here review some of the approaches that I critiqued and extended.

Negotiation as Voting

Within traditions of computer science (or informatics), it is common to model negotiation as a voting process. This is not only a result of the implicit acceptance of rationalist philosophy and of modeling human communication as information processing but arises also for pragmatic implementation reasons:

- Rationalism assumes that people have ideas already existing in their heads (Winograd & Flores, 1986)—in the form of expressible propositions, mental representations, or brain states—that they can then express verbally as opinions on the basis of which they may vote on various issues posed to them.

- Communication theory derived from the information-processing tradition (Shannon & Weaver, 1949) implicitly builds on the rationalist model and construes communication as the transfer of such preexisting opinions (as data) through (error-prone) media.

- Implementation of computer support tends to accept these models because computers necessarily represent explicit information, such as propositional representations of explicit opinions (see chapters 4, 14, and 20). They can easily respond to small numbers of clearly predefined options, such as yes or no votes.

Thus, when we look for examples of support for negotiation in CSCW, we find that they often reduce negotiation processes to voting processes, assuming that the goal is to collect and respond appropriately to a set of opinions that already exist in the minds of the individual system users. In particular, this is true of GDSS systems that frequently include a component for conducting straw votes (Connolly, 1997; Kraemer & Pinsonneault, 1990). Straw votes, by definition, are a means of measuring preexisting personal opinions, with little attempt to influence them or to build group consensus. The goal here is typically to provide support for collecting the opinions of participants about some fixed issue, with the assumption that differences of opinion are based in personal structures of preferences, in differing interests or in limitations of information about the opinions of other participants (Lim & Benbasat, 1993; McGrath, 1993; Nunamaker, Dennis, Valacich, & Vogel, 1991). Thus, GDSS support usually focuses on expressing, collecting, and possibly influencing participant opinions rather than on altering the subject matter under consideration.

Negotiation as Approval of Decisions

Herrmann (Stahl & Herrmann, 1998) proposed a notion of negotiation that goes significantly beyond the simple voting model. He and his students developed an approach to computer-supported negotiation over the years and have designed or prototyped it in a number of software systems (Herrmann, 1995; Herrmann et al., 1996; Herrmann & Kienle, 2002), including a simulation of negotiation (Lepperhoff, 2001). He has reviewed related CSCW and GDSS research and has developed a sociotechnical model for his approach to negotiation. His examples involve group decisions for knowledge management, such as what categories should be used to organize a shared bibliography.

In Herrmann's approach, someone makes a proposal and the other group members can vote on the proposal. They always have an opportunity to comment on their vote. In addition, they can make a counterproposal or call for discussion outside of the computer support system. Although this approach goes beyond a simple yes or no voting system with options for counterproposals and for switching communication media, it is still based on a model of negotiation as voting. This approach serves well to conduct a quick poll to see where agreement does or does not already exist but cannot well support reframing or coconstruction of knowledge. It recognizes the frequent need for people to engage in more complex processes of interaction to settle a negotiation issue, allows people to leave the computer support system to do this, but provides little automated support for their consequent decisions to affect the knowledge in the system.

Negotiation as Access Permission

Wulf (Stiemerling & Wulf, 2000; Wulf, 2001; Wulf et al., 2001) proposed further extensions of the voting model, now applied to function activation rather than decisions. His examples include the right of an individual to access a specific document created by another member of the group. The empirical cases he cites from governmental bureaucracies might best be considered examples of moderated, rather than negotiated, activation. The primary actors do not engage in negotiation with one another but agree to have their interactions mediated by trusted third parties or public procedures, including automated procedures in a computer support system.

Applied to CSCW systems, the issue is whether a particular user should have access to a specific system function, such as editing a document. Wulf has developed a formal Petri net model of negotiation approaches but oriented to the question of activation. This paradigm may work for situations with fixed options, such as access to a defined system function, but not in the general situation in which a group is collaborating to produce group knowledge through exploration and inquiry.

Negotiation as Intertwining of Perspectives

Individual learning, as a process of constructing personal knowledge, takes place within a learner's personal perspective (Boland & Tenkasi, 1995; Nygaard & Sørgaard, 1987) (see chapter 4). Collaborative learning involves an interaction among personal perspectives contributed by the participants and a merging of these into a group perspective definitive of the group discourse. There have been scattered attempts to formulate a conceptualization of perspectives that would lend itself to computer support. The Phidias system was an early attempt to display a database of design rationale notes according to different "contexts" (McCall et al., 1990); this was subsequently reimplemented in Hermes (see chapter 4), where shared contents were displayed within different professional or personal perspectives.

Stahl and Herrmann (1998, 1999) proposed an approach to integrating Herrmann's negotiation and Stahl's perspective mechanisms within a single software system, WebGuide, that they designed specifically to explore these mechanisms. On the one hand, negotiation takes time, and group members may want to continue working on a topic while it is under negotiation. Perspectives allow them to continue to work in their own perspective while contents of a group perspective are being negotiated. On the other hand, within individual perspectives there is a strong tendency for ideas to diverge (Hewitt & Teplovs, 1999). Negotiation is required to bring ideas back into consensus and to promote individual ideas to the status of group knowledge. So it seemed that integrating perspective and negotiation mechanisms—and conceptualizing negotiation as the intertwining of multiple personal perspectives to arrive at a shared perspective—would mutually solve the central problems of these two mechanisms.

While the perspectives mechanism has by now been extensively implemented in WebGuide (see chapter 6), the corresponding negotiation mechanism is still missing in that system. The lack of an appropriate negotiation mechanism was already reported as a serious limitation of WebGuide at the 1999 CSCL, Group, and WebNet conferences (e.g., Stahl & Herrmann, 1999). The delay in implementing negotiation support in WebGuide was largely a result of the feeling that the voting model of negotiation did not seem appropriate for CSCL uses of groupware. Recent reflections on the relation of perspectives to knowledge building suggest that a different, more dialogical, concept of negotiation is called for (see chapter 11).

The Role of Negotiation in Collaborative Learning

To appreciate the role of negotiation in CSCL, consider the centrality of negotiation within each of the different theoretical frameworks that have historically dominated this field.

Small-Group Process

This approach to cooperative (not collaborative) learning maintains a view of learning as transfer of information from teacher to students and conducts experiments to demonstrate the increase in individual learning outcomes through group work in classrooms (Johnson & Johnson, 1989). A typical approach would be to divide up topics within a course and assign the topics to small groups. The small groups would *negotiate* agreed on solutions to their topic, and the different groups would then share their solutions with the larger group—for instance, using procedures like "jigsawing" (Brown & Campione, 1994).

Social Constructivism

Knowledge is socially coconstructed (Vygotsky, 1978) before it may be internalized by children based on what they are capable of understanding. This social coconstruction is a *negotiation* process by which shared understanding is reached about a "knowledge object" or knowledge "artifact" (Bereiter, 2002) (see chapter 15).

Distance Education

Even when peer interaction is possible in distance education (for instance, with threaded discussion software), it is hard to encourage sustained, in-depth knowledge building. Discussions tend to diverge without some form of *negotiation* to bring different people's ideas back together (Hewitt & Teplovs, 1999).

Distributed Problem-Based Learning

Originally developed for medical education, problem-based learning (PBL) is built around problem cases, like patients presenting illness symptoms that a group of about five students and a tutor attempt to diagnose. The group *negotiates* lists of problem statements, key evidence, working hypotheses, and learning issues. Then the individual students research relevant medical theories and come back to the group to *renegotiate* the group understanding. The tutor plays a key role in guiding the negotiation (Barrows, 1994).

Distributed Cognition

Knowledge is not simply a matter of an individual's mental representations but is frequently distributed among the abilities of group members and the artifacts that they use (Hutchins, 1996). Accordingly, knowledge is coconstructed by interactions among people and their shared artifacts, including prominently by means of *negotiation* practices that result in establishing a common ground for understanding.

Situated Learning

This approach views learning in terms of changing relations within the community of practice (Lave & Wenger, 1991). Like situated-action theory (Suchman, 1987) and ethnomethodology (Garfinkel, 1967), the situated-learning approach looks at how people skillfully interact socially to coconstruct and interactively *negotiate* knowledge rather than at individuals as possessors of explicit propositional knowledge.

Cultural-Historical Activity Theory

Learning is viewed as it takes place over extended periods of time and within its broad cultural and historical contexts. It is even possible to track "expansive learning" in which multiple groups *negotiate* changes to the existing social arrangements (Engeström, 1999). Here, again, socially shared artifacts play a significant role in providing a focus to negotiations.

It is possible to conceptualize collaborative learning in different ways, focusing on various units of analysis as seen above. However, in each approach some form of negotiation plays a central role in the learning process. To design computer support for negotiation in collaborative learning, it is necessary to specify an appropriate concept of such negotiation.

Concepts of Knowledge Negotiation for CSCL

Negotiation as Voting

The concept of negotiation as voting seems inadequate for CSCL. In particular, the negotiation of what is to count as new shared knowledge for a group engaged in collaborative knowledge building has different characteristics from other forms of group decision making. Such negotiation might be called "knowledge negotiation" because it is a matter both of selecting among alternative existing states (propositions, proposals, activation functions) and of constructing new knowledge through collaborative interaction and discourse. The new knowledge is typically represented by or embodied in a shared "knowledge artifact," such as a concept, theory, text, or folder of structured information.

There is an important theoretical difference concerning the unit of analysis. We conceptualize knowledge negotiation as a *group* knowledge-building process rather than as a process involving *individuals* and their personal opinions. In CSCW negotiation, such as Herrmann's model, commenting on one's voting serves the purpose of expressing one's supposedly preexisting opinion. In BSCL, engaging in negotiational knowledge building is participating in a group reflection on shared knowledge. This difference can be seen in the thinking types of the notes contributed. In CSCW systems like BSCW, the note format stresses who the author is and may characterize the note as a pro or con opinion. In BSCL, the note must first of all be determined to be a particular aspect of the group's knowledge-building process, such as a problem statement, a working theory, or a summary statement before a student can begin to construct a note. Knowledge negotiation is thereby explicitly structured as part of a collaborative group effort.

Negotiation as Discourse

Knowledge negotiation is at heart quite different from voting. It is, in its paradigmatic forms, a nuanced give and take whose aim is to reach a solution that did not already exist in any participant's opinion but that is ultimately made acceptable to all. It often involves compromises, whereby one participant gives way in part to another's wish to get the other to give in partially to one's own position. Negotiation is a way people respond to nonroutinized, "wicked," or ill-defined problems— where reaching agreement often involves reframing the issues (Rittel & Webber, 1984).

The negotiation process as bargaining is not well modeled as a series of preexisting positions, among which the group must vote. Nor is it well modeled as a series of positions and counterpositions among which the group must choose. In a negotiation process, typically multiple starting positions interact and evolve through a series of changing alternatives until a single consensus position is reached through discourse. The discussion is a subtle political interaction that brings many aspects of power, motivation, and persuasion into play; it is a sophisticated linguistic process that cannot be algorithmically interpreted. In the end, when a consensus is reached (or not), there is often little need for a vote because agreement (or agreement to disagree) has already been established. The purpose of a vote would be to signal within a support system that everyone agreed that a consensus had been reached.

Negotiation as Knowledge Building

Negotiation may be conceptualized as a much broader phenomenon than the process of making a joint decision about prespecified actions (or explicit access permissions). Collaborative knowledge building itself can be viewed as fundamentally a knowledge-negotiation process. Proposed statements of knowledge by individuals are subjected to collaborative interactions, whereby meanings of terms are clarified, alternative related statements are compared, linguistic expressions are refined, warrants are scrutinized, and so on (see chapter 9).

Through these activities, the original suggestion is transformed; through broadening consensus, the resultant expression increasingly takes on the status of socially established knowledge. Simultaneously, this process establishes a "common ground" of understanding concerning the meaning of the accepted expression and its constituent terms (Baker, Hansen, Joiner, & Traum, 1999). This does not necessarily mean that every individual involved fully understands and accepts this common ground in his or her own mind but rather that a group understanding has been established in the discourse of the community in which this knowledge is thereby accepted. The coconstructed knowledge is often embodied in some form of cultural artifact, such as a text or slogan; the common ground provides a basis for the meaning that the artifact encapsulates to be understood in a shared way by the collaborative community.

The shift to understanding group interactions in more dialogical terms as coconstruction within a discourse community has implications for the design of groupware—away from automated selection among alternatives and toward greater emphasis on supporting communication among system users. Accordingly, it is necessary to design an appropriate mechanism for the support of knowledge negotiation in situations of collaborative learning along these lines.

BSCL as an Adaptation of BSCW

BSCL is an adaptation and extension of the BSCW system for collaborative learning applications in schools. It assigns roles of teacher and student that define the available functionality and access rights of the users. Courses are usually split into smaller workgroups (typically comprising about three to seven students) that pursue specific learning goals and produce group products or portfolios.

Each student, workgroup, and course has an associated "virtual learning place"— a folder in which information and ideas are collected, typically in the form of documents, notes, links to Web pages, and discussion threads. Learning places may be hierarchically structured in subfolders. The default structure of learning places supports the concept of perspectives: there are personal, workgroup, and course perspectives for students collaborating in workgroups within larger academic courses. Teachers and students can use BSCW operations to create other kinds of folder structures, but the structure to support typical workgroup collaborative activities is generated automatically by BSCL as the default.

Knowledge Building within BSCL

For the knowledge-building process, students typically collect information and ideas for a learning project in their personal or group learning places. They share and discuss these in the group learning place. The essential task of a workgroup is to produce a group report or "knowledge-building portfolio" from collected materials and the associated discussions and place the report and related materials in the course learning place for students from other groups to view and discuss.

Within an academic setting, such a contribution to the course learning place may count as the group's final product or work portfolio and be displayed as the group's knowledge and shared with the other course members so they can learn from it and comment on it. It may also be evaluated by the teacher or others once it has reached this stage.

In BSCW, any user would be able to copy objects from a group to a course learning place. Because of the requirements of the school setting, a workgroup needs to reach a consensus on what may count as (and be evaluated as) their group product. This requires a negotiation function.

In a CSCW system, access rights and access functions may be specified to an arbitrary degree of precision. This determines whether a given user can execute a given operation under various conditions—or in BSCW it determines whether the operation appears on that user's menus. The rules governing access may even be adaptable so that a group or manager can adjust these rules. However, once set, the rules arbitrate group conflicts silently and invisibly. For instance, if one member of a group workspace wants to delete or edit a document and another member does not want this to happen, then the rules determine whether it can be done or not—but the conflict between the members who do and do not want the operation to be executed is never made apparent. In a given case, no one knows who favors what or if and when there is a conflict of desires, let alone people's reasons. The systems of Herrmann and Wulf have the advantage of making such conflicts visible and providing means for resolving them interactively.

In designing BSCL, I was primarily concerned with transitions of knowledge from the group perspective to the course perspective. Here I wanted to bring to light any conflict within the group about promoting a knowledge artifact to the class perspective as a product of the group.

Approach to Knowledge Negotiation in BSCL

The discussion process within a workgroup may already be considered as an implicit knowledge-negotiation process. However, in the BSCL system, we make this process fully explicit to the users by commencing a formal negotiation when a member of a workgroup proposes to promote a group knowledge artifact to the corresponding course perspective.

Operationally, the difference between the CSCL knowledge negotiation that is proposed here and a voting approach is that *the real negotiation action is in the evolution of the knowledge artifact proposed for agreement and not in the voting process itself.* What is needed is to allow a proposed knowledge artifact to be successively changed by the negotiating parties until all (or a substantial majority) of them agree that the object is now an acceptable representation of the group knowledge. This knowledge negotiation process may proceed as follows:

• A member of the group proposes that a specific knowledge artifact (a set of folders, documents, ideas, or threaded discussion) be promoted to the course perspective. Criteria for the acceptance of the proposal (for example, agreement by 74 percent of the group within two weeks) has already been set by the teacher for the whole class.

• The knowledge artifact is made available for all group members to modify (the object proposed for negotiation has group access rights), within a negotiation interface at the group perspective level.

• A threaded discussion area is made available for the group members to negotiate changes to the artifact, including the statement of reasons and suggestions for acceptable modifications.

• At any point, a member can vote to accept or reject the artifact in its current state. These votes can be withdrawn at any time—for example, when a group member has made a counterproposal that is considered more appropriate or as the knowledge artifact is modified.

• When the preset criteria for acceptance are met, the artifact is automatically published in the class learning place. There is a time limit for group approval; however, this is often moot since the group is usually strongly motivated to agree on final knowledge products to produce their portfolio and complete their work assignment.

In this approach, the voting interface can be extremely simple—for instance, a button for the current user to signify agreement with the current version of the proposed artifact. (See the check and X buttons—for "agree" and "disagree"—of the voting interface in figure 7.4 of the previous chapter.)

The important point for the knowledge-negotiation process is the possibility for a participant to state his or her reasons for withholding agreement in terms of dissatisfaction with the current state of the knowledge artifact. Thus, an adequate interface for the negotiation dialogue is needed, in which students can formulate, exchange, and react to disagreements so that the knowledge artifact can be modified in a direction that is likely to promote consensus. The knowledge-negotiation interface therefore includes its own threaded discussion. The "group negotiation perspective" discussion space that is automatically generated for each proposal is a group knowledge-building area like that in figure 7.3 of the previous chapter. When students vote, they must provide statements explaining their vote; these statements are further discussed. At the conclusion of negotiation, this threaded discussion represents the history of negotiation and implicitly reflects changes that have been made to the knowledge artifact as part of the knowledge negotiation, including the rationale. It can also include summary statements or a minority opinion, for instance.

Support for Knowledge Negotiation
The implementation of negotiation in BSCL is intended to allow teachers to define course learning spaces that contain only shared knowledge. The knowledge in this area is contributed by groups as such, not by individuals. It comes from group learning spaces and represents a consensus of the thinking of the members of that group. In the course area, there is a threaded discussion area where all course members can reflect on the group portfolios and build further shared knowledge on that basis at the level of the course as a whole.

In many cases, such a strict regulation of contributions will prove impractical and cumbersome. Therefore, BSCL gives teachers certain powers to short-cut or override the negotiation procedures. Most important, a teacher can cause a proposal folder to be published to the course without waiting for the voting threshold to be reached. For instance, the teacher might conduct a face-to-face negotiation with the group and then publish the folder on that basis. Going in the other direction, a teacher might feel that an already published portfolio has not been carefully enough discussed and refined and therefore send it back for more work and renegotiation. The teacher can also change the voting threshold for contributions to a course.

Within BSCL, teachers generally have the right to copy items between folders, including student work from group folders into course folders. However, when they do this using the new negotiation functions, the copied items are clearly marked as having been moved by the teacher from the specific group, incorporating the CSCW principle of visibility recommended by Herrmann and Wulf.

Conclusions

The negotiation of what is to count as shared knowledge is an essential aspect of cooperative knowledge work and collaborative learning. When the interaction that creates this knowledge does not take place face to face, computer support for negotiation can play an important role. I have tried to develop an appropriate concept of knowledge negotiation based on a survey of theoretical frameworks for CSCL and a critical review of related concepts of negotiation in CSCW, particularly the concept of negotiation in the systems of Herrmann and Wulf.

The shared knowledge typically aimed at by knowledge-building efforts in CSCL is not taken to be objectively given; it is socially sanctioned within a community. The support implemented in BSCL is designed to scaffold the social process of constituting shared knowledge in a group. Requiring all knowledge in a course workspace to originate in a smaller project group forces the shared knowledge building of the course community to be mediated by the smaller, more tractable working groups. These groups mediate between the individual and the community in a series of manageable steps. The proposal folders that get negotiated by the groups form another layer of organization for ideas and documents, and the proposals themselves function as knowledge artifacts in the making.

In transforming a CSCW infrastructure into a CSCL environment, we have had to give considerable thought to the definition of appropriate roles and activation rights for the different kinds of actors (such as students of different ages, teachers, mentors, and guests) within educational social settings. The workspaces or learning places had to be designed to correspond with these roles and to appropriately house the knowledge-building and knowledge-negotiation processes.

In adapting the concept of negotiation to collaborative learning, we have defined *knowledge negotiation* as a phase of collaborative knowledge building, taken as an activity at the group unit of analysis. This form of negotiation does not simply reconcile multiple personal opinions but helps to construct and confirm new shared group knowledge—and makes it public for the larger community.

The mechanisms for negotiating shared knowledge in face-to-face situations are part of what it means to be human. We need to evolve similar mechanisms that will seem natural and effective in CSCL systems.

II
Analysis of Collaborative Knowledge Building

Studies of Interaction Analysis

Retro-perspective on the Studies in Part I

Looking back on the preceding historical documents—little modified from several years ago when the reported investigations were just winding down—from the perspective of 2005 as I compile this book, the contributions of the individual studies to the overall inquiry becomes more clear.

Study 1: TCA

This effort always seemed ahead of its time. It failed to attract continued funding because while the funding source approved of its goals, the reviewers were worried how the quality of the curriculum content and its indexing could be guaranteed. Similarly, although our contacts at Apple Corporation liked the concept, they could not see how such software would help their quarterly financial bottom line in the near future. In the intervening decade, the National Science Foundation (NSF) has spent millions on a major national science digital library initiative (NSDL) and Apple tried to build its own educational object economy (EOE) online repository of curricular artifacts. Today, the Math Forum, one of the NSDL's most successful digital libraries, consists primarily of content submitted by users, demonstrating the power of community knowledge construction. Large international efforts have gone into trying to define and negotiate standard metadata ontologies (for example, the Dublin Core). They remain incomplete, inadequate, and superficial because systems of interpretive categories cannot be legislated, once and for all, from on high; they must evolve with usage and understanding within specific communities. Ten years of technological advance, the pervasive growth of the Web, and the establishment of digital libraries have changed the way TCA would work today. But they have not eliminated the basic needs that TCA was designed to address. Publishers and teams with NSF funding have meanwhile produced integrated curricula along constructivist principles, but still-isolated teachers have benefited little from the collaboration potential of the Internet. Some of the ideas of TCA have yet to be tried by groups of teachers and to be evolved in response to their usage. In general, the idea of virtual communities of teachers sharing best practices has not really taken off yet, despite various efforts like Tapped-In, Merlot, or ENC.org. Perhaps it is no coincidence that I am now working with the Math Forum and my TCA collaborator, Tamara Sumner, is working with the Digital Library for Earth System Education (DLESE), another major educational digital library project, trying to increase their utility for constructivist learning.

Study 2: Essence
The use of latent semantic analysis (LSA)—explored in this study—is still being pushed as both a panacea for automating student evaluation and as a model of human semantic understanding. This book problematizes the assumptions underlying LSA by discussing many means by which people understand language in non-algorithmic ways: through their life experience situated in specific activities within a meaningful physical, cultural, and historical world; by means of the collaborative negotiation of shared meaning in small groups and communities; through personal, professional, and cultural perspectives; and through subtle processes of contextualized interpretation. The success of LSA in State the Essence is due to the fine tuning that took place as the algorithms, coefficients, and mechanisms were coadapted with the research effort, the teacher presentations, and the student expectations or behaviors. This suggests that it is possible to take advantage of this technology, but only in certain carefully designed applications and through extensive trial and adjustment. The Essence software was originally conceived as a way of evaluating the product of individual work, as LSA is usually applied. However, the study suggests also using such software to stimulate collaborative interactions and to provide feedback and motivation to small groups. This is an approach that deserves further thoughtful exploration in the context of CSCL.

Study 3: CREW
The problem of group formation is one of the first issues I face each term when starting a course organized around small-group projects. Supporting the self-organization of students into effective workgroups is a function that is particularly needed in virtual communities but has not been extensively researched. This has been identified as an important area for exploration in the Virtual Math Teams (VMT) project that is now underway at Drexel, but it is mostly beyond the scope of the present book (see chapters 17 and 21). The approach reported in the CREW study is quite different. It attempts to aid administrators in the formation of astronaut crew groupings by giving them feedback on the probability that given individuals will perform well psychologically under given mission conditions. It develops

a temporal model of individual factors based on case-study data under analogous conditions, using a combination of adapted artificial intelligence (AI) and statistics methods. Pushing this approach to its limits, it shows the enormous requirements such a system has for high-quality data across the whole range of interests. Given that current relevant data are limited, evaluation of its status is difficult, and practical and political barriers to collecting much more data exist, it seems doubtful that this sort of approach can succeed in many realistic situations. Without adequate data, such AI methods are empty promises: garbage in, garbage out. In addition, the expectation that relevant data can easily be collected in an explicit and context-free manner was shattered with the failure of the expert system craze.

Study 4: Hermes

This system suffered the problem of all domain-oriented design environments (DODEs). The effort required to configure a system for a particular application domain is enormous. One must be an expert in that domain, understand the detailed workflow, spot the functions that can usefully be supported, and seed the system with vast amounts of domain knowledge. All this is necessary before anyone would even consider trying out the system. To support the work of a group of domain experts, the system must be complex and sophisticated, combining advanced features as well as all the basics. To develop such a system requires the combined talents of software developers and domain experts, along with a budget on the order of a million dollars—just to produce a system that can be tested by a small community of friendly users. There are engineering and medical applications where such an effort might be financially practical, but it does not seem to be a workable approach in the grossly underfunded education arena.

Study 5: CIE

As the studies of part I progress up through this one, there is a growing awareness that the important information is not just domain-specific and gradually evolving but is specific to each community of practice and is constantly changing and being renegotiated. The studies from this point on try to respond to this finding. The idea of supporting communities of practice with specially tailored computational media seems plausible. The issue then is one of attracting a whole community to a particular platform and getting them in the habit of using that system for their regular community participation.

Study 6: WebGuide

This study confronts the crisis of adoption. Designers can go to great lengths to design systems to provide wonderful tools, but people—even students studying the design and use of such tools—resist using them. WebGuide provided a sophisticated system of interconnected perspectival views on an asynchronous discourse. The intention was to support ongoing knowledge building. But it was underused and at best served to exchange personal opinions. It failed to merge ideas of different people together into effective group cognition.

Study 7: Synergeia

This system added many features, based on a review of what typical CSCL and CSCW systems offered. In particular, it supported group negotiation as well as perspectives and the definition of groups, providing a structure for the interaction of ideas at the individual, small-group, and community levels. As necessary or useful as such features are or could be, the proliferation of features is not sufficient to overcome the barriers to adoption confronted by all collaboration systems. To design more effective media (the goal of part I), we will need better models of computer-mediated collaboration, clearer conceptions of group negotiation, and detailed studies of small-group interactions (as is illustratively undertaken in part II).

Study 8: BSCL

The BSCL study carefully conceptualized negotiation based on current understandings of collaboration. The failure of the BSCL negotiation mechanism to be used as intended showed the need for more detailed analysis of how people actually collaborate and negotiate in normal life. Parts II and III therefore empirically and theoretically investigate how knowledge is actually constructed and negotiated in small-group interactions.

Assessing the Studies in Part I

How should the success of these studies be evaluated? Each study provided a valuable learning experience in the design of groupware. Some never got much past the conceptual design phase—perhaps producing a detailed scenario, a set of interface designs, or a limited working prototype—while others have survived in one form or another.

TCA ended before ever being tried by teachers, but its designers are now deeply involved with major digital library projects that carry on much of that vision. Several versions of Essence were tested in classrooms for two years, eventually demonstrating statistically significant improvement in learning outcomes in controlled experiments reported elsewhere. The technology refined in Essence is now used in scoring various national tests. Essence itself is now being used in dozens of schools in the state of Colorado. The CREW software was turned over to the National Aeronautics and Space Administration (NASA), and its fate is not publicly known. The

Hermes software was further developed and used to deploy NASA's outer-space design rationale manuals as an online hypertext system.

Versions of WebGuide were used in classes as reported in the study, although the final implemented version was never actually deployed. Its perspectives concept reappeared in Synergeia and BSCL, simplified and integrated with negotiation support. Another version of personal, group, and class perspectives on threaded discussion appeared in the Polaris system from the University of Maastricht. I have tried to put all these perspective systems to good effect in my classes, with little success. I now use simple HTML Web sites for student, group, and class repositories, with no computational support. We simply do not know how to design more sophisticated systems that people will really use to support group cognition.

As other researchers have also discovered, threaded discussion and chat systems, as their names suggest, are generally used for the relatively superficial exchange of opinions rather than deep, interactive knowledge building. To the extent that the systems presented here were designed to support group cognition (knowledge building, situated interpretation, intertwining of perspectives, knowledge negotiation), this shows how far we still have to go. The fostering of group cognition is a sociotechnical problem, which is not automatically solved by offering certain functionality in a technical system (Kling & Courtright, 2004). It will require designing whole activity systems or shared worlds around such systems, based on a detailed analysis and understanding of collaboration.

Two releases of Synergeia were fielded in European schools as reported. Extensive surveying of teachers and students who used it showed that they liked it and had no fundamental criticisms of it. However, this form of evaluation provided little guidance for further software development. In particular, it is not clear that the negotiation mechanism was even used in the schools. I used BSCL in two of my Drexel courses on human-computer interaction and had my students design extensions to the negotiation mechanism. In this process, I experienced again how hard it is to adopt the use of that mechanism in an effective manner. The BSCL version of the software has now been integrated as an option of the popular BSCW collaboration system and is being used in many European classrooms.

Groupware is hard to assess. To see how it really supports groups, groups must use it under relatively naturalistic conditions and for a long enough time to become comfortable with it. But this requires building a sufficiently complete and robust prototype for group usage, finding an appropriate group of users, training users in its use, and involving them in a meaningful application of the software that properly exercises the functionality of interest.

Getting a group to use software is not easy, even once all the preconditions have been established. I found this repeatedly when using groupware prototypes in my classes. Users—information science majors who are interested in the design of innovative software, students whose grades depend on entering comments by using the software, and participants in courses whose activities have been designed around the use of the software—are all reluctant to use the software, and they constantly look for more familiar alternatives: meetings, conference calls, e-mail, and instant messaging. Adoption becomes *the* issue. It dominates over all the technical issues of groupware design. The studies in part I make it clear that the problem is to design sociotechnical systems where the technological product is simply an artifact to mediate the important, complex, and poorly understood processes of group collaboration. That brings us to the need to increase our understanding of the social-systems aspects of groupware design through analysis and theory of small-group interaction.

The preceding eight groupware design studies thus supply a sense of the potentials, the issues, and the challenges inherent in the design of collaboration technology. They provide a shared experience to motivate and lead into the parts that follow. Like all case studies, the experiences they offer are limited by their specifics; they should not be looked to for conclusions concerning the effectiveness of their innovations. They may, however, be legitimate and worthwhile explorations of what is possible through investigation of what actually happened under unique and irreproducible conditions. Taken in this sense, the experiences of part I furnish useful occasions for the situated interpretation of what it means today to support collaborative knowledge building and group cognition.

Theoretical Background to Part II

In developing the studies of part II, two analytic perspectives played a major role: sociocultural psychology and communication analysis. I actively pursued an understanding of them to resolve some of the mysteries that arose in my earlier software studies.

Sociocultural Psychology

Lev Vygotsky's thinking had an immediate catalytic effect on me when I first read his *Mind in Society* (1978). I was excited by his deep and original appropriation of Hegel and Marx and by his materialist theory of mind. I was intrigued not so much by what he actually explored in his experiments and what is generally interpreted as a psychology still centered on the individual mind but by the vision he sketched, often between the lines, of a truly socially constructed mind whose consciousness is derivative of the culture in which it was constructed. While my reading of Vygotsky is explicated more in part III, his emphasis on the role of artifacts in mediated cognition is already central to part II. In particular, these studies pursue the question of how people come to understand the meaning or affordances of artifacts and what implications this has for the design of groupware conceptualized as a mediating artifact.

Communication Analysis

In my search to understand perspectives and negotiation, I turned to communication analysis. This choice was also compatible with Vygotsky's emphasis on language and interaction. Colleagues, methods, and ideas from the discipline of communication made possible the analyses of this part, particularly chapter 12. The most relevant work for me was that of ethnomethodology (Garfinkel, 1967) and conversation analysis (Sacks, 1992). In general, I think that interactionist theories of communication have led the way in my understanding of the philosophical and methodological issues that are essential for developing a theoretical framework, empirical analysis, and software support design practice for collaboration.

The Studies in Part II

The five essays in part II try to analyze the nature of small-group interaction as it actually occurs. They

- Propose a model of small-group knowledge building (chapter 9),
- Critique prevalent CSCL methodologies for systematically ignoring the group interactions (chapter 10),
- Suggest new approaches that focus on the group discourse (chapter 11), and
- Conduct microanalyses of small-group interaction, detailing a group decision-making negotiation and looking at its cognitive ramifications for group understanding and activity (chapters 12 and 13).

Chapter 9, a Model

This study started as a tentative working paper when it first occurred to me that we needed to have some kind of graphical representation of the important process called *knowledge building* that I had started to refer to constantly but that seemed only vaguely defined. Gradually, as I circulated the paper for comment, shortcomings of the model became apparent, both in terms of its representation and its content. Nevertheless, the diagram has endured with only minor modifications and continues to prove useful. This paper—with its graphical model—has always been one of my most popular and suggestive writings because it starts to articulate what goes into collaborative knowledge building.

Chapter 10, Rediscovery
When asked to look at a couple of representative CSCL papers, I began to question the adequacy of available analytic methods. In particular, I bumped into the old lamppost problem: people tend to search where it is easiest to see and measure things, even if the important things lie elsewhere. It struck me that some of the most essential phenomena of computer-mediated collaboration were being systematically eliminated by the very methodological procedures that were recommended for rigorously analyzing them.

Chapter 11, Contributions
At the CSCL '02 conference, which I viewed as an occasion for injecting a more theoretical perspective into the field, I proposed a set of four notions that could contribute to a deeper understanding of collaboration: knowledge building, group and personal perspectives, mediation by artifacts, and conversation analysis. By pulling together these four themes, the paper effected a transition from the design issues of knowledge-building support, perspectives mechanisms, and software artifacts to the microanalysis of collaborative interactions.

Chapter 12, a Moment
This study looks closely at a transcript from an intense half-minute interaction among five students involved in an activity with SimRocket, a computer simulation of model rockets. A thick description of this hard-to-interpret discussion shows how the small group constructed group knowledge, which each participant came to share. The phenomenon of group cognition appeared here, where the indexical, elliptical, and projective character of the utterances showed that their meaning only existed at the small-group unit of analysis, not as something attributable to individual cognition. This study provides a pivotal point for the book. Its transcript is repeatedly referred to in the subsequent chapters. In fact, much of the theory presented in part III is derived from this 30-second episode, illustrating how much can be learned from detailed reflection on a brief case study.

Chapter 13, References
The preceding study's analysis is expanded here to dissect the nature of the group cognition that took place around the SimRocket artifact. It is argued that, before the collaborative moment, the group could not see the structure of the SimRocket list of rocket characteristics but that through their interaction they learned to see the new kind of structure and taught each other to see it. This group conceptual change allowed the group to repair the breakdown in relational references of their utterances to the artifact. This incident provides a key case study for the theoretical reflections on group cognition in part III.

9

A Model of Collaborative Knowledge Building

This chapter presents a model of learning as a social process incorporating multiple distinguishable phases that constitute cycles of personal and social knowledge building.[1] It explicitly considers the relationship of processes associated with individual minds to those considered to be sociocultural processes. This model of collaborative knowledge building incorporates insights from various theories of understanding and learning in hopes of providing a useful conceptual framework for the design of collaborative-learning software—specifically, collaborative knowledge-building environments. By identifying a set of cognitive and social processes, it suggests areas for computer support, including a set of specific illustrative knowledge-building environment components.

As we learn more and more about something, what happens?

(a) The questions all get answered.

(b) The questions get easier and easier.

(c) The questions get more and more complex.

   —Adapted from a student survey in Lamon, Chan, Scardamalia, Burtis, & Brett, 1993.

As we learn more and more about the learning sciences, the controversies intensify, the paradigms proliferate, the quandaries deepen, and the foundations shake. This is how knowledge building in a research community advances.

In the book that established the field of computer-supported collaborative learning (CSCL) and presented the state of the art at that time, the editor identified three distinct theories of learning implicit in the community's research (Koschmann, 1996b):

• Neo-Piagetian conflict theory,

• Cultural-historical activity theory, and

• Social practice theory.

Recently, he has proposed two more:

- Deweyan transactional inquiry (Koschmann, 2001), and
- Bakhtinian dialogicality theory (Koschmann, 1999b).

This chapter takes yet another cut at the problem, incorporating insights from these theories and related philosophies.

The model presented here is an attempt to understand learning as a social process incorporating multiple distinguishable phases that constitute a cycle of personal and social knowledge building. The cyclical character of this process allows increasingly complex questions to be posed on the basis of more and more sophisticated understanding.

This model of collaborative knowledge building incorporates insights from theories of understanding and learning within a simplistic schema to provide a useful conceptual framework for the design of CSCL software—specifically, collaborative knowledge-building environments. It is inquiry in the service of practical activities, as Dewey would say (Dewey & Bentley, 1991). In its own terms, this chapter presents a set of personal beliefs, articulated as a contribution to a social knowledge-building process that may lead through collaborative discourse toward the enriched self-understanding of a research community.

A Diagram of Personal and Social Knowledge Building

Despite frequent references to constructivism in the CSCL literature, it is not clear in that literature which cognitive processes are involved in collaborative knowledge building. In particular, it continues to be unclear to skeptical readers of this literature how collaborative group processes relate to individual cognitive processes, despite the fact that each of the theories of learning described by Timothy Koschmann goes to great pains to conceptualize this relationship.

A family of seminal papers in CSCL has formulated a perspective on *learning* as a social process of *collaborative knowledge building* (Brown & Campione, 1994; Lave, 1991; Pea, 1993a; Scardamalia & Bereiter, 1996). However, these papers do not make the set of cognitive processes that underlie such a view explicit in the manner attempted here.

This chapter presents a diagram (figure 9.1) that represents a number of important phases in collaborative knowledge building. The convention in the diagram is that arrows represent transformative processes and that rectangles represent the products of these processes: forms of knowledge. To take this limited representation too seriously would be to reify a complex and fluid development—to put it into boxes and to assume that it always follows the same path. In particular, the diagram gives the impression of a sequential process, whereas the relations among the

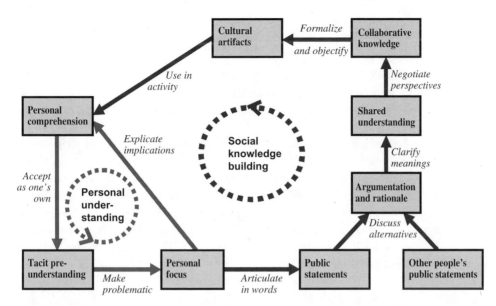

Figure 9.1
A diagram of knowledge-building processes.

elements can take infinitely varied and complex forms (see the afterward at end of this chapter). Indeed, the identification of the particular set of elements is arbitrary and incomplete. Perhaps despite such limitations and potential distortions, the diagram can provide a starting point for discussing a cognitive theory of computer support for knowledge building. It remains to be seen if such a phase model provides the most useful representation.

The diagram attempts to model the mutual (dialectical) constitution of the individual and the social knowledge building as a learning process (Brown & Duguid, 1991; Lave & Wenger, 1991). Starting in the lower left corner, it shows the cycle of personal understanding. The rest of the diagram depicts how our individual personal beliefs that we become aware of in our activity in the world can be articulated in language and how they enter into a mysterious *social* process of interaction with other people and with our shared culture. This culture, in turn, enters into our *personal* understanding, shaping it with ways of thinking, motivational concerns, and diverse influences. Personal cognition and social activity can be separated only artificially, as in a model like this designed for analysis. That is the nature of a relationship of mutually constituting subjects: neither can exist without the other, but it is useful to distinguish them at certain points in their analysis (Hegel, 1967).

The Cycle of Personal Understanding

Martin Heidegger (1996) (an early twentieth-century German philosopher) and Donald Schön (1983) (an influential American theoretician of design) argue that learning starts on the basis of tacit preunderstanding (Polanyi, 1962; Winograd & Flores, 1986) (see chapter 4). Some form of *breakdown* in planning or in our worldly activity renders elements of this tacit understanding problematic on occasion (Dewey & Bentley, 1991). The network of meanings by which we make sense of our world is torn asunder and must be mended. The resolution of the problem proceeds through a gnawing awareness of the problematic nature of some piece of our understanding. We may be able to repair our understanding by explicating the implications of that understanding and resolving conflicts or filling in gaps—*by reinterpreting our meaning structures*—to arrive at a new comprehension. This typically involves some feedback from the world: from our experience with artifacts such as our tools and symbolic representations. For instance, we might learn a new sense of some word or a new application of a familiar tool. More ambitiously, our understanding might undergo a fundamental conceptual change. If we are successful and the problem disappears, this new comprehension gradually settles in to become our new tacit understanding and to provide the starting point for future understanding and further learning.

The process of interpretation that seems to be carried out at the level of the individual mind is already an essentially social process. The network of personal meanings ultimately has its origin in interpersonal language and culture. Interpretation takes place within language (Wittgenstein, 1953), history (Gadamer, 1988), culture (Bourdieu, 1995; Bruner, 1990; Cole, 1996), social structures (Giddens, 1984a), and politics (Habermas, 1984). Our internal thought process capabilities and structures themselves have origins in our previous social interactions (Mead, 1962; Vygotsky, 1978). Our personal interpretive perspective or voice is a consolidation of many perspectives and voices or genres of others we have known (Bakhtin, 1986a; Boland & Tenkasi, 1995). However, social context and social origin are hidden because they have been incorporated into the tacit preunderstandings of the individual. They can be made visible by means of scientific methods, which remove the observer from the primary human engagement with the world and allow objective analysis as a result of such systematic alienation (Heidegger, 1996; Husserl, 1989).

It is not always possible to resolve the problematic character of our personal understanding internally, particularly when it is provoked by other people. Then we may need to enter into an explicitly social process and create new meanings collaboratively. To do this, we typically articulate our initial belief in words and express ourselves in public statements.

The Cycle of Social Knowledge Building

We then enter the larger sequence of processes represented in the diagram. Here we can build on and supplement the cycles of individual learning of several individuals. This happens when someone's personal belief is articulated in words and this public statement is taken up in a social setting and discussed from the multiple perspectives of several participants. The original statements are thereby articulated into a more refined and extensive discussion of the topic, subject to conflicting interpretations. The discussion consists of arguments providing rationales for different points of view. The interchange may gradually converge on a shared understanding resulting from a clarification of differences in interpretation and terminology.

If the communication is relatively free of hidden agendas, power struggles, and undiscussed prejudices, then arguments and clarifications can lead to agreement or at least mutual understanding. If the negotiation of the different perspectives does result in acceptance of a common result, then such a result is accepted as *knowledge*. In this way, collaboration and undistorted communication mediate between personal belief and accepted knowledge.

Underlying the theory of learning defined by this diagram is a *social epistemology*. Individuals generate personal beliefs from their own perspectives, but they do so on the basis of sociocultural knowledge, shared language, and external representations. Further, these beliefs become knowledge through social interaction, communication, discussion, clarification, and negotiation. Knowledge is a socially mediated product.

The fact that knowledge is a product of social communication does not mean that it is ungrounded or arbitrary. The medium of knowledge—language—is grounded in the life experiences of individuals, in our physical embodiment, in our sense of rationality, in the interaction patterns of communicating communities, in cultural traditions, and in the vast background knowledge that is implicitly accepted in every act of understanding or agreement. Furthermore, the communication process that results in knowledge incorporates argumentation that can introduce empirical evidence and logical deduction from other established knowledge. Scientific methodologies have their legitimate and legitimating roles within the communication process of their respective communities. But it is always the case that negotiated agreement on the issues and methodologies as well as on the conclusions is required to promote claims to the status of knowledge. And such knowledge is never absolute—although its character is to be taken as final truth—but always subject to the possibility of future questioning, reinterpretation, and renegotiation.

The public statements that are a result of the discussion, argumentation, and clarification form a shared language created through the communication process.

The communication process takes place on several levels: propositional content, perspective taking, social interaction, repair of misunderstandings, latent connotations, and so on. This process of language and analysis is negotiated by the public group and becomes their shared collaborative knowledge. The resultant understanding exists only in the public communication that took place, although it can subsequently be incorporated into each participant's individual learning process.

Note that the individual mind (left side of the diagram in figure 9.1) is indispensable to the larger cycle, providing both the starting and the ending point—as well as being involved at each social phase in ways not adequately represented in the diagram. Conversely, the individual mind is intimately intertwined with the intersubjective (right side of diagram), solving its problems through the use of public language and constantly internalizing cultural meanings.

From a cognitive viewpoint, there are many skills and subprocesses at work that are not represented in the diagram. These include activities considered personal skills, like summarization, text understanding, critical thinking, and logical structuring of arguments. They also include social interaction skills such as turn taking, repair of misunderstandings, rhetorical persuasion, and interactive arguing. For simplicity sake, the diagram ignores these detailed phases and various other, similar options. It also ignores the unlimited paths that can be followed by the overall process and the manifold interactions of the individual and social levels. A diagram like this is highly selective, illustrating a few prominent processes and ignoring many alternatives and details. The nomenclature for the stages of the processes is particularly inadequate to express what is pictured, for we have only very impoverished ways of talking about these processes and their interactions. Nevertheless, such a diagram may provide a helpful external memory (Donald, 1991), cognitive artifact (Norman, 1993), or "object to think with" (Papert, 1980) in developing a theoretical understanding.

Collaborative understandings are sometimes objectified in external persistent symbolic objects—cultural artifacts—that preserve this understanding as their meaning. The meaning encapsulated in the artifact comes to life when the artifact is used. This coming to life when used by an individual is an interpretive process of the individual's activity in the world. It may take place either consciously or tacitly and may subsequently be integrated into the individual's implicit personal understanding. In this way, among others, social meanings become internalized in personal minds. Another way this may happen is through formalization of the shared understanding in representational schemas that express the shared knowledge. These representations are also cultural symbolic objects that help to transmit and encapsulate collaborative knowledge. Formal representations like mathematical symbol systems or our process diagram provide cognitive supports and help to preserve and communicate meanings, much like physical cultural artifacts, such as sculptures, do in their own way (see chapter 6).

Opportunities for Computer Support

By defining a sequence of typical phases of social knowledge building, the diagram suggests a set of focal points where computer support may be desirable. It thereby provides a conceptual framework for the design, use, and assessment of collaborative knowledge-building environments (KBEs). Table 9.1 proposes a form of computer support corresponding to each phase in the diagram's *social* knowledge-building cycle. Computer support cannot be provided for *individual* cognition per se; personal beliefs must be articulated as public statements before they can interact within computer media. In fact, thoughts must be even more formalized for computer support than for interpersonal interaction (Stahl, 1993a):

• Computer support for learning should facilitate the process of articulating ideas and preserving them in convenient forms. A text *editor* or simple word processor is a minimal instance of this. Some KBEs have tried to introduce procedural facilitation, scaffolding, or prompting to encourage someone to articulate an appropriate expression (Slotta & Linn, 2000). For instance, to start someone articulating their initial belief, an editor might open with the words, "I believe that . . . because . . ." already entered. Other approaches would be to provide an outline editor or a brainstorming area.

Table 9.1
Forms of computer support for phases of knowledge building represented in figure 9.1.

Phase of Knowledge Building	Form of Computer Support
Articulate in words	Articulation editor
Public statements	Personal perspective
Other people's public statements	Comparison perspective
Discuss alternatives	Discussion forum
Argumentation and rationale	Argumentation graph
Clarify meanings	Glossary discussion
Shared understanding	Glossary
Negotiate perspectives	Negotiation support
Collaborative knowledge	Design
Formalize and objectify	Bibliography discussion
Cultural artifacts and representations	Bibliography or other community repository

• Public statements by one person confront those of other people. Computer support can represent the different *perspectives* from which these statements emerge. Perspectives are more general than representations of individuals themselves because one person can offer statements from multiple perspectives and several people can agree on a common perspective. Perspectives can be related to one another, for instance, deriving from a common perspective that they share. Computational representations of perspectives should make explicit the important relationships among personal and group perspectives, as well as providing the means for individuals and collaborative teams to articulate their own perspectives in a KBE (see chapter 5).

• A KBE with support for perspectives should provide *comparison perspectives* in which users can view and contrast alternative perspectives and adopt or adapt ideas from other people's perspectives. A comparison perspective aggregates ideas from various individual or group perspectives and allows them to be easily compared. This is an important source of a union of ideas that fosters convergence of thinking and the sharing of insights or interpretations (see chapter 6).

• The most common element in current KBEs is the *discussion forum*. This is an asynchronous, interactive communication system that allows people to respond to notes posted by one another. Typically, there is a thread of responses to entered notes, with a tree of divergent opinions. A KBE should go beyond superficial undirected discussion to converge on shared understandings and acknowledged ideas (Hewitt, 1997).

• Although every note in a discussion forum is a response to another note, the discussion may have a more complex implicit structure. One note might argue for or against another or provide evidence to back up the claim of another note, for instance. Such an argumentation structure can be made explicit and formalized in a representation of the *argumentation graph*. A component that supported this could contribute to participants' metalevel comprehension of their knowledge-building process, pointing out where additional evidence is needed or where alternatives have not been explored (Donath, Karahalios, & Viegas, 1999).

• An important requirement for constructing group knowledge is the establishment of shared understanding. This can be fostered by clarifying the meaning of important terms used in various competing claims. A *glossary discussion* can make explicit how different participants understand the terms they use. The discussion can go on to converge on common understandings by sharing perspectives or negotiating conventions (see chapter 4).

• The glossary discussion should result in a group *glossary* of the agreed on definitions of important terms. Such a glossary already represents a form of group knowledge. The glossary is subject to future debate and emendation; it may make sense to define the glossary as a particular display of information from the glossary discussion (Stahl & Herrmann, 1999).

• Perhaps the most delicate phase of knowledge building is negotiation. Power differentials of all kinds generally enter at this point. The power of established authority resists the negotiation of change. Computer *support of negotiation* tends, by nature, to make explicit the factors entering into the negotiation process. This can be harmful to the subtle processes of persuasion if not done sensitively. On the other hand, negotiation is critical to helping multiple perspectives to converge on shared knowledge. Computer support can provide a useful tool—as long as it is carefully integrated with other social processes that allow for implicit, culturally established interpersonal interactions (see chapter 8).

• The accumulation of negotiated shared knowledge results in the establishment of a *group perspective*. Like the alternative individual and team perspectives, the group perspective may be represented in a KBE. The content of the group perspective should be inherited by the individual and team perspectives because it is now accepted by them. Individuals can then build on this shared knowledge within their own perspective and even begin to critique it and start the whole cycle over (see chapter 7).

• Shared knowledge is not the final phase in the cycle of social knowledge building. The knowledge can be further formalized. While it must have already been expressed explicitly, at least in written language within the KBE, it can now be represented in another symbolic system or combined into a more comprehensive system of knowledge. For instance, in academic research, knowledge is incorporated in new classroom lectures, conference presentations, journal articles, and books. These venues bring the ideas into broader communities of discussion—widening the social circle that may accept or revise the new knowledge. The discussion of knowledge that has been compiled into publications can be carried out in a *bibliography discussion* component of a KBE.

• Finally, representations of the new shared knowledge in publications and other cultural artifacts are themselves accepted as part of the established paradigm. Although still subject to occasional criticism, ideas in this form more generally provide part of the accepted base for building future knowledge. In academic circles, a shared annotated *bibliography* of such sources might provide a useful KBE component to support this phase of knowledge building.

The preceding suggestions of possible KBE components are simply illustrative of the kinds of supports that might be designed for KBEs based on the analysis of the knowledge-building process outlined above. They are meant to evoke a particular approach to software design.

The Idea of a Computer System to Support the Knowledge-Building Process

A KBE should go beyond a single-purpose system—like a simple discussion forum—and support more than one phase of the social knowledge-building process. It should retain a record of the knowledge that was built up—unlike common chat, newsgroup, and listserv systems that erase contributions after a short period of time. It should therefore probably be built on asynchronous, persistent collaborative technologies and be deployed on the Internet as a Web-based environment.

A KBE should support at least several of the lifecycle phases of knowledge building. It should help people to express their beliefs, discuss them with others, differentiate their own perspectives, adopt those of other people, clarify disagreements or misunderstandings, critique and explicate claims, negotiate shared understandings or agreements, and formulate knowledge in a lasting representation.

Because KBEs are computational, they should provide facilities like searching, browsing, filtering, tailoring, and linking. Beyond that, they could incorporate heuristics that automatically suggest relevant connections, critique problems in the knowledge base, and deliver information automatically when it might be useful.

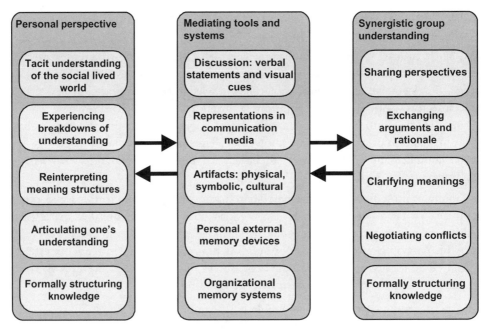

Figure 9.2
The mediation between personal and group understanding.

They can also compile and format sets of notes in convenient displays. KBEs can interface with other software and systems, sending, for instance, e-mails to notify collaborators when important events take place in the environment.

Although there are significant difficulties in implementing and successfully deploying such complex systems, their potential advantages seem extraordinary: they can provide a range of support for what is generally a difficult, painful, and obscure process known as knowledge building. They introduce explicit structures for an otherwise haphazard sequence of uncoordinated events. Not only are the knowledge products made persistent in the computer memory, but much of the process is retrievable later. Historical analyses can be carried out and decision points revisited. The asynchronous nature of the communication allows participants to be more reflective and significantly reduces scheduling problems and time limitations. The computer basis permits computational mechanisms like searching, reorganizing, browsing, filtering, indexing, and matching. An essential requirement of

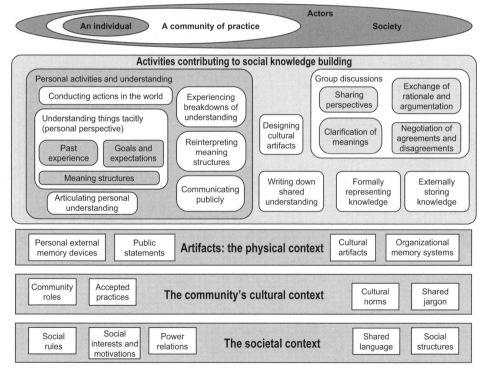

Figure 9.3
Activities contributing to social knowledge building.

collaboration is making things public: a KBE renders public many aspects of the knowledge-building process that otherwise remain hidden from the participants. The social nature of the process and its products is rendered visible, and therefore the fact that the group has the power to evolve the knowledge further is also made evident.

Conclusion

A KBE is a software environment intended to support collaborative learning. The process model of knowledge building presented in this chapter provides a conceptual framework for the design, use, and assessment of such systems by indicating important phases that could be supported.

In broad terms, computer support should provide a workspace in which ideas can be articulated, can come into interaction with other ideas from multiple viewpoints, can be further developed, and can approach consensus. It should afford, facilitate, or even encourage this multiphased community process. It should provide a convenient medium to formulate, represent, and communicate ideas at the various phases. And it should preserve the ideas and their various formulations in its computer-based medium to allow for review, reflection, and continuation at any time or from any place.

As the model suggests, collaborative learning is a complex process. Given the constraints on community members who lead busy, geographically distributed lives, KBEs have the potential to provide computationally supported communication media to facilitate this process that forms a centerpiece of collaborative learning.

Afterward

The model in figure 9.1 was originally circulated informally as part of a working paper. The representation with boxes and arrows may give the false impression that the boxes represent some kinds of objects and that the arrows indicate a necessary full path. Attempts to avoid these misleading suggestions led to the following diagrams, developed in collaboration with Thomas Herrmann. Figure 9.2 models the mediation of various forms of personal and group understanding or knowledge-building moves by different kinds of verbal, symbolic, representational, and computational artifacts. Alternatively, figure 9.3 models the knowledge-building activities engaged in by actors within physical, community, and social contexts. The empirical study described in chapter 11 led to substantive revisions of the model, presented in figure 15.3 of chapter 15.

10

Rediscovering the Collaboration

This chapter was originally published as a commentary to chapters 3 and 4 of *CSCL 2: Carrying Forward the Conversation*.[1] Those two chapters are examples of leading-edge research in computer support for collaborative learning (CSCL) but lose sight of the real phenomena of collaboration due to their use of particular research methodologies that are prevalent in CSCL work. An alternative approach, which analyzes the details of collaborative interactions, is recommended as a supplement to such approaches. In my commentary, I began to reflect on the limitations of CSCL methodologies that are derived from related fields, like education and psychology. It struck me that their drive to quantify data as grist for the statistical mill reduced the richness of the data and eliminated some of the most interesting information for understanding collaboration. While the methodology allowed researchers to make statistically significant tests of specific hypotheses, it obstructed any attempt to follow the processes proposed in chapter 9's model. This insight allowed me to anticipate the proposal of chapter 11 and its implementation in chapters 12 and 13.

The *CSCL2* volume (Koschmann, Hall, & Miyake, 2002) provides a follow-up to the collection that largely defined the field of CSCL six years earlier (Koschmann, 1996a). It compiled a number of key papers from the CSCL '97 conference and was structured with commentaries written in 2001 to spark a knowledge-building conversation within the research community. The present chapter's commentary attempted to suggest a methodological turn for the field of CSCL. That suggestion will be further developed and implemented in later chapters of this book.

Chapter 3 of *CSCL2* ("Computer-Supported Collaborative Learning in University and Vocational Education") was written especially for that edited volume by Frank P. C. M. de Jong, Else Veldhuis-Diermanse, and Gaby Lugens from the Netherlands. Chapter 4 of *CSCL2* ("Epistemology of Inquiry and Computer-Supported Collaborative Learning") was presented at CSCL '97 by Kai Hakkarainen, Lasse Lipponen, and Sanna Järvelä from Finland.

The Ambiguity of CSCL

In the penultimate sentence of their paper, Hakkarainen, Lipponen, and Järvelä correctly point out that CSCL researchers have a complex challenge because they "attempt to promote the educational use of the new information/communication technology while simultaneously trying to implement new pedagogical and cognitive practices of learning and instruction" (p. 153). The naïve, technology-driven view was that tools such as CSILE (Computer-Supported Intentional Learning Environment, the software system used in both studies) would, on their own, make a significant difference in the classroom. The subsequent experience has been that the classroom culture bends such tools to its own interests and that this culture must be transformed before new media can mediate learning the way we had hoped they would. So CSCL research has necessarily and properly shifted from the affordances and effects of the technology to concerns with the instructional context. Thus, the central conclusions of both papers focus on the teacher's role and say little that pertains directly to the role of CSILE or to the consequences of specific features of its design.

Moreover, the papers are concerned with exploring the presence of deep knowledge building within groups, as opposed to more superficial exchange of existing personal opinions or individual offerings of off-the-cuff reactions. Both papers investigate the teacher's role in making a difference to the depth of collaboration and learning. Again, this is an important theme for research, but the methodology seems to miss the core phenomenon of interest to CSCL: instances of collaborative learning and details of their computer support.

The two papers have a similar structure: first, they discuss abstract pedagogical issues from the educational or scientific research literature (e.g., the learner-as-thinker or the scientist-as-questioner paradigm). Second, they present a statistical analysis of the notes in specific CSILE databases. Finally, they conclude that certain kinds of individual student learning took place.

However, in both cases, it could be imagined that the same learning might have taken place in these particular classrooms with their particular teacher *without any computer support and without any collaboration*. While there is no doubt that the concerns expressed and supported in these papers are of vital importance to CSCL research, one wonders what happened to the computer-supported collaboration in CSCL.

The high-level concern of these papers, which ends up ignoring the roles of both collaboration and technology, plays itself out at a methodological level. To see this requires reviewing the analysis undertaken in these papers.

CSCL in the University

The paper by de Jong, Diermanse, and Lutgens raises three central questions for CSCL environments such as CSILE:

- Can these environments be integrated into curriculum at the university level?
- Does their use promote knowledge building?
- What should the role of the teacher be?

Each of these questions would require a book to answer with any completeness—assuming one knew the answers. Research today is really just starting to pose the questions. Any answers proposed either supply the writer's intuitive sense of what took place in an experiment or rely on a methodology whose limitations become obvious in the very process of being applied to these questions. Let us consider each of these questions in turn.

The Cultural, Educational, Learning, and Pedagogical Contexts

Can CSILE (to use this prototypical system as a representative of the class of possible software systems for supporting collaborative knowledge-building) be integrated into curriculum? The first issue implicitly posed by raising this question in the paper was to determine the kind of cultural and educational setting in which a program like CSILE could be integrated. The studies presented here took place in the Netherlands, within the context of a larger European project including Finland, Belgium, Italy, and Greece. Most of the earlier studies of CSILE (Computer-Supported Intentional Learning Environment) were conducted in Canada, where the system was developed (Scardamalia & Bereiter, 1996). However, there is no evidence presented in the paper to say that national culture makes any difference in the adoption of CSILE.

A second aspect of context is to determine the educational level at which CSILE is effective. The paper reports studies at the university level and at a vocational agricultural school at the same age level. The related European studies focused on primary school children 9 to 11 years old. Systems such as CSILE are most frequently used in primary and middle-school classes, although they are increasingly being used in college classes as well. The studies in this paper are not contrasted with other age groups, and there is no reason given to think that educational level makes any significant difference. This is actually a surprising nonresult because collaborative knowledge building might be assumed to require mature cognitive skills. It may be that within modern schooling systems college students have not developed collaborative inquiry skills beyond an elementary-school level.

A third aspect has to do with the learning styles of the individual students. This issue is explicitly raised by the methodology of the first (university) study. Here the students were given tests on cognitive processing strategies, regulation strategies, mental models of learning, and learning orientation. Based on these scores, they were classified as having one of four learning styles: application directed, reproduction directed, meaning directed, or undirected. A statistically significant correlation was found between the application-directed learners and the number of notes entered into CSILE. This was the only significant correlation involving learning styles. This may just mean that students who are generally more inclined to engage in tasks were in fact the ones who engaged more in the note creation task of the study—not a surprising result.

A fourth aspect involves the incorporation of collaboration software into a particular curriculum or classroom culture. As the paper makes clear, CSILE is not intended for a traditional teacher-centered classroom with delivery of facts through lecture. The use of such a technology as a centerpiece of classroom learning raises the most complex issues of educational transformation. Not only do the teacher and student roles have to be rethought, but the curricular goals and the institutional framework need to be as well. If collaborative knowledge building is really going to become the new aim, what happens to the whole competitive grading system that functions as a certification system integral to industrial society? Is it any wonder that "students are not used to sharing their knowledge"? What will it take to change this?

Promoting Collaborative Knowledge Building

The paper's conclusion cites two arguments for the claim that CSILE resulted in much more collaborative learning by the students. First, it contrasts the study with "past courses in which students were directed through the course by closed tasks." No attempt beyond this half sentence is made to draw out the contrast. By definition, a course that has been restructured to centrally include collaborative discussion will at least appear to be more collaborative than its teacher-centered predecessor. But it is important to consider concretely what took place collaboratively and what specific kinds of knowledge were built collaboratively.

The second evidence for collaborative knowledge building comes from an activity that apparently took place outside of CSILE in a noncollaborative manner: the rewriting of educational policy notes. This seems like precisely the kind of collaborative task that could have pulled the whole course together as a joint project. Students could have collected and shared ideas from their readings with the goal of building a group external memory of ideas that would be used in collectively rewriting the educational policy. Instead, the individual students had to retain whatever the group learned using CSILE, combine it with individualized learning from readings, and "transfer" this knowledge to the final individual "authentic" task. Thus, the paper concludes that the use of CSILE "resulted in sufficient transfer of the acquired understanding to work within an authentic problem." There is no evidence of learning or transfer other than a general judgment that the final product was of "high quality."

The remaining evidence for collaborative knowledge building is given by two standard statistical measures of online discussions. The first measure is a graph of the number of notes posted by students and teachers during each week of the course. In the university study, this chart shows a large peak at the beginning and a smaller one at the end—for both students and teachers. There is virtually no addition of new notes for the central half of the course and only a minimal reading of the notes occurs during that time. This is extraordinary, given that the paper calls this period the "knowledge-deepening phase." This is precisely when collaborative knowledge building would be expected to be taking place. As students read, research, and deepen their ideas, they should be sharing and interacting. They know how to use the technology at this point, so if CSILE truly promotes student-directed collaboration, then why is this not taking place? (Raising this question is in no way intended to criticize anyone involved in this particular experiment, as this is an all too common finding in CSCL research.)

The vocational study also presents a graph of the number of notes posted each week. Here, there are peaks in the middle of the course. But as the paper points out, the peaks in student activity directly follow the peaks in teacher activity. This indicates a need for continuing teacher intervention and guidance. The apparently causal relation between teacher intervention and student activity raises the question of the nature of the student activity. Are students just creating individual notes to please the teacher, or has the teacher stimulated collaborative interactions among the student notes? Because the graph shows only the number of created notes, such a question cannot be addressed.

The second statistical measure for the university study is a table of correlations among several variables of the threaded discussion: notes created, notes that respond to earlier notes, notes linked to other notes, notes revised, and notes read by students. The higher correlations in the table indicate that many notes were responses to other notes and that these were read often. This is taken as evidence for a high level of collaboration taking place in CSILE. A nice sample of such collaboration is given in figure 2 of the study. Here one student, Elske, has posted a statement of her theory. A discussion ensues, mostly over three days, but with a final contribution nine days later. This collection of 10 linked notes represents a discussion among four people about Elske's theory. It might be informative to look at the content of this discussion to see what form—if any—of knowledge building is taking place.

The Teacher's Role

The paper ends with some important hints about how CSILE classrooms need to be different from lecture-dominated contexts. The use of the collaboration technology must be highly structured, with a systematic didactic approach, continuing teacher involvement, and periodic face-to-face meetings to trouble-shoot problems and reflect on the learning process. These suggestions are not specific to the studies presented and might surprise only people—if there still are any—who think that putting a computer box in a classroom will promote learning by itself. These are generic recommendations for any form of learner-as-thinker pedagogy, regardless of whether there is collaboration or computer support.

The paper by Hakkarainen et al. comes to a similar conclusion by a somewhat different, though parallel, route. Some of the preceding comments apply to it as well. But it also represents a significant advance in uncovering the quality of the discussion that takes place. In their discussion section, the authors are clearly aware of the limitations of their approach, but in their actual analysis they too fail to get at the collaboration or the computer support.

Hakkarainen et al. are interested in the "epistemology of inquiry" in CSCL classrooms. That is, they want to see what kinds of knowledge are being generated by the students in three different classrooms—two in Canada and one in Finland—using CSILE. To analyze the kinds of knowledge, they code the ideas entered into the CSILE database along a number of dimensions. For instance, student knowledge ideas were coded as either (1) scientific information being introduced into the discussion or (2) a student's own view. Ideas of both these kinds were then rated as to their level of explanatory power: statement of isolated facts, partially organized facts, well-organized facts, partial explanation, or explanation.

Statistical analysis of the coded ideas provides strong evidence that the epistemology of inquiry was different in the three classrooms. In particular, one of the Canadian classrooms showed a significantly deeper explanatory understanding of the scientific phenomena under discussion. This was attributed by the authors to a difference in the classroom culture established by the teacher, including the extent of the teacher's interactions with students via CSILE. Thus, the approach of coding ideas achieved the authors' goal of showing the importance of the classroom culture in determining the character of collaborative knowledge building.

The Epistemology of Science

Hakkarainen et al. review certain philosophers of science and characterize the enterprise of science in terms of posing specific kinds of questions and generating particular kinds of statements. This may be a valid conceptualization of scientific inquiry, but let us consider a different perspective more directly related to collaboration and computer support.

In his reconstruction of the *Origins of the Modern Mind*, Merlin Donald (1991) locates the birth of science in the discovery by the ancient Greeks that "by entering ideas, even incomplete ideas, into the public record, they could later be improved and refined" (p. 342). In this view, what drives scientific advance is collaboration that is facilitated by external memory—precisely the promise of CSCL. Significantly, this framing of scientific knowledge building focuses on the social process and its mediation by technologies of external memory (from written language to networked digital repositories). According to this approach, we should be analyzing not so much the individual questions and statements of scientific discourse as the sequences of their improvement and refinement. Similarly, we can look at the effects of the affordances of technologies for expressing, communicating, relating, organizing, and retaining these evolving ideas.

Reification of Data and its Consequences for CSCL

Unfortunately, Hakkarainen et al. focus exclusively on individual statements. They relate their categorization of statements to CSILE in terms of that system's "thinking types," which the CSILE designers selected to scaffold the discourse of a community of learners. However, the thinking type categories that students select to label their statements in CSILE were designed precisely to facilitate the interconnection of notes—to indicate to students reading the discussion which notes were responses and refinements of other notes.

For purposes of analyzing the use of CSILE in different classrooms, the authors operationalize their view of science. They systematically break down all the notes that students communicated through CSILE into unit "ideas" and categorize these textual ideas according to what kind of question or statement they express. This turns out to be a useful approach for deriving qualitative and quantitative answers to certain questions about the kind of scientific discussions taking place in the classrooms. Indeed, this is a major advance over the analysis in de Jong et al., which could not differentiate different kinds of notes from each other at all.

However, the reduction of a rich discussion in a database of student notes into counts of how many note fragments ("ideas") fall into each of several categories represents a loss of much vital information. The notes—which were originally subtle acts of communication, interaction, and knowledge building within a complexly structured community of learners—are now reified into a small set of summary facts about the discussion. For all the talk in CSCL circles about moving from fact-centered education to experiential learning, CSCL research (by no means just the paper under review here but most of the best in the field) remains predominantly fact-reductive.

The methodology of coding statements is useful for answering certain kinds of questions, many of which are undeniably important. And the methodology can make claims to scientific objectivity: wherever subjective human interpretations are made, they are verified with interrater reliability, and wherever claims are made, they are defended with statistical measures of reliability.

However, it becomes clear here that the coding process has removed all the semantics of the discussion so that we can no longer see what scientific theories have been developed or what critical issues have been raised, and it has also removed any signs of collaboration. We do not know what note refined what other note, how long an important train of argument was carried on, or how many students were involved in a particular debate. We cannot even tell if there were interactions among all, some, or none of the students.

To their credit, Hakkarainen et al. recognize that their (and de Jong's) measures capture only a small part of what has taken place in the classrooms. In their paper, they are trying to make a single focused point about the impact of the teacher-created classroom culture on the scientific level of the CSILE-mediated discourse. Furthermore, in their discussion section they note the need for different kinds of analysis to uncover the "on-line interactions between teacher and students" that form a "progressive discourse," which is central to knowledge building according to Carl Bereiter (2002). For future work, they propose social network analysis, which graphically represents who interacted with whom, revealing groups of collaborators and noncollaborators. Although this would provide another useful measure, note that it too discards both the content and the nature of any knowledge building that may have taken place in the interactions. Methodologically, they still situate knowledge in the heads of individual students and then seek relations among these ideas rather than seeking knowledge as an emergent property of the collaboration discourse itself.

Where to Rediscover CSCL

These two papers represent typical studies of CSCL. The first type provides graphs of note distributions and argues that this demonstrates computer-supported collaboration that is more or less intense at different points represented in the graph. Sometimes, additional analyses of discussion thread lengths provide some indication of processes of refinement, although without knowing what was said and how ideas evolved through interactions during those processes it is impossible to judge the importance of the collaboration. The second type of analysis codes the semantics of the notes to make conclusions about the character of the discussion without really knowing what the discussion was about. It has generally been assumed that the only alternative is to make subjective or anecdotal observations from actually observing some of the discussion and understanding its content—and that this would be impractical and unscientific.

A major problem that we have just observed with the prevalent CSCL assessment approaches is that they throw out the actual computer-supported collaborative learning along with the richness of the phenomenon when they reduce everything to data for statistics.

What we need to do now is to look at examples of CSCL and observe the collaboration taking place. Collaborative knowledge building is a complex and subtle process that cannot adequately be reduced to a simple graph or coding scheme, however much those tools may help to illustrate specific parts of the picture. One central question that needs to be seriously addressed has to do with our claim that collaboration is important for knowledge building. We need to ask where is there evidence that knowledge emerged from the CSCL-mediated process that would not have emerged from a classroom of students isolated at their desks, quietly hunched over their private pieces of paper. Beyond that, we should be able to trace the various activities of collaborative knowledge building: where one person's comment stimulates another's initial insight or question, one perspective is taken over by another, a terminological confusion leads to clarification, a set of hypotheses congeals into a theory, and a synergistic group understanding emerges thanks to the power of computer-supported collaborative learning.

Before we had systems such as CSILE, collaboration across a classroom was not feasible. How could all the students simultaneously communicate their ideas in a way to which others could respond whenever they had the time and inclination? How could all those ideas be captured for future reflection, refinement, and reorganization? CSCL proposes that this is now possible. We have to demonstrate, in showcase classrooms, that it has become a reality—that CSCL systems really can support this and that, thanks to this technology, exciting things really are taking place that would not otherwise have been possible. Only when our analyses demonstrate this will we have rediscovered CSCL in our analysis of classroom experiments.

Making Collaborative Learning Visible

Statistical analysis of outcomes has dominated educational research because it was assumed since Descartes that learning takes place inside people's heads and that we have only indirect access to those processes. Much work in the cognitive sciences, including artificial intelligence, assumes that we can, at best, model the mental representations that are somehow formed or instilled by learning. Whatever we may think of these assumptions as applied to individual cognition, they surely do not apply to collaborative learning. By definition, this is an intersubjective achievement; it takes place in observable interactions among people in the world.

The point is that for two or more people to collaborate on learning, they must display to each other enough that everyone can judge where there are agreements and disagreements, conflicts or misunderstandings, confusions and insights. In collaborating, people typically establish conventional dialogic patterns of proposing, questioning, augmenting, mutually completing, repairing, and confirming each other's expressions of knowledge. Knowledge here is not so much the ownership by individuals of mental representations in their heads as it is the ability to engage in appropriate displays within the social world. Thus, to learn is to become a skilled member of communities of practice (Lave & Wenger, 1991) and to become competent at using their resources (Suchman, 1987), artifacts (Norman, 1993), speech genres (Bakhtin, 1986b), and cultural practices (Bourdieu, 1995). The state of evolving knowledge must be continually displayed by the collaborating participants to each other. The stance of each participant to that shared and disputed knowledge must also be displayed.

This opens an important opportunity to researchers of collaborative learning that traditional educational studies lacked: what is visible to the participants may be visible to researchers as well. Assuming that the researchers can understand the participant displays, they can observe the building of knowledge as it takes place. They do not have to rely on statistical analyses of reified outcomes data and after-the-fact reconstructions (interviews, surveys, talk-alouds), which are notoriously suspect.

Timothy Koschmann (1999b) pointed out this potential, derived from the nature of dialogue as analyzed by Bakhtin, and also cited several studies outside of CSCL that adopted a discourse analytic approach to classroom interactions. According to Mikhail Bakhtin (1986b), a particular spoken or written utterance is meaningful in terms of its references back to preceding utterances and forward to anticipated responses of a projected audience. These situated sequences of utterances take advantage of conventional or colloquial "speech genres" that provide forms of expression that are clearly interpretable within a linguistic community. Explicit cross-references and implicit selections of genres mean that sequences of dialogic utterances display adoptions, modifications, and critiques of ideas under discussion, providing an intersubjectively accessible and interpretable record of collaborative knowledge building.

For collaborative learning processes to be visible to researchers, the participant interaction must be available for careful study, and the researchers must be capable of interpreting them appropriately. In CSCL contexts, learning may take place within software media that not only transmit utterances but also preserve them; the information preserved for participants may be supplemented with computer logging of user actions for the researchers. If communications cannot otherwise be captured, such as in face-to-face collaboration, they can be videotaped; the tapes can be digitized and manipulated to aid in detailed analysis. In either case, it may be possible for researchers to obtain an adequate record of the interaction that includes most of the information that was available to participants. In face-to-face interaction, this generally includes gesture, intonation, hesitation, turn-taking, overlapping, facial expression, bodily stance, as well as textual content. In computer-mediated collaboration, everyone is limited to text, temporal sequence, and other relationships among distinct utterances—but the number of relevant interrelated utterances may be much higher. To avoid being swamped with data that requires enormous amounts of time to analyze, researchers have to set up or focus on key interactions that span only a couple of minutes (see chapters 12 and 21).

The problem of researchers being capable of appropriately interpreting the interactions of participants is a subtle one, as anthropologists have long recognized (Geertz, 1973). A family of sciences has grown up recently to address this problem; these include conversation analysis (Sacks, 1992), ethnomethodology (Garfinkel, 1967; Heritage, 1984), video analysis (Heath, 1986), interaction analysis (Jordan & Henderson, 1995), and microethnography (Streeck, 1983). These sciences have made explicit many of the strategies that are tacitly used by participants to display their learning to each other. Researchers trained in these disciplines know where to look and how to interpret what is displayed. Researchers should also have an innate understanding of the culture they are observing. They should be competent members of the community or should be working with such members when doing their observation and analysis. For this reason, as well as to avoid idiosyncratic and biased interpretations, an important part of the analysis of interaction is usually conducted collaboratively. At some point, the interpretation may also be discussed with the actual participants. Collaboration is an intersubjective occurrence and its scientific study requires intersubjective confirmation rather than statistical correlations to ensure its acceptability.

Observing Computer-Supported Collaborative Learning

If collaborative learning is visible, then perhaps researchers have not observed and reported it because collaborative knowledge building is rare today. I have tried to use systems similar to CSILE in several classrooms and have failed to see them used for knowledge building (see chapter 6). Students sometimes use them to express their personal opinions and raise questions but rarely engage in the kind of ongoing dialogue that Donald (1991) saw as the basis for a theoretic culture or engage in the investigation of "conceptual artifacts" (such as theories) that Bereiter (2002) identifies as central to knowledge building. Of the five classrooms reviewed in the two papers featured here, probably only one of them, a Canadian classroom, advanced significantly beyond the level of chat to more in-depth knowledge building. The exchange of superficial opinions and questions is just the first stage in a complex set of activities that constitute collaborative knowledge building (see chapter 9). Even simple statistics on thread lengths in threaded discussion systems (Guzdial & Turns, 2000; Hewitt & Teplovs, 1999) indicate that communication does not usually continue long enough to get much beyond chatting. Hence, the reviewed papers are correct that the classroom culture and pedagogy are critical, but they do not go far enough.

It is probably important for researchers to set up special learning contexts in which students are guided to engage in collaborative knowledge building. Too much of this was left up to the teachers in the studies we have just reviewed, despite the fact that teachers in CSILE classrooms are trained to foster collaborative learning. Student activities must be carefully designed to require collaboration and to take advantage of computer support for it. For instance, in the Dutch university case, it sounds like the wrong tasks were made the focus of collaboration and computer support. Few notes were entered into the computer system during the long "knowledge-deepening phase" when students were reading. Perhaps through a different definition of tasks, the students would have used the system more while they were building their knowledge by collecting relevant ideas and facts in the computer as a repository for shared information. The final product—the educational policy note—could have been made into the motivating collaborative task that would have made the collection and analysis of all the issues surrounding this meaningful.

A success story about a researcher who set up a CSCL situation is related by Jeremy Roschelle (1996). He designed a series of tasks in physics for pairs of students to work on using a computer simulation of velocity and acceleration vectors. He videotaped their interactions at the computer and in subsequent interviews. Through word-by-word analysis of their interactions, Roschelle was able to observe and interpret their collaboration and to demonstrate the degrees to which they had or had not learned about the physics of motion. He did the equivalent of looking seriously at the actual content of the thread of notes between Elske and her fellow students in the Netherlands. Through his microanalysis, he made the learning visible.

Roschelle analyzed face-to-face communication, and this is in some ways a richer experience than computer-mediated interaction using software such as CSILE. But conversation analysis was originally studied in the context of telephone interactions (Schegloff & Sacks, 1973), so it is possible to interpret interactions where bodily displays are excluded. Computer-mediated collaboration will turn out to look quite different from face-to-face interaction, but we should still be able to observe learning and knowledge building taking place by working out the ways in which people make and share meaning across the network. By making visible in our analysis what is already visible to the participants, we can rediscover the collaborative learning and the effects of computer support in CSCL contexts.

11

Contributions to a Theory of Collaboration

This chapter opens with my *introduction* to the proceedings of the CSCL 2002 conference held in Boulder, Colorado, in January 2002.[1] This introduction was intended to set a tone for the conference's emphasis on theories of collaboration. The remainder of this chapter formed my paper for that conference. It argues that looking at computer support for collaborative learning in terms of collaborative knowledge building, group and personal perspectives, mediation by artifacts, and microanalysis of conversation provides a rich, multidimensional starting point for conceptualizing and studying CSCL. Each of these ideas occupies an important place in CSCL research. The notion of collaborative knowledge building defines a useful paradigm for conceptualizing learning as social practice. The social interactions and knowledge-management activities in which shared knowledge is constructed can be analyzed as the result of interweaving group and personal conversational perspectives. In general, collaborative interaction is mediated by artifacts: sometimes only by transitory artifacts like spoken words or gestures but increasingly by physical or digital artifacts and media. Empirical studies of collaborative knowledge building employing microethnographic analysis of speech, gesture, artifacts, and media can make the details of these collaborative interactions visible, highlighting the interplay of perspectives and artifacts in the transpersonal construction of knowledge. An empirical methodology can overcome the reductionism that was criticized in the previous chapter, as is illustrated in the remaining chapters of part II.

A theoretical framework incorporating models of knowledge building, perspectives, and artifacts—and grounded in an empirical analysis of collaborative interaction—can guide the design of computer-based artifacts and media as a support for collaborative learning with appropriate, elaborated, and unified conceptualizations. This is expanded on in part III.

Foundations for a CSCL Community

A New Era of Learning

Learning takes place in communities and is facilitated by artifacts, which in turn sustain the communities that generate them. Several computer-supported collaborative learning (CSCL) conferences—archived in proceedings artifacts—have been foundational events for a growing CSCL community that has an important role to play in a rapidly and painfully self-transforming global culture.

The CSCL community addresses complex and urgent social issues associated with learning in the information era. Despite its healthy growth curve, this research community is still searching for its foundations. To date, there is little consensus on theory, pedagogy, technology, or methodology—and even less in the broader world of learning stakeholders.

Learning has become a central force of production. Traditional theories and institutions that rose to meet the needs of reproducing knowledge in an industrial world have become fetters on progress: the focus on individual learners obscures the group as the locus of knowledge building and ignores the global interdependence of learning. Fixation on facts distorts the nature of problem-solving inquiry. Modes of thought deriving from the age of rationality and machinery fail to grasp the subtlety of interaction in hypernetworked environments.

CSCL instinctively aims beyond yesterday's concepts. *Collaborative learning* does not just mean that individual learning is enhanced by participation in small groups. It means that the groups themselves learn. Knowledge is a product of the collaboration process: it arises through interaction of different perspectives, heats up in the cauldron of public discourse, is gradually refined through negotiation, and is codified and preserved in cultural or scientific artifacts. Knowledge is not static and otherworldly: it lives, situated—both locally and historically—in groups, teams, organizations, tribes, social networks, and cultural flash points.

Computer support does not just mean automating the delivery and testing of facts. It means supporting forms of collaboration and knowledge building that cannot take place without networked communication media and software tools for developing group understandings. Computers can manage the complexity of many-to-many discussions, allowing multiple perspectives to interact without hierarchical structuring. They can overcome the limitations of human short-term memories and of paper-based aids to generating or sharing drafts of documents. CSCL should enable more powerful group cognition, which can synthesize complex interactions of ideas at different scales of collaboration, from small classroom project teams to global open-source efforts.

A New Paradigm of Learning Research

The keynote talks for CSCL 2002 proposed a new paradigm for a distinctive form of educational research. Timothy Koschmann focused on the micro-level practices that need to be studied, while Yrjö Engeström considered the larger social contexts in which groups interact with other groups to produce learning. Koschmann offers this definition for the CSCL domain:

CSCL is a field of study centrally concerned with meaning and the practices of meaning making in the context of joint activity, and the ways in which these practices are mediated through designed artifacts. (Koschmann, 2002a, p. 17)

For Koschmann, meaning and the practices of meaning making are public, observable, socially shared phenomena, which has foundational implications for CSCL research. Quantitative studies of learning outcomes under controlled conditions may provide important information and ensure empirical grounding, but they can never provide the complete story. CSCL is a human science, concerned with its subjects' own interpretations of their ideas and behaviors. Therefore, CSCL also requires qualitative studies of learning practices—such as thick descriptions that incorporate and explore the understanding of the participants in collaborative learning. As public phenomena, the meanings (learning) generated in collaboration processes can be studied directly, particularly with the help of computer logs and digitized video recordings, rather than just being inferred from posttests.

As already suggested, the description of collaborative learning as meaning making in the context of joint activity does not so much entail looking at *individuals'* practices in social settings as it focuses on the essentially *social* practices of joint meaning making. Even when conducted by an individual in isolation, meaning making is a social act that is based on culturally defined linguistic artifacts and oriented toward a potential public audience. An adequate theoretical foundation for CSCL must explain how individual practices are social without forgetting that the social is grounded in individual activities; concepts of *praxis*, *activity*, *social reproduction*, *structuration*, and *enactment* begin to address this dialectic.

For Koschmann, CSCL includes the study of how meaning-making practices are mediated through artifacts. He sees CSCL technology as a mediational artifact—as software objects designed to support collaborative learning. But this formulation can be taken more generally as raising the question of how meaning making is mediated by all kinds of artifacts—not just by CSCL tools. This is an extraordinarily broad issue, as all human activity is meaning making, and everything in our physical, intellectual, and cultural worlds can be considered an artifact: physical tools, linguistic symbols, cultural entities, cognitive mechanisms, social rules. It is striking that such a fundamental issue has been so little explored. How do different classes of artifacts mediate the creation, sharing, teaching, and preserving of meaning? A clearer understanding of the functioning of nondigital artifacts might help us understand how to design software to more effectively foster and convey collaborative meaning making.

A New CSCL Community

The new era of learning and the new research paradigm call for a community that can integrate results from philosophy, social theory, ethnography, experimentation, and pedagogy. More than this, it must be able to carry out research that integrates the foundations of these disciplines into a coherent and productive field of inquiry. As its conceptual framework and software products mature, the CSCL community must broaden to incorporate educational practitioners, teachers, trainers, lifelong learners, and students around the world. The CSCL 2002 conference aimed to incrementally build the foundations for such a CSCL community.

Four Contributions

I would like to introduce four themes that I have come to be convinced are important for thinking about computer support for collaborative learning:

- Collaborative knowledge building,
- Group and personal perspectives,
- Mediation by artifacts, and
- Interaction analysis.

These themes have been developed in distinct academic literatures—education, psychology, activity theory and conversation analysis, respectively—but I believe they should be brought together for the kind of theoretical and methodological framework required by the complex interdisciplinary field of CSCL.

I present these four themes in terms of hypotheses—or claims—that would have to be investigated further in the future by a theory of collaboration:

- The term *knowledge building* is more concrete and descriptive than *learning* when we are interested in collaboration. It may also help to avoid the baggage of individualistic epistemology in favor of a social practice view.

- Collaborative knowledge building is structured by the intertwining of group and personal perspectives. The role of individual minds should be neither ignored nor fixated on but instead seen in interaction with group understandings.

- The construction of knowledge proceeds on the basis of artifacts already at hand—including linguistic, cognitive, cultural, physical, and digital artifacts—

and creates new artifacts to formulate, embody, preserve, and communicate new knowledge.

- Naturally occurring and carefully captured examples of collaborative knowledge building—such as video recordings of classroom interactions—can be rigorously analyzed to make visible the knowledge-building activities at work, the intertwining of perspectives, and the mediating role of artifacts.

To some extent, these four themes each fly in the face of conventional pedagogical wisdom—oriented toward mental contents of individual students—although they all have their respected advocates as well. Within the limited confines of this chapter, I cannot defend them against all contenders while also demonstrating their relevance and importance to CSCL. I try to explain how they could help to clarify the domain of CSCL.

It should be noted at the outset that these are not intended as four independent theoretical claims but contribute, in a tightly interwoven way, to a single framework or paradigm for thinking about CSCL. Collaborative knowledge building moves away from approaches to learning focused on individual minds in two ways: by focusing on group activities, which necessarily include roles for individuals within the groups, and by noting the importance of artifacts in the world, such as spoken, written, or published texts that capture newly constructed knowledge. The evidence for these views can be found primarily in the kinds of microethnographic studies of learning interactions that have recently become possible with methods of conversation analysis using video. Conversely, when applied to CSCL, such interaction analysis should be guided by an interest in knowledge-building activities, an awareness of contrasting perspectives, and a focus on artifacts—without such guidance detracting from the intersubjective rigor of the analytic methodology. So the four themes shed light on one another and together represent an integral contribution to theory.

One final point should, perhaps, be mentioned up front rather than tacked onto the end as if in apology. That is that the view of CSCL projected here is a visionary one. Collaborative knowledge building may be a way of life on the leading edge of scientific research, but it has proven devilishly hard to foster in contemporary school classrooms. The idea that new technologies will transform learning practices has not yet led to the collaborative ideal. The task of designing effective computer support along with appropriate pedagogy and social practices is simply much more complex than was imagined. An explicit, elaborated, adopted, and actualized theoretical framework is needed to clarify the nature of collaborative knowledge building as a desired goal, indicate how people can participate in it with concrete curricular approaches, design tools to support it effectively in various contexts, and develop methods for observing and assessing it in practice.

Let us look a bit closer at each of the four proposed contributions to CSCL theory.

Collaborative Knowledge Building
There are two troubling problems with the term *learning* for the development of a theoretical framework for CSCL:

• Learning is everywhere. Whenever someone engages in conscious activity, learning takes place. In fact, even nonconscious activity can reinforce tacit competencies.

• Learning is never seen. Only the consequences of learning can be observed, and they generally turn out to be statistically insignificant (Russell, 1999). This approach to evaluating learning is a holdover from behaviorist measurement of changes due to operant conditioning (drill and practice).

In contrast, the notion of collaborative knowledge building seems more tangible:

• It cannot simply be applied everywhere but refers to specific, identifiable occurrences. Cases in which new knowledge is actually constructed by groups—rather than reified facts being recycled—are actually relatively rare in classrooms.

• With care and practice, one can directly and empirically observe the knowledge being built because it necessarily takes place in observable media, like talking. Moreover, it produces knowledge objects or artifacts, which provide lasting evidence and a basis for evaluating the knowledge building.

The term *knowledge building* is attributable to Marlene Scardamalia and Carl Bereiter (1991), who have long advocated the restructuring of classrooms into knowledge-building communities and who have spearheaded the development and testing of computer support for such communities (Scardamalia & Bereiter, 1996).

Their concept borrows explicitly from dominant forms of research in today's scientific communities, where theories are progressively developed through professional discourse and inscription (Latour & Woolgar, 1979)—involving, for instance, peer review and critique of papers published in journals. Here, a scientific community learns about its subject matter by collaboratively building knowledge in the form of documents that gradually define a path of inquiry and successively elaborate theory while also raising issues for future deeper investigation. Conflicting theoretical perspectives are essential to the process, as are the roles of specific participants. Discourse activities—such as questioning, proposing, arguing, critiquing, clarifying, negotiating, accusing, repairing, agreeing—are as important as the artifacts around which, through which, and into which the discourse moves.

Not all important learning is collaborative knowledge building. Bereiter (2002) defines the latter in terms of the development of knowledge objects such as scientific concepts and theories. This does not include the learning of passed-down facts, of practical or social skills, or of techniques of learning itself. However, social discourse about ideas—the core of knowledge building—can certainly motivate and exercise skills like reading, writing, and thinking.

The thrust of collaborative knowledge building is to emphasize the construction and further development of a knowledge object that is shared by the group or learning community. The focus is not on personal learning by the participants, who, it is assumed, retain some of what the group discovered, deepen their collaboration skills, and enjoy positive experiences of inquiry and intellectual engagement.[2]

Many models of curriculum design are compatible with collaborative knowledge building, and the elaboration of appropriate pedagogical practices remains an important area of active research. Progressive inquiry, for instance, dates back to analyses of problem solving by John Dewey and Charles Sanders Pierce. This has led us to an interrogative model of inquiry (Hakkarainen & Sintonen, 2001) based on an analysis of types of questioning according to the philosophy of science (for example, Popper, Kuhn, Lakatos). A systematic approach to having groups of students pursue the posing and investigation of knowledge-building questions is offered by problem-based learning (PBL) (Barrows, 1994). This approach tries to cover the breadth of a domain (such as medical education)—in addition to the depth gained through explorative inquiry—by providing a carefully designed set of cases as problems to be pursued consecutively.

PBL is a form of the case-based method (Collins & Stevens, 1983) but requires students to become self-reliant investigators, with the teacher or tutor facilitating the small-group process. More generally, PBL is a specific approach to project-based learning (Blumenfeld et al., 1991), in which a group of students conducts a project. A potential issue with project-based activities that do not adhere to a model like PBL is that tasks often get divided up so that participants cooperate (as opposed to collaborate) on the overall project but do not collaborate on the knowledge building. They may subsequently share their individual expertise through jig-sawing (Brown & Campione, 1994), but the basic knowledge building takes place outside the group interaction.

For a theory of CSCL, we may want to focus on pedagogical approaches—like PBL—that center on group discussion as the core activity in inquiry. This discussion may take place verbally in face-to-face meetings. However, for the sake of providing computer support (such as searching capabilities or customizable displays) and maintaining persistence of the discourse for subsequent review and reflection, significant parts of the discussions should be captured textually on the computer network—as typed minutes, chat streams, or discussion threads.

Because collaborative knowledge building necessarily involves the use in discourse of concepts whose meaning is continually changing and growing, a trained observer can (given the time and tools) observe how knowledge was built up step by step.

Evidence exists in the interpretation of words, gestures, and documents used. Because the knowledge was built by more than one participant, the changing understandings of the participants had to be shared with one another and may therefore be available to an outside observer as well. Roschelle (1996), for example, has provided an exemplary demonstration of this for a pair of collaborating high school physics students.

The characteristics of collaborative knowledge building just reviewed—that it is typical in modern science, is rarely achieved in classrooms, can effectively motivate other forms of learning, and can be observed in practice—suggest that it might provide a useful pedagogical focus for CSCL. Of course, the main attraction of the notion of collaborative knowledge building is the hope that computer support can significantly increase the ability of groups of people to build concepts, ideas, theories, and understandings together.

Group and Personal Perspectives

After more than 2,500 years of knowledge-building discourse about the nature of ideas and the meaning of meaning—dating back at least to the forum of Athens— we still find the concept of knowledge to be paradoxical and bewildering. However, two things seem clear:

• Wherever meaningful symbols, representations, and artifacts may be found, they are meaningful only for individual minds. Interpretation is necessary, and that is necessarily carried out by individuals within the horizons of their personal perspectives (Gadamer, 1988).

• Isolated from social interaction, physical artifacts, and historical cultures, human brains are poor thinkers and could never have developed into powerful minds (Donald, 1991; Hutchins, 1996; Norman, 1993). In fact, it can be argued that modern minds are simply collections of cognitive artifacts internalized from interpersonal interactions (Vygotsky, 1978). The mental is primordially a social or group phenomenon.

This means that anything like a theory of knowledge building must pay due regard and respect to essential roles of both collaborative groups and their individual members.

The social basis of knowledge is deeply rooted. It is not just a matter of artifacts in the world extending the limited short-term memory of individual minds, like notes scattered about as external memory traces (Donald, 1991; Hutchins, 1996; Norman, 1993). Meaning arises in the historically given, social world. We are, from the start, situated in the shared, meaningful world into which we are born and with which we are engaged (Heidegger, 1996). From the infant's first inkling of intentionality in the mother's gesture (Vygotsky, 1978), to the moment of mutual human recognition (Hegel, 1967; Mead, 1962), to the world-transforming paradigm shifts of expansive learning (Engeström, 1999), meaning springs from interpersonal interaction.[3]

The dilemma between personal and group perspectives plays itself out on the theoretical plane as a dialectic of hermeneutic and social-cultural approaches. Hermeneutics, as the philosophy of interpretation, is concerned with such matters as how one can interpret the text of a distant author here and now. Martin Heidegger's foundational analysis of human existence as an interpretive enterprise carried out on the basis of tacit, situated preunderstanding (Heidegger, 1996) appears at first sight to give priority to the individual as grantor of meaning. However, a closer reading shows that the individual is always essentially engaged in a shared world and that the network of meanings that define the individual's situation are historically, culturally, and socially defined. Thus, in his influential explication of Heideggerian hermeneutic philosophy, Gadamer (1988) argues that the possibility of understanding a text of distant origins depends on the author and interpreter sharing an historical horizon—one that includes the actual historical reception of the text itself.

The analysis that Gadamer applies to communication across the centuries is relevant to face-to-face conversation as well. Ethnomethodology (Garfinkel, 1967) stresses that the meaning of a communicative context is established interactively and is achieved by the participants creating a social order on the fly. That is, the meaning of individual utterances is not given by some preconceived ideas represented in the speaker's mind or from her personal perspective, which are then expressed and conveyed in verbal symbols. Rather, the meaning of the utterances is negotiated by the speaking and responding parties; it exists only in the group perspective that is formed by the intertwining of personal perspectives in the communicative interaction itself. The meaning of a specific utterance may be defined and affected by subsequent utterances, responses, gestures, pauses, repairs, and so on (Sacks, 1992). That is, the meaning of statements made by individuals is constructed or achieved in the discourse of the group and forms the interpretive horizon in which knowledge is shared during the moment of interaction—regardless of whether we choose to attribute individual learning to the participants in the long run.

Discourse is the traditional medium of knowledge building. New ideas—and their interpretation by speakers and hearers—arise in the discourse in ways that transcend any individual's role. Clearly, each word in the discourse can trivially be attributed to an individual speaker. However, the meaning of that word is defined by its position in the discourse context—that is, by its relationship to many other words (by other individuals as well as by the word's speaker) and to the Gestalt meaning of the discourse as a whole, which is the group's.

In Roschelle's (1996) analysis of the physics students, for instance, their collaborative knowledge building coalesced in the phrase, "It pulls it." Roschelle was able to show that the students understood this to mean that the fat arrow (representing acceleration in their computer simulation) caused a specific kind of change to the other arrow (representing velocity). Within the context of their computer model of Newtonian mechanics, this change had a predictable effect on the movement of a particle—and the students understood this. The statement "It pulls it" is an elliptical, indexical statement that has little meaning on its own as an isolated sentence. In the context in which the students were collaborating, however, it amounted to the discovery of the physics principle that acceleration is "the derivative of velocity with respect to time." This latter way of stating it would not have made sense to these students but has meaning only within the context of Newton's theories of motion and calculus. The students' statement made sense to them in terms of the components in their computer simulation, their experience with the simulation, their previous discussion, and their general world-knowledge of pulling.

When I analyzed a discourse among five middle-school students and a teacher (see chapter 12), I was at first mystified by the cryptic interchanges in the transcript of a particularly intense and consequent collaborative moment. Within a matter of 30 seconds, the students exchanged 24 turns at speech, mostly consisting of sentence fragments or single words indicating disagreement or assent. It was clear that the students were intently engaged and shared a common understanding of what was taking place in the discourse: the resolution of a knotty problem for their collaborative inquiry and the achievement of a hard-fought consensus. But my retrospective interpretation of the transcript—which I developed in collaboration with experienced conversation analysts and others—required a careful reconstruction of the argumentation back several minutes as well as an understanding of the details of artifacts active in the knowledge-building context. The meaning of a given utterance was not a simple function of the words used, the prepositional content, the isolated speech act, or even a conversational pair of utterances. Meaning was a shared, collaborative, interactive achievement. It was an ephemeral, rapidly evolving group perspective.

In this analysis, I was also able to track the personal perspective and personality of each participant. The flow of discussion as well as the specific conversational moves derived from the individuals in some sense as well. With different participants contributing from different personal perspectives, the discourse would have been completely different. And yet, the actual knowledge building that took place had "a mind of its own." The group perspective, which unfolded and prevailed, probably had more to do with the conceptual issues that were brought to the fore by the curriculum and the artifacts that formed the shared context and posed the problems to be discussed than with the preexisting ideas, intellectual orientations, or personal values of the individual participants. So while personal perspectives certainly contributed to the discourse and left observable traces there, the interaction achieved a group perspective that determined the meaning of individual contributions and within which knowledge was collaboratively built and comprehended.

Mediation by Artifacts

Knowledge building is mediated by artifacts. The interaction and interweaving of personal and group perspectives is mediated by artifacts. What does this mean? What is mediation, and what are artifacts?

Mediation means that something happens by means of, or through the involvement of, a mediating object. For instance, when a student uses a technical term to construct knowledge or when a class of students uses a software collaboration system to discuss a theme, that term or that system is mediating the activity: it is providing a medium or middle ground through which the students interact with their ideas. The specific form of the mediation generally affects the nature of the activity profoundly, often determining the nature of the task itself; that is, the choice of medium can define the ends or goal as well as the possible means. In Roschelle's example, the metaphor of "pulling" mediated the students' knowledge building and allowed them to formulate a theory, to share their understanding of how the simulation worked, to bring their bodily skills to bear, and to solve some, but not all, of the challenges posed by the teacher.

An artifact is a meaningful object created by people for specific uses. The term *pull*—as elaborated metaphorically by the students and as operationalized by them in manipulating the computer simulation of accelerating forces—functioned as a knowledge-building artifact on several levels. It was a preunderstood concept that they could build on, it provided a tool that they could use for collaborative thinking about the simulated phenomena, and it resulted in a knowledge object that incorporated their new shared understanding.

The concept of artifacts is perhaps most familiar in anthropology, where it refers to discovered objects that were made by ancient people and that still display traces of their intended function or symbolic import. Georg Friedrich Hegel (1967) spoke of artifacts as objects on which meaningful form had been imposed, and he situated the primordial act of artifact creation in the interpersonal interaction in which people recognize each other and themselves as self-conscious actors. Karl Marx (1967a, 1976) took the analysis of artifacts another step to argue that their character was largely determined by prevailing socioeconomic relations so that in our age most artifacts are produced as commodities for monetary exchange. For Hegel, artifacts retain the externalized subjectivity in physical form, and for Marx they retain both concrete human labor that went into producing them and the abstract value of the labor time they required.

These classic analyses of mediation and artifacts are relevant to a contemporary CSCL theory. While theory is now a transdisciplinary undertaking drawing on multiple traditions in the social, human, and natural sciences, the concepts of mediation and artifact can be traced back to the philosophy of Hegel, whose dialectical analyses revealed the mediated and historical dynamic everywhere. Marx critiqued idealist and subjectivist aspects of Hegel's thought and grounded the mediations in concrete analyses of historically specific social relationships. Contemporary theories prevalent in CSCL can be traced back to their roots in Hegel and Marx or later developments based on Vygotsky (activity theory), Heidegger (situated theory), or Dewey (inquiry theory).

Lev Vygotsky (1978, 1986) wanted to supplement Marx's social theory with a psychology of mediated cognition (a perspective on the individual as intertwined with the group perspective). He extended the notion of physical artifact (tool) to encompass linguistic artifacts (symbols) as well. The individual's activity was then seen to be mediated by both varieties of artifact. The human ability to use physical and linguistic artifacts is a cultural development that allowed mankind to evolve beyond its biological basis.

Vygotsky argued—on the basis of empirical psychology experiments—that the meaning of artifacts and our understanding of that meaning are first created in interpersonal contexts, such as mother and child or teacher and student, and subsequently may be internalized in an individual mind. The discussion of learning in a student's *zone of proximal development*, scaffolded by a teacher, is based on this. We can call the internalized result of this process a *cognitive artifact*. For instance, a workgroup might develop a list of tasks or a diagram of a workflow on a white board, and a member of the group might then internalize and later mentally recall that list or diagram to monitor future work. The internal mental representation is then a cognitive artifact that resulted from group knowledge building and that may mediate subsequent knowledge building by the individual or the group. In this analysis, the mental representation is a result of collaborative activities and did not first arise subjectively to then be expressed externally. (The deconstruction of artifacts often shows that things develop in the opposite order from how they now appear. That is characteristic of the reification of meaning in an artifact.)

A complete development of Vygotsky's approach could portray the human mind as nothing but a growing set of cognitive artifacts, internalized by each of us in our personal development from our interactions with those around us and our embeddedness in our cultural world. Vygotsky and others who investigate infant development have suggested how even the most basic senses of intentionality, meaning, and intersubjectivity may arise in interpersonal interaction—as sketched by Hegel theoretically. The folk theories of mind—roundly criticized by Bereiter (2002), Daniel Dennett (1991), and others—can be viewed as metaphors (mind as a container of ideas, a theater of experiences, a homunculus mind within the mind), which may once have served an important purpose but have now outlived their usefulness. Marvin Minsky (1986), for instance, has proposed an alternative "society of mind" metaphor to capture the computational structure of the mind as a decentralized set of cognitive artifacts.

If we adopt a Vygotskian view of mediation by artifacts, then the knowledge-building process can be conceptualized as the construction of knowledge artifacts, involving physical and symbolic artifacts as starting point, as medium, and as product. The process proceeds collaboratively and intersubjectively, within a sociocultural context. The final knowledge artifact may be internalized by one or more of the participants. While the internalized learning outcomes may be problematic to assess, the shared understanding within the collaborative knowledge building is experienced by the participants and may be subject to reconstruction from traces left in various artifacts, including video recordings and their transcripts.

The task of education in this approach is to revive meanings that have been captured and preserved in artifacts. This is the problem of cultural transmission. Culture can be conceptualized as a body of cognitive and other artifacts. In literate society, for instance, culture includes systems of numbers and written language. Schooling is largely the attempt to help young students to internalize the vast repertoire of meaning that has been associated with these artifacts. Although it is often possible for individuals who have mastered certain skills (cognitive artifacts) to develop related knowledge artifacts on their own, it is at other times useful to recreate the intersubjective conditions of knowledge creation in carefully structured contexts of collaboration with well-designed mediational artifacts to scaffold further learning. Within CSCL efforts, this would mean designing software to support the right kinds of interpersonal interaction, of mediation by artifacts, and of knowledge artifact construction.

One does not have to accept Vygotsky's whole approach, as sketched out here, to recognize the importance of an analysis of mediation and of artifacts for a theoretical framework for CSCL. Perhaps the most urgent undertaking at this time is further empirical investigation of how artifacts and their understanding actually function in concrete instances of collaborative knowledge building. For this, we need a methodology of interaction analysis.

Interaction Analysis

Roschelle presented his analysis of two students working with a physics microworld simulation as an instance of student learning as conceptual change, facilitated by collaborative use of a computer artifact (Roschelle, 1996). One could reconceptualize his analysis as an attempt by the students to rediscover the meaning or affordances that were designed into the software artifact as a model of physics. The term *pull*, which they interpreted and developed in this connection, was a linguistic artifact that they collaboratively constructed as a knowledge object and internalized as an expression of their learning. Roschelle used conversation analysis of video tapes as well as interviews of the students to conduct his study of the collaborative knowledge building and the internalized conceptual change.

The question of how people rediscover meaning in artifacts is an important and difficult problem. When artifacts are created, their meaning is shared and relatively accessible. The artifact functions to capture, formulate, and encapsulate that meaning. But the meaning does not remain simply available on the surface of the artifact. As a note in the discussion database from my seminar on artifacts put it:

Thoughts on meaning in artifacts by Bob Craig on Dec. 12, 2000: Do artifacts "embody meaning," or do they embody meaningful traces of human activity? . . . Meaning is not "in" the artifact; rather, it is "in" the total situation that includes artifacts, minds, and social practices.

The meaningful traces transform, reify, distort, and hide the meanings that originally existed in the live human interactions. New minds who encounter the artifacts must recreate the appropriate social practices, reconstruct the cultural contexts, and rediscover the meaning within their own personal and group perspectives.

To investigate how people disclose the meaning of artifacts that they do not understand, I undertook an analysis of how five middle-school students (referred to above) struggled to uncover the structures designed into a rocket simulation (see chapters 12 and 13). I started by trying to follow the students' knowledge-building discussion in a transcript of their discourse. But the most interesting and intense collaborative discussion was particularly hard to interpret. The student utterances did not assume the explicit form of scientific propositions of articulate arguments, nor could the conversational turns be coded as coherent speech acts (Searle, 1969).

Here is the transcript of the pivotal moment of the three-hour long project with the rocket simulation:

1:22:05	Brent	This one's different
:06	Jamie	Yeah, but it has same no . . .
:07		(1.0 second pause)
:08	Chuck	. . . Pointy nose cone
:09	Steven	Oh, yeah
:10	Chuck	But it's not the same engine
:11	Jamie	Yeah it is . . .

:12	Brent	. . . Yes it is
:13	Jamie	⌈ Compare two 'n' one
:13	Brent	⌊ Number two
:14	Chuck	I know
:15	Jamie	Are the same
:16	Chuck	Oh

These one-second utterances make little sense on their own. They are elliptical and indexical—like Rochelle's "It pulls it." By "elliptical" I mean that these are primarily sentence fragments that may complete or be completed by another student's utterance but do not stand on their own. They are fragments of a discussion that is meaningful only at the group level. By "indexical" or "deictic" I mean that they point to or intend something without explicitly stating their referent ("it," "this one"). They index important elements of the shared situation that it would be redundant or superfluous to name. Where words and phrases are repeated, the repetitions play important roles of indicating agreement and shared understanding, which is also signified by the way utterances tend to complete each other.

To understand what took place in these 10 seconds, one must reconstruct the argument that reaches its climax here but that was set up in the previous 10 minutes. (A theoretical foundation for this is given by Bakhtin, 1986b, who argues that an utterance is meaningful only in terms of its references back to preceding utterances to which it responds and forward to anticipated responses of a projected audience, and by Heidegger, 1996, who situates meanings within the extended dimensions of human temporality.) One must also understand the task of the three-hour project and analyze the affordances of the software artifacts that the students are working with. (Activity theory, as formulated by Yrjö Engeström, 1999, proposes general structures of the broader effective context, including societal dimensions as well as the goals and tools of group activities.) In addition, it is necessary to observe closely the bodily orientations, gaze, and gestures of the students.

In figure 11.1, Brent (circled) thrusts his body forward and shifts the group's focus to a rocket description on the monitor, about which he says, "This one's different." The ensuing discussion debates what is the same and what is different about this rocket. The rocket to which "this one" is compared actually shifts here ("compare two 'n' one"), and that shift enlightens Chuck, who has resisted the teacher and the peer group and has long tried to promote his personal perspective. Now, his "Oh" acknowledges a newfound acceptance of the group perspective.

A detailed analysis of this transcript would make visible the knowledge-building process that took place, in which the students displayed for each other verbally and

Figure 11.1
Students discuss a computer simulation artifact. Left to right: teacher, Jamie, Chuck, Brent, Steven, Kelly.

nonverbally their shifting understandings and interactively achieved the creation of shared meaning. This meaning was partially encapsulated in terms like "same" and "different," which took on specific functions in their collaboration (see chapter 13).

More generally, the elements of this kind of interaction analysis have been developed on a rigorous methodological basis by the theory of ethnomethodology (Garfinkel, 1967) and the science of conversation analysis (CA) (Sacks, 1992). With the availability of digital video to capture, manipulate, and facilitate detailed analysis of naturally occurring interpersonal interaction, the CA approach has been combined with the study of gesture, gaze, and bodily orientation into techniques for interpreting detailed behavior (known as microethnography) (LeBaron & Streeck, 2000; Streeck, 1983). Most communication analysis in this tradition has studied pairs or small groups in face-to-face situations without technological mediation, although studies of telephone conversations played a major role in the early years of CA (Hopper, 1992; Sacks, 1992). However, the foregoing observations on the rocket simulation discourse suggest that such methods can be applied to CSCL situations as well—with appropriate adaptation. If this is done, attention must be paid to the central mediational role of digital as well as linguistic artifacts. Also, in cases of collaborative knowledge building, the unit of analysis for meanings should take into account the intertwining of personal and group perspectives by interpreting individual utterances as elements of the larger discourse and activity.

CSCL Foundations and Applications

A theory for CSCL should help us to think about collaborative learning, to structure pedagogy, to design software media, and to study actual occurrences of knowledge building inside and outside of classrooms. I think the four foundational themes discussed here start to address these needs. The notion of knowledge building focuses us on activities associated with knowledge management and the further development of theories. A concern with the intertwining of personal and group perspectives suggests curricular approaches and classroom practices that integrate individual and team efforts. The analysis of artifacts conceptualizes the roles of CSCL systems and their databases as mediators and preservers within processes of creating knowledge objects. Finally, interaction analysis allows one to view and assess the knowledge-building activities, the intertwining of perspectives, and the mediation by artifacts.

The perceived need of these four theoretical contributions arose while I was designing and deploying a CSCL software system named WebGuide (see chapter 6). This system prototyped knowledge creation and knowledge-management functions that extended a conventional discussion forum. WebGuide investigated methods for intertwining notes in personal and group perspectives, which provided interlinked organizations of shared ideas. The effort to reflect on the nature of the WebGuide software I was designing led me to a view of it as a mediating artifact. Rather than trying to analyze the complex interactions of a class using WebGuide, I started by looking at how students learned about a simpler digital artifact, SimRocket (Stahl & Sanusi, 2001)—and that led me to a growing fascination with conversation analysis and microethnography. I believe that the theoretical framework that emerged from my work on WebGuide will prove valuable in designing and deploying the next system I will be working on, BSCL (see chapter 7). Perhaps it can help others as well.

12

In a Moment of Collaboration

The interpretive analysis in this chapter looks closely at an excerpt of a videotape I had made several years earlier when working on the Essence (see chapter 2) system in a middle-school classroom.[1] With the help of trained communication analysts, I conducted the kind of analysis called for in the preceding two chapters and found clear evidence of group cognition. Through a detailed conversation analysis of a half-minute of collaborative interaction, I examine the complexity of communication that takes place among five middle-school students working with SimRocket, a rocket simulation software artifact. In particular, confusion about references to comparable rockets is repaired through a rapid sequence of elliptical utterances, which convey meaning only through the indexing of their interaction context. A group understanding emerges that exceeds the prior understanding of the individual participants and that allows them to derive scientific conclusions together.

Analyzing Collaborative Learning

Quantitative studies of collaboration are indispensable for uncovering, exploring, and documenting communication structures, but they cannot tell the whole story. Although measures of utterances and their sequences—such as frequency graphs of notes and thread lengths in discussion forums—do study the processes in which collaborative learning is constructed and displayed, they sacrifice the meaningful content of the discussion in favor of its objective form (see chapter 10). This reifies and reduces the complex interactions to one or two of their simplest dimensions and eliminates most of the evidence for the studied structural relationships among the utterances. For instance, the content might indicate that two formally distinct threads are actually closely related in terms of their ideas, actors, or approach. Coding utterances along these characteristics can help in a limited way but is still reductive of the richness of the data. Similarly, social-network analysis (Scott, 1991; Wasserman & Faust, 1992) can indicate who is talking to whom and who is interacting in a central or a peripheral way within a network of subgroups, but it also necessarily ignores much of the available data—namely, the meaningful content—that may be relevant to the very issues that the analysis explores. We look at a set of utterances that would be impossible to code or to analyze statistically. The structural roles of the individual utterances and even the way they create subgroup allegiances become clear only after considerable interpretive effort.

The other way in which both traditional experimental method and narrow discourse analysis tend to underestimate their subject matter is to exclude consideration of the social and material context. Some approaches methodically remove such factors by conducting controlled experiments in the laboratory (as though this were not in itself a social setting) or basing their findings strictly on a delimited verbal transcript. Fortunately, countervailing trends are emphasizing the importance of *in situ* studies and the roles of physical factors, including both participant bodily gestures and mediating artifacts. Increasingly, the field is recognizing the importance of looking at knowledge distributed among people and artifacts, of studying the group or social unit of analysis, and of taking into account historical and cultural influences. In our data, it is impossible to separate the words from the artifact that they reference and interpret: We will show that artifacts are just as much in need of interpretation (by the participants and by the researchers) as are the utterances, which cannot be understood in isolation from physical and verbal artifacts.

The study of collaborative learning must be a highly interdisciplinary business. It involves issues of pedagogy, software design, technical implementation, cognitive theories, social theories, experimental method, working with teachers and students, and the practicalities of recording and analyzing classroom data. Methodologically, it at least needs its own unique intertwining of quantitative and qualitative methods. For instance, the results of a thread-frequency study or a social-network analysis might suggest a mini-analysis of the discourse during a certain interaction or among certain actors. Interpretive themes from this might in turn call for a controlled experiment with statistical analysis to explore alternative causal explanations or generalizations. In this chapter, we attempt to uncover, in empirical data, the sort of meaning relationships that other methods ignore but that might enrich their analysis.

What's in a Sentence Fragment?

We naively assume that to say something is to express a complete thought. However, if we look closely at what passes for normal speech, we see that what is said is never the complete thing. Conversation analysts are well aware of this and carefully transcribe what is said, not forcing it into whole sentences that look like written language. The transcript analyzed in this chapter is striking in that most of the utterances (or conversational turns) consist of only one to four words.

Utterances are radically situated. In our analysis, we characterize spoken utterances as indexical, elliptical, and projective. They rely for their meaning on the context in which they are said because they make implicit reference to elements of the present situation. We refer to this as *indexicality*. In addition, an individual utterance rarely stands on its own; it is part of an ongoing history. The current utterance does not repeat references that were already expressed in the past, for that would be unnecessarily redundant, and spoken language is highly efficient. We say that the utterance is *elliptical* because it seems to be missing pieces that are, however, given by its past. In addition, what is said is motivated by an orientation toward a desired future state. We say that it is *projective* because it orients the discussion in the direction of some future, which it thereby projects for the participants in the discussion. Thus, an utterance is never complete in isolation. This is true in principle. To utter a single word is to imply a whole language—and a whole history of lived experience on which it is grounded (Merleau-Ponty, 2002). The meaning of the word depends on its relationships to all the words (in the current context and in the lived language) with which it has cooccurred—including, recursively, the relationships of those words to all the words with which they cooccurred. We show the importance of cooccurrences for determining meaning within a discourse later.

In analyzing the episode that we refer to as "a collaborative moment" in this chapter, we make no distinction between "conversation analysis," "discourse analysis," or "microethnography" as distinct research traditions but adopt what might best be called "human interaction analysis" (Jordan & Henderson, 1995). This methodology builds on a convergence of conversation analysis (Sacks, 1992), ethnomethodology (Garfinkel, 1967), nonverbal communication (Birdwhistell, 1970), and context analysis (Kendon, 1990). An integration of these methods has only recently become feasible with the availability of videotaping and digitization that records human interactions and facilitates their detailed analysis. It involves paying close attention to the role that various microbehaviors—such as turn taking, participation structures, gaze, posture, gestures, and manipulation of artifacts—play in the tacit organization of interpersonal interactions. Utterances made in interaction are analyzed as to how they shape and are shaped by the mutually intelligible encounter itself—rather than being taken as expressions of individuals' psychological intentions or of external social rules (Streeck, 1983). In particular, many of the utterances we analyze are little more than verbal gestures on their way to becoming symbolic action; they are understood as not only representing or expressing but also as constituting socially shared knowledge (LeBaron & Streeck, 2000).

We worked for over a year (2000 to 2001) to analyze a videotape of students learning to use a computer simulation (on March 10, 1988). I say "we" because I could never have interpreted this on my own, even if I had already known all that I learned from my collaborators in this process. The effort involved faculty and graduate students in computer science, communication, education, philosophy, and cognitive science as well as various audiences to which we presented our data and thoughts at the University of Colorado at Boulder. It included a collaborative seminar on digital cognitive artifacts; we hypothesized that this video might show a group learning the meaning of a computer-based artifact collaboratively and hence potentially visibly.[2]

We logged the three hours of video, digitized interesting passages, conducted several data sessions with diverse audiences, and struggled to understand what the participants were up to. Despite much progress with the rest of the learning session, one brief moment stubbornly resisted explanation. The closer we looked, the more questions loomed. In the following sections, we pursue a limited inquiry into the structure of that single moment and try to understand what was meant by individual words and sentence fragments.

The Complexity of Small-Group Collaboration

Conversation analysis has focused largely on dyads of people talking (Sacks, 1992). It has found that people tend to take turns speaking, although they overlap each other in significant ways. Turn taking is a well practiced art that provides the major structure of a conversation. The talk is often best analyzed in conversation pairs, such as a question and an answer, where one person says the initial part of a pair and the other responds with the standard complement to that kind of speech act. These pairs can be interrupted (recursively) with other genres (Bakhtin, 1986b) of speech, including other conversation pairs that play a role within the primary pair (Duranti, 1998).

In much of the three-hour SimRocket tape from which our moment is excerpted, talk takes place between the teacher posing questions and one of the students proposing a response. The teacher indicates satisfaction or dissatisfaction with the response and then proceeds to another conversation pair. This is a typical classroom pattern (Lemke, 1990).

In the specific collaborative moment, something very different from the teacher-centered interaction takes place. In this tape segment, a many-to-many interaction is displayed in which meaning occurs at the group level. The structure of interaction departs from the teacher-centric dialogue and teacher-interpreted meanings. It somehow overcomes the rigid sequentiality of directed turn taking, where one person at a time seems to present his or her own thinking.

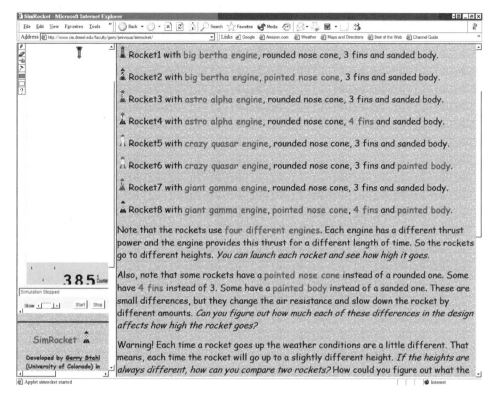

Figure 12.1
The SimRocket simulation and the list of rocket descriptions.

Let us first take a look at this special segment. The group of 11-year-old boys is discussing a list describing eight different rockets that can be used in a rocket-launch simulation (figure 12.1). They are trying to come up with a pair of rockets that can be used experimentally to determine whether a rounded or a pointed nose cone will perform better. During the moment, the students notice that rockets 1 and 2 have the identical engine, fins, and body but different nose cones and that rockets 3 and 4 differ only in their number of fins.

This interaction takes place about an hour and a half into the classroom session. It is initiated by the teacher who poses a question. For the few minutes prior, the teacher speaks primarily with Chuck, who describes some imaginary rockets he would like to design for the simulation to solve the problem of the nose cone. The teacher's question, accompanied by his emphatic gesture at the computer, succeeds in reorienting the group to the list on the screen. After a significant pause, during which Chuck does not respond to this question that interrupted his train of thought, Steven and Jamie utter responses as though talking to themselves and then simultaneously repeat them, as if to emphasize that they had taken the floor. But their response is to disagree with the teacher, something not common in a classroom. So the teacher restates his question, clarifying what it would take to justify an answer. Chuck responds in a confusing way, not directly answering the question but attempting to apply the criteria the teacher has put forward:[3]

1:21:53	Teacher	And (0.1) you don't have anything like that there?
1:21:54		(2.0)
1:21:56	Steven	I don't think so
1:21:57	Jamie	Not with the same engine
1:21:58	Steven	⌈No
	Jamie	⌊Not with the same
1:21:59	Teacher	With the same engine . . . but with a different (0.1) . . . nose cone?=
1:22:01	Chuck	⌈=the same=
	Jamie	⌊=Yeah,
1:22:02	Chuck	These are both (0.8) the same thing
1:22:03		(1.0)
1:22:04	Teacher	Aw⌈right
1:22:05	Brent	⌊This one's different

The teacher pauses at 1:22:03, encouraging student discussion, and Brent jumps in, cuts the teacher off, lurches forward, and points at a specific part of the list artifact (see figure 11.1 in chapter 11), while responding to the teacher's quest for something "different." For the next 16 turns, the teacher is silent, and the students rapidly interact, interjecting very short, excited utterances in a complex pattern of agreements and disagreements. The conversational structure shows that the standard, highly controlled, and teacher-centric dialogue has been momentarily broken and a more complex, collaborative interaction has sprung forth. Normally reticent, Brent excitedly rocks forward off his chair, pushes through a line of students, fills a void left by the teacher, and directs attention pointedly at the artifact.

Dramatically transforming the stage within which talk takes place, Brent has signaled an urgent need to resolve some disturbing confusion. The importance of this move is evidenced in the bodily behavior of Kelly, a student who says nothing during the entire episode. Kelly has been slouched back in his seat, with his head rolling around distractedly, up to this point in the transcript. As Brent leans forward, Kelly suddenly perks up and also leans forward to pay attention to what is transpiring.

At 1:21:53, the teacher opens a conversation pair with a question. It is intended as a rhetorical question—that is, as one that the asker (the teacher) expects to make the conversation partner (the group) see that there is something "like that there" and to answer in the affirmative, signaling that they have seen what the teacher was indicating. We can see that it is intended as a rhetorical question because the negative answers supplied by the students are not accepted. As the first part of an adjacency pair addressed to the plural "you," the teacher's utterance speaks to the students as a group and calls for a response from the group. Various students try repeatedly to produce the projected response on behalf of the group. The three students who try to answer in the negative—first Steven and Jamie simultaneously and later Chuck—repeat their answers, as if to reassert answers that the teacher's question is not projecting. Rather than accepting these answers, the teacher rephrases the question and pauses again for the projected affirmative answer.

Brent responds to the conflict between the expectation given by the rhetorical question and the attempts by the other students to give a negative answer. The section of transcript discussed next can be seen as an attempt by the group to resolve this conflict and provide the affirmative answer that the teacher's question seeks, finally completing the interrupted conversational pair of (rhetorical) question and (affirmative) answer.

The Problem

Brent interrupts the teacher with, "This one's *different*." The word "different" refers back to the teacher's last statement. The teacher's full question, elaborated in response to Steven and Jamie's disagreement, is, "And [0.1] you don't have anything *like* that there? . . . With the *same* engine but with a *different* [0.1] nose cone?" In the meantime, Steven and Jamie have both picked up on the teacher's word "same," as has Brent:

1:22:05   Brent   ⌊This one's different ((gestures with pen at computer 1 screen))

The teacher has used the words, "same" and "different" to clarify what he means by "like." In rhetorically asking, "Don't you have anything *like* that there?," the teacher is suggesting that the list of rockets ("there," where he is directing their attention) includes a rocket whose description is "like" the rocket they needed—namely, one that has the same engine but a different nose cone from the one with which they would compare it.

The teacher's original statement at 1:21:53 is *elliptical* in its use of the term "like." It assumes that the audience can infer from the context of the discussion what something ("anything" "there") would have to be for it to be like the thing under discussion ("that"). After two students respond that they cannot see anything like that there, the teacher tries to explicate what he means by "like." He does this by picking up on Jamie's "Not with the same engine" and defining "like" to mean "with the same engine but with a different nose cone." Scientific talk tries to avoid the elliptical ways of normal conversation. Throughout the session, the teacher models for the students this explicit way of talking, often taking what a student has stated elliptically and repeating it in a more fully stated way. In this instance, the teacher is doing just that. Sometimes one of the students will pick up on this and start to talk more explicitly. Here, Brent picks up on the term "different" as a key criterion for determining likeness.

The problem for us as researchers is that Brent's exclamation, "This one's different," is itself elliptical. In what way is "this one" different?

The Confusion

In analyzing this passage, there is also the interpretive problem of reference or *indexicality*. Brent has just pointed at the list of rocket descriptions, but it is impossible to tell from the video data which description he indicated. Even if we know which one Brent has pointed to, his utterance does not make clear which other rocket he is comparing with the one to which he has pointed. We have to deduce the answers to both these questions from the ensuing discussion to see how the participants themselves took the references.

Jamie's immediate follow-on utterance begins with "Yeah, but," indicating a response that is partially supportive. Because we know that Jamie is responding to Brent, we know that Jamie's use of "it" refers to Brent's "this one." Chuck, in turn, builds on Jamie's response and reclaims the floor by interrupting and completing Jamie's incomplete utterance of the term "nose cone." So Chuck's subsequent utterance—which he ties to the preceding phrase with "but"—uses the word "it's" to refer to Brent's "this one" as well:

1:22:06	Jamie	Yeah, but it has same no. . .
1:22:07		(1.0)
1:22:08	Chuck	Pointy nose cone=
1:22:09	Steven	=Oh, yeah=
1:22:10	Chuck	=But it's not the same engine

At this point, we see the conflict begin to be stated. Chuck's "but" suggests a disagreement with Brent and possibly with Jamie also. In the next second, both Jamie and Brent come back with "yes it is," showing that they have taken Chuck's comment to be a clear disagreement with what they are saying.

Kelly's nonverbal behavior again indicates that something unusual is happening: he rocks forward onto his elbows to follow events more closely. He stays in this position for the rest of the moment.

At this point in our interpretation, we see several shifting factions of opinion. At first, all the students seems to disagree with the teacher. Following Brent's bold gesture, some of the students seem to disagree with other students. In this analysis, we are not yet able to fully work out the basis of this disagreement because of the elliptical and indexical nature of the utterances that form the data.

We can overcome the problem of the elliptical—but not the indexical—character of the utterances by looking closely at how the individual utterances build off of each other, repeat the same words, or use conjunctions like "but" or "yeah" to signal continuity of topic. However, it is harder to know, for instance, which rockets are indexed by pronouns like "it." It seems likely that Jamie and Chuck are, in fact, indexing different rocket descriptions with their use of the pronoun "it." This would certainly cause confusion in the discussion because the repeated use of the same word should signify commonality of reference. To determine which rockets they are each indexing in their utterances, we have to continue our interpretive effort.

The Repair

In the seconds that follow the previous transcription, Jamie and Brent state virtually the same thing simultaneously. This indicates that the state of the group discourse—from the perspective in which Jamie and Brent are viewing it—must be very clear. That is to say, the network of indexical references, as interpreted from Jamie and Brent's utterances, is univocal. Within this set of references, Chuck's claim that "it's not the same engine" is clearly wrong. Jamie and Brent insist that "it" is the same engine.

1:22:11	Jamie	Yeah, It is, =
1:22:12	Brent	=Yes it is,
1:22:13	Jamie	⌈Compare two n one
	Brent	⌊Number two

Jamie and Brent support their counterclaim precisely by clarifying the references: they are talking about similarities and differences between rocket 2 and rocket 1 on the list in the simulation artifact.

Jamie's imperative, "compare two and one," is first of all an instruction to Chuck to look at the descriptions of rockets 2 and 1 on the list. At the same time, it is a reminder that the purpose of the whole discourse is to conduct a comparison of rockets to determine the best nose-cone shape. Jamie's utterance serves both to propose an explicit set of indexical references for the problematic discussion and to reorient the discussion to the larger goal of solving a specific scientific task. His utterance thus serves to state both the indexical basis and the *projective* basis of the discourse. He is saying that the group should index rockets 1 and 2 in the list comparison so that they can then conduct a comparison of rockets 1 and 2 in the datasheet artifact as their projected future task.

Jamie and Brent solve our task of interpreting the indexical references. We might still want to try to reconstruct the networks of references that different participants have at different points in the discourse. We would thereby be retrospectively reconstructing the process of construction that the discourse originally went through to reach this point. We would be "deconstructing" the discourse.

If we go back to the minute of discussion between the teacher and Chuck that precedes our transcript, we indeed find the source of the confusing references. Chuck has switched the discussion from nose cones to fins and has in fact solved the problem of how to determine the best rocket-fin configuration. He says to compare rockets 3 and 4, which are identical, except that rocket 3 has three fins and rocket 4 has four fins. Then Chuck wants to return to the problem of nose cones. He proposes making the simulation software modifiable by users so that he can either change the nose cone of rocket 3 or 4 or else change the engine of rocket 2 to match the engine of rockets 3 and 4. This would create a pair of rockets with the same engine as his baseline rocket (3 or 4) but with different nose cones. So Chuck is actually then already following the theoretical principle of only varying one attribute at a time. However, his description of the changes that he would make gets quite confusing—plus, it makes unrealistic assumptions about the software.

So the teacher's remark at 1:21:53, directing Chuck and the others back to the list on the screen, can be seen as a *projective* attempt to have Chuck recognize that rockets 1 and 2 can be compared as is, without changing one of them to be comparable to 3 or 4. In other words, the list has this built-in structure—that Chuck is not seeing and taking advantage of—that it has been organized to solve the problem of rocket comparisons. Unfortunately, because the discussion has been focused on rockets 3 and 4 as the basis for comparison, none of the students can see at first that 1 and 2 meet the criteria. As Jamie says, there is no rocket with a pointed nose cone, "not with the same engine"; we can see now that the word "same" refers to the same engine as in rockets 3 and 4.

When Brent points to what must be rocket 2 and says, "This one's different," his utterance refers to the fact that rocket 2 has a pointy nose cone, which is different from all the other rockets. At that point in the transcript, Brent's and Jamie's utterances must be taken as comparing rocket 2 to rocket 1 because, when Chuck keeps insisting that "it's not the same engine" (meaning that rocket 2's engine is not the same as the engines in rockets 3 and 4), Brent and Jamie retort "yes it is" and explicitly refer to rockets 1 and 2. As they repeat that they are looking at descriptions of rocket 2 and another rocket with the "same" engine, even Chuck gradually aligns with the reference to rockets 1 and 2. By looking back at the situation prior to our moment in this way, we can reconstruct how our moment develops out of its past, and we can determine a consistent and meaningful interpretation of the utterance references, as understood from the perspectives of the different participants.

The Resolution

In the final segment of our transcript, Chuck responds to Jamie's clarification. When Jamie says, "compare two and one," Chuck actually turns to the computer screen and studies it. With gradually increasing alignment to what Jamie is saying, Chuck says tentatively, "I know." This is the first time during this episode that his utterances are agreements. Jamie goes on to instruct him on how to make the comparison of rockets 1 and 2 by noting how they "are the same." Chuck's "Oh" response indicates a change in interpretation of things. Brent makes even more explicit how Jamie's "are the same" was to be taken—namely, that both rockets have the same kind of engine:

1:22:14	Chuck	(0.2) I know.
1:22:15	Jamie	(0.2) Are the same=
1:22:16	Chuck	=<u>Oh</u>
1:22:17	Brent	It's the same <u>engine</u>.
1:22:18	Jamie	So if you ⌈8compare two n <u>one</u>,
1:22:19	Chuck	⌊Oh yeah, I see, I see, I see
1:22:21	Jamie	(0.8) Yeah. Compare two n one. So that the rounded n- (0.1) no the <u>round</u>ed one is better. Number one.

Jamie repeats his double-edged imperative to "compare two and one." But he precedes it with "so if you." He is not only telling Chuck to look at the two descriptions and to compare them but is also saying that if he does this, then he can go on and do something in the future—namely, he can compare the data that the students collected in the previous hour for these two rockets and determine the best nose cone design. While Chuck is conceding that the descriptions of rockets 1 and 2 meet the criteria that the teacher spelled out at the start of the moment, Jamie starts to look over the data sheet that he has been holding ready at hand during the whole conversation and has brought up to his line of sight at 1:22:13. (Steven has also gone to retrieve his data sheet at 1:22:15, after Jamie first says, "compare two and one" and then checks the list on the screen for a moment.) Then Jamie announces the findings from the data. In the final utterance at 1:22:21, Jamie compares the data from rockets 2 and 1 but not their descriptions. He announces that the rounded nose cone is better based on its performance data. He stops himself in the middle of this announcement to check his analysis, which requires combining information from the list and the datasheet. Finally, he links the conclusion about the rounded nose cone to the rocket description ("number one"). This not only resolves any possible conflict about the references of the discussion but shows how they work to solve the larger task that has been projected for the discourse.

At the end of our collaborative moment, a quiet consensus is reached. Jamie and Steven have moved on to the data sheets, and everyone else is looking intently at the list, having acknowledged the teacher's rhetorical question, "And you don't have anything like that [rocket 1 and 2 descriptions, with the same engine and different nose cones] there [in the list]?" At that point, all the references are aligned with those of the teacher's original question, which brings an end to the breakdown of references and allows the group to affirm the question and move on to solve their task using the newly comprehended list artifact.

13

Collaborating with Relational References

The previous chapter uses a simple concept of reference in which an utterance refers to an identifiable object in the world—a specific rocket description in the simulation list. In this chapter, the analysis is deepened to reveal the same group's learning of a more sophisticated reference that involves pairs of objects compared in a subtle way.[1] Mastering practices that define such references is necessary for conducting collaborative scientific experiments involving controlled variables. This accomplishment is achieved by the group of students as a whole, working with computer-based artifacts under the guidance of an adult mentor. In the previous chapter, the group of students encounter confusion about which rockets they are referring to in their talk-in-interaction. In this chapter, it becomes clear that their task of referring is complicated; it involves a new way of looking at the meanings embedded in the simulation artifact.

This analysis provides a rich case study for the theoretical reflections of part III. By chapter 20, it is shown that the conceptual change that the students' group cognition passed through in this chapter has important philosophical consequences. In chapter 21, the analysis of an excerpt from an online chat provides a complementary case to this one.

Embedding Meaning in Software

Several years ago, I met Tony Petrosino at a conference and was intrigued by his research using model rockets to teach science to disaffected middle-school students in Texas. He explained that the use of model rockets is quite widespread in middle-school curricula and that kits for building model rockets with a variety of rocket engines are readily available. Because we were at a computer-oriented conference, Tony and I started talking about developing a computer simulation of model rockets to supplement his curriculum.

When I returned to my office, I discussed the idea with Alex Repenning, my office-mate at the time and the developer of Agentsheets, a software environment for the end-user programming of simulations. We decided that this would be a good exercise for me to undertake to learn more about Agentsheets. So I got some data from Tony about the effects of different rocket-design options on the flight of model rockets, and I programmed a simulation. Using the Agentsheets visual programming language (Repenning & Sumner, 1995), I defined the behavior of rockets to correspond roughly to Newton's laws, taking into account different air resistances due to rocket shape and texture (based on Tony's data), the thrust of the different rocket engines, and the force of gravity. I translated Newton's laws into difference equations for computing a rocket height at every time slice of the simulation. Then I added a random factor ("weather conditions") to make predictions more interesting. While middle-school students do not know the equations of physics, they can find averages on their calculators to take into account the random noise.

At the time, I was working with two middle-school classes to develop software for them with which to practice writing summaries (see chapter 2). In the spring, these classes broke into special science projects for which parents and community members were encouraged to volunteer. The classroom teachers I was working with invited me to mentor a model rocket group, and I proposed to spend two hour-and-a-half sessions with them using my new simulation.

On one level, I was curious to see what kids in the space age really understand about rockets and the scientific method. In particular, I wondered if they understood the basic principle of experimentation: varying only one attribute at a time while holding the others constant. So I equipped the simulation with seven rockets whose configurations would allow students to measure the effects of each rocket variable and then predict the behavior of an eighth rocket.

On another level, more than just being curious about what a certain group of students knew, I was interested in studying how middle-school students would approach learning about a new software tool. I thought that having them work in a group would make their learning visible to me. I videotaped them to capture a record of their learning.

Based on hours of time spent with video games and similar devices, students these days are adept at using software and at discovering its functionality. However, what I was asking them to learn was different. They had to learn the structure of the list of rockets and learn how to take advantage of that structure to complete certain computational tasks. In other words, I was embedding meaning in the simulation, and they would have to come to understand that meaning. An individual can conceptualize any software program as the embodiment of meanings that were programmed into its appearance and its behavior. For instance, the meaning of certain icons and menu items in a word-processing program has to do with determining fonts for text. To understand that program, users must learn about fonts, their use, and the ways that they can be manipulated using the interface icons.

A computer software program is an artifact that embodies "inferred," "referred," "derived," or "stored" intentionality. That is, the software designer programmed meanings or intentions into the software, and these allow the software to behave in a meaningful way. A clear example of this is given by artificial intelligence (AI). An AI program is supposed to exhibit humanlike intelligence in responding to inputs, but this is possible only if the programmer has reduced some limited domain of intelligent behavior to algorithmic rules (or heuristic rules that are able to mimic human decisions much of the time) and then programmed these into the software. The meaning of the software's behavior is derived from the human software designer's symbolic external representations in the programming language (Keil-Slawik, 1992). The user notices traces of the designer's intention in the form of the operational software artifact. The meaning is referred from its source in the designer to its appearance in the interface, much as "referred pain" appears in a different part of the body from its causal source. The AI software embodies its designer's intelligence in a way that is analogous to how commodities and machinery embody "stored" or "dead" human labor that determine their exchange value according to Karl Marx (1976). In the case of the computer simulation, the temporal behavior of the rocket and also the useful arrangement of the rocket attributes in the list of rockets are intentional artifacts whose meaning was structured by the designer.

Varieties of Meaningful Artifacts

We can distinguish different categories of meaningful artifacts:

- Physical artifacts,
- Symbolic artifacts,
- Computational artifacts, and
- Cognitive artifacts.

By definition, an *artifact* is something human-made. We might typically think of an arrowhead, a pot shard, or a figurine unearthed by an archeologist. The physical artifact is made out of some material that has survived thousands of years. It has a form or outer appearance that displays some purpose or meaning and that shows that it was made by a person—by a designer who embedded that meaning in it. We may not be sure exactly how to interpret the meaning—whether a given figurine is religious, magical, fertility enhancing, artistic, a child's doll, a remembrance of an important individual or a decoration—but we know that we are in the presence of a meaning and that someone at some time in the distant past intended the artifact to have a meaning. We are tempted to attribute some interpretation to the meaning. With our interpretation comes a glimpse into a faint and distant world: a culture within which this artifact was once transparently integrated.

A *physical artifact* embodies meaning in the physical world. Traditional Western theories, influenced by Descartes's conceptualizations, think of meanings as something purely mental, divorced from the physical world. According to this view, meanings are ideas we have in our heads about things in the world. But if we consider the nature of artifacts, we soon realize that the physical world is full of mental meanings, or the world is meaning-full—not because I as an observer apply values and meanings to things I see but because practically everything in our world has been made by people and has been designed to have specific meanings. Our shared culture makes these meanings available to us all. Even the rare glimpses we get of nature are imbued with historical or aesthetic dimensions; they are measured by what it would take for us to climb or touch or paint them; they are framed by the eye of an architect, a landscaper, or an urban planner who purposely left them for us to glimpse. The very concept of nature is so socially mediated that any sharp separation of meaning and the physical object itself is misguided.

And *vice versa. Symbolic artifacts* are not completely ethereal. Words appear in sounds, ink, or pixels. They could scarcely do their jobs as conveyors of meaning from one person to another if they did not appear in the physical world where they could be perceived and shared. Symbols do not come from nowhere, nor are we born with them inside us, like the neurons of our brains. We learn the meaning and use of symbolic artifacts—the words of our languages and of our language games—from our activities in the world, primarily verbal interaction with our caregivers, our siblings, our childhood best friends, our various teachers, and other people.

Once embodied in an artifact, meaning may exceed the original designer's intention. A book or poem may bring together words and images whose interactions and connotations exceed their author's understandings. With computational artifacts, it is well known that software is used in ways never anticipated by the designers. Although meaning may have originally expressed a subjective interpretation, it takes on a life of its own out in the shared world, subject to changing sociohistorical conditions and open to interpretation from various perspectives by different people.

Artifacts have been around as long as humans, although the concept of artifact-as-bridge across the mind and body distinction has played a central role in philosophical ontologies only since Martin Heidegger (1996), Walter Benjamin (1969), and Lev Vygotsky (1978). However, *computational artifacts* are a relatively new phenomenon. An artifact like the SimRocket simulation enlivens with computational power the meaning that is programmed into the software bits. The rocket icon moves with a behavior whose meaning was programmed in by the designer, although carefully designed random and interactive elements make the precise behavior unpredictable, as well as dependent on the user's actions. The computational, interactive artifact has a different kind of complexity than the prehistoric arrowhead (although the crafting of some arrowheads may have been so skilled that they are impossible to duplicate today). While it may be hard to specify precisely how meaning and physicality are merged in the bits of software that can be limitlessly duplicated and reconfigured, it seems clear that effective usage presupposes that the user recover (in his or her own way) the meaning of the software that was designed into the software to empower the user.

In educational contexts, there is an expectation that the meaning will be taken a further step—that the lessons will be *learned* so that whatever meaning is unearthed in the artifacts will be internalized by the student. This expectation does not necessarily entail a return to the view that meanings exist in individual minds. Rather, the expectation is that the student will be able to make use of a meaning that is learned from an encounter with a physical, symbolic, or computational artifact when the student is in a new situation in which that meaning might again be relevant. Without speculating about what might be involved in the student internalizing a meaning, we simply look at the student who interprets the meaning in the original situation and then uses this experience as a resource for constructing some similar form of meaning in a new situation in the world.

Vygotsky recognized that we do have an inner mental life, and he succeeded in relating our mental life to our social life in the world by arguing that our private mental world was an internalization of the primary, shared, social world. We learn to speak, act, and be in the world by interacting with other people and by sharing a culture and a meaningful world with them. As we begin to master these as a young child, we start to talk to ourselves—first out loud and then silently. We follow a similar sequence with reading—and then with debate and other social skills. In each case, when we internalize a skill, it undergoes a complex sequence of transformations and eventually becomes a *cognitive artifact*, a mental tool. For instance, an arrowhead might allow us to kill our prey in the world, the language of hunting allows us to discuss group plans for an expedition, a computer lets us simulate hunting scenarios, and the internalized language lets us imagine a glorious hunt. The nature of the hunt is different depending on whether it is mediated by a physical, symbolic, computational, or cognitive artifact. The silent self-talk that Vygotsky analyzed is the start of the stream of consciousness that forms our private mental life. Various skills like the ability to construct narratives (Bruner, 1990) and to give an account of our actions (Garfinkel, 1967) enrich that life.

In this chapter, we want to observe how a new cognitive artifact can evolve out of social interaction involving a computational artifact. How do the students develop the cognitive skill of comparing experimental cases having different attributes?

The Structure of the Rocket List

The SimRocket applet is a *computational artifact*. It includes the simulation panel of the rocket flight and the rocket list describing the available rockets. Based on Tony's model rocket kits, I designed the simulation rockets to have four variable attributes:

- Nose-cone shape (rounded or pointed),
- Number of fins (three or four),
- Surface texture of body (painted or sanded), and
- Rocket engine (Big Bertha, Astro Alpha, Crazy Quasar, Giant Gamma).

The rockets are paired in the list of available rockets (figure 13.1). There are two rockets with each kind of engine. The first three pairs have identical attributes, except for one difference:

- Rockets 1 and 2 differ in nose-cone shape,
- Rockets 3 and 4 differ in number of fins,
- Rockets 5 and 6 differ in body texture, and
- Rockets 7 and 8 differ in nose cone, fins, and body.

The computer simulation was carefully designed with this particular set of rockets. This set of rockets allows the user to determine the effect of the different attributes on the flight of the rocket by, in effect, holding constant all variables, except one, each trial. Thus, one can determine the effect of nose-cone shape by comparing the flights of rockets 1 and 2, of number of fins with rockets 3 and 4, and of body texture with rockets 5 and 6. These effects can then be combined to predict how rocket 8 will fly, given the flight of rocket 7, which differs from rocket 8 by these three attributes. This describes, from the designer's perspective, the meaning that was embedded in the simulation list artifact.

There are other sets of configured rockets that would allow similar calculations and predictions. Rather than varying attributes in pairs of rockets (let us call this *paired configurations*), one could compare a set of different rockets to one common standard (call this *standard configurations*). For instance, rockets 2, 3, and 4 could

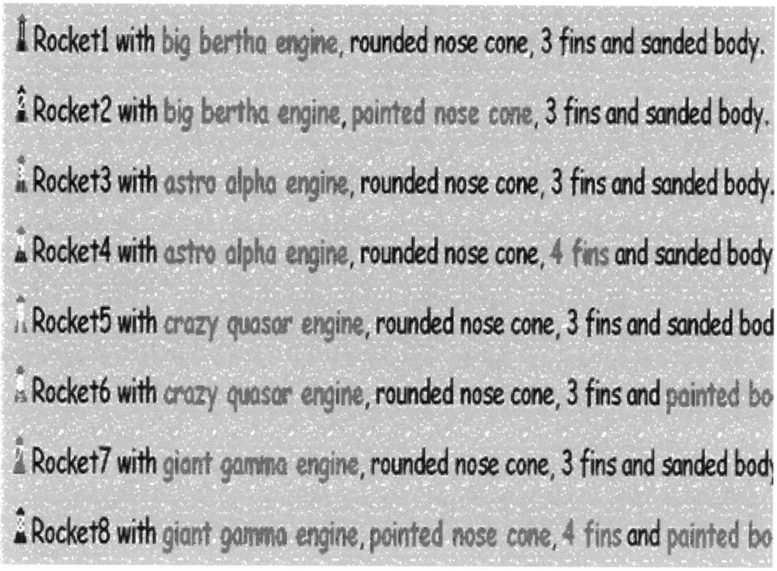

Figure 13.1
The list of rockets. Excerpt from figure 12.1 in chapter 12.

each differ from rocket 1 by a different individual attribute. Then rockets 5, 6, and 7 could be like rocket 1 but have the different engines. This would also allow one to compute the effects of each attribute singly and combine them to predict any configuration of rocket 8. Either this standard configurations combination of rockets or the paired configurations combination above allows one to compute the dynamics of all 32 possible rocket configurations using a set of just seven different rockets.

Using the contrast just made of paired configurations to standard configurations, we can better understand the breakdown analyzed in the previous chapter. The students discovered that rockets 3 and 4 could be compared to determine the best fin configuration because 4 was a variation of 3. They then sought a variation of rocket 3 that could be analogously compared for nose-cone shape. The students were assuming a standard configurations model in which everything is compared to one standard rocket (rocket 3).

However, the rocket list was, in fact, structured with paired configurations. Brent's gesture first drew attention to a pair with the needed difference, using a paired configurations model. The result of the subsequent collaborative interaction was to reach a consensus in which the whole group took a particular pair (rockets 1 and

2) as the focus of comparison, rather than insisting on looking for a variation of the standard rocket-3 engine.

Uncovering Embedded Meaning

At this point, adult readers might understand how the rockets in the SimRocket list should be compared to find out the effects of the different attributes. However, we saw in the last chapter how students' references to rockets to be compared became confused. This confusion presented an occasion for an exceptional interaction to occur among the students to sort out this breakdown in the references. They accomplished this efficiently, with the use of brief, productive utterances that are hard for an observer to interpret but proved to be effective within the discourse. Once the references were resolved and accepted as shared by the group, the students were able to quickly draw the scientific conclusions about rocket characteristics. They then displayed in their talk their mastery of how to compare rockets. They accomplished this not by talking about "controlling variables"—such adult (schooled, professional) terminology was never used—but by making the proper use of their data. They learned the principle of scientific comparison in the practical, situated sense that they could actually carry out the appropriate operations on their data.

The learning that we uncovered in the collaborative moment transcript in chapter 12 played a key role in the larger classroom session. It is now possible to review the larger transcript and find statements in which learning associated with the issue addressed in the collaborative moment is also expressed—following the hermeneutic principle that interpretation must go back and forth between part and whole.

During the 10 minutes surrounding the 30-second "collaborative moment" (from about 1:17:00 to 1:27:00), where the teacher and students discuss how to analyze their rocket data, the group understanding goes from a rather naive and vague sense of how to use the list artifact to a clear and explicit appreciation of the meaning of that artifact and a practical knowledge of how to use it to achieve useful and meaningful results. Following are a series of excerpts from the longer transcript that illustrate this development by presenting significant statements that express the evolving group understanding. They are given here in 10 stages.

Stage 1   Chuck expresses the group's assumption that one could simply adopt all the features of the rocket that flew the highest. When the teacher suggests that a particularly strong engine could mask the differences caused by the other features, the students are at a loss on how to proceed without strong guidance from the teacher, leading up to the collaborative moment with its breakthrough insight:

1:17:01   Chuck   We'll just go with number <u>one</u> uh (.) an that did the best, (.) or something, out of all ours compa:red

Stage 2   After some discussion of statistical analysis, Steven still articulates the same group position as Chuck has, to go with all the features of the best rocket:

1:17:44   Steven   Well we'd look at- (.) we'd look at the <u>graph</u> that we do an see which has (uh) the ↑<u>best</u>. An whichever has the ↑best like rocket one two n three or- so on, (.) .h n whichever has the best we'd look to see if it has a rounded, or a pointed, which (.) which ours shows so far, that a ↑rounded, (.) that a ↑rounded is better?

Stage 3   Jamie suggests seeing whether the set of rockets with pointed noses does better overall than those with rounded noses, assuming that this kind of averaging will cancel the effects of the other features:

1:18:29   Jamie   Well what you do is you take every one that has a rounded nose an every one with a (.) <u>point</u>ed nose. (0.4) an you see which (0.2) one did better overall

Stage 4   Chuck has the idea of manipulating one feature at a time while holding the others constant, but he wants to do this on physical model rockets (made out of soda pop bottles) rather than applying it to the data he has just collected from the simulation:

1:18:36   Chuck   Yeah if you could bring in one that (.) like <u>two</u> two liter pop bottles you know that's (.) make one with a ↑<u>point</u>ed nosecone n one with a ↑<u>round</u>ed nosecone. an see which one did better .hh so then we c'd go with th<u>at</u> one an then add the feature that was on th<u>at</u> one to the <u>other</u> one .hh an whatever features you put on h<u>ere</u>, (.) you leave off of (1.0) that- uh off of the other one .hh that way you c'n j's see which one will fly. (.) 'F the features on this one didn' work then we take th'm off and then go from there.

Stage 5   Jamie is ready to use the data from the simulation but returns to the idea of finding which did "better overall":

1:19:05   Jamie   You can use the simulation by .h finding out (.) j'st which one has a rounded nose and which one has a pointed nose? (.) and which one did better overall. (0.8) Like w- (.) which (.) rockets like (.) if (.) only <u>one</u> rocket with a rounded nose .h did <u>good</u>, then (.) a rounded nose (.) <u>isn't</u> very good, (.) but like if. yeah but like if <u>all</u> the rounded noses are good, (.) compared to the pointed nose, then the rounded nose- noses are good.

Stage 6   Chuck solves the problem for fins, using the simulation and identifying rockets 3 and 4 on the list as having the necessary characteristics for valid comparison:

1:20:30   Teacher   So how would you find out which is better four fins or three fins. (1.0)

           Chuck   By launching ( ) with two different things on it—

           Teacher   —Which one—which two.

           Chuck   one with <u>fou::r</u> (.) n one with three: <u>like</u> (0.6) rocket <u>four</u> an rocket <u>one</u>. (0.8) Err no—(.) Ro:cke:ts, (.) <u>fou:r</u>, n rocket <u>three</u>. Cuz they both have the same <u>engine</u>. (0.8) An they both have the same <u>nose</u>cones.

Stage 7   Chuck wants to change the simulation to create a comparable pair of rockets. He is willing to use the simulation but has not looked carefully through the list to find what he needs:

1:20:03   Chuck   see 'f you guys c'd make one .h wha—with an astro (.) alpha engine four fins and <u>pointed</u> nosecone, (1.6) w'll see if you c'd do, (.) uh <u>cha:nge</u> all this around n stuff so that .hh you might get ( ) you also—.hh have an option of a pointed nosecone like— ((swallow)) .hh you could (.) kinda like in HyperStudio .hh if you were tuh (.) like (.) <u>click</u> on this .h it would <u>give</u> you (.) <u>all</u> kinds of things th't you (.) ought— like (.) on the (.) pointy nosecone (.) .h you c'd switch it to a <u>roun</u>ded nosecone .h and the fins,

Stage 8   This stage is the collaborative moment we analyze in chapter 12. At 1:22:21, Jamie turns to his data sheet and compares the data for rockets 1 and 2, concluding that because rocket 1 went higher than rocket 2 and the only difference between them is that rocket 1 has a rounded nose cone, a rounded nose cone is preferable.

Stage 9   Steven explicitly describes the structure of the list for doing the task for all features of the simulation rockets. He says, "I think it [the structured list] is good how it is," fully appreciating that the necessary pairs have been built into the list:

1:24:46	Steven	What we would do is test (.) test (.) uh- rocket three and rocket four, (.) cuz they both have a rounded nose they both (.) have <u>that</u> astro alpha engine n they- (.) n one has three one has <u>four</u> fins. I think it's good how it is because .hh every rocket has somep'n different. Like if you tested (.) five and six, then it- (.) they have the crazy uh- (.) quasar engine, .h they both have the crazy quasar engine, they both have the rounded .h nose they both have three fins, except th't if- if we uh- if we tested those two, we'd be - testing for thuh- uh painted body or uh—a <u>sand</u>ed body, (.) so I like it how it is.

Stage 10   The whole group agrees about how to use the list, and they are able to collaboratively draw scientific conclusions with its help.

1:26:46	Brent	I would say that ⌈three is better than four
	Jamie	⌊three is better than four ( )=
	Chuck	Yeah, three is better than four so=
	Teacher	=So ⌈your rocket⌉
	Chuck	⌊(we want) ⌋ three fins n a rounded nose ⌈cone
	Teacher	⌊Your rocket three
		goes up higher 'n rocket four=
	students	Yeah ((multiple voices))
	Teacher	So that means that three fins is better 'n four.

By solving a sequence of problems that the teacher guides them through, the students develop an increasingly robust working knowledge of the fundamental principle of scientific experimentation that only one variable should be varied while the others are held constant. Although this principle was built into the simulation's list of rocket descriptions and although the students start the classroom session by reading this list aloud and discussing it, they are not able to use this feature of the list to analyze the data they collect until they work through the preceding 10 stages.

Even as bright, motivated, middle-school students, they were not developmentally able to grasp the principle individually. However, this ability did lie within their zone of proximal development (Vygotsky, 1978), and they succeeded in attaining it as a group through a scaffolded collaborative process.

Articulating Meaning

How was the meaning of the rocket list as a set of paired configurations constructed by the group of students? In reviewing the 10 stages of understanding that evolved in the group during the 10 minutes surrounding the half-minute moment of collaboration, we have seen that the group went from simply wanting to identify the "best overall" rocket, to proposing various methods of comparing rockets, and then—after the intensive collaborative moment—to understanding the paired configuration and using it to complete their task.

Let us return to the transcript in chapter 12 to see in some detail how the pivotal insight developed. Consider the significant pauses of a second or two in the interaction at 1:21:54, 1:22:03, and 1:22:07:

1:21:53	Teacher	And (0.1) you don't have anything like that there?
1:21:54		**(2.0)**
1:21:56	Steven	I don't think so
1:21:57	Jamie	Not with the same engine
1:21:58	Steven	⌈No
	Jamie	⌊Not with the same
1:21:59	Teacher	With the same engine . . . but with a different (0.1) . . . nose cone?=
1:22:01	Chuck	⌈=the same=
	Jamie	⌊=Yeah,
1:22:02	Chuck	These are both (0.8) the same thing
1:22:03		**(1.0)**
1:22:04	Teacher	Aw ⌈right
1:22:05	Brent	⌊This one's different
1:22:06	Jamie	Yeah, but it has same no . . .
1:22:07		**(1.0)**

The teacher starts with a question that references the rocket list to reorient the group to the computational artifact, which Chuck's speculations about alternative software obscured. The students do not respond immediately, but the teacher uses "wait time"—waiting out a long silence and thereby encouraging students to take the floor. Steven begins hesitantly to reject the implication of the teacher's question, hedging his "No" as "I don't think so" at first but then confirms it when backed up by Jamie. Jamie justifies or clarifies the negative response with "Not with the same engine." Jamie then repeats his utterance up to the word "same," making that term focal.

The teacher picks up on Jamie's term "same" to explicate his term "like." By asking, "And you don't have anything like that here?" the teacher is asking if there is a pair of rockets in the list on the computer monitor that can be used to determine the effect of the nose-cone shape the way that Chuck's proposed software variation of rocket 3 or 4 would. Jamie's response points out that there is no rocket in the list that can be paired with rocket 3 or 4 for this purpose because none of the other rockets has the same engine as rockets 3 and 4. So the teacher adds the clarification: "With the same engine, but with a different nose cone," repeating Jamie's "same" as applied to the engine and introducing the term "different" applied to the nose cone.

This expanded version of the question is still ambiguous: it could be applied to either a list of paired configurations or one of standard configurations. After Chuck and Jamie make unsuccessful attempts to respond to the issue of "the same," the group falls silent. This is the point of *aporia* that Plato (1961) considered the catalyst of insight: silent wonder in the presence of a question that one finally understands to be a captivating mystery.

As if suddenly aroused from his intellectual slumber by a muse of scientific thought, Brent dramatically breaks the silence with "This one's different." Jamie does not see what is different and repeats what is the same. Another pause.

Then Steven and Jamie—but not yet Chuck—demonstrate a change of interpretive perspective:

1:22:07		(1.0)
1:22:08	Chuck	Pointy nose cone=
1:22:09	Steven	=Oh, yeah=
1:22:10	Chuck	=But it's not the same engine
1:22:11	Jamie	Yeah, it is,=
1:22:12	Brent	=Yes it is,
1:22:13	Jamie	⌈Compare two n one
	Brent	⌊Number two

At first, they simply register a change of view and alignment with Brent. Then Jamie and Brent make the new comparison explicit: "Compare two and one," "Number two." They continue to explicate, saying, "Are the same," "It's the same engine," "So if you compare two and one," until Chuck sees things their way: "Oh yeah, I see, I see, I see." The crucial move is to look at rockets 1 and 2 as a paired configuration. Then one can see that they both have the same engine (and the same other attributes, except nose cone), so they can be compared for different nose cones.

In this analysis, we see that the terms *same*, *different*, and *compare* become focal to the discourse. These are terms that relate two objects. References that use these terms refer to pairs of objects. The group uses these terms to define the form of relationship that is needed; by repeating, refining, and explicating how these terms are to be used, the group converges on the structure of paired configurations. The discourse breaks down until the reference of the teacher's question can be interpreted by all the students as being directed to the pair of rockets 1 and 2 instead of to a pair based on rocket 3 as a standard.

All the participants in the discourse understand that the teacher's rhetorical question is referencing a set of related rockets. It takes several interactions to shift everyone's understanding from a model of standard configurations to one of paired configurations. Because the reference is to a relationship rather than to a single object, the breakdown in shared understanding cannot be repaired by simply pointing, as Brent tried. It is necessary for Jamie and Stephen to take this further and explicitly name both of the objects, as well as the relationship (*compare*) itself.

Discourse and Understanding

The unfolding of the collaborative moment reveals a subtle interplay between the group discourse and the understandings of the individual participants. This interplay becomes visible during a breakdown in the discourse caused by a nonalignment of the individual interpretations. The character of this interplay does not lend itself to description using traditional conceptualizations of meaning and minds. In particular, we are tempted to say that the students had various ideas in their heads, that they expressed these ideas in their utterances, and that they changed their ideas in the course of the interaction. However, we have no evidence about ideas in their heads beyond the utterances (and other interaction behaviors) themselves. Nor did the participants have any evidence about the mental states of their co-collaborators, other than the same utterances (including intonations and gestures) that we have as observers. The only meanings that we (or they) have access to are those embodied in the utterances of the discourse themselves.

Nevertheless, the question arises as to how some of the participants could (according to our analysis above) understand the shared discourse in different ways, resulting in the breakdown as well as its gradual repair. It seems clear that two different levels of meaning making are taking place—a group level on which meaning is built up through the discourse in which everyone participates and an individual level on which each participant constructs his or her own evolving understanding of the references and other features of the discourse. In particular, the pauses in the collaborative interaction and the arguments in the group discourse seem to stimulate—whether by applying some kind of social pressure or simply by opening up a creative space—reinterpretations by the individuals.

We already observed in the previous chapter that most of the individual utterances had little meaning on their own if viewed in isolation. The meaning was constructed at the level of (in the context of) the group discourse, through the references of words, phrases, gestures, and glances to elements in the discourse, the social interaction, the associated artifacts, and the physical space. A word like *same* derives its lexical meaning from its contrast to *different*, its use in *compare*, and so on. The word also builds up its socially shared meaning from repeated uses of it and related terms. It is common in discourse for one speaker to repeat a term that someone else recently used, as a way of referencing the previous occurrence. In this way, the term takes on a role in the discourse that cannot be attributed to an individual as the expression of a mental idea. The word is better analyzed as a resource for interaction that is shared by the group. While we may not know quite what a certain student intended when uttering a term, we can see how it was interactionally picked up by others and how it came to play a role in the group discourse. The terms used in the discourse gradually form a web of meaning, which specifies and deepens the meaning of the various terms within this context. One can say that the students, as a group engaged in interaction, learn over time to understand these terms more deeply (as quasi-technical terms) and to use them more skillfully (as a fledgling team of scientists). One can say that the group discourse progressively refines the shared group meaning of the terms.

Indeed, in a group it is not clear in what sense we can say what a word meant to its individual speaker as distinct from what it turned out to mean in the group discourse. It is possible that the speaker had mentally rehearsed the word before speaking it. Then we might say that it had a meaning defined by that internal dialog—a very small-group discourse of one with oneself, internalized in silent thought. We could also say that the word had gained a meaning for the speaker through his past personal encounters with that word in a variety of social settings, including texts. One individually builds, refines, and abstracts personal webs of meaning (in some ways analogously to latent semantic analysis; see chapter 2) that approximate cultural lexicons.

The terms *same*, *different*, and *compare* are everyday words used to describe a relational reference that might be discussed in terms of "holding variables constant" in scientific jargon. At different points during the collaborative moment, each student shifted his understanding of this relational reference from a model of standard configurations to one of paired configurations. This shift during the collaborative moment was an important feature of the interplay between the group discourse and the individual understandings.

Through the reconfiguration of the use of the everyday words within a quasi-scientific activity structure involving the computational artifact, the shared meaning of the rocket list underwent a Gestalt transformation from being seen as a shared configuration to being seen as a paired configuration. For this to take place at the group level, every group member had to learn to see or interpret the meaningful list in this new way. To overcome the breakdown in the group discourse, the students eagerly taught each other how to see in the new way. What the students had to learn was not an abstract rule about holding all but one variable constant. They already seemed to have a sense of this rule but did not know how to apply it effectively in practice in the given situation. Chuck, at least, was trying to apply the rule assuming a standard configuration of the rockets in the list. Rather, they had to learn to see the list as already incorporating this rule—but through a paired rather than standard configuration.

Utterances like Brent's pivotal pronouncement "This one's different" refer to artifacts in the activity context. In chapter 12, we argue that different participants in the discourse interpreted Brent's reference differently, causing a breakdown in the shared understanding. The analysis in the current chapter shows that the deictic phrase "this one" does not refer simply to one individual rocket or one line on the list. It is a relational reference to a pair of rockets or descriptions that stand in a salient relationship to each other. The ability to comprehend that relationship—and therefore the ability to see the particular pair of rockets 1 and 2 as a pair (in a contextually meaningful sense)—is reliant on a grasp of the overall list artifact as embodying its meaning through its paired configuration structure.

Individual and Group Learning

The preceding analysis suggests that collaboration may often take place with the following structure:

1. A group is engaged in building shared meaning in its discourse.

2. Each participant develops an individual interpretation of the meaning of the discourse in parallel to the group interaction.

3. Participation in the group interaction is affected by the individual interpretations. The individual contributions to the discourse reflect the distinctive interpretations but simultaneously merge in the creation of the discourse's group-level meaning.

4. Individual interpretations are visible (to other participants and to observers) in the interactions of the participants in the group as nuances in how their contributions are integrated into the discourse. The trajectory of an individual's contributions can be seen as a personal narrative within the history of the group interaction.

Such a structure would have important implications for how individual learning can result from group collaboration. If group learning and individual learning proceed in parallel as different interpretive facets of a single, complexly interacting process, then we can look for both group and individual learning taking place in all collaborative settings and not just those in which an individual division of labor is explicitly introduced. For instance, in the previous chapter's moment of collaboration, the task of isolating the nose-cone effect was accomplished by the group as a whole. Individuals were not assigned subtasks or roles. However, an essential though unstated feature of the collaboration was that each individual had to understand the accomplishment of the group task. Each individual took responsibility for making sure that the others shared a common understanding. This responsibility can be seen to be at work in motivating the various contributions to the discourse. In fact, the intense collaboration in chapter 12 was precisely an attempt to reestablish shared understanding during a breakdown of it. As individuals started to understand the relational reference that was the key to accomplishing the task, they focused on bringing the other participants around to sharing that understanding. Only when all participants acknowledged that their individual interpretations of the group meaning were aligned did the group proceed to look at the data sheet in accordance with the relational reference to rockets 1 and 2 and solve the nose cone task.

The parallel working of group and individual learning is often overlooked when investigating collaboration. Either (usually) researchers focus on the individual learning and miss the group-level phenomena, failing to identify the process as collaborative, or they focus on the group interaction and assume that special interventions (role definitions, task divisions, jig-sawing, interdependence, reflection, reporting) are necessary to stimulate individual effects. In our case study, however, we see that *the participants have spontaneously organized their interaction to ensure that each individual understanding of the meaning of the group discourse was aligned in agreement with each other*. This was necessary for the discourse and the problem solving to proceed. Such agreement is not absolute in any sense but adheres to practical criteria having to do with permitting the collaboration to continue. The result of this natural structuring of the collaborative process is that *the individuals learn in parallel with the group learning*, to the extent needed for the practical purposes of the group activity. Our view of the discourse and the interaction generally made visible the learning at both levels.

The point is not that explicitly introducing individual roles into a group process is necessarily a bad idea; such pedagogical techniques have indeed proved useful in certain settings. Rather, the point is that individual learning may automatically take place within collaborative interactions. This suggests a response to the argument that group learning is irrelevant because the group will eventually break up and that we therefore need to focus on individual learning. On the contrary, it may be that group learning often supplies an essential basis for individual learning, providing not only the cultural background, the motivational support, and the interactional occasion but also an effective mechanism for ensuring individual learning.

In this chapter, we have seen an example of how a process of collaboration required the participants to ensure agreement among their individual understandings. Within the scope of one complex process, the group meaning of the rocket list shifted from a standard configuration to a paired configuration, and each participant learned to make and interpret appropriate relational references and to see, interpret, and discuss the referenced meaning accordingly. We further explore issues of making learning visible, group meaning making, and individual interpretation in part III of this book.

III

Theory of Group Cognition

Studies of Collaboration Theory

Consequences of Part II

Chapter 9 proposes a graphical model of knowledge building that identifies a number of possible phases, at both the individual and social levels. This implicitly raises the question of empirical evidence for such phases. Chapter 10 expresses a concern that widespread CSCL methodologies tend to reduce the data of experiments so that much of the interesting, empirical, detailed information about collaborative interactions is lost. In particular, key phases like those identified in the collaboration model become obscured. Chapter 11 suggests a set of theoretical and empirical approaches to overcome this problem, including the application of conversation analysis. The final chapters of part II follow this suggestion and provide a case study of conversation analysis applied to a collaborative moment. Chapters 12 and 13 identify knowledge building and conceptual change at the group unit of analysis in that moment of collaboration. They show how the shared meaning constructed by the students discussing the computer simulation cannot be attributed to individuals but is essentially a group cognitive phenomenon. The meaning of the indexical, elliptical, and projective utterances is constituted only in situ, across inextricably interwoven utterances by different people and tied to the tasks, artifacts, and social contexts of which they are an integral part.

The empirical discovery of group cognition begs for a theoretical conceptualization. That is the role of part III. Taking as inspiration and guidance the brief case study from chapters 12 and 13, along with a mix of philosophical insights, it sketches a framework for understanding group cognition and provides a series of reflections to make this notion more congenial to readers accustomed to thinking of individual intentions.

Theoretical Background to Part III

This book has been in gestation for some time. My seminars at the University of Colorado on artifacts and mediation were a start. When I went to Germany for a year to work on BSCL and organize the CSCL '02 conference, I had it in mind to prepare myself for writing a book. While there, I was invited to write a theory chapter for an edited book on CSCL; what turned into chapter 15 below was really an outline of a solo book. This encouraged me to think about working out a more detailed, book-length theory of collaboration.

The following year, settled at Drexel, I began to think about first making my scattered publications available in an organized and accessible way. That led to reworking chapters 1 thorough 12, as well as chapter 15. In effect, they constituted the core of the book that I had in mind, for I discovered that these papers had been pursuing a coherent inquiry without my realizing it. They just needed to be properly pulled together and extended. Indeed, this makes for a more honest presentation of a theory, for it presents the historical path of inquiry that leads to the concept of group cognition.

The other eight chapters and the introductory materials were written specifically for this book as it became increasingly clear that the compilation of studies had more to say than the sum of its parts. The theoretical aspects of this subject are where I always assumed I would have the most to contribute to the field, given my background in philosophy. They form part III.

Philosophy

The discipline of philosophy in the past century has followed three mainstreams, which for me are best represented by Karl Marx, Ludwig Wittgenstein, and Martin Heidegger. They might be termed critical social theory, common language analysis, and existential phenomenology. As I mention again later, each of these branches of philosophy undertook a fundamental critique of the positivist, objectivist, behaviorist, individualistic, rationalist, mentalist tradition that goes back to René Descartes—if not to Plato—and that persists in much of our everyday thinking (folk theories) and scientific methodologies.

As an undergraduate math and physics student at MIT, I was well exposed to positivist attitudes. But I also encountered the phenomenology of Edmund Husserl, Martin Heidegger, and Maurice Merleau-Ponty in philosophy courses from Hubert Dreyfus and Samuel Todes. I later followed Todes to Northwestern University—then a unique enclave of European thought in the United States—to earn a Ph.D. in philosophy. During this graduate study, I spent a year at Heidelberg University attending Hans-Georg Gadamer's lectures and two years at the University of Frankfurt studying the roots and heritage of Theodor Adorno and Jürgen Habermas. These were the heady political years of the late 1960s when the classic German universities were transformed into "free universities" in solidarity with the May Days of France in 1968 and in the "new left" spirit. During this period of my life, I gained firsthand experience with the different approaches in contemporary philosophy and their practical application within a society in ferment.

In seeking an alternative foundation to rational cogitation, each of the three mainstreams of twentieth-century philosophy underwent a "linguistic turn." They each looked to language as the central phenomenon for analysis. Extrapolating from Lev Vygotsky (1986) and Mikhail Bakhtin (1986b) as well as from Adorno (1973), Heidegger (1971), and Wittgenstein (1953), one can conceive of the mind as fundamentally linguistic. This has consequences, such as viewing thought or meaning making as something that can take place socially and culturally outside the heads of individuals, primarily in discourse.

Part III on the theory of group cognition tries to take into account the various philosophic advances of our time, which have not completely percolated down to our everyday understanding or our scientific methodologies. It attempts to apply these perspectives to the foundational issues of a theory of collaboration. In particular, it strives to bring about a shift from the traditional focus on the individual to a consideration of the small group as the cell of analysis. Subjecting the focus on the small group to the linguistic turn, it arrives at a concept of group cognition as group discourse.

Activity Theory

In recent decades, the development of theory has taken place largely within niches of the social sciences: anthropology (critical ethnography), communication (conversation analysis), sociology (ethnomethodology), and psychology (sociocultural). This has shifted the focus of theory from the traditional lone thinker to broader sociocultural phenomena. For instance, activity theory (Engeström, 1999) situates the individual firmly in the activity system, which includes other individuals and the mediating artifacts and the community or societal context as a contradictory whole. Artifacts—whether words or tools—are not taken as simply physical or mental but as both meaningful and embodied. Individuals and society are not treated as independent identities but as mutually constituting each other, so that one must take into account both of them in their relations with each other.

Heidegger

The most thorough and systematic critique of the Cartesian tradition was carried out by Heidegger. In my philosophy publications (Stahl, 1975a, 1975b, 1976), I note that the root of Heidegger's tragic political errors was in his failure to take the concrete social context seriously rather than as an abstract principle of historicity. Despite this, I am still convinced that we have much to learn from his philosophy. For this reason, while in Germany, in preparation for writing a book, I reread *Sein und Zeit* (Heidegger, 1996) to get a clearer grasp of his actual and potential contributions. Many of Heidegger's insights have already been translated into important principles for software design (Dourish, 2001; Dreyfus, 1972; Floyd, Zuellinghoven, Budde, & Keil-Slawik, 1994; Schön, 1983; Suchman, 1987; Winograd & Flores, 1986). Most of these are based on specific analyses in Heidegger's early work rather than on his fundamental critique of Western thinking. His writings after what Heidegger calls the "turn" in his "path" open up a rich but quite different view of artifacts and truth (e.g., Heidegger, 1964), which may prove helpful in thinking about software artifacts to open up realms of collaboration. But the later writings build on Heidegger's critique of Western thought in *Being and Time* and that book's analyses of, for instance, human interpretation and how artifacts have meaning.

The Studies in Part III

Part III tries to introduce a certain theoretical perspective to the reader through a series of essays that come at it from different angles. The idea underlying all of the studies is to focus on the group, not primarily the individual. A science of collaboration for computer-supported cooperative work (CSCW) and computer-supported collaborative learning (CSCL) should be centrally concerned with analysis of group interaction, group meaning, group cognition, group discourse, and group thinking. It should not insist on reducing these to cognitive states of individuals. Part I concludes that groupware should be designed as a medium for supporting group discourse—not primarily as a smart tool for individual users. Part II argues for analysis of group interaction and provides an illustrative analysis that did not seek quantitative measures of individual outcomes. Now part III carries the paradigm shift to the theoretical level as a reflection on issues that arose in the previous parts and to help readers overcome the habits of thought that resist the focus on the small group as the agent of collaborative knowledge building. The following questions are raised as part of a reflection on the small-group unit of analysis:

• Can we learn from traditional communication theories and technologies how to support online small groups? (chapter 14)

• Can processes of group cognition and collaborative learning provide a basis for individual cognition and personal learning? (chapter 15)

- Can we identify meaning making and knowledge building at the group unit? (chapter 16)

- Can we understand how group meaning is shared among group members? (chapter 17)

- Can we make learning visible in group discourse, so we do not have to be confined to measuring indirect learning outcomes? (chapter 18)

- Can we say that it is possible for a group as such to think / learn / build knowledge / construct meanings that cannot be attributed to any of the group members individually? (chapter 19)

- Can we develop new conceptions of group discourse that might open up innovative approaches to fostering group cognition? (chapter 20)

- Can we identify rational sequences of reasoning at the small-group unit of analysis, so we can say that the group as such is engaging in high-level thought? (chapter 21)

It is hoped that the view of group cognition that emerges from part III will contribute to the understanding needed to foster computer-supported collaborative knowledge building.

Chapter 14, Group Communication   The theory part of the book opens with a general review of communication theory. This is partially a consequence of the emphasis in part II on conversation analysis and partially a reaction to the linguistic turn in theory. Chapter 14 uses the momentum generated by parts I and II to launch into an analysis of traditional theories of communication and what they can offer for understanding the phenomenon of collaboration. This chapter relates the theory of communication to the needs of groupware design and to theories of learning. It then extends the analysis of communication to begin to cover computer-mediated collaboration.

Chapter 15, Group Theory   This is a lengthy attempt—yet condensed, considering the subject—to present the elements of a social theory of collaboration. The abstract nature of this undertaking at times suggests an exaggerated level of generality, but the suggested theory is intended to apply to instances of small-group collaboration, such as the group of students seen in chapter 12, from which this analysis is in fact derived. The relations of the individual would be much different to a person who is reading alone, to a student sitting in a lecture, or to a designer working with a client. Even keeping in mind the restricted scope of the theory, it seems that much of what is most important, and perhaps most apparent, in the relation of an individual to a group does not manage to come to word in this study. For instance, although it is not stressed in this chapter, it becomes clear in chapter 13 that as the group of students working with SimRocket builds its collaborative knowledge about the list structure, it simultaneously, in parallel, makes sure that each group member also builds a corresponding understanding. Thus, the group view of the list is taken to be established only when the most intransigent student finally acknowledges, "I see. I see. I see." So group cognition processes often enforce parallel individual cognitive processes. It is hard to separate out conceptually the two aspects of the one subtle process.

Chapter 16, Group Meaning   Here, one element of chapter 15 is taken up and expanded on: the relation of meaning and interpretation in collaboration. Again, the scope of the analysis of the relation of group meaning to individual interpretation is intended to apply only to situations of small-group collaboration. The general question of the meaning of meaning is vast. This study simply proposes a distinction within the theory of collaboration—that the term *meaning* be here reserved for use when the unit of analysis is the group and that *interpretation* be used in reference to individual cognition. This does not reduce it to an arbitrary distinction. It still seems to be a rich and useful clarification.

Chapter 17, Group Cognition   This study confronts the question of what could possibly be meant by the phrases *group cognition* and *shared meaning*. It considers a number of alternative interpretations that seem to be implicit in the current literature. Then it addresses the popular discussion of *common ground* as a way of explaining shared meaning. The usual understanding of common ground is criticized as an attempt to reduce a group phenomenon to a sum or overlap of individual cognitions.

Chapter 18, Group Visibility   The methodological question of how to observe and analyze group meaning making is taken up in this chapter. First, the researchers studying the phenomenon need to be distinguished from the agents involved in the studied activity. An approach to video analysis is proposed, based largely on the examples in part II. Policies governing this methodology are adopted from ethnomethodology.

Chapter 19, Group Thinking   The question, "Can groups think?" is reminiscent of the 50-year-long debate in artificial intelligence about whether computers can think. Consideration of three major arguments about computer cognition by Turing, Searle, and Dreyfus concludes that it is misleading to speak of computers as thinking. However, applying the same arguments to collaborative small groups suggests that it is just as reasonable to attribute cognition to these groups as to their individual members.

Chapter 20, Group Worlds   This speculative chapter reflects on the role of discourse as the agent of group cognition. In a sense evoked by Heidegger's later work, the discourse that takes place among group members in their activity situations opens up a world of meaning out of which new group meanings and shared knowledge emanate. To support effective collaboration, we need to design sociotechnical mediating artifacts with social practices that can foster the emergence of productive worlds of group discourse and cognition.

Chapter 21, Group Discourse   The concluding chapter looks at an example of online group chat taken from research that is just starting. A preliminary analysis of collaborative methods of doing math online suggests a research agenda of empirical research guided by the issues raised in this book and focused on analyzing computer-mediated discourse as thinking at the small-group unit of analysis.

Part III ends by introducing a preliminary analysis of computer-supported collaborative knowledge building in a math chat room. Its purpose is to indicate a direction for further empirical exploration. Within a design-based approach, this also means further software innovation and experimentation. This book ends not with a final word but with a call for a serious investigation of group cognition that goes significantly beyond the scope of this text and requires an international collaborative effort. The cycle of design, analysis, and theory illustrated in this book needs to be iterated on a larger scale.

14

Communicating with Technology

When I finished the studies reproduced in part I, I felt a strong need to understand collaborative phenomena like negotiation as communicative interaction. I started to study under, work with, and collaborate with people in the communication sciences. Together, we gradually conducted the analysis in chapter 12. Recently, I hired a conversation analyst to work on the Virtual Math Teams project, and he helped with the analysis in chapter 21. I have been increasingly impressed with the orientation of communication theory to group phenomena. For instance, my methodological recommendations in chapter 18 are based squarely on Harold Garfinkel's ethnomethodology. In this chapter, I review the spectrum of communication theories as they are relevant to this book.[1]

The advent of global networking brings the promise of greatly expanded collaboration opportunities—both for learning together and for working together without geographic limitations. To realize this promise, we need to recognize the different nature of communicating, learning, and working in online settings of collaboration. This chapter looks at groupware as a medium for online communication and collaborative learning. It shows how these differ from traditional conceptions of communication and learning focused on individual cognition and draws consequences for the design of computer-supported collaborative learning and cooperative work systems.

Groupware as Medium of Communication and Learning

Carefully designed groupware and corresponding social practices must be developed if we are to realize the potential of computer-supported small-group collaboration. At the core of this collaboration is an understanding of communication in online groups and how software can support the specific needs of this new form of interaction.

Collaboration can involve the building of group knowledge. In collaborative learning, the explicit goal is to build some knowledge that might answer an initial question posed by the group or provide group members with a deeper understanding of a topic they are studying. In cooperative work, the group generally must build knowledge needed to accomplish a task, if only knowledge about how to divide up and manage the work.

Learning, work, and coordination in groups require communication. This is particularly apparent in online group activities because the subtle forms of communication that we take for granted in face-to-face interaction—such as nonverbal expressions or gestures—must be replaced with explicit forms of communication in online situations.

Groupware to support online work and learning by small groups must function primarily as a communication medium. It must support the particular forms of communication needed in computer-mediated interaction where the participants are separated geographically and possibly temporally as well. This form of communication has special requirements compared to face-to-face conversation and needs its own theory of communication.

Traditional Theories of Communication

There are many general theories of communication. A standard textbook by Littlejohn (1999) lists nine broad categories of communication theories, which can be characterized as follows:

- *Cybernetics* calculates the flow of information between a message sender and a message recipient, allowing for effects of feedback and transmission noise.

- *Semiotics* analyzes the role of signs, symbols, and language in communicative interaction.

- *Conversation analysis* identifies structures of ordinary conversation, such as turn taking and question-response pairs.

- *Message production* considers how message production is determined by the personal traits and mental state of speakers and by the mental processes of producing the message.

- *Message reception* focuses on how individuals interpret the meaning of communicated messages, organize the information they receive, and make judgments based on the information.

- *Symbolic interaction* views group, family, and community social structures as products of interaction among members. The interactions create, define, and sustain these structures.

- *Sociocultural approach*　emphasizes the role of social and cultural factors in communication within or between communities.
- *Phenomenological hermeneutics*　explores issues of interpretation, such as problems of translation and historical exegesis across cultures.
- *Critical theory*　reveals the relations of power within society that systematically distort communication and foster inequality or oppression.

These various kinds of theories focus on different units of analysis—bits of information, words, verbal utterances, communicative messages, social interactions, communities, history, and society. Although traditional communication theories taken together address both individual and social views of communication and take into account both face-to-face and technologically mediated communication, they do not directly address the particular combination of concerns present in groupware. Groupware—software designed to support group interaction and group work—of necessity combines technical, collaborative, and learning issues and does so in novel ways.

Groupware is often divided into computer-supported cooperative work (CSCW) and computer-supported collaborative learning (CSCL), with one typically focusing on workplaces and the other on schools (both presence and distance). This separation is justified by significant differences between these two social contexts. Learning situations at work and in schools are different in several important ways. In a school context, there is generally a teacher who structures the goals and activities of the group to facilitate learning processes. The classroom culture is very different from workplace cultures—for instance, in terms of the social practices and reward systems. Furthermore, members of collaborative learning groups are relative novices with respect to the topic being studied, whereas workers studied by CSCW researchers are experienced professionals.

Nevertheless, both learning and working—broadly understood—take place in both environments. The interactions of online groups collaboratively working or learning reveal workers engaging in many learning tasks and learners doing work of various sorts. Many forms of contemporary work involve building knowledge and sharing it; students learning collaboratively often work hard at establishing divisions of labor; some tasks like negotiating decisions intimately combine working and learning. Because collaboration is a matter of constantly sharing what one knows and maintaining shared understanding, all collaboration can be considered to have the structure of collaborative learning.

The very phrase *collaborative learning* combines social and individual processes. The term *learning* is commonly taken as referring to individual cognitive processes by which individuals increase their own knowledge and understanding. The collaborative aspect, on the other hand, explicitly extends learning to groups interacting together. Recent discussions also talk about organizational learning and community learning. Furthermore, contemporary pedagogical research literature emphasizes that even individual learning necessarily takes place in social settings and builds on foundations of shared or intersubjective knowledge.

Philosophic Theories

Our customary ways of thinking and talking about learning and communication tend to center on the individual as the unit of analysis. This commonsense, or folk theory, view can be ascribed to traditional Western philosophy, which since Socrates, and especially since Descartes, has taken the individual as the subject of thought and learning. The variety of twentieth-century communication theories can be seen as a heritage of different philosophies that arose in previous centuries. Foundational theory used to be the provenance of philosophy but has recently become the task of interdisciplinary social sciences, including communication theory.

As diagrammed in figure 14.1, philosophies prior to Georg Wilhelm Friedrich Hegel provided foundations for the learning sciences focused on the knower as an individual. Hegel (1967), however, tied knowledge to broad social and historical developments. Karl Marx (1976) then grounded this in the concrete relationships of social production, and Martin Heidegger (1996) worked out its consequences for a philosophy of human being situated in worldly activity. Sociologists, anthropologists, computer scientists, and educators have extended, adapted, and applied these approaches to define theories that are now relevant to groupware, cooperative work, and collaborative learning.

Theories of Learning

Different theories of learning are concerned with different units of analysis as the subject that does the learning. Traditional educational theory, such as that of Edward Thorndike (1914), looks at the individual student and measures learning outcomes by testing for changes in the student's behavior after a given educational intervention. From such a perspective, pedagogical communication consists primarily of an instructor conveying fixed knowledge to students.

In the 1950s and 1960s, there was considerable research on learning in small groups (e.g., Johnson & Johnson, 1989). Prior to interest in groupware support for online learning, it was generally assumed that the important learning was what the individual student retained, but there was explicit concern with the interactive processes within small groups of learners working together. Group activities had to be structured carefully to promote cooperation, interdependence, and learning, and

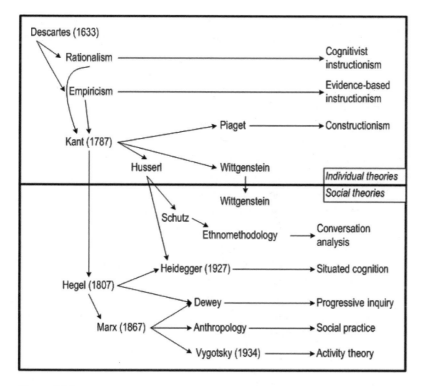

Figure 14.1
Influences on individual theories of learning (top) and social theories of learning (below the line).

participants had to learn how to cooperate effectively as well as learn the subject matter.

A more radical redefinition of learning took place with the analysis of situated learning within communities of practice (Lave, 1991). Here, the life cycle of a community was taken as the primary learning process, and the learning of individual community members was defined by the trajectory of their roles within the evolving community. For instance, even a relatively stable apprenticeship community can be seen as a group learning situation, in which new members gradually become acculturated and promoted. This view spread to the business world as it became concerned with the nature of corporations as "learning organizations" in a knowledge society (Argyris & Schön, 1978). Under these themes, work, learning, and social interactions come together inextricably.

With the rise of the Internet, it became obvious that technology might be useful in providing new communication media for learning communities. CSCL was founded based on the idea that classrooms could be structured on the model of professional communities of practice that collaboratively built knowledge, such as scientific theories (Scardamalia & Bereiter, 1996). New groupware communication environments would structure student contributions to online threaded discussions into knowledge-building processes of collaboration. Work became a model for learning, even as knowledge building became a way of life in workplaces.

The new learning theory was founded on a constructivist theory of knowledge: knowledge was viewed less as a body of facts that teachers could package as explicit messages for reception by students and more as a subtle developmental process in which students had to construct new understanding based on their current conceptualizations (Papert, 1980). Furthermore, following the principles of Vygotsky (1978), knowledge was seen to be generally constructed socially in interactions among people before it was internalized as individual knowing. Vygotsky's followers further developed this social aspect of knowledge generation into activity theory, which emphasizes that individual cognition is mediated by physical and symbolic artifacts and that it centrally involves sociocultural aspects.

The goal of providing effective computer support for collaborative work and learning is complex. Groupware cannot be designed to support a simple model of communication and learning but must take into account interactions among many people, mediated by various artifacts, and pursuing pedagogical goals at both the individual and group unit.

The software itself can be conceptualized as a mediating artifact of collaborative communication and situated cognition: the technology introduces physical constraints as well as sophisticated symbolisms (such as technical terms, icons, and representations of procedures like Web links). This means that students and workers must learn how to use the groupware artifacts and that the technology must be carefully integrated into pedagogical and work activities. Researchers trying to understand how to design classroom pedagogies, workplace practices, computer support, and evaluation methodologies have had to turn to an assortment of theories of communication, education, and cognition, such as collaborative interaction, constructivism, knowledge building, situated learning in communities of practice, and activity theory.

Communication Using Groupware

The circumstances of computer-supported collaborative work and learning introduce a number of significant and interacting factors into the communication process. Most of these factors have occurred before separately: telephones eliminate face-to-face visual contact; letter writing is asynchronous; group meetings exceed one-on-

one interaction; TV and movies add technological manipulation of messages. However, groupware simultaneously transforms the mode, medium, unit, and context of communication.

The Mode of Groupware Communication

Groupware may mix many modes of communication, including classroom discussion, small-group meetings, threaded discussion forums, chat, and e-mail. Typically, it relies heavily on threaded discussion. This mode is asynchronous and allows everyone to participate at their own pace; it can foster reflective responses and equality of participation. However, the volume of communication and the computer context with its restriction to typed text also encourages quick responses with short messages. The asynchronous nature of this mode slows down communication and makes it difficult to make timely group decisions and meet short deadlines. Chat can speed up interaction but increases the pressure to respond quickly. If more than a couple of people are chatting, the structure of responses can become confused. In general, each mode has pros and cons, so that a careful mix of modes is needed to take advantage of the affordances of each.

The Medium of Groupware Communication

The computer-based medium has inherent advantages. First of all, it provides a persistent storage for documents, messages, and interaction archives. A well-integrated collaboration environment can help users to review, browse, and integrate records of related interactions from different modes—and associate them with relevant digital artifacts, like diagrams, graphs, data, pictures, and reports. The computer can also lend computational power, manipulating, organizing, processing, and displaying information in alternative ways. For instance, messages can be displayed by thread, chronology, type, or author. The more functionality a groupware environment offers, the more users have to learn how to use it: how to understand and manipulate its interface and how to interpret and take advantage of its options. The computer environment can be a mysterious, confusing, frustrating, and foreboding artifact with arcane symbols and tricky functions—particularly until one masters the tool. Mastery of the medium often involves understanding some aspects of the technical terminology and model that went into the design of the medium and that is reified in its interface.

The Unit of Groupware Communication

Collaborative learning or working often focuses on the small group of perhaps four or five participants. Groups work and learn by engaging in activities like brainstorming, sharing information, reacting to each other's utterances, discussing, negotiating decisions, and reaching common conclusions. The group may learn something as a group and as a result of the group process—something that no member of the group would have come up with individually and perhaps something with which no member will leave. A group is made up of its members who bring their own backgrounds, perspectives, prior knowledge, and contributions to group discourse and who also take with them what they have learned from the group interaction. So there is an individual unit of learning that is tightly coupled with the group unit. Perhaps just as important, the group activity is embedded in the larger contexts of a classroom or department, a school or corporation, a society or economy. The goals of the group activity (tasks, rewards), its constraints (materials, time), its medium (computer support, meetings), its division of labor (group selection, mix of skills), and its social practices (homework, native language) are given by the larger community beyond the group itself. The individual, group, and community all develop new skills and structures through the influence of one unit on the other; none is fixed or independent of the others; learning takes place at each unit and between them.

The Context of Groupware Communication

Group communication takes place primarily through discourse. Discourse is a sequence of utterances or brief texts in a spoken or written natural language like English. Spoken language is quite different from standard written language: it does not consist of refined, complete, grammatical sentences but includes many halting, ambiguous, garbled phrases. The significance of spoken utterances is largely determined by the subsequent discourse. If some phrase or meaning is problematic for the people interacting, they may engage in a sequence of interactions to repair the problem. Chat tends to be similar to spoken language, but it has its own conventions. Threaded discussion is more like written language, although it is still interactive so that the meaning is determined by sequences or threads of messages from different people. In observing collaborative learning, one should not assume that an utterance is an expression of some well-defined thought in the mind of an individual but should construct the meaning interactively from the ongoing interaction of utterances—much as the members do while collaborating. The discourse context is embedded in the larger activity context, including various layers of community. This larger context includes an open-ended network of physical and symbolic artifacts (including technology and language), whose meanings have been established through histories of use and have been passed down as culture. Collaborative discourse is situated in the shared understanding of the group members, which in turn is historically, socially, and culturally situated.

Empirical Analysis of Collaborative Communication and Learning

The complexity of communication in groupware implies that empirical assessment of collaborative accomplishments should take place on the individual, group, and community levels of analysis and should show how these levels interact. Here are some common approaches.

Individual Outcomes

Perhaps the most frequently used approach for assessing collaborative learning is the traditional measurement of individual learning outcomes under controlled conditions. For instance, individual students might be given a pretest prior to completing a collaborative learning task. Then a posttest is administered to see if there was a statistically significant improvement under various conditions. Extreme care must be taken in defining comparable conditions. For instance, it is probably not possible to compare conditions such as collaborative and individual or computer-mediated and face-to-face because the tasks under those different conditions are necessarily so different: the activity task either involves or does not involve interactions with other group members or with computer software.

Thread Statistics

Group discourse in a threaded forum is often measured by compiling thread statistics. For instance, the number of postings per day or week shows the level of activity during different phases of a project. The distribution of thread lengths can give an indication of the depth of interaction. This kind of communication measure is especially appropriate for comparing similar cases, rather than for making absolute measurements, as thread statistics are dependent on factors like teacher or management expectations and reward schemes. Thread statistics provide a convenient quantitative measure of discourse; they can give some comparative indication of what is going on, although they are not very meaningful in themselves.

Message Coding

A method of quantifying a measure of the quality of discourse is given by coding schemes. Discourse utterances can be coded according to their content or their style. For instance, one could determine the primary topics in a discourse and classify the individual utterances under these topics. Then one could see who discussed what topics when. Or one could classify the utterances according to a set of categories, such as new idea, question, argument, summary, off-topic, or greeting. Analysis of coded utterances can shed light on aspects of a group process, but it cannot follow the development of a group idea in detail.

Conversation Analysis

This is a labor-intensive detailed analysis of an interaction based on a close interpretation of a sequence of utterances. It requires some familiarity with the structure of interaction, such as turn-taking, floor control, and repair strategies. These structures are quite different in computer-mediated modes of communication compared to face-to-face situations, which have been most analyzed. Despite its difficulty, this method of empirical analysis can be pursued when one wants a detailed understanding of the group learning that has taken place. This is because the learning has necessarily been made visible in the discourse. To conduct successful collaboration, the evolving state of knowledge must be visible to all members in the group discourse. This evidence of learning is retained in the traces of discourse if they have been adequately preserved and properly interpreted.

Role of Artifacts

Most collaborative activities involve more than the spoken discourse. The discussions often revolve around coming to increased understanding of a physical or digital artifact—for instance, a printed book or a computer simulation. The artifacts are embodiments of meanings that have been embedded by the artifact designers or creators; new users of the artifact must bring those meanings back to life. This is often an important part of a collaborative task. A full analysis of collaborative learning should consider the role of artifacts in communicating meaning—possibly across generations, from creator to user—and the process by which groups learn to interpret that meaning.

Technological Support of Groups

Computer support of one-on-one communication is relatively well understood. Systems like e-mail may not be perfect, but they do the job for most people. Small-group collaborative communication is much harder to support because it involves sharing across multiple perspectives.

Integrated Design

Collaborative software must allow people to share documents and diagrams and should also allow the collaborators to discuss these artifacts together. For instance, users should be able to annotate segments of text or pictures or even other annotations, thereby potentially constructing threaded discussions of the shared materials.

Shared Meaningful Media

Both the computer support media and the curricular content materials they convey are meaningful artifacts. They embody meanings that group members must learn and come to share. Collaborators can use a software artifact or the documents stored in it only if they can make sense of the documents and of the technology as it was designed. Furthermore, this sense must be constructed collaboratively if it is to work for the group. The software must be designed in a way that permits or fosters this.

Social Awareness

In communication that is not face-to-face, there should be mechanisms to support social awareness so that participants know what other group members are doing, such as whether they are available for chat. Participants should have a presence when communicating and should feel they are engaged in a social experience.

Knowledge Management

A variety of tools should be provided to help groups organize the information and artifacts that they are assembling and discussing. These tools should allow knowledge to be organized by the group as a whole so that everyone can see the shared state of knowledge as well as possible individual arrangements.

Group Decision Support

To arrive at a body of shared knowledge, group negotiation and decision making must be supported. There should be mechanisms that foster both divergent brainstorming and convergent consensus building.

Shared Learning Place

The starting point for a groupware environment is a shared repository and communication center, such as a virtual meeting place.

Pedagogy of Collaboration

The nature of CSCL communication suggests that curricula be structured much differently than traditional didactic teaching, lecturing, rote practice, and testing.

Support for Group Discourse

The centerpiece of collaborative learning practice is the promotion of group discourse. Group members must be able to engage in a variety of modes of discursive interaction. This is the way that knowledge is constructed at the group level.

Scaffolding

The teacher's role is to scaffold the group discourse. This means providing tasks, structure, guidance, and supports. These are offered primarily at the beginning. As the students learn how to direct their own collaborative learning, many of these supports by the teacher can be gradually withdrawn, like the superstructure of scaffolding around a building under construction, which is removed when the building can stand on its own. The teacher functions mainly as a facilitator of learning rather than as a primary source of factual domain knowledge.

Pedagogical Situations

The definition of goals, tasks, media, and resources is critical to the success of collaborative learning. Designing and implementing effective pedagogical situations or opportunities for collaborative learning are the subtle and essential jobs of the teacher. Especially in the early stages, the teacher must also guide the students through the collaboration process, modeling for them how to focus on key learning issues and how to frame manageable tasks. Often, a teacher's guiding question will define an impromptu learning occasion.

Groups and Communities

Ultimately, individual students should grow into positions of skillful leadership within the larger learning community. Practice within small groups builds that capability. In many ways, the small groups mediate between the individuals and the community, providing a manageable social setting for students learning interaction skills and structuring an amorphous community into specialized units.

Learning Artifacts

Artifacts are units of past knowledge building, externalized and made permanent in some physical, digital, or linguistic form. They facilitate the passing down of knowledge from one generation of collaborative learners to another. By learning to interpret the meaning of an artifact, a new group discovers the knowledge that a previous group stored there. Pedagogical situations should contain carefully designed learning artifacts.

Problem-Based Learning

An illustrative pedagogical method for collaborative learning is problem-based learning for medical students (Barrows, 1994). Groups of students work with a mentor who is skilled in collaborative learning but who offers no medical information. During their course of study, students engage in a series of medical cases that have been carefully designed to cover the field of common medical issues. Students discuss a case in a group and then individually research learning issues that their group identifies, coming back together to explore hypotheses and develop diagnoses. Exploration of a case involves in-depth research in medical texts and research literature. The case itself is furnished with rich artifacts like patient test results. Two years of mentored collaborative learning in small student groups prepares the medical students for communicating collaboratively as interns within teams in the hospital.

Implications for Groupware Design

The design and evaluation of software to support online collaboration should take into account the special communication characteristics of online interaction as well as the principles of situated learning. Three recommendations for doing this follow:

- *Focus on group interaction and collaborative learning*   Learning—whether in a classroom or at a workplace—should be seen as an active process of knowledge construction by a group. A deep understanding of a topic is generally developed through critical debate among multiple perspectives and is therefore an inherently social process even if it can be internalized in an individual's head. The development of knowledge content may be inextricably accompanied by the development of increased competence in cooperation, coordination, and collaboration skills. Collaborative learning and cooperative work thereby merge into the model of increasing participation in communities of practice.

- *Recognize the interplay of learning at the unit of the individual, small group, and community*   The classroom teacher or the workplace supervisor must initiate, structure, and guide the group discussion, As leader, facilitator, or moderator, a person in this role has responsibility for supporting and directing the knowledge-building process on both the individual and group levels within the social context. A deep discussion of the content must take place along with the self-organization of the group to promote the goals of the larger community.

- *Conceptualize the software as a communication medium and a knowledge artifact*   A technical environment can offer various collaboration and communication facilities. These constrain how knowledge can be constructed, shared, and preserved by the members of a group. The designers of an application or the people who select and configure software for a particular occasion must be careful to match the advantages of the different synchronous or asynchronous communication possibilities to the task so that selected components integrate well with each other and compensate for each other's weaknesses. The software should be conceived of as a medium for group communication and also as a working knowledge repository in which important learning artifacts can be stored, related to each other, and collaboratively refined. The software environment can itself be viewed as an artifact, whose meaning must be collaboratively interpreted and refined.

The Promise of Communicating with Technology

The nature of online groups holds the potential of enabling forms of collaboration more powerful than are possible in traditional face-to-face collaboration unmediated by technology. The technology overcomes physical limitations, provides computational support, and creates new modes of interaction. We can see this potential of collaboration in the realms of communication, learning, and work.

The Promise of Collaborative Communication

Collaboration depends on the people who come together in a group. The "anytime, anywhere" nature of online, asynchronous communication allows groups to interact without regard for conflicting personal schedules so that everyone who should be included can be included. One can participate in special-interest groups that are so narrow that no one for miles around shares one's passion. More people can be included in groups so that a group can draw the most appropriate participants from around the world. The foundations of the still distant vision of a global village are gradually laid by the formation of small collaborative groups freed from the traditional constraints of family and neighborhood to mediate universally between the individual and humanity.

The technology allows users to express themselves in a neutral, textual format that hides individual physical differences. It also allows users to retrieve and manipulate past messages and to respond to them at will. The fact that one can express one's ideas leisurely, when they occur, even if other group members have moved on to other topics means that people who are hesitant or slower to express their thoughts have more opportunity. Physical disabilities and personal characteristics that restricted participation in the past—immobility, accents, shyness—play less of a role now.

The characteristics of computer-mediated communication transform the mode of interaction. It takes the move from an oral to a literate culture further. Communication in a wired culture can be more reflective, although it is often the opposite. Communicated texts are persistent; they may be archived, annotated, cut-and-pasted, and reconfigured. This increases their power to refer and link to other texts. However, the sheer increased volume of texts drives users to skim more quickly and ponder less frequently. We still lack the computational support to weed through the glut of information and present only that which truly requires and deserves our attention.

The Promise of Collaborative Learning

Collaborative learning overcomes the limitations of the individual mind. When an individual builds knowledge, one idea leads to another by following mental associations of concepts. When this takes place in a group, the idea is expressed in sentences or utterances, with the concepts expressed in words or phrases. As suggested in chapter 13, the mental process can be understood as an internalization of more primary sociolinguistic processes. That is, meanings are built up in discourse—or in internalized dialogue—and then are interpreted from the individual perspectives of the group participants. Online collaborative learning allows more voices to chime in. By taking advantage of a persistent record of discourse, group knowledge building can pay more careful attention to the textual linkages interwoven in the texture of interactions, overcoming the rather severe limitations of human short-term memory for knowledge building.

Computational support could further strengthen a group's ability to construct and refine their understanding or theories. Today's collaborative knowledge management tools are primitive, but already they allow groups to search the Web for information and to scan through their own online conversations. The structure of the Web itself permits hypertext linking of ideas, providing an alternative to linear presentations of text. More sophisticated and adaptive structures are possible by storing short units of text in a database and sorting or arranging them in completely different ways for various presentation occasions, as was done in WebGuide (chapter 6).

Group learning has a qualitative advantage over individual learning. It is not just that two minds are quantitatively better than one or that the whole has a Gestalt that exceeds the sum of its parts. The synergy of collaboration arises from the tension of different perspectives and interpretations. During discourse, a meaning is constructed at the unit of the group as utterances from different participants build on each other and achieve an evolving meaning. For successful collaboration, a high degree of shared understanding must be maintained among the participants. Spoken interaction has many subtle resources for supporting this, and computer-mediated communication must provide a comparable set of mechanisms. Actual discourse is filled with repair activities to reestablish shared understanding when interpretations become too divergent. But the small and ubiquitous divergences of understanding within small groups also have a powerful productive force, often hidden under the label of *synergy*. An utterance is largely ambiguous in meaning until it is fixed by subsequent utterances into the emergent meaning of the discourse. The openness of an utterance to be taken differently by other utterances and to be interpreted variously by different discussants opens up a productive space for interpretive creativity. Combined with the diverse backgrounds and interests of group members and by the complex characteristics of activity structures within which collaborative discourses take place in the raw, the connotations and references of utterances can be incredibly rich. Unanticipated new knowledge emerges naturally from effective situations of group collaboration to an extent that it could not from individual cogitations. In the literate world, new ideas are printed for public critique and refinement. In the wired world, discourses take place in online groups, whose situations and membership can take on virtually limitless forms, resulting in new modes of knowledge building.

The Promise of Collaborative Work

In the information age, work centrally involves knowledge building. The extraordinarily developed division of intellectual labor means that many tasks are much more efficiently accomplished if people can be found who have just the right expertise. This is more likely if one can search the globe rather than simply looking for people in one building. By enormously increasing the choice of people to work together in an online group, one can then assign to each person just the tasks at which they are best. This entails new overhead tasks—bringing the right people together and managing the collaborative product—but in the long run, this should mean that individuals do not have to do so much tedious and routine work and can spend most of their effort doing what they do best. It should also dramatically reduce the total amount of work that has to be done as a result of efficiency increases. Unfortunately, we have yet to see such benefits because the socioeconomic relations of work have not yet changed in response to these potential new forces of production.

Collaborative work should be able to take advantage of the kinds of computer support that individual work has recently gained. So far, most software is designed with a model of work performed by individuals or by sets of individuals who send messages back and forth. There is little software designed for groups, as such. Given the current state of technology, groups tend to take an assignment, break it down into tasks that individuals can do, and then send those individual contributions back and forth to combine them into a group product. What kind of group-productivity software or collaboration environment would allow the group to work collaboratively, and what forms of computational support would facilitate this group work?

The Web, supplemented by the myriad digital libraries now proliferating, provides access to the record of human knowledge—almost. There are still overwhelming barriers to making this a reality. The technology is virtually there, but much of the interesting human knowledge is being held back. In fact, the more valuable and sought after information is, the more tightly it is restricted from public access. This might be termed the contradiction of information access today: world leaders increasingly fan the flames of fear and prejudice to limit global collaboration; employment conditions restrict the sharing of expertise; vigorously defended legal structures prohibit free access to intellectual property, from pop music to academic writings. The ideology of the individual still holds back the promise of the group to benefit from the products of collaborative learning and work.

The task of realizing the promise of communication, learning, and work in online groups sets an ambitious technical, social, and political agenda for our times.

15

Building Collaborative Knowing

This chapter discusses a core phenomenon for a theory of collaboration: meaning making, or the collaborative building of knowledge.[1] Written before I started to use the term *group cognition*, it nevertheless focuses on precisely that phenomenon. This was my attempt to draft a theory that discussed the most important aspects of group cognition, such as the relation of individual to group. At the same time, it reflects on the role of such a theory.

Rather than reviewing, one after another, various theories that are currently influential in the fields of computer-supported collaborative learning and cooperative work, this chapter synthesizes important concepts and approaches from these other sources. The abstract concepts proposed by these theories are illustrated with the example of building collaborative knowing analyzed in chapter 12. It contributes to a social theory of collaboration by unpacking central concepts and by using them to understand the process by which a small group collaboratively builds new meaning. The better we understand how the processes involved in collaborative learning actually work, the better we can design computer support for them and evaluate the effectiveness of both the collaboration and the support.

Elements of a Social Theory of Collaboration

The Need for a Theory of Collaboration
It is often assumed that every professional discipline is founded on a well-developed theory that defines the objects, goals, and methods of its domain. However, when users really begin to implement the theory—such as to guide the design of concrete software to support collaboration—they discover bitter controversies and disturbing questions concerning the fundamentals. This is certainly the case with computer-supported collaborative learning (CSCL): we are still arguing over its very name (Koschmann, 1996b).

Yet one cannot proceed without theory. How would developers, teachers, or researchers know what kind of software or curriculum to develop, how to introduce it into the classroom, or how to assess its effectiveness without at least an implicit theory of CSCL?

Definitions—a starting point for theory—are always contentious. *Computer support*, *collaborative*, and *learning* mean something different every time someone else tries to define them. Even the papers at a CSCL conference might never mention computers, pedagogically innovative software, or collaboration and may be far removed from most concepts of learning. Yet there is a field of CSCL with an active research community and much to recommend its adoption.

This chapter provides a consciously contentious perspective on key elements of theory for computer-supported collaboration. It emphasizes activity and accomplishments at the *group level*. This is what we mean by a *social* theory of learning in contrast to traditional ideas about learning as something that takes place primarily in the minds of individual people. Because the word *learning* often directs attention at psychological or mental processes at the level of the individual participant, this chapter often uses the term *building knowing* in place of *learning*. Rather than saying that a group learns, I say it builds the extent or depth of its knowing. This slightly awkward locution has the added advantage of distancing itself from the idea of accumulating things called knowledge, as in the idea of "learning facts"; what groups learn are often practices, ways of doing things, rather than facts. Roy Pea (1993b) similarly uses the term *distributed intelligence* to avoid the connotations of learning as involving decontextualized mental representations of individuals.

A Core Phenomenon of Collaboration

The term *building collaborative knowing*, coined for this chapter, is derived from the work of Marlene Scardamalia and Carl Bereiter (1996), who did much to found the field of CSCL. As used here, the phrase is intended to point to a core process in collaboration: a particular way in which a group may construct a new degree of understanding about the topic that they are investigating. This new knowing is something that the group creates that cannot be attributed to the mental processes of any one individual. As Bereiter (2002, p. 283) says,

The mark of a really successful design or problem-solving meeting is that something brilliant comes out of it that cannot be attributed to an individual or to a combination of individual contributions. It is an emergent, which means that if you look at a transcript of the meeting you can see the conceptual object taking shape but you cannot find it in the bits and pieces making up the discourse. There are, of course, instances where the design or solution does come from one person, but then you have a different kind of meeting, one that is devoted to grasping, accepting, and elaborating an idea. The result is still a social product, no matter how much it may bear the stamp of an individual.

This emergent group phenomenon is of particular interest to a theory of collaboration. I hypothesize that the building of knowledge, understanding, and meaning—learning, broadly speaking—within a group is central to the activity of both cooperative work and collaborative learning. Thus, it is a core phenomenon for the study of computer-supported small-group collaboration, including both computer-supported cooperative work (CSCW) and CSCL.

There are many ways in which learning can take place: over short and long time periods, in solitude and socially, formally and informally, tacitly and explicitly, in practice and in theory. There are many ways in which people collaborate and learn: by teaching each other, viewing from different perspectives, dividing tasks, pooling results, brainstorming, critiquing, negotiating, compromising, and agreeing. While all these aspects of learning and collaboration may be relevant to CSCW and CSCL, here the focus is on the phenomenon of building collaborative knowing, where group members together invent knowledge and skill that no one member would likely have constructed alone (Fischer & Granoo, 1995; Hatano & Inagaki, 1991; Mead, 1962; Wittgenstein, 1953). The transcript from chapters 12 and 13 (where increased knowing took shape in the group discourse and was not attributable to individual understandings) is again examined.

Collaboration takes place within other activities of learning and cooperation, such as individual meaning making and social enculturation. This chapter focuses on those brief, possibly rare episodes in which group discourse builds meanings, which can then be variously interpreted by the group members or sedimented in artifacts. It may well be in the mining of such gems of interaction that the potential of computer-supported collaboration lies. Too often, this key stage in collaboration is skipped over by theories; either it is treated as a mystery, is seen as an individual act of creativity that is not further explained, or is wrapped up in an abstract concept like synergy, which names the phenomenon without analyzing it. But this emphatically collaborative achievement is a key to comprehending collaboration, for it dramatically sets apart collaboration from individual learning. That is the hypothesis of this chapter. The analysis of such a group accomplishment requires a new way of thinking, a social theory.

A Social Theory of Collaboration

Theory needs to be subject to contending views and arguments and to compete for acceptance. Indeed, the purpose of proposing a theory is to subject it to the discourse of the research community so that it can be refined, critiqued, and negotiated to contribute to that community's collaborative knowing. This is where science gets its real power (Donald, 1991). This book is not an attempt to expound a set of eternal truths but is an effort to engage in a collaborative process of building shared knowing about the field of computer-supported collaboration and its potential. This chapter pulls together threads from an ongoing conversation and contributes a new, tentative, textual artifact into that process in the hope that it will be taken up, critiqued, and modified.

The theories incorporated here are particularly contentious because theoreticians like Lave (1996) and Engeström (1999), for instance, build on a *social* theory tradition that goes back to Hegel (1967), Marx (1976), and Vygotsky (1978). This theory is historically, culturally, linguistically, and politically foreign to many people whose intellectual instincts are shaped by an older, more ingrained tradition that focuses on *individual* minds as rational agents.

Prevalent enlightened thinking about learning owes much to Descartes's (1999) theory of ideas as existing in individual minds isolated from the material and social worlds. Thorndikian educational theories, which still dominate schooling, go back to this philosophic position. The history of philosophy and theory since Descartes has moved toward a more dynamic, social view. Kant (1999) argued that our knowledge of reality was not simply given by the material world but was constituted by the human mind, which imposes a basic structure. Hegel (1967) introduced a developmental view in which this process of constitution evolves through historical changes. Marx (1976) grounded these changes in socioeconomic phenomena. Heidegger (1996) then proposed a view of human being that is more firmly situated in the world than Descartes's approach. Figure 14.1 in chapter 14 provides a graphical representation of how the influences mentioned here led to social and individual theories of learning. This line of thought is developed further in chapter 20.

This Chapter's Approach to Theory
It is difficult for most people to think in terms of group cognition because of the traditional focus on the individual. It is also hard to comprehend the subtle and complex interactions that pass between group and individual knowing or between meaning embedded in an artifact and its interpretation in a person's mind. But such comprehension is necessary for understanding the social approach to a theory of collaboration.

First of all, the right vocabulary is necessary for thinking about phenomena that occur on levels of analysis that we are not familiar with discussing. In addition, we need the appropriate conceptual resources and analytic perspectives. This is what is meant here by *theory*. Philosophy used to provide such intellectual tools, but recently this has become a task for interdisciplinary sciences, such as cognitive science, learning science, CSCW, or CSCL, all of which build on anthropology, communication theory, social theory, and computer science. This chapter draws on theoretical reflections and conceptualizations from these fields to try to explain the phenomenon of building collaborative knowing. *Theory* in this chapter is not meant in the sense of clear and distinct definitions of concepts, empirical laws, rigorous methodologies, and mathematical precision. It is meant to provide a way of looking at social interactions in terms of interrelated phenomena and concepts, such as artifact, situation, meaning, interpretation, tacit knowing, perspectives, negotiation, and internalization. These concepts are not so much defined in unambiguous sentences as they are borrowed from other theories or philosophies and adapted into an emerging conceptualization. The terms glean their definitions from each other as a result of how they are configured together (Adorno, 1958). Hence, these terms should become gradually more meaningful as one reads through the chapter and tries to apply its view to the phenomena presented or to one's own world.

The nature of the interactions involved in building collaborative knowing have scarcely been investigated in any tradition, although they are absolutely fundamental to a possible theory of collaboration. While available philosophies can provide some direction for exploring these interactions, empirical investigations are urgently required. We need to better understand how knowledge and meaning can be encapsulated in a wide variety of artifacts and then how groups of people can come to understand these embedded meanings and effectively interpret them. We need to look carefully at examples of this taking place under real-world conditions. Therefore, this chapter begins with a review of chapter 12 and 13's empirical analyses of an instance of collaboration.

The empirical example introduces the intertwining of individual (psychological) and group (social) processes, through which collaborative knowing can be built. The sharing of knowledge among group participants as well as the building of the group's own knowing is accomplished interactively, primarily through situated discourse processes.

Discourse, which makes things explicit, relies on a background of tacit or practical knowing, and the co-construction of shared knowing in discourse involves the negotiation of tacit meanings—for instance, of the affordances of artifacts. The network of these meanings constitutes the social world in which we live and that we come to understand by building collaborative knowing.

This chapter attempts to suggest the core elements of a social philosophy that could provide a foundation for CSCW and CSCL. Such a theory necessarily involves issues of epistemology, semiotics, hermeneutics, and ontology. *Epistemology* asks how knowledge is possible; social epistemology shows how knowing is interactively constructed within communities. *Semiotics* asks how signs can have meaning; social semiotics shows how meanings of signs and other artifacts are socially constituted.

Hermeneutics asks how we can interpret meaning; social hermeneutics shows how individuals interpret socially shared meaning. *Ontology* asks what kinds of beings exist; social ontology shows how beings are produced and reproduced within a society.

The kind of social epistemology, semiotics, hermeneutics, and ontology proposed here would not provide a complete social theory. For that, we would have to build up from the social as small group to the social as institutions and multinationals, including cultural and historical levels of description, and then return from these abstract social formations to the concrete activities in which people find themselves in any given moment—but this time fully mediated by categories and understandings from the larger sociohistorical context (Bourdieu, 1995; Giddens, 1984a; Habermas, 1984; Marx, 1976; Sartre, 1968). The foundations and concepts for such a full social theory could come in part from the elements presented in this chapter.

A Moment of Collaboration

The theory presented in this chapter emerged through an analysis of the specific example of collaborative learning discussed in chapters 12 and 13. This section reviews that example. The following sections then use the example to illustrate the concepts of the theory.

Why We Need Empirical Examples of Collaboration

Writing about contentious matters like the nature and mechanisms of collaboration is risky. Each reader interprets the meaning of what is said by relating it to his or her own experiences, existing understandings, and interpretations of prevalent folk theories (established wisdom and common worldviews). Paradigmatic examples of small groups building collaborative knowing are still rare these days, and the mechanisms underlying them have yet to be well analyzed. So skepticism and misunderstanding are the expected outcome unless the starting point for the reader's interpretation can be appropriately grounded in shared experience. To this end, I first review the empirical example and some hints for interpreting it. I invite the reader to study the analyses in chapters 12 and 13 and to search for and reflect on other examples (such as Koschmann, 1999a; Roschelle, 1996; Sfard & McClain, 2003) and studies from ethnography, psychology, and ethnomethodology.

This case study is not representative of all collaborative activities, but it provides a particularly useful illustration of the phenomenon of building collaborative knowing. The example here represents some generality, as is suggested by its similarity to what Hatano and Inagaki (1991) describe as "collective comprehension activities" in Japanese classrooms: these take place among small groups of students, involve references to an artifact (or source of confirmation), and include room for comprehension.

The example we present takes place in a middle school and not in the world of work or higher education. This provides a clear view of the collaborative building of an instance of elementary science knowing: the principle of varying only one parameter of an experimental situation at a time. In a higher-education science class or a professional scientific laboratory, most people would have some sense of this principle, but in middle school we can observe such an understanding still under construction. In addition, the discourse is not computer mediated; the face-to-face interaction provides richer, clearer, more intuitive evidence for what is taking place. This is helpful for analyzing the detailed interactions that constitute the building of collaborative knowing, although examples will also need to be studied where the communication is computer-mediated (see chapter 21). The sample interaction is, however, computer-supported by a software rocket simulation so that we can observe how the students increase their knowing about how to use a digital artifact.

Empirical examples are more than mere aids to presentation of a theory. It is necessary to show how theory is grounded in and integrated with empirical studies. Theory can be very abstract and leave the detailed mechanisms undeveloped. Often, these details are crucial for practical application of the theory—such as for guiding the design of technology to support collaboration—and are required for fleshing out the theory itself. Thus, while several recent theories stress the role of artifacts as embodiments of shared understanding (e.g., Dourish, 2001), little has been written about how new users of the artifacts learn to share these stored understandings— a question investigated in a modest way in our example (especially in chapter 13).

The empirical example used in this chapter is not an arbitrary illustration of theoretical ideas that are unrelated to it. The theory in this chapter actually grew out of chapter 12's detailed analysis of this particular collaborative interaction. By presenting the theory within the context of its empirical origin, we try to situate the reader within a concrete understanding of the phenomena being analyzed.

The Experimental Situation

Recall from chapter 12 that five 11-year-old boys were experimenting with a computer simulation of model rockets with different design attributes (different engines, nose cones, fins, and surface textures). The students could fire eight different rockets and record their heights in a datasheet. A list of the attributes of the eight rockets was displayed on the computer screen next to the simulation (see figure 12.1 in chapter 12). Two sessions with the simulation totaled three hours and were video recorded.

The first session began with the students reading the list of rocket descriptions and discussing with the teacher how to figure out which attributes did best in the simulation. Then working in two subgroups, they fired the different rockets multiple times and averaged their heights to adjust for random fluctuations due to simulated weather conditions. After filling in their data sheets, the students were guided by the teacher to figure out which attributes were optimal. Most of the discussion up to this point had been teacher-centric, with the teacher posing questions, evaluating responses, and controlling turn taking, as is typical in school settings (Lemke, 1990).

A key aspect of the experiment is that the list of rocket descriptions was carefully designed to make it easy to compare pairs of rocket descriptions that differed in only one attribute. The relevant pairs were listed consecutively, and the differing attribute was written in boldface type. However, even after having read the list aloud and having worked with the simulation for over an hour—with the list on-screen the whole time—the students were literally unable to see this property of the list.

Preliminary Analysis
At a certain point, after the teacher gestured at the list, the students launched into intense collaborative interaction, which consisted of a brief utterance about once every second. What follows is a transcript of that collaborative moment, beginning with the teacher's directing of the group attention to the list. We can review our analysis from chapter 12 by dividing the interaction in the transcript excerpt into four phases:

Phase 1 The transcript begins at 1:21:53 with the teacher posing a rhetorical question, which was then clarified at 1:21:59 as asking the students to find a pair of rockets on the list that had the same engine but different nose cones. The students responded that there was no such pair in the list. This was not the expected response to a rhetorical question and indicated a breakdown in the group discourse:

1:21:53	Teacher	And (0.1) you don't have anything like that there?
1:21:54		(2.0 second pause)
1:21:56	Steven	I don't think so
1:21:57	Jamie	Not with the same engine
1:21:58	Steven	No
1:21:58	Jamie	Not with the same
1:21:59	Teacher	With the same engine . . . but with a different (0.1) . . . nose cone?

1:22:01	Chuck	the same
1:22:01	Jamie	Yeah,
1:22:02	Chuck	These are both (0.8) the same thing
1:22:03		(1.0)

Phase 2   After a significant pause at 1:22:03, Brent excitedly pointed to what the teacher had asked for: a pair of rockets with a nose-cone difference. Brent lurched forward and physically gestured at the list, forcibly directing the group attention there. This altered the structure of the group. In phase 1, the students were united against the teacher; in phase 2, Brent joined the teacher; in phase 3, other students successively aligned with Brent and the teacher; finally, in phase 4, a new consensus was established:

1:22:04	Teacher	Awright
1:22:05	Brent	This one's different (gestures with pen at computer 1 screen)
1:22:06	Jamie	Yeah, but it has same no . . . (1.0)
1:22:08	Chuck	Pointy nose cone

Phase 3   While Chuck continued to argue against the implication of the teacher's rhetorical question, Steven, Jamie, and Brent successively disputed Chuck's utterances. They pointed to rockets 1 and 2 as a pair with different nose cones:

1:22:09	Steven	Oh, yeah
1:22:10	Chuck	But it's not the same engine
1:22:11	Jamie	Yeah, it is,
1:22:12	Brent	Yes it is,
1:22:13	Jamie	Compare two n one
1:22:13	Brent	Number two
1:22:14	Chuck	(0.2) I know.

Phase 4   Making explicit which rockets to look at on the list finally got Chuck to align with the rest of the group. Chuck had apparently been trying to find a rocket to compare with rocket 3 or 4 and had rejected 2 because although it had a different nose cone it did not have the same engine as 3 or 4. Once everyone saw the pair of 1 and 2, the group could proceed with its task and quickly draw a scientific conclusion:

1:22:15	Jamie	(0.2) Are the same
1:22:16	Chuck	Oh
1:22:17	Brent	It's the same engine.
1:22:18	Jamie	So if you compare two n one,
1:22:19	Chuck	Oh yeah, I see, I see, I see
1:22:21	Jamie	(0.8) Yeah. Compare two n one. So that the rounded n- (0.1) no the rounded one is better. Number one.

Keep this concrete interaction in mind when the discussions become more abstract in the following sections. Each phase presents phenomena that are taken up in later sections.

In phase 1, there was a breakdown in understanding between teacher and students. In overcoming this breakdown, the group built collaborative knowing: by the end, the whole group knew how to find significant pairs of rockets on the list. Such knowing is interactively constructed in groups so that it is available to the group's members (discussed below).

In phase 2 and throughout the collaborative moment, we observed very brief utterances, like "This one's different," "The same," or even "Yeah." Such utterances are meaningful only within the context of the group interaction and not by themselves. They serve mainly to point to other utterances, to reference items in the list, or to engage in the group interaction (e.g., aligning, disagreeing, arguing, or clarifying). Below I explore how meaning—which was not completely present in these utterances of individuals—can be understood only at the group unit of analysis.

In phase 3, there was a concerted effort to realign the shared understanding of the group that broke down in phase 1. At first, the students argued against the teacher. But in subsequent phases, they gradually came to align with him. In the discourse itself (and nowhere else), these shifts could be seen as the individual interpretive perspectives of the different students changed and aligned. Later in this chapter, I distinguish meaning (which exists in the shared social world) and interpretation of that meaning by groups and individuals (chapter 16 discusses this distinction further).

In phase 4, everyone was able to see the descriptions of rockets 1 and 2 in the way implied by the teacher. Although the descriptions were in the list all along, and Chuck had even read them aloud an hour and a half earlier, it took a while for the students to see the meaning that had been designed into the artifact. The final section in this chapter explores how affordances and meanings that are preserved in artifacts and words must be interpreted within concrete and practical situations involving discourse, tasks, and other forms of interaction.

Individual and Group Knowing

Theories of learning and collaboration tend to emphasize either individual or group knowing. It is difficult but important to understand how both take place and influence (or constitute) each other.

Individual and Group Learning in the Example

The data about collaborative learning provided in the previous section were given at the level of a videotaped interaction and transcribed discourse, with some contextual information. To understand the learning that took place, a researcher must analyze it within the context of the small group. That is, the activity system of tasks, artifacts, interactions, symbols, social practices, and roles within the community of practice forms the unit of analysis. In this unit, meaning is constructed, and new ways of knowing are built. The meanings generated within this unit are absorbed into the group's knowing.

As researchers, we can analyze our data either by looking at the group discourse as a whole or by following the trajectories of individuals within the group discourse. That is, we can focus either on the small group (the activity system as distributed among several people engaged with each other and with artifacts in complex ways) or on the individual as the unit of our analysis. We can also reflect on how events at one level affect those at the other; this is, in fact, essential to get a full picture (Fischer & Granoo, 1995; Hatano & Inagaki, 1991). In our example data, there is a breakdown in the group discourse, and individual contributors shift their positions within the group in order to reestablish a healthy group discourse.

Shared and Personal Knowing

Our sample transcript also shows individual utterances that make sense only within the group context and the shared situation. Closer analysis reveals that individual contributions build on what has taken place within the group discourse, on current features in the shared situation, and on future possibilities for joint activity. Thus, the individual utterances rely heavily on the group discourse; we can argue that the group unit of analysis has an epistemological priority in that it provides prior conditions necessary for the knowing that can then take place at the individual unit.

The group unit is particularly significant in *collaborative* learning. In cooperative or coordinated work (as contrasted to collaborative), tasks are often divided so that individuals actually work and build knowledge on an individual basis and then attempt to share the results. However, in collaboration, by definition (Dillenbourg, 1999), the work is done by the group as a whole. For this reason, social approaches to theory are especially appropriate for understanding collaboration. Individual utterances and personal knowing need to be situated within their social context (see next section).

Cognitive and Social Theories

Analyses of learning usually focus either on individual contributions as expressions of psychological states of individual people (the cognitivist or acquisition perspective) or on the collective accomplishments of a community or a society (the sociocultural or participation perspective) (see Sfard, 1998). The *cognitivist* perspective takes utterances to be expressions of preexisting mental representations or ideas of individuals, while the *sociocultural* perspective takes elements of the language used to be social creations or accepted conventions of the culture. By analyzing the transcript data, however, we can see how both the utterances and the terminology they include are interactively constructed in the discourse as a whole—so that there is no need to posit either preexisting mental constructs or fixed structures of social conventions independent of the discourse and causally determining it. Rather, on the contrary, we can see the mental and the social as results or products of previous discourse, now sedimented into meaningful cognitive and linguistic artifacts that function in current activities. Meaning is thereby constructed and interpreted in small-group interaction (see below).

Collaborative Learning as Building Knowing

Collaborative learning can be viewed as the gradual construction and accumulation of increasingly refined and complex cognitive and linguistic artifacts. This takes place primarily in collaborative interaction, but these products of group collaboration and discourse also can be internalized as the internal speech or thought of individuals. The cognitive and linguistic artifacts that develop are tools for knowing. As collaborative learning takes place, both the group in its interactions and the individuals who adopt and internalize these tools build their ability to know the kinds of things in which the group is involved. In the sample data, the group comes to know how to use the list of rockets as an artifact or tool to accomplish their activity. Groups need mechanisms for building collaborative knowing and for helping individuals to understand and internalize what their groups and culture have built (see final section in this chapter).

Situated Discourse

Utterances in the experimental data derive their meaning from the discourse situation, which is constituted by interactions among the utterances.

References to the Situation

The utterances in the example transcript can be characterized as indexical, elliptical, and projective. That is, they are not meaningful in isolation, the way propositions are traditionally taken to be. They are meaningful only through their references to the current physical context, prior utterances, or projected future possibilities within the activity.

Some of the utterances in the transcript can be identified as *indexical*: their meaning depends on their reference to some artifact in the environment, like a rocket or a rocket description (such as "this one"). Other utterances are *elliptical* in that they leave out crucial parts of what would be a complete proposition, assuming that the hearer can fill these in based on previous statements in the discourse history (for example, "Number two"). Finally, some utterances are *projective*: they must be interpreted in terms of a desired future state of the discourse ("So if you compare").

The meaning of these utterances is not self-contained but is constituted by reference to a totality of interconnected artifacts that make up the world of the group. We call this world the *situation* and refer to the discourse as *situated*. Utterances often function as signs, pointing into networks of meaningful terms, artifacts, and activities.

Preserving Knowing in Words and Artifacts

In the example situation, the word *different* plays an important role. In the pivotal utterance, "This one's different," there is an indexical reference to an item on the list artifact as well as to the teacher's previous use of the term *different*. Brent appropriates the teacher's term; in the subsequent group discourse, this reference is extensively developed in terms of what is or is not the "same" and the activity of comparing rockets. Over the course of the transcribed interaction, the participants gradually come to see what Brent referred to as "this one" as "different." The vocabulary of "different," "same," and "compare" serves to point out relationships in the list so that everyone in the group can see them. In the process, the terms preserve this new knowing-how-to-look-at-the-list in their extended meaningfulness to the group. At the end of the collaborative moment, the group knows much better how to use both the terms and the list artifact to which they refer. It is likely that the teacher already interpreted the terms and the artifact this way but that the students had to learn to interpret these meanings as preserved in the terms and artifact.

Brent's interpretation of "this one" as "different" is a first step in articulating a full meaning for the salient differences and similarities among pairs of rockets in the group activity. One can see here the initial phase of the verbal formation of meaning. It is like observing Michelangelo starting to chisel a rectangular block of marble and seeing a human form struggling to emerge from the inert stone in which it is embodied (figure 15.1). Brent may first use the term "different" by mimicking the teacher's speech. As he and his fellow students continue to use it, its meaning becomes more differentiated, articulated, and refined through its connections among more utterances and their circumstances. Eventually, we can say that the students have learned the meaning of the comparison vocabulary as scientific technical terms.

In the next sections, I describe how meaning is embodied in artifacts and sedimented in language so that meanings that may have originally been created in ephemeral spoken utterances become *persistent*. This makes possible the preservation of the meanings over time, and we can say that knowledge has been created as a product that can be effective over time.

Common Ground and Distributed Cognition

We have seen that meaning is given by a shared world that is interactively constructed in collaborative discourse. This is somewhat different from some understandings of common ground that start with individual units of analysis and then try to account for a shared reality (see chapter 17). Common ground is sometimes taken to be an agreement among individuals who all somehow have the same meanings or knowledge as part of their background understanding, and that makes possible further interaction (Clark & Brennan, 1991). But in our theory, the meanings are part of a single world, situation, or activity system in which the individuals all interact. The common ground exists from the start for them as a shared world in which they exist together and is not something that has to be established through some kind of agreement or coordination among mental contents.

This theory is not exactly the same as distributed cognition, which also argues that at least some meaning is "in the world" rather than all being "in people's heads" (Hutchins, 1996). Certainly, meaningful artifacts exist in the physical world. But their meaning is not physically present in the world in the same sense as the body of the artifact itself. The meaning comes from the networks of reference in which the artifact is located (see chapter 16).

An artifact is perceived as meaningful, but this perception is a matter of interpretation. In our example, for instance, we saw that the meaning of the list artifact was not immediately perceptible to the students but that they had to learn how to see it. The common ground, which had broken down, was interactively achieved during and through the transcribed interaction; it was an accomplishment of the group interaction and not a matter of arbitrary agreement among the individuals of preexisting ideas in their heads. The group discourse had to focus on the list as a salient artifact and explicate an interpretation of its meaning. The ability to include

Figure 15.1
Michelangelo Buinarroti, *Slaves: Atlas*, c. 1530, marble, Galleria dell' Accademia, Florence, Italy. Photo: G. Stahl, 2002.

the list artifact effectively in their activity was something that the group had to achieve.

Creating Knowing at the Small-Group Unit of Analysis

Knowing how to use the list artifact was not something that was passed from the teacher to the individual students through propositional instruction. Rather, the group of students evolved that ability by responding to each other's utterances. The teacher had established a context in which this could productively take place by setting up the classroom activity system with designed artifacts, specific activities that required knowing how to use the artifacts, and a pointed question that offered some terminology. The utterances at the start of the transcript disagree with each other ("No. . . . Not with the same. . . ."). Subsequent utterances respond to these, increasingly clarifying differences and justifying views. In the end, there is agreement within the group discourse, established by a process that took place within the group as the actor, subject, or unit of analysis.

Collaborative learning took place as the group increased its ability to talk about the list artifact within the immediate task of responding to the teacher's hypothetical question and within the larger classroom activity of designing effective model rockets. Progress was made through normal discourse processes, specifically repairing a breakdown in shared references to rockets in the list. Overcoming the breakdown involved aligning the interpretations of the individual students with the meanings embodied in the list.

Theories influential within CSCL emphasize assessing learning on the community level and supporting community processes with technology. Scardamalia and Bereiter's (1996) vision of computer-supported learning communities, in which the community as a whole learns, was defining of the field. Lave and Wenger's (1991) situated learning involves changes in the social practices and configuration of the community itself. Engeström's (1999) expansive learning approach even looks at learning taking place when multiple communities interact with each other. In our example, we see an instance of learning unfolding through the communicative interaction of a small group. Here, the discourse is situated not only within a classroom community but more specifically within the activity of the small group (see chapter 21).

Meaning and Interpretation

Collaboration is a process of constructing meaning. Meaning creation most often takes place and can be observed at the small-group unit of analysis. Meaning in the context of collaboration is viewed as an integral part of communication and therefore necessarily as shared within a community. Meaning can be embodied in physical or virtual (computer-based) artifacts or sedimented in words or gestures. Created by groups, institutionalized in communities of practice, and preserved in artifacts, meaning must be reactivated by newcomers to the community as part of their apprenticeship (Lave & Wenger, 1991). Individuals must learn to interpret these meanings, as the students in our transcript learn to interpret the meaning in the list artifact and the meaning in the teacher's use of the term *different*.

Meaning as Use and Knowing in Use

The kind of empirically based social theory being proposed here looks at how groups actually create, share, use, and interpret meaning as an integral part of social interaction. This is quite different from the mainstream tradition. Philosophers have long struggled to understand the nature of meaning by focusing on the individual unit of analysis. They sought the meaning of words in clear and distinct definitions, the meaning of ideas in their correspondence with reality, or the meaning of thoughts in mental representations.

But these attempts to define meaning as a property of individual minds—whose mental representations correspond to realities in the world—did not succeed. In critiquing this tradition, Ludwig Wittgenstein (1953) argued that the meaning of an utterance involved how it is used to accomplish practical moves within "language games" that are part of the speaker's "form of life." John Austin (1952) and John Searle (1969) further developed this view of speech acts as having pragmatic effects within group interaction systems, including social institutions and conventional practices. Functional grammar (Halliday, 1985) took this yet another step, analyzing the grammatical components of a sentence as relationships within a network of meaning.

Using functional grammar as a tool, Jay Lemke (1990), for instance, analyzes the discourse of a science classroom as the construction of a complex network of meaning; this linguistic network constitutes the scientific theory that the students are learning. The collaborative learning of the class consists of the explicit elaboration of this network, and the individual learning of the students consists of their ability to restate parts of this meaningful network. In constructing the network, the teacher and textbooks use a variety of alternative terms and metaphors, so that meanings can be abstracted from the use of multiple phrasings. Students are then expected to be able to talk, write, and reason about parts of the network of meaning in their own words and to understand novel descriptions.

In the sample data, we saw a temporary breakdown in the construction of a network of meaning. Although the students had previously identified rockets with "different" fins, they could not abstract this ability to identify rockets with different nose cones under their specific circumstances. To overcome the breakdown, the students employed gestures, argumentation, peer pressure, the list artifact, clarification, and explication. They also built on their practical experience with their model rockets, the simulation rockets, and their data-collection sheets. Perhaps most significantly, their success in constructing a network of meaning that included consistent references between utterances and rockets on the list artifact came about through group interactions driven by the classroom activity system, including the need to respond appropriately to the teacher's hypothetical question. Thus, the network of meaning grew out of group discourse processes, but these were embedded in contexts of practical social activity. The knowing that the students built was not just a theoretical knowing evidenced by their ability to talk about the rockets consistently but a practical knowing involving the ability to accomplish tasks within the activity structure context.

Tacit and Practical Knowing

It is common to think of knowing as the ability to state facts in propositions. But there is also what Michael Polanyi (1962, 1966) calls *tacit knowledge*, which includes the ability to *do* things—like ride a bicycle—even though one may not be able to put that knowledge into words. *Tacit* means "un-stated" and *explicit* means "stated in words." The students know how to follow nonverbal communication cues like gaze, pauses, and body orientation, as well as to engage in explicit discussion.

Heidegger (1996) showed that tacit or practical knowing actually has an epistemological priority over explicit or theoretical knowing. To understand a proposition requires that one already have immense amounts of background ontological knowing about the world, about people, and about the kinds of objects referred to by the proposition. Language is a form of communication and interaction with other people and with the world. To understand language, one must understand it within the context of a broader tacit preunderstanding of social interaction and of the everyday world of ordinary life.

Interpretation as Making Explicit

In the process of building collaborative knowing, there is interplay between tacit and explicit knowing. In Polanyi's analysis, what is explicit is the current focus of attention. It stands forward against a background of tacit knowing. As attention shifts (for example, as the topic of discourse moves on), what was explicit becomes tacit, and something tacit is made explicit by being put into words. Heidegger calls the process of making something explicit *interpretation* (see chapter 4).

Interpretation is making an implicit idea *x* explicit *as y*. By doing so, it integrates *x* into the situational matrix (as *y*). This *x* is understood as having the meaning *y*, which is defined by *y*'s position in the interpreter's network of references. Discourse is interpretation. It makes things "explicit" or puts them into words. As created embodiments of meaning, words are semiotic artifacts that are part of the network of significations.

When Brent says, "This one's different," he is making explicit what he sees in the list artifact: he points to rocket 2 as different (tacitly, his implication is that rocket 2 is different from rocket 1 in terms of its type of nose cone). According to Heidegger, perception of the world and engagement in the world are always interpretive, even when they are tacit. The process of explicit interpretation takes the existing interpretation and develops it further. At first, Brent and the other students saw rocket 2 as not being comparable with rocket 3 or 4 because it had a different kind of engine. But then he suddenly saw rocket 2 as comparable, but different, from rocket 1. This became explicit as he saw the description of rocket 2 differently, leaned forward, pointed to it, and said, "This one's different." Chapter 13 shows how the group and each of its members shifted from seeing the list as standard configurations to seeing it as paired configurations.

Brent's "Aha!" experience is an instance of what Wittgenstein (1953) calls "seeing as." Among several ambiguous graphical images, Wittgenstein presents a wire-frame cube (figure 15.2). The viewer might first see a cube with its shaded end facing down to the right; then suddenly it appears as a cube with its shaded end facing up to the left. One can see the drawing as one cube or the other or even as a set of lines on a flat surface—but one always sees it *as* something. It is not that there is first an uninterpreted grid of pixels (sense data) that someone subsequently interprets as one of the cubes. Rather, the perception of the image is always given as meaningful and

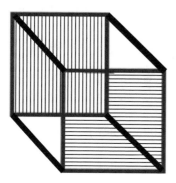

Figure 15.2
Diagram of a cube. First focus on the horizontal stripes as foremost, then on the vertical. Adapted from Wittgenstein (1953, sec. 177).

tacitly interpreted. Then it can be reinterpreted, or the interpretation can be explicated: put into words, made a focus of attention, and further elaborated.

Interpretive Perspectives

Meaning and interpretation are always intertwined. Artifacts and utterances are immediately perceived as being meaningful. They are, from the start, perceived within a certain interpretation—however vague or confused. The interpretation may be made explicit and further elaborated, but it must always be grounded in the given meaning of the artifact or utterance within its context. For the purposes of this chapter's theory, I make a somewhat arbitrary and potentially contentious distinction between meaning and interpretation: the *meaning* is defined for the community involved in the given situation, and the individuals each develop their own *interpretation* of that meaning. (This distinction is worked out in more detail in chapter 16).

How do students learn? In the sample data, we see how the students learn the meaning embedded in the list artifact through their collaborative interpretive processes. They make explicit the features of the list to each other by interpreting it (as "different") and stating references ("compare two and one").

As researchers studying classroom data, we can develop an explicit interpretation of the group meaning by analyzing the network of relationships constructed by the group discourse, taking the group as a whole as our unit of analysis. We call this network the *situation*. Every artifact, action, word, or utterance obtains its *group meaning* from its position within this interactive situation.

Alternatively, as researchers we can develop an explicit interpretation of a specific individual participant's interpretation by analyzing the behavior and utterances observed in that individual's trajectory within the group interaction, taking that individual as our unit of analysis. We call this individual trajectory the *interpretive perspective* of that person. We say that the person interprets the group meanings from that perspective.

Roughly stated, meaning exists in the world, determined by the situation, and participants interpret that meaning individually from their personal perspectives. Both the situation and the perspectives are constructed interactively and may be constantly evolving and interacting with each other. Meanings may be embodied in artifacts and sedimented in language, but they were originally constructed through interpretive processes, and their significance must be reconstructed by new participants who build knowledge with them in the future.

It is not so much that meaning is in the world like a separate set of objects but that things in the world always appear as meaningful. The students saw the list of rockets as meaningful from the start; to them, it was obviously a designed object with human meaning embedded in its form and its content. Brent understood some but not all of its meaning; through interpretation (of one entry *as* "different"), he articulated the initial meaning and thereby increased his understanding of it.

Negotiating Knowledge

Our transcript begins with the teacher asking, "And you don't have anything like that there?" Our analysis of the transcript interprets the meaning of "like that" to refer to a pair of rockets that differ only by nose-cone type, such as rockets 1 and 2. But our analysis also claims that this phrase is initially interpreted differently by the various student perspectives. Because group meaning has to be interpreted by individual participants from their own perspectives, there are many possibilities for divergence and misunderstanding.

The openness to interpretive divergence is a powerful mechanism for creativity in group discourse (Rogers Hall, personal communication). It allows different participants to pursue different interpretive lines of exploration of shared themes. Such divergence can continue until it becomes noticeable, possibly causing a breakdown in communication, and the group sets out to resolve the differences. The various discourse methods for establishing convergence of interpretation can be considered forms of *negotiating* knowing.

In the experimental data, prior explicit focus on comparing rockets 3 and 4 made it hard for the students to see rockets 1 and 2 as the thing "like that" to which the teacher's question was trying to point. The students' negative responses to the teacher's hypothetical question apparently violated the perceived social practices of the classroom and motivated the negotiation that gradually shifted the group focus to rockets 1 and 2. Once those rockets were explicitly named, the various interpretive perspectives aligned their references, and further progress followed rapidly.

The much-touted *synergy* of collaboration has its origin in the negotiation of multiple perspectives. Different viewpoints on the discourse topic interact, are explored, and lead to novel results. This takes place at the group level of interpretation. Individual utterances are open to many possible interpretations due to the ambiguity of their indexical references, the elliptical nature of their expressions, and the openness of their projections. But within the flow of the group discourse, certain of these possibilities are selected. One person's response picks up on one of the possible interpretations of a preceding utterance and establishes that as its meaning within the discourse. Through such discourse processes, the meaning of what is said is determined by the interactions of multiple members of the group, not just by the person who made a particular utterance. In fact, it is not the individual utterance that expresses meaning but the network of consecutive utterances within the situational context. Thus, the meaning is deeply synergistic, arising through the intertwining or negotiation of the individual perspectives within the group situation.

But there are real limits to openness and interpretive creativity. One can attempt to interpret something and fail. This may be due to the resistance of reality: things have meaningful form, particular utility, and specific affordances and cannot be arbitrarily interpreted. Interpretation is a kind of creation/discovery (Merleau-Ponty, 1955) where different things can be tried but will not all work. Interpretation is an ongoing process, incorporating conjectures and refutations, hypotheses and disconfirmations, trials, and revisions. As someone listens to someone or reads a text, he or she constantly and tentatively constructs an interpretation, trying to form a consistent account of the many words, phrases, and references; repeatedly revising and reorganizing as new evidence is taken into account; and quickly forgetting the former interpretations and the process of successive revision.

The objectivity of knowledge arises—gradually and tentatively—through the negotiation with reality and with multiple interpretive perspectives through discourse. This social interaction can, for instance, raise issues of evidence or apply standards of scientific argumentation: science is itself a prime example of continuous knowledge negotiation (Donald, 1991; Latour & Woolgar, 1979). The status of scientific theories, particularly in the human sciences, does not contradict their origin in processes of building collaborative knowing but rather derives from the nature of those processes as methodologically structured and intersubjectively accepted.

Building Knowing

Now that the elements of building collaborative knowing—such as artifacts, situation, meaning, interpretation, tacit knowing, explicit knowing, perspectives, and negotiation—have been introduced, we can outline the process by which groups construct meaning and individuals develop their understanding.

Internalization and Externalization

According to Lev Vygotsky (1978, 1986), human intelligence is formed by individuals internalizing artifacts and language that are generated socially—that is, at the group level. We can think of *internalization* as the generation of *cognitive artifacts* (Hutchins, 1999; Norman, 1991). Here, the term *artifact* refers to symbolic or linguistic as well as physical or digital artifacts. *Cognitive* means that the artifact has been transformed into a mental process.

Suppose that a student took the data sheet with the rocket statistics that the group had compiled. If he remembered the format of the matrix of numbers or some of the key statistics, he could later use this memory to format a data sheet for another project or to make arguments about rocket design. This memory would then be functioning as a cognitive artifact. Its affordances would be different than but derived from the physical data sheet artifact. Similarly, the students were able to internalize the teacher's vocabulary of *different*, *same*, and *compare*. By mimicking the teacher's talk, the students gradually, and with varied success, internalized this language game of rocket science.

This example suggests that human memory, which is commonly considered to be a biological function, is instead a complex involving both inherited capabilities and internalized cognitive artifacts. It is probably built on a biological base of episodic memory, by which many mammals can recall specific events that took place in their past experience and that may be similar to some aspect of a present situation. As part of the specifically human ability to mimic, people also exercise mimetic memory (Donald, 1991), which allows us to imagine things that are not currently present. The human ability to mediate perception, memory, and behavior—especially generating speech, including self-talk and silent internal speech—greatly extends our capacity to imagine and express meanings that reference things not in our immediate perceptual environment (Vygotsky, 1978). In interacting socially to acquire local language and practices through mimesis, human infants develop an extensive array of cognitive artifacts, including more sophisticated forms of memory such as temporally structured narrative memory (Bruner, 1990), which in turn let them develop more complex physical and mental abilities.

Even the concept of self, for instance, can be viewed as a cognitive artifact that is socially constructed and internalized through mimicking. Children learn what is "mine" in contrast to what is someone else's and adopt a view of themselves through the eyes of the other (Levinas, 1998; Mead, 1962). Georg Friedrich Hegel (1967) analyzes the emergence of self-consciousness as a result of the creation of physical artifacts produced for other people, and Karl Marx (1967, 1976) sees self-alienation as a result of the distortion of such social artifact production in commoditization. The modern focus on the individual is an historic product of social organization (Adorno & Horkheimer, 1945; Jaynes, 1976). Hence, the individual as mind is not a primitive element of theory but is itself a socially constructed cognitive artifact.

Externalization has often been considered to follow on internalization, where prior mental representations are expressed in physical forms such as speech or drawing. But in our theory, which does not speculate or hypothesize about mental representations, *externalization* is simply the fact that meaning is embodied in artifacts and sedimented in language. It is unnecessary to speculate on the extent to which that meaning had previously been rehearsed in the internal speech of the people who designed the artifact or uttered the words. In fact, both in terms of the developmental process of the human species and that of each person, meanings are generally internalized first—from some external, interpersonal, group, or social form, according to Vygotsky (1978)—before they can be (re-)externalized. So external meaning generally precedes internal (Hutchins, 1996) rather than the reverse, which is traditionally assumed.

The Interpretation of Signs and the Affordances of Artifacts

The meanings of signs, symbols, terms, and phrases are built up through use. In the transcript, the term *different* takes on a specific meaning through the sequence of its occurrences in the discourse. It is used in conjunction with other terms, in reference to certain rockets, in various functional grammatical roles, and as part of several speech acts. It also brings with it meanings from standard conversational English. All these influences are *sedimented* in the term's meaning for the classroom group, like the layers of sand sedimented in the earth's geology and visible to the knowledgeable eye as traces of ancient history. Just as sand is compressed and transformed into impenetrable rock over time, the past uses of a word are compressed into its meaning (Husserl, 1989). The meaning is shaped by its history long after the details of its episodic uses have been forgotten. Through interpretation, new speakers of the word must learn to read the nuances of its meaning from the occurrences that they experience.

An artifact *embodies* human meaning in its physical form. By definition, an artifact is made for some purpose. Its meaning has been designed into its form by a community for whom that artifact is part of the community's culture. The rocket list artifact, for instance, is a scientific inventory list. It includes a line describing each rocket in the simulation, systematically arranged to facilitate the identification of pairs of rockets differing from each other in only one variable. We say the list *affords* such identification or that the artifact has this *affordance* designed into it. An affordance is not an objective property of an artifact but is part of its meaning for a community of use (Gibson, 1979; Norman, 1990; Wartofsky, 1979). Moreover, it is something that individual interpreters must learn to see as an affordance: only at the end of our transcript can Chuck say, "I see, I see, I see" about the list artifact's affordance.

The Cycle of Knowledge Building and Meaning Making

Building collaborative knowing or constructing shared meaning is a cyclical process with no beginning or end. Any episode starts on the basis of an indefinitely long history of meaning and knowing. It assumes a meaningful language and a world of artifacts, a situation in which everything is already interpreted. Whatever is made explicit was already tacitly known and can be explicated only against an unbounded background of prior understanding. The "hermeneutic circle" (Heidegger, 1996) means that one can interpret only what one already has an interpretation of.

Figure 15.3 represents a number of phases of building collaborative knowing and relates this group process to the individual flow of personal knowing. Here, some of the terminology has been modified from the corresponding figure (figure 9.1) from chapter 9 to incorporate the discussion in this chapter. Individual utterances start the public cycle, triggered by some focus of attention against a background of tacit personal understanding. The cycle can eventually lead to the production of shared cultural artifacts, which can be internalized by individual participants, increasing their resources of cognitive artifacts.

In the small-group discourses that drive building knowing, group meanings intertwine subtly with interpretive perspectives that engage in complex negotiations. Unnoticed, new layers of meaning are sedimented in shared jargon. Periodically, persistent artifacts, like documents or pictures, are produced. Through the mediations of internalization processes, these cognitive artifacts can then persist as personal memories, intellectual resources, mental abilities, and minds.

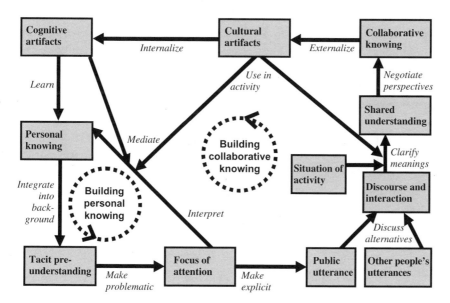

Figure 15.3
A diagram of the cycle of knowledge building. Adapted from figure 9.1 in chapter 9.

Viewed historically, the cycle feeds on itself and spirals exponentially faster. These days, technology mediates the interactions, the artifacts, and the access. Building knowing takes place dramatically differently in a technologically produced environment, interpreted from scientific perspectives. The discourse processes in a CSCL discussion forum, for instance, are very different from those in a face-to-face meeting, partially because they take place in written rather than spoken language. The transition from oral to literate society (Ong, 1998) is taking another major step forward with computer-networked communication. The nature and rate of social interaction and of the building of collaborative knowing are undergoing rapid and continuous transformation.

The Interactive Construction of Knowing, the Situation, Temporality

How is an activity system context interactively achieved by a group discourse? The immediate activity for the collaborative moment in the transcript was established by the teacher's rhetorical question. Both the definition of the immediate task and its accomplishment were carried out discursively. His question was precisely formulated to define a mini activity system that could lead to the desired group knowing. The question was not, however, planned in advance by the teacher but arose spontaneously as his reaction to the ongoing conversation. His skillful use of such questions was a discursive, rhetorical resource that he put to use in the specific context in an effort to further the larger activity. This is an example of how an activity context was created as a natural and integral consequence of the very ongoing discourse that it structured. That is, the context was not a preexisting and immutable institutional structure, nor was it the externalization of someone's prior mental representations or plans (Suchman, 1987).

It is characteristic of persistent objects that they distort or obscure the apparent history of their creation. Marx (1976) pointed this out for commercial products and called it the "fetishism of commodities." He argued that commodities on the market appeared to have an inherent economic value, whereas his historical, socioeconomic analysis showed that their value was based on social relations among the people who produced and exchanged them. Similarly, words seem to have some kind of ephemeral otherworldly meaning, whereas we can deconstruct their meaning and demonstrate how it was constituted in a history of contextualized uses and networks of relationships to other words, artifacts, and activities. Artifacts, too, seem to come with objective affordances, but these were designed into them by their creators and must be learned and interpreted anew by their users.

In our theory, collaborative learning—as the extending of group knowing—is constructed in social interactions, such as discourse. It is not a matter of accepting fixed facts but is the dynamic, ongoing, evolving result of complex interactions, which take place primarily within communities of people. The building of knowing is always situated; the situation grants meaning to the activities, language, and artifacts that define the extended, interrelated context. Such a cyclical, dialectical process in which people construct elements of the very context that conditions their activity and makes it possible is a process of *social reproduction* or *structuration*: the meaningful social situation reproduces itself interactively (Giddens, 1984b). The situation reflects previous social activities and is transformed by current interactions and by projections of the future. Frequently and unnoticed, interactive knowing crystallizes into seemingly immutable knowledge or facts, just as situated action coalesces into habitual practices, conventional rules, and dominant institutions.

Even space and time, as the dimensions within which activities take place, are interactively socially constructed. The utterances in the transcript have been characteringed as indexical, elliptical, and projective, meaning that they referenced unstated elements of the past, present, and future discourse or its situation. In making such references, the discourse weaves an implicit pattern of temporal relations. The interactions of a group narrate the topic of discussion by indexing artifacts in the present situation, elliptically assuming references to past interaction and projecting possible futures. Participants in the discourse interpret and understand this woven temporal pattern as an unnoticed part of their involvement in the discourse. In this way, the situational network of meaning is structured temporally as what Edmund Husserl (1989), Martin Heidegger (1996), and Alfred Schutz (1967) call "lived temporality." Out of the social interaction among people, the following elements get produced, reproduced, and habituated: the group itself as an interactive unit, the individuals as roles and mental subjects, the situation as network of artifacts and space/time as dimensions of reality.

The Larger Social Context as Constituted by Designed Artifacts and Sedimented Language

This chapter focuses on the microprocesses by which the social context is constituted; for instance, how words and artifacts get, preserve, and convey their meaning. From these elemental processes that take place primarily in collaborative group interactions, one could then show how larger-scale social institutions and human cognitive phenomena are built up.

An analysis of the role of artifacts (Bereiter, 2002; Donald, 1991; Geertz, 1973; Latour & Woolgar, 1979; Marx, 1976; Vygotsky, 1978; Wartofsky, 1979) views human culture as consisting of immense collections of linguistic, physical, and technological artifacts. Social theoreticians (Bourdieu, 1995; Garfinkel, 1967; Giddens, 1984a; Habermas, 1984) show how social institutions and behavioral codes arise from elemental processes and become institutionalized into large-scale social structures that seem impervious to human influence. These views could be summarized as arguing that the social context in which we live is constituted by the products and by-products of building collaborative knowing, taken on a global, historical scale. Just as our own behavior and cognitive skills as individuals are products of group interaction, so the large social structures are interactively achieved, reproduced, and reinterpreted in the momentary practices of communities (see chapter 20).

This chapter has attempted to present core elements of a social theory of collaboration. In bringing together terms and approaches from existing theories influential within CSCW and CSCL, it has tried to describe some of the microprocesses (like synergy) that are often left as unexplained mysteries in other writings. I argued for the need to develop collaboration theory, reviewed the empirical example of building collaborative knowing to guide our thinking, and suggested an answer to the epistemological question of how collaborative knowing is possible by pointing to group interaction as its source. After analyzing the semiotics of meaning in terms of the situation as a network of relations among words, artifacts, and activities, I addressed hermeneutic issues of interpretation with the ideas of background tacit knowing, personal perspectives, and knowledge negotiation. Finally, these concepts were brought together to show how knowing evolves through a cycle involving externalization of knowing in artifacts and internalization as cognitive artifacts, all within a broader context of social institutions and community culture. This defines an ontology of meaningful physical objects and human abilities that develop through interaction with other people within a shared meaningful world.

This Chapter as a Theory Artifact

This chapter has not presented a comprehensive and accepted theory but has attempted to point in one possible direction for developing a theory of computer-supported collaboration. Part of this theory is an understanding of how meaning, in group interaction, is collaboratively constructed, preserved, and relearned through the media of language and artifacts. This research complex has barely begun to be explored. For instance, we need careful investigations of how computer-supported discourse differs from face-to-face discourse in daily conversation and how students and workers learn the affordances of CSCL and CSCW artifacts.

If we self-apply our theory of building collaborative knowing to the process of theorizing about collaboration, we immediately see the importance of coining descriptive terminology, designing effective artifacts, and reflecting on these as a collaborative community to achieve the potential of CSCW and CSCL.

16

Group Meaning / Individual Interpretation

For the CSCL 2003 conference, I wanted to present something of my theory of group cognition.[1] I took the theme of meaning and interpretation (see chapter 15) and tied it to the topic of meaning making that has been identified as defining of computer-supported collaborative learning. I deepened the analysis of meaning and interpretation, arguing that *meaning* applied to shared products of knowledge building and *interpretation* corresponded to the individual perspective on such meaning.

Because collaboration and collaborative learning take place through processes of shared meaning making, computer-supported collaborative learning and cooperative work must be concerned with the nature of meaning and social meaning-making practices. Philosophic analysis suggests that meanings are necessarily shared. They persist in linguistic and physical artifacts in our culture and situation, and must be interpreted by individuals. There is a reciprocal relationship between shared meanings and individual interpretations. To engage in collaborative activities, people must come to recognize meanings of artifacts and interpret these meanings from their own perspectives. The interplay between meaning and interpretation has implications for research methodology and for technology design of support for collaboration.

Meaning Making and the Study of Collaboration

Keynote talks at the last three international conferences on Computer-Supported Collaborative Learning—Paul Dourish at Euro-CSCL 2001, Timothy Koschmann at CSCL 2002, and Roger Säljö at CSCL 2003—all emphasized the centrality of the analysis of meaning making to the study of collaboration. In his presentation, Koschmann identified the concept of *meaning*—as it is discussed in the philosophic tradition—as dwelling at the fundamental core of CSCL. Arguing from a close reading of Dewey, he proposed that "CSCL is a field of study centrally concerned with meaning and the practices of meaning making in the context of joint activity, and the ways in which these practices are mediated through designed artifacts" (Koschmann, 2002a, p. 20).

Despite Koschmann's careful crafting of this programmatic statement, it remains open to ambiguous interpretation. As can be seen from the discussion following the keynote (Henderson & Wyman, 2002), *meaning making* can be interpreted as a psychological process that takes place in individuals' minds, and the reference to *designed artifacts* can be understood as narrowly referring to CSCL software systems.

In my introduction to the *Proceedings* that include the keynote, I indicate a possible alternative reading of this definition of the field of CSCL (see chapter 11)—that meaning making can be treated as an essentially social activity that is conducted jointly (collaboratively) by a community rather than by individuals who happen to be colocated. In addition, the mediation of meaning making by artifacts can be seen more generally than just as the transmission of personal opinions through the communication channel of a technological artifact.

The meaning-making practices do not merely take place located *within* a "context of joint activity," the way an armchair philosopher's mental cogitations might take place physically within the four walls of his library. Rather, the context of joint activity *is* those practices: the practices form the joint activity, which constructs the meaning. The meaning is not merely transferred from mind to mind by the activities but is constructed by and exists as those activities.

The practices of meaning making are acts of discourse or interaction; these acts propose, negotiate, display, and define what are to count as the salient features of the setting, the occasion, the social norms. Neither the context nor the meanings are objectively given in advance but are collaboratively constituted or brought in.

Artifacts are not simply instruments for conveying independent meanings but are themselves embodiments of meaning. The process of embodying meaning in artifacts mediates or transforms that meaning. People are necessarily involved in meaning making as interpreters of the meaning, but this does not imply that the meaning exists only in the isolated heads of the individuals. These are some of the issues to be addressed in this chapter.

In my own contribution to a theoretical framework for CSCL at the 2002 conference, I presented four themes that I found helpful for conceptualizing foundational issues of CSCL: collaborative knowledge building, group and personal perspectives, mediation by artifacts, and interaction analysis (see chapter 11). In this chapter, I propose a way of thinking about meaning and interpretation in collaboration by building on Koschmann's statement and on my four themes from CSCL 2002. I hope to thereby clarify my alternative reading of Koschmann's characterization of CSCL. I propose that—particularly in contexts of collaboration—*meaning* exists (as the meaning of artifacts) in the *intersubjective* world and that it is *interpreted* from *personal* perspectives. The meanings of meaningful expressions and objects are intersubjectively established, although they may be interpreted differently by different people, and so, meaning should not be reduced to its interpretation by specific individuals. It is not just a content of individual minds.

The Philosophic Tradition

The nature of meaning has been a hot topic in the 2,500-year-long conversation that we call Western philosophy, since its origin in Socrates's dialogues. In the early twenty-first century, this conversation has spread into the theoretical reflections of the human sciences. It is increasingly filtering into reflections on CSCL. For instance, in his featured paper at the Fifth International Conference of the Learning Sciences (ICLS '02), delivered half a year after his CSCL keynote, Timothy Koschmann explicitly proposed that the history of philosophy—especially the period from Kant to Hegel—was relevant to the learning sciences (Koschmann, 2002c). In particular, he cited a paper that argued that ontology as well as epistemology are central to sociocultural and constructivist learning sciences (Packer & Goicoechea, 2000). This paper focused on how Kant and Hegel had worked to overcome the mind-body dualism introduced by Descartes, where meaning, as something purely mental, is ontologically distinguished from and epistemologically divorced from the physical world. Contemporary learning theories reflect implicit and often unacknowledged philosophic commitments defined at different stages in the history of philosophy, representing different responses to this dualism.

As a discussant to Koschmann's ICLS paper, I reviewed the philosophic relationships among the philosophers and learning theories that Koschmann discussed. I tried to suggest that the timely issue is not so much overcoming the dualism of Descartes but moving beyond his exclusive focus on the *individual* as thinker (the mental *cogito* as seat of cognition and meaning). This is where a nonidealist reading of Hegel proves to be pivotal. Hegel shows how consciousness emerges through activity in the social and physical world. In tracing the historical and personal genesis of mind from the most elemental perceptual awareness to the most sophisticated and acculturated knowledge, Hegel describes the emergence of self-consciousness from within the process of mutual recognition of self and other. In particular, the worker, who produces an artifact in the physical world at the bidding of another, is then able to perceive his labor as externalized and made persistent in the artifact. His self-consciousness emerges through his activity in the social and physical world, where he comes to see himself in his products and through the eyes of others:

Work *gives form* to its object. The worker's transforming relationship toward the object is transformed into the object's form and becomes something *persisting* because for the worker the object gains self-sufficiency. This transforming mediation—the *activity* of forming—is also the *individuality* of consciousness or the pure being-for-itself of consciousness, which in the work process now steps out of consciousness and takes on the character of persistence. The consciousness of the worker thereby arrives at a perception of the self-sufficient artifact as a perception *of his self*. (Hegel, 1967, p. 238, my translation)

In Hegel's paradigmatic parable of meaning making here, the meaning of the arti-fact—the form imposed on the material object—is created in the activity of the worker, which is an intersubjective activity essentially defined within the interaction of worker and master. The meaningful artifact, however, assumes a self-sufficiency in which it is henceforth distinguished from (and to that extent independent of) the worker and his perception of it. The meaning-making process that takes place in the material and intersubjective world endows objects with human meaning that persists with the persistence of the artifacts and thereby distinguishes itself from the momentary intentions and interpretations of the individuals involved. The identity and self-understanding of the individuals are, in turn, determined by the meanings that they then confront in their world as independent and objective meaningful artifacts.

For Hegel's most important interpreter, Marx, the artifact, which is produced by the worker's labor and that externalizes the worker's self by its social relations to other people, is transformed within settings of capitalist production into a com-modity (an artifact produced for sale on the open market) (Marx, 1976). The worker's self-consciousness is alienated because the commodity is no longer his (but the capitalist's who sells it) and because his social relations to potential users of the artifact is transformed into the abstract monetary value of the commodity. The meaning of the labor that went into forming the product undergoes multiple complex transformations as it is externalized into an artifact and as the artifact enters com-modity relations and is reflected back to the worker as monetary value belonging to his boss. This fetishism of the commodity is a real social process in capitalist society and not merely a psychological illusion: the commodity takes on a value and meaning independent of the people who produce it and the social relations in which it is pro-duced. In Marx's analysis, the dominant form of meaning making today (commod-ity production) is one that hides its own social origin and nature.

Marx and Heidegger explicated Hegel's view, showing how meaning is socially produced and situationally interpreted. Their followers developed it further and applied it in many realms, eventually leading to the diverse theories of learning that are influential in CSCL today (see figure 14.1 in chapter 14).

Although it seems clear at a theoretical level that meaning is socially constructed, when it comes to investigations of learning—even in collaborative settings of

CSCL—it is difficult for researchers to stop looking for learned meanings in the heads of students. This is partially a consequence of folk theories that have not kept pace with philosophy (according to Bereiter, 2002; Dennett, 1991), but it is also partially caused by a lack of clarity about the role of interpretation of meaning by individuals. This chapter attempts to clarify the relationship of meaning and interpretation in collaborative activities, showing that although the interpretation of a meaning may be tied to the individual's subjectivity, the meaning itself is shared and observable in the world.

Vygotsky and Mediated Cognition

We start with Vygotsky's programmatic attempt to show how the individual mind—often naively considered to exist "in the head"—is grounded in activity within the physical and social world. His description of the genesis of the pointing gesture illustrates a typical early experience of meaning for a small child. It shows how this meaning is created in the intersubjective world and only then incorporated (internalized) in the child's own sense-making repertoire:

We call the internal reconstruction of an external operation *internalization*. A good example of this process may be found in the development of pointing. Initially, this gesture is nothing more than an unsuccessful attempt to grasp something, a movement aimed at a certain object which designates forthcoming activity. . . . When the mother comes to the child's aid and realizes this movement indicates something, the situation changes fundamentally. Pointing becomes a gesture for others. The child's unsuccessful attempt engenders a reaction not from the object he seeks but from another person. Consequently, *the primary meaning* of that unsuccessful grasping movement *is established by others*. . . . The grasping movement changes to the act of pointing. As a result of this change, the movement itself is then physically simplified, and what results is the form of pointing that we may call a true gesture (Vygotsky, 1978, p. 56, italics added).

Here we see the *genesis of the meaning* of a pointing gesture. The recognized, practical, and formalized gesture becomes an artifact: it embodies meaning in the material world. The meaning is a reference to what is pointed at. The baby intended some object; the mother recognized that the baby intended that object; the baby recognized that the mother recognized this. The multiple mutual recognition entails that the baby and the mother recognize each other as people who can have intentions and who can recognize intentions of other people. This is a first glimmer of self-consciousness, in which the baby becomes conscious of his own and other people's intentionality. (The baby cannot yet express this self-consciousness in any verbal or conceptual sense but only behaviorally.)

The key point for us here is not the birth of intentionality, social recognition, or self-consciousness. It is the creation of an artifact: the pointing gesture. This gesture embodies its meaning in a physical way. As a paradigmatic deictic (pointing) gesture, it already embodies a reference to the intended object as the artifact's very meaning. So we have the first step toward a symbolic artifact representing an intended object. In the origin of the gesture, we already see the basis for intersubjective *shared understanding* of the meaning. The pointing gesture is premised on the mutual recognition of a projected underlying intention.

While there is a mutual assumption of intentionality—that in pointing the child intends to direct shared attention to a certain object—note that this does not imply that the child already had some kind of internal mental representation of the object and is expressing externally a reference to what corresponds to that representation. We know nothing concerning the existence of mental states of the child. By observing the child's physical grasping and pointing behaviors, we know that the child has sufficient perception, attention, and recall skill to interact with physical objects as persistent and as potentially graspable. But Vygotsky's working hypothesis is that the higher, specifically human psychological functions have yet to be developed by the child. The child's intentionality is here purely a matter of physical activity in the world.

Pointing has a clear evolutionary advantage. It establishes a fundamental social bond by shared orientation to a common intended object. It immediately coordinates the orientation of the people involved into the same direction within the world. It thereby provides a practical basis for *collaboration*. It is probably so fundamental to human social experience that it is found in all cultures, although it is not a result of biological instinct. Vygotsky argues that this gesture is used in two general ways, which lead to our extensive repertoire of symbols, artifacts, cognitive skills, external memories, and cultural systems: it is used to control the pointer's own behavior, and it is internalized.

In the original enactment of pointing, the baby achieves *control* over the mother's behavior. He gets the mother to retrieve the intended object that he wanted but could not reach. It is only through success at achieving this control that the baby learns that his failed reach can be recognized by the mother as an intention. As the baby's repertory of gestures and artifacts grows, he begins to use them to control his own behavior as well. We can see this in the behavior of young children playing and drawing, for instance. At certain stages in their behavior, they negotiate or adopt rules and meanings that structure their behavior in ways that may prove useful. The rules and naming originally came after the activity, in reaction to the externalization, but are later used in advance to evoke, structure and control the activity. For instance, a toddler might draw on paper and when asked what she drew retroactively say it is a dog. When she is older, she will intentionally set out to draw a dog.

Language grows out of gesture and is then *internalized*. Names reference objects in a way that extends the pointing gesture. Not that language consists only of names;

rather, many linguistic functions extend other kinds of embodied behavior—and then other linguistic tools may be built on top to perform purely syntactic or pragmatic functions (Halliday, 1985). According to Vygotsky's theory, language begins as spoken communication among people. Clearly, that is how people learn language. At a certain age, when children have learned the fundamentals of a language, kids engage in "self-talk" or "ego-centric talk." This is where they speak aloud to themselves (or to imaginary friends, dolls, and other artifacts). Similarly, early readers initially read aloud. This self-talk evolves into silent internal talk. Internal talk is an important component of what we call *thought*. Thinking often involves talking to ourselves. For instance, silently with ourselves, we rehearse what we plan to say (and control our future behavior and interaction that way), recall what took place in the past, or carry on the kind of conversations that we have aloud with other people. Through this evolution, primal gestures have been transformed into speech, and speech into thought. Meanings and references to things in the world have been internalized into mental forms that still embody some of the functions that they originally had as physical artifacts or bodily gestures.

Externalization in Physical and Semantic Artifacts

As we see in the preceding Hegel, Marx, and Vygotsky stories, meaning may start as an emergent property of activity in an intersubjective physical setting. It begins as an aspect of a collaborative interaction and is then successively transformed into a phenomenon of its own. The worker's effort to prepare something for someone else or the infant's thrust toward an object that requires mother's help takes on a shape that persists or reoccurs. It adopts an increasingly well-defined and shared meaning, ultimately perhaps even becoming a symbol of that meaning.

The object that embodies shared meaning can be further transformed; for instance, it can be named. Either that object or the word that names it can be used to mediate future activity. The infant can use the gradually stylized gesture to indicate things he wants or things that he wants the mother to give him, mediating his interaction with her by means of this gesture. The mother, in turn, can use the gesture to associate names with the thing pointed to, so that both will then use the word with the same reference. Vygotsky generalized the term *artifact* to include symbols like names as well as man-made material objects. He then showed how human activity (as opposed to purely instinctual, biological, animal-like behavior) is generally mediated by such artifacts in complex ways.

When we say that in Vygotsky's theory meaning is *externalized*, we do not imply that some kind of meaning first existed in someone's head and that it was then expressed, represented, or otherwise made to take on a physical existence. On the contrary, the meaning fundamentally emerges in the external, observable, intersubjective world of other people and physical objects. The external meaning can secondarily be internalized. In later developments, internalized meanings can be (re-)externalized. By the time we reflect on the nature of meaning as adults, the origins of meaning in our infancy have long since been covered over in complex layers of successive transformations that can be reconstructed only through careful observations of collaborative interactions and theoretical reflection. That is why we often confuse the origins of cognitive phenomena.

As we have seen in the analyses of Hegel, Marx, and Vygotsky, the creation and use of an artifact (a product, commodity, or gesture) may follow these stages:

• People are involved in some collaborative activity involving their interpersonal relations, social context, physical objects, and so on.

• Some object, bodily gesture, or word becomes associated with this meaning-making activity and acts as a persistent externalization of the constructed meaning.

• The artifact can later be used as an embodiment of the meaning that was created in the previous stages.

In this way, through consistent, intentional use by a community of people engaged in activity together, something—a gesture, a sound, a shaped physical object—becomes a meaningful artifact. Such artifacts intimately combine meaning and physical existence. Through its use in a collaborative activity, an object is meaningful; without having a physical appearance, the meaning could not exist, be shared, and participate in the activity. The very nature of artifacts overcomes Descartes's problem by integrating the conceptual and the physical.[2] It also transcends the individualistic view of meaning by locating the origin of meaning in social interaction, its persistence in artifacts, and its transmission in culture.

Internalization as Cognitive Artifacts

Further transformations can take place, constituting what Vygotsky calls internalization:

An operation that initially represents an external activity is reconstructed and begins to occur internally. . . . An inter-personal process is transformed into an intra-personal one. . . . The transformation of an inter-personal process into an intra-personal one is the result of a long series of developmental events. . . . They are incorporated into this system of behavior and are culturally reconstituted and developed to form a new psychological entity. . . . As yet, the barest outline of this process is known (Vygotsky, 1978, p. 56f).

Although Vygotsky uses Descartes's metaphor of internal (mental) and external (physical) activities, there are essential differences. First, he draws the distinction precisely to overcome the divorce between the two worlds, showing how behaviors can migrate from one realm to the other. Second, Vygotsky gives the temporal priority to the external, whereas for Descartes and his followers, activity is first planned in the mind and then executed in the physical world. Third, Vygotsky emphasizes the interpersonal (or social) as the origin of psychological phenomena, rather than taking the thoughts of the individual as the fundamental activity and as the unquestionable starting point for all analysis.

Vygotsky did not succeed in completely fleshing out the analysis he proposed in *Mind in Society*. However, one can imagine an analysis of the human mind as a complex assemblage of what we might call *cognitive artifacts*: internalized forms of culturally developed artifacts. The term *cognitive artifact* (even in Norman, 1991, and Hutchins, 1999) is sometimes used in a way that is open to a Cartesian reading, where the artifact is a physical object (like a string on one's finger) that is somehow used by an individual's mind to accomplish some cognitive action. Here, on the contrary, the term is being used to indicate an internal artifact that had its origin in the interpersonal world but has since been internalized as a psychological function.

The pointing gesture illustrates how cognitive artifacts might start to form in the activity of an infant, advancing from instinctual movements or learned behaviors to symbolic gestures that involve qualitatively novel ways of interacting with other people, the world, and oneself. Through the mutual recognition that is part of the shared intentionality of pointing, a toddler gradually starts to become aware of the distinction between herself and her social and physical environment. As she gets a little older, the child learns language, the primary form of human social interaction. Spoken language leads to (vocalized) self-talk and finally to (silent) internal speech. The ability to talk to herself proves to be a powerful tool for controlling her actions and for adopting or internalizing the influences of others.

As a core element of thought, learning, and self-reflection, internal speech provides a sense of self-consciousness. It also transforms memory processes, which have already been drastically expanded from the basic inherited memory functions. The child learns to follow and tell stories, eventually internalizing narrative as a cognitive artifact (Bruner, 1990). She can then collect memories of her behavior and internalize other people's views of her, constructing a sense of identity as a person and as a mind with internal dialogue. The concepts of the individual and the mind are not biological givens but emergent cognitive artifacts.

Vygotsky's vision reveals a "society of mind" of many dynamically developing and interacting cognitive artifacts, rather than of Minsky's (1986) computational agents. Mind is not a pregiven cognitive capability (Descartes), a universal schema for structuring reality (Kant), or a biologically developing set of facilities (Piaget) but is the result of internalizing and transforming artifacts that arise in social interaction. This view of human mind as a cultural spinoff of collaborative activity in the social world has implications for how we conceive of meaning and its interpretation. It also grants a certain prominence to the role of collaborative learning in the intellectual development of people and human societies.

Situated with Meaningful Artifacts

The way to avoid the dilemmas of the mentalist and individualist position of Descartes is to recognize that human activity—including contemplative thought—has its origins in our lifelong involvement in a social and physical world that we share with other people and that is imbued with cultural meaning. The term for this is that we are *situated*. The word *situation* does not refer to a simple description of the physical surroundings. Dewey, as quoted in Koschmann's keynote, put it this way:

> What is designated by the word *situation* is *not* a single object or event or set of objects and events. For we never experience nor form judgments about objects or events in isolation, but only in connection with a contextual whole. The latter is what is called a *situation*. (Dewey, 1991, p. 72)

Note that the situation provides a context within which *meanings* are determined, within which we "form judgments about objects or events."

Contemporary theories of situated action can have their philosophic origins traced to Heidegger, as indicated in figure 14.1 of chapter 14. Heidegger's *Being and Time* was a systematic attempt to formulate a nondualistic philosophy of situated human being-in-the-world. According to it, our primary experience of physical objects is as meaningful artifacts. The meaning of an artifact derives from the complex network of artifacts that form our situation:

> For example, the artifact at hand that we call a hammer has to do with hammering, the hammering has to do with fastening something, the fastening has to do with protection against bad weather. . . . What significance artifacts have is prefigured in terms of the *situation* as a totality of relationships of significance. (Heidegger, 1996, p. 78, my translation)

Heidegger discussed the situation as source of meaning of artifacts in terms of our social being-with-others, but he failed to draw the consequences of this in the way that the phenomenologists since him have done, like ethnomethodologists (Heritage, 1984). Unfortunately, having overcome dualism, Heidegger reverted to a fundamentally individualistic approach by relating the meaningful situation to the "authentic" individual rather than the community. He thereby failed to take advantage of the understanding of social phenomena in the tradition of Marx (Nancy, 2000; Stahl, 1975a, 1975b). His later philosophy suffered from not analyzing how meaning is interactively achieved and then externalized and institutionalized. Nevertheless, he was able to develop a philosophy of human being as the ongoing interpretation of meaning-in-the-world (Gadamer, 1988) and describe an evocative artifact-centered view of the situation (see chapter 20).

Individual Interpretive Perspectives

Human understanding, according to Heidegger, is based on a tacit background pre-understanding of the world as a cultural situation consisting of a totality of meaningful artifacts. When we open our eyes in the morning, we are immersed in a meaningful world that we already understand. This world was created by social activity in the past, in which meaning was interactively constructed, externalized, and preserved as the common culture of a community. This culture includes both language, which includes countless symbolic artifacts with complexly interdependent and nuanced connotations of meaning, and tacit social practices. Our contemporary world is composed of an indefinite amount of overlapping cultural heritages.

Each person has a unique situated preunderstanding. People interpret their world and the features of their ongoing activity from this perspective. Interpretation, according to Heidegger, is simply the elaboration of one's preunderstanding, and it is often prompted by a breakdown of that preunderstanding. For instance, I tacitly expected my hammering to pound in the nail, but it did not, so I now explicitly interpret the hammer as "too small" or "broken." Here, the *meaning* of the hammer as a tool for pounding nails is given in the world as part of the culture of carpentry and the equipment of the workshop. But my *interpretation* of the hammer as not only a hammer but as a small or broken hammer is given from the perspective of my circumstances of having failed to pound a nail and my activity of trying to construct a particular new artifact.

The chapters of part I of this book discussed the role of interpretive perspectives in collaboration and of possibilities of computer support for them. This chapter has tried to indicate how meaning—particularly in collaborative contexts—can be taken to be given in the socially shared world, while interpretation stems from an individual's personal perspective. But there is not a sharp divorce between the social and the individual. Groups have interpretive perspectives too. And social meaning is just the persistent externalization of meaning making conducted by interacting individuals. Because neither the distinctions between mind and world nor those between individual and group are absolute and insurmountable, we would not want to claim that the distinction between meaning and interpretation is more than a generally useful analytic artifact, especially useful for clarifying discussions within collaboration theory.

Implications of Theory for Analysis and Design

Because shared meaning exists in the observable world and collaborative meaning making necessarily unfolds there, CSCL researchers can *make learning visible* by interpreting these meanings and practices. As argued in part II of this book, collaborators must make their understandings of what they say, hear, and see public for their partners to work together with them. This does not mean that everything is made explicit. However, people collaborating face to face give frequent feedback to each other through subtle word choices, inflections, gaze, bodily orientations, and gestures. People collaborating through computer mediation must find other ways to share understandings and orientations (see chapter 14). When possible breakdowns occur, indicating a divergence of interpretation, explicit discussion will often ensue to the extent needed to restore a sense of shared understanding. One can see this in the details of discourse—for example, in the analysis by Roschelle (1996) cited in Koschmann's keynote, as well as in the analysis of chapter 12. The clues for making visible the learning that took place during collaboration can generally be found in the externalizations and artifacts that were created.

Researchers must be able to interpret these meanings—for example, through microethnography or conversation analysis (Garfinkel, 1967; Sacks, 1992). This requires that the interpretive horizons (historical and cultural worlds) of the researchers and their subjects overlap sufficiently (Gadamer, 1988). Hermeneutic theory emphasizes the historical context that conditions interpretation. Collaboration science is necessarily a human science, both in the sense that it requires interpretive acts on the part of the researchers and in the sense that it is concerned with the interpretations of the subjects. The basis for possible scientific objectivity lies in the nature of meaning as shared and in the methods of rigorous interpretation that ensure intersubjective validity—including the agreement of interpretations by multiple researchers from their personal perspectives, developed through professional and methodological training.

There are also implications of the foregoing view of meaning for the design of collaboration technologies. A computer environment for supporting collaborative learning is not a characterless channel of communication but is itself a complex designed artifact that embodies its own cluster of meanings. Users must be able to interpret its affordances to realize how it is intended to be used. Again, there must be an overlap of interpretive horizons—between the design and use communities. Computer support for collaboration transforms the interpersonal interactions and the nature of the constructed meanings—for instance, changing the patterns of communication and the formats of textual constructions.

The Relation of Meaning and Interpretation

Koschmann's keynote speech argued that even the most valuable and paradigmatic CSCL studies can and do succumb to statements that frame their findings in terms of concepts like "conceptual change," "shared understanding," or "common ground"—concepts that are open to being construed in terms of mental contents of individuals. Clarity about the distinction between intersubjective meaning and its interpretation from personal perspectives can avoid that confusion and increase the precision of discussions within the theory of collaboration.

This chapter has tried to understand how meaning is constructed, drawing on the framework in chapter 15 and the four theoretical contributions proposed in chapter 11: collaborative knowledge building, artifacts, perspectives, and conversation analysis. The process of meaning making was seen as taking place through collaborative interactions that build group knowledge. The new knowledge was made persistent by being embodied in symbolic and physical artifacts, including discourse and inscriptions. The meaningfulness of objects in the world must be brought to life by human interpretation, which takes place from personal perspectives situated in people's current activities, goals and backgrounds. As is shown in chapter 13, people often must learn how to interpret the meaning embodied in artifacts. For researchers, methods based on conversation analysis can be used to make visible the process of group meaning making, the cultural meaning of artifacts, the personal interpretations, and the learning that goes into making and understanding meaning.

The analysis in this chapter stresses the intersubjective nature of meaning and argues that it cannot be reduced to a matter of mental representations in the heads of individuals. It is true that the meaning making is carried out by people and that the constructed meanings make sense only to people. However, the collaborative meaning-making process itself takes place intersubjectively and is mediated by physical artifacts that grant it its essential persistence in the shared world. Complementing this intersubjective meaning of meaningful artifacts is the psychological process of individual interpretation of the meaning from personal perspectives. Although the interpretive perspectives are derived from shared, culturally transmitted views, they also reflect both the individual situations of the individuals and their personal attitudes, histories, and responses to the artifacts of meaning.

Drawing the distinction between intersubjective meaning and individual interpretation from personal perspectives suggests implications for the theory of mind that go beyond the scope of this chapter. Traditional views confounded meaning, thought, expression, and interpretation, reducing them all to mysterious and inaccessible mental contents. The view presented here identifies thoughts with their expression in meaningful symbolic artifacts like words, gestures, and images. It is not as though meanings already existed as some kind of content in people's heads and were then formed into thoughts that could almost arbitrarily be expressed by symbols used to convey the ideas to other minds. Rather, the thoughts are themselves formed in the very process of being expressed in meaningful words. Having thoughts and expressing them are both aspects of a single meaning-making process. This is a discourse or communication theory of mind (Harre & Gillet, 1999; Wells, 1999). In a collaborative setting, the discourse of thought can take place publicly in a group, or it can take place internalized in the silent dialogue of an individual. In either case, the thought, idea, expression, or meaning is one thing, and its interpretation is another.

Anna Sfard and Kay McClain make the point that this view implies the importance of how one designs artifacts like groupware to mediate the meaning-making and interpretation processes:

> Within the communication approach, it is thus rather senseless to make such statements as "the same thought has been conveyed by two different means" (that, however, does not mean that we cannot interpret two expressions in the same way, with *interpretation* and *thought* being two different things). If thought is discourse, and if the discourse is inseparable from its mediating tools, there is no "cognitive essence" or "pure thought" that could be extracted from one symbolic embodiment and put into another. This conclusion, as philosophical as it may sound, has important practical entailments. One of them is that the nature and quality of thought is a function of the nature and quality of the mediating artifacts, just like the nature and quality of our physical action is a function of the nature and quality of the material tools we use. (Sfard & McClain, 2003, p. 355, italics in original)

Analyzing the discourse of a group of students doing mathematics together, Sfard and McClain argue that the meaning-making process is a collective effort in an essential way that cannot be reduced to the sum of independent individual contributions: "No individual step in the process would be possible without those made earlier by other interlocutors, and, as a result, nobody in particular is entitled to claim an exclusive right to the invention" (ibid., p. 347). A given utterance in a collaborative knowledge-building discourse refers back and responds to previous utterances and to the negotiated sense of the discourse as well as anticipating, projecting, and calling for future responses (see chapter 12). Thus, it is not just the discourse as a whole and its conclusions but every contribution to it that is a group accomplishment and whose meaning is a group construct.

To assess the degree of collaborative interaction in group discourse, Sfard (2002, pp. 39–41) has developed an "interactivity flowchart" that represents which utterances respond to other utterances or invite a response. Arrows show the interrelations among the utterances, with separate representations of each individual's "personal channel" and the overall group interaction. Such a diagram only summarizes the primary thrust of each utterance and cannot show the detailed web of connotations, terminological references, or shared indexing that can be brought out by conversational microanalysis.

The discursive view of collaboration goes back at least to the theory of symbolic interactionism (Blumer, 1969; Mead, 1962). Blumer is quite explicit about the distinction between social meaning and individual interpretation. For him, meaning is constantly negotiated by the group, whereas interpretation is an individual internalized discourse process:

The meaning of a thing for a person grows out of the ways in which other persons act toward the person with regard to the thing. Their actions operate to define the thing for the person. Thus, symbolic interactionism sees meanings as social products, as creations that are formed in and through the defining activities of people as they interact. . . . The use of meanings by the actor occurs through *a process of interpretation.* . . . The making of such indications is an internalized social process in that the actor is interacting with himself. . . . The actor selects, checks, suspends, regroups, and transforms the meanings in the light of the situation in which he is placed and the direction of his action (Blumer, 1969, p. 4, italics in original).

Blumer is clear about the distinction between the joint action of a group and the individual contributions to that joint action by the group members: "A joint action, while made up of diverse component acts that enter into its formation, is different from any one of them and from their mere aggregation" (ibid., p. 17). The joint action has a shared meaning. As a sociologist, Blumer relates this to a theory of social institutions. For instance, a marriage, a stock trade, a war, a governmental debate, or a church service is an action that has public meanings. These social actions are dependent on individuals taking individual actions and making individual utterances, but the social meaning transcends and informs those contributions. In the discourse that goes into instantiating a meaningful social event, the participants negotiate (usually tacitly) that they are engaging in such an event. When a math student says, "How did you get that answer?" she is asking someone to respond with an answer, but she is also negotiating a joint engagement in the activity of doing mathematics—depending on the group context, the sincerity of her utterance, and so on. Other students do not understand her question as simply a request but interpret it as part of a social activity in which they are engaging and whose meaning they have more or less learned through previous participation. Earlier in this chapter, we saw a similar example in Vygotsky's analysis of the infant grasping. Through various moves by the mother and child, the joint action of a child pointing out something for his mother is established as a meaningful gesture.

The relationship of meaning and interpretation is central to an understanding of the mediation of small-group collaboration. This chapter has tried to clarify that relationship with insights from philosophy, social theory, and social research. Small-group processes of collaborative knowledge building can construct meanings of symbolic and physical artifacts like words, gestures, tools, or media. The meanings of these meaningful artifacts are group accomplishments resulting from social interaction and are not attributable to individual participants. The artifacts retain intersubjective meaning, which can be learned or renegotiated later. The meaningful artifacts are interpreted by individuals from within the current situation or activity.

17

Shared Meaning, Common Ground, Group Cognition

Sociocultural theories drawn on in previous chapters suggest that cognition and learning take place at the level of groups and communities as well as individuals. Various positions on the nature of shared meaning have been proposed, and a number of theoretical perspectives have been recommended in the computer-supported collaborative learning literature. In particular, the concept of common ground has been developed to explain how meanings and understandings can be shared by multiple individuals. This chapter takes a critical look at the concepts of shared meaning and common ground as they are generally used and proposes an empirical study of how group cognition is constituted in practice.[1]

The notion of group cognition is defining of the approaches of computer-supported cooperative work and collaborative learning (CSCW and CSCL). In the most influential attempt to define the CSCL paradigm of research, Timothy Koschmann (1996b, pp. 10f) argues that forms of instructional technology research prior to CSCL "approach learning and instruction as psychological matters (be they viewed behavioristically or cognitively) and, as such, are researchable by the traditional methods of psychological experimentation." That is, they focus on the behavior or mind of the individual student as the unit of analysis when looking for instructional outcomes, learning, meaning making, or cognition. By contrast, the paradigm of CSCL "is built upon the research traditions of those disciplines—anthropology, sociology, linguistics, communication science—that are devoted to understanding language, culture and other aspects of the social setting" (p. 11). This radical paradigm shift, focusing on "the social and cultural context as the object of study, produces an incommensurability in theory and practice relative to the paradigms that have come before" (p. 13).

The incommensurability between CSCL and other paradigms of instructional technology becomes clear if we phrase it this way: in the CSCL perspective, it is not so much the individual student who learns and thinks as it is the collaborative group.

Given that we have, over the millennia, become used to viewing learning and thinking as activities of individual minds, it is hard to conceive of them as primarily group activities. This approach does not deny that *individuals often think and learn on their own* but rather states that *in situations of collaborative activity it is informative to study how processes of learning and cognition take place at the group level as well*. In fact, such analysis often demonstrates that even when someone learns or thinks in seeming isolation, this activity is essentially conditioned or mediated by important social considerations.

Koschmann points out that Lev Vygotsky—one of the primary theoretical sources for CSCL—proposed the "zone of proximal development" as "a mechanism for learning on the inter-psychological plane" (p. 12). Vygotsky (1978, p. 85) contrasted his conception of development at the group level to the traditional psychological focus on individual learning, saying, "In studies of children's mental development it is generally assumed that only those things that children can do on their own are indicative of mental abilities." Vygotsky's alternative social conception of development was meant to measure a child's position in the *"process by which children grow into the intellectual life of those around them"* (p. 88, italics in original), as opposed to their mental position in doing tasks on their own. The italicized phrase is strikingly similar to the definition of situated learning in Jean Lave and Etienne Wenger (1991)—another central source of CSCL's theory of learning. Related foundations of the CSCL paradigm include Edwin Hutchins's (1996) presentation of distributed cognition and Lucy Suchman's (1987) discussion of situated action.

Chapter 16 draws on these and other sources to argue for taking meaning that is constructed in successful processes of collaboration as a shared group product, which is, however, subject to interpretation by the individuals involved. As much as the writings on situated action, distributed cognition, social constructivism, activity theory, social practice, and other theories have foregrounded the social nature of learning and thinking, it is still hard to overcome our individualistic conceptual traditions and come to terms with group learning or group cognition. This chapter attempts to further that effort.

The Problem of Shared Meaning

The analysis in chapter 16 tried to provide insight into the nature of the *group perspective*. It argued for a view of both shared group *meaning* and individual *interpretation*. Shared meaning was not reduced to mental representations buried in the heads of individuals. Such mental contents could be inferred only from introspection and from interpretation of people's speech and behavior, whereas socially shared meaning can be observed in the visibly displayed discourse that takes place in group interactions including nonverbal communication and associated artifacts.

This approach does not result in a behaviorist denial of human thought in bracketing out inferred mental states and focusing on observable interaction because of the methodological recognition of interpretive perspectives. People are considered to be interpreting subjects who do not simply react to stimuli but understand meanings.

Only individuals can interpret meaning. But this does not imply that the group meaning is just some kind of statistical average of individual mental meanings, an agreement among preexisting opinions, or an overlap of internal representations. A group meaning is constructed by the interactions of the individual members, not by the individuals on their own. It is an emergent property of the discourse and interaction. It is not necessarily reducible to opinions or understandings of individuals. Chapter 12 presented an example of how this works. The discourse transcribed there is strikingly elliptical, indexical, and projective: each utterance implies and requires a (perhaps open-ended) set of references to complete its meaning. These references are more a function of the history and circumstances of the discourse than of intentions attributable to specific participants. The words in the analyzed collaborative moment refer primarily to each other, to characteristics of the artifacts discussed, and to group interactions. In fact, we can attribute well-defined opinions and intentions to the individual students only after we have extensively interpreted the meanings of the discourse as a whole.

It is not only possible but also habitual to attribute thoughts and intentions to individual actors. We assume that a speaker's words are well-defined in advance in the speaker's mind and that the discourse is just a way for the speaker to express some preconceived meaning and convey it to the listeners. This reveals a conflict. If meaning is socially constructed and shared, why do we feel compelled to treat it as private property? If it takes place in isolated minds, how can it ever be shared and understood collaboratively? The possibility of shared meaning must be somehow explained. This is particularly important in cases of collaborative learning, where the knowledge that is constructed must be shared among the learners.

The term *shared knowledge* is ambiguous. It can refer to the following situations:

• Similarity of individuals' knowledge, where the knowledge in the minds of the members of a group happen to overlap and their intersection is "shared";

• Knowledge that gets shared, where some individuals communicate what they already knew to the others; and

• Group knowledge, where knowledge is interactively achieved in discourse and may not be attributable as originating from any particular individual.

The ambiguity of this term corresponds to different paradigms of viewing group interaction: is it reducible to knowledge held by individual thinkers, or is it an emergent property of the group discourse as an irreducible unit for purposes of analysis?

A Conflict of Paradigms

Research on learning and education is troubled to its core by the conflict of the paradigms we are considering. Anna Sfard (1998) reviewed some of the history and consequences of this conflict in terms of the incompatibility of the acquisition metaphor (AM) of learning and the participation metaphor (PM). AM conceives of education as a transfer of knowledge commodities and their subsequent possession by individual minds. Accordingly, empirical research in this paradigm looks for evidence of learning in changes of mental contents of individual learners. PM, in contrast, locates learning in intersubjective, social, or group processes and views the learning of individuals in terms of their changing participation in the group interactions. AM and PM are as different as day and night, but Sfard argues that we must learn to live in both complementary metaphors.

The conflict is particularly pointed in the field of CSCL. Taken seriously, the term *collaborative learning* can itself be viewed as self-contradictory given the tendency to construe learning as something taking place in individual minds. Having emerged from the paradigm shift in thinking about instructional technology described by Koschmann (1996b), the field of CSCL is still enmeshed in the paradigm conflict between opposed cognitive and sociocultural focuses on the individual and on the group (Kaptelinin & Cole, 2002). In his keynote at the CSCL '02 conference, Koschmann (2002a) argued that even exemplary instances of CSCL research tend to adopt a theoretical framework that is anathema to collaboration. He recommended that talk about knowledge as a thing that can be acquired should be replaced with discussion of "meaning making in the context of joint activity" to avoid misleading images of learning as mental acquisition and possession of knowledge objects.

Although Koschmann's alternative phrase can describe the intersubjective construction of shared meanings achieved through group interaction, the influence of AM can reconstrue meaning making as something that must perforce take place in individual human minds because it is hard for most people to see how a group can possess mental contents. Chapter 16 argues in effect that both Koschmann's language and that of the researchers he critiqued is ambiguous and is subject to interpretation under either AM or PM. A simple substitution of wording is inadequate. It is necessary to make explicit when one is referring to individual subjective understanding and when one is referring to group intersubjective understanding—and to make clear to those under the sway of AM how intersubjectivity is concretely possible.

The problem with recommending that researchers view learning under both AM and PM or that they be consistent in their theoretical framing is that our commonsense metaphors and widespread folk theories are so subtly entrenched in our thinking and speaking. The languages of Western science reflect deep-seated assumptions that go back to the *ideas* of Plato's *Meno* (1961) and the *ego cogito* of Descartes's *Meditations* (1999). It is hard for most people to imagine how a group can have knowledge because we assume that knowledge is a substance that only minds can acquire or possess and that only physically distinct individuals can have minds (somewhere in their physical heads). The term *meaning* as in *shared meaning* carries as much historical baggage as the term *knowledge* in *knowledge building*.

The Range of Views

CSCL grows out of research on cooperative learning that demonstrated the advantages for individual learning of working in groups (e.g., Johnson & Johnson, 1989) but had not yet made the sociocultural paradigm shift. There is still considerable ambiguity or conflict about how the learning that takes place in contexts of joint activity should be conceptualized. While it has recently been argued that the key issues arise from ontological and epistemological commitments deriving from philosophy from Descartes to Hegel (Koschmann, 2002c; Packer & Goicoechea, 2000), I argue in previous chapters that it is more a matter of focus on the individual (cognitivist) versus the group (sociocultural) as the unit of analysis. Theoretical positions on the issue of the unit of learning—such as in the compilations of essays on shared cognition (Resnick, Levine, & Teasley, 1991) or distributed cognition (Salomon, 1993a)—take on values along a continuous spectrum from individual to group:

• Learning is always accomplished by individuals, but this individual learning can be assisted in settings of collaboration, where individuals can learn from each other.

• Learning is always accomplished by individuals, but individuals can learn in different ways in settings of collaboration, including learning how to collaborate.

• Groups can also learn, and they do so in different ways from individuals, but the knowledge generated must always be located in individual minds.

• Groups can construct knowledge that no one individual could have constructed alone by a synergistic effect that merges ideas from different individual perspectives.

• Groups construct knowledge that may not be in any individual minds but may be interactively achieved in group discourse and may persist in physical or symbolic artifacts such as group jargon or texts or drawings.

• Group knowledge can be spread across people and artifacts; it is not reducible to the knowledge of any individual or the sum of individuals' knowledge.

- All human learning is fundamentally social or collaborative; language is never private; meaning is intersubjective; knowledge is situated in culture and history.

- Individual learning takes place by internalizing or externalizing knowledge that was already constructed interpersonally. Even modes of individual thought have been internalized from communicative interactions with other people.

- Learning is always a mix of individual and group processes. The analysis of learning should be done with both the individual and group as units of analysis and with consideration of the interplay between them.

The different positions listed above are supported by a corresponding range of theories of human learning and cognition. Educational research on small-group process in the 1950s and 1960s maintained a focus on the individual as learner (e.g., Johnson & Johnson, 1989; for a review, see Stahl, 2000). Classical cognitive science in the next period continued to view human cognition as primarily an individual matter—internal symbol manipulation or computation across mental representations with group effects treated as secondary boundary constraints (Simon, 1981; Vera & Simon, 1993). In reaction to these views, a number of sociocultural theories have become prominent in the learning sciences in recent decades. To a large extent, these theories have origins in much older works that conceptualized the situated-ness of people in practical activity within a shared world (Bakhtin, 1986b; Heidegger, 1996; Husserl, 1989; Marx, 1976; Schutz, 1967; Vygotsky, 1978). Here are some representative theories that focus on the group as a possible unit of knowledge construction:

- *Collaborative knowledge building*   A group can build knowledge that cannot be attributed to an individual or to a combination of individual contributions (Bereiter, 2002).

- *Social psychology*   One can and should study knowledge construction at both the individual and group units of analysis and study the interactions between them (Resnick, Levine, & Teasley, 1991).

- *Distributed cognition*   Knowledge can be spread across a group of people and the tools that they use to solve a problem and can emerge through their interaction (Hutchins, 1996; Salomon, 1993).

- *Situated cognition*   Knowledge often consists of resources for practical activity in the world more than of rational propositions or mental representations (Schön, 1983; Suchman, 1987; Winograd & Flores, 1986).

- *Situated learning*   Learning is the changing participation of people in communities of practice (Lave & Wenger, 1991; Shumar & Renninger, 2002).

• *Zone of proximal development*   Children grow into the intellectual life of those around them; they develop in collaboration with adults or more capable peers (Vygotsky, 1978).

• *Activity theory*   Human understanding is mediated not only by physical and symbolic artifacts but also by the social division of labor and cultural practices (Engeström, 1999; Nardi, 1996).

• *Ethnomethodology*   Human understanding, interpersonal relationships, and social structures are achieved and reproduced interactionally (Dourish, 2001; Garfinkel, 1967).

One does not have to commit to one of these theories in particular to gain a sense from them all of the range of possible positions on the nature of group knowledge.

Common Ground or Group Cognition?

Within CSCL, it is usual to refer to the theory of *common ground* to explain how collaborative understanding is possible (for instance, Baker, Hansen, Joiner & Traum, 1999). They note that collaboration requires mutual understanding among the participants, established through a process of *grounding*. It is certainly clear that effective communication is generally premised on the sharing of a language, of a vast amount of practical background knowledge about how things work in the physical and social worlds, of many social practices implicit in interaction, and of an orientation within a shared context of topics, objects, artifacts, previous interactions, and so on. Much of this sharing we attribute to our socialization into a common culture or overlapping subcultures.

Most common ground is taken for granted as part of what it means to be human. The phenomenological hermeneutics of Heidegger (1996) and Gadamer (1988)—building on the traditions of Wilhelm Dilthey and Edmund Husserl—made explicit the ways in which human understanding and our ability to interpret meaning rely on a shared cultural horizon. They emphasized the centrality of interpretation to human existence as being engaged in the world. They also considered cases where common ground breaks down, such as in interpreting ancient texts or translating from foreign languages. How can a modern German or American, for example, understand a theoretical term from a Platonic dialogue or from a Japanese poem?

The current discussion of common ground within CSCW and CSCL is, however, more focused. It is concerned with the short-term negotiation of common ground during interactions. Such negotiation is particularly visible when there is a breakdown of the common ground—an apparent problem in the mutual understanding. A breakdown appears through the attempt of the participants to repair the misunderstanding or lack of mutuality. For instance, in Roschelle (1996) as well as in chapters 12 and 13 of this book, much of the transcribed discourse is analyzed as attempts to reach shared understandings in situations in which the group discussion had become problematic.

It is not always clear whether repairs of breakdowns in common ground come from ideas that existed in someone's head and are then passed on to others until a consensus is established or whether the common ground might be constructed in the interaction of the group as a whole. It is possible that shared knowledge can sometimes be best explained in one way and sometimes another. At any rate, it seems that the question of the source of shared knowledge should generally be treated as an empirical question, subject to interpretation in each concrete case. This is what is proposed in the next section of this chapter. But first, let us make this alternative a bit clearer.

The theory of common ground that Baker et al. (1999), Roschelle (1996), and many others in CSCL refer to is that of Herbert Clark and his colleagues. Clark and Brennan (1991) situate their work explicitly in the tradition of conversation analysis (CA), although their theory has a peculiarly mentalist flavor uncharacteristic of CA. They argue that collaboration, communication, and "all collective actions are built on common ground and its accumulation" (p. 127). The process of updating this common ground on a moment-by-moment basis in conversation is called *grounding*. Grounding, according to this theory, is a collective process by which participants try to reach mutual belief. It is acknowledged that understanding (that is, mutual belief) can never be perfect (that is, the participants can never have—and know that they have—beliefs that are completely identical). It suffices that "the contributor and his or her partners mutually believe that the partners have understood what the contributor meant to a criterion sufficient for current purposes" (p. 129). Clark and Brennan then demonstrate how various conversational moves between pairs of people can conduct this kind of grounding and achieve a practical level of mutuality of belief. They go on to show how different technologies of computer support mediate the grounding process in different ways.

Clark's contribution theory—where one participant "contributes" a personal belief as a proposed addition to the shared common ground and then the participants interact until they all believe that they have the same understanding of the original belief, at which point their common ground is "updated" to include the new contribution—is articulated in the language of individual mental beliefs and in the jargon of computer models of rational memories. Thus, it is not surprising that Emanuel Schegloff (1991a) responds polemically to Clark and Brennan by opposing the tradition of ethnomethodology and CA to this theory of mental beliefs. Schegloff points out that Harold Garfinkel asked what exactly might be intended by such notions as "common" or "shared" knowledge. In the days when computers were still UNIVACS, Garfinkel viewed as untenable that notion of common or shared knowledge that was more or less equal to the claim that separate memory drums had identical contents. (p. 151)

Schegloff then presented an analysis of repair in talk-in-interaction that contrasted with Clark's by construing what took place as a social practice following social patterns of interaction. According to Schegloff's approach, repair is a form of socially shared cognition that takes place in the medium of discourse (in the broad sense of social interaction-in-talk, including intonation, gesture, pose, and so on), following established conversational patterns rather than a transfer and comparison of beliefs between rationalist minds.

In a recent critique of Clark's contribution theory of common ground, Koschmann and Curtis LeBaron (2003) present video data of an interaction in an operating room. A resident, an attending doctor, and an intern are discussing the location of internal organs as viewed indirectly through a laparoscopic camera. Koschmann and LeBaron argue that the discourse that takes place does not match Clark's rubric and that the very notion of belief contributions to some kind of common ground storage space is not useful to understanding the construction of shared understanding in this situation. Although the surgery operation is successful and although technology-supported collaborative learning takes place, the beliefs of the individual participants afterward do not agree in Clark's sense.

Perhaps the case of the operating room illustrates Vygotsky's contrast between a person's individual developmental level and his or her social developmental level (separated by the zone of proximal development). The intern was able to participate in the collaborative activity even though he could not correctly identify key items on his own afterward. This might indicate that what takes place in group interactions cannot reliably be reduced to behaviors of the individuals involved. The knowledge and abilities of people in individual and group settings are quite different. *The group cognition of the OR team* would then not be a simple sum of the individual cognitive acts of its members; the group understanding would not be a simple intersection or overlap of individual beliefs or internal mental representations. If one accepts this reading of Vygotsky's distinction between individual cognitive ability and ability within collaborative group settings, then Clark's attempt to reduce group knowledge to individual knowledge may be misguided.

The OR situation was a special case that differed in significant ways from most everyday conversations. Often, interaction can be adequately analyzed as the exchange of personal beliefs. This is particularly true of dyadic conversations, such as those in Clark's examples, rather than in the more complex interactions of small groups of three or more in the OR or in CSCL generally. The practical question for

CSCL is, can sets of students be transformed into groups that learn collaboratively in ways that encourage the emergence of collaborative group cognition in a significant sense?

Empirical Inquiry into Group Cognitive Practices

Based on the issues raised in this book, we have begun an empirical exploration of group cognition (see chapter 21). At Drexel University, we are now starting the Virtual Math Teams (VMT) project, a research project to investigate empirically whether knowledge sharing in community contexts can construct group knowledge that exceeds the individual knowledge of the group's members. Our hypothesis is that precisely such a result is, in fact, the hallmark of collaborative learning understood in an emphatic sense.

This research is based on earlier work that indicated the possibility of observing group cognition. As mentioned above, Roschelle's (1996) study of two students constructing a new (for them) conception of acceleration can be construed as an analysis of shared knowledge building. As Koschmann (2002a) pointed out, the analytic paradigm of that paper is ambiguous. Its focus on the problem of convergence posits the conceptual change as taking place in the minds of the two individual students, while at the same time raising the issue of the possibility of shared knowledge. The SimRocket study reported in chapters 12 and 13 was an attempt to analyze knowledge building at the group level by a group of five students. Our current research project takes this earlier study as a pilot study and aims to generate a corpus of group interactions in which problem solving and knowledge building can be most effectively observed at the group level.

In the VMT project, students engage in collaborative problem solving of challenging mathematics problems. This takes place online at the Math Forum Web site. Students are invited into chatrooms in groups of about four based on similar interests, such as beginning algebra or geometry. They are given a math problem and have about an hour to discuss it. They can later submit a description of their approach to the problem to the Math Forum and receive expert feedback, but during the collaboration there is no adult mentoring.

Like many studies of collaborative learning (but unlike the VMT math study), the pilot study in chapter 12 involved face-to-face interaction with an adult mentor present. Close analysis of student utterances during a period of intense interaction during that study suggested that the group of students developed an understanding that certainly could not be attributed to the utterances of any one student. In fact, the utterances themselves were meaningless if taken in isolation from the discourse and its activity context.

There were a number of limitations to the SimRocket pilot study:

• Although the mentor was quiet for the core interaction analyzed, it might be possible to attribute something of the group knowledge to the mentor's guiding presence.

• The digital videotape was limited in capturing gaze and even some spoken wording.

• The data included only two sessions, too little to draw extensive conclusions about how much individual students understood of the group knowledge before or after the interaction.

To overcome such limitations, we are requiring the following procedures in our current VMT study:

• Mentors are not active in the collaborative groups—although the groups work on problems that have been carefully crafted to guide student inquiry, and advice can later be requested by email from Math Forum staff.

• The online communication is fully logged, so that researchers have a record of the complete problem-solving interaction, essentially identical to what the participants see online.

• Groups and individuals are studied during longer, more multifaceted problem-solving sessions—and in some cases over multiple sessions.

Despite its limitations, the pilot study clearly suggested the feasibility of studying group knowledge. It showed how group knowledge can be constructed in discourse and how conversation analysis can "make visible" that knowledge to researchers. In the VMT project, we will analyze the interactions in the student teams to determine how they build shared knowledge within the Math Forum virtual community.

We are addressing the issue of the nature of shared understanding by studying online collaborative learning in the specific context of Math Forum problems, with the aim of presenting empirical examples of concrete situations in which groups can be seen to have knowledge that is distinct from the knowledge of the group members. By analyzing these situations in detail, we will uncover mechanisms by which understanding of mathematics passes back and forth between the group as the unit of analysis and individual group members as units of analysis.

One example might be a group of five middle-school students collaborating online. They solve an involved algebra problem and submit a discussion of their solution to the Math Forum. By looking carefully at the computer logs of their interactions in which they collaboratively discussed, solved, and reflected on the problem, we can see that the group solution exceeds the knowledge of any individual group members before, during, and sometimes even after the collaboration. For instance, there may be some arguments that arose in group interaction that none of the students fully understood but that contributed to the solution. Or a mathematical derivation might be too complicated for any of the students to keep "in mind" without reviewing preserved chat archives or using an external representation the group developed in an online whiteboard. By following the contributions of one member at a time, it may also be possible to find evidence of how each student interpreted what took place in the collaboration and thereby to follow individual trajectories of participation in which group and individual understandings influenced each other.

While we do not anticipate that group knowledge often exceeds that of all group members under generally prevailing conditions, we hypothesize that it can do so at least occasionally under particularly favorable conditions. We believe that we can set up naturalistic conditions as part of a Math Forum service and can collect sufficient relevant data to demonstrate this phenomenon in multiple cases. The analysis and presentation of these cases should help to overcome the AM/PM paradigm conflict by providing concrete illustrations of how knowledge can be built through group participation as distinct from—but intertwined with—individual acquisition of part of that knowledge. It should also help to clarify the theoretical framing of acts of meaning making in the context of joint activity.

Student discourse is increasingly recognized as of central importance to science and math learning (Bauersfeld, 1995; Lemke, 1990). The analysis of discourse has become a rigorous human science, going under various names: conversation analysis, interaction analysis, microethnography, and ethnomethodology (Garfinkel, 1967; Heritage, 1984; Jordan & Henderson, 1995; Sacks, 1992; Streeck & Mehus, 2003). This method of analysis will allow us to study what takes place through collaborative interactions.

The focus on discourse suggested a solution to the confusion between individual and group knowledge and to the conceptual conflict about how there can be such a thing as group knowledge distinct from what is in the minds of individual group members. Chapter 16 argued that meaning is constructed in the group discourse. The status of this meaning as shared by the group members is itself something that must be continually achieved in the group interaction; frequently the shared status "breaks down" and a "repair" is necessary. In the SimRocket pilot study, the interaction of interest centered on precisely such a repair of a breakdown in shared understanding among the discussants. While *meaning* inheres in the discourse, the individual group members must construct their own *interpretation* of that meaning in an ongoing way. Clearly, there are intimate relationships between the meanings and their interpretations, including the interpretation by one member of the interpretations of other members. But it is also true that language can convey meanings that transcend the understandings of the speakers and hearers. It may be precisely through divergences among different interpretations or among various connotations of meaning that collaboration gains much of its creative power.

These are questions that we will investigate in the VMT project as part of our microanalytic studies of collaboration data, guided by our central working hypothesis:

• *H0 (collaborative learning hypothesis)*   A small online group of learners can—on occasion and under favorable conditions—build collaborative knowing and shared meaning that exceeds the knowledge of the group's individual members.

We believe that such an approach can help researchers maintain a focus on the ultimate potential in CSCL rather than lose sight of the central phenomenon of collaboration as a result of methods that focus exclusively on statistical trends, as argued in chapter 10.

Issues for Future Investigation

Collaborative success is hard to achieve and probably impossible to guarantee or even predict. CSCW and CSCL represent concerted attempts to overcome some of the barriers to collaborative success, like the difficulty of ensuring that everyone in a group can participate effectively in the development of ideas with all the other members, the complexity of keeping track of all the interconnected contributions that have been offered, or the barriers to working with people who are geographically distant. As appealing as the introduction of technological aids for communication, computation, and memory seem, they inevitably introduce new problems, changing the social interactions, tasks, and physical environment. Accordingly, CSCW and CSCL study and design must take into careful consideration the social composition of groups, the collaborative activities, and the technological supports.

To observe effective collaboration in an authentic educational setting in the VMT project, we are adapting a successful math education service at the Math Forum to create conditions that will likely be favorable to the kind of interactions that we want to study. We must create groups by bringing together and matching up students who will work together well, both by getting along with and understanding each other and by contributing a healthy mix of different skills. We must also carefully design mathematics problems and curriculum packages that lend themselves to the development and display of deep math understanding through collaborative interactions—open-ended problems that will not be solved by one individual but that the group can chew on together in online interaction. Further, the technology that we provide to our groups must be easy to use from the start, while meeting the communicative and representational needs of the activities.

As part of our project, we will study how to accomplish these group formation, curriculum design, and technology implementation requirements. This is expressed in three working hypotheses of the project: H1, H2, and H3. Two further working hypotheses define areas of knowledge building that the project itself will engage in on the basis of our findings: H4 draws conclusions about the interplay between group and individual knowledge, mediated by physical and symbolic artifacts that embody knowledge in persistent forms, and H5 reports on the analytic methodology that emerges from the project:

- *H1 (collaborative group hypothesis)*   Small groups are most effective at building knowledge if members share interests but bring to bear diverse backgrounds and perspectives.

- *H2 (collaborative curriculum hypothesis)*   Educational activities can be designed to encourage and structure effective collaborative learning by presenting open-ended problems requiring shared deep understanding.

- *H3 (collaborative technology hypothesis)*   Online computer support environments can be designed to facilitate effective collaborative learning that overcomes some of the limitations of face-to-face communication.

- *H4 (collaborative cognition hypothesis)*   Members of collaborative small groups can internalize group knowledge as their own individual knowledge, and they can externalize it in persistent artifacts.

- *H5 (collaborative methodology hypothesis)*   Quantitative and qualitative analysis and interpretation of interaction logs can make visible to researchers the online learning of small groups and individuals.

We believe that the theoretical confusion surrounding the possibility and nature of group knowledge presents an enormous practical barrier to collaborative learning. Because students and teachers believe that learning is necessarily an individual matter, they find the effort at collaborative learning to be an unproductive nuisance. For researchers, too, the misunderstanding of collaborative learning distorts their conclusions, leading them to look for effects of pedagogical and technological innovation in the wrong places. If these people understood that groups can construct knowledge in ways that significantly exceed the sum of the individual contributions and that the power of group learning can feed back into individual learning, then we might start to see the real potential of collaborative learning realized on a broader scale. This project aims to produce rigorous and persuasive empirical examples of collaborative learning to help bring about the necessary public shift in thinking.

18

Making Group Cognition Visible

How can researchers observe group learning and group cognition? How can these phenomena be made visible for analysis? This chapter addresses the core methodological question for computer-supported collaborative learning, borrowing heavily from Harold Garfinkel.[1] The researcher's interpretive perspective must first be distinguished from and then be related to those of the individual group members, the group as a whole and designers of any technical, pedagogical, or social innovations. Scientific interpretation of group meaning can then proceed in accordance with ethnomethodology's principles that the data for such analysis is everywhere, visible, grounded, meaningful, and situated. The results reveal the structure of the self-organization of group discourse. The discourse is the embodiment of group cognitive processes, and the analysis of that discourse makes the group's learning and meaning making visible and comprehensible.

How is it possible to rigorously analyze collaborative group meaning making in specific case studies? In this chapter, I address the problem of defining a methodology for making group meaning visible to researchers and guide this inquiry with two specific examples. The primary example is the analysis of mediated collaboration in the SimRocket discussion in chapter 12, and the data from the Virtual Math Teams (VMT) project presented in chapter 17 provides an additional example in which the discourse is computer mediated (the VMT data are further analyzed in chapter 21). The SimRocket collaboration was face-to-face and videotaped; it was mediated by the computer simulation of model rockets, including the list of rocket components. The VMT data will consist primarily of chat logs taken directly from the computer software that mediates the online collaboration. The question for this chapter is how we can understand a methodology for analysis of these two kinds of cases within the theoretical framework that is being developed in part III.

Perspectives on Collaboration

The kind of analysis being talked about here is necessarily interpretive. The data are phrases used by people in specific settings and not the kind of thing that can simply be counted up without worrying about what the counted objects meant to the people who uttered and responded to them. Interpretation is perspectival. We argue in chapter 4 that interpretation is necessarily conducted from one interpretive perspective or another. For instance, the perspective from which we are analyzing as researchers is different from the participants' discourse perspectives that we are analyzing. To understand the analysis as a process of interpretation, it is important to distinguish the various interpretive perspectives involved:

- *Individual members* of the group interpret each other's words and behavior as active participants during the live event of collaboration.
- *Small groups* of collaborating people construct group meanings and knowledge artifacts through the interaction of contributions from their members.
- *Communities of practice* preserve and disseminate meanings and artifacts.
- *Collaboration researchers* interpret the behavior of the group and its members by studying data derived from the event, such as video clips and chat logs.
- *Educational innovators* who are interested in the design of technical or pedagogical interventions draw design consequences from the analyses of the researchers.

Accordingly, the following five interpretive perspectives are incorporated in this discussion of analysis methodology: individual group members, the group as a whole, communities of practice providing sociocultural context, researchers studying the communication and collaboration, and designers creating new forms of software, innovative pedagogy, or other social practices for future group members.

Let us consider our central example of analysis. In a moment of collaboration lasting several seconds in a middle-school classroom, a small group of students learned something about the conduct of scientific experimentation using the Sim-Rocket list artifact. The students made this knowledge visible for their group, repairing confusions and establishing a shared understanding. The micro discourse analysis of this moment in chapters 12 and 13 illustrated the complexity of collaborative learning and of its analysis.

To make learning visible as researchers, we deconstructed the references within the discourse. Thus, we conducted the analysis from the perspective of researchers, and our unit of analysis was the group as a whole. The meaning that the group constructed was analyzed as constituting a network of semantic references within the group interaction rather than as mental representations of individual group members. No assumptions about mental states or representations were required or relevant to the researcher's analysis. Collaborative learning was viewed as the interactive construction of this referential network. The group's shared understanding consisted in the alignment of utterances, evidencing agreement concerning their referents.

The list artifact was a focus of the student discourse. Viewed within its activity system, learning is a social process in which artifacts—whether physical, digital, or linguistic—play central roles. Artifacts like the SimRocket software must be understood from all five perspectives: their designers, their users as individuals, their group users, the broader community of stakeholders, and their researchers.

As meaningful objects in the world, artifacts, by definition, both provide persistence across the communities and require interpretation by each community. The artifacts are *boundary objects* (Bowker & Star, 2000) that span different communities or cross the boundaries between them and thereby permit understanding of one from the position or perspective of the other. The design community designs into the artifact meaningful affordances that must be properly understood in practice by the user communities and their group and individual members. To evaluate the success of this undertaking, the research community must interpret the designed affordances and also interpret the users' practical understandings of these.

In chapter 13, particularly, we tried to understand the indexical references to the list artifact in the group discourse—a set of references that was particularly hard to understand from a superficial reading of the transcript. We found that the students were engaged in *making visible* to each other the structure of references within their discourse that had become problematic for them as a group engaged in collaborative learning within a classroom activity structure. In making their learning visible to themselves, they made it visible to us as well. Furthermore, they made visible the central affordance of the artifact, which had until then eluded them and caused their group confusion. The group of students, as a whole, systematically constructed a shared understanding by making increasingly explicit the references from their discourse that had created confusion when different students had constructed divergent interpretations.

The world, situation, or activity structure in which the group of students operates consists of a shared network of references among words and artifacts. To design new artifacts for these worlds, designers must understand the nature of these referential networks, build artifacts that fit into and extend these networks in pedagogically desirable ways, and provide tasks and social practices that will lead students to incorporate the artifact's new references meaningfully into their shared understandings. Researchers who understand this process can analyze the artifact affordances and the situated student discourse to assess the effectiveness of collaboration technologies.

Computational artifacts such as scientific simulations, productivity software, organizational knowledge repositories, and educational systems are designed by one community (such as software developers, educators, domain experts, or former employees) for use by another (end-users, students, novices, or future employees). The two communities typically operate within contrasting cultures; their shared artifacts must cross cultural boundaries to be effective. Diversity among these interacting communities of practice leads to many of the same issues and misunderstandings as cultural diversity among traditional communities.

A computational artifact embodies meaning in its design, its content, and its modes of use. This meaning originates in the goals, theories, history, assumptions, tacit understandings, practices, and technologies of the artifact's design community. A user community must activate an understanding of the artifact's meaning within their own community practices and cultural-historical contexts.

Clarifying the different perspectives and their associated communities sheds light on the distinction between group meaning and individual interpretation outlined especially in chapter 16. Meaning is associated with the small-group unit of analysis and is shared within the group against the cultural background of the group's larger community. Interpretation is associated with the individual unit of analysis and takes place against the background understanding of the individuals. Both units can be subject to analysis from the researcher's perspective, possibly independently of the knowledge-constitutive human interests (Habermas, 1971) and goals of the designer perspective. It is in this sense (that is, for the researcher) that meaning is constructed by small groups, within their discourse communities, and is interpreted by individuals from their personal perspectives, situated in their current activity structures.

Given the diversity between the design and user communities, the question arises: how can the meaning embodied in a computational artifact be activated with sufficient continuity that it fulfills its intended function? A further question for us as researchers is how we as members of a third community can assess the extent to which the designers' intentions (for better or worse) were achieved in the students' accomplishments.

Chapter 13 investigated a process of meaning-activation of a computational artifact through an empirical approach. It conducted a microethnographic analysis of an interaction among middle-school students learning how to isolate variables in a computer simulation. The analytic affordances (paired configurations) designed into the computational simulation of rocket launches were activated through the involvement of the students in a specific project activity. Their increasing understanding of the artifact's meaning structure was achieved in group discourse situated within their artifact-centered activity.

This microethnographic analysis is a scientific enterprise, like viewing under a microscope the world within a drop of water, a world that is never seen while crossing the ocean by boat. We tried to uncover general *structures* of the interaction that would be applicable to other cases and that thereby contribute to a theoretical understanding of collaboration. The conversational structures of small-group collaboration are different from those of two-person dialogue commonly analyzed by conversation analysts, and this has implications for the theory of collaboration.

This approach to studying collaboration differs radically from both traditional educational research and from quantitative studies in CSCL (see chapter 10), both of which can produce useful complementary findings. Experiments in the Thorndikian educational research tradition focus on pre- and post-test behaviors, inferring from changes what kinds of learning took place in between. Such a methodology is the direct consequence of viewing learning as an internal individual mental process that cannot directly be observed (Koschmann, 2002b). However, if we postulate learning to be a social process, then the conditions are very different. In fact, the participants in a collaboration need to make their evolving understandings *visible* to each other; this is the very essence of collaborative interaction. As is shown in chapter 12, when the evolving learning of the group is not displayed in a coherent manner, everyone's efforts become directed to producing an evident and mutually understood presentation of shared knowledge. That is, in the breakdown case, the structures that are normally invisible suddenly appear as matters of the utmost concern to the participants, who then make explicit and visible to one another the meaning that their utterances have for them. As researchers who share a cultural literacy with the participants, we can take advantage of such displays to formulate and support our analyses.

Making Learning Visible

In the transcript of chapter 12, the teacher provides efficient guidance by directing attention to the list artifact (1:21:53), defining criteria of sameness and difference (1:22:00), and then allowing the students to solve the task collaboratively (1:22:04). Brent points the way with a bold gesture to what already exists in the list artifact (the descriptions of rockets 1 and 2) as the solution. Jamie clarifies how to take this as the solution. Through a sequence of brief, highly interactive turns, the students collaboratively move from treating the list as inadequate, irrelevant, and uninteresting to seeing it as holding the key to solving the group task. The sequence ends with a sense of consensus and collaborative accomplishment. In addition to a solution to the nose-cone problem, the group has articulated, accepted, and put into conversational practice a terminology for discussing sameness, difference, comparison, and so on.

By making explicit the references that grant meaning to the discourse ("one and two"), the students make visible to each other the understanding that is being expressed in the interactions. In particular, they make visible the elliptical, indexical, and projective references that had become confused. As researchers, we can take advantage of what the participants made visible to each other to also see what was meant and learned as long as we stand within a shared interpretive horizon with them (Gadamer, 1988). Methodologically, our access to these displays is ensured to the extent that we share membership in the culture of understanding that the participants themselves share. For instance, we are native speakers of English, have experienced middle-school classroom culture in America, have a lay understanding of rockets, but may not be privy to the latest teen pop culture or the local lore of the particular classroom, so we can legitimately interpret much but perhaps not all of what goes on. Intersubjective validity, the analog of interrater reliability, is established by our developing interpretations of the data within group data sessions and presenting those interpretations in seminars and conferences of peers, where our interpretations must be accepted as plausible from the perspectives of a number of researchers.

Interpreting what learning took place in the collaborative moment is considerably harder than interpreting what took place in most of the rest of the three-hour session. When the dialogue format between a teacher and one student dominates (as it did in much of the remaining time), one can assume—unless there is evidence to the contrary—that learning has taken place for the student (if not necessarily for the whole class) if the student's response to the teacher's question has been evaluated as appropriate by the teacher. One basically follows the teacher's displayed interpretation of what is unfolding, assigning learning to students who he indicates have responded appropriately to his questions. In a collaborative moment, there is no authority guiding, structuring, and evaluating the interaction. Deeper interpretation is required to determine what takes place at all, let alone who learns what, when, where, and how. In a CSCL setting, where, for instance, many students may be interacting autonomously within a threaded discussion system on the Internet, one must rely on an analysis of student discourse that has a many-to-many structure rather than having all interaction go through the teacher. The potential here is great because learning can overcome the teacher bottleneck and allow much higher levels of student participation in knowledge-building discourse. The problem is how to assess what learning is taking place.

The factors that have in cases of individual learning been taken to be hidden in mental representations can in cases of collaborative learning be taken to be visible in the discourse. The meaning of utterances—even in elliptical, indexical, and projective utterances—can be rigorously interpreted on the basis of interaction data such as digital video or computer chat logs. Learning—now viewed at the small-group unit of analysis—can be taken to be a characteristic of the discourse itself. In addition to the group's shared understanding, however, one can also determine the interpretive perspectives of the individual members, particularly in cases where there are breakdowns of the shared understanding, individual interpretations diverge, and the group members must make things explicit. The question now is how to specify a methodology for making the group meaning-making process visible for researchers.

Video Analysis

We propose adopting a methodology to analyze collaborative interaction called *video analysis* (Heath, 1986), which has been developed largely through the mediation of digital video. However, it is also applicable to the analysis of collaborative interactions where traces of the discourse are preserved in other forms sufficiently detailed to allow fine-grained microanalysis, such as comprehensive computer chat logs.

This methodology is based largely on a tradition of interaction analysis (Jordan & Henderson, 1995) that is popular among communication scientists and anthropologists. Its roots are perhaps most extensively elaborated under the rubrics of ethnomethodology (Garfinkel, 1967, 2002; Heritage, 1984) and conversation analysis (Psathas, 1995; Sacks, 1992; ten Have, 1999). Ethnomethodology (EM) is a discipline that focuses on the procedures (methods) that participants (members) use in making sense of their own social actions and the actions of others. Conversation analysis (CA) is an area of specialization within EM that focuses specifically on the procedures participants employ in competently producing conversation. It provides a rigorous methodology for studying participants' sense-making practices in the classroom. By studying the sense-making practices of students and teachers, we can document what an instructional innovation means in interactional terms. The pioneers in these fields have focused on discovering the structures of communication (such as turn taking), rather than applying their methods to practical ends, like evaluating learning and designing curricular innovations. So we are borrowing their tools and adapting them within a very different scientific endeavor to the extent that we use these analyses to guide the design of new collaboration technologies and practices.

The method we are recommending is an interpretive (hermeneutic) one. This does not make it subjective. On the contrary, we are interested in analyzing the intersubjective meanings that we find in the physical and visible video or chat record, rather than hypothesizing about what may have taken place in subjective individual minds. Perhaps the hardest thing for newcomers to get used to in CA is the method's strictures against speculating about what participants were thinking when they interacted in certain observable ways. The method relies on the fact that the participants, in interacting with each other, were displaying for each other in visible ways (many of which could be captured on video) words and gestures that made sense to both the actor and the other participants. The record of the interaction typically contains numerous clues as to just what sense this was. Subsequent responses of the participants "take up" this meaning in specific ways. Sometimes it turns out that the meaning of some utterance to the speaker and its meaning to the listener were at odds; this difference becomes visible when the conversation turns to visibly repair the misunderstanding. When no evidence of a misunderstanding appears, the analyst can safely assume that for all practical purposes of that interaction the participants had the same understanding of the interaction. The method of analysis is at pains to ensure that the analyst comes to the same understanding as the participants, given relatively similar access to the same utterances as the participants shared.

According to constructivism, learning is a process of constructing new meanings. But unlike much constructivism, we do not assume that meaning exists only in individual human minds (see chapter 16). The world is full of meaningful things. Most gestures and utterances that people make are meaningful, and their meanings are necessarily visible to other people. Otherwise, they would not be effective means of communication.

When one practices interaction analysis for awhile, it becomes clear that it is not necessary to interpret meaningful human actions as the result of premeditated, fully worked-out plans in their heads (Suchman, 1987). People just interact and respond to each other on the spot. They may sometimes silently rehearse little speeches in advance of saying them, control what comes out, or quickly reflect on what they said so they can retrospectively give an account. But these mechanisms seem to be secondary phenomena. They are not at all trustworthy accounts of what people meant or why they said something. In a deep sense, "actions speak louder" than retroactive words. It may not be so bad that analysts cannot read people's minds: their visible actions are more meaningful. If learning takes place in an interaction, we should be able to observe it by analyzing an adequate record of the interaction. It should show in the changes in the way that participants use words, in the ways they build on each others' utterances, in their expressions, gazes, postures, expressive noises, and in their interactions in similar circumstances later.

Learning is subtle. It rarely expresses itself in syntactically perfect complete propositions, despite textbook presentations of knowledge. It is more likely to reveal itself in how the learner gradually starts to use a term with increasing meaning or begins to approach a problem with greater familiarity. Learning is paradoxical; children acquire vocabulary at an incredible rate, but they only have a glimmer of what a new word means. Learning is situated; someone might be able to use a new resource in the context where it was learned but not yet elsewhere. Analysts can think that they saw visible learning but not be sure what its limits are. Discourse is ambiguous; what is said is often open to multiple consistent interpretations. This opens a creative space in which participants can choose among options for proceeding, and it softens interpersonal commitments to avoid potentially embarrassing social consequences. Analysts must rely on how a given utterance was taken up by other participants—and it still may not be possible to pin down a reading of the utterance with much certainty.

If learning is a process of making new meanings, then instruction consists of forms of interactional practice that foster this process. The instruction's job is to guide the learner or learners in constructing new meaning—that is, in understanding the meaning that is visibly co-constructed in an interaction. The instruction's job is ultimately to facilitate the learner's acquisition of the ability to construct similar meanings in other interactions.

This might take place, for instance, in the manner described by the theory of the zone of proximal development (Vygotsky, 1978). A student who is developmentally capable of participating in a certain kind of meaningful interaction with a teacher, parent, or older sibling may later internalize the learned ability to engage in that form of meaning making and engage in it with a peer or even internally in his or her mental discourse. While the subsequent internal mental transformations and applications may not be directly visible to an observing analyst, the original learning that took place in the interaction is potentially visible. According to Vygotsky, most learning, especially in young children, takes place socially, interactionally. The hidden, internal learning takes place later, building on the social experiences. An analyst may want to investigate interactions among young people or novices, where learning has not yet been internalized as mental cognitive artifacts.

Because instruction consists of forms of interactional practice, it must adhere to the rules of interaction. That is, it must present things in ways that can be seen by participants and whose meaning is made visible to the participants. Because the meanings inherent to instruction must be visibly displayed to the participants, they should be visible to the analyst—under the right conditions. The necessary preconditions are what determine the applicability of the methodology. The conditions can be summed up as the technical preconditions that determine the adequacy of the video record and the hermeneutic preconditions that determine the analyst's ability to interpret the displayed meanings appropriately.

Video analysis requires the meeting of certain technical preconditions. The video analyst owes his or her existence to the development of digital video technology. Ethnographers and other social scientists have observed human interactions for a long time, taking notes by hand and more recently using audio recorders, but the interactions within small groups are too complex and subtle to analyze systematically without a more complete record, which can be returned to repeatedly to study. While analog video provided such a record, the real need was met only when one could put the video on a computer and manipulate it frame by frame, zoom in, loop small segments of the soundtrack, jump around easily to follow lines of inquiry, and easily share clips with coanalysts.

Analysis needs a detailed transcript. Depending on the situation under analysis, the transcript may have to include in addition to the words spoken, indications of other sounds, intonations, pauses, gestures, gazes, and other nonverbal cues that were visible in the tape. Digital video allows repeated and detailed viewing and accurately timed pauses to produce a useful transcript.

In a situation like a classroom, simply capturing the talk of students with each other during collaborative learning sessions strains the ability of the video analyst even with today's digital equipment. Imagine trying to film the utterances, facial expressions, glances, poses, gestures, inscriptions, computer screens, and interactions of a teacher and 30 students in an active, collaborative classroom engaged in an educational innovation. Even with hundreds of cameras and microphones and synchronized recordings, it would not be humanly possible to follow all that was going on. One must design an interaction setting whose analysis is manageable. By confining the interactions to a sequential stream of messages within small groups in chatrooms, for instance, the volume of data is reduced, and a reasonably complete record of everything that the group of participants shared is captured already in a textual format.

Video analysis also requires meeting hermeneutic preconditions. A condition for appropriate interpretation is that the analyst has the proper background understanding to know how the participants would interpret the variety of displayed meanings. For instance, do they speak the same language? Assuming that everyone is speaking English, is the jargon of a subculture unfamiliar to the analyst playing a relevant role? Do the students make reference to people or events that the analyst is unaware of? Is there a culture at work in the classroom that the analyst does not understand and cannot figure out from the record?

Even if a whole classroom session was recorded, the analyst may have focused on a few short but interesting episodes and ignored the rest. The question of where to start and stop these analytic episodes is tricky, for they themselves likely refer back to previous episodes and may be a telling reference for later episodes.

The subjectivity of the interpretation is another important issue. The method responds to this concern by including many points in the analysis where the evolving interpretation is subjected to discussion by groups of analysts—for example, in so-called data sessions where a dozen or so trained analysts brainstorm about specific episodes and repeatedly view the video clips with detailed transcripts in hand. Later, when a final analysis is presented at a conference or in a journal, the original data (videos, transcripts, ethnographic notes, and so on, subject to confidentiality constraints) are made available for alternative interpretations. This approach ensures maximal intersubjectivity of the interpretation.

Five Policies from Ethnomethodology

The goal of video analysis is to analyze the practices by which groups of interacting members construct group meaning. Video analysis is founded on ethnomethodology. Ethnomethodology studies how people (*ethno-*), who are members of communities, construct ways (*method-ology*) of making shared sense of their joint activities. In video analysis, researchers look closely at traces of member activities to study the methods that the members use to achieve meaningful interactions. The meaning-making activities are generally only tacitly understood by the individual members who engage in them, but their meaningfulness is made visible to the group so that it can be shared. Researchers take advantage of this visibility to make the methods explicit. Activities are meaningful in the group perspective. Their meaning is implicitly understood in the individual member perspective and explicitly understood in the video researcher perspective. The phenomenological commitment of ethnomethodology concerns the relationship of the understandings from the different perspectives. Ethnomethodology is a researcher perspective devoted to making explicit the meanings that are understood and taken for granted in the member (individual) perspective and made implicitly visible (for the interacting members as well as for researchers who take the trouble to look) in the group perspective through the utterances, gestures, symbolic artifacts, inscriptions, and so on of the group discourse.

Garfinkel (1967) provided five policies as a starting point for ethnomethodological (EM) studies. These policies are densely worded and complexly interconnected. Therefore, in attempting to summarize them here, I have extracted a key theme from each policy statement and attempted to explain its significance to video analytic research. In particular, I have translated Garfinkel's terminology (*indifference, inspectability, relevance, accountability,* and *indexicality*) into the claim that data for video analysis are *everywhere, visible, grounded, meaningful,* and *situated.*

Policy 1: Data Are Everywhere

An indefinitely large domain of appropriate settings can be located if one uses a search policy that *any occasion whatsoever* be examined for the feature that "choice" among alternatives of sense, of facticity, of objectivity, of cause, of explanation, of communality *of practical actions* is a project of members' actions. Such a policy provides that inquiries of every imaginable kind, from divination to theoretical physics, claim our interest as socially organized artful practices. (Garfinkel, 1967, p. 32)

EM is concerned with the practices people engage in to make sense of each other's activities. Because human interaction always constructs meaningful order, the EM researcher can analyze almost any interaction ("an indefinitely large domain of settings" of "every imaginable kind") and discover interesting processes of meaning construction and order negotiation. Groups use meaning-making methods in all social interactions; these methods can be found in any domain of interactional data. The technical and hermeneutic preconditions for analysis must have been met, but that is not a matter of the choice of interactional case.

Harvey Sacks (1992) elaborates the argument for being able to discover general methods in most any case of interaction. He argues that for people to be able to understand each other within a complex culture, social practices must be relatively standardized and ubiquitous and that this has methodological implications for the researcher:

Then it really wouldn't matter very much what it is you look at—if you look at it carefully enough. And you may well find that you got an enormous generalizability because things are so arranged that you could get them; given that for a member encountering a very limited environment, he has to be able to do that, and things are so arranged as to permit him to. (p. 485)

This means that for society to function and for children to be acculturated fast enough to survive in human cultures, people must structure their interpersonal interactions in ways that can be recognized easily. Member methods—despite their vast variety and extreme subtlety—must be ubiquitous and familiar. Consequentially, a researcher can find member methods in almost any data set. Conversely, the member methods analyzed in an arbitrary interaction can provide generalizable insights into the structure of member methods in a broad range of situations.

This attributes an important role to case studies. A traditional sociological approach seeks out special events (such as examples of best practices) to analyze or imposes laboratory controls on large numbers of cases and computes sophisticated averages. However, the phenomena of everyday practice that are of interest to EM but fall below the radar of other social sciences and conscious folk theories can be studied in depth in arbitrary individual instantiations. Such studies are not "merely anecdotal," as some critics might suggest. Anecdotal evidence is data based on superficial observations of unscientific observers, often generalized excessively. But EM analyses adhere to rigorous, detailed, intersubjective, and inspectable procedures. Furthermore, they claim to demonstrate only how something was achieved in one unique case, although the structure of the methods uncovered may be similar to methods used in many other cases. Case studies are intended not to prove the effectiveness of a specific intervention but to explore what can, in fact, happen and to investigate the characteristics of actual interactions that are unique but interesting. The criticism that case studies are merely anecdotal is misplaced because it assumes that one is trying to make a universal generalization, whereas a case study is really providing an existence proof that may be more surprising than a generalization based on common assumptions (such as assumptions of which cases are "best practices").

For instance, an EM analysis of the SimRocket transcript would not predict that groups of students under such and such conditions would always learn about paired configurations as a list structure. Rather, it would show how the particular students in that case used methods of repair and explication to establish a shared group meaning, methods that are used in many other interactions. The analysis in chapters 12 and 13 was not intended to conclude whether the SimRocket simulation was educationally effective or not. Clearly, the single case could not be generalized to make such a judgment. The case studied was utterly unique. A different group of students might never have engaged in the kind of collaborative discourse that was the focus of the analysis: they might have either seen the list structure immediately or never worked it out. Slight changes in the design of the list (such as using a "standard configuration" rather than a "paired configuration") would have eliminated the problem altogether. If the simulation allowed users to assemble their own rockets (as Chuck in fact proposed), there would have been no list at all to figure out— although the students would eventually have had to construct the equivalent of the list without the help of a list artifact to mediate their work. So even the smallest generalization would be invalid. Nor could one expect to be able to run multiple trials to average—because each would be a unique experience. But despite this extreme limitation, we were able to discover how a real instance of collaboration actually took place. Our observations of this unique brief moment—despite a variety of shortcomings in the technical and hermeneutic preconditions of our analysis and its very tentative and restricted scope—nevertheless motivated much of the discussion of collaboration in this book.

Through a microanalysis of a unique case we were able to discover phenomena that permeate collaborative group interaction but for which our folk theories, intuitions, and training did not prepare us. As Sacks (1992, p. 420) said, one can discover from the details of actual empirical cases phenomena that one would not otherwise imagine take place:

A base for using close looking at the world for theorizing about it is that from close looking at the world you can find things that we wouldn't, by imagination, assert were there: One wouldn't know that they were typical, one might not know that they ever happened, and even if one supposed that they did one couldn't say it because the audience wouldn't believe it.

Because any site is as likely as another to reveal the artful practices of rational action, the EM analyst has great latitude in selecting settings in which to do analysis. In particular, any circumstance, situation, or activity that participants treat as, for instance, one in which instruction and learning are occurring can be investigated for how instruction and learning are being produced by and among participants.

The criteria by which site selection is to be done has to do with how the participants construed what they were doing. The work of the analyst is to conduct an empirical investigation into what participants are doing through their interaction. It is not to impose a theoretical category from outside the interaction. If researchers begin their investigation by seeking out a site that represents "best practice" or "exemplary instruction" or "an example of innovation *x*," they will have begun their investigation by presuming what their investigation is ostensibly designed to investigate. As analysts, we do not presume that we are more informed about learning and instruction than the practitioners who do learning and instruction. It is not for us to bring to the table preconceived notions or theories of learning and instruction and then see if they are operational within a scene. Instead, our analysis should consist of descriptions of the actions that practitioners perform. These descriptions are specifically oriented to display the sequential organization and orderliness that inform these actions and that these actions are designed to produce.

The analyst does not select data as "cases of *x*" but determines what the data are about based on what the data show the participants to be attending to. The researcher's perspective tries to adopt and explicate the member's view. As Schegloff (Prevignano & Thibault, 2003, p. 25) describes the methodology of EM, "The most important consideration, theoretically speaking, is (and ought to be) that whatever seems to animate, to preoccupy, to shape the interaction *for the participants in the interaction* mandates how we do our work, and what work we have to do."

The policy of setting aside or bracketing out externally supplied characterizations of what participants are doing in conducting an analysis is sometimes described as ethnomethodology's studied indifference to members' matters—that is, refusing to impose one's own interests. It is this indifference that makes ethnomethodological input to a project problematic. Video analysis, conducted under the auspices of

Garfinkel's policies, cannot pass judgment on what might serve as good or bad or even representative practice. EM studies are purely descriptive and cannot be used to form prescriptive judgments. Perhaps these problems can be overcome, however, through clarity about the different perspectives of curricular designers, program evaluators, collaboration researchers, and video analysts. EM studies can be used to document, from the research perspective, what members do from their perspective in carrying out educational activities. In so doing, EM studies can produce the data by which designers and evaluators carry out tasks from the design perspective.

Policy 2: Data Are Visible

Members to an organized arrangement are continually engaged in having to decide, recognize, persuade, or make evident the rational, i.e., the coherent, or consistent, or chosen, or planful, or effective, or methodical, or knowledgeable character of such activities of their inquiries as counting, graphing, interrogation, sampling, recording, reporting, planning, decision-making, and the rest. It is not satisfactory to describe how actual investigative procedures, as constituent features of members' ordinary and organized affairs, are accomplished by members as recognizably rational actions in *actual occasions* of organizational circumstances by saying that members invoke some rule with which to define the coherent or consistent or planful, i.e., rational, character of their actual activities. (Garfinkel, 1967, p. 32)

The idea that social practices are a matter of following culturally defined rules is incoherent, as Wittgenstein (1953) had already argued. Tacit practices and group negotiations are necessary at some level to put rules into practice, if only because the idea of rules for implementing rules involves an impossible recourse. Although there is certainly order in social interactions of which people are not explicitly aware but that can be uncovered through microanalysis, this order is an interactive accomplishment of the people participating in the interactions. While the order has aspects of rationality and meaning, it is not the result of simply invoking or complying with a determinate rule. Consider, for instance, the orderliness of traffic flows at stop signs. The smooth functioning in accordance with traffic laws is continuously negotiated with glances, false starts, and various signals. Although we do not usually explicitly focus on how this is accomplished unless we take on an analyst's perspective (because explicit awareness is not usually necessary for achieving the practical ends and may actually distract and impede), the signs that are exchanged are necessarily visible to the participants and accordingly accessible to a researcher with appropriate means of data capture.

If we, as analysts, observe rulelike behavior at stop signs, we cannot causally explain this behavior by simply saying there is a social rule that everyone must follow. The members of the group doing the rulelike behavior are continually negotiating what it means to follow the traffic rules in the current context and how they are going to do that. In innovative classrooms, a similar process of rule adoption takes place. If a teacher is given an instructional innovation, she must work out in her situation how she is going to put that innovation into practice in detail (Remillard & Bryans, 2004) and make that visible to her students.

Participants, "as members to an organized arrangement" (Garfinkel, 1967, p. 32), are continuously engaged in the work of making sense or meaning of their own and others' actions. The imputed sense or meaning of an action or of a sequence of actions is not determinate, however, but is instead endlessly open to new interpretation. As Heritage (1984) explained, "The task of fellow-actors . . . is necessarily one of *inferring* from a fragment of the other's conduct and its context what the other's project is, or is likely to be" (p. 60). In other words, it is the way that actions unfold that gives them the sense they have. Furthermore, actors are selective in what they treat as relevant so that many aspects of an action's sense remain indeterminate. The only requirement that actors themselves place on their sense making is that it be adequate for the purposes at hand. Meaning, therefore, is "a contingent accomplishment of socially organized practices" (p. 33).

Group interactions are rulelike from the researcher's perspective. But from the member's perspective, the rules are not simply given by social laws that must be obeyed like the physical laws of material objects. A member might take an action that to the video analyst looks like a rule-following response to the situation up to that point. But then it is up to other members to take up new action as part of such a rule or not. For instance, there is a conversational rule that questions should be followed by answers. If someone makes an utterance, the determination of whether that utterance is a question (and therefore part of a question-answer pair) may be made by someone else either providing an answer and thereby establishing the rule, or else laughing and thereby establishing that the utterance was a joke—pending the first person's laughter or objection to their response.

The rulelike behavior is always situated and interpreted within a context of history, activities, artifacts, and anticipations. But this context is no more given than the rules that may be followed within it. Members' talk and action has a reflexive character, which is to say that it is simultaneously "context-shaped" and "context-shaping" (Heritage, 1984, p. 242). While the meaning of any action depends crucially on the context within which it is performed, the action itself reshapes the context in ways that will inform the understandability of other actions that follow. This is a mechanism on the micro level of social reproduction, which Giddens (1984b) calls "structuration."

Rules and context can play important roles in the understanding of interactions from both the members' and the researchers' perspective. However, the interpretation of social interaction is a human science and not a physical science (Habermas,

1971), so rules and contextual features are proposed and negotiated within the interaction, rather than being objectively given or analytically proposed. Members may invoke rules as standards within the interactional situation (Pomerantz & Fehr, 1991) to support, justify, rationalize, or generally make their behavior meaningful and accountable. Similarly, the discourse may imply that its setting is a certain kind of occasion involving particular categories of participants. Through such interactional moves, members display what social norms and contextual characteristics are salient to their interactions. Researchers should rely on these displays to guide their explicit analyses. If there are warrants in the discourse for interpreting the members as being oriented toward a social rule, then the researcher may bring in a larger understanding of the structures that define that rule but were not made explicit in the discourse (see the discussion of sources of structural being in chapter 20).

An investigation must rely on the actual practices of the participants as they are engaged in their interactions to provide an adequate description of the context of interaction. Such an analysis would constitute a description of the determinate sense of the situation that members construct through their actions. For example, for a researcher to invoke a rule to explain member actions there must be interactional evidence of an orientation to such a rule by the members. To document members' practices in detail, repeated inspectability of these practices is necessary. Video and computer technology provide for this repeated inspectability. This inspectability serves as the only legitimate basis for making claims about such subtle matters as how groups of people took their methods and contexts from moment to moment. As Emanuel Schegloff (Prevignano & Thibault, 2003, p. 27, interview of Schegloff in 1996) argued, "These days, only such work as is grounded in tape (video tape where the parties are visually accessible to one another) or other repeatably (and intersubjectively) examinable media can be subjected to serious comparative and competitive analysis." In other words, analytical claims about practices must be supported by observable actions of participants, which are evident in the recorded interaction and which establish the facticity and relevance of the claimed matter for the participants themselves. This leads to the recommendation of the remaining three specific research policies.

Policy 3: Data Are Grounded

A leading policy is to refuse serious consideration to the prevailing proposal that efficiency, efficacy, effectiveness, intelligibility, consistency, planfulness, typicality, uniformity, reproducibility of activities—i.e., that rational properties of practical activities—be assessed, recognized, categorized, described by using a rule or a standard obtained outside actual settings within which such properties are recognized, used, produced, and talked about by settings' members. (Garfinkel, 1967, p. 33)

This policy insists on a radical grounded theory approach that derives the categories of the researcher's analysis from the activities of the members. It does not suffice to offer descriptions that depend on categories defined outside of the situation under study (for example, student, teacher, gender, learning-disabled, low-achieving, socioeconomic status, language ability, and so on) as terms for explaining what participants do or don't do. Garfinkel insists that our theories about member practices must not only be substantiated in the observational data but should arise from and be grounded in that data. Specifically, we must "bracket out" our preexisting theories and understandings while constructing our analyses and introducing categories to account for behaviors only when we can empirically demonstrate their relevance as evidenced by the talk and activities of the participants. As Schegloff (1991b, p. 51) observed,

There is still the problem of showing from the details of the talk or other conduct in the materials that we are analyzing that those aspects of the scene are what the parties are oriented to. For that is to show how the parties are embodying for one another the relevancies of the interaction and are thereby producing the social structure.

Further, this policy specifies that actors are not "judgmental dopes" who are incapable of monitoring and acting on their circumstances. They do not simply follow social laws or rules but enact these rules (the patterns that appear to researchers as rule following). They are capable of making choices, and they have a shared, if provisional, sense of propriety with respect to what they both can and cannot do and what they should and should not do. While this sense of propriety may or may not be something actors can account for, it is evident in what they do and the way they do it. The work of instruction and learning, therefore, as it is actually done, is an ongoing sequence of contingent practices commonly shared among and recognizable by participants. Whether or not a situation is an instance of learning and instruction or of successful innovation is not a matter for designers to judge a priori but for video analysts to demonstrate in their empirical analysis of how the participants took their own activities. This does not mean that it is a matter for the participants to address in post hoc surveys, interviews, or focus groups either. For retrospective rationalizations are not the same as the sense making that is enacted in situ. It is up to the video analysis to ground judgments in the traces of the interactive actions of the participants.

Policy 4: Data Are Meaningful

The policy is recommended that any social setting be viewed as self-organizing with respect to the intelligible character of its own appearances as either representations of or as evidences-of-a-social-order. Any setting organizes its activities to make its properties as an organized environment of practical activities detectable, countable, recordable, reportable, tell-a-story-aboutable, analyzable—in short, *accountable*. (Garfinkel, 1967, p. 33)

Groups organize their activities in ways that provide for their intelligibility as reportable and inspectable—that is, as meaningful. EM assumes that people ordinarily do things in ways that are inherently designed to make sense. This is a powerful assumption because it allows us to say that actions and the meanings associated with them are sequential in nature and that this sequential organization produces, sustains, and is informed by members' shared sense of a local social order. This allows members to recognize prospectively and retrospectively that they are engaged in some specific activity as they engage in it.

When Garfinkel refers to behavior as being *accountable*, the word can be understood in at least two senses. First, members are held responsible for their actions and are accountable to their interlocutors for their utterances and actions; they may legitimately be called on to provide an explanation or rationale. Second, Garfinkel is contending that all behavior is designed in ways to give an account of the activity as an instance of something or other—that is, as meaningful. For instance, a group of students might organize their activity to be accountable as a group engaged in doing a class project, in doing a science experiment, in working with a mentor, in being cool, in being teens hanging out. It is the work of the video analyst to document how this making of accountable meaning is accomplished.

Policy 5: Data Are Situated

The demonstrably rational properties of indexical expressions and indexical actions are an ongoing achievement of the organized activities of everyday life. (Garfinkel, 1967, p. 34)

Indexical expressions are those whose sense depends crucially on knowledge of the context within which the expressions were produced. The most obvious examples are expressions that contain deictic terms such as *here, there, I, you, we, now,* and *then*. To make sense of an utterance containing such terms, it will generally be necessary to know who is the speaker, who is the audience, where the speaker and audience are located, when the utterance was produced, and so on. Any sentence containing such elements will have different interpretations or meanings depending on the circumstances in which it is produced. Logicians and linguists "have encountered indexical expressions as troublesome sources of resistance to the formal analysis of language and of reasoning practices" (Heritage, 1984, p. 142). Rationalists strive to eliminate indexicality in favor of "objective" propositions; EM acknowledges indexicality's abiding role in situated discourse.

One of Garfinkel's contributions was to note that deictic terms are not the only ones that have indexical properties. John Heritage (1984) provides the example of the assessment, "That's a nice one," offered while the speaker and the listener are attending to a particular photograph. What qualifies the picture as nice (its composition, color rendering, content) is not made evident by the utterance taken in isolation and must somehow be worked out by the listener by inspecting the object in question. In this way, nondeictic terms such as *nice* are also indexical in use. Similarly, in the SimRocket transcript, when Brent says, "This one's different," each word in this deictic utterance (accompanying a bold, full-body pointing gesture) is itself deictic. As discussed in chapters 12 and 13, the researcher's attempt to explicate the reference of the term *different* is nontrivial but highly relevant.

Socially organized actions also can have indexical properties. Imagine two people standing face to face and one participant reaching out and touching the other. The meaning of this act (as a warning, provocation, greeting, demonstration, empathetic gesture, act of belligerence) depends crucially on context—on the nature of the interaction that immediately preceded and immediately follows the touch. (See the concept of "thick description" developed by Austin, 1952, and Geertz, 1973.)

The fact that the meaning of indexical expressions and actions cannot be determined isolated from the circumstances within which they were produced does not usually present a problem for participants. Brent's indexical exclamation did present problems for his peers, but they managed to resolve this confusion in a few seconds. For starters, participants inhabit the situations within which the expressions and actions are produced and, as a result, are naturally supplied with many resources for resolving their meaning for present purposes. Further, participants have the opportunity to dispel any residual ambiguity through additional sense negotiation. Ultimately, however, all indexical expressions and actions are always contingent and to some degree indeterminate in ways that are deemed acceptable to actors themselves. For Garfinkel, the question of how this indeterminacy is managed in the nonce on a routine basis is at the heart of EM inquiry. It would appear to have similar importance for video-analytic work in the science of computer-mediated collaboration.

The Self-Organization of Group Discourse

A central concept in EM is *accountability*. This term defines an important characteristic of group discourse. Although this characteristic is analyzed from the researcher's perspective, it inheres to the group unit of analysis and provides an essential function within the group perspective. It, in effect, makes the group perspective possible.

Let us look more closely at Garfinkel's (1967, p. 33) policy concerned with accountability:

The policy is recommended that any social setting be viewed as self-organizing with respect to the intelligible character of its own appearances as either representations of or as evidences-of-a-social-order. Any setting organizes its activities to make its properties as an organized environment of practical activities detectable, countable, recordable, reportable, tell-a-story-aboutable, analyzable—in short, *accountable*.

Note that the meaningfulness, sense, or accountability of a group activity structure is a function of that setting itself, not a function of people's mental representations about the setting or even of individuals' interpretations of the setting. The setting itself "organizes its activities to make its properties . . . accountable." This is not intended as a proclamation about the ontology of reality. Rather, "the policy is recommended that any social setting be *viewed* as self-organizing." That is, it is a methodological principle. In other words, a defining premise of EM is that a researcher should focus on the group unit of analysis and make explicit how the group setting organizes itself. (The view of shared group reality as self-organizing—as opposed to a view centered on individual minds—will be pursued in chapter 20.)

The pioneers of EM observed that even the most mundane, everyday social settings are organized in ways that seem meaningful to their members, and they posed as a research agenda the working out of the methods of such self-organization. It is an empirical question whether analyses based on this approach are insightful and useful. So far, video-analysis and conversation-analysis studies seem to offer important views of what takes place in collaborative settings, although their direct aid to design of collaboration support software has yet to be extensively documented.

The relevance of interaction analysis based on EM to CSCL and CSCW has to do with the central role in both fields of meaning making. As expressed in chapter 16, CSCL is supposed to be essentially concerned with the nature of the processes of collaborative meaning making. How do groups make meaning? Garfinkel proposes that *meaning-making* processes consist of the *methods or practices whereby groups make their actions accountable*. This takes place in interaction and discourse. An account of behavior is constructed interactively as people respond to a situation and others take up that response in a particular way, confirming the definition of the context along with an account of the activity. The meaning is constructed not so much by the individual contributions to the discourse as by the ways in which these contributions index, respond to, build on, and take up each other—by the web of interaction.

Let us take two examples from the chapter 12 transcript. First, consider the teacher's utterance, "And you don't have anything like that there?" Initially, the students responded to this as a straightforward question and supplied an answer in the negative. When this did not elicit a response back from the teacher, they reconstrued the question as a rhetorical question and looked at the list to which this utterance situationally pointed—the list that was on the computer screen, to which the teacher gesturally pointed. From there, Brent started to build an account of how something "like that" was there in the list, by pointing toward a pair of rockets that he saw as satisfying this description. But Brent's statement was just a first step in building an accounting that made sense for the whole group.

Brent's own statement (in turn, recursively) went through a similar process of having an accounting constructed. When he emphatically said, "This one's different," the others at first disagreed. Then gradually they clarified which "one" was being pointed to and how it was different. This involved the shift in conceptualizing comparable pairs of rockets as analyzed in chapter 13. Through this discourse process, the group made Brent's statement accountable. The analysis in chapter 13 from the researcher's perspective made explicit what a full accounting might be like. For the participants, it was enough to say things like Jamie: "compare two n one"; Steven: "So I like it how it is"; or Chuck: "Oh yeah, I see, I see, I see."

The methods that the students used included a variety of discourse moves: denying, pointing, answering, clarifying, agreeing, completing each other's utterances, repairing divergent references, pausing, interrupting, gesticulating. Each of these fragmentary moves was itself made accountable and only thereby contributed to the larger meaning making. The account of each move and certainly of the larger accomplishment involved an interplay of the discourse context and multiple actions by the discourse participants. In this sense, it was an accomplishment on the group level of analysis.

The discourse about the list could be said to have organized itself to make itself accountable. It could not have been a successful discourse if it had not done so. The drama captured in the half-minute transcript is the story of how the group discourse organized a story about the list—through the interweaving of contributions from multiple individual perspectives—to the point where Chuck could see the new story, Brent could sit back in his chair relieved that everyone got the story, and Jamie could return to the larger story of designing an optimal rocket. One could feel during the long pause preceding Brent's outburst and the intense student collaboration, while the teacher exercised wait time, the intense pressure on the group to organize an acceptable story or an accounting of the list to which the teacher directed their attention. The activity of this moment in which the group found itself could not succeed without an effort that managed to achieve an accounting.

The EM notion of accountability provides a plausible and operational notion of group meaning. It is, for one thing, a methodological rather than metaphysical notion. That is, it is not so mysterious and counterintuitive as the idea of group meaning might appear from the perspective of empiricist folk theories. It can be observed in the concrete analyses of EM practitioners and judged as to its persuasiveness. In this sense, EM's notion of group meaning as accountability can be judged based on the success of its own accountability.

Garfinkel describes a number of characteristics of *accountability*:

• Accountability is *visible* to members. It is "observable-and-reportable, i.e., available to members as situated practices of looking-and-telling" (Garfinkel, 1967, p. 1). The meaning of social settings is visible to the members of those settings; they can observe and understand that meaning. They can discuss it further themselves and respond appropriately to it. The meaning of a setting is more or less reported to the extent needed for the practical purposes of the discourse interaction. The meaning-making process as a set of member methods is generally taken for granted and not reported in the group discourse. However, traces of those methods and how they have been taken by the group are observable to researchers, who can make them explicit. Thus, group discourse by its nature makes group meaning visible—for both members and researchers, in their own ways.

• Accountability is an *accomplishment* of groups. The meaning is not something distinct and separable from the social settings, activity structure, or group context: "Their rational features *consist* of what members do with, what they 'make of' the accounts in the socially organized action occasions of their use" (p. 4). The accountability is an accomplishment of the ongoing interaction of the occasion; it is an emergent feature of the occasion itself.

• Accountability is *indexical*. Where other sciences try to formulate abstract generalizations, EM insists that meanings of practical group interactions are necessarily tied to concrete contexts that they reflexively specify and that they index. One can try to substitute objective terms for deictic references, but this process is in principle not able to be completed. The scientific attempt to render every description in "objective," quantifiable, classifiable, generalized categories by substituting explicit terms for deictic ones "remains programmatic in every particular case and in every actual occasion" (p. 6).

• Accountability is *reflexive*. Discourse takes place on multiple levels simultaneously. Or discourse can be interpreted in multiple, mutually consistent ways. When a group discusses some content, they are also at work in their discourse making their discourse accountable. For instance, the discussion about comparing rockets was also a discussion about repairing misaligned references and constructing a story about how to analyze the list. The students focused their comments on the rocket content—which numbered rockets had which attributes. The research analysis, by contrast, focused on the meaning-making process. In general, members are little concerned at an explicit level with the account that they are creating—unlike the researchers, who are not much interested in the discourse content except as it reveals the accountability. The reflexivity of accountability has to do with the fact that the two levels are part of a single reflexive process: "members' accounts . . . are constituent features of the settings they make observable" (p. 8).

- Accountability is *tacit*. This is related to the fact that members are not much interested in the methods they use for making their discourse accountable. One can say that the methods of accountability are themselves not accountable. Although member activities accomplish meaning making on multiple levels, "for the member the organizational hows of these accomplishments are unproblematic, are known vaguely, and are known only in the doing which is done skillfully, reliably, uniformly, with enormous standardization and as an unaccountable matter" (p. 10).

- Accountability is *shared*. The EM notion of accountability sheds light on the discussion in chapter 17 of shared meaning, common ground and group cognition. Accountability can be seen as the establishment of a group meaning by reference to rulelike methods. Shared agreement is then seen to be an interactive accomplishment in which a group establishes that the discourse is to be accounted for in terms of a specific method or rule. "To see the 'sense' of what is said is to accord to what was said its character 'as a rule.' 'Shared agreement' refers to various social methods for accomplishing the member's recognition that something was said-according-to-a-rule and not the demonstrable matching of substantive matters. The appropriate image of a common understanding is therefore an operation rather than a common intersection of overlapping sets" (p. 30). Here, the agreement that is so fundamental to social interaction, collaboration and intersubjectivity is clearly not viewed as a matter of overlap among sets of mental representations in members' minds—as the common ground approach seemed to conceive it—but as the successful achievement of accountability of a group discourse.

The EM approach, with its central notion of accountability, provides a plausible way of thinking about how the self-organization of group discourse provides a basis for making group meaning visible.

19

Can Collaborative Groups Think?

Can the thinking in collaborative groups really be attributed to the group as a whole?[1] What forms of cognition can small groups engage in? What is the relationship of group cognition to the cognition of the individuals who are in the group? The question suggests a widening of the notion of cognition from one conventionally based on the individual human. It is hard for many people to accept this rethinking of thinking.

A similar attempt to extend the definition of cognition with artificial intelligence eventually concluded that computers cannot think because they could not convincingly imitate intelligent human behavior, they could not understand the symbols they manipulated, and they could not act intelligently in the world. Applying these criteria to small groups, however, suggests that groups *can* think as entities distinct from their individual human members. Many people became accustomed to considering computers as potential cognitive agents during the half century in which the claims of artificial intelligence were debated. Perhaps this receptivity to a broader definition of cognition can now be transferred to human group cognition, even as it has been denied to computers.

Cognition by the group should be looked at as a unit of analysis, both because individual thought is derived in crucial ways from group cognition and because the meaning created by groups often makes sense only within the group-discourse context as the analytic unit. Group discourse is thus seen as an important source of shared meaning and as the locus of collaborative cognitive processes. This provides an evocative framework for conceptualizing computer-supported collaborative learning and cooperative work.

From AI to CSCL

Alan Turing (1950) famously posed the question "Can machines think?" For 50 years after that, the field of artificial intelligence (AI) was driven largely by Turing's framing of the quest for computer-based (artificial) cognition (intelligence). In recent years, this quest has migrated into the development of technologies that aid or augment human intelligence. As the collaborative technologies of computer-supported cooperative work (CSCW) and computer-supported collaborative learning (CSCL) become more important, the trend may be even more to design computationally intensive media to support communication among people, making their—human but computer-mediated—group efforts more intelligent (see part I of this book).

It has become increasingly clear that computers do not "think" in the way that people do. As has been repeatedly stressed in the past decade or two, human cognition is essentially situated, interpretive, perspectival, and largely tacit. Computer symbol processing has none of these characteristics. Computers manipulate information that has meaning not for the computer but only for the people who configured or use the computer. Without meaning, there is no need or possibility to reference a situation, interpret symbols, view from a perspective, or link to tacit background understanding. Only the combination of people (who understand meaning) with computers (that help manipulate information) involves computers in thinking.

In this chapter, I pose a question analogous to the classic AI question: can groups think? In keeping with the priorities of CSCW and CSCL, I am interested in the potential of small groups that are collaborating effectively with technological mediation. Chapter 15 argued that collaborative knowledge building was a central phenomenon for collaboration, and chapter 16 extended the argument by claiming that meaning making in collaborative contexts took place primarily at the small-group unit of analysis. Perhaps the question of group cognition can help to set an agenda for future work in computer-supported collaboration, much as Turing's question propelled AI research in the past. CSCW and CSCL may provide a positive answer to the question, taking advantage of what AI learned in the process of arriving at its negative conclusion. After all, many technological pursuits within CSCW and CSCL have been inspired by AI.

In the following, I want to explore the sense in which small groups of people collaborating together can, under propitious conditions, be said to be thinking as a group or engaging in group cognition. I start with the simpler issue of whether small groups can *learn*, drawing on a study by Cohen and colleagues, and then take up the three major arguments by Turing, Searle, and Dreyfus about whether computers can think, applying their considerations to group cognition.

Can Groups Learn?

Learning is considered closely related to thinking. Perhaps a first step in addressing the question of group cognition would be to ask if groups can learn. This seems like a concrete question capable of being operationalized and explored empirically.

We saw in chapter 13 that the group of students working with SimRocket learned something as a whole: the group learned to see the list structure as a "paired configuration." Utterances from individuals indicated that they did not see the list this way before the moment of collaboration, but afterward they were able to appreciate this structure (Steven at 1:24:46) and to use it to compare rockets (Brent, Jamie, and Chuck at 1:26:46).

Educational researchers often prefer to argue for hypotheses based on statistically significant differences between experimentally controlled conditions, applying results of pre- and posttests. Where discourse is brought in as data, utterances are coded, and the number of utterances in certain categories are quantitatively compared across conditions. An interesting analysis using such a methodology was recently conducted about whether groups can learn by a team of educational researchers at Stanford. We now turn to their findings.

An Empirical Test

The team's research has been reported under the title "Can Groups Learn?" (Cohen, Lotan, Abram, Scarloss, & Schultz, 2002). It designed an experiment to assess the role of small groups as learners. The authors note that social scientists who have studied groups often claim that a group is greater than the sum of its individual parts. However, they continue,

There has been a tendency in assessment to regard the potential for performance in a group as the sum total of the amount of information, skills, and abilities that *individuals* bring to that group. Through the creative exchange of ideas, groups can solve problems and construct knowledge beyond the capacity of any single member. Thus it is possible to talk about the concept of *group learning* that is a result of the interaction of the group members and is not attributable to one well-informed person who undertakes to create the product or even to a division of labor in which different persons contribute different pieces of the product. (p. 1046)

Here the authors have identified the problem to be one of assessment at the group unit of analysis, which is distinct from treating the group learning as measurable by the sum of individual member learning. They suggest that groups can build knowledge as a group because of the potential of group discourse. The authors define the concept of group learning as something that is not attributable to one person or to a division of labor resulting in multiple individual products. (Unfortunately, the authors characterize the building of group knowledge at the individual unit of analysis as "the creative exchange of ideas," where ideas presumably come from the individuals and it is ambiguous whether the creativity is conceived as that of the group discourse or that of the individual participants.)

A carefully planned experiment was conducted with 39 small groups of four or five students. The groups were located in five different sixth-grade classrooms. The 163 students were from a linguistically, ethnically, and racially diverse student body in California, including children of immigrant workers. All five of the teachers were highly trained in instructional strategies of complex instruction, and the classes were tested to confirm that the teachers and students were all equally proficient at engaging in group work. The class work involved a week-long focal unit on Egyptian concepts of an afterlife, including group discussions, rehearsed group skits, and individual written reports.

The experimental design was an ingenious attempt to distinguish individual and group phases of learning and to assess them separately to see their relationship. The controlled variable was that only three of the five teachers gave explicit instructions to the students in the groups. For instance, for a skit about the heart, the evaluation criteria were, "Skit includes at least 2 sins, 2 virtues, and 1 spell; Skit gives good reasons for whether or not the deceased entered the afterlife; Skit is well rehearsed and believable." All classrooms participated in skill-builder exercises designed to improve the general quality of group discussion, but the explicit evaluation criteria were included in the exercises for only three groups—the experimental condition. The unit included a number of group discussions and activities like the skits. At the end, students wrote individual essays, where they were clearly instructed to use what they learned in the group activities.

The following measurements were taken:

1. A pretest of individual knowledge of the subject matter of Egyptian concepts of an afterlife,

2. Whether the group was trained with the explicit evaluation criteria,

3. The percentage of group discussion coded as evaluating the group product,

4. The percentage of group discussion coded as related to the content of the group product,

5. The percentage of group discussion coded as off topic,

6. The quality of the group product (a skit), based on the explicit evaluation criteria,

7. The quality of the individual essay (language skills were factored out), and

8. A posttest of the student's knowledge of the subject matter.

A path model of the causal relations between instructional variables and these assessment measurements was constructed by running several regression analyses.

Pretest scores (item 1 on this list) were not a predictor of the quality of the group products. The better group products (6) were the result of focused group discussion (3 and 4) and shared awareness of evaluation criteria (2), not the result of superior individual knowledge brought to the group. The same proved true for the individual essays (7). Prior individual knowledge was not a predictor of the quality of the individual essay. The better individual essays (averaged for each group) were the result of the group's discourse on evaluation considerations of the group product and the quality of the group product itself.

Perhaps equally surprising, the experimental condition of providing training on the explicit evaluation criteria (2) had no *direct* effect on the individual cognitive performance (7). The individual effect was mediated by the group work: "Evaluation criteria had no effect on essay score. It is through the increase in self-assessment (talk that is evaluation of product) and through the superior product that evaluation criteria affect the final essay" (p. 1062). Figure 19.1 represents all of the statistically significant causal relationships with arrows. Individual knowledge as measured by pre- and post-tests was not a significant determinant of either individual or group performance. Furthermore, the difference between the control and the experimental difference exerts an effect only by means of its effect on the group performance. In the terms of the experiment's paradigm, this demonstrates an empirically quantifiable phenomenon of group learning as distinct from the sum of individual member learning.

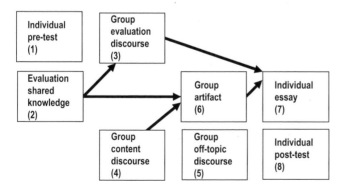

Figure 19.1
Path model of instruction, group work and assessment. Adapted from Cohen, Lotan, Abram, Scarloss, & Schultz (2002, p. 1062).

Curiously, the authors turn the conclusion around at the end of their paper to argue that individual assessments can be used for assessment at the group level, as though teachers and others are primarily concerned about group performance: "The fact that individual performance in the last analysis was affected by both quality of group product and self-assessment shows that teachers can feel confident about using individual assessment to measure the instructional outcome of group work. Individuals greatly benefit by exposure to the discourse and the creative process in groups" (p. 1066). At least this addresses the more usual concern that people have for group learning benefiting the individual students.

How Do Groups Learn?

Given its title and its opening remarks about group learning being assumed by social scientists but rarely assessed, the research paper based on the study described above seems to be positioning itself as a study of group learning. The authors, in a series of three central hypotheses of the experiment, speculate about the mechanisms of group learning. For instance, in motivating their first hypothesis, the authors suggest that the use of explicit criteria and feedback from the whole class should "prepare groups to produce better group products," should "improve the quality of the discussion and thus promote group learning," and should "make the group more task focused" (p. 1048). In connection with the second hypothesis, they note that certain conditions are ordinarily necessary for group work to have a positive effect on individual learning but that when such conditions are met, for instance, "when there is a true group task that cannot be well done by one individual, the process of creating a group product will add to the understanding and ability to articulate knowledge on the part of all group members" (p. 1049). Finally, their third hypothesis is, "The better the quality of the group discussion and product, the better will be the individual performance of group members" (p. 1050).

These suggestions concerning group learning and its relationship to individual learning are reasonable and are largely confirmed by the empirical support discovered for the path model shown in figure 19.1. This confirmation, coupled with the disconfirmation of a significant correlation between pretest scores and group performance, leads the authors to conclude that learning "came about through reciprocal exchange of ideas and through a willingness to be self-critical about what the group was creating. . . . Learning arose from the group as a whole" (p. 1064).

But these specific characterizations of what happened are unjustifiable interpretations based largely on the authors' assumptions as expressed in their hypotheses. The method they followed obfuscated the discourse mechanisms at work in the group sessions (similar to the studies critiqued in chapter 10). There is no data analysis concerning exchanges of ideas or willingness of students to be self-critical. These interpretations are imposed on the evidence by the researchers and are not grounded in their empirical analyses. They are interpretations that do not emerge from a rigorous interpretive methodology such as that of video analysis as proposed in chapter 18.

Statistical correlations can at best indicate that one condition caused another (to a high probability). They are rarely able to show the mechanisms at work. The authors of the study speculate in their hypotheses that certain mechanisms are at work, such as discussion quality, task focus, increased understanding, articulation of knowledge, and product quality. In their conclusions, they repeat their assumptions that mechanisms like reciprocal exchange of ideas and willingness to be self-critical are responsible for superior performances. However, their methodology does not allow them to make these factors visible to us in the sense discussed in chapter 18. They count how many utterances in a group expressed ideas related to the topic and how many expressed opinions critical of content ideas, but the utterances are treated as self-contained units, attributable to individuals. Even the authors' wording betrays this attribution of the utterances to the individual students: "reciprocal exchange" and "willingness." The study concludes that the experimental effects are not attributable to individuals because the study aggregated all the discourse and the aggregated pretests did not correlate with the aggregated essays. This is rather indirect evidence. All sorts of relationships could be hidden in all this aggregation.

Another complicating factor is the nature of the experimental condition. The independent variable was training in evaluation criteria. But these evaluation criteria were to be applied to the group work, not to the individual reports. So the fact that the condition impacted the group work directly and that the discovered individual effects were consequently mediated by the group work should be no surprise.

It would be interesting to be able to look at the group interactions carefully and see how the training in evaluation criteria actually played itself out in the different groups. How does the "reciprocal exchange of ideas" take place interactionally— through question-and-answer pairs or through key terms gradually accruing more meaning? Do some students play leading roles in developing or critiquing ideas, or do the ideas emerge and evolve through intense, indexical, elliptical, projecting, mutually completing gestures, and utterances (as is shown in chapter 12) that would not be interpretable in isolation? Statistical parameters give us little insight into the nature of group learning and its intimate relationship with individual learning. They can be useful in locating episodes in the data where group learning seems to be talking place, so that qualitative microanalysis can then be applied to these data to understand it better.

Nevertheless, this paper does define a sense in which group learning can be defined, operationalized, and quantified. It concludes that there is an important phenomenon of group learning in this sense and demonstrates its presence in a real school setting. Having reviewed this empirical argument that groups can learn, we now ask if groups can think. To explore this more philosophical question, we investigate whether we can adopt the arguments from AI concerning whether computers can think. We address the main reaction against the idea of group cognition and then turn to the arguments of Turing, Searle, and Dreyfus about what it means to think.

A Group Does Not Have a Brain

The commonsense objection to attributing thought to small groups of people is that groups do not have something like a "group brain" the way that individual people have brains. It is assumed that cognition requires some sort of brain—as a substrate for the thinking and as an archive for the thoughts.

Thought as Software

The idea of a substrate for thinking was developed in its extreme form in AI. Here, the analogy was that computer hardware was like a human brain in the sense that software runs on the computer in the way that thinking takes place in the brain. Software and its manipulation of information was conceptualized as computations on data. Projecting this model back on psychology, the human mind was then viewed in terms of computations in the brain. Originally, this computation was assumed to be symbol manipulation (Newell & Simon, 1963), but it was later generalized to include the computation of connection values in parallel distributed processes of neural-network models (Rumelhart & McClelland, 1986).

Thought as Content

Thought has also traditionally been considered some kind of mental content or idea objects (facts, propositions, beliefs) that exist in the heads of individual humans. For instance, in educational theory the application of this view to learning has been critically characterized as the pouring of content by teachers into the container heads of students (Freire, 1970). Again, this has its analogy in the computer model. Ideas are stored in heads like data is stored in computer memory. According to this model, the mind consists of a database filled with the ideas or facts that a person has learned. Such a view assumes that knowledge is a body of explicit facts. Such facts can be transferred unproblematically from one storage container to another along simple conduits of communication. This view raises apparent problems for the concept of group cognition. For instance, when the notion of group learning is proposed, the question of what happens to group learning when the members of the group separate is often raised. To the extent that group members have internalized some of the group learning as individual learning, then this is preserved in the individuals' respective heads. But the group learning as such has no head to preserve it.

Groupware as Group Memory

One tact to take in conceptualizing group cognition would be to argue that groupware can serve as a substrate and archival repository for group thought and ideas. Then one could say that a small group along with its appropriate groupware, as an integrated system, can think. However, this argument is not entirely satisfactory.

Discourse as Cognition

The view that is proposed here is somewhat different, although related. Here *discourse* is viewed as providing a substrate for group cognition. The role of groupware is a secondary one of mediating the discourse—providing a conduit that is by no means a simple transfer mechanism. Discourse consists of material things observable in the physical world, like spoken words, inscriptions on paper and bodily gestures. The cognitive ability to engage in discourse is not viewed as the possession of a large set of facts or ideas but as the ability to skillfully use communicative resources. Among the artifacts that groups learn to use as resources are the affordances of groupware and other technologies. The substrate for a group's skilled performance includes the individual group members, available meaningful artifacts (including groupware and other collaboration tools or media), the situation of the activity structure, the shared culture, and the sociohistorical context. In a sense, the cognitive ability of a group vanishes when the group breaks up because it is dependent on the interactions among the members. But that cognitive ability is not simply identical to the sum of the members' individual cognitive abilities because the members have different abilities individually and socially (according to Vygotsky's (1978) notion of the zone of proximal development as the difference between these) and because group cognitive ability is responsive to the context, which is interactively achieved in the group discourse (Garfinkel, 1967). Both of these points make sense if the abilities of members are conceived of primarily as capacities to respond to discursive settings and to take advantage of contextual resources and if intelligence is not conceived of as a store of facts that can be expressed and used in logical inferences. To the extent that members internalize skills that have been developed in collaborative interactions or acquire cognitive artifacts that have been mediated by group activities, the members preserve the group learning and can bring it to bear on future social occasions, although it might not show up on tests administered to the individuals in isolation.

In exploring the sense in which small groups can be claimed to think or engage in group cognition, I take up the three major arguments of Turing, Searle, and Dreyfus about whether computers can think and apply their considerations to group cognition.

A Turing Test for Groups

In a visionary essay that foresaw much of the subsequent field of AI, Alan Turing (1950) considered many of the arguments related to the question of whether machines could think. By *machines*, he meant digital computers. He was not arguing that the computers that he worked on at the time could think but that it was possible to imagine computers that could think. He operationalized the determination of whether something is thinking by assessing whether it could respond to questions in a way that was indistinguishable from how a thinking person might respond. He spelled out this test in terms of an imitation game and predicted that an actual computer could win this game by the year 2000.

The original imitation game is played with three people: a man and a woman, who respond to questions, and an interrogator who cannot see the other two but can pose questions to them and receive their responses. The object of the game is for the interrogator to determine which of the responders is the woman, while the man tries to fool the interrogator and the woman answers honestly. (It may be considered ironic that Turing's most famous proposal is based on deceptions about gender, considering the circumstances of the tragic end of his life.)

Turing transposed this game into a test for the question of whether computers can think, subsequently called the Turing test: "I believe that in about 50 years' time it will be possible to programme computers, with a storage capacity of about 10^9, to make them play the imitation game so well that an average interrogator will not have more than 70 percent chance of making the right identification after five minutes of questioning" (p. 442). The test reduces the question of whether a computer can think to the question of whether a (properly programmed) computer could produce responses to a human interrogator's probing questions that could not be distinguished from the responses of a (thinking) human.

Turing, who was largely responsible for working out the foundations of computation theory, specified what he meant by a computer in terms of a "discrete state machine." This is a theoretical machine that is always in one of a number of well-defined states and that moves from one to another of these states based on a state-change table that specifies a new state given any legal input signal and the current state.

It is generally accepted that no computer passed the Turing test by the year 2000. Computer programs have been developed that do well on the test if the interrogator's questions are confined to a well-defined domain of subject matter but not if the questions can be as wide-ranging as Turing's examples. The domain of chess is a good example of a well-defined realm of intelligent behavior. A computer did succeed in beating the best human chess player by around 2000. But it did so by using massive numbers of look-ahead computations in a brute-force method, quite the opposite of how human masters play.

Can a Group Pass the Turing Test?

Turing argued that his test transformed the ambiguous and ill-defined question about computers thinking into a testable claim that met a variety of objections. His approach has proven to be appealing, although it is not without its critics and although it has not turned out to support his specific prediction.

To determine what we can borrow from the Turing test for the question of whether collaborative groups can think, suppose that an interrogator communicated questions to a thinking individual person and to a collaborating small group of people. Could the group fool the interrogator into not being able to distinguish to a high probability that the group is not a person? A simple strategy would be for the group to elect a spokesperson and let that person respond as an individual. Clearly, a group can think in the same sense as an individual human according to the Turing test.

In a sense, the Turing test, by operationalizing the phenomenon under consideration, puts it in a black box. We can no longer see how thoughts (responses to the interrogator) are being produced. It is reminiscent of the limitation shown in chapter 10 of many quantitative CSCL studies of learning. An operational hypothesis is either confirmed or denied, but the mechanisms of interest are systematically obscured. We do not really learn much about the nature of thought or learning—whether by individuals, groups, or computers—by determining whether their results are indistinguishable or not. One would like to look inside the box.

A Chinese Room for Groups

John Searle's (1980) controversial Chinese-room argument takes a look inside the box of an AI computer, and he is disappointed. Writing in an article on "Minds, Brains, and Programs," Searle reviews many leading views on whether computers can think, attracts even more views in commentaries, and ends up leaving most readers in more of a quandary than when they started.

Searle's argument revolves around a thought experiment that can be traced back to Turing's paper. In describing a computer as a discrete state machine, Turing starts out by saying that a digital computer is "intended to carry out any operations which could be done by a human computer" (Turing, 1950, p. 436). By "human computer" he has in mind a person who follows a book of fixed rules without deviation, doing calculations on an unlimited supply of paper. In a digital computer, the book of rules, paper, and human are replaced by an executive, store, and control—or, in modern terms, software, digital memory, and computer processor. Searle reverse engineers the computer to ask if digital computers consisting of software, memory, and processors think by asking the same question of the "human computer" that Turing imagined being asked of the digital computer. In his thought experiment, Searle imagines that he is the human who follows a book of fixed rules to do computations on paper.

The key argumentative move that Searle makes is to note that the computer follows the rules of its software without interpreting them. To get a feel of the computer's perspective on this, Searle specifies that the symbols coming into the computer and those going out are all in Chinese. As Searle (who knows no Chinese) sits inside the computer manipulating these symbols according to his book of rules (written in English, of course), he has no idea what these symbols mean. The software that he executes was cleverly programmed by someone who understood Chinese, so the outputs make Chinese sense as responses to their inputs, even though Searle, who is manipulating them inside the computer, has no understanding of this sense. From the outside, the computer seems to be behaving intelligently with Chinese symbols. But this is a result of the intelligence of the programmer, not of the human computer (Searle) who is blindly but systematically manipulating the symbols according to the program of his rule book.

According to Searle's "thought experiment" (note that from the start Searle modestly characterizes his own behavior as thinking), a computer could, for instance, pass the Turing test without engaging in any thoughtful understanding whatsoever. Human programmers would have written software based on their understandings, human AI workers would have structured large databases according to their understandings, and human interrogators or observers would have interpreted inputs and outputs according to their understandings. The computer would have manipulated bits following strict rules, but with no understanding. The bits might as well be in an unknown foreign language.

Searle's reformulation of the question is whether the instantiation of some AI software could ever, by itself, be a sufficient condition of understanding. He concludes that it could not. He argues that it could not because the computer manipulations have no *intentionality*—that is, they do not index any meaning. If a sequence of symbols being processed by the computer is supposed to represent a hamburger in a story about a restaurant, the computer has no understanding that those symbols reference a hamburger, and so the computer cannot be described as intelligently understanding the story. The software programmer and the people interacting with the computer might understand the symbols as representing something meaningful, but the computer does not. Searle distinguishes the perspective of the computer from that of its users and attributes understanding of the processed information only to the users. He says of machines including digital computers that "they have a level of description at which we can describe them as taking information in at one end, transforming it and producing information as output. But in this case it is up to outside observers to interpret the input and output as information in the ordinary sense" (Searle, 1980, p. 423).

Searle concludes that there is necessarily a material basis for understanding, which no purely formal model like a software program can ever have. He says that he is able to understand English and have other forms of intentionality

because I am a certain sort of organism with a certain biological (i.e., chemical and physical) structure, and this structure, under certain conditions, is causally capable of producing perception, action, understanding, learning and other intentional phenomena. And part of the point of the present argument is that only something that had those causal powers could have that intentionality. (p. 422)

For Searle, "intentionality" is defined as a feature of mental states such as beliefs or desires by which they are directed at or are about objects and states of affairs in the world.

Putting Searle into a Group

Searle is convinced that computers cannot think in the sense proposed by strong AI advocates. Do his arguments apply to the thinking done by groups?

Applying Searle's thought experiment, analysis, and conclusions to the question of whether a collaborative group could think is tricky because of the shift of unit of analysis from a single physical object to a group of multiple objects or subjects. What would it mean to remove the individual Searle from his hypothesized computer and to put him into a collaborative group? It would make no sense to put him into a Chinese-speaking group. Such a group would not meet the hermeneutic precondition of shared background knowledge and would not be a collaborative success. But we are not asking if every possible group can be said to think, understand, or have intentional states. Can it be said of *any* collaborative group that it thinks? So we would put Searle into a group of his English-speaking peers. If the group started to have a successful knowledge-building discourse, we can assume that from Searle's insider position he might well agree that he had an understanding of what was being discussed and also that the group understood the topic.

Would he have to attribute understanding of the topic to the group as a whole or only to its members? If the utterances of the members made sense only as part of the group discourse, or if members of the group learned only by means of the group interactions, then one would be inclined to attribute sense making and learning to the group unit. This would be the attribution of intentional states to the group in the sense that the group is making sense of something and learning about something—that is, the group is intending or attending to something.

Another move that Searle considers with his human computer experiment is to have the person who is following the rules in the book and writing on scraps of paper then internalize the book and papers so that the whole system is in the person. In Searle's critique of Turing, this changes nothing of consequence. If we make a similar move with the group, what happens? If one person internalizes the perspectives and utterances of everyone in a collaborative group, that person can play out the group interactions by himself. This is what theoreticians of dialogue—for example, Bakhtin (1986b) and Mead (1962)—say happens when we are influenced by others. Vygotsky (1978) sees this process of internalization of social partners and groups as fundamental to individual learning. When someone plays out a debate on a topic, that person can certainly be said to be thinking. So why not say that a group that carries out an identical debate, conceivably using the same utterances, is also thinking?

The only issue that still arises is that of agency. Someone might insist on asking *who* is doing the thinking and be looking for a unitary physical agent. The group itself could be spread around the world, interacting asynchronously through e-mail. Perhaps collaboration takes place over time, such that at no one time are all the members simultaneously involved. Where is the biological basis for intentionality, with its causal powers that Searle claims as a necessary condition for intentionality, understanding, and thought? Certainly, thought went into formulating the individual e-mails. That can be explained as the result of an individual's biology, causality, intentionality, understanding, and so on. But in addition, the larger e-mail interchange can be a process of shared meaning making, where the meaning is understood by the group itself. Comments in a given e-mail may make sense only in relation to other e-mails by other members.

The group may rely on the eyes of individuals to see things in the physical world, and it may rely on the arms of individuals to move things around in the physical world because the group as a whole has no eyes or arms other than those of its members. But the group itself can make group meaning through its own group discourse. The interplay of words and gestures, their inferences and implications, their connotations and references, their indexing of their situation, and their mediating of available artifacts can take place at the group unit of analysis. These actions may not be attributable to any individual unit—or at least may be more simply understood at the group level.

Searle, who wrote the ground-breaking text on speech acts (Searle, 1969), has overlooked in his discussion of thinking the power of language itself to be the agent of thought. This may not affect his critique of AI (for in outputting words, computers do not engage in intentional speech acts, except in the eyes of others), but it is crucial for our question of group thinking. For when we say that a group thinks, we are not postulating the group as a unitary physical object but are focusing on the unity of the group's discourse—the fact that effective collaborative discourse is best understood at the level of the group interaction rather than by focusing on the contributions of individual members. The group discourse has a coherence, and the references of the words within it are densely, inextricably interwoven. Furthermore, the group can act by means of its speech acts.

Although Searle sounds like he is making a materialist argument for biological structures and causal properties that do not map directly to collaborative groups, his discussion is primarily one about language. It has more to do with the nature of Chinese and programming languages than it does with hamburgers and neurons. He is basically arguing that computers do not understand their programming languages the way people understand their mother languages. The difference has more to do with the languages than with the computers or people. Even if a human computer executes a "story understanding" AI program in a software language, there will be no understanding of the story; there will be only a lot of rote following of meaningless rules.

Searle's case hinges on the argument that knowing a lot of rules about something is not equivalent to understanding it. For instance, in manipulating rules related to stories about visits to restaurants, the rules about symbols for menus, ordering, food, eating, paying, tipping, and so on do not make for an understanding of restaurant stories because the computer does not understand that the symbol "hamburger" represents a hamburger: the symbol manipulation lacks intentionality. Let us consider this argument further.

Why would someone ever have thought that having large sets of rules constitutes understanding? Perhaps they thought this because we often learn by being given explicit rules. For instance, I learned German by memorizing rules about word order, endings, spellings, uses, and relationships. So why wouldn't Searle understand Chinese after internalizing all the rules? Searle might respond that German was my second language and that I learned it by relating it to my mother tongue but that I learned English the way that Vygotsky's infant learned the pointing gesture—by interacting with the world and other people, with intentionality (Vygotsky, 1978).

What about more abstract understanding than that of restaurants? Don't we learn chess by learning rules for legal moves, strategies, and common positions? Surely being able to see and move the little wooden pieces is not of the essence. We can play chess blindfolded or online, and computers can play chess better than we can. It is, indeed, interesting that computers do not display the kind of expert understanding—or "professional vision" (Goodwin & Goodwin, 1994)—that the best chess players do (Dreyfus & Dreyfus, 1986). But that does not mean that they have no understanding or that understanding does not come through internalizing rules and therefore might not come to Searle inside his Chinese room.

Consider students who are learning mathematics—for example, basic algebra. Algebra is not about hamburgers or apples and oranges. It is about symbols and rules for manipulating the symbols. In learning algebra, students learn algorithmic procedures for manipulating mathematical symbols. They learn to stick to the fixed rules rigidly and to carry out the manipulations quickly. Once they know a book full of rules and can carry out the manipulations strictly according to the rules, we say that they have learned algebra, that they know algebra, that they understand algebra, and that they can think algebraically.

Some teachers of mathematics in recent years might say that memorization of procedural rules is not enough. Students need to be able to talk about the math. They should be able to demonstrate a "deep understanding" of the math. But what does a deep understanding consist of here? Well, they might say, the student should be able to explain how she arrived at her answer. Perhaps she should be able to solve a given problem by a number of alternative methods, thereby exploring the nature of the problem. But isn't this just a matter of internalizing more rules and being able to state them? The given problem can be solved by applying various sets of rules and manipulations, and one can express these rules in knowledgeable-sounding utterances. Perhaps knowing how to select the right rules to solve a given problem is a sign of mathematical understanding. But software often includes rules for making such decisions. In fact, problems in logic and mathematics can be solved by computer programs quite a bit better than by ninth graders. What is it that these programs do not understand that the ninth graders do?

Perhaps the answer to this question will have to wait for the results of future empirical studies of collaborative discourse involved in math problem solving. Rather than speculating on this matter, we should look closely using the methods of video analysis or conversation analysis to see just what goes on in the discourse of groups who display a deep understanding of the mathematics they are collaborating on and the discourse of groups who display patterns of manipulating mathematical symbols with little understanding. Such an approach can get behind the comparison of outputs to inputs (such as an algorithmic solution to a given math problem) to make visible the reasoning that goes on within the problem-solving group. In this way, the thinking of groups would provide a window on how individuals think.

An investigation of the thoughtful understanding and the meaning making that takes place in the events simulated in AI programs or quantified in educational experiments—but lost through the behavioristic or operationalizing procedures of simulating or quantifying what takes place—might get at the nature of collaborative thought and human deep understanding. In the end, Searle recommends that AI purge itself of the approach already established by Turing of ignoring the phenomena that are not immediately observable by certain experimental methods: "The Turing test is typical of the tradition in being unashamedly behavioristic and operationalistic, and I believe that if AI workers totally repudiated behaviorism and operationalism much of the confusion between simulation and duplication would be eliminated" (Searle, 1980, p. 423).

Being-in-the-World as Groups

The third "critique of artificial reason" that we want to consider is that of Hubert Dreyfus (1972, 1991; Dreyfus & Dreyfus, 1986). Dreyfus agrees with Searle that AI has emerged from the attempt to push a specific philosophic position too far, to the detriment and confusion of AI. Dreyfus calls this extreme position "representationalism" and argues that it ignores much of what accounts for human understanding. It in effect reduces our complex engagement in the world, our sophisticated social know-how, and our subtle sense of what is going on around our embodied presence to a large database of symbols and books of explicit rules:

Rationalists such as Descartes and Leibniz thought of the mind as defined by its capacity to form representations of all domains of activity. These representations were taken to be theories of the domains in question, the idea being that representing the fixed, context-free features of a domain and the principles governing their interaction explains the domain's intelligibility . . . mirrored in the mind in propositional form. (Dreyfus, 1992, p. xvii)

Representationalism reduces all knowing, meaning, understanding, cognition, and intelligence to the possession of sets of facts, ideas, or propositions. It matters little whether these explicit formulations of knowledge are said to exist in an ideal world of nonmaterial forms (Plato), as purely mental thoughts (Descartes), as linguistic propositions (early Wittgenstein), or as data stored in database entries (AI). Wittgenstein's early *Tractatus*, which reduces philosophy to a set of numbered propositions, begins by defining the world as "the totality of facts, not of things" (Wittgenstein, 1974, sec. 1.1). From here, via the work of the logical positivists, it is easy to conceive of capturing human knowledge in a database of explicit representations of facts—such as Searle imagined in his books of programmed instructions for manipulating Chinese symbols.

The problem with representationalism, according to Dreyfus, is that it ignores the diverse ways in which people know. The consequence that Dreyfus draws for AI is that it cannot succeed in its goal of reproducing intelligence using just formal representations of knowledge. Dreyfus highlights three problems that arose for AI in pursuing this approach: sensible retrieval, representation of skills, and identification of relevance.

Retrieval

The AI approach has proven unable to structure a knowledge base in a way that supports the drawing of commonsensical inferences from it. For instance, as people learn more about a topic, they are able to infer other things about that topic faster and easier, but as a computer stores more facts on a topic its retrieval and inference algorithms slow down dramatically.

Dreyfus details his critique by focusing on Lenat's Cyc project, a large AI effort to capture people's everyday background knowledge and to retrieve relevant facts needed for making commonsense inferences. Dreyfus argues that the logic of this approach is precisely backward from the way people's minds work:

The conviction that people *are* storing context-free facts and using meta-rules to cut down the search space is precisely the dubious rationalist assumption in question. It must be tested by looking at the phenomenology of everyday know-how. Such an account is worked out by Heidegger and his followers such as Merleau-Ponty and the anthropologist Pierre Bourdieu. They find that what counts as the facts depends on our everyday skills. (Dreyfus, 1992, p. xxii)

Skills

AI representations cannot capture the forms of knowledge that consist in skills, know-how, and expertise. People know how to do many things—like ride a bike, enjoy a poem, or respond to a chess position—that they are unable to state or explain in sentences and rules. The effort within AI to program expert systems, for instance, largely failed because it proved impossible to solicit the knowledge of domain experts. An important form of this issue is that human understanding relies heavily on a vast background knowledge that allows people to make sense of propositional knowledge. This background knowledge builds on our extensive life experience, which is not reducible to sets of stored facts: "Human beings who have had vast experience in the natural and social world have a direct sense of how things are done and what to expect. Our global familiarity thus enables us to respond to what is relevant and ignore what is irrelevant without planning based on purpose-free representations of context-free facts" (Dreyfus, 1992, p. xxix).

Relevance

A fundamental interpretive skill of people is knowing what is relevant within a given situation and perspective. This sense of relevance cannot be programmed into a computer using explicit rules. This ability to focus on what is relevant is related to people's skill in drawing inferences (retrieval) and builds on their expert background knowledge (skills):

> The point is that a manager's expertise, and expertise in general, consists in being able to respond to the relevant facts. A computer can help by supplying more facts than the manager could possibly remember, but only experience enables the manager to see the current state of affairs as a specific situation and to see what is relevant. That expert know-how cannot be put into the computer by adding more facts, since the issue is which is the current correct perspective from which to determine which facts are relevant. (Dreyfus, 1992, p. xlii)

In all three points, Dreyfus emphasizes that *facts* are not what is immediately given in human experience and understanding. Rather, what is to count as a fact is itself mediated by our skills, our situation in the world, and our perspective as embodied and engaged.

Dreyfus's critique shows that computers cannot think in the most important ways that people do. Arguing on the basis of a Heideggerian analysis of human being-in-the-world as situated, engaged, perspectival, skilled, and involved with meaningful artifacts, Dreyfus provides the basis for understanding the failure of computers to pass the Turing test and to exhibit the kind of intentionality that Searle argues is a necessary condition of cognition. Explicit, propositional, factual knowledge is not an adequate starting point for analyzing or duplicating human cognition. There are a number of factors that come first analytically and experientially: tacit know-how, practical skills, social practices, cultural habits, embodied orientation, engaged perspective, involvement with artifacts, social interaction, perception of meaningfulness, and directedness toward things in the world. Heidegger's (1996) analysis of human existence, for instance, begins with our being involved in the world within situational networks of significant artifacts. Our relationship to things as objects of explicit propositions and our expression of factual propositions are much later, secondary products of mediations built on top of the more primordial phenomena. Similarly, Maurice Merleau-Ponty (2002) stresses our orientation within a meaningful social and physical space structured around our sense of being embodied. Because AI representations lack the features that are primary in human cognition and try to reduce everything to a secondary phenomenon of factual propositions, they ultimately fail to be able to either imitate human cognition to the degree envisioned by Turing or to capture the sense of understanding sought by Searle.

Being-with-Others in Groups

I now turn to the question of whether the proposed notion of group cognition fares any better against these standards than did the AI notion of computer cognition. Clearly, the individual members of a group bring with them the skills, background, and intentionality to allow a group to determine what are the relevant facts and issues. But in what sense does the group as a whole have or share these? The group is not defined as a physical collection of the members' bodies. It might exist in an online, virtual form, physically distributed across arbitrary spatial and temporal distances. Rather, the group exists as a discourse, perhaps recorded in a video, chat log, or transcript. So we need to ask whether such a group discourse reflects such tacit skills, commonsense background knowledge and intentionality.

Recall a key utterance from the group discourse in chapter 12:

1:22:05   Brent   This one's different

This utterance reveals intentionality. The deictic phrase "This one" indexes some part of the simulation list artifact. The attribute "different," which the utterance associates with its subject, connotes background knowledge. The attribution of difference is necessarily from a specific perspective. Any two things can be considered different from some perspective of relevance (Rittel & Webber, 1973). To make this utterance is to assume a particular perspective and to assume that it is part of the group perspective. The fact that others did not agree with the utterance at first signals that this perspective had not yet been established as a shared group perspective. It precipitates an intense moment of collaboration in which the students repair the breakdown of the group perspective and establish the perspective proposed by this utterance through group negotiation and clarification. A close conversation analysis shows how subtle this particular perspective was and how the group had to go through a complex learning process to adopt it.

Similarly, look at the utterance from 20 seconds later that consolidated the group perspective and moved on within that perspective:

1:22:21   Jamie   Yeah. Compare two n one. So that the rounded n- (0.1) no the rounded one is better. Number one.

Here we see again the group intentionality in how the list artifact is being indexed. Now the specific detail of the artifact is named: "two n one." In addition, the discussion of which rockets to compare, with its question of determining which nose cone performs better, is relocated within the larger context of the design situation.

It should now be clear that the group discourse is itself engaged in a group activity, embedded within a context of tacitly understood goals and situated in a network of meaningful artifacts. The discourse itself exhibits intentionality. It builds on tacit background knowledge of the experiential world. It adopts—sometimes through involved group processes of negotiation and enactment—perspectives that determine relevance.

Group Discourse as Emergent Thinking

This chapter has argued that small collaborative groups—at least on occasion and under properly conducive conditions—can think. It is not only possible but also quite reasonable to speak of groups as engaging in human cognition in a sense that is not appropriate for applying to computer computations, even in AI simulations of intelligent behavior. When we talk of groups thinking, we are referring not so much to the physical assemblage of people as to the group discourse in which they engage.

To some social scientists, such as Vygotsky, the group level (which he calls *social* or *intersubjective*) is actually prior in conceptual and developmental importance to the individual (intrasubjective) level. So why does the notion of group cognition strike many people as counterintuitive? When it is recognized, it is generally trivialized as some kind of mysterious "synergy." Often, people focus on the dangers identified by social psychologists as "group think"—where group obedience overrides individual rationality. At best, the commonsensical attitude acknowledges that "two heads are better than one." This standard expression suggests part of the problem: thought is conceived as something that takes place inside of individual heads, so that group cognition is conceived as a sum of facts from individual heads rather than as a positive cognitive phenomenon of its own.

An alternative conceptualization is to view group cognition as an *emergent* quality of the interaction of individual cognitive processes. Here, one can choose to view things at the individual unit of analysis where traditional individual cognition takes place *or* at the group unit of analysis. The individual mechanisms are taken as primary and the group phenomena are seen as emergent. This is not the view of group discourse as primary and individual thought as a mediated, internalized, derivative version of the primary social cognition. However, it is still worth considering this emergent conception.

Emergence occurs on various scales; it has quite different characteristics and mechanisms in these different guises (Johnson, 2001). I distinguish three scales: large-scale statistical emergence, midlevel adaptive system emergence, and small-group emergence.

Statistical Emergence

Chemical properties can often be viewed as emergent phenomena that arise out of large numbers of particles, each following laws of physics. For instance, thermodynamic phenomena involving billions of atoms exhibit higher-level characteristics, such as molecular movement appearing as heat. The lower-level behaviors of the individual molecules are covered by the laws of physics. But their mass interactions exhibit qualities such as temperature and pressure, which are studied by chemistry rather than quantum mechanics. This transformation of individual motions to group qualities can be modeled by statistical analysis. The distinction in levels of analysis gives rise to distinct sciences, each with its own methodologies: biology cannot be reduced to chemistry, or chemistry to physics.

Adaptive System Emergence

Thousands of ants each following simple rules of behavior and interaction exhibit metalevel behaviors, such as efficient work organization and group foraging strategies. The lower-level rules are biologically evolved through success at the metalevel. These connections can be modeled by parallel computational systems encoding simple rules, such as StarLogo, SimCity, and AgentSheets. In such systems, simple units exhibit behavior that follows small sets of simple rules. The rule-governed behaviors interact in ways that allow groups of these units to follow patterns of behavior and to adapt to their context. In this way, group-level behaviors emerge from interactions at the lower level.

Small-Group Emergence

Traditional human social interaction typically takes place among up to 150 people. It differs from the other kinds of emergence in that it does not involve statistically significant numbers of individuals and the rules they follow or the rules by which they interact are not simple. Small-group interaction is governed by complex, subtle, interpreted, negotiated, mutually constituted rules. These depend on the following:

- Biologically evolved capabilities of human brains to interpret the behavior of other people, to recognize individuals, and to maintain models of their minds;
- Culturally transmitted social practices that have accumulated over millennia;
- Language as a medium for conducting social interaction;
- Language as a tool for interpreting social interaction; and
- Education, training, and the experiences of a lifetime.

As is shown in the critique of AI, the determinants of human group behavior cannot even be made explicit and stated as rules. Nevertheless, human groups exhibit behaviors that cannot be predicted from an understanding of the individuals involved. For instance, families, neighborhoods, villages, and cities emerge with complex structures and behaviors. Sociology cannot be reduced to psychology, let alone to biology.

Discourse

The emergence of group cognition is somewhat distinct from the emergence of social phenomena as discussed above. Conversation is the interaction of utterances, gestures, and so forth from a small number of people. Often it involves only two people. Internal discussion or thought is generated by one person, although it may incorporate multiple internalized perspectives. The interaction can nevertheless be extremely complex. It involves the ways in which subsequent utterances respond to previous ones and anticipate or solicit future ones. Individual terms carry with them extensive histories of connotations and implications. Features of the situation and of its constituent artifacts are indexed in manifold ways. Syntactic structures weave together meanings and implications. Effective interpretations are active at many levels, constructing an accounting of the conversation itself even as it enacts its locutionary, perlocutionary, and illocutionary force (Searle, 1969).

Yes, small groups can think. Their group cognition emerges from their group discourse. This is a unique form of emergence. It differs from statistical, simple-rule governed, and social emergence. It is driven by linguistic mechanisms. Understanding group cognition will require a new science with methods that differ from the representationalism approach of AI.

Group Cognition and CSCL

Many methodologies popular in CSCL research focus on the individual as the unit of analysis: what the individual student does or says or learns. Even from the perspective of an interest in group cognition and group discourse, such methods can be useful and provide part of the analysis because group thinking and activity is intimately intertwined with that of the individual members of the group. However, it is also important and insightful to view collaborative activities as linguistic, cognitive, and interactional processes at the group level of description. This involves taking the group as the unit of analysis and as the focal agent and then analyzing how a group solves a problem through the interplay of utterances proposing, challenging, questioning, correcting, negotiating, and confirming an emergent group meaning. One can see how a group does things with words that have the force of accomplishing changes in the shared social world. Some things, like electing an official, can be done only by groups—although this obviously involves individuals.

Other things, like solving a challenging problem, may be done better by groups than by individuals—although the different perspectives and considerations are contributed by individuals.

CSCL is distinguished as a field of inquiry by its focus on group collaboration in learning; it makes sense to orient the methods of the field to thinking at the small-group unit of analysis. This may require rethinking—as a research community—our theoretical framework, such as the conceptualization of cognition that we have inherited from the representationalism of cognitive sciences oriented overwhelmingly toward the individual.

Opening New Worlds for Collaboration

The philosophy of Martin Heidegger has appeared briefly but frequently throughout this book. Here, I consider his multifaceted but problematic influence in some detail.[1] I argue that by avoiding certain dangers in his approach, we may be able to use what is deeply innovative there to find ways out of the habits of thought that limit our understanding of group cognition and collaboration.

The international, multidisciplinary field of computer-supported collaborative learning needs to transcend the boundaries of narrow and incompatible cultural and academic traditions based exclusively on individual psychology, technological engineering, or physical science methods. We need new ways to conceive of artifacts that open worlds for collaboration and of group cognition as a phenomenon in its own right. Where do we get our ways of looking at the world, at data, and at research challenges? How can we develop new ways, appropriate to the unique promises of CSCL? This chapter discusses ideas from Heidegger, Karl Marx, and others that address these questions and may open up a new conceptualization of the CSCL enterprise.

The Diverse Traditions of CSCL

In the past decade, computer-supported collaborative learning (CSCL) has grown willy-nilly out of various theoretical and methodological traditions that are mutually incompatible but that seem to contribute important insights individually. As is typical in exciting new fields, CSCL research has demonstrated—perhaps above all else—that relatively straightforward extensions of traditional approaches imported from other domains are inadequate for addressing the intertwining issues raised by CSCL. Researchers in CSCL have come to the field from diverse disciplines and have brought with them disparate methodological traditions. It may be helpful to reflect on the traditions that have been brought to the field and to consider whether CSCL needs to develop its own theoretical framework, appropriate for defining the phenomena and methods of a unique field that transcends academic and cultural boundaries of the past and that becomes a truly international and multidisciplinary endeavor in the next decade.

When I was invited to be an American guest speaker at a German conference on e-learning in 2003, I started to think about the difference between American and German philosophies and how they had influenced work on both sides of the Atlantic in CSCL, computer science, and artificial intelligence (AI). It occurred to me that it might be useful to bring to the German audience (consisting largely of people trained in engineering) something of German philosophy (which I had studied as an American graduate student in Germany). In particular, I felt that Martin Heidegger's philosophy still had potential contributions to make—despite the fact that some of his ideas have already been taken up and despite the serious problems that inhere to his thinking and writing. In addition, I felt that Karl Marx's philosophic method might help to overcome an ideology of individualism that limits insights into the nature of group collaboration. Together, these traditions of German philosophy might help to move from an American-style engineering mentality to a mentality open to what could be most innovative in CSCL.

In this chapter, I would like to consider how we might fashion a tradition that is appropriate and effective for CSCL by considering certain contributions that I think Heidegger and Marx can make to how we look at the world. Ultimately, this will bring us to some thoughts about where traditions come from and how they affect how we do science. I will start by contrasting caricatures of the American engineering mentality, which has influenced CSCL through computer science and artificial intelligence, with German philosophy, which has influenced CSCL through situated action and sociocultural theory.

The American engineer Claude Shannon developed a mathematical theory of technical communication that helped to design efficient telephone systems (Shannon & Weaver, 1949). He conceived of communication as the transfer of information from a sender to a receiver. This model is often applied to education, which is seen as a transfer of information from a teacher to a student. It is tempting to view computer support in this way—as a neutral channel for the conveying of educational information from distributed database sources to online student recipients.

In contrast, German philosophy sees education as an intellectual process of personal development (*Bildung*), not as the simple accumulation of received factoids. There is the crucial matter of understanding (*verstehen*). In the case of Heidegger's philosophy (1996), language is not a neutral medium for transferring bits of information but an active source of truth that opens up new worlds for us. According to this, we might suspect that CSCL's job is to design computer-supported environments and media that create new collaboration spaces to bring together people and ideas in ways that stimulate and nurture the building of increased shared meaning and knowledge.

Past efforts at developing computer support for learning started with the engineering model and moved from there to increasingly divergent approaches. Timothy Koschmann (1996b) identified the following historical phases of this research:

- Repetitive student drill of atomic facts and algorithmic procedures (computer-assisted instruction, from the 1960s),

- Tutoring based on cognitive models of individual learning (intelligent tutoring systems, from the 1970s),

- Hypertext information sources and Logo programming environments for individual exploration (constructivist discovery learning, from the 1980s), and

- Support for collaborative learning and group discourse (CSCL, from the 1990s).

Computer-assisted instruction took a strongly engineering-type approach, and intelligent tutoring focused on individual cognition from an AI perspective. Discovery learning started to talk about opening worlds (virtual miniworlds) for creative exploration, and CSCL necessarily involves shared worlds. While each of these has its legitimate role in education, the last one seems to hold the most intriguing and intransigent research challenges for us.

What I am here caricaturing as the American engineering mentality is the technology-driven approach. In its naive form, it reappears in every software design course where a student is struck by the power of some technical mechanism and then designs based on that idea rather than on an investigation of how that mechanism would actually be used by people in real situations. The whole human-centered design emphasis of human-computer interaction (HCI) was developed as a field to combat this disastrous tendency. In the more sophisticated form of the engineering approach, subtle AI techniques are implemented to scaffold learning. The research community around the "AI and Education" conferences and publications was quite influential in early CSCL research. The technology-driven approach was still quite apparent at the 2003 e-learning conference in Germany where I presented the ideas of this chapter. As in all contexts of fundamental paradigm shifts, the fact that practitioners adopt a user-centered or sociocultural jargon does not necessarily mean they have fully overcome the practices that these terms were invented to counteract.

Today's combination of fast computers, global networks, distributed databases, and powerful communication software does have the alluring potential to support interactions among groups of people, relieved of the limitations of the past. Group interaction need no longer be moderated by a teacher or hierarchical authority:

people can interact with others around the globe, contributions can be made whenever inspiration strikes, and the record of discussions can be preserved and reflected on. Imagine the Open Source development model (Raymond, 2001) scaled up to learning in all kinds of student and virtual communities. However, attempts to design software environments to support cooperative work and collaborative learning bump into formidable barriers. In many CSCL software design studies, social issues of adoption and community practices have overwhelmed the technical innovations. This is typical of applications that try to support interaction and communication in groups.

Consider e-mail, the major success in groupware to date. It has taken a good decade for e-mail to attain widespread adoption. And look how hard it still is, even for expert computer users, to deal with e-mail: spam, privacy, security, contact lists, message management, and many other hassles continually plague users. It takes incredible amounts of time, energy, reorganizing, and worry to maintain our e-mail lives. If each new tool for collaboration is going to continue to be this much work for every user, then innovative software will always face insurmountable resistance from users. These are largely cognitive, organizational, and social issues and not simply technical ones.

CSCL systems of the past decade have tried to push to its limit the engineering approach in the extreme form of artificial intelligence algorithms (see part I of this book). These attempts revealed deep-seated problems in the engineering paradigm. Many software designs required the systematic collection of a volume of explicit representations of domain knowledge that far exceeded what was practical. The attempt to formulate heuristic rules based on the tacit practices of experts similarly proved to be misguided, despite the fact that in each of the explored domains people are fluent at problem solving and sharing knowledge in face-to-face settings.

So the software-design approach moved toward supporting cooperation and collaboration within human groups. These efforts faced "wicked problems" (Rittel & Webber, 1984) that could not be managed with traditional engineering methods. There were no clear sets of functional requirements, measurable goals for success, or even pools of subjects who could meaningfully test prototypes. The evaluation methods of the science of interface design—like heuristic evaluation and cognitive walkthrough (Preece, Rogers, & Sharp, 2002)—focus more on details of appearance and individual navigation than on the more consequential social issues of groupware and the mediation of human-human interaction. Taking a design-based research approach (Design-Based Research Collective, 2003), software studies explored specific technical solutions to arrive at a clearer understanding of the problems they were designed to solve. Because the problems could not be well defined in advance, the assumptions necessary for quantitative evaluation methodologies were not present. Due to the costs of building working prototypes adequate for group use, iterations were limited. My own attempts to develop CSCL software faced these problems. For me, at least, they convinced me of the need for analyses of group interaction, for theoretical studies of group cognition, and for a view of collaboration environments as sets of artifacts that mediate group cognition. In other words, I concluded, we need a new theoretical framework for conceptualizing the phenomena and issues of our field.

An Appropriate Framework for CSCL

We need to drastically expand the traditional engineering model that focused on technical issues of transmission and that left the interpretation, use, and sharing of all content to the unproblematized individual recipient. We have learned that collaborative interaction does not follow the model of rational agents making independent decisions but involves complexly interdependent processes of group meaning making. In the next period of CSCL research, we need to focus on such nontechnical matters as how groupware systems can and do the following:

- Create and structure communities,
- Define and generate educational realms of knowledge,
- Give form to intentions and meanings, helping users to come to an understanding of the system's designed affordances,
- Impose new tasks and transform existing social practices, and
- Make life more rewarding, if also more complex.

To accomplish this, the CSCL research community should develop appropriate new methods for design, evaluation, and theory building. In the past, we have tried to make use of traditional approaches taken over from other fields: technical engineering, cognitive psychology, single-user productivity software, and teacher-centered pedagogy. Significant further progress in supporting collaboration may now require that we recognize the social, collaborative basis of learning and rethink the role of digital artifacts and virtual media within the social practices that constitute learning and other activities. This does not mean throwing away all the methods we know from the past. However, it does mean questioning them, defining their limits, and integrating them with complementary views from other perspectives within a larger picture of what is unique to CSCL.

Working with colleagues in the CSCL community and drawing heavily on writers in relevant fields, I have recently been trying to sketch the needed theory of mediated collaboration through analysis of the phenomenon of *group cognition* (see part

III). First, I tried to indicate how online communication differs from face-to-face communication and how both are more complex than Shannon's model (chapter 14). In particular, I viewed collaborative communication as integral to group cognition. I presented a general discussion of the concepts related to group cognition in terms of building collaborative knowing (chapter 15). Then I explored the notion of group meaning in more detail and distinguished it from individual interpretations of this meaning (chapter 16). I further developed the notion of group cognition as central to CSCL's distinctive focus on collaborative knowledge building in chapters 17, 18, and 19. Now I want to speculate on a direction for future development of the concept of group cognition.

The future is likely to see a proliferation of alternative approaches and methodologies within CSCL, some complementary and others mutually inconsistent. Clarity about the bigger picture may help us to choose among methodologies, adapt them, and integrate them effectively. Perhaps an innovative reading of German philosophy, with its social focus, can play an important role as a balance to American-style engineering centered on the individual user.

The final stage in German philosophy—before it merged into social science with the Frankfurt School—can probably be identified with Heidegger's later work. It offers a systematic critique of the theoretical presuppositions underlying the engineering paradigm. It also suggests an alternative way of conceptualizing thought, meaning, and being. Although it has influenced a generation of social science theoreticians, such as Pierre Bourdieu and Jacques Derrida, it has still not percolated down to more widespread views.

This chapter presents a reading of Heidegger from the perspective of group cognition as an alternative to the traditional focus on the individual. From this vantage point, Heidegger can be seen as part of a lineage of German philosophers reacting against René Descartes's position. Individualism as a focus of philosophy and as a social ideology can actually be traced back to the earliest writings of Western culture, even to the oral epic poems of Homer, with Odysseus as the paradigmatic individual searching for his identity (Adorno & Horkheimer, 1945). The centrality of the individual reached its zenith when Descartes (1999) concluded that the only thing he could be certain about, given his radical questioning, was his own individual existence.

German idealism's reaction to Descartes started with Immanuel Kant's (1999) "Copernican revolution," which reversed the relation between the individual mind and the world. It continued through Georg Friedrich Hegel's (1967) detailed social history of the development of mind: from simple awareness through human mind, to group cognition and world spirit. Karl Marx (1967a, 1976) began the transition from philosophy to social science by relating the Hegelian development of mind to political economy and the relations of production and by carrying out a critique of individualism as social ideology.

The three mainstreams of twentieth-century Western philosophy—based on Marx, Ludwig Wittgenstein, and Heidegger—all transitioned from an individualist to a social or group focus. The early writings of Marx (1967a, 1967b) considered alienated labor as a consequence of capitalist relations for the individual, while his later writing (1976) analyzed the capitalist relations as a social system. Wittgenstein's later *Investigations* (1953) soundly rejected his earlier vision in the *Tractatus* (1974) of propositions in the individual mind in favor of viewing language as social interactions—language games within a social form of life.

Heidegger's work can also be broken into contrasting early and late periods. Heidegger himself talks of a crucial reversal or "turn" (*Kehre*) in the "path" of his thinking after the publication of *Being and Time*. The reversal is in the relation of human existence (*Dasein*) to the world. Heidegger's early work focuses on the individual in an effort to interpret human being in a way that overcomes the duality of Descartes's system. Rather than starting from the solitary thinker as a mind separated from physical reality, Heidegger systematically considers human existence as thoroughly involved in a meaningful world of engagement.

This is where Heidegger's characterization of artifacts as ready-to-hand enters. Artifacts are not simply present-at-hand, as though a self-contained mental self could stare at them in a material world divorced from meanings. Rather, they are integrated into one's skillful being. Moreover, they are meaningful in terms of their being situated in our already meaningful world; we do not have to somehow project a mental meaning onto a physical substrate:

For example, the artifact at hand which we call a hammer has to do with hammering, the hammering has to do with fastening something, fastening has to do with protection against bad weather. What significance artifacts have is prefigured in terms of the *situation* as a totality of relationships of significance. (Heidegger, 1996, p. 84)

This analysis of artifacts, situation, and possible breakdowns has had a widespread influence, including within the theory of software design (Dourish, 2001; Dreyfus, 1972; Ehn, 1988; Floyd, Zuellinghoven, Budde, & Keil-Slawik, 1994; Suchman, 1987; Winograd & Flores, 1986; Winograd, 1996).

The world of *Being and Time* is a social world, with shared meanings and social relationships: "On the basis of this being-in-the-world with others, the world is always the world which I share with others. The world is always the shared world. Being in the world is being there with others" (Heidegger, 1996, sec. 26). At this point in his analysis, Heidegger briefly overcomes the tradition of individualistic philosophy and can analyze situated meaning and language as based in the community.

Unfortunately, in the very next section of *Being and Time*, Heidegger rejects the social basis of human being in favor of an "authentic" stance of the individual toward his own finitude as the basis of meaning. Theodor Adorno, in his *Jargon of Authenticity* (1973), tied this move to a politically conservative ideology. One can see this as a source of Heidegger's infamous and concerning political problems, as well as his philosophical problem of not understanding the social basis of phenomena like language and history (Nancy, 2000; Stahl, 1975a, 1975b).

Up to this point, Heidegger had successfully and rigorously forged an alternative to Descartes's individual, cut off from the material and social world. He had assembled the philosophic tools to begin to analyze language, culture, practices, and habits as meaning structures that are given in our shared world and that we interpret from our personal circumstances and concerns (see chapter 16). But instead of building on this, Heidegger fell back on his conservative heritage and reversed these relationships into projections based on the most individualistic of sources: one's personal relationship to one's own mortality (*Angst*). Heidegger's reversal from the resulting apotheosis of individualism came just a few years later but too late to save him from entanglement in fascism. I now skip ahead to review briefly the promising social aspects of Heidegger's later work.

Opening Shared Worlds

The later Heidegger is perhaps best represented by his discussion of the work of art as a special kind of artifact (figure 20.1):

Van Gogh's painting is an opening-up of that which the artifact, the pair of farmer's boots, in truth is. This being moves into the unconcealment of its being.... There is a happening of truth at work in the work, if an opening-up of the being takes place there into that which and that how it is. (2003, p. 25)

This quotation refers to two very different artifacts: a pair of shoes and a painting of them. What has van Gogh's painting revealed about the shoes? It makes visible the nature of the shoes as artifact. The shoes, which in daily life sit unnoticed in a dark corner, are themselves the center of the nexus of people, places, activities, history, hopes, skills, materials, and affordances that are made visible by the working of the artwork. Works of art are not objective mathematical dimensions or sources of sense data pixels but are networks of meaningful relationships as structured by personal, group, and social activities and concerns.

The painting itself evokes the life of the farmer who wears these boots as she trudges through the plowed field in them and then places them aside at the end of a weary day. The remarkable quality of artwork is that it makes visible the very nature of the things that it displays; it sets their truth in work by unconcealing them

Figure 20.1
Vincent Van Gogh, *Farmer's Shoes*, oil painting, Van Gogh Museum, Amsterdam, the Netherlands.

from their taken-for-granted invisibility in everyday life. Heidegger's analysis of the work of art rejects the dominant view that centers on the role of the individual person who experiences the work. Traditional aesthetics—even that of Hegel or Dewey—talks about the active role of the observer as source of the work's power, value, and connotations. Heidegger reverses this perspective and sees the work as itself an agent that sets things into work.

The sculpture of a human figure by Alberto Giacometti, although standing alone on a small pedestal, defines a human space of movement around it (figure 20.2). It opens up a space for activity, for life, for other people, and for the artifacts that go with them according to Heidegger: "Sculpture: an embodying bringing-into-work of places and with this an opening up of realms of possible living for people, of possible persisting for the things which surround and concern people" (1969, p. 13).

Works of art are special kinds of artifacts. Thanks to their unique capability, they make visible for Heidegger and others the nature of artifacts. All artifacts have some of the same power as works of art, just not so dramatically visible. In fact, their

Figure 20.2
Alberto Giacometti, *Standing Figure*, bronze, Pompidou Center, Paris, France. Photo: G. Stahl, 2001.

hidden, taken-for-granted, tacit mode of working is often necessary for their effectiveness. Artifacts can generally play an active role of opening up a world and gathering together the material, social, and artifactual furniture of that world. Heidegger extends the artifact-centered view of the world to bridges, jugs, and other artifacts.

A bridge, such as the renowned Alte Brücke of Heidelberg, joins the banks of the Neckar river, defining their separation and carrying people across. Its massive red stone construction anchors the bridge in the river valley, while relating it to the castle and cliffs above of the same stone. The sculptures carved into the pillars evoke the history and ancient leaders of the town. The elements of running water below, blue sky above, durable stone building blocks underneath, and human commerce across are brought together harmoniously in the meaningful space that the bridge opens up and structures for them (Heidegger, 1967a).

A ceramic jug for wine opens a similar kind of world. The jug gathers within itself the fruits of the labor of skilled vineyard workers, long hours of summer sun, and drenching rains. The porous container chills and aerates the wine properly. Its carefully crafted spout transfers the wine to glasses without spilling a drop, while its handle allows it to be manipulated effortlessly with balance and grace. Both jug and contents contribute to a hard-earned end of the workday or to a festive pause in the life of the village (Heidegger, 1967b).

Heidegger's favorite art form is poetry. Poetry makes language visible (see Heidegger, 1971). Poetry is a source for the creation of new expressions and new forms of speech. Poetry also opens up worlds, and it can name the elements that it brings together in those worlds. For Heidegger, language speaks (*Sprache spricht*). It is not so much that people use words to express their ideas but that *language speaks through us.*

Consider the collaborative discourse that was analyzed in chapters 12 and 13. What took place there happened largely through the power of language, the mechanisms of discourse. Utterances built on each other. Words gathered richness of meaning through repetitive usage. The discourse itself provided an opportunity for all this to happen.

Or consider this book. It is not a "brain dump" of ideas that already existed in my head. The writing of the book opened a world for the development of the ideas it contains. Its gradually developing manuscript provided a persistent artifact that elicited diverse thoughts and joined together various ideas—far more than I could ever keep in mind. The Heideggerian approach helps us to overcome the subjective view of writing as an externalization of mental contents and to see the book itself as opening a world of discourse and as gathering within itself a multitude of ideas. To the extent that it is an effective work, the book makes issues visible to an audience and invites readers and writers to reconfigure its meanings from their own interpretive perspectives.

This view of artifacts as opening up worlds of meaning and interaction contrasts with the technological or engineering approach that dominates the modern world view. Engineering looks at artifacts as instruments and raw materials to be rationally organized by people to meet their material and economic needs. The methods of modern science and technology correspond to the ontology of our epoch of the history of being, and Heidegger looks toward a postindustrial ontology that would be less alienating (Heidegger, 1967c).

Heidegger's analysis suggests an approach to CSCL that conceives of collaboration environments as active worlds rather than one that assumes that individual people are the only interesting source of meaning-making agency. How can we go about developing a methodology for CSCL research in keeping with this shift in the locus of agency?

A Methodology for Analysis

The approach taken by Marx in his life's work provides a model of abstracting from empirical analyses and then using the abstract categories, structures, concepts, and insights to return to concrete observation with deeper understanding, interpreting the phenomena from the newly acquired theoretical perspective. In his early studies, Marx dealt with historical instances of revolution and counterrevolution. He found that there were social forces at work that were not adequately understood but that posed barriers to significant liberation and social change.

In his middle studies, Marx conducted detailed grounded research into the development of capitalist forms of production. During this period, he formulated his methodology in his rough draft (*Grundrisse*) study. He dismissed the commonsense approach of simply accepting what seems to be empirically given in favor of deriving analytic concepts from the given phenomena and using these to build up a rich analysis of the concrete as complexly mediated:

It appears to be the correct procedure to start with the real and the concrete, with the real precondition, thus e.g. in economics to begin with the population. . . . But if I were to begin with population, it would be a chaotic representation of the whole and through closer determination I would arrive analytically at increasingly simple concepts; from the represented concrete to thinner and thinner abstractions until I reached the simplest determinations. From there it would be necessary to make the journey back again in the opposite direction until I had finally arrived once more at the population, but this time not as the chaotic representation of a whole, but as a rich totality of many determinations and relationships. (1939, p. 21)

Then in his late study of *Capital*, Marx began with the "cell form" (1867, p. 15) of capitalist society, writing in the opening section of the original edition: "The *form of value of the product of labor* is the most abstract, but also most general *form* of the *bourgeois* mode of production, which is thereby characterized as a specific kind of social mode of production and is thus simultaneously historically characterized" (1867, p. 34). For Marx, the analytic cell of capitalist society is the mediation of the value of the *commodity* (an artifact produced for sale). Any commodity in modern society has both a use value (based on its affordances) and an exchange value (based on the labor time necessary to produce it). For instance, the components of activity systems for learning and working (such as schools and factories) have their exchange-value (political and economic) aspects. In particular, supports for collaboration have their considerations of power and profitability that have not been made thematic here but that must not be ignored in a fuller analysis. The critique of the ideology of individualism, the private-property relations of information and the intellectual division of labor are all part of this.

For Vygotsky (1978), the analytic cell of human cognition is the mediation of thought by linguistic and physical *artifacts*. For this book, the analytic cell of collaboration is the mediation of *group cognition as discourse*. This result has emerged gradually from my work in CSCL during the past decade. I have certainly not yet provided a systematic analysis of this mediation, but perhaps I have supplied a number of theoretical terms that could contribute to such an analysis. I have undertaken a journey from concrete experience with groupware prototypes to an abstract understanding of collaborating with technology. The analysis itself requires much more empirical study—the equivalent of Marx's years of self-sacrificing research in the British library or the years of experimentation that Vygotsky would have needed to flesh out his vision if he had not died so young. From such a more fully developed theory of collaboration, one could then ascend back to a concrete understanding of collaborative learning and working—but this time as a rich totality of visible mediations—that could guide the design, analysis, and deployment of collaboration software and associated social practices. This suggests an agenda for the next decade.

The path of research in this book roughly followed the sequence of Marx's work. The shift of approach to providing computer support for collaboration through fostering group cognition—seeing the group, rather than the individual, as agent—took place gradually through the three parts of the book:

• In part I, case studies of software design increasingly took the form of viewing software as a medium that opens up and supports group communication and collaboration—or fails to do so. This led to an attempt to experience and understand how innovative software prototypes function (for the user as well as the designer) as mediating artifacts.

• In part II, the analysis of interaction was approached as the making visible of that which happens in discourse, without objectifying and reifying utterances as quantifiable expressions of individuals' thoughts. This took the form of a microethnographic study of a small group of students collaboratively learning about the meaning or affordances of a digital artifact with which they were working.

• In part III, theoretical reflections explored the concept of shared meaning and group cognition as related to the speaking of language in discourse. A network of related concepts was explored, including artifacts, situation, mediation, meaning, interpretation, tacit knowing, explicit knowing, perspectives, and negotiation.

While I think that systematic empirical study of small-group, computer-mediated collaboration is necessary for advancing work in CSCL, compiling facts and statistics about those facts is not enough. When Marx poured over the detailed financial ledgers and other documents that revealed the formation of capitalism in England, he not only collected data, but he uncovered layer upon layer of social mediations through which the meaning of the data about the prices of linen and working conditions contributed to a history of social transformation resulting in commodity production and the private ownership of the means of social production. The socially established meanings and institutional structures that Marx analyzed through a combination of empirical data collection and brilliant critique of prevailing ideologies provides a theoretical framework that is still essential (taking into account subsequent social mediations) for understanding today's phenomena like agribusiness, globalization, or technology-driven progress. That sort of theory is needed for CSCL: a theory of collaboration that provides an appropriate conceptual framework for designing groupware and analyzing its use.

Differenz, Differánce, Different

In Heidegger's terminology, we need to investigate being as well as beings. For instance, it is not enough to compare software environment A with system B as empirical things that may influence learning outcomes. We need to think about the being of those artifacts: How do they function within the collaborative interactions that pass through them? What kind of space do they open up for collaborative learning? Do they structure time and space effectively for their users? Are their environments conducive to social interaction, creativity, fun, and learning? If we are focusing on group discourse, then we want to know how CSCL environments open up a world of discourse and how they structure it. From conversation analysis (CA), we know the importance for interaction of discourse structures like turn taking (Sacks, Schegloff, & Jefferson, 1974) and repair (Schegloff, Jefferson, & Sacks, 1977). From our experiences with CSCL, we know that these structures are drastically transformed through computer mediation. Different systems transform them differently. For instance, in chat and threaded discussions, strict turn taking is not required. In chat among several active participants, this can lead to confusion, while the threads of asynchronous forums are designed to avoid such confusion.

Heidegger's later work dwells on what he calls the "ontological *Differenz*": the relationship between beings and (their) being. (Ontology is the study of being.) Already, in his early *Being and Time*, Heidegger (1996) contrasted a view of artifacts like hammers as meaningful components of a network of useful and ready-to-use tools with a Cartesian view of them as physical objects extended in space and simply present to our passive perception. As we saw above, the hammer is an integral part of a lived world, which opens up a space for our human activity. The being of the hammer as something usefully available for a range of possible applications involves the network of other artifacts and human purposes that make up our human and social world. The relationship of a being to its being is even clearer in the later examples like the jug and bridge discussed above. The being of the jug is not its clay materiality, its having been crafted by a potter, or its presence in front of a user. It is its work of opening up a space in which it brings together within the user's life the wine as a gift of the heavens and earth that have nurtured the vineyard. The being of the bridge across the Neckar similarly opens a world in which the banks of the river appear and are spanned, allowing the townsfolk to pass back and forth, under the ever-changing skies and above the flowing waters. The being of the jug or the bridge is a dynamic process that plays a unique role in structuring and making available a lived and shared world, a humanly meaningful environment within nature.

The ontological *Differenz* is not a solved problem according to Heidegger but, rather, the most challenging task for reflection today. A jug and a bridge are both part of our lived world, but they are not identical. The possibilities that are opened by the being of a jug are not those opened by the being of a bridge. How is it that the one has the being of a jug and the other that of a bridge? Or viewed along another dimension, how is it that the jug may under different historical conditions have the being of a spatiotemporal manifold, a formed lump of clay, a craftsman's creation, a commodity worth 13 euro, a source of wine, or an heirloom?

Analogously, we can ask, what is the being of a given CSCL environment? Is it the technological functionality of the software? Is it the affordances of the user interface? Is it a role in a larger activity system? Is it involved with how group discourse is mediated within the environment? Does it have to do with the place of technology within modern life? Is it the opening of a world where groups that never before existed can come together and interact? Is it an unending network of meaning and meaning-making possibilities? Perhaps Heidegger's question of being and his problem of the ontological *Differenz* blend into our question of CSCL theory and our problem of how to conceptualize group mediation to guide system design. For instance, if the being of a CSCL system is taken as involving how it mediates group cognition instead of how it can be used as an instrument to optimize individual learning, then that would have significant implications for the design, adoption, and assessment of the system.

Jacques Derrida (1984) takes up the problematic of the ontological *Differenz* in his reflections on *differánce*. He relates it to Ferdinand de Saussure (1959) and his distinction between (spoken) speech and (formal) language. Speech is the kind of thing that CA studies or that we analyze when we look at the talk in interaction captured in a video transcript, a discussion forum, or a chat log. Language, on the other hand, is the formal system of structures that defines a natural language like English that is used in speech. In a sense, a formal language does not exist in the world; it is an abstraction from a great many instances of speech that can be said to take place in that language. Noam Chomsky (1969) made this particularly clear by developing mathematical models of languages and in defining linguistic competence as distinct from actual speech. It took a revolutionary reversal by CA to start analyzing actual speech utterances rather than sentences invented by linguists, which were supposed to appeal to one's linguistic competence. Derrida's point is that a speech utterance—despite its empirical priority—depends entirely on a system of language for its meaning or its being.

Language can be viewed as a massive system of distinctions, or *differánce*. When someone makes an utterance—even a silent utterance of consciousness expressing self-awareness—that act relies for its meaning on the whole structure of this complex language. Derrida agrees with Heidegger's critique of the Cartesian view of being as (physical, temporal) presence and concludes that the being of beings is determined by formal systems of distinctions. For example, the meaning of a particular utterance is determined by language as a system of differentiations:

Thus one comes to posit presence—and specifically consciousness, the being beside itself of consciousness—no longer as the absolutely central form of Being but as a "determination" and as an "effect." A determination or an effect within a system which is no longer that of presence but of *differánce*. (Derrida, 1984, p. 16)

Sources of Being

Language is only one of the structures that determines the being of beings. Society is another one—or a set of such structures. Society is not a being that can be found somewhere present in the material world; it is an immense and evolving set of distinctions, rules, institutions, and meanings that make some actions possible and others impossible, which condition the actions that we do make and give them their significance and consequences. Just as a language is continually being created by the population that speaks that language, so society is being reproduced and transformed by the activities that take place within it. In trying to make sense of radical social change (and its failures), Marx noted,

> Men make their own history, but they do not make it just as they please; they do not make it under circumstances chosen by themselves, but under circumstances directly encountered, given and transmitted from the past. The tradition of all the dead generations weighs like a nightmare on the brain of the living. And just when they seem engaged in revolutionizing themselves and things, in creating something that has never yet existed, precisely in such periods of revolutionary crisis they anxiously conjure up the spirits of the past to their service and borrow from them names, battle cries and costumes in order to present the new scene of world history in this time-honoured disguise and this borrowed language. (1963, p. 15)

Here Marx has identified the recursive nature of the being of beings. History is neither something divorced from historical activities nor identical with them, neither simply determinate of them nor determined by them. Rather, history is made by people and it simultaneously delimits and defines those new activities that could transform it. When someone introduces a new term into the language, that term is defined by the very language that it is changing. In a sense, the language itself is speaking through the poet and transforming itself; society is acting through the social activist and evolving itself. Both Harold Garfinkel (1967, p. 33) and Anthony Giddens (1984b, p. 25) identify the reflexive and recursive nature of being that defines and delimits the beings through which being comes to be and to evolve.

The history of CSCL provides a relatively simple example of the dialectic of being and beings. Methodologies, definitions of data, and key terminology have been brought into this multidisciplinary domain by researchers and authors from diverse fields. But somehow, certain terms have been accepted and not others. Jean Lave and Etienne Wenger's (1991) influential book, for instance, proposed terms like "peripheral legitimate participation," "social practice," and "situated learning," but the terms that stuck were "communities of practice" and "sociocultural." This may have been a result of how the book entered into group interactions within CSCL gatherings and related community discussions. Some terms simply have greater resonance within a body of discourse; they are adopted by practitioners and become guiding concepts, buzz words, hype, or jargon. The being of individual contributions merge into the being and *differánce* of a discipline. This being is then reified and acts as an autonomous institution that provides a conditioning context for subsequent beings.

In discussing linguistic or social "structures" as analyzed by Heidegger, Derrida, Garfinkel, or Giddens, I do not intend to conjure up immutable forces or abstract relationships divorced from social interaction. This is not a variety of structuralism. These structures are historically evolving aspects of the sociocultural context. Their rules and preferences are results of small-group interactions and are made relevant and interpreted within these interactions. Taken for granted as rules of polite society, for instance, socially accepted values and rules can be used as resources in accounting for behavior (Garfinkel, 1967). In other words, these "rules" are not unmediated causes of human and group behavior but socially constructed habits (Bourdieu, 1995). They are not predictive like the laws of physics but reflect patterns of the expectations and rationalizations that people often use in their interactions with other people. The appearance of structures as objective, ahistorical edifices is an illusion that must be deconstructed by critical theoretical analysis.

Although Garfinkel's ethnomethodology arose largely as an alternative to structuralism, it still must recognize the role of structural properties of the concrete context. As a matter of research methodology, it insists that features of the context can be considered only to the extent that they have been made relevant by the interactions of the members who are acting in the context. But that insistence on grounding the analysis in the interactional data does not eliminate the problem of describing the structural properties of the context that are made relevant by the members. For instance, if racism or sexism is referenced in the interaction, then issues are thereby brought in that go beyond the immediate interaction. Similarly, conversation analysis has worked out organizational features of talk and interaction based on empirical utterances and conversations. However, if they demonstrate a pattern of organization or a preference for certain interactions over others (e.g., Sacks, Schegloff, & Jefferson, 1974; Schegloff, Jefferson, & Sacks, 1977), then one can still ask where these patterns or preferences come from. What is the being—the system of distinctions, the historical pattern—that delimits how people behave in their concrete interactions?

A variety of answers can be given as sources of being. The structure of conversational turn taking seems to be a natural response to the fact that our auditory attention and short-term memory cannot deal well with more than one person speaking at a time; therefore, our conversational speech has developed simple conventions for indicating when and how sequential turns can change. These conventions were practiced as we began to engage in social interactions and are part of our socialization. Many techniques that support communication and intersubjectivity are established through mechanisms like, for instance, peek-a-boo games between mother and infant or the kind of mutual-recognition interactions that led to the pointing gesture in Vygotsky's (1978, p. 56) analysis of the genesis of symbolic artifacts. Lakoff (1987) details how much of the underlying meaning of our mother tongue is grounded in our being embodied within the world and in metaphors that extend our bodily sense of orientation. Jürgen Habermas (1984) argues that there is an ideal speech situation and that many conversational patterns aim to approach this ideal or to follow its logic; others reflect forces that systematically distort that goal. Then there are what Marx referred to above as the "traditions of all the dead generations," sedimented in the tacitly understood connotations of the words of our language. There are many languages, dialects, and jargons of cultures, subcultures, and groups; these bleed into each other, contributing to each other's expressiveness, shaping how reality reveals itself to communities, and passing on ways of conceiving.

The question of the origin of being is not just an academic matter. Members to conversations take up this question themselves. As Garfinkel (1967, p. 33) puts it, actions that violate conversational norms are "accountable." For instance, someone who violates the preference for self-repair may be taken to account for being rude. Violators of other norms may be considered aggressive, shy, or—in extreme cases—insane. People commonly account for conversational behaviors by appeal to standards of politeness or manners. These standards play the role of a folk theory of the being of conversational utterances.

It is also possible to empirically investigate the source of being in this sense. In fact, this is just what chapter 13 did, analyzing a collaborative interpretation of a list artifact in a computer simulation of rockets. The discourse analyzed there pivots around the exclamation, "This one's different!" Brent, normally a quiet, reserved boy, thrust his body forward past his fellow students and pointed with his whole body, lifting himself out of his chair and gesturing resolutely at the computer screen, with his pencil extending his body almost into the monitor. Everything, his body, demeanor, gaze, arm, pencil, and words pointed at a spot on the screen. The teacher had asked, "You don't have anything...?" and the students had unanimously responded, "No" (there isn't anything). Then Brent emphatically pointed out that there was one: "This one's different." His actions and the deictic phrase "this one's" served to open a space for shared consideration and to focus the group discourse on it. As if Brent had studied Heidegger on ontological *Differenz* and Derrida on *différance*, he characterized his discovery simply as "different."

The ensuing collaborative moment involves the small group of students interactively explicating what is here meant by "different" and confirming this as an acceptable description of something on the computer screen. The characterization of a rocket pair on the monitor as different started as a personal interpretation by Brent. As Heidegger defined it, interpretation is a matter of laying something out *as* something. This involves making explicit something that was already there in one's tacit preunderstanding (see chapter 4 in this book). Brent made explicit that the rocket pair should be seen *as* different. The group discourse then went on to make matters even more explicit. The term "different" pointed back to the teacher's explication of "anything" *as* same engine, *different* nose cone. The group made explicit that they were now talking about rockets one and two, and that these rockets had the same engine (but different nose cones) as required. The group developed a shared understanding through the development of a logical argument using a sequence of cognitive moves: proposals, arguments against, clarifications, explications, arguments for, agreements, conclusions. The rational sequence of argumentation was made by the group as a whole. Through their collaborative interaction, the group learned to see the list as structured in a way that they had not previously been able to see it. That is, the being of the list in the sense of its structural properties was transformed by the group discourse. The meaning of the beings in the list (the individual rockets and their descriptions) was created or revised in this interaction. The system of differentiations and relationships among the rockets was literally transformed when Brent dramatically declared that a key one was "different" and the group took up his proposal, explicated it, and adopted it as shared meaning.

The reinterpretation of the list was not arbitrary. The list could not simply be interpreted in terms of *any* differentiations that anyone came up with. The differentiations of the first boy were systematically compared with the reality of the simulation list and with the differentiations of the teacher's guiding question, and found to be lacking validity. The list artifact talked back to the group. This "back-talk" (Schön, 1992) of reality was essential to the process of "creation/discovery" (Merleau-Ponty, 1955) that created a new structure. It uncovered the structure as visible to the group by discovering it in the list, so that in the end the first boy could say, "I see. I see. I see." Retrospectively, the group took the list structure as having always already been there: they created this meaning and interpreted it as a discovery.

This is a layperson's example of respect for the empirical. As a science, CSCL must be founded on a systematic respect for the empirical. However, this does not mean blindly accepting narrow methodological definitions of the empirical from sciences that investigate very different realms of reality—for instance, realms in which human interpretation, interpersonal interaction, and shared meaning do not play such a central role.

A New World for CSCL

Given a Heideggerian view of artifacts as agents for opening worlds of interaction, meaning, and being, what are the implications for collaboration design, analysis and theory? One aspect of Heidegger's artifact-centered approach is to minimize human willful agency: let the artifact do its work and be itself (*Gelassenheit*); let the event of mediation (*Ereignis*) unfold and become what it wants to be by gathering together and appropriating what is appropriate to itself. There is a shift of agency. For CSCL, this could mean shifting from individual rational actors to the group discourse as the primary unit of analysis.

My work—like that of others (e.g., Linell, 2001; Wegerif, 2004; Wells, 1999; Wertsch, 1985) concerned with CSCL theory—has increasingly focused on a conception of group cognition as shared discourse. Collaborative knowledge is built not so much by individuals or even sets of individuals but by effective instances of group discourse. Shared knowledge is built not so much through deductive sequences of people's mental ideas as through the workings of language and social interaction. The way to foster this involves designing and creating artifacts, social settings, activity systems, cultural standards, community practices, and societal institutions that open up worlds of structured group discourse. Let the discourse unfold. Let it gather together elements, concepts, and perspectives that can mix productively. Let group cognition emerge from the working of the discourse through which the cognition is mediated.

According to this focus on group cognition as discourse, computer support for collaboration in the next decade should attempt the following:

• Focus *software design* on user communities and interacting groups rather than primarily on individual users and their personal psychology. That is, groupware should be designed to meet the social needs and support the actual and potential practices of communities by opening effective worlds for collaborative knowledge building. It should provide powerful artifacts for mediating their group discourse.

• Develop *evaluation methodologies* for collaborative learning based on the group unit of analysis. Suggestions for doing this and examples have been advanced by video analysis and ethnomethodology (see chapters 10 and 18 along with chapters 12, 13, and 21).

• Articulate a *theoretical framework* that situates software in its sociotechnical context, drawing on traditions of German philosophy and social thought. Approaches to this have been offered by derivates of the three mainstreams of philosophy: Marx's methods as developed in activity theory, Wittgenstein's philosophy of language as applied in conversation analysis and Heidegger's analysis of artifacts as interpreted in terms of group cognition and shared worlds.

This chapter has tried to open up the discourse concerning support for collaborating with technology by bringing together diverse traditions and by situating the topic within a theoretical framework of mediating group cognition. The hope is that this discourse continue and help to open up new opportunities for effective CSCL work in the coming years and for a more collaborative world generally.

21

Thinking at the Small-Group Unit of Analysis

After I had put most of this book together, I offered a seminar on computer-supported collaborative learning at Drexel University in the spring of 2003 based on the manuscript. The responses from students of different backgrounds underscored for me how hard it was for most people to accept the notion of group cognition. I subsequently wrote the introduction and chapters 19 and 20 to scaffold the cognitive change that I was asking of individual learners and of groups of readers.

In preparing for a European CSCL symposium a few months later, I decided to try to present an overview of my research through the lens of the notion of group cognition that emerged in the book. I wanted to stress the empirical basis of this work, so I showed several video clips and transcripts, including the old SimRocket clip and data from my current Virtual Math Teams project. In putting these data sets next to each other, I realized that they showed nicely complementary examples of higher-order scientific and mathematical thinking at the small-group unit of analysis. I presented the same talk at several European research labs and had stimulating discussions that led me to expand and clarify various points. I then included the presentation as the final chapter of this book.[1]

This chapter wraps up the view of group cognition that emerged in the previous chapters. In particular, it discusses the approach of taking the collaborative group rather than the individual group member as the unit of analysis in making visible knowledge-building achievements. This is largely a methodological concern: how can researchers analyze and understand collaborative learning and cooperative working, particularly when it is computer supported? Consideration of this issue suggests a research agenda for going forward from the preceding studies. Initial observations from work that continues beyond the scope of this book are presented here to point the way for further exploration of the issues raised. The book ends by indicating the kind of empirical investigation needed to explore the world of group cognition that has been opened in the book.

The title of this chapter—"Thinking at the Small-Group Unit of Analysis"—can be interpreted in various ways:

- *Methodological*   How should researchers be thinking? Should their thinking be focused on what is happening at the small-group unit of analysis?

- *Analytic*   What is the nature of group thinking? Can what takes place at the small-group unit of analysis really be considered thinking?

- *Theoretical*   Is this notion of group cognition an innovative idea? Is thinking at the small-group unit of analysis a new conceptualization of distributed cognition?

All three of these senses are pursued in the chapter as a way of gathering together what has emerged in the book about group cognition. First, I argue that computer-supported collaborative learning (CSCL) researchers should focus less on the individual and more on the group as agent of collaborative knowledge building. Then I anticipate the kind of research that I think is needed in the future by analyzing an empirical instance of group cognition in a computer-supported collaborative learning context and argue that the group there is engaged in mathematical argumentation and problem solving through the group interactions rather than primarily through individuals' thoughts. Finally, I conclude by briefly discussing the relation of the concept of group cognition as it has emerged here to recent notions of distributed cognition.

How Should We Understand Collaborative Learning?

Considered in the terms presented in chapter 20, this book has moved from concrete case studies of technology to abstract conceptual reflections. It is now time to use the theoretical framework of group cognition to return to empirical data and to use the theory for developing a rich understanding of the data. Then, conversely, detailed empirical applications of the theory can serve to clarify and refine the conceptual framework.

In this final chapter, I want to share some initial glimpses into the data we are starting to collect in the Virtual Math Teams (VMT) project as a way of indicating a direction for future research. Up to this point, the book has primarily presented studies of software, analysis and theory from before I moved to Drexel University in September of 2002. Since then, I began the VMT project (introduced at the end of chapter 17) with colleagues at Drexel. This project is concerned with investigating how students can collaborate on mathematical problem solving with the help of technologies like chatrooms. The research takes as its primary unit of analysis the collaborative small group—its group discourse and its group cognition. By investigating collaborative math problem solving, the VMT project targets the analysis of high-level cognitive accomplishments by small groups of students.

It should have already become clear that the focus on the group unit of analysis is not meant predominantly as an ontological commitment to group mind as some kind of physical or metaphysical thing. Rather, it is an alternative way of looking at subtle linguistic interactions that our preconceptions and our languages are not capable of grasping readily as such. In the Heideggerian imagery of chapter 20, group cognition is not a being but the form of being of a group, in which a network of semantic references are gathered together to form a coherent meaning.

The focus on the group is largely an attempt to defocus the individual—recognizing that the thinking individual is really a complexly mediated process, a product of social and cultural forces, despite its visual appearance as associated with a simple physical entity. To exclusively consider the individual and to treat the social interactions that involve the individual as secondary environmental influences (Vera & Simon, 1993) is problematic enough in learning theory generally. But when analyzing technologically mediated *collaboration*, such a strong focus on individuals necessarily misses or undervalues interactional and group-level phenomena.

Collaboration itself is an essentially group-level phenomenon, not an individual behavior or attribute. It is possible to define CSCL as an area of learning research and to adhere to the traditional conceptions and methodologies oriented toward individual learners—merely measuring the effects of computer-based tools and collaborative experiences on the learning outcomes of individual subjects, as was generally done in social psychology, cooperative learning, and small-group studies in the past (Johnson & Johnson, 1989; Stahl, 2000). But this book has tried to take CSCL seriously as a new paradigm of theory and research rigorously centered on collaboration. It has tried to affect a shift in thinking and observing. The reflections in the previous chapters of part III, in particular, have been designed to critique the exclusive consideration of individual-level phenomena and to overcome widespread initial resistance to thinking at the small-group unit of analysis.

The recommendation of prioritizing the group unit is primarily a methodological suggestion rather than an ontological commitment. It hypothesizes that it will be productive to analyze collaborative sense making—the creation of shared meaning—as something that takes place at the group level, as a form of group cognition. Because it is centrally concerned with promoting collaborative knowledge building (see chapter 17), *CSCL should try to comprehend meaning making at the small-group unit of analysis and should design software to support group cognition as such.*

What is meant here by a methodological recommendation? A basic methodological question for the daily practice of CSCL research is "how can we analyze instances of collaborative learning?" For instance, if we have a video clip or chat log of students collaborating, how do we go about determining what they are doing and what they are learning? If we say that the group members have certain "methods" for accomplishing whatever it is they are doing, then what are *our methods* as researchers for identifying and analyzing *their methods?* Ultimately, researchers in CSCL want to understand, evaluate, and redesign educational interventions and technological media. If we are using a design-based research approach to do this, then what analytic methods should we incorporate in this approach to understand and critique the learning practices that take place under various conditions?

In particular, if we are investigating learning under conditions of collaboration, we need to have methods to analyze both the individual and the group levels of description. In analyzing group-level behaviors, we can treat the group as the sum of its members and analyze it from the individual perspective, but we can also view the group as an emergent phenomenon with its own set of ideas and behaviors.

Multiple Units of Analysis

The tradition in educational and psychological research has been to focus primarily on the individual person as the unit of analysis. Group behavior is seen as the interplay of actions that are ultimately understood as the behavior of the individual members. In these traditions, the questions that the researcher poses when looking at data might be, *What is this or that individual person doing, thinking, intending, or learning?*

In sociology or anthropology, by contrast, methodology focuses on the social unit or the shared culture as the unit of analysis. Researchers in these traditions might ask, *What are the norms, institutions, values, rules, or methods that dominate behavior in the society or culture of the studied group?*

This book has proposed a middle ground between the extremes of individual and society: the small group as unit of analysis. It suggests that fields like CSCL and computer-supported cooperative work (CSCW) should focus their empirical analysis on what is happening at the small-group level of description. Remember that the small group exists primarily not as a set of physical objects (the bodies of the members) but as a shared discourse (where discourse may include gaze, physical gesture, body posturing, and intonation or may be computer mediated in a virtual space). Chapter 20 talked about this as looking at how language speaks through us rather than how we speak using language—viewing the discourse as the site of agency. Key questions here might be, *What is taking place interactionally? How are particular utterances contributing to the group discourse? How is shared meaning being constructed?*

Conversation analysis based on ethnomethodology adopts a phenomenological stance. Following the method of Edmund Husserl—founder of phenomenology and teacher of Martin Heidegger—this approach restricts itself to the given data without relying on theoretical constructs and inferences. In analyzing a chat log, we are justified only in interpreting the posted texts as sequentially given. We cannot speculate on intentions, mental models, or internal representations of the participants except insofar as these are expressed or made relevant in the sequential texts themselves. Other scientific approaches might argue from theories of human behavior, even from theories of neuron firings, cognitive loads, sociological forces, and so on.

As noted in chapter 18, chat participants are typically also restricted to interpreting the chat on the basis of the temporally appearing sequence of posted texts. That puts the researchers on a nonprivileged equal basis with the group members. The interpretation by the researcher relies on a hermeneutic competence shared with the subjects but takes advantage of a nonengaged, reflective attitude and the opportunity to repeatedly review the log.

Since the meaning of the indexical, elliptical, projective texts in the log spans multiple texts contributed by multiple participants and constituting a small-group interaction, it is appropriate to interpret the log primarily at the small-group unit of analysis. Individual utterances are fragmentary. To ascribe meaning to them one must see them either as part of the larger group interaction or else as expressions of mental representations or mental models (such as models of the topic under discussion, of the other participants, or of the group process). But mental representations are not visible; they are speculative constructs of the researcher based on psychological or folk theories. It is often tempting to assume some individual intentions or mental states causing the utterances that are observable—because we are so familiar with the use of these theoretical constructs in giving retrospective accounts of human behavior. But these construals go significantly beyond the evidence given in conversational data. Conversation analysis discusses what is happening interactionally within the group discourse; it does not make causal claims about why participants are doing their individual actions that produce the group interaction.

It may often be possible to reduce the analysis of an interaction in a small group to a series of actions of individuals, each responding to what they perceive and interpret. This is particularly plausible when the interaction has not effectively constituted a functional knowledge-building group but remains at the level of several individuals exchanging their own personal opinions. However, when deep collaborative learning takes place within a group that has been constituted by its participants as the subject or agent of knowledge building, then the group cognition has properties that are different than the sum of the individual cognitions. In general, collaboration is an interactive phenomenon with meaning-making properties at the group unit of analysis. These important properties are easily lost through methods that focus on phenomena at the individual unit of analysis.

To analyze small-group discourse, one must be prepared to integrate many considerations. An utterance gathers together previous utterances, it references artifacts, and it projects future activity possibilities. So the utterance's topic implies a much broader, potentially unbounded target for interpretation involving an interplay between (1) individual and (2) community, figure and ground, text and context. On the one hand, specific utterances are contributed primarily by individual speakers (although sentence completions of one person's utterance by another person are common, and all utterances must be understood as responses to the group history and situation). So the small group incorporates its individual members, and one can attempt to reduce one's interpretation of each utterance to the psychological state of its individual speaker (as secondarily influenced by the other speakers). On the other hand, discourse takes place within the language of a culture, and the content of discourses typically reference social and cultural issues and traditions. How we interact in general is a cultural matter. So the small-group discourse is essentially embedded in a much larger sociocultural context that must be taken into account when analyzing the small-group unit.

Although the individual, group, and community levels are inextricably intertwined, it is useful for purposes of analysis to distinguish them explicitly. Table 21.1 summarizes the five perspectives that have played a major role in this book and that were defined in the beginning of chapter 18.

The first three perspectives in the table are those of the agents at the different units of analysis just discussed: the *individual*, *small group*, and *community of practice*. The other two perspectives are those of *research teams*, where the perspectives of analysts who are describing what takes place in their data can be distinguished from the perspectives of *educational innovators* when they are oriented toward design issues involving curricular or technical interventions. These perspectives are different viewpoints for analyzing empirical interactions; they signify alternative knowledge-constitutive human interests (Habermas, 1971); they allow for making

Table 21.1
Analytic perspectives and their activities.

Perspective	Activity
Individual	Interpretation
Small group	Meaning making
Community of practice	Social practice
Research team	Analysis
Educational innovators	Design

different sorts of analytic or interpretive claims about what is taking place in the data.

Each perspective has its own vocabulary of technical terms corresponding to the interests of that perspective. Chapter 16 proposes that we talk about *meaning making* taking place at the small-group level, based on *interpretations* of the shared meaning that take place at the individual level. To that distinction we can add that the meaning making takes place through methods that enact *social practices* that have been defined and are shared at the level of communities of practice. *Analysis* and *design* take place within the activities of different phases of design-based research cycles (Design-Based Research Collective, 2003). These distinctions and their associated analytic vocabularies allow us to avoid confusions. For instance, if we do not confine talk of meaning making to the group level, then the term *meaning* could get construed in very different ways by different people—as mental content in individual heads, as shared understanding of groups, and as widely accepted conventions in communities—and thereby cause misunderstanding and arguments based on people's different assumptions about (interpretations of) what is being discussed (meanings).

Groups Rock!

Groups are where the meaning-making action is. They are the engines of knowledge building. Accordingly, this book has come to recommend that analysis of collaboration focus on the small group. The small group is seen as an intermediate level of description between that of the individual and the community. Let us see how the prominent theories of collaboration conceptualize the role of small groups.

Three general approaches to a theory of collaborative learning in CSCL can be distinguished:

• Vygotsky's (1978, 1986) theory is often read as focusing on the psychology of the individual. Internalization of the social by the individual is the key form of mediation.

• Lave's theory (1988, 1991, 1996; Lave & Wenger, 1991), in contrast, is read as a sociological focus on the community, where mediation takes place primarily through changing participation patterns within social practices.

• This book has tried to outline a theory at the intermediate level, in which small groups mediate between the individual and larger social formations.

In a sense, the central role of small groups is implicitly acknowledged in studies by both Vygotsky and Lave. Vygotsky's (1978) analysis of the infant's grasping and pointing gesture discussed in chapter 16 treats the mother and infant dyad as a small group in which the interpretive perspectives of the two individuals are dissolved in a process of shared meaning making. Similarly, the apprenticeship studies reported by Lave and Wenger (1991) all involve small groups, typically consisting of one mentor and several apprentices or even just a small group of apprentices who learn together. In these examples, the small group mediates between the individual learning and social institutions of professional language and economic production.

The same point can be made about activity theory studies (e.g., those in Engeström, Miettinen, & Punamäki, 1999; Nardi, 1996). To discuss communities of practice, such studies actually analyze behavior in small groups—for instance, Engeström's discussions of "knotworking" as fluidly changing group formations (Engeström, Engeström, & Vähäaho, 1999). However, the theory itself does not acknowledge the crucial role of small groups. For instance, Engeström (1999) stresses the importance of conducting analyses at both the individual and community units of analysis and of relating these to each other, but he does not emphasize the intermediating role of the group unit of analysis. Furthermore, his popular representation of activity theory's extended triangle of mediations fails to represent the group, despite the central role of small groups within the concrete studies.

Figure 21.1 contrasts the activity theory triangle with a simple representation of the mediation of group cognition. On the left side of figure 21.1, we see how the idea of a relatively simple perceptual or communication channel connecting a subject and an object (Shannon & Weaver, 1949) was supplemented by Vygotsky (1978) to include the mediation by a physical or symbolic artifact and then extended by Engeström (1999) to include a layer of sociocultural mediations. On the right, a representation of a dialogical relation of two (or more) subjects connected by discourse is supplemented to explicitly indicate the mediation by their group discourse and then extended to include artifacts, a community of practice, a discourse community, and other contextual features made salient in their discourse. The point of the contrast is that the activity theory representation fails to acknowledge the role of the small group, group discourse, or group cognition as a central agent of mediation. This book's contribution is to make the role of small groups explicit and prominent and to begin to develop an associated concept of discourse as group cognition.

If we want to advance the third alternative for a theory of collaborative learning, here are some research hypotheses for future empirical investigation and for a theory of small-group cognition grounded in such analysis:

• The *small group* is the primary unit that mediates between individual learning and community learning.

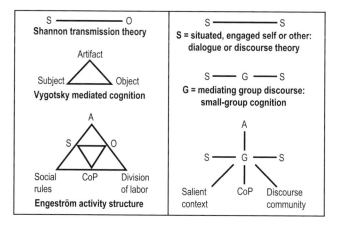

Figure 21.1
Comparison of representations of activity theory (left) and of the mediation of group cognition (right).

- *Community* participation takes place primarily within small-group activities.
- *Individual* learning is acquired largely through participation in these small-group activities.
- Individual *identities* are formed and acknowledged through small-group activities.
- Community *practices* are enacted and reproduced through small-group activities.

These hypotheses motivate my latest research.

Varieties of Collaboration

Having proposed the centrality of small groups and articulated the concept of group cognition, the next step is to use this to guide empirical analysis of actual instances of collaboration. The Virtual Math Teams project was designed to begin this effort. It started by gathering examples of collaboration under different conditions. Although the VMT project has completed only the first of its five years, the VMT team is already observing instances of group cognition in its data. We have not yet undertaken thorough analysis of this data guided by the theory in this book, but we can begin to see the richness of such data from this perspective.

Our first experiment was to go into a middle-school classroom in an urban public school and videotape a collaborative math problem-solving lesson. The VMT project is concerned with collaboration that is neither face to face nor tied to a school context; however, we wanted to start with this kind of traditional experience as a baseline for understanding—by analogy and by contrast—what takes place in the virtual setting.

We videotaped four girls sitting around a table in the classroom and working on a task. The collaboration that took place was very different from that of the five boys with the SimRocket simulation discussed in chapters 12 and 13. The girls sat facing each other, but each worked on her own piece of paper. Each pursued the assignment herself, despite the fact that the group's explicit assignment had been to produce one paper to hand in and that the girls were supposed to take different roles in producing that paper. As they worked, they softly spoke out loud—but as if thinking to themselves—about what they were doing. They counted aloud, complained in frustration that they were confused ("lost"), or expressed pain ("headache"). They took turns looking up to see how the others were doing and to review each other's progress on their papers. This running commentary on their problem solving provided a continuous social intercourse. They periodically judged themselves and each other as smart or lost, articulating social and intellectual identities. When one person was particularly lost, someone would point at that person's paper and help them through the computation step by step. It was clearly important to all the participants that everyone maintain pace and complete each major phase of the task before the others could continue.

In this case study, collaboration took place through highly synchronized parallel work. We might term this "parallel," "indirect," or "multivocal" collaboration (Cobb, 1995, p. 42). This was a different form of collaboration than in the SimRocket case. In the latter case, the boys worked as a group and solved the task jointly within a single discourse. The intense collaborative moment that the boys engaged in was concentrated on making sure that each participant had the same understanding about which rockets were being discussed and that everyone agreed that the rockets were different in the relevant sense. The girls looked like they were working individually, although closer inspection showed that they also put considerable effort into ensuring that they all had the same results and a similar understanding. The relationship of the group work to the individuals was different. Where the boys' utterances alternated so that the group discourse was a sequence of sequential statements that built into one line of argument, the girls' talk proceeded more in parallel, seemingly independently, although they did respond to each other's comments and reused each others' terms and phrases. In both cases, the end result was that the task was accomplished through a blending of contributions from all the participants—what chapter 7 called intertwining of perspectives—and everyone shared the same basic understanding of what had been accomplished.

In the VMT project, we have begun to characterize the differences between the way the group of boys collaborated and how the girls did as a difference of *exploratory* versus *expository* knowledge building. We notice this alternative as a quite general pattern, with some groups switching between the two methods during a single session. In exploratory collaboration, the group investigates proposed lines of inquiry together, as the group of boys did. In expository processes, one member at a time narrates their finding or solution, explaining and justifying it enough to garner agreement, much as the girls did. The difference in these two group methods is apparent in both quantitative (coding statistics) and qualitative (conversation analytic interpretations) comparisons of video transcripts as well as of chat logs. It was also anticipated in Bereiter's quote in chapter 15.

In other face-to-face experiments, 10 groups of three or four students working together on a relatively open-ended geometry problem were videotaped. Although the styles of interaction of these groups were extremely diverse, they all included patterns of proposals being offered for consideration and then being discussed, checked, critiqued, and either accepted, rejected, or modified. This is a process that was called *negotiation* in part I, especially in chapter 8. Negotiation methods are ways in which contributions from individuals can be accepted into a group's shared knowledge. This gives group members opportunities to react to the contribution and to influence what is adopted. It thereby involves the group members in the development of ideas and keeps the individuals synchronized with the group and with each other—to the extent required and in the ways needed for the practical purposes of the group discourse and group interaction. The negotiation process can be conducted through a broad range of methods, with members adopting various implicit or explicit roles.

The way in which group discourse grows through negotiation provides for its potential strength. Through proposals by many members, the group discourse incorporates and benefits from insights from multiple personal perspectives (backgrounds, interests, skills, emphases). By means of checking one person's proposal with others from their different perspectives, proposals are subjected to critical review, and weaknesses can be uncovered and corrected. In such ways, the group cognitive process gathers together strengths of the individual minds and can overcome some of their weaknesses.

In the data we have started to collect, we can begin to see how small groups actually negotiate shared knowledge. Analysis of this data should inform our understanding of how to design software to support knowledge negotiation and small-group collaboration generally to avoid the problems met by the software prototypes discussed in part I of this book. We particularly need to study methods that groups use to negotiate when they are collaborating online.

Chatting about Math

The video data discussed so far recorded face-to-face interactions. However, the Virtual Math Teams project is most interested in computer-mediated online collaboration. We have just begun on a small scale to invite students to a chatroom to work on math problems in virtual teams of two to five students. An excerpt from near the beginning of the chat log from one of our first sessions is shown in figure 21.2. The math problem for this chat is as follows:

If two equilateral triangles have edge lengths of 9 cubits and 12 cubits, what is the edge length of the equilateral triangle whose area is equal to the sum of the areas of the other two?

From an educational innovator's or a mathematician's perspective, the most elegant solution to the problem is to consider the proportions of the triangles. Because the three triangles are all the same shape two-dimensional figures, their areas will be proportional to each other in the ratio of the squares of any given linear dimension. The two smaller triangles have corresponding sides in the ratio of $9:12$, which is $3:4$. It is well-known (for instance from the 3/4/5 right triangle) that the squares of 3 and 4 add up to the square of 5. So the three triangles should have sides in the ratio of $3:4:5$ or $9:12:15$. The answer of 15 might well pop into a mathematician's head when she sees the problem, based on this consideration of proportions.

Even if one did not have this insight into the problem, the most effective algebraic approach to solve the problem is to use an argument about proportions to avoid computing the numeric length of the altitude. Since the triangles are all the same shape, the ratio of the altitude to the base will be the same in each triangle, some constant k. So $h = kb$, and the formula for the area of the triangle will be as follows:

$$\text{Area} = 1/2 \, bh$$
$$= 1/2 \, b(kb)$$
$$= (1/2 \, k)b^2$$

Given that the sides of the squares are 9, 12, and x and that the area of the third equals the sum of the other two,

$$(1/2 \, k)x^2 = (1/2 \, k)9^2 + (1/2 \, k)12^2$$
$$x^2 = 9^2 + 12^2$$
$$x = 15$$

The group of students whose work is excerpted in the chat-log segment did not adopt this perspective. Their chat is interesting both for the skillful methods they

1. Avr (8:21:46 PM): Okay, I think we should start with the formula for the area
of a triangle
2. Sup (8:22:17 PM): ok
3. Avr (8:22:28 PM): A = 1/2bh
4. Avr (8:22:31 PM): I believe
5. pin (8:22:35 PM): yes
6. pin (8:22:37 PM): i concue
7. pin (8:22:39 PM): concur*
8. Avr (8:22:42 PM): then find the area of each triangle
9. Avr (8:22:54 PM): oh, wait
10. Sup (8:23:03 PM): the base and height are 9 and 12 right?
11. Avr (8:23:11 PM): no
12. Sup (8:23:16 PM): o
13. Avr (8:23:16 PM): that's two separate triangles
14. Sup (8:23:19 PM): ooo
15. Sup (8:23:20 PM): ok
16. Avr (8:23:21 PM): right
17. Avr (8:23:27 PM): i think we have to figure out the height by ourselves
18. Avr (8:23:29 PM): if possible
19. pin (8:24:05 PM): i know how
20. pin (8:24:09 PM): draw the altitude'
21. Avr (8:24:09 PM): how?
22. Avr (8:24:15 PM): right
23. Sup (8:24:19 PM): proportions?
24. Avr (8:24:19 PM): this is frustrating
25. Avr (8:24:22 PM): I don't have enough paper
26. pin (8:24:43 PM): i think i got it
27. pin (8:24:54 PM): its a 30/60/90 triangle
28. Avr (8:25:06 PM): I see
29. pin (8:25:12 PM): so whats the formula

Figure 21.2
Excerpt of $3\frac{1}{2}$ minutes from a one-hour chat log during which three students chat about a geometry problem. Line numbers have been added and screen names anonymized. Otherwise, the transcript is identical to what the participants saw on their screens.

employed in constructing a problem-solving strategy and for the weaknesses we can identify in their ability to take full advantage of all their collective resources. By seeing how real students actually interact in a specific social, technical, and mathematical context, we can understand the collaborative knowledge-building activity that we are trying to support and can make use of breakdown phenomena to suggest design improvements to the group formation, math task formulation, and software environment.

A first impression of the chat log is that it looks similar to a transcript of students talking. As in the face-to-face SimRocket dialogue analyzed in chapters 12 and 13, one can see that the individual contributions to the online chat log are indexical, elliptical, and projective. They *index* features of the problem with which they are situated ("that's two separate triangles"), and they point back to previous postings ("o" or "I know how"). They are *elliptical*, relying on other postings to round out their meaning ("I see" or "proportions?"). They *project* responses or future activities ("i think we have to figure out the height by ourselves" or "how?"). Even at the utterance level, meaning is constructed across multiple postings by multiple contributors. As is shown below by an analysis of the larger problem-solving process, thinking through the mathematics is accomplished by the group as a whole: it is an interactive accomplishment achieved in the group discourse. It is an instance of group cognition. This log is an example of precisely the kind of data that need to be analyzed to see how group cognition works in detail.

Perhaps the first thing one may notice here is a pattern of proposals, discussions, and acceptances similar to what takes place in face-to-face discourse. Proposals about steps in solving the math problem are made by Avr in lines 1, 3, 8, and 17 and by Pin in lines 20 and 27. These proposals are each affirmed by someone else in lines 2, 6, 10, 19, 22, and 28, respectively.

Another thing to note is that the turn-taking conventions of face-to-face discourse (Sacks, Schegloff, & Jefferson, 1974) do not exist in chat in an unmediated way. Chat is a quasi-synchronous medium in which everyone can be typing at the same time, and the messages of other people appear sequentially after the posting has been completely typed and sent (Garcia & Jacobs, 1998). In larger groups, this can result in considerable confusion. Even in the small group of three members in this example, one must be careful to check time stamps when interpreting the threading of postings because they do not always follow each other immediately in a simple response sequence the way they do in conversation, which is constrained by the turn-taking patterns of face-to-face discourse. Thus, line 21 responds to line 19, while line 22 responds to line 20. The timestamps show that lines 20 and 21 effectively overlapped each other chronologically: Avr was typing line 21 before she saw Pin's line 20. Similarly, lines 24 and the following were responses to line 20, not line 23.

So online chat is similar to face-to-face conversation in some ways and different in others. The characteristics of the technological medium have specific effects on the mediation of the discourse. It is plausible to expect that groups need to meet most of the same fundamental interactional requirements whether computer-mediated or not. For instance, they need to be able to determine what utterance is a response to what other utterance. The methods for accomplishing this in different media may differ in interesting and consequential ways. Applying a conversation analysis approach to an online environment necessitates determining what are the similarities and differences between chat and face-to-face conversation. In addition, conducting math problem solving in a VMT chat room is not exactly the same activity as engaging in informal social conversation. Students have to officially register for the event and show up at the right time and place. Math topics automatically bring in elements of the school context, even if VMT takes place outside of the institutions of formal schooling. The problems are given to the students in the context of an institutional authority, and the students are acting as students, watched over by adults. So there are social as well as technological constraints that mediate the interaction and transform conversational methods.

Many students are accustomed to using chat technology for socializing freely with their peers, and they have to adopt a rather different behavior when participating in a VMT chatroom. Their methods of interacting reflect this. Normal conversation defines a baseline system of institutionally unconstrained discourse, which has to be adapted to in discourse contexts that have particular definitions, conventions, constraints, goals, or structures (Garcia & Jacobs, 1999). The fact that chat is a text-based medium, in which brief texts are posted in a temporal sequence, makes it quite different from interactive, embodied talk in interaction. The VMT context adds even more differences.

In addition, mathematical discourse has a number of specific features. Some of these are visible in the chat log excerpt displayed above. Methods of making various sorts of mathematical *proposals* are of central concern. Methods of critiquing and otherwise responding to these proposals require a considerable grasp of math content and conventions. As in any human argumentation, math discussions involve complex techniques of persuasion, one-upmanship, and verbal sparring as well as the officially sanctioned math reasoning skills taught in math textbooks. Furthermore, the VMT chats provide a social occasion that is important to the participants; the sociality and identity-building aspects of the interaction are necessary if the students are going to return for future chats. As is shown below, the social and the mathematical characteristics of interaction may be inextricably fused. A given brief posting may be playing multiple sophisticated roles in the chat; its interpretation by a researcher may be a complex, tricky, multilayered, open-ended, and ultimately ambiguous undertaking.

A Failed Proposal

For instance, try to interpret line 23 where Sup says simply "proportions?" What is this line a response to? Why does it occur at precisely this point in the discourse? What work is it doing—or failing to do—in the discourse? Is it posing a question, or is it making a proposal? If it is a question, what is it asking? If it is a proposal, how is it suggesting using proportions? One approach for a researcher faced with such an ambiguous posting is to see how it is taken up by the group members. In this case, this approach is frustrating for the researcher because the posting does not seem to be taken up by Sup's peers at all. First, Avr's next line overlaps Sup's with the identical time stamp. It is not completely clear what Avr's posting refers to, but it is likely a response to Pin's "draw the altitude." Avr is apparently having trouble drawing the altitude of a triangle on paper near her computer. The following remarks by Pin continue his discussion thread from line 20. (If we, as researchers, draw an equilateral triangle on our own piece of paper and then draw the altitude of the triangle, we can see that the altitude divides it into two 30/60/90 triangles. The chat software did not include a shared whiteboard for the students to display such a drawing, so it took them quite a while to share this insight later in the chat.) Sup's contribution on line 23 is lost as a result of its overlap by Avr.

The loss of Sup's contribution from the discussion is consequential from the analyst's point of view, considering the mathematics of the problem. As discussed above, a focus on relations of proportionality might have been useful in solving the problem.

The group discourse ignores Sup's suggestion of using proportions and heads down a different road, one that does not ever reach an answer. One can argue from an educational analyst or software designer perspective that this demonstrates a negative possibility of collaboration (sometimes called "group think"), where the group discourse goes off in a direction that prevents an individual from going in a better direction. In fact, Sup effectively dropped out of the chat for a long time. More than an hour later, after he returned, he symbolically computed the value of the ratio of the altitude to the side and proposed again, "i think it is gunna be in proportions." Unfortunately, his proposals continued to have little effect on the group problem solving.

Certainly, collaboration is not always perfect or even helpful. It remains an empirical hypothesis that collaboration is even appropriate to mathematical problem solving. Some people have the feeling that math is precisely the kind of thing that is best done in isolated concentration, far from the kind of peer pressure that is felt in a chat environment, where one constantly has to keep up with the flow of other people's contributions and of the group's movement. On the other hand, math educators argue that math discourse is important for building deep understanding, as opposed to rote application of formulas and computational algorithms. The resolution of this debate requires detailed analysis of mathematical discourses. We need to determine what methods people actually use—both individually and collaboratively—to "do" mathematics, particularly outside the context of textbook drill and practice exercises (Hall & Stevens, 1995; Lave, 1988).

In conducting our experiments, the VMT project is very aware that a simple chat interface is woefully inadequate for supporting effective collaborative math problem solving and discussion. However, the nature of the inadequacy is not clear, and the technical solutions for overcoming it are not obvious. Exploratory inquiry is required. One of the most effective investigatory techniques is to zero in on breakdowns and other problems that arise in practice. That is why phenomena like line 23 should be given careful consideration.

From a designer's perspective, is important to know why line 23 was ignored, particularly given that it might have led to an effective strategy for the group. We would like to know how promising but failed proposals can be supported in the group process so that they can be more effective in the collaborative problem solving.

Sup's posting has the appearance of a question. Superficially, it has the same form as Avr's question in line 21: a single word followed by a question mark (figure 21.3). In line 17, Avr made the proposal "i think we have to figure out the height by ourselves," to which Pin responded in line 19 by saying, "i know how." Avr then asks in line 21, "how?" While she is asking, Pin continues his response in line 20 ("draw the altitude"), thereby, in effect, answering Avr's question before even seeing it. When Avr sees Pin's answer, she says in line 22, "right"—aligning with him. This is a nice example of close coordination between Pin and Avr, which contrasts with Sup.

Sup's line 23 "proportions?" can be interpreted as a question in parallel to Avr's question in line 21. That is, he could be asking Pin if he plans to use some kind of calculation of proportionality to figure out the height of the triangles. However, line 23 comes too late to simply pose this question because Pin has already announced that his plan is to draw the altitude. Sup could be asking if Pin plans to use proportional reasoning in conjunction with the altitudes of the triangles once they are drawn, but this goes beyond asking a simple question like Avr's, and in effect it

17. Avr (8:23:27 PM): i think we have to figure out the height by ourselves
18. Avr (8:23:29 PM): if possible
19. pin (8:24:05 PM): i know how
20. pin (8:24:09 PM): draw the altitude'
21. Avr (8:24:09 PM): how?
22. Avr (8:24:15 PM): right
23. Sup (8:24:19 PM): **proportions?**
24. Avr (8:24:19 PM): this is frustrating

Figure 21.3
Part of the chat log excerpt in figure 21.2.

would be making a proposal for a further problem-solving strategy. So perhaps Sup's posting should be evaluated as a proposal.

One way of pursuing this interpretation from a conversation-analysis perspective is to look at the conversational *method* used for making the proposal in line 23 and to ask why it was less effective than the other proposals in the chat. Two features of Sup's method have already been mentioned: its lack of clarity and its bad timing. Several other problems are also apparent.

All the other proposals (1, 3, 8, 17, 20, and 27) were stated in relatively complete sentences. Additionally, some of the proposals were introduced with a phrase to indicate that they were the speaker's proposal (1: "I think we should . . . ," 17: "I think we have to . . . ," 20: "i know how . . . ," and 27: "i think i got it . . ."). The exceptions to these were simply continuations of previous proposals: line 3 provided the formula proposed in line 1, and line 8 proposed to "then" use that formula. Line 23, by contrast, provided a single word with a question mark. There was no syntactic context within the line for interpreting that word, and there was no reference to semantic context outside of the line. Line 23 did not respond in any clear way to a previous line and did not provide any alternative reference to a context in the original problem statement or elsewhere.

The timing of line 23 was particularly unfortunate. We already noted that it overlapped a line from Avr. Because Avr had been setting the pace for group problem solving during this part of the chat, the fact that she was following a different line of inquiry at the time of line 23 spelled death for an alternative proposal. Pin seemed either to be continuing his own thread without acknowledging anyone else at this point or to be responding too late to previous postings. So a part of the problem for Sup was that there was little sense of a coherent group process—and what sense there was did not include him. If he was acting as part of the group process (for instance, posing a question in reaction to Pin and in parallel to Avr), he was not doing a good job of it, and so his contribution was ignored in the group process. A possible advantage of text-based interaction like chat over face-to-face interaction is that there may be a broader time window for responding to previous contributions. In face-to-face conversation, turn-taking rules may define appropriate response times that expire in a fraction of a second as the conversation moves on. In computer-based chat, the turn-taking sequence is more open. However, even here, if a participant is responding to a posting that is several lines away, it is important to make explicit somehow to what they are responding. Sup's posting does not do that. It relies purely on sequential timing to establish its context, and that fails in this case.

Sup's posting 23 came right after Pin's proposal 20 to "draw the altitude." Avr had responded to this with posting 22, "right," but Pin seems to have ignored it.

Pin's proposal had opened up work to be done, and both Avr and Pin responded after line 23 with contributions to this work. So Sup's proposal came in the middle of an ongoing line of work without relating to it. In conversational terms, he made a proposal when it was not time to make a proposal. It is like trying to take a conversational turn when there is not a pause that creates a turn-taking opportunity. Now, it is possible—especially in chat—to introduce a new proposal at any time. However, to do so effectively, one must make a special effort to bring the ongoing work to a temporary halt and to present one's new proposal as an alternative. Simply saying "proportions?" will not do it.

To get a response to a proposal, one must elicit at least an affirmation or recognition. Line 23 does not really solicit a response. For instance, Avr's question at line 21 "how?" called for an answer. It was given by Pin in line 20, which actually appeared in the chat window just prior to the question and with the same time stamp. But Sup's posting does not call for a specific kind of answer. Even Sup's own previous proposal in line 10 ended with "right?," which at least required agreement or disagreement. Line 10 elicited a clear response from Avr at line 11 ("no"), which was followed by an exchange explaining why Sup's proposal was not right.

Other proposals in the excerpt are successful in contributing to the collaborative knowledge building or group problem solving in that they open up a realm of work to be done. One can look at Avr's successive proposals on lines 1, 3, 8, and 17 as laying out a work strategy. This elicits a response from Sup trying to find values to substitute into the formula and from Pin trying to draw a graphical construction that will provide the values for the formula. But Sup's proposal in line 23 neither calls for a response nor opens up a line of work. There is no request for a reaction from the rest of the group, and the proposal is simply ignored. After no one responded to Sup, he could have continued by doing some work on the proposal himself. He could have come back and made the proposal more explicit, reformulated it more strongly, taken a first step in working on it, or posed a specific question related to it. But he did not—at least not until much later—and the matter was lost.

Another serious hurdle for Sup was his status in the group at this time. In lines 10 through 16, Sup made a contribution that was taken as an indication that he did not have a strong grasp of the math problem. He offered the lengths of the two given triangles as the base and height of a single triangle (line 10). Avr immediately and flatly stated that he was wrong (line 11) and then proceeded to explain why he was wrong (line 13). When he agreed (line 15), Avr summarily dismissed him (line 16) and went on to make a new proposal that implied his approach was all wrong (lines 17 and 18). Then Pin, who had stayed out of the interchange, reentered, claiming to know how to implement Avr's alternative proposal (lines 19 and 20), and

Avr confirmed that (line 22). Sup's legitimacy as a source of useful proposals had been totally destroyed at precisely the point just before he made his ineffective proposal. Less than two minutes later, Sup tried again to make a contribution but realized that what he said was wrong. His faulty contributions confirmed repeatedly that he was a drag on the group effort. He then made several more unhelpful comments before dropping out of the discourse for most of the remaining chat.

Does this mean that Sup was an inferior mathematician or a poor collaborator? Collaboration is a group process, not an individual attribute. One could say that Sup's low status as mathematician and contributor to the group was produced by the group. Avr is an aggressive leader of the group process, as was evident throughout the hour-long chat log. She is skilled at techniques and conventions of chat as an interactional format. Pin exercised various behaviors to maintain his collaboration with Avr. Sup was considerably less successful at this. It may be possible that Sup has strong mathematical intuitions but is not skilled at formulating them or at making proposals based on them. Perhaps different forms of group facilitation, group formation, or group support would allow him to participate more effectively in collaborative math problem solving and to engage more productively in the production of group cognition. A group process that was more supportive for Sup might allow him to work better as a collaborative mathematician. Vygotsky (1978) argued that a student's ability to perform within a group was at a higher developmental level than the same student's ability to perform alone—as measured by the zone of proximal development that separates these distinct capabilities. But the higher ability assumes a properly supportive group process. What takes place (and its analysis) on the individual level is derivative of what takes place (and its analysis) at the group unit.

Sup's misguided attempt to use the lengths of the two triangle sides as the values of the base and height of a single triangle is not as surprising as it might seem. It is an instance of a strategy that is commonly used by students (Verschaffel, Greer, & Corte, 2000). Many students have been trained in school to solve problems by simply plugging given numbers into an available formula. Often, a school math session will consist of practicing computing a given formula with many sets of values. Avr had presented a formula that called for values of base and height (line 3), so Sup took the two numbers given in the problem statement and proposed using them in the formula just because they were at hand, perhaps without thinking deeply about their role in the mathematics of the problem (Hall, 2000).

It is also possible that Sup was trying to work with the two numbers as part of his intuition about proportionality of the triangles, not just because they were the only numbers given in the problem statement. As discussed above, the mathematically elegant approach to the problem builds on the proportional relation $9:12$. Sup may have felt inclined to build on this relation but been unable to work it out. Perhaps if Avr and Pin had combined their skills at making proposals with Sup's intuitions, then the group cognition would have solved the problem quickly.

Pin thought through the problem carefully along the shared group-strategy approach and drew in the missing altitude that was needed for Avr's formula of the area of a triangle. He then correctly identified the result as forming a standard 30/60/90 triangle. His next step (line 29) was to ask "so whats the formula." At this point, he too fell into the school pattern of expecting to apply a standard formula to solve a problem.

These are methods of math problem solving that are reinforced in many math classes: identifying a handy formula and plugging in available numbers. The problems used in the VMT project are typically not problems that can be solved with these rote methods. They generally require reflection on the structure of the situation and some discussion of how to approach the problem. Note how the problem in this chat could be elegantly solved with the considerations of proportionality described earlier in the chapter.

The method used in arithmetic that must be overcome when students learn algebra is numeric calculation. This method ultimately sidetracked Pin and Avr later in the chat. Rather than keeping their formulas in symbolic, algebraic format, they both insisted on substituting numeric values for square roots and multiplying everything out on their calculators. Particularly because they were working at a distance and not sharing one calculator, they wasted a substantial part of the chat hour arguing over insignificant decimal place values. This became a major point of contention and a power struggle between them. As far as the problem-solving process goes, numeric values made it much harder to solve the problem. As we saw above, maintaining everything in symbolic format allows one to cancel out all of the square roots and multiplicative constants. By engaging in numeric computations, one loses track of the overall strategy and gets bogged down in unnecessary and error-prone detail. As a consequence, the group in this chat never solved the problem.

Chat as Group Cognition

A conversation analysis can highlight the various methods that students engage in, both mathematical and interactional. For instance, it can track the level of abstraction of their discourse. Abstraction is an essential dimension of mathematics, and learning algebra requires significant shifts in cognitive abilities to deal with abstraction (Sfard & Linchevski, 1994). This applies to group cognition as well as individual cognition in beginning algebra. We can make this visible by looking at the language used in postings about math (Sfard, 2002). In the excerpt we are considering, the students move between discussing "a triangle" (line 1) or "proportions" (line 23) in general, specific formulas for specific kinds of triangles (line 29), concrete values (line 10), and numeric computations (later).

Consider line 1: "Okay, I think we should start with the formula for the area of a triangle." With "Okay," Avr takes charge of the group discourse and announces that she is making a proposal of a strategy for the group to follow. She says, "I think," indicating that this is a proposal from her individual perspective but one that she is sharing with the group. She continues, "we should start," constituting the group of chat participants as a plural subject, as a group agent that should undertake some action. "With the formula" defines the action as a mathematical task and the strategy to be one that uses a particular standard formula. "The area of a triangle" is an abstraction from the three particular triangles of known and unknown size and shape; it references the completely general triangle figure. "A triangle" is quite abstract, but some things are known about triangles in general, including a formula for their area, which Avr gives in her next posting.

After starting with the abstract concept of "a triangle" and proposing a method for working with it (namely, to use the formula for area), Avr proposes in line 8 a step toward making it more concrete by applying the formula to the three specific triangles in the problem to "then find the area of each triangle." As we have seen, Sup thereupon takes the next step in concretizing by providing concrete candidate values for the abstract variables of the formula, b and h or base and height. The rest of the excerpt remains at the intermediate level of abstraction, making proposals about the particular kinds of triangles in the problem but not yet supplying numeric values. The proposals reference "*two* separate triangles," "*the* height," "*the* altitude," "*a* 30/60/90 triangle," and "*the* formula" (for a 30/60/90 triangle). The exception to this is line 23, where Sup makes the very abstract proposal, "proportions?" Unfortunately, he does not state more concretely which proportions he is referring to. This is another way that Sup displays his inability to join the group: at line 10 he made a proposal that was too concrete, and now at line 23 he makes one too abstract.

As we have seen from this preliminary look at an initial chat log, members' postings constitute the group discourse as such and orient to it as salient. For instance, individuals make proposals to be shared by the group. These proposals are often explicitly presented as the individual's personal opinion (such as lines 1, 4, 17, 19, and 26), but acceptance by another group member makes it part of the shared flow of considerations and sets it up for being built on by anyone in the group. Subsequent postings reference them, identifying them as integral to the group discourse. By prefacing a proposal with something like "I think we should . . ." (line 1), the proposer indicates that she is a group member and also calls on the rest of the group to respond and confirm (or deny or critique) the proposal. Stating the first part of an adjacency pair (like question and answer) that elicits a response from someone else can be directed to a whole group (Lerner, 1993). It thereby constitutes the group, as such, as a participant in the conversation and designates the group as the projected respondent. This means that any of the other group members can take the next turn and respond to the proposal on behalf of the group. This is a pattern that we see repeatedly in the chat excerpt, except for Sup's failed proposal, which did not succeed in eliciting a response.

Some methods of contributing proposals are effective, and others are not. We have seen several problems with Sup's line 23:

- Its lack of semantic clarity (what is he proposing about proportions?) and its weak syntactic structure (is it even a proposal?),

- Its unfortunate timing in being followed immediately by line 24,

- Its inability to interrupt the ongoing work,

- Its failure to elicit a response,

- The absence of any proposed work to be done,

- Sup's history of distracting from the flow of the group problem solving rather than contributing to it, and

- Sup's lack of alignment with the group in terms of level of abstraction.

These may have all contributed to the failure of the posting. Line 23 was simply not properly formulated or presented as a proposal that calls for uptake by the group. At best, it is a suggestion vaguely offered to the other group members for their consideration. Given the rapid flow of proposals and responses in chat, it is too weak to have an effect on the problem solving and is ignored.

Due to the quasi-synchronous nature of the chat medium, there is a competition to time and to structure postings and social relationships so as to increase the likelihood of the posting being taken up into the group discourse (Garcia & Jacobs, 1998). Line 23 fared poorly in this competition. In considering this empirical case in its concrete context, we have noted some of the considerations involved. Methods for doing math collaboratively integrate skills of text chatting (typing, abbreviating, posting quickly, referencing other postings, and so on), socializing (establishing roles, legitimacy, and social relations), formulating proposals mathematically (proper level of abstraction, use of symbols, strategies, and explanations), and interacting (making effective proposals, leading the group discussion, and eliciting desired responses). We have seen problems along all these dimensions with line 23 compared to line 1, for instance.

Many common sorts of methods of doing math appeared in this chat: selecting levels of abstraction, using formulas, and substituting numeric values. The mathematics of the chat-mediated group discourse bears strong resemblance to cognitive processes attributed in the math education literature to individual students working on their own. Students are likely to grasp at available formulas or pursue numeric computations with whatever numbers are at hand. Some of the math methods we observed are simultaneously methods of interacting socially and constituting group identity (such as who can play what role and whose proposals will be taken seriously). In particular, leadership in the group interaction seems to be both defined by and controlled by the making of effective math proposals. Avr's self-identity as a leader in the group is maintained by her attempts to control the proposal making and is reflected by her success in making effective proposals that set the group agenda.

Design Support for Group Cognition

In the chat excerpt involving Avr, Pin, and Sup, we have seen several examples of a three-step pattern:

1. A proposal for the group to work on is made by an individual: "I think we should."
2. An acceptance is made on behalf of the group: "Ok," "right."
3. There is an elaboration of the proposal by members of the group. The proposed work is begun, often with a secondary proposal for the first substep.

This suggests that collaborative problem solving of mathematics may often involve a particular form of what conversation analysis refers to as adjacency pairs (like question-and-answer pairs). We can define a *math proposal adjacency pair* with this structure:

1. An individual makes a proposal to the group for the group's work.
2. Another member of the group accepts or rejects the proposal on behalf of the group.

Many adjacency pairs allow for recursive insertion of other pairs between the two parts of the original pair, delaying completion of the pair. With math proposal adjacency pairs, the subsidiary pairs seem to come after the completion of the original pair, in the form of secondary proposals, questions, or explanations that start to do the work that was proposed in the original pair.

The centrality of math proposal adjacency pairs in collaborative math problem solving argues for the importance of analyzing thinking at the small-group unit. If one focuses just on individual postings as speech acts, then one is tempted to reduce them to expressions of individual cognitions: "In general, speech act theory takes individual speech acts produced by individuals as its unit of analysis" (Duranti, p.

253). In contrast, math proposals elicit responses and further work by the group. "Adjacency pairs are thus important mechanisms for establishing *intersubjectivity*, that is mutual understanding and coordination around a common activity" (Duranti, p. 255, emphasis in original). Initiated by individuals, math proposals constitute the group as the agent to accept the proposal as shared and to do the problem-solving work as a group activity. The proposal-and-acceptance pair is itself the linguistic accomplishment of at least two members of the group and is clearly situated in the activity of the group as a strategy for continuing that group's activity. Successful adjacency pairs are group accomplishments, not individual acts.

At this time, the notion of math proposal adjacency pairs is just a preliminary proposal based on a brief chat log excerpt. It calls for extensive conversation analysis of a corpus of logs of collaborative online math problem solving to establish whether this is a fruitful way of interpreting the data. If it turns out to be a useful approach, then it will be important to determine what interactional methods of producing such proposals are effective (or not) in fostering successful knowledge building and group cognition. An understanding of these methods can guide the design of activity structures for collaborative math.

For instance, if the failure of Sup's proposal about proportions is considered deleterious to the collaborative knowledge building around the triangles problem, then what are the implications of this for the design of educational computer-based environments? One approach would be to help students like Sup formulate stronger proposals. Presumably, giving him positive opportunities to interact with other students, like Avr and Pin, who are more skilled in chat proposal making would provide Sup with models and experiences that he can learn from—assuming that he perseveres.

Another approach to the problem would be to build functionality into the software and structures into the activity that scaffold the ability of weak proposals to survive. As students like Sup experience success with their proposals, they may become more aware of what it takes to make a strong proposal. For instance, functionality could be built into an extended chat system to support the indexical, elliptical, and projective nature of group discourse.

Professional mathematics relies heavily on inscription—the use of specialized notation, the inclusion of explicit statements of all deductive steps, and the format of the formal proof—to support the discussion of math proposals. This can take place on an informal whiteboard, on a university blackboard, or in an academic journal. Everything that is to be indexed in the discussion is labeled unambiguously. To avoid ellipsis, theorems are stated explicitly, with all conditions and dependencies named. The projection of what is to be proven is encapsulated in the form of a proof, which starts with the givens and concludes with what is proven. Perhaps most important, proposals for how to proceed are listed in the proof itself as theorems, lemmas, and so forth. All of the elements of this system are organized sequentially.

One could imagine a chat system supplemented with a window in which participants could maintain an informal list of their proposals in a format analogous to the steps of a proof. After Sup's proposal, the list might look like figure 21.4. When Sup made a proposal in the chat, he would enter a statement of it in the proof window in logical sequence. He could cross out his own proposal when he felt it had been convincingly argued against by the group.

There are many design questions and options for doing something like this. Above all, would students understand this functionality, and would they use it? Here it is meant only to be suggestive. The idea is that important proposals that were made would be retained in a visible way and be shared by the group.

Another useful tool for group mathematics would be a shared drawing area. In the chat environment used by Sup, Pin, and Avr, there was no shared drawing, but a student could create a drawing and send it to the others. Pin did this 12 minutes after the part of the interaction shown in the excerpt. Before the drawing was shared, much time was lost due to confusion about references to triangles and vertices. For math problems involving geometric figures, it is clearly important to be able to share drawings easily and quickly. Again, there are many design issues, such as how to keep track of who drew what, who is allowed to erase, how to point to items in the drawing, and how to capture a record of the graphical interactions in coordination with the text chatting.

In our next iteration of the VMT project experiments, we will experiment with a chat system that allows students to link their postings explicitly to other postings, to items in the shared drawing system, and to elements of a proposals list. The links

Given: 2 equilateral triangles of edge length 9 cubits and 12 cubits

Formula for a triangle: A = 1/2 *bh*
Area of each triangle = ?
b, h = 9, 12
Draw the altitude.
Use proportions for ratio of altitude to base.

Find: The edge length of the equilateral triangle whose area is equal to the sum of the areas of the other two triangles.

Figure 21.4
A list of proposals.

will appear as lines connecting the currently selected posting to the items that its author linked it to. Because postings may be linked to the statements that they respond to, the chat can optionally be displayed as a threaded discussion, avoiding some of the "chat confusion" that comes from postings appearing in a chronological order that obscures their response structure.

In general, mathematical group cognition may benefit from software features that support indexicality through displayed linking, shared drawings, and threaded displays; compensate for ellipsis by maintaining memory lists that can be referenced; and aid projecting by making the status of open proposals explicit. In addition, ideas that were explored in the software prototypes of part I of this book—carefully selecting people to work together in groups, merging interpretive perspectives, and structuring knowledge negotiation—can be applied to chat environments for group cognition.

Online methods tend to parallel face-to-face methods, but technical mediation makes a difference, making some things easier (like working in parallel) and other things harder (reconciling computational differences, repairing losses from overlap). Design of the sociotechnical mediation based on analysis of group interaction can improve the likelihood of desirable collaborative knowledge building. Whether face-to-face or online, the flow of the discourse from one proposal to the next, from method to method, and from problem to strategy to subproblem to solution defines the logic of mathematical group discourse—a unique form of group cognition.

The Rationality of Group Discourse

The science of conversation analysis discovered the *sequential* order inherent in ordinary talk (Sacks et al., 1974). Ethnomethodology explored the sense of *accountability* produced by conversational moves (Garfinkel, 1967). The concepts of sequentiality and accountability are closely related to the definition of *rationality* and high-level *thought*. This becomes particularly clear in mathematical discourse.

Mathematics can be considered a model of rational cognition. In modern times, logic itself has become a subdomain of mathematics. The form of the mathematical proof is held up as a paradigm of pure thought.

A proof combines its own special forms of sequentiality and accountability. A proof begins with known facts (the givens of a problem), proceeds step-by-step through a rigorously defined sequence of propositions that are either themselves axioms (true by definition), results of previous proofs (such as theorems), or logical consequences of preceding steps. Each step is accountable: the person who proposes it must be prepared to demonstrate that it is true by virtue of being an axiom, theorem, or consequence. The interesting part of the proof is not the individual propositions that make it up but their strategic sequential flow from the givens to what is to be proven (QED, *quod erat demonstrandum*).

In the triangles problem discussed above, the mathematically interesting feature is neither the given values of the sides of the smaller triangles nor the answer of the length of the larger triangle but the way one goes from the former to the latter: whether by elegant proportional reasoning, efficient algebraic manipulation, or brute-force numeric computation. To be considered mathematically valid, all of these strategies must adhere to a mathematical version of accountable sequentiality.

The difference in sequentiality and accountability between normal conversation and mathematical logic is one of degree. Logic is an abstraction from the flow of conversation, and proof is derivative from how we hold our conversational partners accountable to certain expectations of sense making. Thought is speech turned inward. The standards of logical cognition are derived from the patterns of social intercourse: rationality is derived from rationalization, not vice versa.

In the SimRocket transcript of chapter 12, we saw that the meaning of fragmentary utterances resulted from the sequentiality of their responsiveness to each other and to their strategic situation. Brent, in proposing that one pair of rockets was "different," was thereby made accountable for convincing the other group members that what he said made sense in the context. This, in turn, led to the group recognizing a different sequentiality (called *paired configurations* in chapter 13) to the rocket descriptions in the simulation list.

The mathematical discourse of the chat log in this chapter (see figure 21.2) followed quite closely the sequential format of a proof. Student proposals were strategic steps in a proof that would, if successfully completed, derive an answer to the problem from its givens (see figure 21.4). The accountability of each step meant that the group could not continue after a proposal was made until that proposal was accepted (with the second part of a proposal adjacency pair). Permissible responses to a proposal were to accept it because one recognized it as legitimate, to reject it, or to question it. If one rejected it, then the rejecter was accountable for providing a convincing reason for rejection. The epistemic status of a proposal was determined by the group through a negotiation method (similar to that in chapter 9's model of collaborative knowledge building). Candidate proposals were offered to the group from individual perspectives as tentative beliefs or, better, as questions posed to the group. The determination of a proposal as knowledge had to be made by the group—by a response in the name of the group to a proposal addressed to the group. Such knowledge is always subject to future critique and revision but is in the meantime taken as knowledge that can be built on.

Part of learning math is learning to enact methods that meet the standards of sequentiality and accountability. As we saw, Avr and Pin were much more skilled than Sup at participating in and contributing to such group methods. The group process progressed through multiple sequences of math proposal adjacency pairs building on each other systematically. This group process of math cognition formally parallels at the group level the classic Socratic dialogue method of math instruction in the *Meno* (Plato, 1961), frequently imitated by classroom teachers (Lemke, 1990).

Considered at the small-group unit of analysis, the groups of students discussed in this chapter accomplished cognitive achievements. The groups underwent cognitive change, and they solved math problems. They reflected on and selected problem-solving strategies. They built knowledge and fashioned symbolic artifacts. They thought as groups. Viewing their behavior as a thinking group constituted by interacting interpretive individuals, we could make visible how shared meaning was constructed. Rather than focusing on hidden processes of individual cognition, we analyzed the group discourse and looked at issues of sequentiality, accountability, sociality, and shared meaning making through the negotiation and acceptance of proposals. Many of the questions concerning mathematics education and thinking that arise for individual students presented themselves at the small-group unit of analysis as well.

If we accept that sequentiality and accountability are the hallmarks of high-order rational thought, then we see that group discourse meets the criteria for being considered an important form of cognition. Moreover, we have reason to hope that computer-supported collaboration can produce high-order cognitive achievements that rival and ultimately surpass those of individuals. This is not to deny the problems that can arise in groups, which may even hold back individual accomplishments. Nor is it to claim that current technologies provide the required forms of support. But it does point to a potential that transcends the limitations of the individual human mind and allows people to think together, to collaborate online in ways that effectively mediate group cognition.

Group Cognition and Distributed Cognitions

The notion of group cognition developed here may be considered a strong form of distributed cognition. It goes considerably beyond Norman's (1993) argument that the individual mind extends outside the head to artifacts in the world as forms of external memory, like a reminder string on the finger. Many discussions of distributed cognition (as surveyed by Perkins, 1993) start from the individual and gradually add on elements of the person's physical environment as cognitive aids or factors. Artifacts that extend perception (like the tip of a blind person's cane) are often considered first, followed by external memory devices (notes on scraps of paper), or computational tools (calculator). A danger of this approach is that one is always tempted to fall back on the individual mind as the central locus of cognition.

The concept of group cognition in this book takes the collaborative interaction (such as a math proposal adjacency pair) as a starting point. The collective discourse is primary, and the individual appears as a node of the group, a contributor of pieces of the whole, and an interpreter of the shared meaning. An individual act that is not part of a group process—for instance, an utterance that is ignored by the group—is not a core part of the cognition. It does not contribute to the problem solving, knowledge building, or meaning making. The search for the nature of collaborative knowledge building motivated by the breakdowns in the software studies of part I, culminated in the discovery in part II that the knowledge created by the boys working with the SimRocket program was constructed at the group-level discourse. This was paralleled in the chat-log analysis in this chapter, where the problem solving was seen to be accomplished through adjacency pairs in the group discourse. The sense making occurs at the group unit of analysis and cannot be reduced to the individual level without losing its meaning. "Proposal?" remained an individual act—and was therefore consigned to irrelevance.

The view of meaning making as a group achievement is adopted from the social sciences, particularly ethnomethodology and conversation analysis. In the context of this book, the focus on group discourse is reflected on as a methodological principle, and the implications are drawn out for a theory of computer-supported collaboration.

This approach is closely related to what is called "distributed cognition" within the academic literature of CSCW, CSCL, and the learning sciences. But distributed cognition is still a contentious term. Roy Pea (1993b) proposed a version that is compatible with group cognition. For instance, he recognized the relation of knowledge building to the merging of perspectives at the group level when he said that "Knowledge is commonly socially constructed, through collaborative efforts toward shared objectives or by dialogues and challenges brought about by difference in persons' perspectives" (p. 48). He preferred the term *distributed intelligence* to *distributed cognition* because he was interested in how intelligent behavior is accomplished with resources that are distributed across people, environments, and situations. He did not want to attribute cognition to the tools involved—just designed intelligence. Because the analysis of group cognition in this book is concerned primarily with the distribution of knowledge-building activities across people, Pea's concern is less relevant—as discussed in chapter 19, where it is argued that groups of people can think even though computers cannot.

In an edited volume of papers that helped to popularize the concept of distributed cognition (Salomon, 1993a), the editor, Gavriel Salomon, felt moved to defend individual cognition against the theory that his book was promoting (Salomon, 1993b): "The individual has been dismissed from theoretical considerations, possibly as an antithesis to the excessive emphasis on the individual by traditional psychological and educational approaches" (p. 111). It should be clear that the conception of group cognition developed in this book has paid careful explicit attention to the role of the individual (from personal perspectives in part I, to parallel collaboration in part II, to interpretation in part III), without, however, allowing group phenomena to be reduced to the individual unit of analysis. It is both necessary and difficult to protect against reductionism precisely because of excessive emphasis in the past. One could accept the fall-back position offered by Salomon that this book's focus on the group is a one-sided corrective, albeit one that is particularly appropriate in that the book has collaboration as the object of its analysis. However, to do so would be to underestimate the power of the group cognition view, allowing it to be conceived as a secondary effect, when in fact individual cognition is the subsidiary product.

Salomon himself unintentionally provides a series of examples of how easy it is to slide back into the traditional outlook. His paper is a carefully structured text with three major points and four arguments to the first of his points. In the first of these arguments, claiming that people's cognitions in daily life are not always distributed, he writes, "Sitting at my desk thinking about the arguments I want to present in this chapter, I cannot but rely on my own cognitive repertoire; there is little in this austere surrounding that affords much cognitive distribution of any notable quality" (p. 114). This sentence could have been written by Descartes himself 400 years ago. Salomon's chapter was surely developed on a computer surrounded by printouts of chapter outlines, notes, books, and other chapters. He explicitly cites 41 published works: were they all in his head or were they in his austere surrounding? But more important, his entire thinking is completely situated in the circle of debates, positions, and controversies to which his edited volume contributed. The concepts of cognition that he is thinking about could not be thought without the words, claims, and issues that other people contributed. Even if, for the moment, he is actively using only resources from this complex social process that he managed to internalize, his thoughts cannot be separated from their community context. Furthermore, the very reason he is engaging in these private cogitations is to present his chapter to the public that is engaged with these issues. His social identity, his job, and his collaboration with the other contributors to his volume are all at work. His individual thinking is but one narrow analytic perspective within the group cognition that produced his whole book.

For his second argument, Salomon makes use of Searle's Chinese-room argument (see chapter 19). He turns Searle's argument around to argue that joint systems cannot have distributed understanding, only the person inside the box can. While this may apply to systems of external memories and external representations, as Pea suggested, the argument does not apply to groups of people, each of whom can intend meanings. This argument raises more problems for traditional cognitive scientists, who are focused on representations, than it does for group cognition.

In Salomon's third argument, he tries to rescue a role for individual mental representations after acquiescing to the basic position of situated cognition from Heidegger as summarized by Terry Winograd and Fernando Flores (1986). He renders the concept of "thrownness"—a cornerstone of Heidegger's analysis of human temporality—in an explicitly atemporal way and then picks up on how we gradually build up an understanding after a breakdown. This is a flawed gloss on Winograd and Flores's summary of Heidegger's theory of situated interpretation (see chapter 4). Salomon (1993b) interprets it within his own set of very non-Heideggerian assumptions:

This understanding can be stored only as a representation that will be brought to the fore when a subsequent "concernful action" of ours with the system breaks down, requiring us to reflect again. One would expect such reflection, based as it is on representations. (p. 119)

Winograd and Flores present Heidegger's philosophy precisely to show that one can have a coherent theory of human understanding without relying on representations. Yet Salomon assumes here that understanding "can be stored only as a representation" and that reflection must be based on representation and cannot be a hermeneutic process of situated interpretation. With the help of this misconstrual, Salomon reaches the conclusion he was aiming for: "one cannot but consider the role that individuals' representations play" (p. 119). He assumes the centrality of the role of the individual as well as the role of representations. In contrast, we saw in chapter 13 that a group of students could reflect on a breakdown situation within a group discourse, requiring neither representations nor individual reflections.

Again, in the fourth argument, Salomon assumes what is to be proven. He refers to situations in family therapy and organizational change, where group interaction is clearly central, and he states that "change is brought about by affecting the cognitions or behaviors of one or another member" (p. 119). But the whole point of something like family therapy is that the problems are systemic and the system as such must change to overcome the problems that present themselves through the individuals. What the therapist has to transform is precisely the nature of the interactions at the group unit of analysis: that is why it is called family therapy, not family-member therapy.

The preceding look at Salomon's chapter demonstrates how hard it is for people steeped in Western cognitive theories—particularly in the traditions of education and psychology—to accept the principles and approaches of distributed, situated, group cognition and how easy it is for them to fall back into mentalist assumptions about individual thought and learning.

Writers from traditions of pragmatism (Dewey & Bentley, 1991; Mead, 1962), German philosophy (Habermas, 1984; Hegel, 1967; Heidegger, 1996; Marx, 1976), ethnomethodology (Dourish, 2001; Garfinkel, 1967; Sacks, 1992; Schegloff, 1991b), anthropology (Donald, 1991; Geertz, 1973; Hutchins, 1996; Lave, 1991), and dialogism (Bakhtin, 1986b; Harre & Gillet, 1999; Levinas, 1998; Linell, 2001; Wegerif, 2004; Wells, 1999) seem much more comfortable thinking at the group unit of analysis. But most of them are not much concerned with the design of computer support for collaborative learning. I have tried to apply some of their thinking to examples that are of relevance to CSCL; to draw out their consequences for a methodology for studying computer-supported collaboration; and to sketch a theory of collaborative knowledge building. I have entitled the result "group cognition"—to show its relatedness to distributed cognition while differentiating it from varieties of distributed cognition that are more focused on the use of external memory artifacts than on thinking at the group unit of analysis. While the focus of many discussions of distributed cognition is on tacit understanding and skillful use of artifacts by individuals, I have specifically explored scientific reasoning and mathematical argumentation by small groups.

Future Work on Understanding Group Cognition

This book has tried to pose some fundamental questions about how to understand the mechanisms and potentialities of group cognition and to suggest ways to take on the task of responding to these issues through empirical studies. The Virtual Math Teams project has been organized as one small effort in this direction. The goal of the project is to identify and analyze common practices of online collaborative mathematical problem solving at the level of beginning algebra or geometry. What interactional methods do group members engage in to do math? How are these methods proposed, negotiated, and shared? This analysis is oriented toward informing the design of collaboration environments for supporting math practices—including the design of software, training, curriculum, scaffolding, facilitation, feedback, and so on.

The VMT project proceeds through iterative cycles of design-based research. We started with a simple commercially available chat system that was already familiar to many students. We conducted a number of small-group sessions of math problem solving using that chat system and observed what took place, including the chat log excerpt discussed earlier in this chapter.

We are acting as both analysts of computer-mediated collaborative math methods and designers of online environments to support communities of math discourse. The design-based research approach requires these perspectives to work in a coordinated and unified way. We are using—in tandem—both qualitative methods like conversation analysis and quantitative methods involving a multidimensional coding scheme to conduct rigorous and detailed analyses of chats and to compare results across chats. As we gain insight into how to make improvements, we will modify the software support system, the design of the service, the kinds of scaffolding provided, the training of group participants and leaders, the character of the math problems, and the procedures for forming small groups. We have already added a shared whiteboard to allow the groups to make drawings. We plan to improve the drawing and pointing capabilities and add functionality to the chat to make it easier for students to be successful in making proposals to the group—adding explicit graphical support for referencing parts of a drawing or previous postings from a new posting and including a persistent list of proposals offered. As we deepen our understanding of effective student methods of "doing" collaborative online math, we will evolve the VMT service. We will also collect examples of effective and ineffective group cognition and refine the theory of technology-mediated collaboration.

The VMT project is pursuing the empirical investigation of issues raised explicitly and implicitly in this book. We are analyzing the methods that small groups use in collaborating with technology and designing technology to support the effective use of those methods. We are exploring the methods that teams of students use to discuss mathematics and are building communities for such discourse. We are fleshing out a theory of how group discourse mediates the collaboration of individuals in communities and using this theory to guide our practice.

The commercial software that we have used to support chat provides generic communication support. It was designed primarily for informal chatting and socializing or for coordinating schedules, not particularly for the interaction activities of collaborative knowledge building. Our conversation analysis of online math problem solving is starting to uncover questions that may suggest specific forms of software support for group cognition. For instance, how does a small group

- Initiate its interaction, form into a group, and establish intersubjectivity?
- Decide on a joint task to undertake and define and refine the task?

- Start to undertake the task and make proposals?
- Negotiate, persuade, question, and explain?
- Adopt roles, socialize, and define identities?
- Change activities, take turns, and terminate interaction?

This chapter has suggested ways of proceeding beyond what has been said in this book. Avr's opening proposal in the chat log excerpt provides a nice example of the initiation of group cognition that could be replicated and further analyzed: "Okay, I think we should start with the formula for the area of a triangle." This proposal in the group chat explicitly relates an individual perspective ("*I* think") to a group action ("we should *start*") and to a community artifact ("the *formula*"). The posting constitutes the group as an agent ("*we* should start") as well as positing the group as recipient of the proposal and therefore anticipating that the group itself should respond through one of its members. The posting can also be taken as an element of an already existing group activity, the chat. As such, the proposal partakes in the ongoing mediation between the individuals participating in the chat and the institutions or communities of practice of school mathematics that provide the content, goals, and context of the chat. The proposal—by instantiating a method of doing math in a specific technological medium—illustrates how group discourse mediates between participants and their culture. Avr's proposal "I think, we should" thereby contrasts starkly with Descartes's "I think, therefore I am," which failed to escape the solipsistic individual perspective to constitute a collectivity.

The discourse-based conception of group cognition as proposed here rejects Descartes's notion of thinking as a mental activity of individuals. Methodologically, it suggests looking in great detail at fine-grained interactions, lasting perhaps a minute or less, within groups. Rather than looking for learning effects that may affect an individual for a lifetime, it looks at brief episodes of meaning making that contribute to knowledge building within the group discourse as an activity. These episodes are characterized as "cognitive" because they display the requisite characteristics of sequentiality, accountability, and sense making—not because they are extensions of individual cognition. Group cognition is a phenomenon at the group unit of analysis, not a derivative of either individual thinking or community-level establishment of cultural resources. It is the source of knowledge constructed collaboratively—and is therefore an appropriate foundation for CSCL and CSCW.

Individual learning enters the picture secondarily. Because collaboration requires shared understanding, processes of group cognition ensure that all participants keep pace with the group to the extent needed for the group discourse's practical purposes. This causes individuals to develop and alter their interpretations of constructed meaning and perhaps internalize cognitive artifacts based on the products of group cognition, such as meaningful texts.

Brent's dramatic gesture ("This one's different") in chapter 12, like Avr's opening proposal in this chapter, mediated through his individual interpretive perspective the group discourse dilemma and the scientific community. His contribution to the small-group interaction transformed shared meanings and uncovered for the group cognition a realm of differentiations belonging to the sociocultural structure of the scientific world.

The exploration of more examples like Avr's and Brent's are needed to help to describe in both concrete and theoretical ways how group cognition is accomplished as a linguistic achievement. More rigorous conversational analysis of multiple chat studies will lead to an improved understanding of the methods that students use to constitute and structure group interaction and to engage in math problem solving. The VMT project is designed to generate and capture rich episodes of online group cognition as data for such exploration. The detailed interactional analysis of these episodes and their comparison to each other will increase our understanding of the following issues:

- How is *mathematics* done by online small groups of students such that we can say, for instance, that the group is displaying deep mathematical understanding versus simply manipulating things algorithmically without such understanding?

- What methods are used systematically by small groups in *online*, *text-based* environments for taking turns, keeping interaction flowing, repairing mistakes or misunderstandings, opening and closing sessions, constituting the group as a collectivity, and so on?

- Can online events, activities, and environments be *designed* to stimulate group cognition and to lower the barriers to participation and group success?

- How can math discourse communities be *catalyzed*, *grown*, and *sustained* by networks of small groups interacting with each other?

Addressing these issues will help to refine the notion of group cognition introduced in this book.

The Beginning

The quotation introducing chapter 9 made the point that as we build knowledge about something, the questions do not so much get answered as get more and more complex. Perhaps this book has turned group cognition from a simple conundrum into a far more complex mystery. Hopefully, however, it has shown that it is a meaningful and important subject of inquiry that we have just begun to probe.

The book started with the promise of the Internet to overcome the limitations of individual cognition. Networked computers not only allow global access to information but could also facilitate collaborative knowledge building within online communities. Case studies in the beginning of the book showed that even in virtual environments intentionally designed to support knowledge building, discussions were generally limited at best to the sharing of personal opinions. Commercial systems provide media for generic communication or transmission of information but no specific support for the phases of more involved collaboration—such as those modeled in chapter 9. Driven by the marketplace demands of corporate users and educational institutions, the designs of these systems aim to structure and control individual access and usage rather than to scaffold group cognition.

Part I illustrates that computer support for collaborative knowledge building is a tricky undertaking. Software designs are explored there to provide support for group formation, interpretive perspectives, and knowledge negotiation. The barriers to success that these investigations encountered were typical of CSCW and CSCL systems that try to establish innovative supports for group cognition.

The middle part of the book identifies the need to better conceptualize collaborative knowledge building as a set of group processes and the discovery of group cognition as a phenomenon of small-group discourse. Contributions to collaborative knowledge-building discussions do not typically express meanings that already existed in mental representations of individual participants. The utterances are indexical, elliptical, and projective in the sense that they contribute to meaning at the group unit of analysis by virtue of their embeddedness in the group situation, discourse, and activity. The meaning and the knowledge are originally constructed through group cognition. Individual cognition may later result from internalization or retrospective accounts. Accordingly, evidence of collaborative learning is to be found in the brief episodes of shared meaning making in which group knowing is constituted, rather than in traces of lasting capabilities of individuals, which are subject to numerous psychological factors.

Part II suggests the need for empirical research at a micro level of conversation analysis to determine how people actually form themselves into groups; intertwine personal, group, and community perspectives; and negotiate shared knowledge products. Example analyses in chapters 12 and 13 as well as in the present chapter illustrate the level of interpretation required to make visible the details of collaborative meaning making.

Part III draws on these experiences to develop a notion of group cognition that involves thinking at the small-group unit of analysis, where meaning is constructed that cannot be attributed to any individual, although it is constituted out of individual contributions and is reliant on individual interpretations. Chapters in this part try to overcome widespread resistance to the term *group cognition* and to suggest ways of conceptualizing collaborative processes that make it easier for us all to talk about group cognition.

In particular, conversation analysis was proposed as a methodology for making group cognition visible. Interpretations like those in chapters 12, 13, and 21 focus on thinking at the small-group unit of analysis. They look at intersubjective interactions like turn taking, knowledge negotiation, adjacency pairs, and conversational repair. Through such analysis, we see that the basic components of collaborative knowledge building are not actions of individuals but are methods of small-group activity. Through them, shared meanings are proposed, adopted, and refined. The processes of group cognition incorporate contributions by individuals, based on individual interpretations of the emerging and evolving group meanings. But these individual utterances are essentially fragmentary; they become meaningful only by virtue of their contributing to the group context. That is why computer support for collaborative knowledge building must be centrally concerned with group cognition.

The cycle of software prototyping, conversation analysis, and theoretical reflection must be iterated repeatedly. Many innovations of CSCL and CSCW systems will have to be prototyped and tried out, developing a whole field of technology for use in supporting collaboration. The interactions that take place online in these and other contexts must be analyzed systematically to catalog methods that people use to accomplish their group work, learning, communicating, and thinking. The technology and the analyses should be conceptualized within a vocabulary adequate for making sense of them.

The comprehension of how thinking takes place at the small-group unit of analysis will guide the design of more effective computer support for collaborative knowledge building. Then the potential of group cognition can blossom around the world. This will require a global effort, itself a major instance of group cognition. The task of CSCL and CSCW has just begun.

Notes

A primordial form of collaboration is that of man and woman. Throughout the decade covered by this book, I have thrived in the collaboration with my Bliss, who supported me, tolerated my long hours at the computer, and taught me a great deal about the nature and joys of collaboration, in both theory and practice.

This book also benefited in numerous ways from my collaborators at the Virtual Math Teams project and Drexel University while I assembled and refined the text. They provided essential feedback, continuous stimulation, and new insights. I received valuable insights into the manuscript's difficulties from my students. The series editors and the MIT Press staff gently steered the book's evolution in helpful ways. David Tietjen read the entire manuscript and improved its details. Despite all this help, any flaws that the book retains are solely my contribution.

Chapter 1   Share Globally, Adapt Locally

1. Previously published as G. Stahl, T. Sumner, & R. Owen (1995), Share globally, adapt locally: Software to create and distribute student-centered curriculum, *Computers and Education*, Special Issue on Education and the Internet, 24(3), 237–246.

This chapter, originally published with coauthors Tamara Sumner and Robert Owen, describes work done at Owen Research with support by the U.S. Department of Energy (DOE) and the National Science Foundation (NSF). Michael Wright and Carla Selby also worked on this project. The project received encouragement from Len Scrogan, technology specialist in the Curriculum and Instruction Division of Boulder Valley Public Schools, and Jim Spohrer of Apple Computers. The design environment approach grew out of research at the Center for LifeLong Learning and Design, University of Colorado.

The research reported in this chapter and several others was supported in part by the NSF; any opinions, findings, and conclusions or recommendations expressed in this book are those of the author and do not necessarily reflect the views of the National Science Foundation.

Note that this paper was written in 1995, when the Internet was available but the World Wide Web was not yet popular and browsers like Netscape and Internet Explorer did not exist. The technical implementation of TCA and the distribution of resources on servers and desktops would be designed differently 10 years later. Although digital libraries of educational resources have been created meanwhile—such as <www.mathforum.org>—they lack several of TCA's affordances.

Chapter 2   Evolving a Learning Environment

1. This chapter is based on a previously unpublished manuscript: G. Stahl (1999), Evolution of an LSA-based interactive environment for learning to write summaries. It was originally written for submission as a companion piece to (Kintsch et al., 2000) in the special issue of *Interactive Learning Environments* on latent semantic analysis (LSA) but was never submitted.

The research reported here was supported in part by a grant from the Cognitive Studies in Educational Practice Project of the McDonnell Foundation. The principal investigators on the grant were Walter Kintsch, Gerhard Fischer, and Thomas Landauer. The initial versions of State the Essence were developed by the author, with assistance from Rogerio dePaula and David Steinhart. Steinhart developed a later version, named Summary Street, as part of his dissertation. In addition, Eileen Kintsch, Darrell Laham, and Maureen Schreiner also participated in this LSA Research Group. Cindy Matthews and Ronald Lamb team-taught the sixth-grade classroom at Platt Middle School in Boulder, Colorado, where the software was used in 1997 and 1998. The teachers were more than helpful, and, as always, the kids were great. The views expressed in this chapter are those of the author and are not necessarily shared by Walter Kintsch, Tom Landauer, and Eileen Kintsch, who provided the primary project leadership.

2. See the special issue on LSA in *Interactive Learning Environments*, 8(2) and the LSA Web site at <lsa.colorado.edu> with interactive displays and publications.

Chapter 3   Armchair Missions to Mars

1. Previously published as: G. Stahl (1996a), Armchair missions to Mars: Using case-based reasoning and fuzzy logic to simulate a time series model of astronaut crews, In S. Pal, T. Dillon, & D. Yeung (Eds.), (2000), *Soft computing in case-based reasoning* (pp. 321–344) (London: Springer Verlag). This was an extended version of a paper published in 1996 in *Knowledge-Based Systems*, 9, 409–415.

The research was conducted at Owen Research, Inc. (ORI) in Boulder, Colorado, during a two-year SBIR grant from NASA in 1993 to 1995. ORI is a small research laboratory founded and run by Robert Owen, a physicist specializing in laser optics. He also has a Ph.D. in anthropology, and his dissertation in that field led to this research in modeling small-group behavior using AI techniques. I developed the technical approach and programmed the system. Brent Reeves assisted with the fuzzy-logic algorithms. To help collect and analyze social science literature related to small groups in isolated conditions, we worked with Russell McGoodwin of the anthropology department at the University of Colorado (CU) and his student, Nick Colmenares. In addition, I conducted several interviews with an experienced astronaut, Mike Lounge, and discussed our project with him. I also discussed this work and that of the following chapter with Gene Cernan, the last man to walk on the moon.

This research was sponsored by the Behavioral and Performance Laboratory at Johnson Space Center in Houston, Texas, part of NASA's Astronaut Support Division. We worked closely with NASA researchers Joanna Wood and Albert Holland on the design of the software and the data. At the end of the project, we delivered the software to them to continue the work.

Chapter 4   Supporting Situated Interpretation

1. Previously published as G. Stahl (1993b), Supporting situated interpretation, In *Proceeding of the Fifteenth Conference of the Cognitive Science Society, 1993 (CogSci '93), Boulder, Colorado* (pp. 965–970). Hillsdale, NJ: Lawrence Erlbaum.

This chapter is indebted to Gerhard Fischer, Ray McCall, Kumiyo Nakakoji, Jonathan Ostwald, and Tamara Sumner, who helped to focus it, and to the Center for LifeLong Learning and Design (L3D) research group at the University of Colorado, whose ideas and systems it tries to ground theoretically and extend practically. The Hermes system was a rewrite of McCall's Phidias system, an object-oriented implementation of his contexts as computational perspectives. The chapter reports on main themes in my computer science dissertation.

Chapter 5   Collaborative Technology for Communities

1. Previously published as G. Stahl (2000b), Collaborative information environments to support knowledge construction by communities, *AI & Society, 14*, 1–27.

The earlier research on collaborative information environments (CIEs) for design was a collaboration of the author with Gerhard Fischer and Jonathan Ostwald. We would like to thank the other members of L3D, particularly the Organizational Memory and Organizational Learning group, including Jay Smith, Scott Berkebile, Sam Stoller, Jim Masson, and Tim Ohara, who worked on the WebNet system. Our knowledge of local-area network design benefited from our domain investigators John Rieman and Ken Anderson and local informants Kyle Kucson and Evi Nemeth. The more recent research on CIEs for knowledge construction involved the author with Rogerio dePaula, Thomas Herrmann and his students at Dortmund, Ted Habermann and his group at the National Oceanic and Atmospheric Administration, Dan Kowal and his middle-school students, the collaborators in the Readings in Cognitive Science seminar, and the researchers in the Articulate Learners project. The work reported here was supported in part by grants from the Defense Advanced Research Project Agency, the McDonnell Foundation, and the National Science Foundation. NetSuite Advanced Professional Design is a trademark of NetSuite.

An early version of this chapter was published in 1998 as "Collaborative Information Environments for Innovative Communities of Practice" in *Proceeding of the German Computer-Supported Cooperative Work Conference (D-CSCW '98): Groupware und organizatorische Innovation, Dortmund, Germany* (pp. 195–210). Stuttgart: Teubner.

Chapter 6   Perspectives on Collaborative Learning

1. Previously published as G. Stahl (2001), WebGuide: Guiding collaborative learning on the Web with perspectives, *Journal of Interactive Media in Education (JIME)*, 2001(1). Available at <www-jime.open.ac.uk/2001/1/>.

This chapter grew out of the author's Readings and Research in Cognitive Science seminar, Spring 1999, on Computer Mediation of Collaborative Learning, which included the following participants: Kirstin Butcher, John Caron, Gabe Johnson, Elizabeth Lenell, Scott Long, Rogerio dePaula, Paul Prestopnik, and Tammy Sumner. The WebGuide research is a collaboration of the author with Rogerio dePaula and other L3D members, Ted Habermann and his group at the National Oceanic and Atmospheric Agency, Dan Kowal and his middle-school students, the participants in my WebGuide seminars, Thomas Herrmann and his group at Dortmund, and the researchers in the Articulate Learners project at the Institute of Cognitive Science (University of Colorado).

The first major version of this chapter was in response to Ricki Goldmann's invitation to submit to a paper session at the 1999 American Educational Research Association conference in Montreal. Earlier posters, demos, and papers on WebGuide were presented at CSCL '97, CILT '98, CSCW '98, ICLS '98, Interaktion in Web: Innovative Kommunikationsformen '98, WebNet '99, GROUP '99, CSCL '99, and CILT '99. While incorporating some of the content of these other presentations, the current chapter is based primarily on the final *Journal of Interactive Media in Education* version. The *JIME* reviewers—Helen Chappel-Hayios, Hans van der Meij, and Gary Boyd—provided supportive and stimulating reflections. Their comments were incorporated in the *JIME* publication and are summarized in the present version.

The research was supported in part by grants from the National Science Foundation, the McDonnell Foundation, and the University of Colorado's Lab for New Media Strategy and Design.

Chapter 7   Groupware Goes to School

1. Previously published as G. Stahl (2002c), Groupware goes to school: Adapting BSCW to the classroom, *International Journal of Computer Applications Technology (IJCAT)*, 19(3/4), 162–174.

The ITCOLE (Innovative Technology of Collaborative Learning and Knowledge Building) project—funded by the European Commission School of Tomorrow framework grant IST-00-III.2—was a collaboration of many people from universities and schools throughout Europe. The project was conceived largely by people at the Centre for Research in Networked Learning and Knowledge Building at the University of Helsinki and at the Media Lab at the University of Art and Design Helsinki. Much of the Synergeia user interface was designed by the Media Lab group. MapTool was implemented at the University of Murcia in Spain. The implementation of most of the features described in this chapter was done by the BSCW group at Fraunhofer Institute for Applied Information Technology (FIT), near Bonn, Germany, especially by Rudolf Ruland and me. To carry out the adaptation of a complex system like BSCW in a way that takes advantages of the strengths of its design and does not contradict its philosophy would not be possible without detailed guidance from the BSCW development staff, including Thomas Koch, Elke Hinrichs, Wolfgang Appelt, and Gerd Woetzel, in addition to Rudolf. I am grateful to all the people at FIT who made my year there possible, productive, and enjoyable.

Parts of this chapter originally formed a user manual for Synergeia. An early version of this chapter was presented at the C-R International Workshop on Groupware (CRIWG '02) in La Serena, Chile, September 1–3, 2002. A number of CRIWG reviewers and participants made suggestions that significantly improved this chapter.

Chapter 8   Knowledge Negotiation Online

1. Previously published as G. Stahl (2003b), Knowledge negotiation in asynchronous learning networks, Paper presented at the Hawaii International Conference on System Sciences (HICSS '03), Hawaii, HA.

The concept of knowledge negotiation grew out of discussions at Fraunhofer-FIT, where I had the pleasure of working in 2001 and 2002. The BSCL system was implemented there with the help of the BSCW development team (especially Rudolf Ruland and Thomas Koch) as part of the European Commission's ITCOLE Project IST-2000-26249. My interest in negotiation goes back to discussions begun in 1997 with Thomas Herrmann and his students, both in Boulder and in Dortmund. The chapter has also benefited from personal communications with Volker Wulf, as well as from comments by several HICSS reviewers.

Chapter 9   A Model of Collaborative Knowledge Building

1. Previously published as G. Stahl (2000c), A model of collaborative knowledge building, in *Proceedings of the Fourth International Conference of the Learning Sciences (ICLS '00), Ann Arbor, Michigan, June 14–17, 2000* pp. 70–77 (Mahwah, NJ: Lawrence Erlbaum).

This chapter was motivated by modeling sessions with Thomas Herrmann and Kai-Uwe Loser during a visit to the University of Dortmund in June 1999 and exchanges with Tim Koschmann while he was a visiting professor in Boulder. The alternative models appended to the end of the chapter use the conventions of Herrmann's SeeMe editor. The original paper benefited from comments by collaborative in my fall 1999 seminar on knowledge-building environments, participants in the CSCL '99 workshop on knowledge-building environments, and reviewers for ICLS 2000.

Chapter 10   Rediscovering the Collaboration

1. Previously published as G. Stahl (2002d), Rediscovering CSCL, in T. Koschmann, R. Hall, & N. Miyake (Eds.), *CSCL 2: Carrying forward the conversation* (pp. 169–181). Hillsdale, NJ: Lawrence Erlbaum.

The view of collaborative learning as visible in interaction is itself a collaborative product that has emerged in interactions of the author with Timothy Koschmann as well as with Curtis LeBaron, Robert Craig, Alena Sanusi, and other members of a fall 2000 seminar on CSCL.

Chapter 11   Contributions to a Theory of Collaboration

1. Previously published as G. Stahl (2002b), Contributions to a theoretical framework for CSCL, in *Proceeding of the International Conference on Computer-Supported Collaborative*

Learning (CSCL '02), Boulder, Colorado, January 7–11 (pp. 1–2, 62–71) (Hillsdale, NJ: Lawrence Erlbaum).

The ideas in this chapter grew out of collaborative knowledge building mediated by WebGuide in a series of seminars on CSCL at the University of Colorado. I would particularly like to thank participants Alena Sanusi, Curt LeBaron, and Bob Craig from the Communication Department as well as the teachers and students at Platt Middle School in Boulder who were involved with SimRocket. The introduction part of this chapter is taken from the introduction to the CSCL '02 *Proceedings* (Stahl, 2002a). The remainder was a paper I presented at that conference; Jeremy Roschelle was the discussant.

2. Koschmann, in his keynote address, would no doubt prefer the term *meaning making* to *knowledge building* because *knowledge* carries Cartesian connotations of mental objects. But so does *meaning*—or any terms in which learning has been conceptualized in mainstream modern Western thought. Carl Bereiter's (2002) focus on knowledge objects underlines their intersubjective, publicly accessible character. His easily misinterpreted reference to Popperian ontology is best replaced by an analysis of artifacts as physical objects embodying meaning—as Bereiter now does (personal communication, June 25, 2004).

3. The interpersonal nature of learning is established in the relationship of a young child with his or her parents. The social can be very personal. Throughout the duration of my relationship with my parents, they motivated my attitude toward the generation of knowledge as social praxis. I wrote the introduction to these *Proceedings* on November 19, 2001, the final day of my parents' living relationship with me, and in my mind this chapter is dedicated to the memory of that relationship.

Chapter 12   In a Moment of Collaboration

1. Previously published as G. Stahl (2002e), Understanding educational computational artifacts across community boundaries, Paper presented at the Conference of the International Society for Cultural Research and Activity Theory (ISCRAT '02), Amsterdam.

Thanks to Tim Koschmann, who has long pushed me in the direction of this kind of analysis, and to Curt LeBaron and Bob Craig, who opened up the communication-based microethnographic approach to me. Much of the transcription and many of the insights into the interaction were due to Alena Sanusi. Support for the original research while at the Center for Life Long Learning and Design at Colorado was from the McDonnell Foundation, the National Science Foundation, and Omnicom. The analysis and writing continued while I was in the CSCW group of Fraunhofer-FIT near Bonn, Germany. This work was presented in various formats at ISCRAT '02, ICLS '02, and Ethnography in Education '01 and '03.

2. The materials from this seminar are still available as of this writing at <http://www.cis.drexel.edu/faculty/gerry/readings>. This includes logs, digitized clips, transcripts, SimRocket, reading lists, and related documents. The learning moment itself can be viewed at <http://www.cis.drexel.edu/faculty/gerry/readings/simrocket/collab_short.mov>.

3. Note on the transcription: Numbers in parentheses indicate length of pause in seconds. Brackets between lines indicate overlap. An equal sign between utterances indicates a lack of pause between them. An underscore indicates verbal emphasis.

Chapter 13   Collaborating with Relational References

1. Previously published as G. Stahl (2004c), Collaborating with relational references, Paper presented at the workshop on representational guidance at the American Educational Research Association (AERA 2004), San Diego, CA.

Rogers Hall made two suggestive observations related to the SimRocket data at a workshop on video analysis at the International Conference of the Learning Sciences (ICLS 2002), where I presented the data from chapter 12: (1) that divergent interpretations of a group discourse might open a space for group creativity and (2) that the deictic relation of "This one's different" is not to a simple rocket object but to a more complex relationship among objects and that such a complexity caused problems for both the students and the analysts. I have attempted to explore these suggestions (1) by trying to understand the interaction of group meaning and individual interpretation in later chapters and (2) by looking at the relational character of the reference in this chapter.

Chapter 14   Communicating with Technology

1. A condensed version of this chapter, translated and revised by Angela Carell, was previously published as G. Stahl & A. Carell (2004), Kommunikationskonzepte (The role of communication concepts for CSCL pedagogy), in J. Haake, G. Schwabe & M. Wessner (Eds.), *CSCL-Kompendium* (pp. 229–237). Munich: Oldenbourg.

Chapter 15   Building Collaborative Knowing

1. Previously published as G. Stahl (2004a), Building collaborative knowing: Elements of a social theory of CSCL, In J.-W. Strijbos, P. Kirschner, & R. Martens (Eds.), *What we know about CSCL: And implementing it in higher education* (pp. 53–86). Boston, MA: Kluwer.

This chapter was originally written as the theory chapter for the edited volume in the Kluwer CSCL series. As a result of working with Jan-Willem Strijbos on that project, I invited him to work on my research at Drexel for five months in early 2004. During his visit, we celebrated the publication of his book, intertwined our contrasting methodological proclivities and discussed the first draft of this book.

Chapter 16   Group Meaning / Individual Interpretation

1. Previously published as G. Stahl (2003c), Meaning and interpretation in collaboration, in B. Wasson, S. Ludvigsen, & U. Hoppe (Eds.), *Designing for change in networked learning environments* (pp. 523–532). Boston: Kluwer.

This chapter was the final plenary presentation at CSCL '03 in Bergen, Norway, where it was well received. Subsequent comments from students in Dan Suthers's class and in my CSCL seminar led me to expand several central points.

2. The analysis of the artifact eliminates the need to hypothesize the neo-Platonic "third-world" objects attributed to Karl Popper (1972), in addition to physical and mental objects.

There is only one world, consisting of various kinds of meaningful artifacts and people who interpret their meanings. The fact that something like a theory or a musical composition can have a *meaning* that transcends any particular *interpretation* or instantiation of it merely reflects the nature of meaning as a distillate or emergent Gestalt that abstracts from the sum of its concrete manifestations. As shared within a community, meaning exists at a different level of analysis than its interpretation by individuals, but not in a different world.

Chapter 17   Shared Meaning, Common Ground, Group Cognition

1. Previously published as G. Stahl (2004b), Can community knowledge exceed its members'?, *ACM SigGroup Bulletin, 23*(3): 1–13.

Parts of this chapter began life within one of the Virtual Math Teams research proposals coauthored with Stephen Weimar, Wesley Shumar, and Ian Underwood of the Math Forum @ Drexel. Early versions were presented at the Communities and Technology 2003 Conference in Amsterdam and at GROUP 2003 on Sanibel Island, Florida.

Chapter 18   Making Group Cognition Visible

1. The central section of this chapter is based on T. Koschmann, G. Stahl, & A. Zemel (2005), The video analyst's manifesto (or the implications of Garfinkel's policies for the development of a program of video analytic research within the learning sciences), in R. Goldman, R. Pea, B. Barron, & S. Derry (Eds.), *Video research in the learning sciences* (Mahwah: Lawrence Erlbaum). That document adhered more closely to the terminology of ethnomethodology (Garfinkel, 1967). My coauthors are not responsible for the liberties taken in reinterpreting their ideas here. After so much e-mail-mediated collaboration on the text and the influences of the sources indexed or the effects of resituating the argument in the context of this book, it is no longer possible to attribute most of the ideas to any one author, and this chapter should particularly be considered a product of group cognition, although my cothinkers would reject many of the formulations in this text.

The distinction of five perspectives (returned to in chapter 21) originated in a talk I gave at ISCRAT '02 in Amsterdam on "Understanding Educational Computational Artifacts Across Community Boundaries." (Most of the rest of that talk is presented in chapter 12.)

Chapter 19   Can Collaborative Groups Think?

1. Ideas for this chapter were previously published as G. Stahl (2005), Group cognition: The collaborative locus of agency in CSCL, Closing plenary paper presented at the international conference on Computer-Supported Collaborative Learning (CSCL '05), Taipei, Taiwan. Comments by anonymous reviewers for CSCL 2005 prompted minor clarifications in this and the next chapter.

Chapter 20   Opening New Worlds for Collaboration

1. Previously published as G. Stahl (2003a), Keynote talk: The future of computer support for learning: An American/German DeLFIc vision, in A. Bode, J. Desel, S. Rathmeyer, & M. Wessner (Eds.), *DeLFI 2003, Tagungsband der 1. e-Learning Fachtagung Informatik, 16–18 September 2003 in Garching bei München* (pp. 13–16). Bonn: Köllen-Druck.

I began to explore these themes on the occasion of a keynote talk that opened the first German computer science conference on e-learning, DeLFI 2003 in Munich. Discussions of other chapters from part III with Rupert Wegerif at the Kaleidoscope CSCL Symposium 2004 in Lausanne and with Sten Ludvigsen and his colleagues at InterMedia in Oslo pushed me to extend the considerations. Translations of the Heidegger and Marx quotations have been taken from my philosophy dissertation (Stahl, 1975b), where they are discussed more thoroughly.

Chapter 21   Thinking at the Small-Group Unit of Analysis

1. Previously published as G. Stahl (2004d), Thinking at the group unit of analysis, Paper presented at the CSCL-Sig Symposium of Kaleidoscope, Lausanne, Switzerland.

This chapter is based on a paper delivered at the first Symposium of the CSCL Sig of the Kaleidoscope Network of Excellence of the European Union, in October 2004. It was the final paper presentation there and was well received. Versions of that talk were also presented at Drexel University in Philadelphia, Knowledge Media Research Center in Tübingen, Intermedia in Oslo, and Fraunhofer-FIT near Bonn. The analysis of the chat excerpt was subsequently extended with help from Alan Zemel and his conversation-analysis seminar at the Virtual Math Teams project. The VMT project is supported in part by grants from the National Science Foundation.

References

Ackerman, M. S. & McDonald, D. W. (1996). *Answer garden 2: Merging organizational memory with collaborative help*. In *Proceedings of the Sixth Conference on Computer Supported Cooperative Work (CSCW 96): Cooperating Communities, Boston, November 16–20, 1996* (pp. 97–105). New York: ACM.

Adorno, T. W. & Horkheimer, M. (1945). *The dialectic of enlightenment* (J. Cumming, Trans.). New York: Continuum.

Adorno, T. W. (1958). Der essay als form (The essay as form). In *Noten zur literatur I* (pp. 9–48). Frankfurt am Main, Germany: Suhrkamp.

Adorno, T. W. (1984). The essay as form. *New German Critique, 32*(2), 151–171. (Original work published in 1958).

Adorno, T. W. (1973). *The jargon of authenticity*. Evanston, IL: Northwestern University Press. (Original work published in 1964).

Adorno, T. W. (1967). *Prisms* (S. S. Weber, Trans.). Letchworth, UK: Neville Spearman.

Alexander, C. (1964). *Notes on the synthesis of form*. Cambridge, MA: Harvard University Press.

Ambach, P., Perrone, C., & Repenning, A. (1995). Remote exploratoriums: Combining networking media and design environments to support engaged learning. *Computers & Education, 24*(3), 163–176.

American Astronomical Society. (1966). *Stepping stones to Mars meeting*. Washington, DC: American Institute of Aeronautics and Astronautics.

Appelt, W. (1999). WWW-based collaboration with the BSCW system. In Jan Pavelka, Gerad Tel, & Miroslav Bartosek (Eds.), *Proceedings of the Twenty-sixth Annual Conference on Current Trends in Theory and Practice of Informatics (SOFSEM '99), Milovy, Czech Republic* (pp. 66–78). Berlin: Springer-Verlag.

Appelt, W. & Klöckner, K. (1999). Flexible workgroup cooperation based on shared workspaces. In *Proceedings of the Third World Multiconference on Systems, Cybernetics, and Informatics (SCI '99) and the Fifth International Conference on Information Systems Analysis and Synthesis (ISAS '99), Orlando, Florida, July 30 to August 3, 1999 (5 vols.)* (pp. 34–39). Orlando, FL: International Institute of Informatics and Systemics.

Argyris, C. & Schön, D. A. (1978). *Organizational learning: A theory of action perspective.* Reading, MA: Addison-Wesley.

Austin, J. (1952). *How to do things with words.* Boston, MA: Harvard University Press.

Baker, M., Hansen, T., Joiner, R., & Traum, D. (1999). The role of grounding in collaborative learning tasks. In P. Dillenbourg (Ed.), *Collaborative learning: Cognitive and computational approaches* (pp. 31–63). Oxford, UK: Pergamon.

Bakhtin, M. (1986a). *Speech genres and other late essays* (V. McGee, Trans.). Austin: University of Texas Press.

Bakhtin, M. M. (1986b). The problem of speech genres (V. McGee, Trans.). In C. Emerson & M. Holquist (Eds.), *Speech genres and other late essays* (pp. 60–102). Austin: University of Texas Press.

Barrows, H. (1994). *Practice-based learning: Problem-based learning applied to medical education.* Springfield: Southern Illinois University School of Medicine.

Bauersfeld, H. (1995). "Language games" in the mathematics classroom: Their function and their effects. In P. C. H. Bauersfeld (Ed.), *The emergence of mathematical meaning: Interaction in classroom cultures* (pp. 271–289). Hillsdale, NJ: Lawrence Erlbaum.

Benjamin, W. (1969). The work of art in the age of mechanical reproduction (H. Zohn, Trans.). In H. Arendt (Ed.), *Illuminations* (pp. 217–251). New York: Schocken Books. (Original work published in 1936).

Bereiter, C. (2002). *Education and mind in the knowledge age.* Hillsdale, NJ: Lawrence Erlbaum.

Birdwhistell, R. (1970). *Kinesics and context.* Philadelphia: University of Pennsylvania Press.

Blumenfeld, P., Soloway, E., Marx, R., Krajcik, J., Guzdial, M., & Palincsar, A. (1991). Motivating project-based learning: Sustaining the doing, supporting the learning. *Educational Psychologist, 26,* 369–398.

Blumer, H. (1969). *Symbolic interactionism: Perspective and method.* Berkeley: University of California Press.

Boland, R. J. & Tenkasi, R. V. (1995). Perspective making and perspective taking in communities of knowing. *Organization Science, 6*(4), 350–372.

Borghoff, U. & Parechi, R. (1998). *Information technology for knowledge management.* Berlin, Germany: Springer Verlag.

Bourdieu, P. (1995). *Outline of a theory of practice* (R. Nice, Trans.). Cambridge, UK: Cambridge University Press. (Original work published in 1972).

Bowker, G. C. & Star, S. L. (2000). *Sorting things out: Classification and its consequences (inside technology).* Cambridge, MA: MIT Press.

Brown, A. & Campione, J. (1994). Guided discovery in a community of learners. In K. McGilly (Ed.), *Classroom lessons: Integrating cognitive theory and classroom practice* (pp. 229–270). Cambridge, MA: MIT Press.

Brown, J. S. & Duguid, P. (1991). Organizational learning and communities-of-practice: Toward a unified view of working, learning, and innovation. *Organization Science, 2*(1), 40–57.

Bruner, J. (1990). *Acts of meaning.* Cambridge, MA: Harvard University Press.

Buckingham Shum, S. & Hammond, N. (1994). Argumentation-based design rationale: What use at what cost? *International Journal of Human-Computer Studies, 40*(4), 603–652.

Buckingham Shum, S. (1998). Negotiating the construction of organizational memories. In U. Borghoff & R. Parechi (Eds.), *Information technology for knowledge management* (pp. 55–78). Berlin: Springer Verlag.

Bush, V. (1945). As we may think. *Atlantic Monthly, 176*(1), 101–108.

Caron, J. (1998). Wide area collaboration: A proposed application. Paper presented at the 1998 Association for Computing Machinery (ACM) Conference on Computer Supported Collaborative Work (CSCW 98), Seattle, WA, November 14–18.

Chomsky, N. (1969). *Aspects of a theory of syntax.* Cambridge, MA: MIT Press.

Clark, H. & Brennan, S. (1991). Grounding in communication. In L. Resnick, J. Levine, & S. Teasley (Eds.), *Perspectives on socially shared cognition* (pp. 127–149). Washington, DC: APA.

Cobb, P. (1995). Mathematical learning and small-group interaction: Four case studies. In P. C. H. Bauersfeld (Ed.), *The emergence of mathematical meaning: Interaction in classroom cultures* (pp. 25–129). Mahwah, NJ: Lawrence Erlbaum.

Cohen, E. G., Lotan, R. A., Abram, P. L., Scarloss, B. A., & Schultz, S. E. (2002). Can groups learn? *Teachers College Record, 104*(6), 1045–1068.

Cole, M. (1996). *Cultural psychology.* Cambridge, MA: Harvard University Press.

Collins, A., & Stevens, A. R. (1983). Goals and strategies of inquiry teachers. In R. Glaser (Ed.), *Advances in instructional psychology* (pp. 65–119). Hillsdale, NJ: Lawrence Erlbaum.

Collins, D. (1985). *Psychological issues relevant to astronaut selection for long duration spaceflight: A review of the literature.* Texas: USAF Systems Command, Brooks Air Force Base.

Connolly, T. (1997). Electronic brainstorming: Science meets technology in the group meeting room. In S. Kiesler (Ed.), *Culture of the Internet* (pp. 263–276). Hillsdale, NJ: Lawrence Erlbaum Associates.

Cox, E. (1994). *The fuzzy systems handbook.* Boston: Academic Press.

Crook, C. (1994). *Computers and the collaborative experience of learning.* London: Routledge.

de Saussure, F. (1959). *Course in general linguistics* (W. Baskin, Trans.). New York: Philosophical Library.

Dennett, D. C. (1991). *Consciousness explained.* Boston: Little Brown.

dePaula, R. (1998). Computer support for collaborative learning: Understanding practices and technology adoption. Master's thesis, Telecommunications Department, University of Colorado, Boulder, CO.

Derrida, J. (1984). Différance. In *Margins of philosophy* (pp. 1–28). Chicago: University of Chicago. (Original work published in 1968).

Descartes, R. (1999). *Discourse on method and meditations on first philosophy.* New York: Hackett. (Original work published in 1633).

Design-Based Research Collective. (2003). Design-based research: An emerging paradigm for educational inquiry. *Educational Researcher, 32*(1), 5–8.

Dewey, J. (1991). Logic: The theory of inquiry. In J. A. Boydston (Ed.), *John Dewey: The later works, 1925–1953* (Vol. 12, pp. 1–5). Carbondale: Southern Illinois University Press. (Original work published in 1938).

Dewey, J. & Bentley, A. (1991). Knowing and the known. In J. A. Boydston (Ed.), *John Dewey: The later works, 1925–1953* (Vol. 16). Carbondale: Southern Illinois University Press. (Original work published in 1949).

Dillenbourg, P. (1999). What do you mean by "collaborative learning"? In P. Dillenbourg (Ed.), *Collaborative learning: Cognitive and computational approaches* (pp. 1–16). Amsterdam: Pergamon, Elsevier Science.

Donald, M. (1991). *Origins of the modern mind: Three stages in the evolution of culture and cognition.* Cambridge, MA: Harvard University Press.

Donath, J., Karahalios, K., & Viegas, F. (1999). Visualizing conversation. *Journal of Computer Mediated Communication, 4*(4). Retrieved from <www.ascusc.org/jcmc/vol4/issue4/donath.html>.

Dourish, P. (2001). *Where the action is: The foundations of embodied interaction.* Cambridge, MA: MIT Press.

Dreyfus, H. (1972). *What computers cannot do.* New York: Harper & Row.

Dreyfus, H. & Dreyfus, S. (1986). *Mind over machine: The power of human intuition and expertise in the era of the computer.* New York: Free Press.

Dreyfus, H. (1991). *Being-in-the-world: A commentary on Heidegger's* Being and Time, *division I.* Cambridge, MA: MIT Press.

Dreyfus, H. (1992). *What computers still can't do: A critique of artificial reason.* Cambridge, MA: MIT Press.

Duranti, A. (1998). *Linguistic anthropology.* Cambridge, UK: Cambridge University Press.

Ehn, P. (1988). *Work-oriented design of computer artifacts.* Stockholm, Sweden: Arbetslivscentrum.

Engeström, Y. (1999). Activity theory and individual and social transformation. In Y. Engeström, R. Miettinen, & R.-L. Punamäki (Eds.), *Perspectives on activity theory* (pp. 19–38). Cambridge, UK: Cambridge University Press.

Engeström, Y., Engeström, R., & Vähäaho, T. (1999). When the center does not hold: The importance of knotworking. In S. Chaiklin, M. Hedegaard, & U. J. Jensen (Eds.), *Activity theory and social practice: Cultural-historical approaches* (pp. 345–374). Aarhus, Denmark: Aarhus University Press.

Engeström, Y., Miettinen, R., & Punamäki, R.-L. (Eds.). (1999). *Perspectives on activity theory.* New York: Cambridge University Press.

Fischer, G., Nakakoji, K., Ostwald, J., Stahl, G., & Sumner, T. (1993). Embedding computer-based critics in the contexts of design. In S. Ashlund (Ed.), *Human Factors in Computer Systems: Interchi '93, Proceedings of the Interchi '93, Amsterdam, the Netherlands, 24–29 April 1993* (pp. 157–164). Retrieved from <www.cis.drexel.edu/faculty/gerry/publications/conferences/1990-1997/chi93/CHI93.html>.

Fischer, G. (1994). Domain-oriented design environments. *Automated Software Engineering,* 1(2), 177–203.

Fischer, G., Lemke, A. C., McCall, R., & Morch, A. (1996). Making argumentation serve design. In T. Moran & J. Carrol (Eds.), *Design rationale: Concepts, techniques, and use* (pp. 267–293). Mahwah, NJ: Lawrence Erlbaum.

Fischer, G., Nakakoji, K., Ostwald, J., Stahl, G., & Sumner, T. (1998). Embedding critics in design environments. In M. T. Maybury & W. Wahlster (Eds.), *Readings in intelligent user interfaces* (pp. 537–561). New York: Morgan Kaufman. Retrieved from <www.cis.drexel.edu/faculty/gerry/publications/journals/ker/index.html>.

Fischer, G., Grudin, J., McCall, R., Ostwald, J., Redmiles, D., Reeves, B., & Shipman, F. (2001). Seeding, evolutionary growth and reseeding: The incremental development of collaborative design environments. In G. M. Olson, T. W. Malone, & J. B. Smith (Eds.), *Coordination theory and collaboration technology* (pp. 447–472). Mahwah, NJ: Lawrence Erlbaum.

Fischer, K. & Granoo, N. (1995). Beyond one-dimensional change: Parallel, concurrent, socially distributed processes in learning and development. *Human Development, 1995*(38), 302–314.

Floyd, C. (1992). Software development and reality construction. In C. Floyd, H. Zuellinghoven, R. Budde, & R. Keil-Slawik (Eds.), *Software development and reality construction* (pp. 86–100). Berlin: Springer Verlag.

Floyd, C., Zuellinghoven, H., Budde, R., & Keil-Slawik, R. (1994). *Software development and reality construction.* Berlin: Springer Verlag.

Freire, P. (1970). *Pedagogy of the oppressed.* New York: Continuum.

Fu, M. C., Hayes, C. C., & East, E. W. (1997). Sedar: Expert critiquing system for flat and low-slope roof design and review. *Journal of Computing in Civil Engineering, 11*(1), 60–68.

Furnas, G. W., Landauer, T. K., Gomez, L. M., & Dumais, S. T. (1987). The vocabulary problem in human-system communication. *Communications of the ACM, 30*(11), 964–971.

Gadamer, H.-G. (1988). *Truth and method.* New York: Crossroads. (Original work published in 1960).

Garcia, A. & Jacobs, J. B. (1998). The interactional organization of computer mediated communication in the college classroom. *Qualitative Sociology, 21*(3), 299–317.

Garcia, A. & Jacobs, J. B. (1999). The eyes of the beholder: Understanding the turn-taking system in quasi-synchronous computer-mediated communication. *Research on Language and Social Interaction, 34*(4), 337–367.

Garfinkel, H. (1967). *Studies in ethnomethodology.* Englewood Cliffs, NJ: Prentice-Hall.

Garfinkel, H. (2002). *Ethnomethodology's program: Working out Durkheim's aphorism.* Lanham, MD: Rowman & Littlefield.

Geertz, C. (1973). *The interpretation of cultures.* New York: Basic Books.

Gerosa, M., Fuks, H., & de Lucena, C. (2001). Use of categorization and structuring of messages in order to organize the discussion and reduce information overload in asynchronous textual communication tools. In *Proceedings of the Seventh International Workshop on*

Groupware (CRIWG '01), September 6–8, 2001, Darmstadt, Germany (pp. 136–141). Los Alamitos, CA: IEEE Computer Society.

Gibson, J. J. (1979). *The ecological approach to visual perception.* Boston: Houghton Mifflin.

Giddens, A. (1984a). *The constitution of society.* Berkeley: University of California Press.

Giddens, A. (1984b). Elements of the theory of structuration. In *The constitution of society* (pp. 1–40). Berkeley: University of California Press.

Goldman-Segall, R. (1998). *Points of viewing children's thinking.* Mahwah, NJ: Lawrence Erlbaum.

Goodwin, C. & Goodwin, M. H. (1994). Professional vision. *American Anthropologist, 96*(3), 606–633.

Greenbaum, J. & Kyng, M. (1991). *Design at work: Cooperative design of computer systems.* Hillsdale, NJ: Lawrence Erlbaum.

Greeno, J. (1993). For research to reform education and cognitive science. In L. Penner, G. Batsche, H. Knoff, & D. Nelson, (Ed.), *The challenge in mathematics and science education: Psychology's response* (pp. 153–192). New York: APA Press.

Grudin, J. (1990). Why CSCW applications fail: Problems in design and evaluation. In F. Halasz (Ed.), *Proceedings of the Third Conference on Computer Supported Cooperative Work (CSCW '90), Los Angeles, California, October 7–10* (pp. 85–93). New York: ACM.

Guzdial, M. & Turns, J. (2000). Effective discussion through a computer-mediated anchored discussion forum. *Journal of the Learning Sciences, 9,* 437–469.

Habermas, J. (1971). Knowledge and human interests. In *Knowledge and human interests.* Boston: Beacon Press. (Original work published in 1965).

Habermas, J. (1971). Labor and interaction: Remarks on Hegel's Jena philosophy of mind. In *Theory and practice* (pp. 142–169). Boston: Beacon Press.

Habermas, J. (1984). *Reason and the rationalization of society* (Vol. 1) (T. McCarthy, Trans.). Boston, MA: Beacon Press. (Original work published in 1981).

Hakkarainen, K. & Sintonen, M. (2001). The interrogative model of inquiry and computer-supported collaborative learning. *Science & Education, 11*(1), 25–43.

Hall, R. & Stevens, R. (1995). Making space: A comparison of mathematical work in school and professional design practices. In S. L. Star (Ed.), *The cultures of computing.* Oxford, UK: Blackwell Publishers.

Hall, R. (2000). Work at the interface between representing and represented worlds in middle school mathematics design projects. In L. R. Gleitman & A. K. Joshi (Eds.), *Proceedings of the Twenty-second Annual Conference of the Cognitive Science Society (CogSci 2000), Institute for Research in Cognitive Science, University of Pennsylvania, Pennsylvania, August 13–15, 2000* (pp. 675–680). Mahwah, NJ: Lawrence Erlbaum.

Halliday, M. A. K. (1985). *An introduction to functional grammar.* London: Edward Arnold.

Harre, R. & Gillet, G. (1999). *The discursive mind.* London: Sage.

Harrison, A., Clearwater, Y., & McKay, C. (1991). From Antarctica to outer space: Life in isolation and confinement. *Behavioral Science, 34,* 253–271.

Hatano, G. & Inagaki, K. (1991). Sharing cognition through collective comprehension activity. In L. Resnick, J. Levine & S. Teasley (Eds.), *Perspectives on socially shared cognition* (pp. 331–348). Washington, DC: APA.

Heath, C. (1986). Video analysis: Interactional coordination in movement and speech. In *Body movement and speech in medical interaction* (pp. 1–24). Cambridge, UK: Cambridge University Press.

Hegel, G. W. F. (1967). *Phenomenology of spirit* (J. B. Baillie, Trans.). New York: Harper & Row. (Original work published in 1807).

Heidegger, M. (1996). *Being and time: A translation of Sein und Zeit* (J. Stambaugh, Trans.). Albany, NY: SUNY Press. (Original work published in 1927).

Heidegger, M. (1964). The origin of the work of art (A. Hofstadter, Trans.). In A. Hofstadter & R. Kuhns (Eds.), *Philosophies of art and beauty* (pp. 647–701). New York: Modern Library. (Original work published in 1935).

Heidegger, M. (2003). Der Ursprung des Kunstwerkes. In M. Heidegger (Ed.), *Holzwege*. Frankfurt A. M., Germany: Klostermann. (Original work published in 1935).

Heidegger, M. (1967a). Das Ding. In *Vorträge und Aufsätze II* (pp. 37–60). Pfullingen, Germany: Neske. (Original work published in 1950).

Heidegger, M. (1967b). Bauen Wohnen Denken. In *Vorträge und Aufsätze II* (pp. 19–36). Pfullingen, Germany: Neske. (Original work published in 1951).

Heidegger, M. (1967c). Die Frage nach der Technik. In *Vorträge und Aufsätze I* (pp. 5–36). Pfullingen, Germany: Neske. (Original work published in 1953).

Heidegger, M. (1971). *On the way to language*. New York: Harper & Row. (Original work published in 1959).

Heidegger, M. (1969). *Raum und Kunst*. St. Gallen, Switzerland: Erker Verlag.

Henderson, B. & Wyman, J. (2002). *CSCL 2002 DVD*. Mahwah, NJ: Lawrence Erlbaum.

Heritage, J. (1984). *Garfinkel and ethnomethodology*. Cambridge, UK: Polity Press.

Herrmann, T. (1995). Workflow management systems: Ensuring organizational flexibility by possibilities of adaption and negotiation. In *Proceedings of the ACM Conference on Organizational Computing Systems 1995 (COOCS '95, Milpitas, California, August 13–16)* (pp. 83–94). New York: ACM Press.

Herrmann, T., Wulf, V., & Hartmann, A. (1996). Requirements for a human-centered design of groupware. In D. Shapiro, M. Tauber, & R. Traunmüller (Eds.), *Design of computer supported cooperative work and groupware systems* (pp. 77–99). Amsterdam: Elsevier.

Herrmann, T. & Kienle, A. (2002). Kolumbus: Context-oriented communication support in a collaborative learning environment. In Tom J. van Weert and Robert Munro (Eds.), *SInformatics and the Digital Society: Social, Ethical, and Cognitive Issues. Proceedings of the Open Conference on Social, Ethical, and Cognitive Issues of Informatics and Information and Communication Technology, Dortmund, Germany, July 22–26, 2002)* (pp. 251–260). Amsterdam: Kluwer. Retrieved from <iugsun.cs.uni-dortmund.de:2048/pub/bscw.cgi/d219854/30206.pdf>.

Hewitt, J. (1997). Beyond threaded discourse. In *Proceedings of the Second World Conference of the World Wide Web, Internet, and Intranet (WebNet '97), Toronto, October 31–November 1997*. Norfolk VA: Association for the Advancement of Computing in Education (AACE). CD-ROM.

Hewitt, J., Scardamalia, M., & Webb, J. (1998). Situative design issues for interactive learning environments Retrieved from <csile.oise.on.ca/abstracts/situ_design>.

Hewitt, J. & Teplovs, C. (1999). An analysis of growth patterns in computer conferencing threads. In *Proceedings of the Conference on Computer-Supported Collaborative Learning (CSCL '99), Palo Alto, California, December 12–15, 1999* (pp. 232–241). Mahwah, NJ: Lawrence Erlbaum.

Hopper, R. (1992). *Telephone conversation*. Bloomington: Indiana University Press.

Husserl, E. (1989). The origin of geometry (D. Carr, Trans.). In J. Derrida (Ed.), *Edmund Husserl's origin of geometry: An introduction* (pp. 157–180). Lincoln: University of Nebraska Press. (Original work published in 1936).

Hutchins, E. (1996). *Cognition in the wild*. Cambridge, MA: MIT Press.

Hutchins, E. (1999). Cognitive artifacts. In *MIT encyclopedia of the cognitive sciences*. Cambridge, MA: MIT Press. Retrieved from <cognet.mit.edu/library/MITECS>.

Jaynes, J. (1976). *The origin of consciousness in the breakdown of the bicameral mind*. Boston: Houghton Mifflin.

Johnson, D. W. & Johnson, R. T. (1989). *Cooperation and competition: Theory and research*. Edina, MN: Interaction Book Company.

Johnson, S. (2001). *Emergence: The connected lives of ants, brains, cities, and software*. New York: Simon & Schuster.

Jordan, B. & Henderson, A. (1995). Interaction analysis: Foundations and practice. *Journal of the Learning Sciences, 4*(1), 39–103. Retrieved from <lrs.ed.uiuc.edu/students/c-merkel/document4.htm>.

Kant, I. (1999). *Critique of pure reason*. Cambridge, UK: Cambridge University Press. (Original work published in 1787).

Kaptelinin, V. & Cole, M. (2002). Individual and collective activities in educational computer game playing. In T. Koschmann, R. Hall, & N. Miyake (Eds.), *CSCL2: Carrying forward the conversation* (pp. 297–310). Mahwah, NJ: Lawrence Erlbaum.

Keil-Slawik, R. (1992). Artifacts in software design. In C. Floyd, H. Züllighoven, R. Budde, & R. Keil-Slawik (Eds.), *Software development and reality construction* (pp. 168–188). Berlin: Springer Verlag.

Kendon, A. (1990). *Conducting interaction: Patterns of behavior in focused encounters*. Cambridge, UK: Cambridge University Press.

Kintsch, E., Steinhart, D., Stahl, G., Matthews, C., Lamb, R., & LSA Research Group. (2000). Developing summarization skills through the use of LSA-backed feedback. *Interactive Learning Environments, 8*(2), 87–109. Retrieved from <www.cis.drexel.edu/faculty/gerry/publications/journals/ile2000/ile.html>.

Kling, R. (1999). What is social informatics and why does it matter? *D-Lib Magazine, 5*(1).Retrieved from <www.dlib.org/dlib/january99/kling/01kling.html>.

Kling, R. & Courtright, C. (2004). Group behavior and learning in electronic forums: A socio-technical approach. In S. A. Barab, R. Kling, & J. H. Gray (Eds.), *Designing for virtual communities in the service of learning* (pp. 91–119). Cambridge, UK: Cambridge University Press.

Klöckner, K. (2001). Preparing the next generation of learning: Enhancing learning opportunities by Web-based cooperation. In *Learning without Limits: Developing the Next Generation of Education. Proceedings of the European Distance Education Network (EDEN) Tenth Anniversary Conference, Stockholm, June 10–13, 2001* (pp. 330–335). Stockholm: EDEN.

Kolodner, J. (1993). *Case-based reasoning.* San Mateo, CA: Morgan Kaufmann.

Koschmann, T. (Ed.). (1996a). *CSCL: Theory and practice of an emerging paradigm.* Hillsdale, NJ: Lawrence Erlbaum.

Koschmann, T. (1996b). Paradigm shifts and instructional technology. In T. Koschmann (Ed.), *CSCL: Theory and practice of an emerging paradigm* (pp. 1–23). Mahwah, NJ: Lawrence Erlbaum.

Koschmann, T., Ostwald, J., & Stahl, G. (1998). Shouldn't we really be studying practice? Paper presented at the International Conference on the Learning Sciences (ICLS '98), Atlanta, GA. Retrieved from <www.cis.drexel.edu/faculty/gerry/publications/conferences/1998/icls98/ICLS Workshop.html>.

Koschmann, T. & Stahl, G. (1998). Learning issues in problem-based learning: Situating collaborative information seeking. In *Proceedings of the Association for Computing Machinery (ACM) Conference on Computer Supported Cooperative Work (CSCW'98), Seattle, Washington, November 14–18, 1998.* New York: ACM Press. Retrieved from <www.cis.drexel.edu/faculty/gerry/publications/conferences/1998/cscw98/cscw_workshop.html>.

Koschmann, T. (1999a). Meaning making: Special issue. *Discourse Processes, 27*(2).

Koschmann, T. (1999b). Toward a dialogic theory of learning: Bakhtin's contribution to learning in settings of collaboration. In *Proceedings of the Conference on Computer Supported Collaborative Learning (CSCL '99), Palo Alto, California, December 12–15, 1999* (pp. 308–313). Mahwah, NJ: Lawrence Erlbaum. Retrieved from <kn.cilt.org/cscl99/A38/A38.htm>.

Koschmann, T. (2001). A third metaphor for learning: Toward a form of transactional inquiry into inquiry. In D. Klahr & S. Carver (Eds.), *Cognition and instruction: Twenty-five years of progress.* Mahwah, NJ: Lawrence Erlbaum.

Koschmann, T. (2002a). Dewey's contribution to the foundations of CSCL research. In G. Stahl (Ed.), *Computer support for collaborative learning: Foundations for a CSCL community. Proceedings of CSCL 2002* (pp. 17–22). Boulder, CO: Lawrence Erlbaum.

Koschmann, T. (2002b). Dewey's critique of learning as occult. Paper presented at the Annual Meeting of the American Educational Research Association (AERA '02), April 1–5, 2002, New Orleans.

Koschmann, T. (2002c). Differing ontologies: Eighteenth-century philosophy and the learning sciences. Paper presented at the Fifth International Conference of the Learning Sciences (ICLS '02), Seattle, Washington, 2002.

Koschmann, T. & LeBaron, C. (2003). Reconsidering common ground: Examining Clark's contribution theory in the operating room. In K. Kuutti, E. H. Karsten, G. Fitzpatrick, P. Dourish, & K. Schmidt (Eds.), In *Proceedings of the Eighth European Conference on Computer Supported Cooperative Work (ECSCW '03), Helsinki, September 14–18, 2003* (pp. 81–98). London: Springer.

Koschmann, T., Hall, R., & Miyake, N. (Eds.). (2002). *CSCL2: Carrying forward the conversation.* Mahwah, NJ: Lawrence Erlbaum.

Koschmann, T., Stahl, G., & Zemel, A. (2005). The video analyst's manifesto (or the implications of Garfinkel's policies of the development of a program of video analytic research within the learning sciences). In R. Goldman, R. Pea, B. Barron, & S. Derry (Eds.), *Video research in the learning sciences.* Mahwah, NJ: Lawrence Erlbaum.

Koyeve, A. (1969). *Introduction to the reading of Hegel* (J. James Nichols, Trans.). New York: Basic Books. (Original work published in 1947).

Kraemer, K. & Pinsonneault, A. (1990). Technology and groups: Assessment of the empirical research. In J. Galegher, R. Kraut, & C. Egido (Eds.), *Intellectual teamwork: Social and technological foundations of cooperative work* (pp. 375–405). Hillsdale, NJ: Lawrence Erlbaum.

Kreindler, L. & Zahm, B. (1992). *Mathfinder sourcebook: A collection of resources for mathematics reform.* New York: Learning Team.

Lakoff, G. (1987). *Women, fire, and dangerous things.* Chicago: University of Chicago Press.

Lamon, M., Chan, C., Scardamalia, M., Burtis, P. J., & Brett, C. (1993). Beliefs about learning and constructive processes in reading: Effects of a computer supported intentional learning environment (CSILE). Paper presented at the Annual Meeting of the American Educational Research Association (AERA '93), Atlanta, Georgia, April.

Landauer, T. K. & Dumais, S. T. (1997). A solution to Plato's problem: The latent semantic analysis theory of acquisition, induction and representation of knowledge. *Psychological Review, 104*(2), 211–240.

Landauer, T. K., Foltz, P. W., & Laham, D. (1998). Introduction to latent semantic analysis. *Discourse Processes, 25*(1), 259–284.

Latour, B. & Woolgar, S. (1979). *Laboratory life.* Thousand Oaks, CA: Sage.

Lave, J. (1988). *Cognition in practice: Mind, mathematics and culture in everyday life.* Cambridge, UK: Cambridge University Press.

Lave, J. (1991). Situating learning in communities of practice. In L. Resnick, J. Levine, & S. Teasley (Eds.), *Perspectives on socially shared cognition* (pp. 63–83). Washington, DC: APA.

Lave, J. & Wenger, E. (1991). *Situated learning: Legitimate peripheral participation.* Cambridge, UK: Cambridge University Press.

Lave, J. (1996). Teaching, as learning, in practice. *Mind, Culture, and Activity, 3*(3), 149–164.

LeBaron, C. & Streeck, J. (2000). Gesture, knowledge and the world. In D. McNeill (Ed.), *Language and gesture* (pp. 118–138). Cambridge, UK: Cambridge University Press.

Leinonen, T., Hakkarainen, K., Appelt, W., Dean, P., Gómez-Skarmetav, A., Ligorio, B., et al. (2001). ITCOLE project: Designing innovative technology for collaborative learning and knowledge building. Paper presented at the World Conference on Educational Multimedia, Hypermedia and Telecommunications (Ed-Media 2001), Tampere, Finland.

Lemke, J. (1990). *Talking science.* Norwood, NJ: Ablex.

Lenell, E. & Stahl, G. (2001). Evaluating affordance short-circuits by reviewers and authors participating in on-line journal reviews. In P. Dillenbourg, A. Eurelings, & A. Hakkarainen (Eds.), *Proceedings of the European Conference on Computer-Supported Collaborative Learning (E-CSCL '01) Maastricht, Netherlands, March 22–24, 2001* (pp. 406–413). Maastricht: University of Maastricht. Retrieved from <www.cis.drexel.edu/faculty/gerry/publications/conferences/2001/ecscl2001/ecscl.html>.

Lepperhoff, N. (2001). Sam: Untersuchung von Aushandlungen in Gruppen mittels Agentensimulation (Analysis of negotiation in groups: An agent-based simulation). Ph.D. dissertation, Informatics Department, University of Dortmund, Dortmund, Germany.

Lerner, G. (1993). Collectivities in action: Establishing the relevance of conjoined participation in conversation. *Text, 13*(2), 213–245.

Levinas, E. (1998). *Otherwise than being or beyond essence* (A. Lingis, Trans.). Pittsburgh, PA: Duquesne University Press. (Original work published in 1974).

Lim, L.-H. & Benbasat, I. (1993). A theoretical perspective on negotiation support systems. *Journal of Management Information Systems, 9*(3), 27–44.

Lindstaedt, S. (1996). Towards organizational learning: Growing group memories in the workplace. In M. J. Tauber, V. Bellotti, R. Jeffries, J. D. Mackinlay, & J. Nielsen (Eds.), *Proceedings of the Conference on Human Factors in Computing Systems (CHI '96): Common Ground, Vancouver, British Columbia, Canada, April 13–18, 1996* (pp. 14–18). New York: ACM.

Lindstaedt, S. & Schneider, K. (1997). Bridging the gap between face-to-face communication and long-term collaboration. In S. C. Hayne & W. Prinz (Eds.), In *Proceedings of Group 97: International ACM SigGroup Conference on Supporting Group Work—The Integration Challenge, Pheonix, Arizona, November 16–19* (pp. 331–340). New York: ACM.

Linell, P. (2001). *Approaching dialogue: Talk, interaction and contexts in dialogical perspectives.* New York: Benjamins.

Littlejohn, S. (1999). *Theories of human communication* (6th ed.). Belmont, CA: Wadsworth.

Marx, K. (1967a). Alienated labor. In L. G. K. Easton (Ed.), *Writings of the young Marx on philosophy and society* (pp. 287–300). New York: Doubleday. (Original work published in 1844).

Marx, K. (1967b). Theses on Feuerbach. In L. G. K. Easton (Ed.), *Writings of the young Marx on philosophy and society* (pp. 400–401). New York: Doubleday. (Original work published in 1845).

Marx, K. (1963). *The eighteenth brumaire of Louis Bonaparte.* New York: International Publishers. (Original work published in 1852).

Marx, K. (1939). *Grundrisse der Kritik der politischen Oekonomie (Rohentwurf).* Frankfurt, Germany: Europische Verlagsanstalt. (Original work published 1858).

Marx, K. (1867). *Das Kapital: Kritik der politischen Oekonomie* (Vol. 1). Hamburg, Germany: Otto Meisner.

Marx, K. (1976). *Capital* (B. Fowkes, Trans.) (Vol. 1). New York: Vintage. (Original work published in 1867).

Maturana, H. R. & Varela, F. J. (1987). *The tree of knowledge: The biological roots of human understanding.* Boston: Shambhala.

McCall, R., Bennett, P., d'Oronzio, P., Ostwald, J., Shipman, F., & Wallace, N. (1990). Phidias: Integrating cad graphics into dynamic hypertext. In A. Rizk, N. Streitz, & J. Andre (Eds.), *Hypertext: Concepts, systems and applications. Proceedings of the European Conference on Hypertext (ECHT '90)* (pp. 152–165). Cambridge, UK: Cambridge University Press.

McDowall, D., McLeary, R., Meidinger, E., & Hay, R. J. (1980). *Interrupted time series analysis.* Beverly Hills, CA: Sage.

McGrath, J. (1993). A typology of tasks. In R. Baecker (Ed.), *Readings in groupware and computer-supported cooperative work: Assisting human-human collaboration.* San Francisco: Morgan Kaufmann.

McKay, C. (1985). *The case for Mars II.* San Diego: American Astronomical Society.

Mead, G. H. (1962). *Mind, self and society.* Chicago: University of Chicago Press. (Original work published in 1934).

Merleau-Ponty, M. (2002). *The phenomenology of perception* (C. Smith, Trans.) (2nd ed.). New York: Routledge. (Original work published in 1945).

Merleau-Ponty, M. (1955). *Visible and invisible.* Evanston, IL: Northwestern University Press.

Miller, P. L. (1986). *Expert critiquing systems: Practice-based medical consultation by computer.* Berlin: Springer Verlag.

Minsky, M. (1986). *Society of mind.* New York: Simon & Schuster.

Mittal, S., Bobrow, D., & Kahn, K. (1986). Virtual copies at the boundary between classes and instances. In N. Meyrowitz (Ed.), *Proceedings of the Conference on Object-Oriented Programming Systems, Languages, and Applications (OOPSLA '86), Portland, Oregon, October 1986* (pp. 159–166). New York: ACM Press.

Muukkonen, H., Hakkarainen, K., & Leinonen, T. (2000). *Introduction to FLE2 pedagogy.* Retrieved from <fle2.uiah.fi/pedagogy.html>.

Nancy, J.-L. (2000). *Being singular plural* (R. Richardson, Trans.). Palo Alto, CA: Stanford University Press.

Nardi, B. (Ed.). (1996). *Context and consciousness: Activity theory and human-computer interaction.* Cambridge, MA: MIT Press.

NCTM. (1989). *Curriculum and evaluation standards for school mathematics.* Alexandria, VA: National Council of Teachers of Mathematics.

Nelson, T. (1981). *Literary machines.* New York: Mindful Press.

Newell, A. & Simon, H. A. (1963). GPS, a program that simulates human thought. In A. Feigenbaum & V. Feldman (Eds.), *Computers and thought* (pp. 279–293). New York: McGraw Hill.

Norman, D. (1990). *The design of everyday things.* New York: Doubleday.

Norman, D. (1991). Cognitive artifacts. In J. Carroll (Ed.), *Designing interaction.* Cambridge, UK: Cambridge University Press.

Norman, D. A. (1993). *Things that make us smart*. Reading, MA: Addison-Wesley.

Nunamaker Jr., J., Dennis, A., Valacich, J., & Vogel, D. (1991). Information technology for negotiating groups: Generating options for mutual gain. *Management Science, 37*(10), 1325–1346.

Nygaard, K. & Sørgaard, P. (1987). The perspective concept in informatics. In G. Bjerknes, P. Ehn, & M. Kyng (Eds.), *Computers and democracy: A Scandinavian challenge* (pp. 371–393). Aldershot, UK: Avebury.

O'Malley, C. (1995). *Computer supported collaborative learning*. Berlin: Springer Verlag.

Ong, W. (1998). *Orality and literacy: The technologizing of the world*. New York: Routledge.

Orlikowski, W. (1992). Learning from notes: Organizational issues in groupware implementation. In J. Turner & R. Kraut (Eds.), *Proceedings of the Fourth Conference on Computer-Supported Cooperative Work (CSCW '92), Toronto, October 31–November 4, 1992* (pp. 362–469). New York: ACM.

Orlikowski, W., Yates, Y., Okamura, K., & Fujimoto, M. (1995). Shaping electronic communication: The metastructuring of technology in the context of use. *Organization Science, 6*(4), 423–369.

Orr, J. (1990). Sharing knowledge, celebrating identity: War stories and community memory in a service culture. In D. S. Middleton & D. Edwards (Eds.), *Collective remembering: Memory in society*. Beverly Hills, CA: Sage.

Owen, R., Holland, A., & Wood, J. (1993). A prototype case-based reasoning human assistant for space crew assessment and mission management. In U. Fayyad & F. Uthurusamy (Eds.), *Applications of artificial intelligence 1993: Knowledge-based systems in aerospace and industry* (pp. 262–273). Bellingham, WA: SPIE.

Packer, M. & Goicoechea, J. (2000). Sociocultural and constructivist theories of learning: Ontology, not just epistemology. *Educational Psychologist, 35*(4), 227–241.

Pal, S., Dillon, T., & Yeung, D. (Eds.) (1996). *Soft computing in case-based reasoning*, London: Springer-Verlag.

Papert, S. (1980). *Mindstorms: Children, computers and powerful ideas*. New York: Basic Books.

Papert, S. (1993). *The children's machine: Rethinking school in the age of the computer*. New York: Basic Books.

Pea, R. (1993a). The collaborative visualization project. *Communications of the ACM, 36*(5), 60–63.

Pea, R. (1993b). Practices of distributed intelligence and designs for education. In G. Salomon (Ed.), *Distributed cognitions: Psychological and educational considerations* (pp. 47–87). Cambridge, UK: Cambridge University Press.

Perkins, D. N. (1993). Person-plus: A distributed view of thinking and learning. In G. Salomon (Ed.), *Distributed cognitions: Psychological and educational considerations* (pp. 88–110). Cambridge, UK: Cambridge University Press.

Plato. (1961). Meno. In E. Hamilton & H. Cairns (Eds.), *The collected dialogues of Plato* (pp. 353–384). Princeton, NJ: Princeton University Press. (Original work written in 350 BC).

Polanyi, M. (1962). *Personal knowledge*. London: Routledge & Kegan Paul.

Polanyi, M. (1966). *The tacit dimension.* Garden City, NY: Doubleday.

Pomerantz, A. & Fehr, B. J. (1991). Conversation analysis: An approach to the study of social action as sense making practices. In T. A. van Dijk (Ed.), *Discourse as social interaction: Discourse studies, a multidisciplinary introduction* (Vol. 2, pp. 64–91). London: Sage.

Popper, K. (1972). *Objective knowledge: An evolutionary approach.* Oxford, UK: Clarendon Press.

Preece, J., Rogers, Y., & Sharp, H. (2002). *Interaction design: Beyond human-computer interaction.* New York: Wiley.

Prevignano, C. & Thibault, P. (2003). *Discussing conversation analysis: The work of Emanuel A. Schegloff.* Amsterdam: John Benjamins.

Psathas, G. (1995). *Conversation analysis: The study of talk-in-interaction.* Thousand Oaks, CA: Sage.

Radloff, R. & Helmreich, R. (1968). *Groups under stress: Psychological research in Sealab II.* New York: Appleton Century Crofts.

Raymond, E. (2001). *The cathedral and the bazaar: Musings on Linux and open source by an accidental revolutionary.* New York: O'Reilly.

Remillard, J. & Bryans, M. (2004). Teachers' orientations toward mathematics curriculum materials: Implications for curricular change. *Journal for Research in Mathematics Education, 35*(5), 352–388.

Repenning, A. (1994). Programming substrates to create interactive learning environments. *Journal of Interactive Learning Environments, Special Issue on End-User Environments, 4*(1), 45–74.

Repenning, A. & Sumner, T. (1995). Agentsheets: A medium for creating domain-oriented visual programming languages. *IEEE Computer. Special issue on visual programming, March.*

Resnick, L., Levine, J., & Teasley, S. (Eds.) (1991). *Perspectives on socially shared cognition.* Washington, DC: American Psychological Association.

Ricoeur, P. (1976). *Interpretation theory: Discourse and the surplus of meaning.* Fort Worth: Texas Christian University Press.

Riesbeck, C. & Schank, R. (1989). *Inside case-based reasoning.* Hillsdale, NJ: Lawrence Erlbaum.

Rittel, H. & Webber, M. (1973). Dilemmas in a general theory of planning. *Policy Science, 4,* 155–169.

Rittel, H. & Webber, M. M. (1984). Planning problems are wicked problems. In N. Cross (Ed.), *Developments in design methodology* (pp. 135–144). New York: Wiley.

Robbins, J. E. & Redmiles, D. F. (1998). Software architecture critics in the argo design environment. *Knowledge-Based Systems,* 47–60.

Roschelle, J. (1996). Learning by collaborating: Convergent conceptual change. In T. Koschmann (Ed.), *CSCL: Theory and practice of an emerging paradigm* (pp. 209–248). Hillsdale, NJ: Lawrence Erlbaum.

Rumelhart, D. A. & McClelland, J. L. (1986). *Parallel distributed processing: Explorations in the microstructure of cognition* (Vols. 1–2). Cambridge, MA: MIT Press.

Russell, T. (Ed.). (1999). *The no significant difference phenomenon.* Mindspring Press. Retrieved from <cuda.teleeducation.nb.ca/nosignificantdifference>.

Sacks, H., Schegloff, E. A., & Jefferson, G. (1974). A simplest systematics for the organization of turn-taking for conversation. *Language, 50*(4), 696–735. Retrieved from <www.jstor.org>.

Sacks, H. (1992). *Lectures on conversation.* Oxford, UK: Blackwell.

Salomon, G. (1993a). *Distributed cognitions: Psychological and educational considerations.* Cambridge, UK: Cambridge University Press.

Salomon, G. (1993b). No distribution without individuals' cognition: A dynamic interactional view. In G. Salomon (Ed.), *Distributed cognitions: Psychological and educational considerations* (pp. 111–137). Cambridge, UK: Cambridge University Press.

Sartre, J.-P. (1968). *Search for a method* (H. Barnes, Trans.). New York: Random House.

Scardamalia, M. & Bereiter, C. (1991). Higher levels of agency in knowledge building: A challenge for the design of new knowledge media. *Journal of the Learning Sciences, 1,* 37–68.

Scardamalia, M. & Bereiter, C. (1996). Computer support for knowledge-building communities. In T. Koschmann (Ed.), *CSCL: Theory and practice of an emerging paradigm* (pp. 249–268). Hillsdale, NJ: Lawrence Erlbaum.

Schank, R. (1982). *Dynamic memory.* Cambridge, UK: Cambridge University Press.

Schegloff, E. (1991a). Conversation analysis and socially shared cognition. In L. Resnick, J. Levine, & S. Teasley (Eds.), *Perspectives on socially shared cognition* (pp. 150–171). Washington, DC: APA.

Schegloff, E. (1991b). Reflections on talk and social structure. In E. Boden & D. Zimmerman (Eds.), *Talk and social structure: Studies in ethnomethodology and conversation analysis* (pp. 44–70). Berkeley: University of California Press.

Schegloff, E. A., Jefferson, G., & Sacks, H. (1977). The preference for self-correction in the organization of repair in conversation. *Language, 53*(2), 361–382. Retrieved from <www.jstor.org>.

Schegloff, E. & Sacks, H. (1973). Opening up closings. *Semiotica, 8,* 289–327.

Schön, D. (1992). Designing as reflective conversation with the materials of a design situation. *Knowledge-Based Systems Journal, Special Issue on AI in Design, 5*(1), 3–14.

Schön, D. A. (1983). *The reflective practitioner: How professionals think in action.* New York: Basic Books.

Schutz, A. (1967). *Phenomenology of the social World* (F. Lehnert, Trans.). Evanston, IL: Northwestern University Press.

Scott, J. (1991). *Social network analysis: A handbook.* Thousand Oaks, CA: Sage.

Searle, J. (1969). *Speech acts: An essay in the philosophy of language.* Cambridge, UK: Cambridge University Press.

Searle, J. (1980). Minds, brains and programs. *Behavioral and Brain Sciences, 3,* 417–424.

Senge, P. (1990). *The fifth discipline, the art and practice of the learning organization.* New York: Currency Doubleday.

Sfard, A. & Linchevski, L. (1994). The gains and the pitfalls of reification: The case of algebra. *Educational Studies in Mathematics, 26,* 191–228.

Sfard, A. (1998). On two metaphors for learning and the dangers of choosing just one. *Educational Researcher, 27*(2), 4–13.

Sfard, A. (2002). There is more to discourse than meets the ears: Looking at thinking as communicating to learn more about mathematical learning. In C. Kieran, E. Forman, & A. Sfard (Eds.), *Learning discourse: Discursive approaches to research in mathematics education* (pp. 13–57). Dordrecht, Netherlands: Kluwer.

Sfard, A. & McClain, K. (2003). Analyzing tools: Perspectives on the role of designed artifacts in mathematics learning. Special issue. *Journal of the Learning Sciences, 11*(2 & 3).

Shannon, C. & Weaver, W. (1949). *The mathematical theory of communication.* Chicago: University of Illinois Press.

Shumar, W. & Renninger, K. A. (2002). Introduction: On conceptualizing community. In K. A. Renninger and W. Shumar (Eds.), *Building virtual communities* (pp. 1–19). Cambridge, UK: Cambridge University Press.

Simon, H. (1981). *The sciences of the artificial* (2nd ed.). Cambridge, MA: MIT Press.

Slotta, J. D. & Linn, M. C. (2000). The knowledge integration environment: Helping students use the internet effectively. In M. J. Jacobson & R. Kozma (Eds.), *Learning the sciences of the twenty-first century.* Hillsdale, NJ: Lawrence Erlbaum.

Stahl, G. (1975a). The jargon of authenticity: An introduction to a Marxist critique of Heidegger. *Boundary 2, III*(2), 489–498. Retrieved from <www.cis.drexel.edu/faculty/gerry/publications/interpretations/jargon.htm>.

Stahl, G. (1975b). Marxian hermeneutics and Heideggerian social theory: Interpreting and transforming our world. Ph.D. dissertation, Department of Philosophy, Northwestern University, Evanston, IL. Retrieved from <www.cis.drexel.edu/faculty/gerry/publications/dissertations/philosophy>.

Stahl, G. (1976). Attuned to being: Heideggerian music in technological society. *Boundary 2,* 4(2), 637–664. Retrieved from <www.cis.drexel.edu/faculty/gerry/publications/interpretations/attuned.htm>.

Stahl, G., McCall, R., & Peper, G. (1992). Extending hypermedia with an inference language: An alternative to rule-based expert systems. In *Proceedings of the IBM ITL Conference: Expert Systems, October 1992, Yorktown Heights, New York.* (pp. 160–167). Retrieved from <www.cis.drexel.edu/faculty/gerry/publications/conferences/1990/1997/ibm92/ExtHyper.html>

Stahl, G. (1993a). Interpretation in design: The problem of tacit and explicit understanding in computer support of cooperative design. Ph.D. dissertation, Department of Computer Science, University of Colorado, Boulder, CO. Retrieved from <www.cis.drexel.edu/faculty/gerry/publications/dissertations/computer>.

Stahl, G. (1993b). Supporting situated interpretation. In *Proceedings of the Fifteenth Conference of the Cognition Science Society, 1993* (CogSci '93), Boulder, Colorado (pp. 965–970). Hillsdale, NJ: Lawrence Erlbaum.

Stahl, G. (1995). *Supporting personalizable learning* (No. CU-CS-788-95). Boulder, CO: Department of Computer Science, University of Colorado. Retrieved from <www.cis.drexel.edu/faculty/gerry/publications/techreports/personalize>.

Stahl, G., Sumner, T., & Owen, R. (1995). Share globally adapt locally: Software to create and distribute student-centered curriculum. *Computer and Education, 24*(3), 237–246.

Stahl, G., Sumner, T., & Repenning, A. (1995). Internet repositories for collaborative learning: Supporting both students and teachers. In *Proceedings of the International Conference on Computer Support for Collaborative Learning (CSCL '95), Bloomington, Indiana, October 17–20, 1995* (pp. 321–328). Mahwah, NJ: Lawrence Erlbaum. Retrieved from <www.cis.drexel.edu/faculty/gerry/cscl/papers/ch06.pdf>.

Stahl, G. (1996a). Armchair missions to Mars: Using case-based reasoning and fuzzy logic to simulate a time series model of astronaut crews. In S. Pal, T. Dillon, & D. Yeung (Eds.), *Soft computing in case-based reasoning* (pp. 321–344). London: Springer Verlag.

Stahl, G. (1996b). *Personalizing the Web* (No. CU-CS-836-96). Boulder, CO: Department of Computer Science, University of Colorado. Retrieved from <www.cis.drexel.edu/faculty/gerry/publications/techreports/www6/PAPER82.html>.

Stahl, G. & Herrmann, T. (1998). Verschrankung von perspectiven durch aushandlung (The sharing of perspectives by means of negotiation) (G. Stahl, Trans.). In M. Sommer, W. Remmele, & K. Klockner (Eds.), *Proceedings of the Interaktion im Web: Innovative Kommunikationsformen, Berichte des German chapter of the ACM, Marburg, Germany, May 12–13, 1998* (pp. 95–112). Stuttgart: Teubner. Retrieved from <www.cis.drexel.edu/faculty/gerry/publications/conferences/1998/verschrankung/index.html> and <www.cis.drexel.edu/faculty/gerry/publications/conferences/1998/sharing/sharing.html>.

Stahl, G. & Herrmann, T. (1999). Intertwining perspectives and negotiation. In *Proceedings of the International ACM SIGGROUP Conference on Supporting Group Work (Group '99), Phoenix, Arizona, November 14–17, 1999* (pp. 316–324). New York: ACM Press. Retrieved from <www.cis.drexel.edu/faculty/gerry/cscl/papers/ch07.pdf>.

Stahl, G. (2000a). Review of *Professional development for cooperative learning: Issues and approaches* [book review]. *Teaching and Learning in Medicine: An International Journal, 12*(4). Retrieved from <www.cis.drexel.edu/faculty/gerry/cscl/papers/ch18.pdf>.

Stahl, G. (2000b). Collaborative information environments to support knowledge construction by communities. *AI & Society, 14*, 1–27.

Stahl, G. (2000c). A model of collaborative knowledge building. In *Proceedings of the Fourth International Conference of the Learning Sciences (ICLS '00), Ann Arbor, Michigan, June 14–17, 2000* (pp. 70–77). Mahwah, NJ: Lawrence Erlbaum.

Stahl, G. (2001). WebGuide: Guiding collaborative learning on the Web with perspectives. *Journal of Interactive Media in Education (JIME)*, 2001(1). Available at <www-jime.open.ac.uk/2001/1>.

Stahl, G. & Sanusi, A. (2001). Multi-layered perspectives on collaborative learning activities in a middle school rocket simulation project. Paper presented at the Twenty-second Annual Ethnography in Education Research Forum, Philadelphia, PA. Retrieved from <www.cis.drexel.edu/faculty/gerry/publications/conferences/2001/ethnography2001/ethnography.pdf>.

Stahl, G. (Ed.). (2002a). *Computer support for collaborative learning: Foundations for a CSCL community. Proceedings of CSCL '2002, Boulder, Colorado, January 7–11.* Hillsdale, NJ: Lawrence Erlbaum. Retrieved from <isls.org/cscl/cscl2002proceedings.pdf>.

Stahl, G. (2002b). Contributions to a theoretical frameword for CSCL. In *Proceedings of the International Conference on Computer-Supported Collaborative Learning (CSCL '02),* Boulder, Colorado, January 7–11 (pp. 1–2, 62–71). Hillsdale, NJ: Lawrence Erlbaum.

Stahl, G. (2002c). Groupware goes to school: Adapting BSCW to the classroom. *International Journal of Computer Applications Technology (IJCAT), 19*(3/4), 162–174.

Stahl, G. (2002d). Rediscovering CSCL. In T. Koschmann, R. Hall, & N. Miyake (Eds.), *CSCL2: Carrying forward the conversation* (pp. 169–181). Hillsdale, NJ: Lawrence Erlbaum.

Stahl, G. (2002e). Understanding educational computational artifacts across community boundaries. Paper presented at the Conference of the International Society for Cultural Research and Activity Theory (ISCRAT '02), Amsterdam.

Stahl, G. (2003a). Keynote talk: The future of computer support for learning: An American/German DeLFIc vision. In A. Bode, J. Desel, S. Rathmeyer, & M. Wessner (Eds.), *DELFI 2003, Tagungsband der 1. e-Learning Fachtagung Informatik, 16–18 September 2003 in Garching bei München* (pp. 13–16). Bonn: Köllen-Druck.

Stahl, G. (2003b). Knowledge negotiation in asynchronous learning networks. Paper presented at the Hawaii International Conference on System Sciences (HICSS '03), Hawaii.

Stahl, G. (2003c). Meaning and interpretation in collaborative. In B. Wasson, S. Ludvigsen, & U. Hoppe (Eds.), *Designing for change in networked learning environments* (pp. 523–532). Boston, MA: Kluwer.

Stahl, G. (2004a). Building collaborative knowing: Elements of a social theory of CSCL. In J.-W. Strijbos, P. Kirschner, & R. Martens (Eds.), *What we know about CSCL: And implementing it in higher education* (pp. 53–86). Boston: Klumer.

Stahl, G. (2004b). Can community knowledge exceed its members'? *ACM SigGroup Bulletin, 23*(3), 1–13.

Stahl, G. (2004c). Collaboration with relational references. Paper presented at the workshop on representational guidance at the American Educational Research Association (AERA '04), San Diego, California.

Stahl, G. (2004d). Thinking at the group unit of analysis. Paper presented at the CSCL-Sig Symposium of Kaleidoscope, Lausanne, Switzerland.

Stahl, G. & Carrel, A. (2004). *Kommunikationskonszepte* (The role of communication concepts for CSCL pedagogy). In J. Haake, G. Schwabe, & M. Wessner (Eds.), *CSCL-Kompendium* (pp. 229–237). Munich: Oldenbourg.

Stahl, G. (2005). Group cognition: The collaborative locus of agency in CSCL. Paper presented at the international conference on Computer-Supported Collaborative Learning (CSCL '05), Taipei, Taiwan.

Steinkuehler, C., Derry, S., Woods, D., & Hmelo-Silver, C. (2002). The step environment for distributed problem-based learning on the World Wide Web. In *Proceedings of the Conference on Computer-Supported Collaborative Learning (CSCL '2002), Boulder, Colorado, January 7–11, 2002* (pp. 217–226). Hillsdale, NJ: Lawrence Erlbaum.

Stiemerling, O. & Wulf, V. (2000). Beyond "yes and no": Extending access control in groupware with awareness and negotiation. *Group Decision and Negotiation, 9*, 221–235.

Streeck, J. (1983). *Social order in child communication: A study in microethnography.* Amsterdam, NL: Benjamins.

Streeck, J. & Mehus, S. (2003). Microethnography: The study of practices. In K. F. R. Sanders (Ed.), *Handbook of language and social interaction.* Mahway, NJ: Lawrence Erlbaum.

Suchman, L. (1987). *Plans and situated actions: The problem of human-machine communication.* Cambridge, UK: Cambridge University Press.

Sumner, T. (1995). The high-tech toolbelt: A study of designers in the workplace. In I. R. Katz, R. Mack, L. Marks, M. B. Rosson, & J. Nielsen (Eds.), *Proceedings of the Conference on Human Factors in Computing Systems (CHI '95), Denver, Colorado, May 7–11, 1995* (pp. 178–185). New York: ACM Press.

ten Have, P. (1999). *Doing conversation analysis: A practical guide.* Thousand Oaks, CA: Sage.

Thorndike, E. L. (1914). *Educational psychology* (Vols. 1–3). New York: Teachers College.

Tomasello, M., Kruger, A. C., & Ratner, H. (1993). Cultural learning. *Behavioral and Brain Sciences, 16*, 495–552.

Turing, A. M. (1950). Computing machinery and intelligence. *Mind, 59*, 433–460.

van Aalst, J., Burtis, J., Teplovs, C., & Scardamalia, M. (1999). Latent semantic analysis and data analysis in computer supported collaborative learning. Paper presented at the annual conference of the American Educational Research Association (AERA '99), Montreal, Canada, April, 1999.

Vera, J. & Simon, H. (1993). Situated action: A symbolic interpretation. *Cognitive Science, 17*(1), 7–48.

Verschaffel, L., Greer, B., & Corte, E. D. (2000). *Making sense of word problems.* Lisse, Netherlands: Swets & Zeitlinger.

Vogel, D., Nunamaker, J., Applegate, L., & Konsynski, B. (1987). Group decision support systems: Determinants of success. In *Proceedings of the Seventh Conference on Decision Support Systems (DSS '87): Crisis Support Systems—Tools for Action, June, 1987* (pp. 118–128).

Vygotsky, L. (1978). *Mind in society.* Cambridge, MA: Harvard University Press. (Original work published in 1930).

Vygotsky, L. (1986). *Thought and language.* Cambridge, MA: MIT Press. (Original work published in 1934).

Wartofsky, M. (1979). Perception, representation, and the forms of action: Towards an historical epistemology. In M. Wartofsky (Ed.), *Models: Representation and the scientific understanding* (pp. 188–210). London: D. Reidel. (Original work published 1973).

Wasserman, S. & Faust, K. (1992). *Social network analysis: Methods and applications.* Cambridge, UK: Cambridge University Press.

Wegerif, R. (2004). A dialogical understanding of the relationship between CSCL and teaching thinking skills. Paper presented at the Kaleidoscope CSCL Symposium, Lausanne, Switzerland, October 7–9, 2004.

Wells, G. (1999). *Dialogic inquiry: Towards a socio-cultural practice and theory of education*. Cambridge, UK: Cambridge University Press.

Wertsch, J. V. (1985). *Vygotsky and the social formation of mind*. Cambridge, MA: Harvard University Press.

Winograd, T. & Flores, F. (1986). *Understanding computers and cognition: A new foundation of design*. Reading, MA: Addison-Wesley.

Winograd, T. (1996). *Bringing design to software*. New York: ACM Press.

Wittgenstein, L. (1974). *Tractatus logico philosophicus*. London: Routledge. (Original work published in 1921).

Wittgenstein, L. (1953). *Philosophical investigations*. New York: Macmillan.

Wulf, V. (2001). *Zur anpassbaren gestaltung von groupware* (Tailorable design of groupware) (Vol. 10). Sankt Augustin, Germany: GMD Research Series.

Wulf, V., Pipek, V., & Pfeifer, A. (2001). Resolving function-based conflicts in groupware systems. *AI & Society, 15*, 233–262.

Yates, J. & Orlikowski, W. (1992). Genres of organizational communication: A structurational approach to studying communication and media. *Academy of Management Review, 17*(2), 299–326.

Zuboff, S. (1988). *In the age of the smart machine*. New York: Basic Books.

Name Index

Subject Index